Gangster PLANET

Daniel Hopsicker & Linda Minor

Published by:
Trine Day LLC
PO Box 577
Walterville, OR 97489
1-800-556-2012
www.TrineDay.com
trineday@icloud.com

Library of Congress Control Number: 2024944720

Hopsicker, Daniel & Minor, Linda, .Gangster Planet—1st ed.
p. cm.

Cloth (ISBN-13) 978-1-63424-479-4
Epub (ISBN-13) 978-1-63424-481-7
Trade Paper (ISBN-13) 978-1-63424-480-0

1. Organized crime United States. 2. Political corruption United States History 20th century. 3. Drug dealers United States. 4. Seal, Barry, 1939-1986. 5. Trump, Donald, 1946- Friends and associates. 6. True Crime 7. SOCIAL SCIENCE / Criminology. I. Hopsicker, Daniel & Minor, Linda. II. Title

.

FIRST EDITION
10 9 8 7 6 5 4 3 2 1

Distribution to the Trade by:
Independent Publishers Group (IPG)
814 North Franklin Street
Chicago, Illinois 60610
312.337.0747
www.ipgbook.com

Publisher's Foreword

Come writers and critics
Who prophesize with your pen
And keep your eyes wide
The chance won't come again
And don't speak too soon
For the wheel's still in spin
And there's no tellin' who
That it's namin'
For the loser now
Will be later to win
For the times they are a-changin'
–Bob Dylan, ©Universal Music Publishing Group, 1963

You want to know what this was really all about? The Nixon campaign
in 1968, and the Nixon White House after that, had two enemies: the
antiwar left and black people.... You understand what I'm saying? We
knew we couldn't make it illegal to be either against the war or black,
but by getting the public to associate the hippies with marijuana and
blacks with heroin, and then criminalizing both heavily, we could dis-
rupt those communities. We could arrest their leaders, raid their homes,
break up their meetings, and vilify them night after night on the evening
news. Did we know we were lying about the drugs? Of course we did.
–John Ehrlichman, aide to President Nixon, *Harper's Magazine*, 1994

What can I say? I am a hippie and as such learned a few things about "drugs" and the how they move around. I bought my first kilo of marijuana illicitly in 1967 for $80. Now in 2024 I grow it for myself legally. Much happened in between.....

The late 1960's were heady times, I was a college student, founded a record store, managed a band, put on rock-n-roll dances, got married, had a kid ... and was generally having a good time.

Then my ex-spook father told me some things I didn't understand. It took me years to comprehend his revelations and the search sent me deep into "conspiracy-theory land." While on that journey I had the good fortune to meet Daniel Hopsicker.

We met on an email list called "CIA-Drugs" in the late 1990s. The list was a raucous one, Bob the moderator tried but the list imploded. I had been running an email list, CTRL, (Conspiracy Theory Research List) and so I started up a new CIA-Drugs list. It grew into a good-size community – writers, researchers and interested folk. And it was on this list where Daniel began decrying that a book that he had spent three years writing, had now been with an agent for two years and nobody was going to print it. After hearing that for a couple of weeks, I told Daniel that I had a computer on my desk and had been told that I could make a book.

Daniel came out to Oregon, and we put together *Barry & 'the Boys.' The CIA, the Mob and America's Secret History* for MadCow Press. Daniel was journalist. He had had a business show aired internationally by NBC. He had written, produced and voiced several documentaries. Once he stumbled upon the subject of CIA-Drugs, it ruined him professionally. His Hollywood agent told him bluntly that his 1999 documentary, *Secret Heartbeat of America: The CIA and Drugs,* would not air. We went to a local bistro with an open mike, Daniel got up on stage and screamed, "There is no free press in America" – several times. It was cathartic.

I then watched, and sometimes helped, Daniel in his career. I saw him break amazing news over and over again. *He was ignored.* As a journalist he had little patience for outlandish "truther" rhetoric, but also produced one of the most insightful rejoinders to the official story of the 9/11 attack, *Welcome to Terrorland: Mohamed Atta & the 9-11 Cover-up in Florida*

Daniel has passed, but his work lives on. Esteemed researcher Linda Minor worked tirelessly to complete his magnum opus, *Gangster Planet: Where "Being Connected" Means Never Having to Say You're Sorry* a tale of corruption, deceit, and lies. We are honored to have known Daniel Hopsicker!

Everybody must get stoned
– Bob, Dylan, Rainy Day Women #12 & 35, 1966©Dwarf Music

Onward to the Utmost of Futures,
Peace,
R.A. Kris Millegan
Publisher
TrineDay
September 9, 2024

Daniel Harold Hopsicker
July 16, 1951– August 22, 2023
R.I.P.

CONTENTS

Rogues' Gallery

Planes:

Cocaine One: DC9 (tail number N900SA) busted with 5.5 tons of cocaine at an airport in Ciudad del Carmen in the state of Campeche, Mexico in April 2006. Plane was registered to "Royal Sons LLC," a Florida air charter company, that gave plane's location as Venice, Florida Airport, same address used in 2001 as infamous flight school Huffman Aviation, which trained Saudi pilots Mohamed Atta and Marwan al-Shehhi.

Identical DC9 (tail number N12ONE): FAA registration showed it had also been owned by Royal Sons LLC, before being transferred by Ramy El-Batrawi's Genesis Aviation, Inc. to Finova Capital Corporation in Scottsdale, Arizona. I recognized Finova as the CIA front company set up in Arizona and headquartered in Canada. Finova also ended up as owner of the Beechcraft 200 Barry Seal leased from Greyhound Leasing of Phoenix. The CIA works through cutouts to maintain plausible deniability.

Cocaine Two: Gulfstream II (tail number N987SA), owned by Donna Blue Aircraft Inc, a front company for a Florida-based Tampa ICE undercover operation named Operation Mayan Jaguar. It flew out of a St. Pete-Clearwater hangar and was transferred to front men for World Jet, Inc. in Fort Lauderdale, controlled by Whittington brothers, at the time it crashed in the Yucatan on September 24, 2007, carrying 4 tons of cocaine.

Learjet: (tail number N351WB) owned by Plane 1 Leasing, a charter jet service wholly owned by Wallace J. Hilliard, was busted in July 2000 at Orlando Executive Jet Airport carrying 43 pounds of heroin. Passengers Edgar Valles and Neyra Rivas, both of Caracas, Venezuela, had the heroin hidden in tennis shoes. The charter was called a "milk run" because it made 39 weekly down-and-back runs from Orlando to Caracas. In a hearing on November 3, 2000, Federal Magistrate Judge James Glazebrook denied Hilliard's motion to get his Lear back.

Ships:

MSC Gayane: ship busted by Homeland Security at Port of Philadelphia with 16.5 tons of cocaine on June 17, 2019, from Freeport, Bahamas bound for Rotterdam, the Netherlands. The crew members from Kotor, Montenegro were part of a Balkan drug cartel, possibly a satellite of Oleg Deripaska's Russian mob connection. Historically it was linked to "Group America," a CIA connection from the 1980s.

COMPANIES:

Argyll Equities LLC: Numerous entities were set up by Douglas A. McClain (Jr. and Sr.) and their associates using the Argyll label. Argyll Equities made "loans" to other companies in an arrangement more akin to money-laundering than to traditional lending operations. Through Argyll Biotechnology, the Mc-Clains also became involved in the fraudulent sale of stock related to the patent for SF-1019, touting it as a cure for multiple sclerosis and other diseases.

EBI Securities, Inc. (formerly Eastbrokers, formerly Czech Industries, formerly Global Capital Partners): brokerage company involved in financial fraud as a front for CIA in Eastern Europe during fall of Soviet Union. It had connections to former NSC and CIA operative Robert "Bud" McFarlane after he was involved in Iran-Contra. It was also linked to organized crime network of Douglas McClain, Sr.

Genesis Aviation, Inc.: Ramy El-Batrawi was sole shareholder of the company, created as a subsidiary of GenesisIntermedia.com, Inc. (GENI) (according to 1999 SEC filing for parent Company). Ramy claimed the stock price of the parent company rose at an average of 1600% a year until September 11, 2001, when the stock collapsed, coincident with the buildings in the Trade Center. Ramy blamed "corrupt FBI agents [who] worked for "illegal naked short sellers" of the GENI stock.

Industrial Biotechnology Corporation (IBC): a public corporation once headed by Andrew Badolato of Sarasota, Florida, which claimed to produce ethanol from Brazilian sugar cane. Badolato teamed up with Jonathan Curshen, also of Sarasota, in a pump and dump and a scheme, in which Curshen was arrested in New York. for paying undercover cops posing as brokers to sell worthless stock to alleged clients.

Jetborne International, Inc.: Delaware corporation created in January 1987 as a public vehicle for Jetborne, Inc., a Florida corporation set up in 1980 by two Israeli brothers named Blattner, along with their brother-in-law, to engage in the sale of aircraft parts and components. Deed records show they bought the building in 1985 from U.S. Industries, Inc. After bankruptcy, controlling stock in the Florida company was purchased by Finstock Investments, Inc., of London, which leased the building at 4010 NW 36TH Avenue in Miami to Aircraft Modular Products, Inc. ("AMP") for its offices and manufacturing facilities. Roger Koch was a principal in AMP.

Ringling Circus: the world's larges circus, which was started in Wisconsin by the Ringling family, eventually headquartered in New York with winter quarters in Sarasota (1927) and in Venice, Florida from 1959 until it closed.

Royal Sons, Inc.: The Royal unofficial trademark had been used in the St. Pete, Florida, area by the Geffon family, who sold rugs. When Fred Geffon joined the business, he added a boat sales division, later expanding to aircraft sales and charters. He claims to have been suckered into Brent Kovar's scheme to invest heavily in Skyway Communications, trading an airplane or two for shares in Skyway.

Sky Way Aircraft, Inc.:Clearwater, Florida-based Nevada corporation developing a unique ground-to-air in-flight aircraft communication network that it claimed would provide anti-terrorism support, real time in-flight surveillance, WIFI access to the Internet, telephone service and enhanced entertainment service for commercial and private aircraft.

SkyWay (or Skyway, both as one word) Communications Holding Corp. (OTCBB: SWYC): a Delaware corporation, had been known since 1998 as Mastertel, Inc., which traded on the NASDAQ as an over-the-counter (OTC) stock. In late 1999, the Company changed its name to i-Teleco.com, Inc. and on April 17, 2003, it changed again to SkyWay (or Skyway) Communications Holding Corp. The following month it acquired Sky Way Aircraft, Inc. as a wholly owned subsidiary. The purpose of the change, in addition to issuing new shares to pay off debt, was to enable shareholders to engage in a pump and dump scheme involving its stock.

TMM (Transportacion Maritima Mexicana, S.A.): a transportation company founded in Mexico in 1958 and allied with U.S. shipping and trucking firms. It began trading its shares publicly on Mexican stock exchange in 1981, and in 1982 it bought the Tex-Mex Railroad in the U.S. Jose Serrano Segovia became chairman of TMM following the 1991 purchase by Grupo Servia, S.A. de C.V., a family corporation owned by the Hank family.

PEOPLE:

Andy Badolato: Florida-born son of Italian Catholic family from New York, who grew up in Sarasota, graduate of Cardinal Mooney High School in Sarasota and St. Thomas University in Miami. Most notable company he chaired was Industrial Biotechnology Corp. (IBC), whose stock Jonathan Curshen was attempting to promote when arrested in 2008. IBC changed its name – on the same day Curshen's indictment was unsealed – to The Renewable Corporation. Badolato developed a business relationship with Steve Bannon in 2003, working on various stock promotions, and was indicted with Bannon and Brian Kolfage in the "We Build the Wall" fraud.

Joey Barquin: Florida man who provided information to author Daniel Hopsicker about a variety of financial frauds in which Jonathan Curshen and Andy Badolato of Sarasota, Florida, were involved. Barquin had received a substantial personal injury court settlement he wanted to invest and was invited to hang out with "investment managers," whom he personally witnessed engaged in illegal activity.

William P. Barr: Republican attorney with an impressive resume, which he gave to Congress during 2019 confirmation hearing for Attorney General in Donald Trump administration: B.A. in government (1971), master's degree in Chinese studies and government (1973) from Columbia University. Analyst for the Central Intelligence Agency (1971-1977) during graduate and law school in New York and Washington, D.C. Law Clerk to Judge Malcolm Richard Wilkey at U.S. Court of Appeals for the D.C. Circuit, 1977-1978, Senior Policy Advisor/Deputy Assistant Director, Office of Policy Development for the White House under Pres. Reagan, 1982-1983. Assistant Attorney General under Richard Thornburgh (Pres. Reagan) in 1989 and Attorney General in 1991-1993 under Pres. George H. W. Bush. During the gap period (1978-1982) he used the "connected" law firm Shaw, Pittman, Potts and Trowbridge – one of whose partners was president of the Military Air Transport Association – as cover for CIA activities in Mena, Arkansas, operating under the code name "Robert Johnson."

Wolfgang Bohringer: friend and "brother" of Mohamad Atta, principal subject of author Daniel Hopsicker's previous book, *Welcome to TerrorLand*, whom fans of the MadCow website sighted and notified the author when Bohringer showed up on a yacht at tiny and remote Fanning Island, which lacks much basic infrastructure suitable for a flight training school – not even an airfield. Later arrested, Bohringer exclaimed he worked for the CIA.

Michael Francis Brassington: Guyanese copilot of Lear jet (N351WB) charter plane, registered to Hilliard's company, Plane 1 Leasing, which flew 39 weekly runs between Florida and Venezuela during 2000 until it was busted with 43 pounds of heroin aboard. The author spent years searching for the name of the copilot before it was furnished to him by a former employee of Customs in Florida, who had met Brassington, and was fired for stopping him after seeing his name flagged by DEA in the Customs computer. The Brassington family in Guyana was also involved in the sale of bauxite to Oleg Deripaska.

Stuart Burchill: Tampa-born "businessman and accountant," who worked for Wallace Hilliard in Naples, who claimed to have his start in business working for McFaddin Ventures.

Kenneth Burnstine: Chicago born and educated man who joined the Marine Corps shortly after the Korean War, who lived first in Alabama and moved to Fort Lauderdale around 1960. He became one of the first well-known businessmen who left the real estate business to become a drug smuggler. He used a surplus P-51 military plane to fly marijuana from the Bahamas, and later began to fly cocaine before being busted and used as a witness against men with more powerful connections.

D. Harold Byrd: wealthy scion of family from Dallas, who in 1941 founded the Civil Air Patrol (CAP). He founded Temco Aircraft, which in 1961 merged with a Ling electronics company and with aircraft manufacturer, Chance Vought Corporation, to form Ling-Temco-Vought (LTV). Graduate of University of Texas and close friend of Lyndon Johnson, both of whom were founding members of Mt. Kenya Safari Club, later sold to Adnan Khashoggi. Byrd also owned the Dallas building leased to the Texas State Book Depository, where it was claimed Lee Harvey Oswald fired the single bullet that killed President Kennedy and wounded Governor John Connally. Others have furnished credible evidence that Malcolm "Mac" Wallace's fingerprint was found on the rifle found near the 5th story window of the building.

Claire Chennault: Louisiana native who was trained to fly in Army bases in San Antonio during WWI. Chennault led a group of aerial acrobats and barnstormers in the years between the wars. He resigned from the military to work for the Chinese Air Force in training Chinese pilots to fight in their war with Japan. Later he led American pilots (the "Flying Tigers") after the U.S. entered the war. His second wife, Anna Chan Chennault, became after his death a social butterfly and fundraiser as part of the "China Lobby."

Jonathan Curshen: grandson of a Jewish merchant (Curshenberg) who emigrated from London UK to Toronto, where his father became involved in selling pornographic materials before moving the family to New Jersey in the U.S. Jonathan claimed dual citizenship. He moved to Sarasota, Florida, and set up an insurance company to engage in fraudulent activity. Later he created Red Sea Management, Ltd., a Costa Rican investment company used to launder dirty money

Oleg Deripaska: Russian oligarch who married the daughter of Boris Yeltsin's top adviser, who was married to Yeltsin's daughter at one time. He hired American political strategist Paul Manafort, former partner of Roger Stone and Rick Gates, to get a pro-Putin candidate elected President of Ukraine in 2005-2006. Manafort said he was employing unidentified legal experts at the Center for Strategic and International Studies (CSIS) to help. Deripaska had emerged as the winner in the "aluminum wars" that began after the fall of the Soviet Union in 1991.

Ramy El-Batrawi: Tampa man who wormed his way into becoming a "lieutenant" in financial operations of CIA-connected arms dealer Adnan Khashoggi in the mid-1980s as Iran-Contra was exploding in the press. He acted as front man in GenesisIntermedia, a public company whose stock was underwritten by Millenium Financial Group's Michael Roy Fugler, who had once acted as attorney for Barry Seal.

Michael D. Farkas: an attorney in Miami thought to have links to Israeli intelligence, who created corporations with public trading rights to sell as off-the-shelf corporations to companies wishing to take their companies public. He was involved with Holiday RV Superstores, Inc.

Samuel Drew Fife, Jr.: a Florida-born man who served in the military and founded the "Christian" Move of God cult in New Orleans in the 1960's. One member, Vennie Kocsis, said it was "evangelical, socialist, extremely abusive, trafficked humans from around the globe, limited our education, and more. Many of us children suffered sexual abuse, extreme physical abuse, exorcisms, mind control, and child labor." She named as participants "Sam Fife. Tom Rowe. Buddy Cobb. Joe McChord. Douglas McClain. Donald McClain. Bill Grier. Jay Cheshire. Jane Miller."

Michael Roy Fugler: Baton Rouge attorney who sued author of *Barry and 'the Boys,'* Daniel Hopsicker, to have his name removed from that book. In 1998 Fugler was the Representative of Millennium Financial Group, Inc., underwriter of securities issued by Genesis Media Group, Inc. and its chairman, Ramy El-Batrawi, on behalf of majority shareholder Adnan Khashoggi.

Frederic Geffon: Principal shareholder and chairman of Royal Sons, Inc., which sold a DC9 valued at $7 million to Skyway Communications Holding Corp. in exchange for worthless stock falsely appraised at equal value.

Carlos Hank Gonzalez: half German Mexican citizen who served in Mexican congress and as party leader in PRI, and adviser to President Carlos Salinas de Gortari. A report from the National Drug Intelligence Center (NDIC), leaked in 1999 to the *Washington Post*, noted that Hank González's alleged involvement in drug trafficking and money laundering at one time posed "a significant criminal threat to the United States," and that Hank Gonzalez committed political corruption, tax evasion, bribery and vote-buying. The report was naturally disavowed by the Clinton Administration.

Carlos Slim Helú: In 2015 Carlos Slim (born to both Maronite Christians from Lebanon's Bekaa Valley) was said to be the biggest shareholder of A shares in the *New York Times*, although it was B shares held by the Ochs-Sulzberger family which controlled the newspaper. He was recently listed on *Forbes'* List as the 11th-richest person in the world, with a net worth of $105 billion. Because of his importance to the *New York Times*, perhaps, there's no mention of his wealth stemming from the illicit drugs industry, estimated in 2019 to be valued at half a trillion dollars.

Wally Hilliard: Everything we know about him was written in *Welcome to Terror-Land*, which we suggest you read as soon as possible.

Adnan Khashoggi: Saudi-Arabian citizen, educated at Chico State University in California and Stanford in the 1960s. Because of his connections with the Saudi Royal Family, he acted as a go-between with defense contractors previously represented by the CIA's Kim Roosevelt, in selling U.S. made weapons to oil-rich countries willing to pay big bucks for them. He was used by the Reagan-Bush National Security Council (NSC) to act as mediary for funds in the Iran-Contra Scandal. Afterwards, Khashoggi became involved in financial fraud on a massive scale – both in Eastern Europe and in the U.S.

Arik Kislin: American citizen (grandson of Semyon Kislin of New York) who emigrated from Russia as a teen in the 1990's. Identified in an Interpol report as being a front for Ismailovskaya, Russian organized-crime group. As owner of Air Rutter International (ARI), a company that provided charter services for individual plane owners, he managed planes owned by William Achenbaum, one time owner of the Gulfstream II, once registered to Donna Blue Airlines (aka Cocaine Two). He also partnered with Achenbaum in developing Hotel Gansevoort in the Meatpacking District in Manhattan. Hotel Gansevoort also built a resort at the site of the original Third Turtle Inn in Turks and Caicos, the first hotel and restaurant on Providenciales, opening in the 1960s, closed in 1989.

Brent Kovar: President and CEO of Satellite Access Systems, Inc. (SAS), Sky Way Aircraft, Inc. and Skyway Communications Holding Corp. based in Clearwater, Florida.

Glenn Kovar: New Jersey man who got degrees in Arizona in the 1950s before relocating to Pasadena, California, and spent a career in the U.S. Forestry Service, division of film and publicity. Worked with stars of *Lassie* TV series. Divorced from Joy Carson Kovar, he moved to St. Thomas for a while, sailing a pirate's boat back and forth to Florida. Settled in St. Petersburg area to help his son, Brent Kovar, pursue his own career in broadband services and technology.

Asher M. Leids: California attorney at Donahue, Mesereau & Leids, LLP, 1900 Avenue of the Stars, Suite 2700, Los Angeles, California 90067, who represented Genesis Media Group, Inc. (created in late 1993) in issuing public securities underwritten by Fugler's company in 1998.

James J. Ling: master electrician, trained in U.S. Navy., who built an Altec Electronics plant in Anaheim, California in 1959, which D. Harold Byrd bought and turned into a subsidiary of Ling-Temco-Vought (LTV), a company that fired Regulus missiles from Venice Airport in 1959. Ling moved to Dallas where LTV went bankrupt. He then sold the home he'd bought from Lamar Hunt to Gene Phillips, who headed another notorious conglomerate called Southmark.

David Breed Lindsay, Sr.: son of George Lindsay, owner of Marion, Indiana newspaper. David Sr. was a pilot in WWI, stationed in south Florida before moving to North Carolina, where he bought a newspaper. He relocated to St. Petersburg, Florida, and later to Sarasota, buying more newspapers, hiring his father George Lindsay as editor. He rejoined the Army Air Force in WWII, later the OSS, where he ran the Far East station for Claire Chennault.

David Breed Lindsay Jr.: son of David Breed Lindsay, Sr. and his first wife, who divorced when their son was young. He grew up in North Carolina but returned to Indiana for college. He worked for his grandfather's and father's newspapers and succeeded David Sr. as head of the *Herald-Tribune*, which was later sold to the *New York Times*. As a sideline to publishing, in 1958 he set up Trans Florida Aviation with the intent of refurbishing the ex-military P-51s into civilian aircraft, changing the name to Cavalier Aircraft Corp., which also made Mustang planes.

Douglas McClain, Sr.: son of Donald and Muriel, who grew up in the cult they helped found in Massachusetts and in Alaska. As an adult, he got involved in serious financial fraud. With his son, he founded the Argyll Group, parent of several subsidiaries such as Argyll Equities and Argyll Biotechnology. In Boerne, Texas near San Antonio, he was involved in swindling members of the community out of their life's savings under the guise of being a Christian.

Donald and Muriel McClain: Connecticut residents who became members of the "Move of God" cult led by Sam Fife. The cult was suspected of crimes throughout the western hemisphere, possibly involving child abuse and financial fraud.

Lance McFaddin: Texan who formed numerous night clubs in Austin, Houston and Dallas under the name McFaddin Ventures. In Austin he met and became partners with Texas State Representative Charlie Wilson and his childhood friend Buddy Temple, of Lufkin, Texas. The Temples' lumber company was bought by Time, Inc. in 1972 – same company that owned the Zapruder film showing JFK's assassination.

Mike Misick: Premier of Turks and Caicos Islands (TCI) who dated Omarosa, a woman who appeared on Donald Trump's reality show, *The Apprentice*, before he married LisaRaye McCoy, a model and sitcom television actress. Misick hired Michael Brassington as his personal pilot, thus furnishing a kind of immunity for Brassington, who was the copilot on Wallace Hilliard's plane carrying heroin in 2000. Misick's lavish lifestyle called attention to massive corruption of using government funds for personal expenses, including the hiring of Brassington to fly a jet leased from Jeffrey Watson, a former aide to President Bill Clinton. The UK conducted an Inquiry that resulted in returning TCI to government by a governor appointed by the Crown. Misick was prosecuted but fought extradition for years.

Henry Ringling North: nephew of John N. Ringling. Became executor of the uncle's estate with his brother, John Ringling North, after the death of John N. Ringling. Together they fought the codicil which bequeathed the circus and the Ringling assets, including the buildings and artwork, to the state of Florida. Henry served in WWII in the OSS under William J. Donovan's "McGregor" Mission.

The missions' Commander was John M. Shaheen, former Republican party publicity director in Illinois. (*OSS, War Report of the OSS, Overseas Targets*).

William Pawley: organizer of the "Flying Tigers," an American team of pilots who fought in China during WWII. After the war, Pawley's company was incorporated as Civil Air Transport, also known as "Air America."

John N. Ringling: the youngest son, ran the circus for decades prior to his death in 1936. He made millions in the Healdton Oil Field in Oklahoma, which he used to buy artworks in Europe while traveling there with the circus with his wife, Mabel. In Sarasota, he built an Italianate palace to store his artworks, which was bequeathed to the State of Florida in an addendum (codicil) to his will, which had appointed his nephews as executors.

Kermit "Kim" Roosevelt, Jr.: grandson of President Theodore Roosevelt, who, in 1953, engineered the coup that toppled Iranian prime minister Mohammed Mossadegh and restored the Shah to Iran's Peacock Throne. As a specialist in Middle Eastern affairs, he set up numerous front companies through which the CIA funneled funds. Retiring from CIA in 1958, he worked undercover for oil and defense contractors based primarily in California, using Adnan Khashoggi as a cutout for arms deals.

Barry Seal: Subject of author Daniel Hopsicker's first book, *Barry and 'the Boys.'* which revealed Seal's career as a pilot for CIA drug operations and protection for his own personal drug operations. After his arrest in Florida during Operation Screamer, he "worked off his beef" by cooperating with the Drug Enforcement Agency. As a consequence, information was leaked by the Reagan White House that resulted in his assassination in 1986.

John K. "Jack" Singlaub: Major General in the U.S. Army, who served in the Office of Strategic Services (OSS) and CIA. In 1977 he criticized President Carter in public and was reprimanded. He retired, and in 1979 founded a private intelligence network that was later implicated for supplying weapons to the Contras during the Iran–Contra affair. Singlaub was a founder in 1981 of the United States Council for World Freedom, the U.S. chapter of the World Anti-Communist League (WACL). Associated Press (AP) reported that "Singlaub's private group became the public cover for the White House operation."

Charlie Wilson: After returning from U.S. Navy service, Wilson entered politics in Lufkin, Texas, sponsored by lumberman Arthur Temple. Once elected to Congress, he met and became a close friend of Houston socialite Joanne (Herring) King, honorary consul for Pakistan. Together they worked to send Israeli weapons to the Mujahadeen in Afghanistan, an act credited with assisting Presidents Reagan and George H. W. Bush in bankrupting the Russian military, resulting in the collapse of the USSR in 1991.

PREFACE

"It is difficult to get a man to understand something when his salary depends on his not understanding it."
— Upton Sinclair: *I, Candidate for Governor* (1934)

Organized crime is a candy store in Brooklyn selling bolita tickets and maybe doing a little loansharking, with sometimes a couple guys peddling swag that fell off the back of a truck.

Transnational organized crime is a three-football-field long container ship sliding into port carrying twenty tons of cocaine.

Russiagate is about transnational organized crime. There's nothing Good Fellas-y about it.

Where to look to see this collusion? Fifth Avenue? Brighton Beach?

Yes, and yes, as we'll see later.

But where I saw it – without even looking for it – was in Florida. More specifically, on the Gulf Coast of Florida. In Sarasota County, which includes Venice, where I have lived since 2001, shortly after completing the writing of *Barry and 'the boys'* and only months after 9/11 occurred.

Still somewhat focused at the time on Seal's drug trafficking for the CIA, I could not have chosen a better place to observe such operations up close.

As it happens, I had gone to Venice to visit my parents, who'd retired there decades earlier, and my decision to stay awhile was meant to be temporary. The timing seemed so perfect, however, that I rented an apartment. It was less than a mile from where Mohamad Atta had registered for flight training in the summer of 2000. Soon I discovered 9/11 was as closely tied to drug smuggling as Barry Seal had been, and. I ended up writing my second book there. *Welcome to TerrorLand* was published in 2004.

I moved to Texas, just selling books and reporting for *The Mad Cow Morning News*, my own website. But I went back to Venice in 2006, after events described in this book began to occur.

The arrest of the DC-9 in the state of Campeche, Mexico, carrying 5.5 tons of cocaine was my own Siren's Song. Without a crew to tie me to the ship's mast – as in Homer's classic *Odyssey* – I chose to be lured back. To Venice, Florida, where Sirens sang to me:

> *We'll teach you wisdom,*
> *We'll give you love, sweeter than honey.*
> *The songs we sing, soothe away sorrow,*
> *And in our arms, you will be happy.*
> *Odysseus, bravest of heroes,*
> *The songs we sing, will bring you peace.*

As I write this, I am rereading Homer's work, which I read as a sophomore English Lit major at UCLA in the early '70s. In those days, with reddish blond hair on my head and face, I had aspirations of being a writer of literature and dreams of living on a peaceful planet without war.

Was I being lured even then by Sirens who promised my generation that drugs would provide us wisdom and peace? Then, as now, was it all just one big psy-op?

What I learn from Homer is that even before the days of Christ our planet was peopled by tragic figures manipulated by gods – individuals like me who wanted love, beauty and peace to rule a world riddled with evil intent, lust, greed, and the desire for power.

It makes my pitiable tale of woe seem small in the telling. But tell it I must. Gangster Planet is my own Odyssey, metaphorically speaking.

Our story here begins with a DC-9 based at St. Petersburg-Clearwater International Airport, busted with cocaine in Mexico in April 2006. That's where my own investigation began. The book follows my own steps in the order I learned details, each leading me to another aspect of the way the drug smuggling network behind this DC-9 operated.

I labeled the micro-network managing that drug operation a "hyena pack," but you should note, it's not the only one out there. There are hundreds of them – maybe more – all over the world. What makes their success possible is what P. T. Barnum once said allowed his traveling freak show to succeed: "There's a sucker born every minute."

Package an idea just right, and it will sell every time.

Barnum, incidentally, sold his three-ring circus in 1919 to the Ringling family, now almost totally identified with Sarasota, Florida, where much of our story takes place. John N. Ringling and his wife set a stage for what later took place in their fair city on the bay. We discuss Ringling's role in the chapter titled "Art and Circuses," which is a primer on how Republican politics got mixed up with financial fraud. *Remember Teapot Dome?*

President Warren Harding's administration wasn't the first time, however, that Republicans used Sarasota, Florida, as a setting to stage their dreams of grandeur. First there was Bertha Honore Palmer, whose sister, Ida Honore, happened to have married the son of President Ulysses S. Grant. Ida Grant's daughter, who was actually born in the White House in 1876, was destined to marry a White Russian prince.

Who knows where history would have placed them if the Bolshevik Revolution had not intervened to destroy what could have been a glorious royal reign in – where else – Sarasota's regal palace, C' D'Zan?

The best laid plans, alas, they do go awry.

The first dozen or so chapters of this book describe one covert operation perpetrated on the stock-buying public. We begin with a tale of a drug bust in Mexico that took place on a DC-9 (N900SA) owned by Skyway Communications, busted in April 2006. Likening the plane to Air Force One because of its blue, gold, and black insignia, early on, I dubbed it Cocaine One.

SkyWay Aircraft was set up by a somewhat innocuous family named Kovar, transplanted from southern California to Florida. They claimed to own a patent to an invention made by the son, Brent Kovar, which they said a huge defense contractor was interested in buying.

SkyWay Aircraft soon morphed into a public corporation called Skyway Communications through a corporate procedure then known as a reverse merger. They found a shell corporation being sold by a Miami attorney named Michael Farkas, which had public trading rights. Farkas merged his company into an acquisition company – they now call such companies SPACs (special purpose acquisition company), as we show later – with its name simultaneously changed to Skyway Communications.

Voila! Skyway was now a public corporation with all the public trading rights of the shell. Skyway then found itself in need of, not just one, but two DC-9s. We trace the FAA title of both DC-9's to determine how the planes had previously been used and by whom.

How did the buyers pay for the planes? An FAA title includes copies of Liens, Leases, and Transfers, all smushed together into a folder that must be examined to determine the state of the plane's title. It is often confusing.

When a second plane, a Gulfstream II, crashed in Mexico in September 2007, we were intrigued by the fact it had been sold out of a hangar at the St Pete-Clearwater Airport, allegedly to buyers in Fort Lauderdale, only two weeks before it crashed while carrying huge quantities of cocaine bound for the United States. Plane-spotters linked the Gulfstream to CIA renditions.

The drug busts led to the arrest of a man authorities claimed was the primary money launderer for Joaquin Guzman, "El Chapo," leader of the Sinaloa cartel. Wachovia Bank in North Carolina was outed as the international banking empire used by El Chapo's dirty money network.

I linked the Gulfstream, allegedly owned by a mystery company called "Donna Blue Aircraft," to a corrupt U.S. Customs operation being run out of Florida. A fired Customs official contacted me to say that his former employers were reportedly protecting a drug pilot named Michael Francis Brassington of Guyana, whose records showed he had co-piloted the plane owned by Wally Hilliard's company, busted in Orlando in 2000 carrying "heavy weight," 43 pounds of heroin.

Brassington also owned a charter business called Platinum Jet, based in Florida, previously named in an incident in which a Bombardier Challenger CL-600 jet ran off a runway at Teterboro Airport and crashed into a warehouse.

But as of February 2009, when I published my first story about Brassington, no American news medium had noticed he had been the co-pilot on a plane that made drug smuggling history in Central Florida on a Wally Hilliard-controlled Learjet.

My reporting clearly spooked some spooks. A Fort Lauderdale lawyer, purportedly acting on behalf of Guyanese pilot Brassington, whom I had linked to a "massive corruption scandal roiling U.S. Customs in South Florida," filed a lawsuit against me in a Florida court.

I'd been searching forever for the Learjet's co-pilot without knowing his name. Now I knew it. He was the client of the lawyer suing me. I always know I'm on the right track when I get handed a summons. It emboldens me to keep going.

Maybe that's what Homer would have called "hubris."

Wally Hilliard owned the Learjet through Plane 1 Leasing – which, a year prior to 9/11, carried heroin into Orlando. Through Brassington, we could link the 9/11 pilots trained in Venice to the drug network operating out of Clearwater-St. Pete Airport.

The ramifications of that discovery were enormous. Remember Tony Blair's profound words to Parliament shortly after September 11, 2001: "Al Qaeda is a terrorist organization with ties to a global network."

Discovering that Brassington had been Wallace Hilliard's unnamed heroin co-pilot at Orlando Executive Airport would also lead us to RussiaGate. Brassington's family was involved in the sale of a huge aluminum plant in Guyana to Oleg Deripaska, one of Vladimir Putin's richest oligarchs.

It also led to our finding out he was also the No. 1 pilot of Turks and Caicos' Premier Michael Misick, a fact that would have provided him with diplomatic immunity during his days of drug smuggling.

It's all a part of transnational organized crime – what we call "Gangster Planet."

Skyway Communications – the scam involving the Kovar family – was only the tip of a much bigger, hidden iceberg, we discovered. The hidden iceberg was a money-laundering network that used a company called Argyll Equities based in Boerne, Texas and LaJolla, California.

Investigating the Argyll fraud also gave us a shocking glimpse of a cult involved in pedophilia, foreign missions, and biomedical testing. Along the way we learned about goats' blood, SF-1019, Stanford Research Institute, Myron DuBain, Fireman's Fund Insurance. And yes, even American Express had a role. "Don't leave home without it!"

Staring at the "Big Picture" before us, we had to compare it with what we already knew about the CIA's inglorious past while asking ourselves: "Is this how the world really works?"

It's long been my opinion that once the CIA acquires an airplane, it doesn't sell it. Often the plane is just "parked" with someone with whom it has an ongoing relationship – knowing there will always be another need for a jet at a later date.

That "someone" may be a leasing company like the one that furnished planes to Barry Seal. It could also be an insurance company, or even a company that holds title through a long-term lease. The contracts denoting these interests in the plane all show up as part of the FAA documents, which resemble old real estate Abstracts of Title – with one document after another crammed between two covers.

It requires a legal professional to read and interpret each document to give an opinion of the owner, lienholder, and rights of any other parties in the airplane. Linda Minor, my coauthor, spent her legal career examining such documents in the field of real property (land).

What put me onto the trail of a "hyena pack" based in Sarasota County was a combination of reporting by Chris Anderson of the *Sarasota Herald-Tribune* and a call from a local man named Joey Barquin.

Anderson wrote an article for his paper on April 24, 2018, which quoted from Sarasota County Sheriff's reports filed after visits to Andrew Badolato's residence at Casey Key, an island off the mainland of Venice and Nokomis, Florida:

> "*Male resident refused to pay housekeeper unless she performed sexual favors.*"

> "*This is part of your job. Think of yourself as my dirty slut.*"[1]

The Sheriff 's reports indicated three or more women made allegations of rape against Andy Badolato between 2006 and 2010. One was a babysitter, and two were hopeful models who clearly did not know what they were getting into when they flew thousands of miles to Sarasota for a "photo shoot on the beach," only to be forced to commit sexual acts for Badolato's gratification.

Joey Barquin, who had been victimized as an orphan, found Andy's behavior so abhorrent, he began telling what he knew about the so-called investment manager's other activities. None of it was pretty or impressive.

Through Joey's first-hand encounters, I learned that a transnational criminal network of American Mobsters, Florida Republicans, and Russian gangsters had been engaged in massive financial crime for decades in Sarasota County.

Grifters and criminals, with ties to Donald Trump, included Steve Bannon, Andrew Badolato, and Jonathan Curshen. To name only a few. You'll meet them in subsequent chapters.

Adnan Khashoggi, who died in 2017, was still alive when most of the events mentioned in this book occurred, and he was well acquainted with wealthy and powerful men – offhand I can't name a single woman except Maggie Thatcher – involved in the global network.

The CIA began "using" Khashoggi in the early 1960s to help it accomplish the foreign policy goals of whichever party had control of the White House. Those goals always included sales of weapons systems, Adnan's specialty.

Adnan's reputation has since been plastered over, all but forgotten. Google the name "Khashoggi" today and you bring up his nephew Jamal, seemingly far removed from Adnan's notorious past.

In the mid-1980s Adnan took on a protégé, Ramy El-Batrawi, who acted as a cutout for the Khashoggi enterprises after Adnan was prosecuted with Imelda Marcos by none other than Rudy Giuliani in New York. Adnan then sought to cash in on the fall of the Soviet Union, teaming up with global fraudsters who found their way into the Skyway covert operation.

Before Khashoggi came on the scene, Claire Chennault, William Pawley and other operatives built and financed an American-controlled Chinese Air Force, intended to strengthen the US position against Japan before WWII. They used the Asian division of the Office of Strategic Services (OSS), which, in the process, "discovered" the opium pipeline in that area and passed the information down to the CIA, created in 1947.

Roosevelt's "boys" who designed the legal infrastructure for proprietary companies fronting for China Airways left a model for future corporatization of covert activities carried out for the decades that followed. Paul Helliwell, George Doole, and William Barr each had roles in keeping the CIA's hand on the tiller – as well as helping Republicans win elections.

In building up the Southeast Asian opium pipeline, the CIA had neglected to pay attention to what had been so carefully protected when the Marshall Plan had funneled American dollars to Europe by the process of "counterpart" funds.

In fact, the CIA had fucked up so badly by the time Richard Nixon came to office in 1969 that the global monetary imbalance required the CIA to take drastic steps to protect the US economy then suffering from horrific inflation.

The opium pipeline had to be transported from Asia and France into the sphere of influence of the United States. With advice from Nelson Rockefeller, Nixon learned how to train American pilots like Kenneth Burnstine to import drugs into the US, not from the port in Marseilles, but from Colombia, South America by way of Mexico and the Caribbean.

The cover for the operation was Nixon's own "War on Drugs," a psychological operation worthy of CIA praise. They should have won an international prize for the name. Something equivalent to the Nobel "Peace" Prize named for the family famous for manufacturing TNT.

Or maybe the Pablo Escobar "Anti-Drugs" Prize?

Psy-ops deserve appropriately ironic names.

Covert operations stem from their planners' arrogance and deceit, as they manipulate huge markets of goods traded all over the world. They tinker with global currencies, often bankrupting entire countries. These handlers feel no need to explain their actions to anyone.

For centuries those engaged in this arrogant deception have called it "the Great Game." The game is outside the role of democratic governance, and the players' names have never appeared on any ballot. We, the people, are told nothing about what they do in our name.

The public has no "need to know," we are told. It's none of our business.

In our own way, Investigative reporters are equally arrogant. We do not accept at face value what we've been told. We dig deeper. We ask questions. We even look under the rocks where slime and vermin tend to hide.

Much of the drug trafficking profiled in this book can be traced back to Clearwater-St. Petersburg International Airport, located in Pinellas County, a few miles north of where I lived after 2001.

The financial fraud I discovered, which related to washing the drug profits–commonly known as money- laundering–was taking place much closer to my home in Sarasota County.

If you manage to discover hidden secrets, you'll learn just how difficult it becomes to talk about the secrets, let alone publish your work in print. Gary Webb – may he rest in peace – learned that lesson. He called the collusion a "dark alliance" between the CIA and its drug smuggling friends.

To this day, so much obfuscation exists that most people still don't know what to believe about his articles and the books about him. He's even credited with a posthumous movie, *Kill the Messenger*, which we hope his family collected royalties on. I wrote *Barry and 'the boys'* and collected not one red cent when *American Made* came out, credited to a different author. But at least I had the satisfaction of knowing my version was true.

There are questions that journalists – uniformly, in countries around the world – are strongly encouraged not to ask. Many – if not most – concern the drug trade, an illicit industry that, in its contribution to world trade, dwarfs any other. Its tentacles can be seen slithering into the legitimate economy, even into major media companies.

When Mexican Drug Lord Carlos Slim bought a piece of the *New York Times* a few years back, it wasn't because he saw a great future in print media.

Most of us know instinctively that we will not "succeed" by telling the unvarnished truth. So, we fib a little, or a lot. Our continued salary, as Upton Sinclair was quick to remind us, depends on it.

During the Great Recession that hit in the fall of 2008, the official at the UN in charge of the yearly global drug report declared in interviews that, if it were not for huge pools of drug money constantly being laundered through the banking system, every major Western bank would have failed.

Drug money, he said, in so many words, provided the world's banks with their only source of liquidity. It's a frightening reality.

Fast fact: Drug trafficking is the most widespread and lucrative organized crime activity on our *Gangster Planet*. It accounts for as much as one-half of the revenue of transnational organized crime –which is what we see all around us today.

Part of this book is about how proceeds of criminal activity have turned a planet once composed of separate nations into one global interdependent mass of money-movers. Transnational organized crime seems to have control.

If you're considering a career in transnational organized crime, and looking for an area of specialization, consider the mountain of cash proceeds from drug trafficking, which reaches dizzyingly skyward into the death zone.

That revenue dwarfs the proceeds of all other criminal activities of organized crime combined: extortion, loan sharking, bribery, sex trafficking, and human trafficking. It's the elephant in the room. It's the biggest slush fund on the planet. It buys anything it wants. The revenue from such criminal activity makes transnational organized crime stronger than any single nation-state on Planet Earth. It's that revenue which has helped to make our planet a *Gangster Planet.*

I saw it in action, at least on the micro level. Because of my investigative focus on drug trafficking, with my base in Florida, it played out before my eyes, though I did note that some of the members of the Florida network had out-of-state connections.

In his book *Disloyal,* Michael Cohen, Donald Trump's former personal attorney, revealed that he grew up hanging around the El Caribe Country Club, owned by his Uncle Morty a few miles east of Brighton Beach. There 'made guys' were frequent visitors.

His Uncle Morty's joint, Cohen then tells us casually, was also – coincidentally?– the headquarters of the Russian Mob in America. Trump's attorney and fixer Michael Cohen could pick up the phone and reach out to Russian gangsters he may have known since he was a kid. They were fingertip-close. Who knew?

This fact added a completely different spin on RussiaGate. It also brings Russia directly into the focus of our story, as we will show.

The "deep state" is supposed to be sinister, according to Donald Trump. He says it's the Deep State that's out to take him down. But in sunny Palm Beach Florida we saw little that was sinister, until we started seeing stacks of classified files stored in Mar-a-Lago's gold-plated bathrooms.

Before the first ballot had been cast in 2016 Donald Trump was worrying out loud that "they" – the deep state – were going to steal the election. That was said, of course, to protect his position if he lost. Like the boy who cried 'wolf,' however, Trump and his minions began to repeat it so often, the term lost its import to most of us.

I knew, however, on election night 2020 Trump was hatching a coup. I told my coauthor, who was in Venice to work on the book and watch election returns. She reminded me later I'd been so adamant about it, she left early to drive to Texas before the hurricane du jour crossed her path.

"You were so sure," she said, "that I couldn't see how we'd get anything else done on the book until it was all over."

Not until after January 6, 2021, did Linda – politically savvy in her own right, even if less instinctive than me – realize a coup had long been in progress. When I'd first heard mutterings of stopping the ballot count on election night, I just knew something sinister was in the works. Everything that happened between then and January 6 just confirms it.

Daniel Hopsicker

June 14, 2023

CHAPTER ONE

POLITICS OF CONTRABAND

The sailors and the pilots,
The soldiers and the law
The payoffs and the rip-offs,
And the things nobody saw.
— Glenn Frey, "Smuggler's Blues"

It was 3 o'clock in the morning – literally the middle of the night. Except if you knew me, you'd know I generally work nights and take naps during the day, so it was all good. My phone was ringing. A tipster I won't identify had just heard the news and immediately thought of me. Something big had just happened, he said. There was a huge seizure of cocaine in Mexico yesterday. But that wasn't what was so urgent.

The plane involved, he said, was connected with Venice, Florida – where I lived.

"Read your email," he told me quickly before hanging up.

An American-registered DC-9 was caught with 5.5 tons of cocaine... the email began.

The company the plane was registered to, wrote the tipster, is someone named Frederic Geffon, and lists an address in its ads in *Trade-A-Plane* [a trade magazine] as 224 E. Airport Avenue at the Venice Airport.

That's your area, son.

My friend had clearly been tracking the information as it happened, then looked up the tail number to get the owner's name.

The address at Venice Airport, I already knew, was the hangar where the now-defunct Huffman Aviation used to park its planes. And what he meant by "your area" – it's in my "area" – my remit, my beat. It's arcane information to anyone else. Huffman Aviation flight school – remember the blue awning in the background of thousands of newsclips in the days after 9/11 – had been owned by Wally Hilliard, whose legend, or cover story, was as a retired insurance executive from Green Bay, Wisconsin.

Oddly for a recent Florida retiree, just a few months after moving to Naples, he'd purchased 30-40 jets, according to his jet manager. Without putting too fine a point on it, that's a lot of planes for a retired guy.

I let the information sink in, deciding I'd pick up some coffee on my way to the airport. I wondered if I'd detect any changes since I'd been there last.

A half-hour later, after throwing on some sweatpants, I was cruising the perimeter at the silent Venice Municipal Airport. There was something strange and vaguely sinister about the place that night, though I couldn't put my finger on why. From where I'd parked at the northeast side of the airport, I could hear trapezes at the old Ringling circus grounds swishing and banging in the wind, emitting an eerie chime that sent a chill down my spine.

It just felt wrong, especially at 4 A.M., with not a soul around. The only movement came from the runway lights blinking on and off, pointing a neon finger over the hundred-mile-thick black waters of the Gulf of Mexico in the middle of the night.

What it was, was *spooky*.

I knew there were some nice big shade trees planted along the airport apron, and I'd at times wondered what Mohamed Atta thought about them as he taxied by, while practicing touch-and-goes. I couldn't see them in the dark. There was nothing to see, so I went home.

* * *

Years earlier, when I'd interviewed the Police Chief of Venice, the first thing he did as he got up from his desk was to throw his hands up in a universal "wasn't me" gesture.

"Don't blame us for what went on," he said, shaking his head. "We had no jurisdiction out there. It was strictly a federal deal."

"The Venice Municipal Airport," he said slowly, "has always been the kind of place where everything's dead quiet all night, and then a Blackhawk helicopter swoops in, lands, and takes off again thirty seconds later." It could have been the ghosts of those helicopters that spooked me.

The next day, following my tipster's lead, I found the plane ads for *Royal Sons, LLC,* a company registered at a hangar at the Clearwater-St. Petersburg Airport, and owned – according to the Florida Division of Corporations – by Frederic Geffon. The tip was, it seemed, dead on.

The FAA registration for the DC-9 airliner carrying tail number "N900SA," once I got my hands on it weeks later, would also list Frederic Geffon as the Royal Sons owner. Tail numbers are similar to license plates, but they're far less accurate.

The government knows far more about a VW camper stopped at the border with a few pot seeds than it does about the ownership of huge forty- million dollar Gulfstreams, and other luxury jets.

This is not, by the way, incidental information. It's not a glitch. It's a feature. The government wants it that way.

Anyway, Frederic Geffon. An *American*. This should be interesting.

DC-9 That Couldn't

Monday, the 10th of April 2006, had already been a bad day for an aging DC-9 jetliner bearing tail number N900SA. After taking off shortly after 12:00 noon from Maquieta Airport outside Caracas, Venezuela, the plane had returned … twice.

The third departure had put the DC-9 way behind schedule. Most major drug busts begin with mechanical difficulties as their root cause. This flight, we at first thought, fit that profile.

It was like a scene out of a spy movie. The airliner based at a hangar at St Petersburg, Florida, had been flying weekly charter flights to Venezuela and back … for 39 straight weeks. Then the routine is broken, causing the plane to make an emergency stop at an airport in the state of Campeche, Mexico, three hours from the nearest city of any size.

What's up with that?

In 2006 the small airport at Ciudad del Carmen closed every night at 6 P.M, and it was already well past that time, half an hour past closing time, with the last rays of sunlight glinting off the wings of the sleek silver American DC-9 airliner, circling the airport, waiting for permission to land.

The city, on the edge of a jungle as vast as an ocean, is turning from green to purple in the twilight – no doubt a picturesque scene from the air. Ciudad del Carmen below cannot be confused for a posh resort like Cancun, located 350 miles to the east on Yucatan's more fashionable Caribbean coast. It's a hardscrabble oil town on the Gulf of Mexico, sweltering and smelling of crude oil.

You won't see tourists being towed around in the air by speedboat. It's called the PEMEX Riviera. Oil drilling rigs outnumber ancient Mayan ruins.

It's the last place you'd expect to see big-time *Miami Vice*-style drug trafficking. Maybe that's what made it perfect for the scene about to play out below.

"SHROUDED IN MYSTERY"

We know for a fact that the DC-9 jetliner bearing tail number N900SA, based at Clearwater-St. Pete International, had left Florida on April 5th, bound for Venezuela and, ultimately, its rendezvous with destiny, to repeat a hackneyed but catchy phrase. That destiny was finally playing out five days later.

My first story about this flight appeared at the *Mad Cow News* website on April 17, 2006 – only a week after the bust. My knowledge was limited at first. Known was the fact the bust netted 5.5 tons of cocaine, seized on an American plane registered to Royal Sons, LLC, a Florida entity set up by Ron Gregory, attorney for Frederic J. Geffon, filed with the Secretary of State on September 13, 2005. Royal Sons gave its address as 15875 Fairchild Drive in Clearwater, a hangar where the airport's fixed based operator, Jet Executive Center, was situated.

News reports about the drug bust barely trickled out of Mexico or Venezuela and were almost non-existent in the United States. One exception: The *Tampa Tribune* had published several full pages almost a month after the event, stating ominously that the plane's "journey is shrouded in mystery."

Thanks to Google Translate, I had been able to follow foreign-language sources such as the excellent coverage by *Proceso*, a news magazine in Mexico. In an impromptu press conference held early the next morning, Alejandro Jacinto Carro Bautista, commander of the 33rd Military Zone, announced the arrest of three pilots. One had been aboard the DC-9 and was a Venezuelan named Miguel Vicente Vázquez Guerra. The other two pilots arrested were from Mexico. He stated also that the cocaine seized was "allegedly destined for various cartels."

Each of the various groups at the scene was reportedly suspicious of the others. *Proceso* quoted the commander having said: "The one who arranges the planes in Ciudad del Carmen is probably one of those involved, since he had illuminated signs in his hands to guide the plane to land near the Falcon, and he told my sergeant that the man with him was a PFP (Policía Federal Preventiva) agent, which I doubt."[3]

Proceso also indicated the presence at the press conference of a contingent of personnel from the Attorney General's Office (PGR), as well as two sections of soldiers from the 10th Infantry Battalion, based in Campeche, and the 11th Motorized Cavalry Regiment, based in Escárcega, to help unload and transport the cocaine to the 33rd Military Zone headquarters.

There's no doubt that this press conference had a role in the decision to freeze information coming out of the PGR office. President Vicente Fox was running for reelection in July, and the party in power did not want any negative news about possible involvement in drug trafficking by anyone in his administration leaking out before then.

Three months after I'd begun my investigation, Proceso finally announced in mid-July that the freeze had been a "strategy of the federal government to hide the alleged involvement of senior officials of the PFP in one of the largest drug trafficking operations in this six-year term."[4]

The La Policía Federal Preventiva (PFP), a police force trained by the FBI at Quantico, whose main mission, ironically, was to enforce Mexico's laws against drug trafficking, had been a total failure during its short seven years of life, as the DC-9 bust soon revealed. According to *Proceso's* unnamed sources who furnished the investigation file, Mexico's *entire airport network was being operated in the service of the drug cartels.*[5]

WHERE IS THE AMERICAN PABLO ESCOBAR?

On April 11, a day after the big bust, Mexican General Carlos Gaytan showed up and held a second news conference. His soldiers, who were ringing the airport in Ciudad del Carmen the previous day, had unfortunately been unable to apprehend the plane's pilot, he told reporters. The "disappeared" pilot had slithered through a crack in the line of soldiers and escaped. Or so the story went.

The captain of the DC-9 had left the aircraft to do an errand concerning flight plans, then managed to evade authorities by climbing over the airport perimeter fence. Somebody in a Volkswagen picked him up, and he was gone.

Unfortunately, he apparently had the presence of mind to take his name with him when he fled. Ten days later, he remained unidentified.

In the press briefing, General Gaytan quickly pointed out that his men had, at least, managed to arrest the plane's Venezuelan co-pilot, as well as two Mexican pilots who showed up early at the airport in a Falcon 20 business jet, filled out forms and paid fees to enable the DC-9 to land, and then just hung around, spending a day slouching around the airport.

The Falcon jet belonged to the Mexican government's Federal Water Commission. The pilots – Fernando Poot and Marco Aurelio Perez – were government employees. The two men had a lot in common. Both were ex-military, and both had gone to prison in 1999 for flying drugs through the airport of Toluca.

I wondered: so how come the General can't get them to give up one name? Couldn't the General's people just rough them up a little? Just till they remembered the name of the escaped pilot?

Apparently not.

That's when I began to get upset. Americans seem to do okay in other areas of organized crime. Our stock swindlers and fraud merchants are the envy of the Underworld. But we apparently have neglected to nurture any home-grown American Drug Lords, and once again ambitious young Americans looking for role models for future careers, had been disappointed.

Were we fated to import our Drug Lords from South America forever, like we do with junior welterweights?

When the DC-9 was busted, I thought, at last! At long last we're going to get an American Drug Lords. Americans yearned for a few drug kingpins who weren't named "Pablo" or "Juan."

After all, the plane had come from St. Petersburg in the sunny orange-juice-filled state of Florida. The DC-9 was even American-registered.

Other countries had even been taunting us.

"Where is the Pablo Escobar of Texas?" Colombian Vice President Francisco Santos had once asked with a knowing wink on a visit to Houston. "I would love to know."[6]

Former Mexican President Vicente Fox shared Santos' concern. "That is the question I always ask myself," said Fox, during a speaking tour of the U.S. "Who permits the drugs to cross the border, and who transports the drugs to the markets of this great nation?"[7]

We were being mocked to our face.

And that's when I learned a bitter lesson about my country. We aren't ever going to have any Drug Lords of our own. I don't know why. Ask the DEA.

MAIQUETÍA, NEAR CARACAS, VENEZUELA

Intrigue was intense before takeoff, according to a file *Proceso* obtained from the Sub-Prosecutor's Office for Specialized Investigation in Organized Crime (SIEDO) in Mexico.[7] We later learned the witnesses had lied – surprise, surprise – changing names to protect the guilty.

Captain Jose Lopez was the pilot, we were incorrectly informed by this file, who had hired Venezuelan co-pilot, Miguel Vicente Vázquez Guerra only two days earlier for this trip. *Proceso* reported these details as fact, relying on the investigation file containing raw data that had not been thoroughly vetted.

"Let's go to Mexico, friend. It's a cargo flight and there will be good pay," Vazquez Guerra quoted the man who hired him, trying to make himself look less culpable. They'd arrived at a figure of $200 per hour on top of $250 a day, plus travel expenses and special treatment upon his arrival in Mexico, including accommodation in a luxury hotel. He even paid him $2500 in advance.[8]

At around noon, the pilots headed to the DC-9 (N900SA), parked at the Venezuelan airport. While the captain was in contact with the drug traffickers, Miguel Vázquez Guerra conducted the required inspections: He checked the tires, measured the amount of fuel, walked around the aircraft to check if it had any dents or any damage, and then made his way up to the cabin.

Miguel claimed in his statements that he did not ask anything about the contents of 128 suitcases which he observed inside the plane, nor did he inquire why there were no passengers.

He simply settled into his seat. The plane's turbines started up without any problem.

Meanwhile, in Mexican Airports

Respected Mexican reporter and author Ricardo Ravelo, who still writes for *Proceso*, traveled to Ciudad del Carmen in the days following the drug seizure. He interviewed airport personnel and eyewitnesses, trying to get their varied stories straight.

The stories told by witnesses, who reported both to Ravelo and to official investigators, led them to conclude that the airport was swirling with intrigue several days before the DC-9 showed up on April 10.

"The strangest thing was the behavior of some agents of the Federal Police PFP who showed up unannounced in the terminal," an airport employee told Ravelo. "They seemed highly agitated."[9]

Ravelo, author of several books on drug cartels in Mexico, would turn out to be one of the best sources on what happened that day and the following few months.[10]

Airport official Jorge Perez Ochoa told Ravelo, "On the evening before the DC-9 came in, Ramon Gonzalez Virgen, a member of the intelligence wing of the Federal Police (PFP) showed up at the airport." He was there, said Perez, to install software which automatically registered landings. With some urgency, he said he needed to meet with all officials working in the terminal.[11]

"They told us we were going to be receiving an American-registered flight coming from Mérida," an anonymous airport employee told Ravelo, and "since it was an internal flight, it wouldn't need to clear Customs."[12]

The airport employee asked not to be named, Ravelo wrote. They all did, everyone out at the airport wanted to be invisible. When they spoke, it was in a low tone of voice, amid frequent nervous furtive glances. Most of the airport's regular security detail made themselves scarce. The smart ones – including several suspected of involvement in drug trafficking, called in sick.

Ramon Gonzalez Virgen, the alleged intelligence man from PFP, wanted to discuss with Perez Ochoa an "economic adjustment" to allow the DC-9 to land the next day, he claimed, though neglecting to mention it was loaded with 5.5 tons of cocaine.

Two other agents had traveled with Ramon to the city from their headquarters but never showed up at the airport. "Someone back at their hotel had stolen their briefcases," Perez Ochoa related, a fact seemingly unrelated to the subject. [13] But who knows?

"Get Some Pepper for the Drug-Sniffing Dog"

As many as a dozen Federal PFP officers may have been working to ensure the success of this one drug move – five of them in Cuidad del Carmen alone. Instead of working against the drug move, which was their official job, they were there to facilitate the flow by preventing airport personnel from calling in the Mexican military.

At least four PFP officers were stationed at the flight's scheduled destination – Toluca Airport in Mexico – on the morning of April 10. Their role was to reach an "economic arrangement" with – or, in simple terms, to bribe – the tax and military police to allow the DC-9 with its huge shipment of drugs to land there without any inspection.

A couple of hours before takeoff was scheduled in the early afternoon, PFP officers were nervous. All their efforts with the Fiscal Police had been refused. Offers had climbed as high as $1,500 per kilogram of cocaine, they later told investigators. The reason? The bribes were not enough money for such a huge risk. But none of those approached had ratted out the bribers. Perhaps they were thinking toward the future.

That same morning at Ciudad del Carmen PFP agents arrived in force. The airport had just gotten a K-9 officer with a trained drug dog to sniff out narcotics. José Ángel Uc May, the handler for the dog, named "Destreza," told investigators that at around four in the afternoon he had noticed three men, each wearing the distinctive uniform of the PFP – white guayabera shirts with a star pinned to the right front pocket and dark trousers – just loitering in the airport.

"One I had seen in the airport before, asking about our drug-sniffing dog, things like what drugs could he detect? What aromas does he identify? Could the dog identify the aroma of urine, marijuana and cocaine?"[14]

A second PFP agent had seemed extremely nervous as he moved from one place inside the airport to another, asking the staff members at Airports and Auxiliary Services (ASA) questions. Uc May described him as having a dark complexion and being of average height, 170 cm (5'7").

Uc May had walked away from him, only to meet the third PFP-uniformed man. Seeing so many officials on the same day was suspicious enough, but the questions they asked made him especially wary.

PLANE WITHOUT PASSENGERS

At least the airport is still open almost an hour past closing time and is cleared to land. As it approaches the main runway, smoke is visible around one of the tires. Firefighters rush to the plane, which lands, then taxies past the main terminal, coming to rest in a remote darkened corner of the tarmac.

A gold-bordered blue stripe runs down the fuselage with an official-looking blue-and-gold Seal over the cockpit door. The motif seems familiar: an American eagle clutching an olive branch in its talons. But there the resemblance ends. The words running around the outside of the seal are distinctly non-governmental: "Skyway Aircraft: Protection of America's Skies."

Could this plane, observers may have wondered, be carrying government diplomats or potentates flying back to Washington from a recent conference at a posh hotel in Cancun, ironically, on drug interdiction?

The pilot waves the fire fighters away, insisting on refueling immediately – a request that makes no sense if the aircraft is on fire.

Realizing he is unsuccessful in keeping the firemen and other intruders at bay, the pilot quickly disappears, taking his name with him.

Although the DC-9 is listed as a charter flight, soldiers who board with guns drawn quickly notice there are no passengers onboard. The charter flight with no passengers carries only 128 identical black leather suitcases. Each suitcase bears a stamp on its side: "Privado."

It was a warning. Much like the signs you see on fences saying, "Posted, Keep Out." Each suitcase, they found, was stuffed to bursting with tightly packed kilos of cocaine. Each package was stamped with a symbol – a scorpion, a star, a horse – meant to identify its owner.

The DC-9 carried what was until then an almost unheard-of quantity of cocaine: 5.5 tons. It was the biggest coke bust on an airplane – at least for a time – in the history of Mexico, a benighted country located, as its citizens say, "So far from God, so close to the USA."

THE BACK STORY

Why was this particular plane, which had been making what's known in drug parlance as a "milk run," since around July 1, 2005, without incident, interdicted on April 10, 2006? Although I didn't know it at the time, that question was to form the central point of my drug investigation for the remainder of my life.

July 2005, I learned, preceded Geffon's creation of Royal Sons, LLC, but not Geffon's own involvement with this plane, based at a hangar at Pinellas International Airport – with call letters PIE – more commonly known as St Pete/Clearwater International Airport, though it had a yet-unknown connection to another hangar located at Venice Municipal Airport.

"Royal Sons Motor Yacht Sales, Inc. DBA Royal Sons" had joined with Skyway Communications Holding Corp., in procuring a $1.5 million loan from United Bank and Trust Company in St. Petersburg, Florida, seemingly as part of the purchase price for the DC-9 from HW Aviation's Jeff Wolfson in Chicago, along with Skyway stock allegedly worth $2.5 million, the *Tampa Tribune* had reported on May 4, 2006. Copies were included in the FAA title abstract.

The public corporation, then called Skyway Communication Holding Corp., had been in the middle of losing $40 million between 2002 and its last annual report before filing bankruptcy in January 2005.

I had to ask how a company that deep in the red could afford one DC-9, let alone two, as I discovered later. Brent Kovar, Skyway's president, must have been expecting the planes to bring in some revenue that would justify purchasing two jets valued in the multi-millions.

This flight, it must be emphasized, was not an ordinary flight. It was singularly exceptional because it still holds the record as the biggest coke bust on an airplane in the entire history of the benighted country of Mexico, which its citizens say is located "so far from God, so close to the USA." That had to be a pretty steep hill to climb. It even, for a time, made the list of the Top Ten Drug Seizures in World History.

"Cocaine One"

Today drug seizures making news are usually much bigger: 6-ton, 12-ton, even 33-tons of cocaine. But in 2006, this was not yet commonplace. The idea that somebody was flying boxcar-sized loads of cocaine into Mexico was still a novelty. The role of the drug trade in our national life is a big taboo and way bigger than anyone will admit.

Street value is how the DEA usually figures the worth of a load in its own press releases ... except in those rare cases when it's trying to minimize things, as had been done in this case.

It would become the emblematic drug story of our times. This particular cocaine bust, as we will see, was only the first in a series of them that took so many surprising turns that, were it a Hollywood pitch, it would be rejected out of hand as not being believable enough.

Among its many mysteries is why the seizure of such a mountain of cocaine met with such stony silence in the U.S. media. No one in the US major media ran with the story.

I quickly dubbed the plane "Cocaine One." To my surprise, the name stuck. For the next year and a half, I was the only one investigating, at least in the U.S. I had the field to myself. It was like I had a secret. *And it felt a little lonely.*

Endnotes

1   Howard Altman and Karen Branch-Brioso, *Tampa Tribune*, May 04, 2006, pp. 1,6.

2   "Plane with 5.5 tons of cocaine seized in Campeche," *Proceso*, April 12, 2006. https://www-proceso-com-mx.translate.goog/nacional/2006/4/12/decomisado-en-campeche-avion-con-55-toneladas-de-cocaina-42519.html?_x_tr_sl=auto&_x_tr_tl=en&_x_tr_hl=en&_x_tr_pto=wapp}

3   Ibid.

4   Ibid.

5   Editor, "The hidden history of the narcoplane," *Proceso*, July 16, 2006 (as translated). https://www-proceso-com-mx.translate.goog/nacional/2006/7/16/la-historia-oculta-del-narcoavion-1237.html?_x_tr_sl=es&_x_tr_tl=en&_x_tr_ hl=en&_x_tr_pto=sc (accessed 12/26/2022).

6   Ibid.

7   Dane Schiller, "Where are the big drug bosses this side of border?" *Houston Chronicle*, Oct 9, 2007. https://www.chron.com/news/houston-texas/article/Where-are-the-big-drug-bosses-this-side-of-border-1622364.php

8   Ibid.

9   Editor, "La historia oculta del narcoavión," *Proceso*. https://www.proceso.com.mx/nacional/2006/7/16/la-historia-oculta-del-narcoavion-1237.html

10   Ibid.

11   Gustavo Cano, Ph. D., Director of the Transnationalism Research Project, mentions Ravelo in a bibliography prepared for the Mexican Research Network published January 9, 2015. He states: "The work of Ravelo (2011), mostly the historical part, is very important to understand the formation and consolidation of narco-trafficking of organized crime in Mexico." The reference is to his book published only in Spanish in 2011 entitled *El narco en Mexico. Historia e historias de una guerra,* which was published in Barcelona by Grupo Editorial Grijalbo, an imprint of Random House.   https://www.publishersweekly.com/pw/print/20010723/39385-grupo-editorial-random-house-mondadori-launched.html (accessed 12/26/2022).

12   Ibid.

13   "The hidden history of the drug plane," July 16, 2006. *Proceso* (as translated). https://www-proceso-com-mx.translate.goog/nacional/2006/7/16/la-historia-oculta-del-narcoavion-1237.html?_x_tr_sl=es&_x_tr_tl=en&_x_tr_hl=en&_x_tr_pto=sc (accessed January 12, 2023).

14   Ibid.

Chapter Two

Right Here In Pinellas County

> *Well, ya got trouble, my friend, right here,*
> *I say, trouble right here in Pinellas County.*
> *— The Music Man*, paraphrased

At least, I commiserated with myself, "if the Central Intelligence Agency (CIA) couldn't own the drugs, our government could at least own the planes that carried them."

Clearwater's Skyway Owns A Drug Plane

The DC-9 had been registered to Frederic Geffon's Royal Sons, LLC in St. Petersburg, Florida. So I began there. It was close to home.

Geffon eventually told reporters he had sold the DC-9 (N900SA) to an airplane broker from Simi Valley, California named Jorge Corrales – a man totally unknown in the business. The market for DC-9's, I quickly learned, is not a hot one. There were only three airplane brokers in the U.S. who sold them.

The man who told me that was one of the three. And he'd never heard of Jorge Corrales.

U.S. authorities made no statements identifying the organization involved in the massive drug move. Nor did they address serious questions with obvious national security implications. Five questions came to my mind, just for starters:

- Why was an airliner allowed to impersonate an official Dept of Homeland Security aircraft?

- How did it then end up being owned by crooks boasting of American intelligence connections?

- How did it become involved in drug smuggling?

- On whose behalf did all that coke take wing?

- How is it that the owner of an airliner carrying 5.5 tons of cocaine remains unidentified?

You could almost hear the leather shoe soles of FAA officials creaking, as they back-pedaled away from the case as fast as their little feet could carry them. Nobody was talking. Not the FAA. And not the former owner of the plane, who had at first coyly refused to divulge the name of the buyer to whom it was sold.

More than ten weeks (that's two and a half months!) after the seizure, the FAA finally released ownership records for the plane.

The reason for the FAA's foot-dragging became immediately clear. They did not want to have to admit that the document informing the FAA that the DC-9 had been sold and exported to Venezuela wasn't submitted until the *day after* its drug seizure in Mexico.

Roland Herwig, FAA spokesman, had told Howard Altman of the *Tampa Tribune* the FAA received a copy of a letter *dated April 7*, sent by Royal Sons asking that the plane be exported to Venezuela.[1]

After the massive cocaine bust, the FAA officially took Royal Sons' name off the books.

FAA officials, however, carefully avoided stating when change of ownership documents were actually *received* by the FAA, citing merely the date typed on the letter, April 7,[th] as if that provided definitive proof.

But ... the change of ownership docs *were not mailed* to the FAA. They were *faxed*. Fax numbers at the bottom of the letter indicate it was faxed to Geffon and Corrales just minutes after being submitted to the FAA – on April 11, a day after the bust.

The documents submitted by Geffon had been *backdated!*

FAA registration information available online when the story first broke indicated that the DC-9 (N900SA) was registered to Frederic Geffon's Royal Sons, Inc., an aircraft sales company set up by his father in 1995. Seven years after Stanley Geffon died in 1998, Fred Geffon created Royal Sons, LLC, an air charter company, as a subsidiary.

The FAA listed it as the last registered American owner of "Cocaine One." When questioned, however, Geffon would say nothing except to mention bankruptcy proceedings in Tampa involving Skyway Communications, whose principals were Brent and Glenn Kovar.

In particular, he wouldn't say why his own company, Royal Sons LLC, had given its address in an ad in *Trade-A-Plane* as the same Venice Airport hangar where Huffman Aviation had parked its planes five years earlier. Was that simply a typo? Or was there a more sinister connection?

So, we asked around Venice Airport. No one there admitted to having heard of the company Royal Sons, nor did the names of its two principals – Frederic Geffon or Ron Gregory – ring any bells.

In an exclusive interview with me before the May 2, 2006, edition of the *Mad Cow Morning News*, Geffon couldn't, or wouldn't, say who bought the plane from him, merely stating, "The DC-9 was no longer my concern when it left the general aviation terminal at Clearwater-St. Pete on April 5th, heading for Caracas."[1]

The FAA had accepted back-dated documents claiming falsely that the plane had been exported before the bust, but it would not say to whom the title had been transferred. They didn't care what you did with the planes, they shrugged. They just registered them. Or, in the case of a plane sold to someone with a foreign address, de-registered them.

The DEA was even worse. They deliberately low-balled the value of the 5.5 tons of cocaine that had been seized, estimating its value as $100 million. The United Nations Office on Drugs and Crime (UNODC), in contrast, valued a bust in Ecuador the previous March at more than a half billion dollars. A $446 million discrepancy!

Asked if they were investigating the American side of the 5.5 ton bust, the Tampa DEA office issued a terse "no comment."

That was still pretty much where things stood four months after the April seizure in Mexico of more than five tons of cocaine. The story had reached a stalemate, for everyone but me.

VEIL COVERING BLACK HOLE LIFTED

By the first week of August, I was off and running with what I'd found out, working on my own in little Venice, Florida. Remembering not to bury the lead, I titled my next story, "Cocaine One Bust Lifts Veil on Global Narcotics Cartel." Was that too subtle?

> A DC-9 registered to a company which once used as its address the hanger of Huffman Aviation, the flight school at the Venice, FL Airport which trained two terrorist pilots who crashed planes into the World Trade Center, was caught in Campeche by the Mexican military April 10th carrying 5.5 tons of cocaine destined for the U.S.
>
> Beyond a few half-hearted stabs at pinning blame for the crime on "scapegoats du jour" like the FARC in Colombia or Hugo Chavez in Venezuela, authorities in Mexico and the U.S. have had virtually nothing to say about the case. In the more than three months since, the massive seizure has slipped into a black hole.[2]

My investigation, I continued, was "beginning to pierce the heavy curtain behind which the biggest taboo in the U.S. mainstream media has remained hidden: the identities of the until-now anonymous American Drug Lords."

What I had discovered within those four months was how the money laundering inside an American drug cartel worked. How to explain it, though, was a whole 'nuther thing.

Kovar's "A Scammer"

"All I had to go on at first was a man named Frederic Geffon, born and raised on one of the keys west of Clearwater and St. Petersburg. His grandfather, a Russian immigrant to the United States, and his father, Stanley Geffon, a handsome man who once won a Mario Lanza-lookalike contest, had started a rug selling and cleaning business as early as 1935 in that part of Florida.[5] Stan expanded the business, known as Royal Rug Co., in the late '50s as his sons were born and brought into the business.[6]

Fred, the youngest, worked with his dad in the original shop, which he later took over. When Fred added an aviation business to the family stable of companies, Royal Sons, Inc., he set up a limited liability company under that umbrella.

Royal Sons ran ads in *Trade-A-Plane*, an aviation magazine, using the Venice, Florida, address of 224 E Airport Avenue, which I recognized as soon as I first heard it. I could see the tiny Venice, Florida, airport in my mind and knew the address was that of the hangar where Huffman Aviation parked their planes. Huffman offices were at 400, and 224 was the second hangar to the right, as you faced the office.

Suddenly, the DC-9 drug bust became a big deal. It linked Royal Sons to the same company where Mohamed Atta practiced touch and go's in July 2000, possibly at the same time DEA agents toting sub-machine guns were busting the Learjet belonging to Huffman Aviation flight school owner, Wallace J. Hilliard.

Numerous local news clippings, some reprinted in *Welcome to Terror-Land*, proved that fact beyond a shadow of a doubt. Yet the record-breaking Orlando heroin bust in July 2000 was totally ignored in discussions of Hilliard's flight school's role in the 9/11 attack.

It seemed to me some powerful force was diverting attention from the obvious linkage between the two events.

I was, after weeks of delay – about the same length of time information had been frozen in Mexico because of the election – able to acquire

N900SA's FAA history, which verified that the last registered American buyer/seller of "Cocaine One" was Royal Sons Inc./LLC, the LLC being a subsidiary of Geffon's family's corporation. That's when I again approached Fred Geffon.

"Their company is a scam and he's a scammer. I got sold a bill of goods about his stock. Everybody out here at the Clearwater-St. Pete International airport invested with him, and we all lost it all," he angrily told me. Asked the name of the Venezuelan buyer he sold the plane to, Geffon responded, "I'm not at liberty to say. I've been asked not to say to whom the plane was sold."

Who asked him not to say?

"I've been asked not to say who asked me not to say," he said.

Could he tell us, then, who was piloting the plane when it flew out of Clearwater? "No, because I wasn't looking out the window," he replied. "I was focused on business."

Could the confusion be deliberate? An aviation executive in Venice thought so...

"When it comes to registering airplanes, it's the Wild West out there," he explained. "An airplane is a mobile, big ticket item. Yet there are no airport police doing ramp checks or checking N umbers at airports."[7]

My source continued: "The FAA system for registering airplanes is little changed from when it was started back in the good ol' boy days of the 1930's. Each plane has a paper folder, for example, stuffed with all correspondence regarding airworthiness and ownership relating to that plane. "It's an antiquated system which some feel is kept deliberately in place to encourage a certain ambiguity when a plane is interdicted. When a change of registration is mailed in, the FAA places a plane's folder in what they call 'suspense.'

"That's a tremendous inducement to anyone with a chance of having a plane nabbed to keep floating sales in progress. The CIA, for example, is very adept at keeping files on its planes 'in suspense,'" he added with a look I took to be a smirk.

Did Somebody Say … CIA?

Reading the story today, some fifteen years later, or more, makes me realize how focused I had been at the time. Focus is a sometimes-difficult thing for me. In the late 1980s, after my second divorce, I was diagnosed with attention deficit disorder (ADD), for which the doctor prescribed Adderall. It helped a lot with my ability to focus. So much so, in fact, that I was careful to keep the prescription filled for thirty years or so.

Until, that is, the DEA was put in control and saw fit to cut off the supply for everyone diagnosed with the same or similar condition. That's just one more strike against the DEA in my little black book.

If you ever are lucky enough, as I was, to stick your head into a black hole and emerge from the experience intact, as I did, I hope you can interpret what you saw better than I did at my website on August 23, 2006. Had I missed my Adderall that day? Or was I simply more focused than anyone else on the scene?

What I wrote was pretty much the crux of the story as I then saw it. Repeating for emphasis what the aviation source in Venice I'd consulted told me with an unmistakable smirk, an airliner mistaken for one belonging to the U.S. Government would have definite advantages for a drug smuggler.

"Glenn Kovar told everybody he was with the CIA," Frederic Geffon had told us. "A lot of people at the airport believed him and became investors in his scam."

The question of whether there might be a Central Intelligence Agency connection to a plane loaded with 5.5 tons of cocaine is, to some – you know who you are – like asking if the Pope might be Catholic. Or if a writer about the CIA's role in drug smuggling might be a "conspiracy theorist." I then concluded that one of two things must be true:

> 1. We were either looking at a pattern of systematic ambiguity meant to protect the privacy of the rich and famous, to keep their options open – a pattern which plays right into the hands of unscrupulous drug dealers, and/or, worse yet, terrorists. *Or,*

> 2. We were just fantasizing, and what the FAA was telling us was true. …Thus, the fact that "Cocaine One" passed through several owners before and after being owned by the scamsters at Skyway, was in no way germane to a story about 128 suitcases filled with cocaine baking in the heat on a runway in the Yucatan. If the FAA was telling the truth, all we had been doing was wasting our readers' time – your time. You could have had a V8. Or been surfing for Internet porn.

I chose option one. That's why I wrote "5.5 Ton DC-9 Coke Bust Fallout: Worse Than Snakes on a Plane," my interpretation of what I knew about events by August 23, 2006.

Home Free with a Big Wad and a Bottle of Jack

Some of what I based that story on was instinct, in addition to the experience I'd acquired in writing my first two books. You can believe it or not. It was consistent with the reporting by *Proceso* as well as other newspapers in Mexico which supported the Vicente Fox government. The latter tended to feel Hugo Chavez had probably personally supervised the loading of the 128 suitcases, and that probably there were FARC guerrillas standing around with machine guns watching.

Venezuelan newspapers denied drugs had been aboard the American plane when it left Caracas. The DC-9 must have stopped in Colombia to pick up the load, before heading down to Mexico.

Each of us sees events through our own set of eyes, it seems.

Proceso had quoted a control tower employee, who had been approached by a man about 40 years old, with blond hair, a deep tan, and a green polo shirt. He sounded to me like a gringo – possibly an American – who'd been helping an airport employee guide the plane to landing, motioning for it to be parked with the cabin pointing towards a maintenance hangar of the Mexican Aviation Company, about 50 meters away and perpendicular to the very expensive Falcon-20 business jet, which had arrived at least a day earlier.[7]

This same man, cliché that he is, carried a Big Wad of dollars, which he offered to numerous airport employees if they would allow the plane to land. He also asked the tower to "certify the flight," to allow it to continue its journey into Mexico as a domestic flight. No need to go through customs. "He indicated to me that the plane would just refuel and then head towards Toluca," the employee stated.

Everyone at the airport seemed to sense that it would be too risky on that particular day. His money was in dollars, the controller explained later, and the airport operations office doesn't take foreign currency. They didn't want his bribe. His offer was refused.

Nevertheless, these same maneuvers, we knew, had been working for 39 straight weeks. What was different on April 10?

From Drug Smuggling to Massive Financial Fraud? Before going bankrupt, the company which painted the plane to look like it belonged to the U.S. Government, Skyway Communications, was clearly up to no good. They had no use for one DC-9. Yet they controlled two. The Chairman of Skyway, Glenn Kovar, was a retired employee of the U.S. Forest Service, who claimed to have been a long-time CIA associate.

Was he ever taken in for questioning?

Perhaps government complicity in the protected drug trade may be easier to spot in Mexico, not because its more prevalent, but because it's easier to imagine the worst when dealing with foreigners.

By November, I had begun to zero in on San Diego defense contractor Titan Corporation as being at the "center of a private intelligence network engaged in a broad range of criminal activities with seeming impunity, everything from drug trafficking to white collar crime that includes massive stock fraud cumulatively totaling billions."[8]

> The network involves elements from the military, as well as intelligence agencies like the CIA and Mossad, in combination with Gulf and Saudi financiers like the notorious Adnan Khashoggi, and individuals who give off more than a whiff of international organized crime.
>
> However, with the recent conviction and sentencing of California Republican Congressman Randy "Duke" Cunningham, the influence-peddling scandal involving a nest of San Diego defense and intelligence contractors that includes Brent Wilkes, Titan Corp. and SAIC (now its official name but which was created as Science Applications International Corporation), may be losing momentum before getting anywhere close to the dark heart of corruption beating just below the surface.[8]

If I say so myself, I waxed eloquent. Everything seemed to be pointing to what Tony Blair in his speech to Parliament shortly after 9/11 called the global financial network which funded the terrorists.

But if that was true, then we must have had America's Pablo Escobar in our sights!

I wrote on August 7 about that network:

> What local officials blundered into at a remote airport in the farthest corner of Mexico's Yucatan may have earth-shaking reverberations felt around the world… if the true story of what happened there becomes widely known.
>
> The seizure in Ciudad del Carmen has exposed the links of a global narcotics cartel that may be the most powerful political force on the planet.
>
> Based on court documents, SEC filings, records of incorporation, and interviews with eyewitnesses, the elements which comprise this global narcotics cartel – all of which will be named and covered in this series – include the following:
>
> Rogue U.S. defense contractor Titan Corp in San Diego; CIA proprietary airlines; "fugitive" Saudi billionaires, Gulf States Sheiks and financiers; the Israeli Mossad and right wing Israeli political parties identified with Jewish settler interests; "retired" officers of the CIA and U.S. military intelligence; Texas Republican kingmakers and private investment banks; member of U.S. organized crime…

Also ... stock swindlers in Vancouver, Canada responsible for multi-billion dollar financial fraud; officials from the party of Mexican President Vicente Fox; Colombian and Mexican drug cartels; Florida air charter companies which enjoy – as did the Florida aviation companies associated with the terrorist hijackers–apparent official immunity from prosecution; and Lebanese "industrialists" in Mexico known to the Mexican press as the "Narco-Pederastas," for their penchant for molesting children, with apparent immunity from prosecution, both boys and girls, as young as four.[9]

Had I left anyone out?

PEDDLING PROSTITUTES TO SAUDI ROYALTY

I was just getting wound up. For more lurid tastes, the best was yet to come, but I barely skimmed the surface on that occasion. Could it have been modesty that prevented me from quoting sensational tales from *News of the World*?

> The tabloid tale of "Lord Macca" and "Lady Mucca" reached its lurid climax on Sunday [6/11/06] when *News of the World* published claims that Paul McCartney's estranged wife, Heather Mills McCartney, had been a high- priced prostitute specializing in lesbian and group sex.
>
> ""Under the headline, 'Bisexual Heather sold body to Arabs for years," two ex-prostitutes and a former private secretary to arms dealer Adnan Khashoggi said the former model, now Lady Heather Mills McCartney, was paid £5000 to take part in a threesome with a call-girl and a member of the Saudi royal family.
>
> She was alleged to have worked as a prostitute about 15 years ago, seven or eight years before she met McCartney, whom she married in 2002. The *News of the World* says her *secret encounters with Mr Khashoggi* took place in Marbella, Spain and at the Lanesborough, Hilton, Dorchester and Grosvenor House hotels in London's Mayfair.
>
> The allegations, denied by Mills McCartney, followed last month's report in the *Sun* that the former Sun page-three girl had taken part in a 1988 German porn video, *Die Freuden der Liebe* (The Joys of Love), in which she performed various acts, sucked strawberries from her co-star's mouth and "licked whipped cream off his manhood."[10]

After we've cooled down, maybe had a refreshment and a nap, we'll continue shortly.

It's hard to top that visual.

Endnotes

1   Daniel Hopsicker, "Mystery of 5.5 Ton Coke Flight Deepens," *Mad Cow Morning News*, May 2, 2006. https://www.madcowprod.com/2006/05/02/mystery-of-5-5-ton-coke-flight-deepens/

2   Daniel Hopsicker, "Cocaine One Bust Lifts Veil on Global Narcotics Cartel," *Mad Cow Morning News*, August 7, 2006. https://www.madcowprod.com/2006/08/07/cocaine-one-bust-lifts-veil-on-global-narcotics-cartel/

3   Howard Altman, "Facts on Sale of Jet in Drug Case Disputed," *Tampa Tribune*, 05 May 2006, Pages 19 and 24.

4   Obituary for Stanley Geffon, *Tampa Bay Times*, September 21, 1998.

5 "Mario Lanza's Double Is Top Winner," *St. Petersburg Times*, June 21, 1958.

6   Author interview of Frederic Geffon, April 2006.

7   Mexican Aviation Company had originally been created in the 1930s as a subsidiary of Pan American Airways, whose history had a strong connection to the CIA. See Yesenia González Flores and Susana Esquivel Ríos, "The Impact of Aviation in Strengthening the Mexican Tourism Industry," International Journal of Science and Research (USR), 2022.   https://www.ijsr.net/archive/v13i2/MR24210042326.pdf

8   Daniel Hopsicker, "Cunningham Scandal Far From Over," November 3, 2006. https://www.madcowprod.com/2006/11/03/cunningham-scandal-far-from-over/

9   "Tabloids turn up heat on Beatle's wife," *The Age*, June 13, 2006. https://www.theage. com.au/world/tabloids-turn-up-heat-on-beatles-wife-20060613-ge2i92.html

10   Ibid.

CHAPTER THREE

IS THERE A WIZARD SCHOOL
IN PASADENA?

Funny way to get to a wizard's school, the train. Magic carpets all got punctures, have they?

— *Harry Potter and the Sorcerer's Stone*

Profit Connect Wealth Services, Inc., a corporation shut down by the Securities and Exchange Agency in 2021 for fraudulently raising more than $12 million from at least 277 retail investors was not Brent Kovar's first rodeo.[1] It wasn't his second rodeo. Nor even his third. Yet he somehow escaped from a series of financial scandals unscathed.

This raises a series of questions both simple and central – to this book, certainly, and perhaps the Western World: *Don't people go to jail for financial fraud anymore?*

How did Brent Kovar get away with committing felonies with utter impunity, on a schedule regular enough to define the word "recidivist?"

And assuming Brent Kovar doesn't turn out to be a once in a millennium magician with special Marvel superhero powers, who or what was behind him?

What's the name of the powerful organization behind him that's greased his path from the penthouse office of Plaza Tower, downtown St Peterburg's most recognizable icon?

MEET THE KOVARS, AND LASSIE, & WOODSY OWL

What does any of this have to do with Pasadena, California? That's an interesting question, not least because it may be one of only a few questions which has a satisfactory answer. So let's take it first.

Brent, his mom Joy, and dad Glenn were at one time a typical American nuclear family in Pasadena, California. Brent Carson Kovar was born in 1966 in Los Angeles, and attended John Marshall Fundamental School in Pasadena, which may well be where things began to go wrong.

Pasadena was not just an all-American city in the middle of the all-American Century, hosting the Rose Bowl which came on right after the Rose Parade every January 1st, it was also a center of intrigue during the Cold War.

It was at Pasadena's famous Jet Propulsion Laboratory (JPL) that America's rocket program was born. Jack Parsons, and junior rocket scientists like him, had been launching home-made rockets from remote arroyos and canyons in Pasadena's foothills since he was a teenager.[2]

But that wasn't all the eclectic scientist saw being born in Pasadena. Parsons was a close associate of L. Ron Hubbard, who was busy hatching a new science-fiction religion called Scientology while he was also busily seducing Parson's girlfriend at the time.[3]

Hubbard created the first version of Scientology in Arizona in 1952, revising it a few years later in California. Later he moved his headquarters offshore to a large yacht. Finding himself denied admission in one port after another, he established a new headquarters in 1975, having one in Clearwater, Fla., and another in southern California.[4]

Within a year his wife and ten associates were indicted in Washington, D.C. after one Scientologist was arrested with fake federal credentials in a government office building, and thousands of documents were seized in raids of Scientology offices.[5]

Two years before Hubbard died, a Los Angeles judge who tried a lawsuit against what he called the cult, said of Mr. Hubbard: "The evidence portrays a man who has been virtually a pathological liar when it comes to his history, background and achievements," and who seemed gripped by "egoism, greed, avarice, lust for power, and vindictiveness and aggressiveness against persons perceived by him to be disloyal or hostile."[6]

Sound like anyone else you know?

* * *

It seemed almost too coincidental that Hubbard was living only a few miles from Glenn and Joy Kovar in the early '50s when they were students in Tempe, Arizona. Hubbard then relocated in 1956 to Pasadena just before they did. But coincidences do happen.

Joy Kovar taught speed reading in Pasadena during the Cold War, holding classes at JPL. "Her early experience in personnel work was gained during 1957 to 1960 for the Department of Agriculture and later with the Air Force in 1963 and 1964. In 1960, Mrs. Kovar started Communication Skills Laboratory, in Pasadena, California, conducting classes for hundreds of businesspeople."[7]

She did that while her husband, Glenn Kovar, worked for the U.S. Forest Service in the Hollywood area, creating public service announcements with Smokey the Bear and Woodsy Owl. He was also a consultant on "Lassie."

The Kovars had met while each was a student at Arizona State University in Tempe, Arizona in the mid '50s, before relocating to Pasadena.[8] Glenn was hired to set up the National Media Office, based out of the Washington, D.C. Office, but actually located in Pasadena. It was called the U.S. Forest Service Network Radio & Television studios, designed "to increase its visibility in the media. The most famous and lasting result of this initiative was the Lassie program. The famous collie and her forest ranger friends appeared every Sunday night on CBS for nearly a decade."[9]

DAVID VS. GOLIATH

One financial reporter – some referred to him as David versus the Goliath of Wall Street – seemed to understand what was going on, pretty much in real time: Christopher Byron. He wasn't a gonzo journalist, just a deadpan sober business reporter with a wicked sense of humor.

About Donald Trump, Byron once wrote:

> The disappointing thing about most phonies is that they don't have staying power. Once they get caught, they give it up and skulk off into the night, never to be heard from again. Think of Rosie Ruiz, say, who pretended to win the Boston Marathon by sneaking out of a crowd of bystanders ahead of everybody in the last half-mile of the race.

"That's why I like Donald Trump so much. When it comes to pretending to run marathons, he never quits," Byron wrote in 2011, years before Trump began the campaign that put him in the White House. [10]

For the blatant criminality of the thieves and swindlers who were plundering the stock market with seeming impunity, Byron pointed a finger at the CIA, even though blaming the CIA has long been a prescription for career suicide in America journalism (see Webb, Gary).

What Byron thought was going on had a certain ring of truth to it – suggestions that the CIA had invaded Wall Street like a plague of locusts, pumping and dumping poorly traded stocks of unknown companies in the OTC (over the counter) market. All things considered, being a wolf plundering Wall Street was a dream job. It paid well, was easy work, with no downside. Martin Scorsese even made a movie about it. Make money, and vacay in the Turks & Caicos.

Then things changed – just like that – when the CIA decided it wanted a piece of the action. According to Byron, the Agency spun off a holding company called In-Q-Tel, to manage the Agency's more speculative investments.

Who is Q?

They were off to the races. And haven't stopped yet. Science writer Eric Hal Schwartz wrote in 2020 that the CIA was heavily invested in artificial intelligence, and he may even have provided a hint for who could be behind alt-right conspiracy theorist QAnon:

> Deepgram isn't In-Q-Tel's first dip in investing in speech technology. In 2005, the VC [venture capital] firm invested in CallMiner and its speech analysis software for phone calls, followed in 2009 by a deal to invest in speech recognition tech startup Carnegie Speech. In-Q-Tel's portfolio history notes plenty of investment in related technology, such as handwriting recognition and instant translation software.
>
> The breadth of technology [that] In-Q-Tel has been interested in makes sense, considering its roots in the CIA and the fact that the Q in the name refers to the ever-inventive provider of high-tech tools for James Bond. The deal with Deepgram doesn't mean secret agents will use the start-up's tech to transcribe conversations among spies, though, at least not yet. First, the tech will undergo some tests to see how it might fit into the government.[11]

One of the companies Byron had profiled was Ionatron. "A year ago," Byron reported in 2011, "this column drew back the curtain on a fishy IN-Q- TEL investment, a defense-sector start-up called Ionatron Inc., financed out of the black box budget of the CIA."[12]

America's spook establishment, Byron reported – though he didn't say "spook" – was secretly funneling hundreds of millions of dollars through Wall Street's murkiest back alleys. Byron lived in Connecticut. Lots of ex-spooks lived there. But even he was gobsmacked at how easily they got away with it. His columns always spoke of the caper in a tone of awed respect.

Ionatron sounded – to me – uncannily like SkyWay. It was as if Ionatron came from the same stable, or that In-Q-Tel may have even been channeling SkyWay.

SkyWay was selling a black box that let you beam live, they told investors, down to and up from a DC-9. They sold it as a Nat-Sec play. It would be handy for when the terrorists rushed the cockpit. But you could also use the black box to stream movies as an add-on source of revenue. It was airborne HBO Max. Another twofer! Ionatron's sales pitch used a golf cart they said would protect American troops in Iraq from IED's.

"Ionatron used a cash infusion from In-Q-Tel to promote itself around Washington," Byron said, "as the developer of a laser-equipped, remotely-controlled device the size of a golf cart that can patrol highways in Iraq, as well as ferret out and detonate insurgent land mines ahead of troop movements."[13]

Supplying U.S. forces in Iraq with anti-IED devices was something of a boom market at the time. Congress was complaining that the Pentagon was dragging its feet on up-armoring Humvees to keep U.S. servicemen being blown to bits. So just in case the golf carts didn't work, the company had a fallback position: They had a raygun that zapped roadside explosives buried by insurgents.

SkyWay also owned a fleet of Humvees, decorated with the same logo SkyWay put on their planes. Probably got them at a discount after Ionotron became a defendant in a class action lawsuit.[14]

Like SkyWay, Kovar's Satellite Access Systems (SAS) had also touted an imaginatively packaged gee-whiz product.

If these guys would just go straight, they'd have enough imagination and stick-to-itiveness to found a sci-fi religion. It appeared to be a burgeoning field. I sometimes wondered if that was why the Kovars located SkyWay at an office building in St. Petersburg, within stone's throw from the headquarters of Scientology.

TWOFERS ARE THE BEST

In 2003, father-son duo Glenn and Brent Kovar helped get Sky Way Aircraft up and running. They weren't scientists. They were specialists in the arcane practice of penny stock fraud.

While still living in California, Brent had set up Satellite Access Systems (SAS), which they will sell after moving to Florida. Touting the same technological invention, Brent and his mom then set up a local Internet service provider in Florida, while, at about the same time he started selling shares in SkyWay Communications.

SkyWay was seemingly created to enable the Kovars to smuggle drugs while acting simultaneously as a money laundering device. You get a better bang for your buck with a twofer.

Investors (like Fred Geffon and others) lost $40 million on SkyWay, according to the US District Bankruptcy Court in Tampa. Most of investors' money ended up in "the boys" pockets, I surmised. For their earlier venture, Satellite Access Systems (SAS), the SEC fined Brent Kovar $36 million for lying about the proprietary "black box" technology the company was said to possess.

But Kovar didn't pay any of it. The SEC doesn't have a very efficient enforcement and collection arm, we've observed.

The SEC said, not only did Brent Kovar's new company (SkyWay) not have the rights to the black box which Satellite Access Systems' (SAS) buyers were now claiming to own, but even if he *had* still owned it, it didn't work. Presumably, it had never worked, despite the patent application he made for a compression algorithm.

But all that came out later. In the moment, which was all that counted, SAS was soaring into the penny stock stratosphere. It all ended badly. When the stock collapsed, it was worth three one-thousandths of a penny – that's $0.003 – per share.

"Holy Grail" of Internet Speed

Brent Kovar stood before a giant movie screen in the penthouse theater of his Plaza Tower in St Petersburg, Florida. Playing on the screen was an excerpt from the movie *Top Gun*, with stars Tom Cruise and Anthony Edwards yelling "we have the need – the need for speed!"[15] Kovar told the group of investors sitting in front of him that he had found speed. He had invented the most promising advance in Internet communications on the planet.

His "magic" black box could compress massive amounts of data and transmit it faster than ever before, Kovar said.

Using an antenna in a nearby control room, he told investors, the movie had been sent to a satellite in the sky, then back down. It took only seconds at a time when transmitting a movie by dial-up took almost half a day.

The investors were spellbound.

"There was an aura around you that I'm involved in something gigantic here," said B. Scott Limehouse, Kovar's vice president of sales.

Scam artist Brent Kovar's companies raised $22M from investors, including from a group in Kuwait and Saudi Arabia ($13M), and even from his own mother-in-law ($40K) – perhaps I should say "former" mother-in-law.

Needless to say, once the stock price plummeted, so did his marriage. He was now living alone in his big house at Tierra Verde, just outside St. Pete. Brent had a keen sense of timing. Both companies seemed to ride the edge of the technology frontier. One expert called his invention the "holy grail" of Internet communication. Kovar knew he had everyone's attention.

He bragged to investors, sometimes in newsletters and brochures, that he had the interest of high-profile players like AOL-Time Warner, American Airlines, Bill Gates and Donald Trump.

Kovar said he had met one-on-one with Tom Ridge, head of Homeland Security; gone to dinner with President Bush; and that Vice President Dick Cheney wanted to discuss "various homeland security initiatives."

Reported the July, 2007 *Tampa Times*, "Representatives for the three men say they've never heard of Kovar."[16]

Brent Kovar had the spending habits of a confidence man. He spent elaborate amounts on his fleet of Humvees, all of which appeared to be impersonating vehicles from the Dept of Homeland Security, until the local police made them take the seals off.

THE APPLE DOESN'T FALL

"Some men follow their dreams. Glenn Kovar chased the 28th parallel. Which is primarily why several weeks ago the 64-year-old president of Satellite Access Systems moved his company from Pasadena, Calif., to St. Petersburg," the *Tampa Business Journal* reported in 1996.[17] "Of the umpteen imaginary lines encircling the globe, the northern hemisphere's 28th happens to be among the most popular parallels for high-flying communications satellites, SAS' electronic lifeblood."

"We needed to be close to the 28th parallel because we would have access to 24 satellites instead of the one or two we usually had (in Pasadena)," the Long Island native explained at his offices atop the 16-story Plaza Towers, near the St. Petersburg Pier.

"And if you look at a globe, there aren't that many cities in the world on the 28th parallel that are nice to live in. St. Petersburg is."[18]

In the same interview, Glenn said he'd just "spent six storm-tossed days aboard a research vessel at the site" of the sunken S.S. *Titanic,* and he was in talks with the "salvage team that last month worked on an abortive effort to raise a 21-ton chunk" of the ship that was the subject of the 1997 film starring Leo DiCaprio.

• • •

I used to live in Newport Beach, California, where several large satellite companies, like Loral, were headquartered. Because of my proximity to the aerospace industry, I had met and become friends with Richard Freeman, who designed satellites for Hughes, the world's leader in satellite technology. I asked him what he thought about Glenn Kovar's quote about the 28th parallel.

"*It's utter horseshit,*" he told me bluntly. "The man obviously doesn't know the first thing about satellites."[19]

Maybe Paul Abercrombie was a little embarrassed after this interview with Glenn was published. Only a year later in 1997, the *Business Journal* reporter was backtracking. The first sentence in a new article stated: Glenn Kovar "apparently hasn't always lived up to his word."[20]

"In an interview late last year, Kovar told the *Business Journal* that he had worked for five U.S. presidents as director of special projects; his actual title was director of special projects for the U.S. Forest Service. Kovar also told the *Business Journal* that he had managed the joint Soviet-American Apollo-Soyuz space mission."[21]

Abercrombie pushed back, stating that "Kovar downplayed the significance of any of the inconsistencies: 'Irrelevant. (SAS) has got nothing to do with that. That was 10 years ago. (What happened in Dunedin) was political This is stirring old things up and (SAS) has nothing to do with that.'"[22]

Unfortunately, the Kovars would persist for another decade in the Tampa Bay market before they'd be thoroughly outed in the special report splashed across three pages in the *Tampa Bay Times* on Jul 1, 2007. It would finally make the connection between the blatant financial fraud, and the flagrantly criminal drug smuggling being carried out on the company's airplanes. By "splashed," I mean it had pictures of soldiers unloading 128 suitcases at the airport in Ciudad del Carmen.

Being Connected Means ...

Individuals involved in the SkyWay operation, it will turn out, have extensive and wide-ranging connections to each other which pre-date the brief life span of the company – thus revealing the outlines of a larger and previously secret organization, as we learn simply by reading documents filed with the SEC.[23]

First of all, by 2003, SkyWay, like a caterpillar emerging from its cocoon as a butterfly, had become an entirely new corporation. It even moved from the Plaza Tower in St. Petersburg to a building owned by St.

Pete college in Clearwater, which has since been sold as surplus.[24] The new location was less than three miles from the St. Pete-Clearwater Airport (designated PIE).

As in pie-in-the-sky? Glenn set up Sky Way Aircraft, Inc. first in Nevada, then filed to have it authorized for business in Florida – all this in the spring of 2002. The Kovars had already brought James S. Kent aboard, according to his biographic blurbs in SEC filings. He worked for SAS beginning in 1998, hired from Booz Allen Hamilton (BAH), an IT Consulting firm based in McLean, Virginia. That in itself aroused suspicion. Prior to BAH, Kent had worked nearly 20 years in "government contract management positions supporting projects of the Department of Defense, National Security Agency, and Department of the Navy."

His job at SkyWay was to oversee the merger with a shell corporation being bought from the Miami law firm headed by Michael Farkas, who had the shell of a public corporation all ready for them to turn into a pump-and-dump machine.

Farkas also had ties to Adnan Khashoggi and his lieutenant, Ramy El-Batrawi. As we describe later, they headed a corporate network that fell under the code name Genesis, through which Skyway acquired one of the two DC-9's to be used in SkyWay's new operation – drug smuggling.

Both Khashoggi and El Batrawi went on the lam in 2001 when their $300 million Stockwalk scam precipitated what news reports called the "largest brokerage industry failure in more than 30 years."[25]

GenesisIntermedia was put together in a complicated deal by El-Batrawi, shortly after he'd worked with Michael Farkas on Holiday RV Super Stores, which we'll also explain in another chapter.

The original underwriter for GenesisIntermedia was an investment bank called Millennium Financial, later known as I-Bankers Securities, whose principal (at least one of them) was a man from Baton Rouge named Michael Roy Fugler. Before becoming an investment banker and broker of note, Fugler worked as a criminal defense lawyer for a time, handling the increasingly-byzantine narcotics-related cases of pilot Barry Seal.

Fugler had sued me – and won, unfortunately – settling the lawsuit only when I agreed to remove disparaging references to him from *Barry & 'the boys.'*

My colleague and publisher laboriously blacked out Fugler's name from every copy of the first printing of my first book not already sold. Linda Minor likes to boast that she'd got her copy early, and it still has all the names, unredacted. Probably worth a fortune today.

Maybe we have no free press. But at least in our country they let you live.

For the record, Fugler avers that he had absolutely no involvement with Barry Seal … except to represent him in two criminal cases involving narcotics in Florida, and a series of what he described as "routine civil actions" elsewhere, and he says he never met and did not know Adnan Khashoggi.

Both Barry Seal and Adnan Khashoggi, however, were "assets" of the Central Intelligence Agency (CIA). An asset, by definition, is a property a person or company owns. It has value.

The CIA used its assets – I'm guessing it still does – to make money. With Seal, it made the money on the drugs he imported for them. With Khashoggi, it made money on financial fraud.

As Republican Senator Everett Dirksen famously (and sonorously) intoned, "A billion here, a billion there, and pretty soon you're talking real money."[26]

Endnotes

1   "SEC Shuts Down Fraudulent Mother-Son Offering Involving Purported Supercomputer," Litigation Release No. 25144 / July 20, 2021. https://www.sec.gov/litigation/litreleases/lr-25144

2   Elías Martínez. "Sex, Drugs and the Occult: An Introduction to Jack Parsons," *Cult Nation*, August 13, 2015. https://cvltnation.com/sex-drugs-and-the-occult-an-introduction- to-jack-parsons/

3   John Carter (Author), Robert Anton Wilson (Introduction), *Sex and Rockets: The Occult World of Jack Parsons*, Feral House, March 10, 2005.

4   Robert Lindsey, "L. RON HUBBARD DIES OF STROKE; FOUNDER OF CHURCH OF SCIENTOLOGY," Special To the *New York Times*, Jan. 29, 1986. https://www.nytimes.com/1986/01/29/ obituaries/l-ron-hubbard-dies-of-stroke-founder-of-church-of-scientology.html

5   Bette Orsini, "Centerpiece," *Tampa Bay Times*, 18 Feb 1979, Sun · Page 199.

6   Robert Lindsey, "L. RON HUBBARD DIES OF STROKE; FOUNDER OF CHURCH OF SCIENTOLOGY," Special To the *New York Times*, Jan. 29, 1986. https://www.nytimes.com/1986/01/29/ obituaries/l-ron-hubbard-dies-of-stroke-founder-of-church-of-scientology.html

7   SKYWAY COMMUNICATIONS HOLDING CORP. Information Statement. https://www.sec.gov/Archives/edgar/data/1128723/000110801703000460/skyway.htm

8   Bonita Granville Wrather and Jack Wrather: An Inventory of Their Papers The Harry Ransom Center. https://norman.hrc.utexas.edu/fasearch/findingAid.cfm?eadid=00155

9   "The Unmarked Trail: Managing National Forests in a Turbulent Era, Forest Service," Pacific Southwest Region, U.S. Department of Agriculture, 2009. https://digitalassets.lib.berkeley.edu/roho/ucb/text/unmarked_trail_vol2.pdf. Also see Bonita Granville Wrather and Jack Wrather: An Inventory of Their Papers at The Harry Ransom Center. https://norman.hrc.utexas. edu/fasearch/findingAid.cfm?eadid=00155. The Wrathers were creators of the *Lassie* television show.

10   Christopher Byron, "Is Trump playing us for suckers?" Special to CNN, April 19, 2011. https://www.cnn.com/2011/OPINION/04/19/byron.trump.president/index.html

11   Eric Hal Schwartz, "US Intelligence-Backed VC Firm In-Q-Tel Invests in Speech Tech Start-up Deepgram," Voicebot.AI, June 4, 2020. https://voicebot.ai/2020/06/04/us-intelligence-backed-vc-firm-in-q-tel-invests-in-speech-tech-startup-deepgram/

12   Christopher Byron, "Is Trump playing us for suckers?" Special to CNN, April 19, 2011. https://www.cnn.com/2011/OPINION/04/19/byron.trump.president/index.html

13   Ibid.

14   Noah Shachtman, "Shareholders Zap Lightning Gun Maker," *Wired*, Jul 25, 2007. https://www.wired.com/2007/07/investors-in-re/. See also https://www.wired.com/2007/07/if-you-write- an/.

15   Leonora LaPeter Anton, "Invention Was Too Good to Be True," *Tampa Bay Times*, St. Petersburg, Florida, Jul 01, 2007, Pages 1, 8, 9. https://www.tampabay.com/archive/2007/07/01/ invention-was-too-good-to-be-true/

16   Ibid.

17   Paul Abercrombie, "Satellite firm scans universe of new markets," *Tampa Business Journal*, Sept. 16, 1996. https://www.bizjournals.com/tampabay/stories/1996/09/16/story3.html

18   Ibid.

19   Personal interview with Richard Freeman.

20   Paul Abercrombie, "Tech firm boss has padded file; Claims cost him job in Dunedin," *Tampa Bay Business Journal*, Jun 30, 1997. https://www.bizjournals.com/tampabay/stories/1997/06/30/story7.html

21   Ibid.

22   Ibid.

23   SKYWAY COMMUNICATIONS HOLDING CORP. FORM 10-KSB, June 20, 2003. https://www.sec.gov/Archives/edgar/data/1128723/000110801703000595/skyway.htm

24   https://www.myfloridalands.com/st-petersburg-college-building

25   "MJK Clearing was the branch of Stockwalk that had been involved in a stock deal gone sour, when the price fell on the stock of GenesisIntermedia, owned by arms dealer Adnan Khashoggi, and MJK and Stockwalk couldn't come up with the money to back their loan for the shares." A

trustee in bankruptcy was appointed on September 27, 2001, three days after the brokerage was declared insolvent. Nicole Garrison-Sprenger, "Deutsche Bank to pay $270M in Stockwalk settlement, *Minneapolis/St. Paul Business Journal*, Dec 21, 2005. https://www.bizjournals.com/ twincities/ stories/2005/12/19/daily35.html

26   https://dirksencenter.org/research-collections/everett-m-dirksen/dirksen-record/bil- li-on-here-billion-there

CHAPTER FOUR

THE KOVARS AND KHASHOGGI'S CLIQUE

I was initially recruited while I was in business school back in the late sixties by the National Security Agency, the nation's largest and least understood spy organization; but ultimately I worked for private corporations.

— John Perkins, *Confessions of an Economic Hit Man*

Into the Florida swamp of corruption, California native Brent Kovar slithered, locating himself first in the area of Clearwater, where his father, Glenn, had been known to hang out years earlier.

In fact, Glenn Kovar had literally been swept into a boat slip at 100 Pierce Condominiums in 1985 by Hurricane Alicia – a feat documented in the *Tampa Times* that October.

This is, coincidentally, the same October 1985 that Adnan Khashoggi was facilitating a sale of TOW missiles to Iranians to free hostages in Lebanon.

Small world.

The only reason Kovar made the news was that "Hurricane Alicia" also swept a young teenage boy into the bay, and Glenn saved him from drowning. Reporters rushed to the scene and interviewed the heroic Kovar – complete with photos of his boat and exotic costume.[1]

Two years later, Brent (then 27) visited his father in the Virgin Islands of St. Thomas, where they made a decision to go into business together, Brent told reporters.

Brent had grown up in gated neighborhoods located a mile or so from the Jet Propulsion Laboratory in Pasadena, California. However, in 1972, when he was 12, Brent's parents – Glenn and Joy Kovar – divorced.

Glenn had been producing films for the television show, *Lassie,* and Brent still had fond memories of romping on the living room floor with the dog star.

At John Marshall Fundamental High School in the early 1980s, his interest in computers took over everything else. Brent's mother transported him to night classes, later bragging, he'd received his Bachelor of Science degree the same time he finished high school. She claimed he went to Caltech, but SEC records reported it was the less iconic Devry Institute.

In 1986 Brent started his career as an "Internet engineer" at a cable television company in Pasadena, later moving up to Jacobs Engineering. He was ready to start his own business at the age of 24 – a company called simply PC, Ltd – where Brent designed specialized remote-controlled devices. After six years of self-employment, he formed a new company – Satellite Access Systems, Inc., (SAS), which Glenn registered in Nevada.

By this time Brent had moved to Florida, living along the north border of Sarasota County. Remarkably, Andy Badolato, a Sarasota man we will meet later in the book, was himself working nearby, having recently bought a minor-league basketball team called the Sharks with a couple of other guys. Maybe Brent took in one a Sharks game at some point. Maybe the two men never met. We don't know.

At any rate, Brent was busy spending money he did not have to lease the entire 16th floor of the Plaza Tower and Courtyard Shops Building on NE Second Avenue in St. Petersburg in July 1996. The realtor bragged about the huge commission in the local paper.

Three years later in 1999 the Kovars – no doubt needing rent money – sold all their SAS stock, apparently promising the buyers the data-compression software the Kovars claimed Brent had invented.

But only a year after the sale, Brent applied for a patent (US6587887B1) for data-compression software – an invention that claimed to accomplish what he said SAS had done. Then while he was trying to market the same invention as part of SkyWay Communications (more later on that), Satellite Access Systems' buyers were going through all kinds of crazy shenanigans.

"SEE IT, DO IT, AND GET OUT"

The buyers merged SAS into a shell corporation called Corsaire, Inc., which changed its name to Corsaire Snowboards, Inc., and in short order to Net Command Tech, Inc.

Rene Hamouth and William Roger Dunavant, who now owned the stock, both had sordid histories of fraud in Canada and had been blacklisted by the Vancouver Stock Exchange.

Business writer Brent Mudry comically detailed in the summer of 1999 what the two Canadians had done before they got together to form Net

Command Tech out of Kovar's invention. Quoting my two favorite writers, Christopher Byron and David Baines, Mudry reminded their readers that *Forbes* magazine had labeled Dunavant in 1996 as a "persuasive scoundrel" who'd actually plundered a company called Straight Arrow – Dunavant's self-acclaimed biggest success story.

"Dunavant took control of the family-run horse shampoo firm in 1989 and expanded the market to humans, while allegedly milking the company dry. Even Forbes fell for Mr. Dunavant's new pitch of "Mane 'n Tail" in 1994."[2]

Citing *Miami Herald* reporter James McNair, he then wrote:

> Dunavant jumped from horse shampoo to high-tech video compression technology. At a computer pornography convention in Las Vegas in 1997, the entrepreneur, then the president of Summus Technologies, an affiliate of Verinet, told a *San Francisco Chronicle* reporter that Verinet's software was great for fast porno site downloads.[3]
>
> "People want to see it, do it and get out of a site fast," Mr. Dunavant told the reporter. A year later, the Mane 'n Hair and porno pitchman hooked up with Mr. Hamouth in Corsaire.[4]

REPRISE OF "THE ENTERPRISE"

One company which had invested in Hamouth's Net Command Tech (NCT) was an investment bank called EBI Securities, which had a sordid history of its own, as we'll see later.

EBI sued the sellers, accusing them of … what was it they called it? "Wrongfully realizing short-swing profits from trading Net Command Tech common stock," a violation of section 16(b) – a big no-no for insider shareholders who've hired an investment manager.

EBI Securities had been through as many lives as a blind cat with three legs. The first life began in 1993 – four years after the Berlin Wall collapsed, two years after the USSR disintegrated and BCCI collapsed.

Michael Sumichrast, "a native of Czechoslovakia who fought the Nazis and later fled the Communists" – chief economist for the National Association of Home Builders (NAHB) in Washington, D.C. from 1965 to 1986 – founded the Czech Fund, *ostensibly* to help the newly created Czech Republic convert to a capitalistic economy.[5] But it was really a cover for intelligence operations. How do we know this? We look for the tells. The first was that Iran-Contra insider Robert C. "Bud" MacFarlane – an old pal of Ollie North – was involved.

As one of his last acts before leaving office, on Christmas Eve 1992, the lame duck President George H.W. Bush pardoned his faithful retainer "Bud" MacFarlane, who'd been President Reagan's National Security Adviser back in 1982-83, the same years Bush was in charge of, you know, just about everything from getting hostages back to overseeing the drug trade.

Under the guise of selling American-style homes to Czechs, "The Czech Fund" had the job of traveling throughout Eastern Europe to observe, report back, and possibly given a license to loot whatever it could. Shortly thereafter the name was changed to Czech Industries. MacFarlane joined their board in 1993.

WOLVES OF WALL STREET

Money came in through shares issued by the unknown Republic Securities in Chicago, which had no marketing department. Instead, the job of selling the stock was assigned to a "fake" brokerage company called Stratton Oakmont, led by Jordan Belfort, who would later be depicted in the movie *Wolf of Wall Street*.

In an *Esquire* article in 2013, author Michael Maiello noted that Stratton Oakmont "started as a phone bank in the show room of an abandoned car lot in Queens." Jordan Belfort, its founder, did not relish having a job description as "something that sounds like a colonic procedure" ("pump and dump"), so he insisted on being called a "stock manipulator" instead. He thought it sounded much more reputable, according to Maiello.[6]

Josh Shapiro, who worked for Belfort's Stratton Oakmont for several years, claimed that his colleagues boasted they "used to get a couple of bums off the street, throw them in the shower, put a suit and tie on them, and say, 'Listen, buddy, for the next couple of hours, you're the president of Czech Industries.'"[7]

Stratton Oakmont's collapse for fraud in 1996 seemed to have no effect on Czech Industries, however. It was still flush enough with funds to buy up much of the stock of a Viennese stock brokerage – Eastbrokers Beteiligungs AG – and thereby establish a new American company called Eastbrokers International, Inc. Eighty percent of the capital injected into Eastbrokers came from Czech Industries, according to SEC filings for Global Capital Partners, Inc.[8]

We'll run into these companies again in a later chapter which shows EBI Securities Corp., had previously been called Cohig & Associates, located in Denver, and it was owned by Viennese firm called East Broker International.

I'm sure it would help to have a whiteboard to draw it all out on, but we're just doing the best we can on paper.

The US-incorporated company, which used the Wolf of Wall Street to whip up the stock value, paid cash to Wolfgang Kössner for a block of stock in the former Austrian corporation, giving him in exchange 38% of the stock in the merged company, now called Eastbrokers International, Inc.

Included with the stock Eastbrokers got from Wolfgang was a 49% interest in WMP-Bank AG – later called General Commerce Bank, Austria's then largest private stock brokerage company listed on the Vienna Stock Exchange.

What we are describing here is what today's intelligence agencies do in our name. They hire these crooks to cheat the stock-buying public and use the proceeds of fraud to take over foreign banks. All under the guise of national security.

Perhaps it is in our national security, but that doesn't make it legal. Unfortunately, we're not cleared to see the big picture.

"TROUPE OF DAZZLING, INTERNATIONAL FINANCIAL ARTISTS"

One WMP shareholder was a smaller bank, Hypo-Alpe-Adria Bank (HAA Bank) of Liechtenstein. After Khashoggi was introduced to HAA Bank's president in late 2000, he got control of it. He was assisted in the endeavor by "a troupe of dazzling, international financial artists," according to an article in a European magazine called *Format*.[9]

Format then explained that "a US company called Global Capital Partners Inc. took on a dominant role" by diluting the percentage of shares held by Wolfgang Kössner from 40 to nine percent. Kössner declared, "There are increasing indications that a clique of major criminals has nested in the bank."[10]

Calling them "extremely dazzling, international financial artists," he listed those who had assisted Adnan Khashoggi, including:

- Canadian-born Raoul Berthaumieu,
- Californian, Regis Possino, and
- Rakesh Saxena, from India.

Eastbrokers, located in Rockville, Maryland – 12 miles north of the CIA headquarters at Langley, Virginia – meanwhile changed its name to EBI Securities, eventually becoming Global Capital Partners. As Global

Capital Partners (GCAP), it also changed its headquarters to Charlotte, North Carolina.

Prior to October 10, 2011, Michael Sumichrast, founder of the Czech Fund was suspended. Why was GCAP located in this particular location? Stay alert. That will be explained as we reveal how South and Central American drug cartels brought down Wachovia Bank.

Christopher Byron – my favorite business writer, as I may have said before, but it bears repeating – explains Adnan Khashoggi's role in the story more succinctly than I can, in an article titled "Kiosks, Cocaine, and Khashoggi." [11] But the story is rather more complicated than most readers can take in. You may have to read it more than once.

CHRISTOPHER BYRON MADE THE CONNECTIONS

Let's start with the largest single shareholder in Genesis: an outfit called Ultimate Holdings, which turns out to be an investment vehicle for a Saudi arms merchant named Adnan Khashoggi, who played a key role in helping broker illegal weapons traffic from the United States to Iran during the Iran/Contra affair.

Incidentally, Khashoggi and Imelda Marcos, former first lady of the Philippines, were jointly tried and acquitted of federal fraud charges in New York, but, as of November 26, 2001, Adnan was a fugitive from a bank fraud warrant in Thailand. More on that later.

Chris Byron wrote:

> Genesis's original underwriter was an outfit bearing the name Millennium Financial. The firm – now known as I-Bankers Securities – is run by a fellow named Michael Roy Fugler. Prior to becoming an investment banker and broker, Mr. Fugler worked as a criminal defense lawyer – in which capacity he handled narcotics-related cases for an Arkansas pilot named Barry Seal.
>
> Seal kept a plane at a rural airport in Mena, Ark., which was eventually cited in news stories as a base of operations for alleged CIA drug trafficking in connection with covert U.S. support for the Contras. Seal is widely reported to have worked as a contract pilot for the CIA in that effort, smuggling arms to the Contras in Nicaragua and returning to Mena with cargoes of cocaine and other drugs. Seal was murdered in 1986 in Louisiana by Colombian cocaine cartel hit men. Mr. Fugler says he had absolutely no involvement with Seal except to represent him in two criminal cases involving narcotics in Florida, and a series of more routine civil actions elsewhere. He says he has never met and does not know Mr. Khashoggi. [12]

MORE FROM ARKANSAS

B yron continued his tale:

> Another company that Millennium took public was Netivation.com, which has a curious history with an Arkansas politician named Asa Hutchinson, a Republican. In 1982, Mr. Hutchinson was appointed by then-President Ronald Reagan as U.S. attorney for the district in which Mena is located. Mr. Hutchinson has publicly stated that he began researching 'evidence of money laundering' in Mena when he was U.S. attorney, but that he re-signed before the probe was complete. In 1999, Netivation signed a business contract with Mr. Hutchinson, by then a U.S. congressman, to undertake fund-raising for his re-election. Mr. Hutchinson now serves in the Bush administration as the head of the U.S. Drug Enforcement Administration.
>
> The co-underwriter of Netivation, along with Millennium, was an investment bank known as EBI Securities, which began in 1993 as the Czech Fund. One of the company's founding board members was Robert McFarlane, who had served as Mr. Reagan's National Security Advisor during the Iran/Contra scandal. In 1994, the Czech Fund changed its name to Czech Industries, and in 1995, it sold stock to the public courtesy of a Wall Street investment firm called Stratton Oakmont. By 1996, Mr. McFarlane had left Czech's board. Stratton Oakmont was subsequently shut down by the U.S. Securities & Exchange Commission for fraud and stock-rigging activities.[13]

Byron concluded by saying:

> But don't we really know enough already? With more than 5,000 public companies to choose from, why waste an- other minute on this sort of dreck?
>
> Alas for the public, too few did their homework. Instead, they simply went chasing after this barking dog as it howled and growled from $6 to $25, then collapsed right back down to $6 all over again- at which point the National Association of Securities Dealers halted trading in the stock entirely.
>
> It will be interesting indeed to see what 'additional information' the regulators squeeze from this mutt before trading in Genesis's shares resumes – if it ever does.[14]

"THEY ALL KNOW EACH OTHER"

U ltimately, Global Capital Partners, Inc., a Delaware corporation trading as GCAP, in 2000 moved its physical address to Charlotte,

North Carolina, which will become more significant when we talk later about Wachovia Bank.

Dr. Alexander von Paleske alleged in articles he wrote, posted at *Silicon Investor*, that under the new management GCAP was turned into what's known as a "boiler room."[15]

That takes us back to the lawsuit filed by Canadian Rene Hamouth and William Dunavant, the horse shampoo salesman – purchasers in 1999 of Brent Kovar's company – Satellite Access Systems (SAS).

They changed the name from Satellite Access Systems to Net Command Tech, Inc. and hired an investment manager, EBI Securities, Inc. (formerly Eastbrokers, formerly Czech Industries, formerly Global Capital Partners). Then these horse shampoo salesmen and their assorted corporations as Plaintiffs, sued the Kovars, who had sold Satellite Access Systems (SAS) to them.

EBI was also defending itself in a different lawsuit filed by an insurance company called National Care Life, according to an amended SEC filing in March 2000 by Global Capital Partners.

This is where the weirdness starts to get exponentially strange.

National Care claimed it had been scammed in 1994 by none other than Robert Colgin Wilson, friend and colleague-in-fraud of a man we will soon introduce you to, Douglas McClain, Sr.

Wilson used a variety of companies to perpetrate that particular fraud in 1994. A Wilson corporation had opened a trading account at EBI to trade U.S. Treasuries, by buying the securities on margin, but taking the loan in the full amount.[16]

"At margin" means that Wilson borrowed the securities' total value even though only 10% of the face amount had been paid. That gave Wilson 90% of the loan proceeds, which he deposited in accounts set up at private banks on offshore islands. EBI/GCAP then sued Wilson and his companies to force him to turn his profits from the fraud over to them. It was like the CIA suing The Mafia. It was a case of fraudsters calling out fraudsters.

Kelley, Drye & Warren, outside attorneys for Global Capital Partners (GCAP) had been awarded two directors' seats on its board. One director was Jay Schifferli, a partner in the firm. Kelley, Drye proudly traced the law firm's ownership back to 1836 through a series of attorneys who, going back close to two hundred years, had invisibly represented only the most powerful men in the country.

In no way did GCAP appear to fit that description. Unless – and this is where we escalate to a higher level of weird, which we'll label as eerie –

unless GCAP could have been a cutout of a three-letter intelligence agency which shall remain unnamed.

Jay Schifferli went to law school at Georgetown University in Washington, D.C. back in 1986 with Asher Leids, where both men were associate editors for *The Tax Lawyer*, a professional journal sponsored by the American Bar Association. Asher Leids later became the Los Angeles tax attorney hired by Ramy El-Batrawi to represent Khashoggi's GenesisIntermedia in its 1999 IPO.

Another attorney represented the U.S.-based securities underwriter, Millennium Financial, which also had a European branch. That attorney was from Baton Rouge, Louisiana, and his name... – drum roll, please – was Michael Roy Fugler.[17]

It's a small world after all.

Endnotes

1   *Tampa Bay Times*, 01 Sep 1985, Page 2. https://www.newspapers.com/article/45722193/glenn-kovarclearwater-resident-1985/. Three weeks later he was interviewed in costume. *Tampa Bay Times*, 23 Sep 1985, Page 37.

2   Brent Mudry, "Net Command's Dunavant, Hamouth had colourful pasts," Street Wire, June 15, 1999.

3   Ibid.

4   The above cited article by Brent Mudry from Street Wire in 1999 was copied in full at Silicon Investor. https://www.siliconinvestor.com/readmsg.aspx?msgid=17253865.

5   Sumichrast will be suspended from trading on NASDAQ on October 10, 2001, less than a month after 9/11.

6   Michael Maiello, "The Wolf of Wall Street is Real, and I've Been Reporting on Him for Years," *Esquire*, December 23, 2013. https://www.esquire.com/entertainment/news/a26702/real-wolf-of-wall-street/.

7   Josh Shapiro, "I Worked for the Wolf of Wall Street," *New York Post*, December 8, 2013. https://nypost.com/2013/12/08/former-stock-pusher-reveals-life-in-wolf-of-wall-street-boiler-room/.

8   For example, see https://www.sec.gov/Archives/edgar/data/899627/000110801701500397/gcap10k.htm.

9   Hannes Reichmann, "Waffenhändler Khashoggi kontrolliert kleine Bank in Wien," *Format Magazine*, March 11, 2001. https://www.ots.at/presseaussendung/OTS_20010311_OTS0012/format-waffenhaendler-khashoggi-kontrolliert-kleine-bank-in-wien

10   Ibid.

11   Christopher Byron, "Kiosks, cocaine, and Khashoggi: The tangled world of GenesisIntermedia.com," Contrarian column at RED HERRING, November 26, 2001. https://www.siliconinvestor.com/readmsg.aspx?msgid=16705561; and https://www.deepcapture.com/wp-content/uploads/General-Commerce-Bank-Chris-Byron.pdf

Chris Byron died recently, and his obituary says all the things I would like mine to say. Written by Susan Antilla, "'Guardian' Angel' to Investors Christopher Byron Has Died: An Appreciation," *The Street*, Jan 12, 2017. "Over a 40-year career as a financial journalist, Christopher Byron exposed corporate scoundrels, dissed Donald Trump and gave Martha Stewart a giant migraine." https://www.thestreet.com/opinion/guardian-angel-to-investors-christopher-byron-has-died-an-appreciation-13949639

12   Ibid.

13   Ibid

14   Ibid.

14   To: StockDung who wrote (516) 3/19/2006 3:00:40 a.m.. From: Dr. von Paleske, Head, Department of Oncology; Princess Marina Hospital; Gaborone/Botswana/Africa; Ex-Barrister-at-Law, High Court Frankfurt (M) E-Mail avpaleske@botsnet.bw *Silicon Investor*, https://www.siliconinvestor.com/readmsg.aspx?msgid=22273715.

15   Buying on margin refers to the initial payment made to the broker for the asset – for example, 10% down and 90% financed. Only the amount actually paid should be used as collateral, not the full value.

16   I'll add the endnote for those who read only the paperback edition of my first book, Barry and the boys. Fugler sued me after the hard book was published and forced me to recall the unsold books and take out his name. He had, of course, grown up in the same town as Barry Seal and had acted as his criminal defense attorney for drug smuggling.

CHAPTER FIVE

THE MAN WHO LOST A DRUG PLANE

Most folks here got rules 'bout trespassing. Warning shot's fired right close to the head. Get they's attention. Next shot gets a lot more personal. Now I'm too old to waste time firing a warning shot.
    – David Baldacci, *"Wish You Well."*

This book is about a half dozen or so major drug moves that occurred over a span of fifty years, moves that tell a story about how much the drug trade has changed. And – even more – how much it hasn't.
Because it hasn't changed, all that much. You'll see evidence that the criminal organization visible during the 1970's became the mainline of the industry during the 1980's and is still recognizable as essentially the same organization involved in the iconic drug busts of the 21st Century.

And yet – and here's the sticky part – during those years mainstream news of the drug trade was constantly filled with stories portraying drug trafficking as a dog-eat-dog industry.

Who's up and who's down. As if drug trafficking was a horse race. Medellin. Cali. Sinaloa. The Zetas. The enemy du jour.

This cartel or that one was in serial danger of being smashed to bits through the vigilant efforts of – and the active cooperation with – international law enforcement.

"Did you see, they got Escobar."

"They let El Chapo slip away – again?"

Was it all just the product of the mainstream media narrative we imbibe, no matter our disdain for it?

Certainly, from the perspective of the "five major drug moves" this book is about, it was all just so much hooey.

The reality is something else entirely. Something much more unchanging with the same recognizable organization featuring at least some of the same people, carrying forward across decades. It's an organization which, as I see it, exhibits a remarkable continuity. Fifty years after America declared the War on Drugs, cocaine and heroin are distributed as efficiently as Charmin bathroom tissue, at least before the coronavirus epidemic made that a questionable comparison.

This is not my first rodeo.

I've been covering drug trafficking for over thirty years. In terms of foreign trade, it is the biggest industry in the world.

Discretionary funds are always available – "What do you need?" – for whatever's necessary.

So, I have zero interest in pretending that the organizations and networks busily restocking the shelves of Illegal Drug Supercenters nationwide aren't already well-known to the public at large.

On this *Gangster Planet* which we all call home, nation-states as powerful as the U.S. have lost their autonomy in dealing with international drug trafficking.

But you probably already know all that, too.

THE REAL PICTURE

So. Where were we? "Let me put you into the picture."

Right. Let me put you into the *real* picture. Where abstract concepts become lived experience. The point where the wave collapses. Where Schrodinger's Cat – c'mon, already, decide! – lives or dies.

It was a spring day in Florida in 2006, and I was staring at Brent Kovar. One of the "little people" of organized crime. Six inches away from his big round white face, which looked like it could have played a full moon in a grade school play with kids dressed like sunflowers.

Brent Kovar was the President and CEO of a company called Skyway Communications, headquartered on a sprawling college campus in St. Petersburg, Florida, in a building recently vacated by a government-connected Israeli telecommunications company.

Unusual for a corporation of its size, Skyway had just "lost" a DC-9 to Mexican soldiers, who surrounded it on a runway in the Yucatan and seized 5.5 tons of cocaine.

On the spur of the moment, just out of curiosity, I had decided to look him up.

I'd never encountered anyone who'd just lost 5.5 tons of cocaine. Tons of cocaine that somebody was going to have to make good on, unless or until appropriate leverage could be applied. That's a lot of coke to watch slip from your grasp. Would he be all mopey? Or did he "get" the funny parts? (Because there were funny parts.) But that wasn't the real reason I was peering intently at Skyway Communications CEO Brent Kovar.

It was because he had me in a headlock.

It wasn't a tap-out-or-feel-your-eyes-pop-out-of-your-head type of headlock. More of a "Don't move till I say you can" headlock.

For an "inventor" and corporate executive, he was surprisingly strong. One burly damn CEO.

What had happened – before I found myself staring into his flaming nostrils with his arms twisting my neck up for an amazing view of his nose hairs – was that I had driven up his circular driveway just as he was standing in his front doorway to accept a delivery from a Fed Ex driver.

He clearly saw me over the Fed Ex guy's shoulder as I got out of my car and hustled up the driveway. He took the package from the Fed Ex guy, then spun around and closed the door in my face, all in one fluid motion. I didn't get to say, "Hey, wait a minute," let alone prepare an embarrassing question to shout at his back. Something memorable that would hang menacingly in the air until he was forced to come out of the house to respond.

ESTABLISHING FOOTAGE WITH A HANDICAM

Having a door slammed in your face can feel mildly non-life-affirming. So, what I did then was, well, I sort of overreacted. I snuck around the back of his mini-mansion and then nonchalantly strolled across his lawn, making my way surreptitiously, I thought, towards the raised veranda running along the back of the house, as if I had all the time in the world to shoot a little establishing footage with my Sony Handycam. Just, you know, getting good coverage.

That was when he blindsided me. Which is how I came to be in a headlock. Before I'd been so rudely interrupted, I'd been mentally composing a *medium shot* in my head. It would have featured the imposing facade of Kovar's $1.3 million dollar waterfront mansion on Tierra Verde, an island near the mouth of Tampa Bay.

Much of my lifetime career had centered around writing plays or producing commercial films in Los Angeles, so composing camera shots was a habit of mine. Cut to the grassy patio. That's where Kovar and I were panting with exertion on a thin strip of grass, sandwiched between the raised rear veranda and his boat slip, where even then, his boat – or somebody's – was tied up. Brent Kovar – as I also would later learn – registered at least 17 separate "recreational watercraft"... just in the state of Florida.

Was he some kind of boat-collecting marine enthusiast? Or were watercraft important in some way toward achieving the goals of corporations in Tampa Bay?

I never got a chance to ask. I was out of breath from the headlock. Also, this was his moment to gloat a little. He knew who I was. And he knew that I knew that he had me dead to rights for trespassing on his property.

I was embarrassed at getting caught. Even more so at the unexpected headlock and feeling desperate to retain a little dignity.

Especially having a girlfriend present; not right there, but still, too close for comfort, waiting in the car in front of the house.

The question was, after he released my head from his suffocating grip, what were we going to do next? Words were unnecessary. In a gesture as old as time, he motioned for me to proceed up the steps through the back door of the house.

I could see at that point we were going to call the police.

I realized I should probably feel more nervous. I was facing a shameless crook. A classic sociopath. But it was the crook who was about to call the law on me!

POINTS OF A PSYCHOPATH

One of the first ten employees to work at SkyWay would later tell me, "In identifying psychopaths, there are 20 signs, and Brent Kovar fits all of them."[1]

If I'd known that at the time, I may have hesitated about just barging into the back yard. Part of the truth would come out later at his trial, held in June 2007, but it would not be reported in the *Tampa Bay Times* until a year and three months after the bust of the DC-9.

That's when the *Tampa Bay Times* put the story all together – the drugs along with the massive financial fraud he had personally engaged in.

> He got his new bride's family – including his new wife's sister, who invested her husband's death benefits – to invest more than a half-million dollars in a company with no income, no products, and no prospects. I mean, he knew it was a dog!
>
> He even conned his next-door neighbor, who said he didn't want to invest with him. Brent told him he just needed $300,000 for a few days. The neighbor's never seen a dime back. I just don't know how he sleeps at night.[2]

I tried to view him objectively, after he'd released my head from his bulky arms. For someone who'd recently lost 5.5 tons of cocaine, Brent Kovar looked pretty okay with it. I expected that maybe he'd look a little crestfallen. But he didn't.

He motioned for me to go inside without having to say much, so I entered through the door off the veranda and sat down at his kitchen table. It had a nice, elevated view of the harbor, I noticed while we waited for a patrol car to roll up. It appeared they'd already been alerted.

That was in the spring of 2006, when it seems only the loyal fans of my website would learn of Brent Kovar's connection to the cocaine found in Mexico. I had my questions all ready to ask him:

- What was Kovar's connection to Fred Geffon, head of Royal Sons, who had listed his address at Huffman Aviation in Venice?

- Why did Texas Republican Tom DeLay give Brent an award "in recognition of his valuable contributions and dedication to the Republican Party"? Was he splitting his drug take with a political party?

- But most important was why was his company's DC-9 carrying 5.5 tons of cocaine?

WAITING GAME

Time for a little conspiracy theorizing while waiting...

Successful drug moves require careful planning. So does successful financial fraud. They are intentional conspiracies. They don't happen by themselves. Somebody has to make them happen.

On October 29, 1929, known as "Black Tuesday," the Dow Jones, after peaking at 381.17 on September 3, 1929, had fallen to just 41.2, its lowest level of the 20th century.

Of the wealth of America that had been invested in stocks, 89% percent was gone. Vaporized into thin air.

In the Savings and Loan Scandal in 1986, more than a thousand of the 3,234 savings and loan associations or "thrifts" – financial institutions that accepted savings deposits and made home loans to individual members – failed. More than 1,000 bankers – like Charles Keating Jr., whose failed Savings and Loan cost taxpayers $3.4 billion – were convicted and sentenced to jail.

Then came The Great Recession of 2006-2009, which is sometimes called the Sub-Prime (or housing bubble) Loan Scandal – the one revealed right in the middle of the 2008 election.

Economists calculate its cost was between $12.8 trillion and $25 trillion dollars and cost every American alive at least $20,000. American workers' average lifetime incomes fell by almost $150,000. The broader impact could raise the price tag to $120,000 for every man, woman, and child in the United States, enough to pay for a 4-year college education.[3]

If financial regulators made criminal referrals to the Justice Department, no one ever heard about them. No bankers went to prison. There was a book written and a movie made about it, called *The Big Short*.

Somehow, though, the country bounced back much more quickly than ever before. Why?

The answer is that the drug-trade moves, which happened at the same time trillions of dollars began to disappear from the American financial system, brought enough cash into the coffers of banks to balance out the losses.

The drug bust of the Skyway plane occurred on April 10, 2006, at the onset of what came to be known as "The Great Recession." That date was one week to the day before I published my first piece about Brent Kovar at my website, the *Mad Cow Morning News*, opening with a line that I'm still proud of today:

> One of the two owners of the DC-9 (tail number N900SA) busted at an airport in Ciudad del Carmen in the state of Campeche, Mexico last week freighted 5.5 tons of cocaine had been appointed in 2003 to the Business Advisory Council of the National Republican Congressional Committee by then-Congressional Majority Leader Tom Delay, The MadCow Morning News can exclusively report. It was an unheralded and unnamed corporal who first stumbled onto a scene whose reverberations would be felt around the world.[4]

Further down the page was this:

> The DC-9 was purchased several years ago in a partnership between 'Royal Sons Motor Yacht Sales, Inc. DBA Royal Sons' and a company owned by Brent Kovar called Skyway Communications Holding Corp, which jointly signed a loan with United Bank and Trust Company in St. Petersburg, FL. for $1.5 million.
>
> Skyway Communication's principal Kovar must have been looking well forward to justify the purchase; the company was then in the middle of losing $40 million in less than three years, between 2002 and its last annual report before bankruptcy in January 2005.[5]

Notice the date. It took the *Tampa Bay Times* almost a year and a half to publish all the details.

What I had written fifteen months earlier was what led me to Tierra Verde, Florida.

It was my curiosity that got me gripped in a headlock. The same curiosity gets a cat killed, so at least I was ahead of the feline population.

Kovar Kitchen Table

B ack at the kitchen table, waiting for the cops to arrive, I rehearsed what I could say in my defense, to the cops or, heaven forbid, a judge. "Yes, I knew it was private property, and I was trespassing, Your Honor.... But when he slammed the door in my face, I saw red, and I momentarily forgot the sanctity of private property. It was a momentary lapse of reason, Your Honor. I'm much better now."

I doubted it would work. But I toted up the pros and cons as they presented themselves. I even visualized myself in jail.

First, when the white Tierra Verde squad car rolled up, its siren wasn't screaming. Nor did it screech to a halt.

So, I thought, there's that.

On the other hand, when the lawman entered the house, it was clear that he and Brent Kovar were singing off the same page. Stern faced, he read me my rights, then, before asking questions, gave me to understand I just "might could" be in big trouble.

We were looking at trespassing, he told me. I could do time.

During all this, the man in uniform and Kovar were both stealing glances at my Handycam, which I had been cradling like a football with my body when Kovar tackled me. My football training from high school in Chicago Heights must have kicked in unconsciously. The camera contained what little illicit footage I'd been able to shoot before being flung to the ground.

It was sitting like an open invitation on the kitchen table. Kovar and the cop were looking from it … to me, then back again.

Now it was my turn to look seriously pissed. Any idiot could see the deal on the table: Would I turn over my camera and let them erase my ill-gotten footage? Or did I want to take a trip downtown?

It was, for me, pretty much a no-brainer. I've got what the experts and educators label "attention deficit disorder," or ADD, as I may have mentioned earlier. I can't do time. I can't even watch commercials on TV. The terms of the deal seemed to pass wordlessly between us. It was at that very moment – when all that remained in closing the deal was a handshake – that my girlfriend, who had been sitting in the car parked out front and must have seen the patrol car roll up – chose to make her presence felt.

I saw her standing in the open doorway, wearing a simple shift over running shoes, exhibiting an expensive Nikon with an impressive telephoto lens, slung over her shoulder.

In a dexterous yet graceful motion, she unslung the camera and pointed it through the open door. I could hear clicking.

Both the cop and Brent Kovar exclaimed "Hey!" at one time.

Eyes on me, she ignored them. Regarding me curiously, as if for the first time, she said, "I don't suppose you noticed there are surveillance cameras on every corner of this house? Like this is some kind of miniature Fort Knox?"

I had not noticed, but I couldn't find my voice to admit it. It explained how I'd been blindsided. Kovar had fled inside after slamming the door in my face and had been lying in wait to see what I would do next.

I tried to show no emotion on my face, but I'm not very good at poker. I tend to bite my bottom lip when I'm nervous, and my mouth was in overdrive. Kovar gloated in triumph at my predicament.

"You can't take pictures in here, ma'am" said the cop. "It's private property."

"I'll keep that in mind, officer," she replied saucily.

My girlfriend was a petite, red-haired environmentalist from Austin. She was passionate about protecting the local aquifer in the Hill Country of Texas. They take their watershed very seriously in that part of the world. She and her organization created photo-ops and got themselves arrested several times every few years. It was a tactic she employed with relish. It was their main fundraising device.

Now I began to see – just from the tone of her voice – that there might be trouble ahead, as she ignored the cop and continued snapping pictures. She was looking right at me. She said, slowly and distinctly, putting stress on every syllable, "He shouldn't have slammed the door in your face."

Gentlemen's Agreement?

While the three of us – Kovar, the cop, and I – had stared at the camera on the table, I felt sure that we were about to come to some kind of gentlemen's agreement that would forestall my having to go to court on the trespassing beef. Maybe I wouldn't even have to go down- town!

Couldn't she see that?

I said to her, "We were just coming to an understanding here."

But she may have been looking for a fight. It's hard to know sometimes, with women. Maybe she envisioned a cover for "Save Our Springs Alliance," her favorite quarterly magazine.

Brent Kovar hadn't committed any environmental outrages to speak of – except for drug trafficking, that is, which was, arguably, carbon neutral.

Trespassing at the home of a well-connected drug kingpin in Florida seemed – just then – several orders of magnitude more serious than contaminating the Edwards Aquifer.

This was my freedom being bartered here. Anyone can buy bottled water.

As I sat dithering in silence at Brent Kovar's kitchen table, she continued snapping shots of the interior of Brent Kovar's home. Her presence had definitely introduced a new element into the mix. If the cop wanted *her* footage, too, the tiny Tierra Verde branch of law enforcement might soon be dialing its partners in regional law enforcement for back-up.

But I couldn't tell him that, just in case he hadn't thought of it yet. The cop eyed me curiously. "What do you think?"

I was thinking that a peaceful end to these proceedings may be beyond reach. It wasn't just because she was a redhead, though – don't get me wrong – I'm sure it didn't hurt. That was just how she rolled.

Covering the drug trade attracts a certain fringe element. And I fit right in.

I guess that's why I have no pictorial footage to show. Needless to say, my questions remained unanswered.

Drug Lord 1 Hopsicker 0

* * *

Endnotes

1   Later I looked it up and found he was spot on. https://www.choosingtherapy.com/signs-of-a-psychopath/

2   Leonora LaPeter Anton, "Invention Was Too Good To Be True," *Tampa Bay Times*, 01 Jul 2007, Sun · Page 8.

3   T. van Treeck, "Is there a link between rising inequality and the "Great Recession"?" As noted by *The Economist* (22/01/2011, p. 11).

4   Daniel Hopsicker, "Aircraft's Owners in 5.5 Ton Cocaine Bust Include Tom Delay Appointee, 'Royal Sons LLC," April 17, 2006. https://www.madcowprod.com/2006/04/17/owners-of-plane-seized-with-5-5-tons-of-cocaine/.

5   Ibid.

CHAPTER SIX

ARGYLL EQUITIES – FROM CULTS TO ORGANIZED CRIME

There is a cult of ignorance in the United States, and there has always been. The strain of anti-intellectualism has been a constant thread winding its way through our political and cultural life, nurtured by the false notion that democracy means that "my ignorance is just as good as your knowledge."

– Isaac Asimov[1]

For Skyway, bankruptcy was inevitable. The millions that had been invested in the company's stock hadn't been enough – Kovar lied to his investors – even to get started on the promises made to them.

One lawsuit claimed Plaintiffs who had invested an aggregate of $7.4 million, only a third of their total contract to buy Skyway Communications shares, by August 2004 had quit paying. There were no positive results shown from the infusion of money. What Kovar was doing with the money he took in was a total mystery.

Had he thrown it into a black hole?

Skyway Communications' bankruptcy documents solved part of the mystery. By the time Skyway filed its petition, the second-largest shareholder/creditor listed was Argyll Equities LLC, owning nearly 21 million shares of Skyway Communications stock. Its value was totally worthless.

Skyway had pledged the stock to Argyll, which was in the business, stated their glossy literature, of providing "creative financial solutions globally." It was a fancy money-laundering technique that never quite worked. "Pledged," in this sense is a legal term meaning the stock was loaned out as collateral for a loan received by Argyll. We'll furnish more detail on that loan later.

Argyll claimed to provide what it called "specialized services," which we discovered were offered to drug trafficking operations. One perfect example of Argyll's lending services was shown in a loan to Grupo TMM in Mexico, which we'll get to shortly.

Argyll had just finished up that transaction before we noticed it was the biggest creditor in Skyway's bankruptcy.

ARGYLL'S CREATIVE SOLUTIONS

Douglas Arthur McLain, Sr., then in his-mid 60's, was the unbalanced brain behind Argyll. He was a man with a spectacularly checkered past before we tracked him down in San Antonio, Texas, where he was busy defrauding elderly customers of their life's savings.[2]

Douglas McClain was a soulless fraudster with no remorse and no empathy for the people he harmed. He deserved whatever he had to endure. Masquerading as a Christian, he mouthed all the right words that convinced others to trust him. That has since become the ploy used by MAGA Republicans who want to convince constituents to donate money and do their bidding.

How did he turn out like that, I wondered. So I did a little investigating. Doug's father, Donald Freeland McClain, had lived most of his life in Manchester, Connecticut, after graduating from Duke University in 1934. He was a salesman for the Pratt & Whitney Co., which built jet engines for airplanes, before being acquired by Raytheon some years later.

Donald left the job in 1960 to take his NYSE's licensing exam. Once he became licensed by the stock exchange, he worked for Shearson, Hamill & Co.[3]

As a securities trader, Donald McClain was wealthy enough by 1967 to send Douglas, his youngest child, to Cushing Academy, a private boarding school about 90 miles away from their home, but apparently only for his freshman year. Doug graduated from Manchester High, a public school in 1969, where he played football, was on the track team, and was also a wrestler.

Donald and his wife Muriel had by then become devout followers of a charismatic former Baptist preacher named Sam Fife, whose Pentecostal cult branched out nationally, allegedly even into South America.

Thanks to research by one victim of the cult, we know that in 1972, Donald McClain, with two other men, acquired a 280-acre tract of land halfway between his home and the Cushing Academy, and they put title in the name of Mt. Bether Bible Center, Inc. It was one of many congregations controlled by Sam Fife's cult.[4]

The author of *Cult Child*, Vennie Kocsis, was quite young when her mother first joined the cult. She writes from her vague, ghost-like memories: "Life before we leave for the U-Haul trip comes in chunks of memory and corroborating stories from my siblings. My father is a retired Naval officer turned civilian government employee at the naval station in Miramar, California where we move in 1970, one year after my birth. He is contracted to work on a project designing a fighter plane called the F-14 Tomcat."[5]

Donald McClain had bought the land and was getting the destination ready for the cult from Hemet, California, to move to. At the same time the convoy of cars dragging trailers behind set out, Donald and Muriel McClain and other members of their family were putting the finishing touches on the property. Many of the cult members in the Hemet church – located about halfway between the secret Naval Base at Miramar and Indio – were linked somehow to the Naval base at Miramar.[6] These converts of "The Move of God" – a cult originally created by Sam Fife in New Orleans around 1950 – were on their way to a new home in Massachusetts.

A CULT IS GOOD COVER

S amuel Drew Fife, Jr. also had connections to the Navy. Born in Miami, Florida, in 1925, his own father had recently been discharged from the Navy after serving on the USS *Martha Washington* in WWI. Sam Jr. would follow in his steps when the next war rolled around, serving on the S.S. *LaJeune* until 1945, when he'd become a truck driver with two children by 1950.

Sam grew up as a member of the Little Flock Primitive Baptist Church in northwest Miami before moving to New Orleans to attend the Baptist Bible Institute, from which he graduated in 1957. Its purpose "was centered on missionary work, and initially established as gateway to Central America."[7] Still living in Metairie in 1959, he lost his home for failure to pay paving liens filed against it. Rev. Fife returned to Miami for revival meetings at Calvary Bible Church but by then he was ready to move on.

Fife's cult is said to have consisted of more than 10,000 members who lived on farms and ranches in remote corners and wilderness areas of Colombia, Peru, and Guatemala. According to an account in the *New York Times*, Both Donald and Douglas McClain, Sr. were active in the cult for more than a decade and maintained cordial relations long afterwards.

Incidentally, the cult also owned its own fleet of planes. That little detail got our attention. We know about what one retired insurance executive, Wally Hilliard, did with his fleet of planes. What would an itinerant preacher do with his?

Sam Fife's Cult

The father of Angela "Vennie" Kocsis, was stationed at Miramar when his wife decided to leave him, taking their children to Ware, Massachusetts. Vennie later discovered a deed signed by Donald McClain and two other men in 1972, as well as a later document showing title in Mt. Bether Church.

The land in Massachusetts was tax exempt from 1972 until sixteen years later – on June 14, 1988. Just over 128 acres was sold, resulting in a tax bill for almost $4,000, which then had to be paid.

Vennie also found evidence that Douglas Arthur McClain in 1980 had title to land in Alaska held in his name. Was this just a scam for men to hold land for a number of years tax free until it was ripe for development? It's a worthy subject for research.

Or was it even more sinister? Was it a ruse to allow these men to play out their vile pedophilia fantasies on innocent children? Donald McClain and his family are described several times in *Cult Child*:

> Sister Muriel's trailer sits on a big, green yard on the other side of the driveway," the author writes. "Sister Muriel has her own trailer, not only because her husband helped buy the land for the church, but also because her son, Brother Douglas McClain Sr., is part of the Father Ministry and their family has given a lot of money to the church. When people have a lot of money, they get special privileges. Sister Muriel and her husband are two of those people.[8]

Donald was living in Forsyth, North Carolina, in 1986 when he died – presumably having left his wife, Muriel at least temporarily before the rest of the family moved with the cult to Alaska in 1988.

Doug McClain also moved to North Carolina for a time. Several sources said he planned to set up his own church there. But by 1989 we find him living in Wellington, Florida. A birth announcement for a son, Patrick Sterling McClain, born to Debra Alloe, was announced in Palm Beach County. Douglas' first wife – Doug Jr.'s mother – had died years earlier.

The so-far unanswered question about him is where he first acquired powerful patrons whose clout could – and did – keep him out of jail despite his record for flagrant financial fraud for years before he set up Argyll, and for and money-laundering services for drug smugglers through that company.

INTERNATIONAL PROFIT ASSOCIATES

While the ultimate answer may not yet be clear, for sheer greed, bra- zen theft and raw carnality – committed with the protection and apparent blessing of former leaders in both major political parties – it would be hard to top McClain's stint during the early 1990's at International Profit Associates (IPA) in Chicago.[9]

All three of the top officers at IPA boasted felony convictions. The company chairman, John R. Burgess, was a disbarred lawyer from New York, with a criminal record for larceny and patronizing a 16-year-old prostitute in a company board room.[10]

Charles W. "Bill" Morton was convicted of a misdemeanor in 1988 for stealing Hummell figurines from three Pittsburgh stores. Seriously.

A year later Bruce Tulio pleaded guilty to involvement in the manufacture of a major ingredient of methamphetamine.[11]

The highlight event at every year's IPA Christmas Party was a speech by a famous U.S. politician – former President Gerald Ford, Bob Dole, and later both Bush President and both Clintons. What was that about?

The company was also the scene of what a prosecuting attorney called "the most egregious case of sex harassment that Chicago has ever seen," a case in which 113 women employees were victimized.[12]

IPA was where Douglas McClain would hook up with key associates with whom he collaborated during the next two decades in a "hyena pack" that went from one success to another in a series of lucrative financial scams.

"HIS HORIZONTAL RIVALS HIS VERTICAL"

Following in Donald's footsteps, Douglas also got a degree that enabled him to deal in securities of public corporations. It was just enough to get Doug McClain, Sr. into an organized crime ring we mentioned earlier, that was run by Robert Colgin Wilson, according to a *Wall Street Journal* article published on February 24, 1997.

Author Jim McTague described 600-pound six-foot-five-inch Wilson as a con man "whose horizontal rivals his vertical."[13]

Wilson's pack of hyenas fast-talked investors in the U.S. and Canada out of somewhere between 60 and 100 million dollars.

"Wilson dazzled his victims by treating them to jaunts to Las Vegas and the Cayman Islands on his luxurious corporate jets, promising super-high returns in supposedly risk-less investments, and employing high-profile, unwitting company directors–among them Chip Carter, son of the former President, and Carter budget chief Bert Lance," Tague wrote.[14]

In each case McClain was connected to there was a scheme to defraud a group that included entities and individuals in the United States, Canada, Barbados, Ireland, Switzerland, the Channel Islands, and numerous other locations throughout the world, making Wilson's organization the very definition of transnational organized crime.

Doug McClain, as one of Robert Wilson's henchmen, had learned of a template – which dates all the way back to the 1950's – used by members of organized crime to defraud and "bust out" coal companies. It came in handy for McClain's M3 Energy scam.

In 2002 Doug Sr. moved from Florida to Boerne, Texas, a quaint town just north of the Bexar County line, the gateway into the Texas "Hill Country."

Doug Jr. was finishing college in Florida as his father and stepmom moved to Texas, to be near where her parents, Richard Paul and Margaret Mary Alloe – both now deceased – were living.

After college, "Dougie" moved to Savannah, Georgia, according to a deposition he gave contesting jurisdiction in Texas. But that wasn't quite the whole truth, as we'll learn.[15]

McClain's Radiating Social Network

One case the SEC prosecuted gives us a window into how Wilson's scam team operated. In the SEC's case against Jack Kenny, an associate of McClain and Wilson, the judge spelled out with methodical precision what each member of the team did and where they did it.[16]

Jack Kenny had brokerage licenses in at least 20 states during a career that began in 1981, and he was working in St. Louis for Dean Witter when Douglas McClain, "acting" as the Director of Robert Colgin Wilson's Euro America Insurance Company Limited, appeared there, posing as a potential client. In short order, McClain introduced Kenny to Wilson, a man with impressive credentials.

Wilson helps set Kenny up in his own office, which then becomes an integral part of Wilson's "hyena pack.

"One item that captured our attention was about a different client of McClain's – Albert Norman Kaufman – a former non-commissioned military man who had retired in Boerne. Early in 1995, McClain advised Kaufman to open a brokerage account at Cohig and Associates in Denver, a company we found little about without looking under a few rocks.[17]

Set up by a stockbroker named James "Jim" Cowdery Cohig, the company had never been registered to issue or even sell securities. Jim Cohig, born in Denver in 1929, had an individual broker license for a time but was suspended by the National Association of Securities Dealers (forerunner of FINRA) in 1983. Back in 1969, Cohig's employer, McDonnell & Co. was bought up by Shearson Hammill & Co., and his job was terminated. FINRA's investigation showed Cohig had been asked to resign from the Shearson partnership, but he told investigators that "he forgot to" because he had been hospitalized for six weeks, then went on vacation for a month. His excuse was almost as convincing as "the dog ate my homework."

Cohig & Company, Inc., unlicensed, operated as an agent for Wall Street West, Inc. – licensed only in Colorado, although it was illegally operating in numerous other states as well without authorization. It was fined in 1983 for misrepresenting itself.[18]

One of those states was Missouri, where the Kansas City Chiefs employed Wall Street West's broker, Bill Kenney as starting quarterback in 1980-81.[19] In 1996, when Kenney ran as a Republican for Missouri lieutenant governor, his work history was brought up against him in attack ads.[20] Bill Kenney and Jim Cohig were both selling stocks for Wall Street West at the same time, and Kenney was also working directly with Lamar Hunt, owner of the Kansas City Chiefs.

As we'll detail later, Hunt had around this time owned the DC-9 (N900SA), later acquired by Skyway to smuggle drugs. Surely just one of the many coincidences that keep piling up. Ya think?

We mentioned quite a few anomalies connecting Cohig and Eastbrokers in a previous chapter which you might want to review to save our repeating it here. The facts are so confusing, we are tempted to believe it's by design. That's probably why bad guys don't get put away as often as they commit crimes.

* * *

In 1996, at the same time Brent Kovar leased the entire top floor of the Plaza Tower building in St. Pete, he sold his satellite company, SAS, planning to start fresh with Skyway Communications. Only it didn't quite work out as he planned. He was sued for selling the same invention twice – an invention which had never even existed at all.

The dodgy guys who bought SAS (Roger Dunavant and Rene Hamouth) – who'd sold horse shampoo to humans – merged SAS into a shell corporation called Corsaire, Inc., which then changed its name to Corsaire Snowboards, Inc., and in short order to Net Command Tech, Inc. (NCT).[21]

EBI Securities Corp. then bought a large percentage of Net Command Tech stock and sued Hamouth on behalf of Net Command shareholders. Czech Fund aka Czech Industries, Inc., which had been set up as a cover for Bud McFarlane to travel to eastern Europe in the aftermath of the collapse of the Soviet Union, had links to Adnan Khashoggi and the Viennese bank, WMP. It was the remnants of this spooky company which bought the assets of Eastbrokers in Vienna and hired Wolfgang Kossner of Austria as a consultant.[22]

EBI also has links to Adnan Khashoggi and Ramy El-Batrawi through GenesisIntermedia, whose original underwriter was an outfit bearing the name Millennium Financial before it became I-Bankers Securities, a company where Michael Roy Fugler worked, as we're reminded by Christopher Byron's "Red Herring" essay, which we quote at length previously.[23]

Byron also pointed out the connection between Millennium Financial and Netivation.com, which he said had "a curious history with an Arkansas politician named Asa Hutchinson." Netivation had two underwriters – Fugler's Millennium (I-Bankers) and EBI Securities (the former Cohig & Associates, Inc.).[24]

* * *

Need I remind you who Asa Hutchinson was? Before he became a failed candidate for the Republican Presidential nomination in 2024, Asa was the Governor of Arkansas from 2015 to 2023.

A graduate of Bob Jones University, the craven Southern Baptist manqué Asa Hutchinson was the U.S. Attorney for the Western District of Arkansas, where he specialized in looking the other way while Barry Seal was bringing cocaine back from Honduras in a CIA military cargo plane to Mena airport. It was only the biggest cocaine smuggling operation in recorded history, allowed to hum along right outside his office window.

Terry Reed's first-person account of the operation, told by a friend of mine, John Cummings, pulled back the curtain to reveal how an undercover CIA operation worked in real time. In the pages of *Compromised: Clinton, Bush and the CIA*, the book they wrote together, Cummings clearly exposed how an elite Republican (George H. W. Bush) mentored an ambitious Democrat (Bill Clinton) in the dirty work of campaign finance *à la* drug money, provided by the CIA's most profitable sideline.

Bush's friends in the operation included Oliver North, William P. Barr and U.S. Attorney at the time, Asa Hutchinson.

As a reward for not prosecuting anyone involved in the Mena CIA-drug operation, Asa was named by George W. Bush as head of America's DEA, where he totally fit the necessary qualifications – lack of interest in stopping drug smugglers affiliated with the CIA.

I was criticized for having a brief excerpt of *Barry and 'the boys'* published in the newsletter put out by the old right-wing Liberty Lobby, but I thought, "Hey, if we're ever going to reach these folks – now we call them 'Trump's MAGA base' – we've got to deliver the unvarnished facts to them through a medium they might read." Just saying. Since then, I've started to wonder if they read at all.

Here's part of what I said back then, pulling no punches:

> Hutchinson has served as a member of the House Speaker's Task Force for a Drug-Free America. The task force has a mandate "to seek out new and more effective approaches to combating the threat of drug use among the nation's youth." Hutchinson made some tough-talking speeches to community groups in Arkansas about cleaning up what even he had been forced to acknowledge was "a haven for international drug trafficking," where Seal had continued to operate from an airfield in Mena, just a few miles from Hutchinson's office.
>
> Maybe the sound of the big C-123s rumbling overhead had scared him, but observers of Hutchinson's lack of performance grew increasingly skeptical of his crime-fighting credentials. Hutchinson's action never once matched his rhetoric.
>
> Former IRS agent William Duncan had been the first to take his information on Hutchinson public. In a deposition for the Arkansas attorney general, Duncan was asked, "Are you stating now under oath that you believe that the investigation in and around the Mena airport of money laundering was covered up by the U.S. attorney?"
>
> Duncan replied: "It was covered up."[25]

William Duncan's name had also appeared in the *New York Times* in 1989. When invited to testify by the House Judiciary subcommittee on crime, the IRS general counsel told him not to mention the name of a senior official who was suspected of laundering drug money. He resigned from his IRS job and testified truthfully.

A Democratic chairman of another subcommittee he testified for blasted IRS officials, calling them "the wizards" in the "land of Oz." The Times, unfortunately, entirely omitted Hutchinson's name as well as the name of the IRS officials.[26]

After more than 20 years, I'm left to wonder if it even matters. Hutchinson was one of only two candidates for the Republican nomination who said, if elected, he would not pardon Donald Trump for all of the 91 crimes he's been indicted for. He's almost become one of the few good guys.

How far our country has fallen. The cited articles are further evidence of the CIA's involvement in protecting Barry Seal's drug smuggling, but that protection ended once Seal turned on the Agency for allowing him to be arrested along with his crew in Florida in 1984 during Operation Screamer, as I described in *Barry and 'the boys.'*

One intrepid reporter named Michael Haddigan in a small town in Arkansas – after Barry Seal's old C-123 cargo plane he'd used to fly cocaine into Mena, crashed with Eugene Hasenfus and other CIA operatives aboard – was able to document that the "Fat Lady" had been "parked" at the airport in Mena for a year before the crash. His reporting is additional evidence that confirms Terry Reed's story.[27]

Asa Hutchinson simply resigned as U.S. Attorney in November 1985, three months before Barry was gunned down, to run unsuccessfully for the U.S. Senate.

He had no Federal Government job again until 1997 when he was elected to the Congressional seat vacated by his brother, Tim Hutchinson. Just as Asa's term was ending, out of all the seasoned political direct-mail companies available, he hired a brand-new unknown dot-com – Netivation.com – to handle fund-raising for his re-election. Did he know something nobody else knew at the time?

Netivation.com was intent on gaming the system, according to a lawsuit it filed against Yahoo in 2000. It sued Yahoo for taking its money and not doing what they contracted to do – manipulating its search engine to bring up Netivation banner ad when certain key words were typed into the search box.

It was a forerunner of what happened with Facebook and Twitter in the 2016 election. The technology was changing faster than the everyday consumer could keep up. But the experts were just waiting in the wings to bring it all out.

Our book about Barry Seal – I used to call him America's first drug lord – offered overwhelming evidence that one drug pilot flew drugs into the United States for the Central Intelligence Agency. The evidence has never been refuted. The scope of *Gangster Planet* is much broader, branching out to show more details of how the organizations we now call transnational organized crime works.

There are eighteen intelligence agencies buried inside the U.S. federal government – all operating in our name.[28] Yet they are seemingly completely unsupervised because of "national security." Their work is "classified," and we are not "cleared" to know what it is they do.

Endnotes

1   "A Cult of Ignorance," *Newsweek*, January 21, 1980.

2   John Tedesco "Scam suspect claims he's paying back $200,000," *My San Antonio*, Dec. 14, 2012. Felony fraud charges were filed against McClain for swindling $200,000 from a 74-year-old neuropsychiatrist who'd been paralyzed in a motorcycle accident in 2012. The article also says McClain owned a "3,600-square-foot home in Fair Oaks Ranch appraised by the county at nearly $410,000." https://www.mysanantonio.com/news/local_news/article/Scam-suspect-claims-he-s-paying-back-200-000-4119612.php

Also see John Tedesco, " Doctor pays for helping friend," *My San Antonio*, August 24, 2012. https://www.mysanantonio.com/news/local_news/article/Doctor-pays-for-helping- friend-3814336.php

3   Wikipedia comes through again to give us the history of this securities brokerage company which went through a series of changes in the early to mid '70s, just as its Manchester, Connecticut representative was getting involved with Sam Fife's cult. https://en.wikipe- dia.org/wiki/Shearson

First, the company Donald McClain represented, Shearson, Hammill & Co., a classic partnership, was bought by a newly incorporated investment bank called Hayden Stone, Inc. – becoming Shearson Hayden Stone – headed by Sanford I. Weill. A concise history of the merged firm to this point is available: http://www.fundinguniverse.com/company-histories/shearson-lehman-brothers-holdings-inc-history/

"By 1977, Shearson's holdings were consolidated, resulting in the seventh largest investment banking firm in the country. Its revenues had more than tripled since 1972, to $134 million in 1977, and employees now numbered more than 4,000."

4   As recounted in the book, *Cult Child*: "Life before we leave for the U-Haul trip comes in chunks of memory and corroborating stories from my siblings. My father is a retired Naval officer turned civilian government employee at the naval station in Miramar, California where we move in 1970, one year after my birth. He is contracted to work on a project designing a fighter plane called the F-14 Tomcat.[4] We will always brag about that, [siblings] Leis, Jeremy, and I. "Remember when we lived by the base and waved at the jet planes going over 'cuz we thought it was Dad doing fly by's and test flights for the F-14, Sila?" … "Lenny Nerbonne and Dad are longtime friends from the Navy, having known each other for many years. Lenny has a tall, big, bony wife named Esther. She has a stern face complete with thin, pursed lips and dark piercing eyes. Esther has been around since before the time I am born. Their family moves to California shortly before we move…. It is during this time while my father is gone working long hours for the military, that Esther invites Mama to start attending church in the town of Hemet, California. Kocsis, Vennie. *Cult Child* (pp. 22-25). Kindle Edition.

After living on the farm in Ware, Massachusetts, the cult moved to Delta Junction, Alaska, shortly after the Trans-Alaska Pipeline was started. "Preconstruction work during 1973 and 1974 was critical and included the building of camps to house workers, construction of roads and bridges where none existed, and carefully laying out the pipeline right of way to avoid difficult river crossings and animal habitats. Construction of the pipeline system took place between 1975 and 1977." Wikipedia.

"Living Word Ministry, what will be called 'Dry Creek, 'The Land' or 'The Farm' is an incredibly vast compound." Kocsis, Vennie. *Cult Child* (p. 124). Kindle Edition.

"Peace River commune awaits imminent apocalypse" read the headline in the *Vancouver Sun* on Sept 22, 2003.

We found additional evidence of Doug McClain's leadership in the cult in a history of the Alaska settlements centered around Delta Junction: "Members of a church group in Claremont, New Hampshire were looking for land on which to establish a community. A man named Doug McClain living in Dry Creek, Alaska was in contact with the New Hampshire group known as "Whitestone Community Association." http://whitestonecommunityassociation.net/history.html

5   Kocsis, Vennie. *Cult Child* (p. 22). Kindle Edition. The Tomcat was first tested by the Navy in 1970, but by 1973 they were calling what the Pentagon had done a repeat of the TFX. The Navy had never been happy with the TFX aircraft design, which they had to tweak to meet what the Air Force wanted. The TFX contract was the last decision President Kennedy announced in Fort Worth the morning he was murdered. Indio was where Michael Riconosciuto lived. See Inslaw, Inc. v. USA, Case No. 85-00070

U.S. District Court, Washington, D.C. Bankruptcy case. https://newtotse.com/oldtotse/en/conspiracy/casolaro/inslwmjr.html The move of this Move Cult predates by almost a decade the subjects that arose during the Reagan administration's secret going-on described by J. Orlin Grabbe at https://rense.com/general16/tim.htm

6   Wikipedia. https://en.wikipedia.org/wiki/Sam_Fife and https://en.wikipedia.org/wiki/New_Orleans_Baptist_Theological_Seminary

7   Kocsis, Vennie. *Cult Child* (p. 108). Kindle Edition.

8   Intriguingly the deceased parents of McClain's wife Debra Alloe also had connections to John R. Burgess.

9   "International Profit Associates, Inc.," Encyclopedia.com. https://www.encyclopedia.com/books/politics-and-business-magazines/international-profit-associates-inc

10   Ibid.

11   Ibid., with reference to *New York Times*, May 2006.

12   James McTague, "Same-Old Same-Old," *Barron's*, Jan. 19, 1998. https://www.barrons.com/articles/SB884993439376072000#wilson

13   Ibid.

14   We learned from a lawsuit filed in Kendall County, Texas, that the address in Boerne, Texas, was inserted into loan documents, mandating Boerne (Kendall County) as the venue where lawsuits must be brought. When that first lawsuit was filed in the old historic courthouse, however, the case was dismissed as to all defendants, each successfully fighting jurisdiction because none of them had sufficient contacts within the county.

15   Initial Decision of an SEC Administrative Law Judge, In the Matter of John 15 J. Kenny and Nicholson/Kenny Capital Management, Inc. FILE NO. 3-9611; August 6, 1999. https://www.sec.gov/litigation/aljdec/id147slg.htm#body1

16   Ibid.

17   https://law.resource.org/pub/us/case/reporter/F2/718/718.F2d.973.82-1125.html

18   https://en.wikipedia.org/wiki/Bill_Kenney AND SEE PHOTO at https://www.chiefs.com/photos/photo-gallery-lamar-hunt-18262546#6b19ff1c-d5c8-4edc-9a0d-f1e6c372cbbe

19   Virginia Young, "Ads in Wilson-Kenney race put spin on truth," *St. Louis Post-Dispatch*, 13 Oct 1996, Page 52. https://www.newspapers.com/article/st-louis-post-dispatch-bill-kenney-bro/139810363/

20   https://miamiherald.newspapers.com/image/617873199/?clipping_id=135931494&fcfToken=eyJhbGciOiJIUzI1NilsInR5cCI6IkpXVCJ9.eyJmcmVlLXZpZXctc-WQiOjYxNzg3MzE5OSwiaWF0IjoxNzAyODUxNTA1LCJleHAiOjE3MDI5Mzc5MDV9.LwfZ196naXIL9ICLWOQ5IBen4Q4kSYyxSrnqwmZ9wls

21   https://www.lawinsider.com/contracts/2WYe3n2swJm

22   Christopher Byron, "Kiosks, Cocaine, and Khashoggi," December 6, 2001. http://www.redherring.com/Article.aspx?a=5463&hed=Kiosks%2c+Cocaine%2c+and+Khashoggi.

23   Ibid.

24   Daniel Hopsicker, "New head-honcho at DEA protected drug smuggler," Spotlight. The article was undated, but it was written at some point after Asa Hutchinson was appointed by President Bush and confirmed by a unanimous vote of the U.S. Senate in January 2003. http://www.libertylobby.org/articles/2001/20010528dea_honcho.html

25   Susan F. Rasky, "Chief of Panel Says I.R.S. Tried to Impede Its Inquiry," Special To the *New York Times*, July 28, 1989. https://www.nytimes.com/1989/07/28/business/chief-of-panel-says-irs-tried-to-impede-its-inquiry.html

26   https://www.dni.gov/index.php/what-we-do/members-of-the-ic

27   Alexander Cockburn, Jeffrey St. Clair, *Whiteout: The CIA, Drugs, and the Press*, Verso 1998, p. 325.

28   https://www.dni.gov/index.php/what-we-do/members-of-the-ic

CHAPTER SEVEN

ARGYLL'S DRUG VIBES HINKY

"Drugs and covert operations go together like fleas on a dog," said former CIA analyst David MacMichael. "When congressional probers scratched the surface of the drug trade, it became clear that certain cocaine and heroin dealers were okay by the CIA, as long as they snorted the anticommunist line. Anything goes in the fight against communism."
– Martin A. Lee & Bruce Shlain, *Acid Dreams*

Manuel Vicente Losada Martinez's original ambition had not been to become a drug smuggler but a professional tennis player. With a tennis scholarship to Austin Peay University in Clarksville, Tennessee in the early '70s, Losada was conveniently away from Chile when duly elected Salvador Allende was ousted by "strong-man" General Augusto Pinochet, perhaps with a little help from the CIA.

Correction: We can now say unequivocally there was no "perhaps."[1] President Joseph Biden in August 2023 declassified CIA records, clearing almost all previous redactions, making it clear that U.S. military (both Army and Navy units) were involved in the *coup d'etat* against Allende and the installation of the brutal dictator Augusto Pinochet into power a year before Nixon resigned.

Soon after the military coup, Losada – a college tennis player from a family who lived in a mini-palace in Valparaiso – opined in an interview by the *Clarksville Leaf-Chronicle*, that Allende had "tried to move too fast with socialism."[2]

He was being well-trained at the time in capitalism.

As a boy in 1967 Manuel won the tennis title of National Vice-Champion, before going off to college in Tennessee, where he ultimately received a degree in engineering and an MBA (Master of Business Administration) from the University of Tennessee.

Back home in Chile a couple years later, Losada Martinez was becoming a discreet but well-recognized figure of Chilean high society. His family was notable in the maritime trade and the breeding of thoroughbreds.[3]

Losada soon gets in touch with the new regime. He finds he can do a little business with Augusto Pinochet's niece, now in charge of mining. She happens to be married to the head of Chile's central bank, which no doubt corresponds with Nelson Rockefeller's family's banks in the U.S. – part of the New York Fed.

Nelson Rockefeller, once in charge of the South American desk – it was called the Office of the Coordinator of Inter-American Affairs (CIAA), before it was handed over to the newly minted CIA – had hopes in the early '70s of becoming President through a back door, as *New York Times* reporter Sam Roberts has reminded us.[4]

Later in this book, we will show how drug smuggler Kenneth Burnstine worked through a domestic corporation controlled by the Rockefeller family in the '60s and 70's, also working in Florida with a Rockefeller-connected building contractor, Ken Behring, who moved to the Pacific Northwest and bought a Seattle football team. Behring also owned one of our Skyway drug planes for a few years. It was all part of a RICO operation before there was a Racketeer Influenced and Corrupt Organizations (RICO) Act.

Nixon learned from Rockefeller how to replace the Europeans' "French Connection" with a similar one throughout South and Central America. The CIAA, created within Office for Emergency Management, was under direct control of the Office of the President from 1940 until 1945. After Franklin Delano Roosevelt's death, it was moved to State Department oversight – as the Office for Inter-American Affairs (OIAA) – then quickly abolished when the CIA was created. [5]

Rockefeller had an unofficial channel through which the movement of illegal drugs could be supervised under control of the covert section of the CIA.[6] All Nixon had to do was to announce a "war on drugs," so the CIA could step in. In cases where the CIA was involved in the trafficking, the CIA could overrule the Drug Enforcement Administration (DEA), which the Nixon Administration had set up a year or two before he resigned in 1974.

NEPOTISM – A GOOD SYSTEM, IF YOU'RE CONNECTED

Pinochet's favorite niece, María Teresa Cañas," we were told by *Ciper Chile*, "is one of the largest owners of mining concessions in Chile. In addition, she, together with her husband Jorge de la Barra, created a large number of companies in the most diverse areas in the last 30 years: agricultural, financial, fishing and forestry. One of their companies did business with Manuel Losada Martínez, convicted of drug trafficking in 2009."[7]

You can't read *Ciper* Chile's articles anymore online, unless you risk being infected with malware. Just sayin'.

The *Official Gazette* informed that the Barra-Losada partnership (South Pacific Fishing) obtained loans for almost a million dollars from Chile's equivalent of Enterprise Florida, called "Corfo."[8] All Losada then needed was official approval to proceed, which could be obtained from his partner's wife – Pinochet's favorite niece – which was granted on February 6, 1989.

Once the government authorized the "fishing" company to engage in business *outside Chile*, the drug operation was off and running. Deliveries through the newly approved route through Mexico continued from that date on.

Nepotism ("being connected") always helps.

In 1991 the company we have been following, Argyll Equities, had arranged for a $17 million loan to a Mexican businessman named Jose Serrano Segovia, an owner of Grupo TMM, a Mexico-based international shipping line.

At least part of the "loan proceeds," according to *The Santiago Times*, an English language newspaper in Chile, were passed to Segovia, most likely as part of a merger of their two businesses. [9]

AQUATIC INTERLUDE

Fast forward three years later…

It is January 5, 1992, and a U.S. Coast Guard cutter is slicing through the Windward Passage, the sweep of warm blue Caribbean Sea separating Cuba from Haiti.

The Coast Guard boat, the *Campbell*, is looking for a Chilean freighter called the MV *Harbour*, steaming for Baltimore under a Panamanian flag carrying a cargo of zinc. Drug agents think a shipment of cocaine may be aboard.

It is close to midnight when the *Harbour* heaves into sight of the Coast Guard boat *Campbell*, just off Guantanamo, Cuba, within the U.S. Coast Guard's jurisdiction. The *Campbell* radios for permission to board, but the *Harbour* douses its lights and radios back, "We're on fire and sinking." The crew is abandoning ship, intent upon scuttling the *Harbour* before U.S. Coast Guard crewmen can scramble aboard. The crew had also opened two sea valves. Three feet of water had accumulated below deck by the time the Coast Guard arrive and put out the fire in the engine room. Another few minutes and the ship would have sunk. The flooding is stopped just in the nick of time. Just like in the movies.

Like trained drug dogs, the Coasties begin digging through the zinc. Lo and behold, they strike pay dirt – five tons of cocaine – at the time the Coast Guard's third-largest cocaine seizure ever.

When the *Harbour* sailed from Peru, it was known as the *Golden Hill*. Once it crossed into Chile, it was re-registered and renamed the *Harbour* by a Chilean shipping magnate and former tennis professional, Manuel Losada.

As co-owner of South Pacific Fishing, S.A., Losada's partner in Chile is Jorge de la Barra, married to Uncle Augusto's favorite niece. The U.S. has had a lot of history with Uncle Augusto since the CIA's operations in the mid-1970s.[10]

It's always nice to have connections. Though they're not always fool- proof.

Those aboard were taken to Tampa, which already had an ongoing investigation, not fully revealed until 2001.[11]

* * *

The State Defense Council (CDE) in Chile investigated for six years, finally deciding they had sufficient evidence to charge 13 of the persons aboard. Manuel Losada Martinez was detained in Valparaiso, Chile, in May 1998, and formally charged with drug trafficking and money-laundering.

The Court in Valparaiso soon heard the case, finding "the businessman Losada and the other 12 prosecuted by his court are responsible for the crimes of illicit association for money laundering and illicit association for drug trafficking."

The defendants then had another six years to prove they were innocent, according to a report by Cooperativa.cl dated June 1, 2004.[12]

It was five years and three months later when Losada's sentence for money-laundering and drug trafficking was reduced by the Valparaíso Court of Appeals – from ten years to time served – that is, to less than two years. Since money-laundering hadn't been made a crime in Chile until 2005, a year after his conviction, Losada was immediately released. The 541 days he'd served was applied to his conviction for illicit association (conspiracy to engage) in drug trafficking.[13]

They ordered the government to return to Losada his "real estate and personal property, such as motor vehicles, money, commercial papers and personal securities."

What a deal. Manuel Losada was back in business.

The delay had worked to the benefit of Argyll Equities, Losada's lender, which was already gearing up for its next big deal: The Skyway loan would be Argyll's third business endeavor.

As they say, the third time is the charm.

MAD COW NEWS DATED JANUARY 19, 2011:

Hank Gonzalez was the richest man in Mexico.

He uses his post in the federal government to amass a fortune, steering state money to his trucking firm. He is the essence of power in Mexico: wealth based on graft, on pillaging the national treasury.

The rumor for decades has been that he is the link between the drug business and the government. The President of Mexico between 1988 and 1994 was Carlos Salinas. During that time forty-six reporters are murdered in Mexico.

A major drug figure, Juan Espattagozo, alias "El Azul" went to work for Carlos Hank Gonzalez's family's trucking and shipping company, TMM, in 1992. Mexico's biggest drug baron at that time was Amado Carrillo. He died during botched plastic surgery. But while he was alive, he is the Lord of the Skies His-Ownself.

Along with Carlos Hank Gonzalez, Amado was a major investor in Grupo TMM, according to U.S. intelligence.

A truck from Grupo TMM entered California with 4.5 tons of cocaine. Another was caught in Jalisco with 2 tons. According to the DEA, a TMM boat in 1998 offloaded a ton of cocaine in the Florida Keys.

The two men also had a big stake in Mexico's biggest airline.

OPERATION WHITE TIGER

Hank Gonzalez's son is Carlos Hank Rhon. The thing to remember about him is: Hank loves wildlife. After a sojourn in Asia, he lands in Mexico City with twelve suitcases filled with jewels, animal pelts, and ivory tusks. He keeps a rare white Siberian tiger as a pet.

When a Tijuana gossip columnist makes fun of him in print, Jorge's bodyguards cut him down with Uzis.

The bodyguards are marched off to prison. Not Hank.

A DEA investigation of the Hanks, called "Operation White Tiger," accuses the family of having illicit business partnerships with some of the world's most infamous drug smugglers. The report accuses the Hank family of being narco-kingpins who launder money through Laredo National Bank.

The *Washington Post*, quoting parts of the report, says the Hank family "poses a significant criminal threat to the United States."

In 1993 a Catholic Cardinal is murdered in his car at the airport in Guadalajara. Afterwards the killers of Cardinal Jose Ocampo saunter over to board a Mexicana flight. It is being held at the gate for their arrival.

Onboard is Hank Rhon. The men fly back to Tijuana together. When the killers are caught, Hank is not charged.

Lucky Hank!

SOLILOQUY STAGE LEFT

We take a brief pause here for a personal aside, like in a Shakespeare play when a narrator comes on stage to tell the audience the back-story that explains the action taking place now. It's like a flashback in a novel.

When Linda Minor and I were first doing research together back in the early 2000s or so, she was deep into studying Texas railroads. She once said something totally off the wall like, "It *all* goes back to the Texas Railroad Commission."

Even today, when she tells me she has the answer to the question we're researching, I tell her I already know: It goes back to the Texas Railroad Commission.[14]

Being connected means hooking up with people who have the wealth and political power to keep you from getting in trouble. They are your protection. In Russia that protection is call "krysha," or roof, which we will get to soon.

When Linda was following railroads back in the day, she already knew about the Bush family's connection to Brown Brothers Harriman and to G.H. Walker & Co. and to Walker's Thyssen connection through Harriman Fifteen. You can find it all now in Wikipedia. But she did not realize Walker had been heavily involved in railroad stock, which he'd handled for St. Louis millionaires. When his clients' investments were in danger of being lost in 1913, squat and pudgy Bert Walker – like Clark Kent entering a phone booth and emerging as Superman – stepped forward to rescue them from bankruptcy.

He protected their investment in a railroad built from New Orleans through the southern tip of Texas to the Mexican border and preserved it for the future. In so doing, he negotiated a merger with the Missouri Pacific, which had a long-range plan to cross into Mexico.[15]

Prescott Bush was good at hooking up. He went to Yale and got tapped to Skull and Bones. Then he married the daughter of the man from St. Louis (G. H. "Bert" Walker), who had planned to move to New York in 1920 to handle investments for Morgan Guaranty Trust, but instead joined up with the two sons of the biggest railroad tycoon of all – old E.H. Harriman.

Walker became a partner in W.A. Harriman & Co. in New York, buying an estate among super-wealthy capitalists at Wheatly Hills, Old Westbury, Long Island, NY – smack dab in the heart of horse breeders and bankers who had more money and power than God.[16] In his spare time, Bert bred racehorses, served as head of the Jockey Club, and financed the upgrade of Madison Square Garden.

Walker's firm, G.H. Walker & Co., invested $60 million in the Brownsville Syndicate, along with his friends and associates in St. Louis, who had millions more in the rail network that bordered Mexico.

When Bert died in 1953, his stock portfolio still included shares of the old St. Louis-based railroad syndicate, held in Missouri Pacific receivership until 1956. The syndicate had quietly been renamed Westag corporation.

Bert's son, G. H. Walker, Jr. (G.H.W. Bush, "Poppy") called him "Uncle Herbie." Herbie was at that same time helping Poppy start his career in West Texas oil fields. That's when Herbie finds the yellowed stock certificates, which still had a few assets remaining – worth in the neighborhood of a cool million, in the '50s, when you could buy both a hot dog and a Pepsi for a nickel.

Thanks to Uncle Herbie, credited in Bush's book, *Looking Forward*, this old stock became Poppy's basis in Zapata Petroleum, and later Zapata Offshore, in 1956.[17]

That's where our trail goes dead.

All that's left are questions about what Uncle Herbie did with his daddy's stock portfolio after 1953. Like this big query: Did he start cooperating with the likes of the Hank family, who was accused of smuggling drugs?

End of soliloquy: (Narrator exits stage).

From Aiding Cali Cartel in Mexico to Skyway

TMM (Transportcion Maritima Mexicana) was founded in 1958, two years after Zapata, and it included investors from two wealthy Mexican families – the Hank-Rhon family and the members of Serrano-Segovia family.

In 1991 the families merged their shares in the business by issuing new stock as Grupo TMM.

A decade prior to the merger, since about 1982, TMM owned a Delaware-incorporated subsidiary called Mex-Rail, Inc., whose history was discussed in a paper delivered at a conference for professional railroad researchers, reprinted at a Mexican website.[18]

Railroad researchers apparently concern themselves with the historical owners and creditors – shareholders and bondholders – and government ownership of assets. Their work covers the financial minutia of what was the dull, everyday business of railroad transactions of the past.

It's great bedtime reading for insomniacs, true. But if you can stay awake for it, the history does explain why TMM needed to borrow money, and why they might have been willing to deal with a shady company like Argyll. My best guess?

The boys in the back room arranged it, and then flubbed it up.

It's not within the scope of *Gangster Planet* to analyze the historical transactions that might explain any link between Bert Walker's railroad and the Mexican lines that were privatized at auctions in the '80s. The authors are too old ... and tired ... to accomplish that task. We leave it to the youngsters of today.

My best advice to said youngsters:

Just follow all the breadcrumbs wherever they may lead. Don't make assumptions. Some things can never be proved or disproved, especially when secret government agencies are involved. Warning: Plausible deniability works against transparency.

Above all: *Follow the money.*

One-third of the shares in TMM – the company the Mexican government sold at auction to Carlos Hank in 1982 – were sold in 1991 to Grupo Servia, S.A. de C.V., controlled by the Serrano Segovia family. The result was that Grupo TMM (the Serrano Segovia shares) became a subsidiary of TMM. On the day after Christmas 1991, Jose Serrano Segovia was named chairman of the parent company, TMM.

A year later Bill Clinton was elected President of the U.S. and worked hard to get NAFTA through Congress in 1994. It was the most controversial issue of the time. Five years after NAFTA, the *Washington Post* reported:

> "Allegations that significant sums of foreign drug money are being invested in the United States are extremely serious," the [Clinton administration] official said.
>
> The report said the Hank family "has begun to extend its interests from Mexico to the United States. [It] has purchased or exercises control over several U.S. banks, investment firms, transportation companies and real estate properties."

The report mentioned, for example, that Carlos Hank Rhon purchased shares of Laredo National Bankshares, the holding company of two Texas banks, through two of his own holding companies. It also gave examples of the family's efforts to gain influence over U.S. gambling businesses.[19]

SEC filings of Grupo TMM are available online, and, like the Mexican railroad history just cited, are highly recommended if you're looking for an Ambien substitute. I tried it and found it quite efficient as a sleep aid.

I also discovered that the general counsel for Jose and Ramon Serrano Segovia's various entities, including the one which borrowed money from Argyll Equities, was Haynes & Boone, a law firm with offices in several cities in Texas, in Mexico City – well, actually, all over the world.

The lawyer defending Argyll Equities was based in tiny Boerne, Texas. But Argyll also brought in another attorney from Dallas named Samuel L. Boyd, who today has a squeaky clean reputation.[20]

Linda happened to notice she had been in her last year of Texas Tech Law School during his first year there. She never met him, but his educational credentials were very impressive to both of us.[21]

Not only that. Boyd had a previous career in the military that was perhaps even more imposing. In 1971 Boyd graduated from the U.S. Army John F. Kennedy Special Warfare Center and School (SWCS)–known informally as "Swick."[22]

The Dallas attorney, Samuel L. Boyd, was also linked to both Doug McClain of Argyll and his mentor, Robert C. Wilson, through frauds in Denver, Florida and North Carolina.[23]

THE ARGYLL LOANS

Argyll had arranged for a $17 million loan to Jose Serrano Segovia, chairman of the shipping line called Grupo TMM (for Transportcion Maritima Mexicana), according to filings with the SEC. The loan to help finance a merger, was announced in December 2001.

At least two members of the Segovia family, holding the majority of shares in TMM Group and subsidiaries, had sought out Argyll Equities for a loan just before the merger was to take place – offering ADRs (American Depositary Receipts) as collateral. [24]

Losada's shipping company, Intermares, was just then getting set to merge with TMM Group – GRUPO TMM SA (NYSE:TMM), owned by Mexico's Segovia family. The loan was to work like this:

SEC jargon: In June 2004, a TMM subsidiary, Servicios Directivos Servia, S.A. de C.V. (SDS) appointed Argyll through a Pledge Agreement, to be its proxy with power to trade the pledged stock.[25] This was reported to the SEC as part of a Schedule 13D/A filing.[26]

Translation: Servicios, the subsidiary, "loaned" the stock to Argyll in exchange for $17 million from Argyll to Servicios. The deal was that Argyll could trade the stock until the loan was repaid.

El Universal de Mexico had connected Losada to the Juarez Cartel (linked to Jorge Hank Rhon of Mexico), referring to Losada as "the Chilean narcotics trafficker, way back in September 1997," the *Santiago Times* reported, then added more to the story.[27] The *Times'* English edition in Chile reported on May 5, 1998, that Segovia, after receiving the $17 million loan, had then "provided significant capital to Chilean narcotics trafficker Manuel Losada, who has connections with both the Cali and Juarez Cartel."

The *Times* reminded readers of Losada's 1998 conviction after a ship he owned had been caught with "five tons of cocaine, which U.S. drug enforcement officials in Miami intercepted on the vessel Harbour, as it headed toward Guantanamo Bay."[28]

On June 2, 1999, the DEA, the FBI, the CIA, US Customs and Interpol issued a joint report, published in the *Washington Post*, alleging that Carlos Hank González and his two sons, Carlos Hank Rhon and Jorge Hank Rhon, were drug traffickers, money launderers and "a threat to the internal security of the United States."[29]

Now that's one big fat PR problem, seemingly for all concerned. But somehow Losada's attorney got him out of prison on a technicality, had all his assets restored, and set him up to continue business as usual by 2004. Argyll was then free to move on to its next project – Skyway Communications.

Again, clear sailing for a year or two. Then on April 10, 2006, something went very wrong. Skyway's DC-9 was busted in Ciudad del Carmen.

In the late spring of 2006, the Segovia attorney showed up in court in tiny Kendall County, Texas, demanding an injunction against Doug McClain and his entity, Argyll Equities, to whom their stock shares were pledged. Argyll must immediately stop trading TMM and subsidiary stock, the lawyers demanded, and return the ADRs to the Segovias.

The injunction was granted on June 30, 2006.[30]

It was all very short and sweet. No questions. No answers.

But it was only the beginning of problems for Argyll. At the same time Skyway was also beginning to "go through some things," as we'll learn later.

Endnotes

1   Editor's note: I was editing the chapter when – lo and behold! as they say – up pops this unredacted CIA record from 1973. The CIA was working with the U.S. Navy to oust Allende and put Pinochet in power. Says it right there, clear as day. Edited by Peter Kornbluh ,"The Coup in Chile: CIA Releases Top Secret 9/11/1973 President's Daily Brief," Briefing Book #838, Published: Aug 25, 2023. https://nsarchive.gwu.edu/briefing-book/chile/2023-08-25/coup-chile-cia-releases-top-se-cret-9111973-presidents-daily-brief

2   Richard McFalls, "Allende Tried to Move Too Fast with Socialism," Clarksville, TN *Leaf-Chronicle*, 12 Sep 1973, Page 1.

3   Jean-Francois Boyer. *La guerre perdue contre la drogue*, Chapter 9. https://www. cairn.info/la-guerre-perdue-contre-la-drogue--9782707132864.htm

4   Sam Roberts, "Serving as Ford's No. 2, Rockefeller Never Took His Eye Off Top Job," *New York Times*, Dec. 31, 2006. https://www.nytimes.com/2006/12/31/nyregion/31rocky.html

5   Roosevelt's middle name is included here because his Delano family goes back to the earliest days of drug smuggling operations in the U.S. – when the Delanos were partners in the Forbes operation absorbed into the Russell Trust. See Linda Minor's essay at https://wherethego-ldis.blogspot.com/2012/01/following-forbes-money-trail.html Also see Kris Millegan's article at https://www.iviewit.tv/CompanyDocs/skull1.pdf

6   Henrik Krüger and Jerry Meldon, *The Great Heroin Coup*, Trine Day 2016. https:// www.overdrive.com/media/2553643/the-great-heroin-coup

7   Ciper Chile on May 16, 2011. When attempting to access in November 2023, Malwal-bytes warned against the site. The information, fortunately, had been preserved in another source: https://anales.cl/canas-pinochet-maria-teresa/

8   Jane Bussey, "In Chile, scandal shakes financial moorings," *Miami Herald*, April 10, 2003.

9.   *Santiago Times*, Santiago, Chile, May 5, 1998.

10   https://www.cia.gov/readingroom/docs/CIA-RDP77-00432R000100340005-5.pdf

11   Paula Christian and Pat Minarcin, "Years of Drug Boat Seizures set the stage for Tampa's most ambition drug case ever," *Tampa Tribune*, June 17, 2001. https://www.newspapers.com/ arti-cle/the-tampa-tribune-chile-drug-case-2001/136102561/

12   https://www.cooperativa.cl/noticias/pais/judicial/jueza-dicto-cargos-contra-involucra-dos-en-la-operacion-oceano/2004-06-01/125910.html

13   "Court reduces sentence and orders property returned to Manuel Losada," Diario Impre-so, La Tercera, Sep 12, 2009. https://www-latercera-com.translate.goog/diario-impreso/corte-re-baja-condena-y-ordena-devolver-bienes-a-manuel-losada/?_x_tr_sl=auto&_x_tr_tl=en&_x_tr_hl=en&_x_tr_pto=wapp

14   Linda never let my amusement stop her from following her instinct, however removed it seems from what is happening today, no matter how boring it is. Since nobody will listen, she writes her ideas in her blog in as many words as it takes. Quixotic Joust – the title alone gives you an insight into how she sees her own musings. In fact, she had another blog called "Minor Musings."

15   The New Orleans, Texas & Mexico Railway owed money on bonds. The bondholders ap-pointed St. Louis investment banker, George Herbert Walker, to be the receiver (like a bankruptcy trustee) to collect the bonds out of the railroad's assets. As receiver he incorporated in 1916 a new company with virtually the same name to hold the securities of four railroads: (1) New Orleans, Texas & Mexico; (2) Beaumont, Sour Lake & Western; (3) Orange & Northwestern; and (4) St. Louis, Brownsville & Mexico Railroads. New officers elected were the new chairman, Frank Andrews of Houston, Texas, and vice president G.H. Walker, a banker in St. Louis.

The Missouri Pacific (MP), a Gould railroad, acquired these four railroads in December 1924, plac-ing them in its hierarchy as MP's Gulf Coast Lines Division. This acquisition now gave the Missouri Pacific access to the southern portions of Texas in competition with the Southern Pacific Railroad and its Atlantic Lines Division.

To further expand the "Spider Web Rail Network" in the Rio Grande Valley, the Missouri Pacific acquired the Rio Grande City Railway under the New Orleans, Texas & Mexico Railroad in 1926, and in 1941, the Port Isabel & Rio Grande Valley railway, which was acquired by the St. Louis, Brownsville & Mexico. But in 1933 the MP was placed under control of a trustee for creditors, which lasted until after G.H. Walker's death in 1953.

Also see Linda Minor's essay called "The Presidents Bush: Walker Genealogy, Part VI." https://quixoticjoust.blogspot.com/search/label/George%20Herbert%20Walker?m=0

16   Most of the Walker story still exists at Linda Minor's various blogs. Doug Wead's biography of Bert's grandson, *The Raising of a President*, indicated the Walker move may have begun as early as 1919.

17   George Bush, *Looking Forward*, Doubleday; First Edition (August 18, 1987). https:// www.newspapers.com/image/574406428/?match=1&clipping_id=136915655

18   "The debts of the National Railroad and the Texas Mexican Railroad," *Digital* magazine, Jan-Apr 2018. Paper presented on October 26, 2017 within the XI National Meeting of Railway Researchers, organized by the National Center for the Preservation of Railway Cultural Heritage, through the Center for Railway Documentation and Research (CEDIF) and the National Museum of Railways. Mexican Railways in the City of Puebla, Pue. https://www-miradaferroviaria-mx.translate.goog/las-deudas-del-ferrocarril-nacional-y-el-ferrocarril-texas-mexican-the-debts-of-the-national-railway-and-the-texas-mexican-railway/?_x_tr_sl=es&_x_tr_tl=en&_x_tr_hl=en&_x_tr_pto=wapp

19   Douglas Farah, "Prominent Mexican Family Viewed As Threat to U.S.," *Washington Post* Foreign Service, June 2, 1999; Page A1. https://www.washingtonpost.com/wp-srv/inatl/longterm/mexico/stories/hank060299.htm

20   https://www.samboydlaw.com/attorneys/samuel-l-boyd/

21   B.A. in Mathematics, with highest honors, Texas Tech University, 1974; M.B.A., Texas Tech University, 1977; J.D., with high honors, Texas Tech University, 1977. Phi Kappa Phi, Beta Gamma Sigma, Order of the Coif, Phi Delta Phi, National Mock Trial Team, Texas Tech University School of Law, 1975-1977, Member and Managing Editor, Texas Tech Law Review, 1975-1977, Member, National Order of Barristers, Texas Tech University School of Law, Member and President, Texas Tech Slovo (Russian Language) Club,1973. He was also in 1994 admitted to the Bar of the U.S. Virgin Islands.

22   Ibid. Also see: https://en.wikipedia.org/wiki/John_F._Kennedy_Special_Warfare_Center_and_School

23   Sarah Okeson, "County looks at pricey swamp," *Florida Today*, 29 Jun 2008, Pages 1, 3.

24   https://www.sec.gov/divisions/corpfin/cf-noaction/grupotmm062702.htm

25   Grupo TMM, S.A.B - ADR - Series A, on Letterhead of Argyll Equities. See agreements   at   https://fintel.io/doc/sec-segovia-jose-f-serrano-1163560-ex9913-2005-december-29-18764-2859 and https://fintel.io/doc/sec-segovia-jose-f-serrano-1163560-ex9921-2005-december-29-18764-6918

26   https://www.sec.gov/Archives/edgar/data/1163560/000095012308007437/y62054e20vf.htm

27   *Santiago Times*, May 5, 1998. https://web.archive.org/web/20050114190312/http:/ ssdc.ucsd.edu/news/chip/h98/chip.19980505.html#a0

28   *Santiago Times*, May 5, 1998.

29   Douglas Farah, "Prominent Mexican Family Viewed As Threat to U.S.," *Washington Post* Foreign Service, June 2, 1999; Page A1 https://www.washingtonpost.com/wp-srv/inatl/longterm/mexico/stories/hank060299.htm

30   https://fintel.io/doc/sec-segovia-jose-f-serrano-1163560-ex9926-2006- june-28-18764-4661

CHAPTER EIGHT

BUSTING OUT ALL OVER

Fans of the Sopranos will remember the "bust out" as a mob tactic in which a business is taken over, loaded up with debt, and driven into the ground, wrecking the lives of the business' workers, customers and suppliers. When the mafia does this, we call it a bust out; when Wall Street does it, we call it "private equity."

—Cory Doctorow

LAS VEGAS TO HOLLYWOOD

There's no telling how many times Kenny Rogers had sung the words to "The Gambler," the song that became his claim to fame and fortune before he bought his own private jet to tour in. During the '70s most of his singing engagements were in Las Vegas, where he appeared at Steve Wynn's Golden Nugget.

"Kenny Rogers was a big deal at the Golden Nugget. Bigger, even, than blackjack," John Katsilometes of the *Las Vegas Review-Journal* wrote in Rogers' obituary in 2020.[1]

His public awaited him worldwide. It was time he had a jet of his own. Kirk Kerkorian, the Las Vegas "financier," who was one of the big five corporate owners of gambling in Nevada in the '60s, bought a Mc-Donnell-Douglas DC-9 in 1979 under the name of his holding company, Tracinda Investments, through which Kerkorian owned his shares in Caesar's Palace, International Hotel and MGM Grand.[2] Undoubtedly, he knew Steve Wynn, who also owned the Golden Nugget, possibly working through him to sell the jet to Kenny in 1984.

At the same time he acquired the plane, Kenny and his wife Marianne moved to West Hollywood and built an entertainment Center at 8730 Sunset Boulevard.[3]

WHAT A TRUE COINCIDENCE LOOKS LIKE

Ironically, the Kenny Rogers Building was only four or five blocks – a short walk, except nobody walks in West Hollywood – from the Tiffany Theater where my play, "Marooned in Malibu," would run for a year almost a decade later.[4]

I merely mention this personal detail to give an example of what a true coincidence is. While Kenny was wailing about what condition his condition was in with the First Edition, I was still groovin' to the Grateful Dead. Maybe Kenny just had a bad trip. Go figure.

My college major at UCLA, a decade before Kenny made it big as a sole act, had been creative writing and English Lit, and I'd been so enamored of Shakespeare, I took a semester off college just to study Hamlet on my own. A couple years after completing my degree, I married in 1974 a sweet girl from Malibu named Cathy Sue, who worked to pay the bills, while I was writing a play that never quite made it. She was too sweet to hold that against me, and we divorced amicably in 1983.

After my second marriage ended in 1987, I saw a doctor. What was wrong with me? The medical term was attention deficit disorder – ADD – and the remedy was a drug called Adderall. It was, for me, a miracle cure. It helped me focus. I resumed the play, which at this late date I now dedicate to Cathie Sue and Adderall.

Little did I know in the summer of 1993, when my play was being performed at the Tiffany on Sunset Boulevard, that Kenny Rogers had been so close in distance, but so far away in time, from my own tiny claim to fame.

A mere coincidence.

FROM DC-9 N900SA FAA TITLE DOCUMENTS

Kenny Rogers and his wife realized after two years of touring it was time to walk away, so they folded their cards. In April 1986, they transferred the jet to a corporation called Syntek, created in the late '70s by Gene E. Phillips in Greensboro, North Carolina.[5]

Phillips later bought Atlanta-based Southmark Properties, a real estate trust, and turned it into his holding company for Syntek, as well as a plethora of limited partnerships set up by his partner, William Friedman, a New York lawyer who specialized in tax shelters. The money came from junk bonds issued by Drexel, Burnham, Lambert – the flagship of Michael Milken.

Syntek owned the jet but leased it back to Southmark, which used the leased jet as collateral for a new loan from The CIT Group in New York, paying off a $4.3 million loan with California First Federal.

The mid '80s were the vulture capital years – Milken's heyday. Even more importantly, Barry Seal was murdered, and then a short time later Iran-Contra exploded in the press.

Coincidences? Not on your life.

When I finally received the documented title from the FAA of the DC-9, N900SA, I discovered these celebrities had been among the jet's former owners, immediately noticing that what they had in common was gambling and entertainment – possibly a close association with organized crime figures.

During that period of the plane's use, Republicans were, of course, in charge of the country, and the CIA played a big part in the party's financial maneuvers. Despising Jimmy Carter's high moral tone, at the same time, Republican strategists came to realize they could use Evangelical Christian leaders to steer voters toward them.

A review of Russ Baker's book, *Family of Secrets,* is quoted here in length because of its importance in understanding how Republicans took control of the Christian Right:

> Baker's chapter titled "The Conversion" features startling revelations that challenge the well-known narratives of the Bush family's religious history – including the way they crafted a strategy for winning over the religious right, and the creation of a conversion legend for George W. Bush. The purpose of the latter was not only to position him as a religious and political man of his time, but to neutralize the many issues from his past that threatened to undermine his future in politics (and possibly that of his father as well). The plan probably worked far better than anyone could have hoped. "I'm still amazed," Doug Wead, a key architect of the Bush family's evangelical outreach strategy told Baker, "how naïve so many journalists are who have covered politics all of their life."
>
> **Poppy and W. Learn Evangelical Lessons**
> In the early 1980s, Vice President George H.W. Bush faced a political problem of historic proportions. The religious right, driven by politically energized evangelical Christians had altered the political landscape, helping deliver both the 1980 GOP nomination and the presidency to Ronald Reagan. How could the tragically preppy Poppy – a product of Andover and Yale, and secretive former director of the CIA – adjust to the new political reality in order to run for president in 1988? The answer to this question is part of the Bush family's slow motion transition from old line Yankee blue bloods to good ol' Red State politicians.
>
> The story begins with Doug Wead, a former Assemblies of God minister turned what Baker terms a "hybrid marketer-author-speaker-historian-religious-political consultant," who by

1985 had apparently been vetted and groomed to shape the Bush approach to the religious right. "Instinctively," Baker writes, "he [Poppy Bush] was uncomfortable with pandering to the masses, and uncomfortable too with ascribing deep personal values to himself. For that matter, he didn't like to reveal much of anything about himself, which was partly patrician reserve and partly perhaps an instinct reinforced by his covert endeavors over the years."

If Poppy was going to be president, Wead advised, he needed to learn about "these people." Eventually, Wead drafted a lengthy memo outlining a way for Bush to surf the rising wave of the religious right to the presidency. "This was the beginning," according to Wead. But not only for their political strategy. Wead felt that Poppy himself had embarked on a spiritual journey, reworking his own spiritual identity even as he studied the evangelical world and developed a political approach for his 1988 presidential campaign.

All of this would be crucial since Representative Jack Kemp (R-NY), a well-known conservative evangelical, and televangelist Pat Robertson also planned to run for the GOP nomination, forcing Bush to compete for the evangelical vote. The three first clashed in the Michigan GOP caucuses, which preceded the usually first-in-the-nation Iowa caucuses. (Bush ultimately won after a critical court ruling.)

But Wead revealed to Baker how the "covert operator" orientation of the Bush camp played out on the ground. "I ran spies in our opponents' political camps," Wead said, including elected Robertson precinct delegates in Michigan. These Bush agents made headlines when they abandoned Robertson and publicly threw their support to Bush. "We helped them win… and totally infiltrate the Robertson campaign," Wead declared. "I ran them essentially for [Lee] Atwater, but W. knew about them."

"The spy argot here is suggestive," Baker writes. "In the Bush milieu, an intelligence mentality spills over not just into politics but even into dealings with the church-based right. Domestic political constituencies," he warns, "have replaced the citizens of Communist countries as a key target of American elites. They seek to win hearts and minds of devout Christians through quasi-intelligence techniques."[5]

Money-laundering techniques were being tweaked and fine-tuned. What is telling about those years is that the financing institutions providing funds to purchase this particular jet, SkyWay's Cocaine One, both before and after it was sold by Syntek, would eventually be rolled into the "patsy" bank that went down for laundering money for El Chapo's Sinaloa Cartel. Rest assured, Wachovia was not the only bank involved in the scheme.

Wachovia Corporation, based in Charlotte, North Carolina, was a stone's throw from where Gene Phillips created Syntek with help from a North Carolina bank then in the planning stage to expand before being consumed by bigger banks in New York or San Francisco.

NationsBank in Charlotte had merged with C&S/Sovran Corporation of Atlanta, the company that sold Southmark to Gene Phillips.[6]

North Carolina bankers in the early '90s had already decided to become New York's primary financial rival for international customers. Then they made the dream happen. Almost like magic. It all started happening right after Bill Clinton's inauguration in January 1993. The city of Charlotte, North Carolina proudly announced a merger allowing it to "leapfrog over San Francisco" and become "the No. 2 U.S. banking center."[7]

In that deal, First Union Bank paid $5.4 billion to acquire First Fidelity Bancorporation, New Jersey's largest bank.[8] Not far from Donald Trump's Atlantic City empire of casinos, First Fidelity held mortgages on those properties.

In Pamela L. Moore's article in the *Charlotte Observer*, she wrote that First Union bankers began "holing up" in a classy hotel in October 1993 for two full days a month, making plans to change the face of the southern bank into an investment bank rivaling Wall Street's biggest banks in the New York Fed. The first step was to create First Union Capital Markets Group in January 1994.[9]

Almost at the same time Charlotte's largest bank, NationsBank, began to plan for a future merger with San Francisco-based Bank of America in October 1998.[10]

Deposits also began pouring in through Mexico's casa de cambios to Wachovia Corporation in Winston-Salem – one of the cities making up North Carolina's so-called 'Triad'. Then on September 4, 2001, Wachovia merged into First Union of Charlotte, but maintained the wealth-management sector, as well as the Carolinas-region headquarters in Winston-Salem.[11]

It was all very complicated. That's why they almost got away with it.

SOUTHMARK RISING

Gene Erlo Phillips had risen, as Pete Brewton wrote, "from the ashes of the biggest personal bankruptcy in South Carolina history, took a busted-out real estate investment trust in Atlanta called Southmark and transformed it into a $9 billion company in Dallas."[12]

Ever since wildcatters found oil in the East Texas field and turned Texas oilmen into caricatures for movies and TV, people have been mocking wealthy Texas eccentrics. Gene Phillips was not a Texas oilman in that sense. Neither was a Dallas man named James J. Ling. They were scavengers of the wealth that had been tossed aside, wealth that dribbled from the bulging pockets of oilmen to be scooped up into their holding companies.

What Phillips and Ling had in common is that both lived at different times in the same house. Not only that. Both had links to the same DC-9 in a weird sort of way.

The house – a mansion really – was built around 1937 by Cipriano "Dick" Andrade, described by Shad Rowe in *Texas Monthly* as "an oil-field wheeler-dealer who might hit it big and go broke all in a week's time. If he wasn't betting on oil wells, he was betting on cards or horses."[13]

Andrade, as Texans would say, "might could have" taught Kenny Rogers a thing or two about gambling, if he'd lived, that is.

The mansion, Rowe tells us, was "situated in Preston Hollow on a street named Gaywood near North Dallas, arguably the most prestigious residence in the city."[14] Andrade lived there until New Year's Day 1961. The New Year's Eve party the night before had, presumably, been so rowdy he only survived a few hours after singing "Auld Lang Syne".

LING'S LTV AND E-SYSTEMS – "CHUMMY" WITH CIA

That same year (1961) the North Dallas mansion was sold to James J. Ling, famous for building a conglomerate called Ling-Temco-Vought (LTV). I was familiar with LTV because it had a huge connection to the Venice "missile launch complex" situated right next to the Venice Airport.[15] The same airport where two pilots involved in 9/11 took flight lessons.

You know the one.

Ling had taken his first company, Ling Electric, public in 1955, issuing new stock to acquire a bunch of electronics companies.[16] That's probably our first CIA tell. The "boys" love to rip off innocent investors who believe in American capitalism – i.e., Wall Street.

It's a way to make big bucks fast. All it requires is a little PR work called "pumping" to get the stock price higher. Once the paper value of the stock has risen, the manipulators can target a company to buy.

In this case, it was Texas Engineering and Manufacturing Corporation (TEMCO) of Dallas, bought by Ling in 1960. A year later Chance Vought Aircraft was in his sights.[17] The merged corporation was named LTV for Ling-Temco-Vought.

LTV spun off Electro Systems in 1972, later called E-Systems. Three years later, E-Systems bought Air Asia from the CIA. For the $1.9 million it spent, E-Systems acquired a huge aircraft repair facility in Taiwan, where Claire Chennault's old airline ended up after being chased across China by both the Japanese and the Red Chinese. In 1975 Air Asia was said to be worth $3.2 million, so it was quite a profitable deal for LTV.

John Mintz, a reporter in 1994, said, "If Big Brother ever took control of the United States, E-Systems Inc. would surely be its prime contractor."[18] E-Systems, located between Dallas and Fort Worth, near DFW Airport, Mintz continued "is almost indistinguishable from the CIA because it operates so secretly, lacks accountability and is loaded with retirees from the CIA and other intelligence agencies."[19]

Chance-Vought Installs Missiles in Venice, FL

Along the way, Ling's business partner had been a man we've all heard of – D. Harold Byrd – one-time Mr. Big in both the Dallas branch and the national Civil Air Patrol (CAP).[20] CAP was where both Barry Seal and Lee Harvey Oswald learned to fly, with help from CAP pilot David Ferrie. I wrote about this years ago at my website[21] and in *Barry and 'the boys.'*[22]

Under a headline reading **"Air Force Keeps Range In Venice,"** the *Sarasota Herald Tribune* on Dec 4, 1959, reported, "As the result of talks between the Air Force and Chance-Vought Aviation of Dallas the missile firing range at the Venice Airport may be given semi-permanent status." Similar information was published that year in St. Petersburg: **"Regulus Missile Fired at Venice."**[23]

Several weeks later, under snapshots of CAP student pilots being trained by the National Guard, appeared possibly the most hyberbolic headline ever for a dateline Venice story:**"1959 Has Been the Best Year for Venice Since City's Birth."** The body of the article announced that the city had "received national publicity as the site of the launchings of the Regulus II guided missiles or drone target planes manufactured by the Chance-Vought Aircraft Corp. which has set up installations on the Venice Airport."[24]

Just like Brent Kovar, Jimmy Ling had earlier been called a wizard in electronics. He did not finish high school, let alone college – getting his knowledge from working in his father's shop and that of Oscar Emerson in Dallas before World War II.

He returned from the Navy in 1947 with big ideas and some important military contacts, including D. Harold Byrd, whose marriage in 1935 to

Mattie Caruth, the daughter of one of Dallas' wealthiest and most prominent families, added to his power as the head of the Civil Air Patrol in Texas and nation-wide.

Ling formed Ling Electronics in Anaheim, California, California, hiring Cameron George Pierce of Menlo Park, California, in 1956 as president. [25]

In 1941 Pierce had been working on a project with Professor Felix Bloch, a Swiss-born physicist and Dr. Ernst O. Lawrence – building Stanford University's first cyclotron.[26] Any time nuclear power is mentioned, you know we're talking about highly classified information protected by the three-letter agencies.

There were two Navy Reservists who spent a couple of years in California during the war, as we've been told in *Book Four* of Robert Caro's biography series on Lyndon Johnson, though he wasn't quite sure what they did there. More than likely, he was building up a Democratic base there with future Governor Pat Brown, who was elected Governor in 1958 and later re-elected in 1962 over his opponent, former Vice President Richard Nixon.[27]

By the mid-'50's Pierce was in radio and television, rising to be the chief engineer of the Western Division for American Broadcasting Company (ABC).

Robert McCulloch had been president of Temco in Grand Prairie, Texas, since the 1940s and brought D. Harold Byrd onto Temco's board of directors by 1952. He served there until all his stock was bought out by Ling in 1965 – four years after Ling-Temco merged with missile-maker Chance Vought to form LTV.

Ling was wealthy enough by 1961 to buy a magnificent mansion. He lived in splendor in the North Dallas mansion on Gaywood Street from 1961 until he was forced to sell it in 1970, when the bloated LTV conglomerate began crashing down around his feet.

That's called, in CIA parlance, a "bust-out," the end result of any public corporation 'the boys' find themselves involved in. A bust-out is not failure, in their eyes; it's the goal. The people who cause the bus-out, therefore, don't always end up poor.

Mansion-buyers weren't hard to find in oil-rich Dallas. Who would appear to rescue Ling from poverty but one of H. L. Hunt's larger-than-life sons, Lamar Hunt, without quibbling over the $1.5 million purchase price.[27]

JUST PLAIN FOLKS

For a man who had just run his conglomerate into the ground, Ling found employment quickly. Dallas banker Robert H. "Bob" Stewart

III – the same man who would, would hire George H. W. Bush in 1977, when Jimmy Carter shunned him as Director of the CIA – hired Ling straightaway.[28]

Bob Stewart's grandmother Ada Rauch Clark, as it happens, was a widow with a nine-year-old daughter when she married Robert Henry Stewart, Sr. in Dallas in 1893.[29] That daughter, Earle Clark, was the older half-sister of Bob Stewart's dad, Robert Henry Stewart, Jr.

When Earle Clark grew up, she married the biggest landowner in the whole Dallas region – Will Caruth – and they lived on Swiss Avenue among the other wealthy citizens of Dallas at the time.[30]

"It was in this home that Will and Earle's daughter, Mattie Caruth, married D. Harold Byrd. The Caruth family had once grown cotton, raised cattle, and operated a dairy on a vast 11,000-acre spread that comprised much of what is now North Dallas. The gradual sale and lease of the family land for commercial and residential development over the past 50 years is thought to have earned the Caruths about $1 billion," according to one historical website.[31]

The other families living on their street make up a who's who of Dallas society and wealth at that time. Many of them are related to others on that street by marriage. Dallas isn't the only place like that.

D. Harold Byrd, the business partner of James J. Ling, just happened to be married to banker Bob Stewart's first cousin – the former Mattie Caruth.

The Preston Hollow mansion owned by James Ling, then Lamar Hunt, then Gene Phillips was in a subdivision of land once owned by Mattie Caruth's father, whose family had been "Old Money" from Virginia.[32]

Lamar Hunt, who had bought Ling's mansion in 1970, years later sells it to Gene Phillips. On Valentine's Day 1989, Gene gets himself arrested for trying to strangle his wife, Roxanne, who tells police she feared he'd resume his chokehold if they left him in the mansion.[33]

Odds are he also forgot to buy her Valentine candy and roses. Although she filed for divorce, she dropped it. There were rumors that they were giving up the mansion – Southmark had been dealt a brutal blow by the 1987 stock market crash, it was said – but Gene and Roxanne lived the rest of their lives there on Gaywood Street.[34]

The jet Phillips owned was another story. Phillips sold the jet he bought from Kenny Rogers to the Seattle Seahawks, a National Football League team, in 1989. Only a few months earlier, the Seahawks had been acquired by Ken Behring, who we'll return to in another chapter.

Was it a coincidence that, eighteen years earlier (1970), Lamar Hunt worked a deal to merge the American Football League he had created into the NFL? We can only guess whether he still owned enough stock in the league to be instrumental in its decision-making.[35]

* * *

Behring's team (also operating as the Seattle Seahawks, sells the jet in late 1997 to KEB Aircraft, which transfers it a month later to JRW Aviation Inc. That transaction brings us back to Lamar Hunt. Why? Because Lamar's niece, Alinda Hunt Hill Wikert, was married to James R. Wikert, owner of JRW Aviation. In each of the previous sales the tail number was changed, but the serial number (45775) remained the same. When Wikert sends it in January 2001 to a repair company in Chicago, the tail number got changed to N900SA, but it was the same DC-9 carrying 5.5 tons of cocaine in Mexico in 2006.

We'll pick up at that point in a later chapter. For the moment, however, we want to go back to the Ling-Hunt-Phillips mansion in Dallas.

In 2008, George Walker Bush bought two tracts that adjoined the east property line of the Gaywood mansion, where Gene Phillips continued to live until his death in 2019.[36] The backyards of the two houses would have made it convenient for the occupants to get together without being seen by pubic spectators.

Oh, to be a fly at their backyard picnics!

Dallas to Wachovia Via Clearwater-St. Pete

In 1954 Americans replaced the French in IndoChina. Kris Millegan has often told his personal story about his CIA dad and General Lansdale having a picnic in the middle of a meadow in Vietnam where a battle was supposed to be taking place. There was no battle. There was a decision made to bring in the "Secret Society" boys who had known how to import and distribute opium since the early days at Yale and Harvard in the mid-1800s. It had already been decided to move poppy fields and heroin refineries.[37]

That's when money-laundering began to be America's leading industry. Earlier we quoted from Pamela Moore's feature story about Gene Phillips. Notable is the fact that he created Syntek from a Greensboro, N.C., lumber company that he owed $150,000. Yet he managed to buy out his employer in a leveraged buyout and moved his new company, renamed Syntek, to Dallas.[38]

Phillips' "next target was Atlanta-based Southmark Properties, a real estate investment trust with $90 million in assets, spawned by Citizens & Southern National Bank. He and his former lawyer, Bill Friedman, waged a successful takeover," Moore wrote: "From there, they bought and sold undervalued properties, spinning them off into hundreds of limited partnerships. Along the way, they purchased Houston's San Jacinto Savings Association, which was nearly insolvent, and began dealing with the granddaddy of the junk bond market: Drexel Burnham Lambert."

H. R. "Bum" Bright, a Dallas millionaire who also owned the Dallas Cowboys NFL team for a few years, said in 1987, "I think the loans that Texas banks have on real estate and oil, well, by comparison [to loans in Zimbabwe], that collateral looks like gold."[39]

Bum Bright was being quoted in *D Magazine* by Sally Giddens, who interviewed a number of Texas bankers for her article. She begins with a catchy subtitle: "Since the new banking laws took effect January 1, Texas banks have been waiting for their princes to come. And waiting..."[40]

Clearly, the implication was that the bankers had something up their sleeves. Would they pull a rabbit out of a hat?

Bum Bright, Giddens wrote, had "initiated the Republic-InterFirst deal." He was a RepublicBank director who "wasn't too fond of the idea of cozying up to those New York bankers," she said.

She also quoted the Dallas banker we were just discussing – Robert H. Stewart III:

"InterFirst Chairman Robert H. Stewart III (who will become First RepublicBank Corp's chairman of the board pending regulatory and shareholder approval of the acquisition), says being the country's twelfth largest banking institution gives First RepublicBank Corp. a 'unique opportunity' in the marketplace."

The merged bank would be a huge holding company for 35 banks, controlling about 40 percent of its market. Before the big meltdown that was soon on its way, optimist Stewart thought his bank deal had "protected itself from acquisition and ensured itself a place in the Big Bank competition that is to come."[41]

Stewart's grandfather had worked for several banks in Dallas before retiring as chairman of the First National Bank in Dallas, which would merge in 1972 with the Citizens Bank and Trust of Houston to form First International Bancshares.[42] For decades they were the bankers for the Hunt family. They hired George H. W. Bush, known by his family as "Poppy," when he got a pink slip from Jimmy Carter. It's easy to be optimistic when the next U.S. President used to be your employee, I suppose.

Poppy Bush was in his last term as Vice President, and about to ascend to the highest elected position in the country. Stewart had a right to feel cocky.

Stewart did not then know what was about to happen, even though he had a big hand in causing it. We call it the Savings and Loan Scandal. It hit Texas very hard, as the bubble in real estate values began to burst. Or should we say "bust," since we're talking Texan?

RepublicBank Corporation in 1987 merged with InterFirst Bank Corporation, also based in Dallas, creating First RepublicBank Corporation, but it quickly began to fail, requiring the FDIC to pump $1 billion into it without success. It eventually broke the Federal Savings and Loan Insurance Corporation (FSLIC).

When First Republic failed on July 29, 1988, the FDIC accepted a bid made by Hugh L. McColl Jr., chairman and chief executive of NCNB Corporation from Charlotte, North Carolina. The merger doubled NCNB's assets and vaulted it from the 17th-largest bank in the country to the 10th-largest in one stroke. [43]

Fast forward twenty years. Ask yourself, "Why did Charlotte's other bank, Wachovia, decide to launder money for the Sinaloa Cartel?

You may also want to ask who El Chapo was really working for?

Endnotes

1   John Katsilometes, "In Las Vegas, Kenny was King of the Golden Nugget," *Las Vegas Review-Journal*, March 21, 2020. https://www.reviewjournal.com/entertainment/entertainment-columns/kats/in-las-vegas-kenny-rogers-was-king-of-golden-nugget-1987877/

2   https://www.justice.gov/media/1185776/dl?inline

3   https://www.newspapers.com/image/633610448/?match=1&clipping_id=133817900

4   *L.A. Weekly*, September 23, 1993. I had actually titled it "Los Angeles is Burning!" or something similar but, after the Rodney King riots in 1991, I was advised the title should be changed.

5   Frederick Clarkson, "New Book Reveals How Faith is Like a Covert Operation for the Bush Family," Religion *Dispatches*, June 16, 2009. https://religiondispatches.org/new-book-reveals-how-faith-is-like-a-covert-operation-for-the-bush-family/

6   https://greensboro.com/newspaper-says-developer-got-loans-from-former-boss/article_e757eb9b-bcc9-5cf3-ba4c-779689c9e6b2.html

7   Wendy Johnson Bilas, "NationsBank Corporation," Encyclopedia.com. https://www. encyclopedia.com/books/politics-and-business-magazines/nationsbank-corporation

8   David Mildenberg, "First Union Tackles Northeast," *Charlotte Observer*, 20 Jun 1995, Page 28.

9   Pamela L. Moore, "Treading on Wall Street Turf," *Charlotte Observer*, June 18, 1995.

10   Ibid. NationsBank became the name of the Charlotte-based NCNB bank in 1991 when it acquired C&S/Sovran Corp. – thus creating a regional bank in North Carolina with assets in Georgia, Virginia and South Carolina. Acquiring the San Francisco Bank of America a few years later seemed highly inconsistent.

11   "Wachovia Completes Merger Integration On Schedule, Under Budget, With Added Convenience For Customers" (Press release). Wachovia Corporation. 2003-08-18. Archived from the original on 2007-10-22. Retrieved 2007-10-14. Wikipedia.

12   Pete Brewton, *The Mafia, CIA & George Bush* (New York: Spi Books, a division of Shapolsky Publishers, Inc., 1992), p. 34.

13   Frederic E. "Shad" Rowe, Jr., "If These Walls Could Talk," *Texas Monthly*, January 1989. https://www.texasmonthly.com/news-politics/if-these-walls-could-talk/

14   Ibid.

15   *Sarasota Herald-Tribune*, May 21, 1960

16   During the 1950s the company employed quite a controversial figure, as we learn from reading "The Mac Wallace Story," by Walt Brown, an essay published in the *JFK Deep Politics Quarterly*, Volume 3 Number 4 (July 1998):

"On September 22, 1952, the arrest record of Malcolm E. Wallace is transmitted to Luscombe Airplane Corp., a wholly owned subsidiary of TEMCO by the Austin Police Department. In 1952 a SECRET security clearance was issued to Mac in spite of his criminal record. There are over a hundred pages of Office of US Naval Intelligence (ONI) files, 1952-1965, directly addressing his security clearance with the recommendations that it be revoked, but it stayed in effect until the mid 1960's. At the end of his tenure at LTV-Electrosystems he still held the same managerial position, but his security clearance had finally been canceled.

"This was never normal procedure for a civilian employee of a major governmental contractor. On November 15, 1952, Mac had been arrested in Georgetown, Texas for being "drunk in a Judge's Office," fined $18, and released from the Williamson County Jail the following day. NOTE he did NOT acknowledge this (or any subsequent arrest(s) in his personal security questionnaire for his secret clearance with TEMCO aka LTV-Electrosystems." Some of these details appear in the Spartacus Educational website. https://spartacus-educational.com/JFKwallaceM.htm.

John Simkin, Spartacus owner, added:

"In 1961, [Malcolm E. "Mac"] Wallace left Texas to go to Anaheim, Calif., to work for Ling Electronics. The change of jobs is what prompted the 1961 background check, said one of the former Navy intelligence officers. The officer, who conducted the background check, said 'There was an investigation; that I can verify.' He asked that his name not be used. The second Navy intelligence officer, who supervised the Texas end of the background check and now works in Dallas, confirmed that the report was compiled and forwarded to Washington.

"Wallace had been active in politics while at the University of Texas, and authorities who investigated the [Doug] Kinser murder said they found information linking Wallace to Communist Party activity in the United States, according to one investigator, who also wished that his name not be used. Former Texas Ranger Clint Peoples, who investigated the Kinser murder, said the Navy intelligence officer who compiled the background report indicated to him in November 1961 that Johnson may have been a factor behind Wallace's employment with the defense contractors. 'I was furious that they would even consider a security clearance for Wallace with the background he had,' said Peoples, who is a U. S. Marshal in Dallas. 'I asked him (the intelligence officer) how in the world Wallace could get the security clearance and he said 'politics,' Peoples said. 'I asked who could be so strong and powerful in politics that he could get a clearance for a man like this, and he said, 'the vice president.'"

The allegation that Mac might could be a Commie was, of course, invented out of whole cloth. Mac was obviously as committed to capitalistic pursuits as his sponsors, James Ling and D.H. Byrd. His politics mirrored those of Lyndon Johnson and his cronies in Dallas.

17   The corporate history is all available at Wikipedia and can be fully explored by jumping from link to link.

18   John Mintz, "THE SECRET'S OUT: COVERT E-SYSTEMS INC. COVETS COMMERCIAL SALES," *Washington Post*, October 24, 1994. https://www.washingtonpost.com/archive/politics/1994/10/24/the-secrets-out-covert-e-systems-inc-covets-commercial-sales/3deadc17-4bd2-41bd-b607-9fa493458fb8/.

19   Ibid.

20   "Aerospace: Ling increases holdings in LTV; firm sets up 3 subsidiaries," *Los Angeles Times*, 14 Jan 1965, Page 47.

21   Daniel Hopsicker, "Ferrie, Oswald, Seal: 'Committing Journalism' in New Orleans," https://www.madcowprod.com/2015/10/13/committing-journalism-in-new-orleans-witnesses-to-jfk-plot/

22   Daniel Hopsicker, *Barry and 'the boys': the CIA, the Mob and America's secret history*, Mad Cow Press, 2001.

23   *Tampa Bay Times*, 04 Sep 1959, Page 2.

24   Woody Thayer, "1959 Has Been the Best Year for Venice Since City's Birth," *St. Petersburg Times*, December 29, 1959.

25   *Los Angeles Evening Citizen News*, 04 May 1955, Page 11.

26   *Press Democrat*, Santa Rosa, California, 20 Jun 1941, Page 9.

27   Leslie Wayne, New York Times News Service, "James Ling: the legend endures," *Fort Worth Star-Telegram*, 28 Jul 1981, Page 34.

28   It helped Bush that Stewart was a director of Dresser Industries, the Dallas-based oil supply company, where Bush family friend, Neil Mallon, was installed as president in 1950 by the Skull and Bones partners of Wall Street investment bank, Brown Brothers, Harriman. Stewart's grandfather had worked for the bank since its inception.

29   https://texashistory.unt.edu/ark:/67531/metapth41244/m1/210/

30   https://www.sahd.org/history; see also https://www.dallashistory.org/wp-content/uploads/2019/04/Caruth-Family-Papers.pdf

31   https://www.exp1.com/blog/what-to-see-in-the-swiss-avenue-historic-district-in-dallas/

32   Ruth Miller Fitzgibbons, "DALLAS' FIRST FAMILIES: Old Money Still Survives," *D Magazine*, August 1, 1982. https://www.dmagazine.com/publications/d-magazine/1982/august/dal-las-first-families/

33   Ashley Cheshire, "Ex-Southmark executive charged in attack on wife," *Fort Worth Star Telegram*, February 14, 1989.

34   It was then placed in FGH, a beneficial trust handled by a Dallas lawyer who's now suing a neighboring property owner who recently acquired the mansion lawyer Tom Hicks owned.

35   https://en.wikipedia.org/wiki/Lamar_Hunt#Ownership_and_NFL_merger

36   http://www.dfwfreeways.com/dnt/roadside-bush-residence.

37   Linda Minor wrote about this problem at her blog. https://quixoticjoust.blogspot.com/2013/12/the-great-heroin-coup-foreword-and.html

38   Spartanburg, *S.C. Herald Journal* Staff Writer, "BORN TO DEAL; Phillips rides high-energy wave of success before Southmark crash," *USA Today*, July 29, 1990. https://www.goupstate.com/story/news/1990/07/29/born-to-deal-phillips-rides-high-energy-wave-of-success-before-south-mark-crash/29526724007/

39   Sally Giddens, "BUSINESS Interstate Banking: Fable and Reality," *D Magazine*, March 1, 1987. https://www.dmagazine.com/publications/d-magazine/1987/march/business-inter-state-banking-fable-and-reality/

40   Ibid.

41   Ibid.

42   https://www.tshaonline.org/handbook/entries/interfirst-corporation

43   Kathleen Day, "NCNB'S AGGRESSIVE BID TO WIN FIRST REPUBLICBANK," *Washington Post*, July 31, 1988. https://www.washingtonpost.com/archive/politics/1988/07/31/ncnbs-aggressive-bid-to-win-first-republicbank/ff9d3f72-feed-446f-bdac-476ed6253447/

CHAPTER NINE

CREATING A GLOBAL NETWORK

The fictionalized images of organized crime are far from the truth. The reality is less Hollywood and far more about fluid organized criminal networks profiting from the sale of illegal goods wherever there is a demand. These international illegal markets are anonymous and more complex than ever and each year generate billions of dollars.
            – United Nations Office on Drugs and Crime

The real reason for *Gangster Planet*, as I've said in different ways at different times, all goes back to Tony Blair's October 2, 2001, speech to the House of Commons in which he acknowledged that "Al Qaida is a terrorist organization with ties to a global network." He then added that the global network:

- had been in existence for over 10 years,

- was founded, and has been led at all times, by Osama Bin Laden.

- Bin Laden and Al Qaida have been engaged in a jihad against the United States, and its allies.

- One of their stated aims is the murder of US citizens, and attacks on America's allies.

- Bin Laden and Al Qaida have been based in Afghanistan since 1996,

- but have a network of operations throughout the world.

- The network includes training camps, warehouses, communication facilities and commercial operations able to raise significant sums of money to support its activity.

- That activity includes substantial exploitation of the illegal drugs trade from Afghanistan.

What Blair did not say was that as people in the network die off, or are killed, other people take their place. The global financial network keeps changing.

The Bin Laden Bros

It all began with oil, under Saudi Arabian sands Americans had discovered lots of clean light crude. The US government struck a deal to create an oil company called Aramco to drill it, promising to train Saudis and give them the option to buy the US out over time.

Mohammad bin Laden was a bricklayer for Aramco in 1931, when he founded what was to become the Binladen Group.[1] After his death in a helicopter crash in 1968, his son Salem was named his successor.

The Binladin Group owners were also trained and educated in Western cities in the United States and Europe.[2] Mohammad had numerous wives and concubines and hundreds of children. When he died in 1967, he was succeeded by his son Salem, who had friends in Texas.[3]

On May 29, 1988, Salem was checking out an Ultralight plane to buy from a seller near New Braunfels, Texas, a short hop from San Antonio, when he made a mid-air turn into power lines and was killed instantly.[4]

Another brother named Bakr was named to succeed Salem. Bakr had a degree in civil engineering from the University of Miami and also owned a large estate west of Orlando, purchased in 1980.[5] So the bin Laden brothers had lots of ties to Texas and Florida.

They also had a half-brother named Osama, who got an engineering degree in 1979, but did not join the family firm. Instead, he joined the mujahadeen in Afghanistan which was invaded by the USSR that same year. This is where stories begin to diverge.

The official version is that, when Bakr was named as Salem's replacement, Osama was angry enough to organize rebel fighters into a military force to take over Sudan. As he grew more and more radical, he started to raise funds for jihad through his years of fighting alongside the Taliban, which was said to control Afghan poppy fields. Then he used the poppies to make heroin to fund his rebel cause against the western world.

Voila! You have instant financing of global terror. But is it true?

Danny's Dictum: "Whoever Controls the Poppy..."

The Taliban has not just once, but twice eradicated. Afghanistan's poppy cultivation, at times the world's largest source of heroin. Despite western accusations, it has never been the Taliban behind the Afghan drug industry, *but only ever the US and its allies*, with billions in profits breezily laundered through the global financial system."[6]

From his study of the Afghan drug trade, while quoting extensively from Alfred W. McCoy and Peter Dale Scott, author William Van Wagenen reminds us of "the intricate connections between geopolitics, illicit economies, and global finance...."[7]

He says "the simplistic narrative that the Taliban largely controlled the Afghan drug trade," is flawed because "the dominant role [was] played by the US-backed Afghan government and its allies in the CIA."[8]

Let's winnow it down even more succinctly. Our entire planet is a *Gangster Planet* ruled by whoever has control of the drug market.

"Danny's Dictum" is easy to remember. Memorize and repeat:

> *In every country on this Gangster Planet that hosts a significant local market, the people who control the market are the same people who control the country.*

Here's even more proof that the dictum is true. Since President Biden withdrew military and intelligence forces from Afghanistan, the poppy crop there has been almost totally eradicated.[9]

What this means is that, if Osama had been using poppy farmers and their crop to raise funds for the jihad, he wasn't collaborating with the Taliban to finance a global terror network. So, if not the Taliban, then who?

ADNAN, STUDENT APPRENTICE

When Adnan Khashoggi's photo appeared in the Chico, California, newspaper in 1954, it's something of a miracle his name was spelled correctly in the caption. He was then just another unknown Arab student.

When he returned to California in 1966 with his entourage, lodging in rooms at the Beverly Hills hotel, which Queen Elizabeth II and the Prince had recently occupied, his name was spelled as Khashoggi, still an unknown Arab based in Beirut. [10]

How had he become so rich and so powerful so fast?[11]

"COVERT STATECRAFT 101"

We have to go back to the days of LBJ and Nixon to find the beginnings of Saudi influence in the United States. To Adnan Khashoggi, who was the first Saudi to work openly with the CIA.

The best introduction to Adnan, in my opinion, was written by his son-in-law spy, Larry J. Kolb, recruited and trained by Miles Copeland. Kolb was cleared to write about some of his experiences working for the CIA in connection with Adnan Khashoggi in a book called *Overworld*:

> Adnan's father was a doctor. Court physician to King Abdul Aziz, the founder of Saudi Arabia. Adnan grew up at court, in Riyadh.

Playing marbles in the dirt with young *Prince Sultan, who would later be Saudi Minister of Defense.* And befriending young Prince Fahd, who would be King. Adnan's father was also an entrepreneur. He brought electricity to Riyadh. Lit up the mud-walled palace of the King for free. Sold electricity to everyone else.

The court physician and owner of Saudi Arabia's first power company sent teenaged Adnan to Egypt, to Iskandria, which we call Alexandria and was once the seat of all the knowledge in the world, to attend Victoria College. There, all classes were taught in English, and boys caught conversing in Arabic were caned in fine English boarding school style. At Victoria, one of Adnan's classmates and best friends was Crown Prince Hussein, latterly known as King Hussein, of Jordan. Another was Hussein's Hashemite cousin from Baghdad, the Crown Prince of Iraq.[12]

When it came time for Adnan to attend university, his father, a practical man, decided Adnan could best serve his country by becoming a petroleum engineer. So he was enrolled in the Colorado School of Mines, in Golden, Colorado, where, upon his arrival, in a blinding snowstorm, Adnan noticed it was somewhat chillier than he was used to. He sent word to his father that he couldn't stand it, then sat by a fire and awaited further instructions. When they came, his next stop was Northern California. Where the climate was more agreeable and Adnan enrolled in Chico State University, chosen because it had a small community of Arab students.

At Chico, Adnan parlayed his modest college allowance into what seemed to be a fortune. He made his first big score selling trucks, manufactured by the Kenworth Motor Truck Company of Seattle, Washington, to one of his father's patients back home in Riyadh – a construction tycoon named Mohamed bin Laden, who was so rich he used to loan money to the King.

When the deal was done, Adnan, who was about nineteen years old, maybe twenty, received a fifty-thousand-dollar commission. With which Adnan hired a secretary to help him with his homework and his business letters. Bought himself a fancy car. Hired a chauffeur. Moved into a hotel. And threw a hell of a party..."

Life was good, and Adnan no longer had time for school. He went home and set up for business, bringing American and European products and services to the Kingdom of Saudi Arabia. Got himself Riyadh's Post Office Box No. 6, which might be seen as an indication of how early he got in on what was to be the Saudi development boom. To his agency rights for Kenworth Trucks, he added the exclusive Saudi agencies for Rolls-Royce engines, Marconi electronics, and Fiat and Chrysler automobiles. Saudi Arabia needed these things. More checks flowed in.

On a sunny day in 1962, young Adnan was summoned to the palace of Crown Prince Faisal, who was running Saudi Arabia in the stead of his debauched brother King Saud. Down in Yemen, royalist guerrillas were fighting to take back the country from the Communists. The royalists needed guns and trucks, and the House of Saud wanted them to have them. But *not to be linked* to their supply. Covert Statecraft 101.

Adnan's education was continuing. Faisal gave Adnan a check for one million pounds sterling. Told him to get a specified number of rifles and trucks to certain parties in Yemen. From where the goods came or how they got there, Faisal didn't care, *as long as no one knew Saudis were involved*. Adnan did what he was told. Adnan's first masterstroke. Then he went to his old friend Prince Sultan, who was now the Saudi Minister of Defense, and gave Sultan the change from the million-pound check. Asked Sultan to give it to Faisal. No, said Sultan, the rest is for you. No, said Adnan, I did this for my country. For my King. Not for money.

After that, as torrents of oil money washed into the Saudi coffers, Sultan gave companies represented by Adnan almost every major contract as Saudi Arabia built itself a modern defense system. Before he was thirty, Adnan had netted over two billion dollars in commissions by putting together American or European sellers and Saudi buyers of everything from trucks and towels to fighter jets, tanks, radar systems, schools, and hospitals. People called him an arms dealer, but Adnan called himself a "merchant banker."[13]

Larry Kolb should know. He was an intimate of the Khashoggi family for years before Adnan's death. But he refers to himself as a "reluctant spy."[14]

ADNAN, AN MI6 ASSET

Adnan left Chico State without completing his degree and moved to London, where in 1960 he met a British girl, born to an unmarried working-class mother. At the time Sandra Patricia Jarvis Daly was 19, introduced to Adnan by his "cousin," whom author Ronald Kessler left unnamed in his 1986 book.[15]

They married in late April 1961, when the Earth seemed like a different planet than today's. We're pretty sure Adnan Khashoggi and his associates over the years were responsible in a major way for those changes.

Living in Riyadh and Beirut, the short, dark – I hesitate to add "handsome" – Saudi was undoubtedly working with the CIA's Arabists stationed in Lebanon.

Kermit "Kim" Roosevelt (grandson of President Theodore Roosevelt) and his sidekick Miles Copeland had known each other since their days in the OSS in the Middle East Branch during and shortly after World War II. What really changed the world was when the Arabists got together with former OSS officers stationed in China in the area around Kunming.

The baby girl was given up for adoption in Leicestershire, England, where Sandra lived. Years after being adopted, Kim Patrick was discovered by a private detective (hired by Soraya) in South Africa, living with the couple who'd adopted her. They had moved when she was nine.

Kim was 14 when Soraya first met her in London, according to Kolb. That would have been around 1973, some months after Adnan divorced Soraya after hearing from MI-5 that she was having an affair with President Gaafar Nimeri of the Sudan.

"By the time she saw [divorce lawyer Marvin] Mitchelson, she had been divorced for more than five years. In fact, she had since remarried and had that marriage annulled. Her second marriage, two years earlier, was to Richard J. Coombes," 20-year-old Kim's then-boyfriend. Soraya was 35.

From Kolb we also learn that Sandra had been friendly with Khashoggi's favorite sister, Samira, who was married to Mohamed al-Fayed. Dodi, their son, was a first cousin of the Khashoggi children. Dodi was killed in a car crash with Princess Diana at the Pont de l'Alma tunnel in Paris in August 1997.

Some said MI6 staged the crash to prevent Diana from marrying Dodi.

By 1970 Adnan's commissions from Lockheed totaled $106 million, but he was still seeking to expand sales. An introduction to Northrup came by way of Kermit "Kim" Roosevelt. Kim had retired from the CIA's Middle East division in 1955. He then moved into what he called the "private sector," by becoming the first "director of government affairs for Gulf Oil." The title alone connotes "being connected." His business was a consulting and lobbying operation that specialized in hooking up U.S. firms which did business in the Middle East with foreign governments seeking to buy.

According to his obituary in the *Washington Post*:

> Over the years, according to Northrup officials, he helped Northrup obtain more than $1 billion in Middle East business. Ac-

cording to business sources, he also represented Raytheon Corp. in Saudi Arabia and Lebanon, and he was a Washington lobbyist for several foreign governments, including the Shah's. He retired [from this second career] in the late 1970s.[16]

BYRDS, PLANES AND MISSILES

The Navy and Air Force each wanted to build a new fighter plane while President Kennedy was in office. The Defense Department Secretary Robert McNamara had his hands full. While he was trying to keep Southeast Asia tamped down, he had to decide how to keep both the Air Force and Navy officials from rioting.

They'd have to share the same plane, he told them – combining the best of what each wanted into one plane called the "tactical fighter experimental," or TFX.

The final plan for the TFX was, in fact, the subject of President Kennedy's last speech, which he gave in Fort Worth the morning before he was murdered in Dallas.[17]

Only two companies remained after bids had been sorted through. Boeing in Seattle and General Dynamics (with Grumman's assistance) in Texas. They were fighting tooth and nail for the contract. Boeing was favored to win. The Lockheed and Chance-Vought designs (in a bid submitted by Republic Aviation) had already lost.

People involved in missile-maker Chance-Vought Corp., nevertheless, had other irons in the fire. Vice President Lyndon Johnson's friend, D. Harold Byrd, had quietly joined forces with James J. Ling in buying up shares of Chance- Vought until they attained control. They'd been threatening a proxy fight to take over management if a merger didn't occur.[18]

The Vought Co. had a long history of making Corsair fighter planes both for the Navy and Air Force. That was why General Dynamics acquired the company in 1954.

During World War II the Texas plant had been a highly classified facility owned by the U.S. Government (Air Force Plant 4),[19] which made B-24 bombers for Consolidated Vultee Aircraft Company (later Convair). [20] Convair also had a plant near San Diego, which built planes for the Navy.[21]

In 1959 a Florida corporation called Double-Chek, located just north of Miami International Airport, was set up. Its name popped up after the failed Bay of Pigs Operation, when widows of pilots killed began receiving checks every two weeks signed by its president. Senator Barry Goldwater promised an investigation to find out where the money for the "mystery trust" came from.

The CIA was silent.

Years later, the Church Senate Committee Report listed Double-Chek as a proprietary of the CIA.[22] It also acted as a paymaster for activities at the Convair plant – such as installation of Regulus missiles at the tiny airport in Venice, Florida.

CORPORATE SHENANIGANS

The same process General Dynamics used to gain control of Convair was repeated a few years later by two Dallas men, James J. Ling and D. Harold Byrd of Temco-Ling Electronics. They wanted to merge with this highly-classified company, Chance-Vought, now operating in a county next-door to Dallas.

There had always been a rivalry between Fort Worth and Dallas, not only during Friday night football games. Their Chambers of Commerce also fought each other for new business.

Suddenly the two Dallas men at Ling-Temco had huge sources of funds with which to buy shares in the Chance-Vought company of Fort Worth – enough shares to put them over the top and give them control. The merger that created LTV occurred in August 1961. The General Dynamics design would, therefore, be manufactured at the Corsair plant, now managed by LTV, at tiny White Settlement, Texas, west of Fort Worth.

Fifteen months after LTV was created, the Secretary of Defense chose General Dynamics over Boeing. "General Dynamics planned to build the aircraft at its Convair plant in Fort Worth, Texas."[23]

Chance-Vought was operating out of the Convair plant at the same time it had installed Regulus II missiles at Venice Airport in 1959. The same missiles brought down by Boeing's drones in the testing.

One would have thought the winner of that test would get the contract. But no. Tempers flared.

Complaints were immediate, followed by a Senate investigation. At stake: *"production orders were estimated eventually to be worth more than $6.5 billion and involve 20,000 jobs and 1,700 planes–the largest tactical airplane contract since World War II."* [24]

It was huge.

All eyes then turned to Secretary of the Navy Fred Korth, a Texan.[25] Did he have an insider interest? Wasn't he a friend of LBJ and the Vice President's other Texas friends?[26]

OPERATION BIG SAFARI

On the day of the JFK assassination D.H. Byrd was conveniently "away from his desk." He was out of the country on a two-month safari in Africa. When he returned in January, his good friend Lyndon Johnson was the new President of the United States, and Byrd's School Book Depository building had become famous in his absence. A huge juicy defense contract was waiting on his desk, awarded to his company to build fighter planes, and to be paid from the 1965 Congressional budget ... even though it had not yet been approved by Congress.[27]

Back in 1956 both LBJ and his Dallas friend and donor, D. H. Byrd, an enthusiastic safari and game hunter, had become members of the Mt. Kenya Safari Club.

We called on a source, now retired and possibly deceased, who had worked in the American aerospace industry, building satellites for NSA for several decades. He might have known General Harry Byrd, we figured. He had ... in fact, he had worked at LTV.

And in between anecdotes that are colorful, but neither here nor there, he mentioned that, oh, by the bye, did we know that ...

When Byrd's defense aerospace firm LTV "went big" after the JFK assassination, he told us, it had become a big part of an overarching Air Force Operation...

For years afterward, he said, every self-respecting big-time Air Force defense program – everyone who was anyone, in other words – came under the overall rubric of an Air Force Operation whose declassified code-name – he paused here, for dramatic effect...

It was called Operation Big Safari.

DEMOCRATIC FUNDRAISING

In 1972 the Democratic National Committee's chiefs, Lawrence O'Brien and Robert R. Straus, selected Edward Kiper Moss to be the exclusive agent for furnishing campaign supplies to Democratic candidates nationwide. Moss was president of a subsidiary corporation within the DNC, and his partner in the enterprise was his long-time mistress Julia Cellini, sister of Mafia dons Dino and Eddie Cellini. They opined the company might make $1 million, with a kickback to the DNC.

CIA files on Moss indicated his role in his government jobs had been as liaison between the Mafia and government contracting, as a means of laundering dirty profits into legitimate business. His business office at 1025 Connecticut NW in Washington, D.C. was actually run as a secretarial service by his girlfriend, Julia Cellini, whose brothers ran casinos at various times in Cuba, Miami and the Bahamas.

It may not have been the same office, but it would have been walking distance from the office of B. R. Fox Electronics – aka Bernie Spindel – who planted bugs for Mafia dons and Teamsters presidents. And others. Anyone who would pay.

Moss had long been a member of the African Safari Club originally set up in 1959 by actor William Holden, former Indiana oilman Raymond John Ryan, who built up Palm Springs out of nothing, and banker Carl (or Karl) Hirschmann of Switzerland. Senator Lyndon Johnson was a founding member of the Mt. Kenya club, along with Sir Winston Churchill and Prince Bernhard of the Netherlands.[28]

Rich American, British and Dutch adventurers who frequented the Mt. Kenya Safari Club – all were white, of course – and viewed Adnan Khashoggi as they would a trusted concierge. Moss recommended him as the "white knight" to rescue the owners from their varied financial problems. Perhaps the members just assumed they could use his money to vamp up their club to accomplish their own ends without losing their place in the world order. After all, he wouldn't have become so rich without the commissions made from selling *their* weapons.

In 1970 Mt. Kenya's management was exposed for giving secret memberships to known gangsters.[29] The kind of men we've always called gangsters – before the white-collar version took over.

They got rid of the mobsters left over from the Bugsy Siegel and Lucky Luciano era in favor of new blood. In corporate takeovers, they call new blood "white knights." In 1977 Adnan Khashoggi became the white knight for Ray Ryan, who died in a car bombing in his hometown under very strange circumstances.

Ryan, according to writer John Kamau, "worked with the Italian Mafia, at least the Chicago-based underworld, also known as the Mob, and they had turned the Mt Kenya Safari Club into one of their African hideouts."[30] Ryan's biggest other shareholder was actor William Holden, who attracted Hollywood types as members of the Club. He too would meet a mysterious death a few years later.

The beginning of the best times for Khashoggi began in late 1976 when he bought the Safari Club at Mt. Kenya near Nairobi, Africa.

His numerous companies under the Triad umbrella, headquartered in Utah, hired a public relations consultant in 1976 – the same Edward K. Moss who brokered the deal at Mt. Kenya. Moss was pictured in newspapers, a rare event for him, in September 1978. As chairman of the private group, Moss was quoted saying, "We think our Mount Kenya Safari Club is the jewel in the crown of Kenya's tourism."[31]

Moss, a Pennsylvanian educated at Culver Military, Yale, and George Washington University, had been in public relations work since FDR's administration in 1940 until 1952. When Eisenhower took office, Moss started his own firm, which, in 1960, merged with Howard Chase Associates, a similar firm with ties to Republicans.

Edward K. Moss had been cleared by the CIA for public relations uses in 1959 and 1962 under Project ZRMAJOR – a CIA program that "exploited" the use of political consultants by covert action staff, according to a report in 1967 issued by the CIA's inspector general.

If he wasn't one of the boys, he clearly was working for them.

OUR LITTLE SECRET, PROPPING UP THE FED WITH SAUDI OIL

The transfer of the Mt. Kenya Safari Club to Saudi ownership occurred just as American politicians and bankers were hoping for infusions of money from Arab oil just as the Saudis were buying back their Aramco shares. That could only double the value of petrodollars flowing into the Saudi economy.

Our leaders were jealous, envious. It didn't seem fair that non-white desert rats could be so rich while the U.S. was drowning in debt.

The last thing Richard Nixon accomplished before allowing George Bush to talk him into resigning was to get the Saudi king to sign a document agreeing to bail out the U.S. Fed. Nixon met the Saudi King in June 1974 and concluded a verbal agreement.

He then sent William E. Simon, his "energy czar," – before rising to that glorified title, had been a mere broker in U.S. Treasury securities for Salomon Brothers – to work out the details in Saudi Arabia. Simon had, therefore, been at the right place at the right time to replace John Connally when he got himself indicted in the milk fund scandal.

According to Bloomberg, the basic framework of the agreement was simple. The U.S. would buy Saudi Arabia's oil and also provide the Saudis with military aid and equipment. "In return, the Saudis would plow billions of their petrodollar revenue back into Treasuries and finance America's spending."[32]

Elsewhere in this book you'll hear mention of the secret "28 pages." This agreement was what that term refers to. It was Gerald Parsky who hashed out the final the terms of the two leaders' verbal agreement.[33] The one real sticking point was this: "King Faisal bin Abdulaziz Al Saud demanded the country's Treasury purchases stay *'strictly secret,'* according to a diplomatic cable obtained by Bloomberg from the National Archives database."[34]

SAUDIS FINANCE U.S. DEBT SPENDING AFTER 1974

By the time the American public learned about the Saudis' secret acquisition of U.S. Treasuries, our debt to them was disclosed as $117 billion – a figure some experts said was less than half of what the kingdom really owned. "Some analysts speculate the kingdom may be masking its U.S. debt holdings by accumulating Treasuries through offshore financial centers, which show up in the data of other countries," Bloomberg revealed.

These disclosures came amid lawsuits filed by victims of 9/11 and their families and numerous FOIA requests in the last months of Obama's second term. Threats came from Saudi Arabia in April 2016, warning *"it would start selling as much as $750 billion in Treasuries and other assets if Congress passes a bill allowing the kingdom to be held liable in U.S. courts for the Sept. 11 terrorist attacks,* according to the *New York Times."*

The threats meant little, as there was "a renewed push by presidential candidates and legislators from both the Democratic and Republican parties to declassify a 28-page section of a 2004 U.S. government report that is believed to detail possible Saudi connections to the attacks," Bloomberg said.[35]

In May 2004 I'd made my first reference to 28 pages of the Intelligence Committee Report that would have told the American people about the foreign government sponsorship of the terrorists, which President George W. Bush had classified, saying, "It would reveal sources and methods."

What it would have revealed more than anything was that the U.S. Government and the Federal Reserve were owned by Saudi Arabia, and the only people who had known about the secret deal made in 1974 were Republicans, who would continue making secret deals with Saudis for many years to come – just to get elected, or re-elected.

KHASHOGGI KEEPS THE SECRET

That secret deal, made just before Nixon boarded his helicopter and rode off into the sunset in 1974, was part of the reason Adnan Khashoggi agreed to buy the Safari Club in Kenya two or three years later. The Saudis weren't satisfied just owning the U.S. Fed. They had international interests.

One of the first groups to meet at Khashoggi's new African digs in September 1976 was "a coalition of nations including Morocco, Egypt and France – that ran covert operations around Africa at a time when Congress had clipped the C.I.A.'s wings over years of abuses."[36]

The funding provided by this "international club," who also called themselves the "Safari Club," was meant to be secret, so the CIA had to develop a cover story to hide the source of funds being poured into the White House sponsored activities of Col. Oliver North and his cronies. Mazzetti and Apuzzo explained that:

> In 1984, when the Reagan administration sought help with its secret plan to sell arms to Iran to finance the contra rebels in Nicaragua, Robert C. McFarlane, the national security adviser, met with Prince Bandar, who was the Saudi ambassador to Washington at the time. The White House made it clear that the Saudis would "gain a considerable amount of favor" by cooperating, Mr. McFarlane later recalled.
>
> Prince Bandar pledged $1 million per month to help fund the contras, in recognition of the administration's past support to the Saudis. The contributions continued after Congress cut off funding to the contras. By the end, the Saudis had contributed $32 million, paid through a Cayman Islands bank account.
>
> When the Iran-contra scandal broke, and questions arose about the Saudi role, the kingdom kept its secrets.

That is, until the secret came out in the middle of the long hot summer of 2016. By then we'd only been waiting fifteen years. A whole generation had grown up since 9/11.

BILLIONS WITH A "B" IN BACKSHEESH, OR BRIBES

You may have detected a slight hint of sarcasm that overcame me when I heard the news and posted my opinion at the time.

By Daniel Hopsicker – July 15, 2016

Leading up to today's release of the redacted 28 pages from the Intelligence Committee Report on the 9/11 Attack, national security officials have beat out a steady drumbeat proclaiming "conspiracy theorists" would be sorely disappointed by the "inconclusive evidence" long-rumored to implicate Saudi Arabian government officials in the 9/11 attack.

Nothing, as it happens, could be further from the truth.

And no bigger Big Lie in recent memory has issued from the mouth of an official representative of the U. S. Government as that which White House press secretary Josh Earnest uttered today.

"The release doesn't shed any new light or change any of the conclusions about responsibilities for the 9/11 attacks," Earnest dissembled. "It should put to rest longtime speculation that the Saudi government had a role."

Were that in any way true, the pages would not have been slipped out the door late on a Friday afternoon. And certainly not in the middle of summer, days before the two parties begin holding their conventions.

Whistling past the graveyard has long been part of any White House press secretary's role. But Earnest's performance today – given the tremendous loss of life America suffered that fateful day – seems particularly shameless.

In fact, the inescapable conclusion from a first reading of the pages is that to get the kid glove treatment they were afforded at every step of the way, the Saudis must have passed out billions of dollars – that's billions with a "b" – in baksheesh, or bribes, up to and including the President of the United States of America, who obligingly classified the 28 pages.

The reputations of both former President George W. Bush and Prince Bandar bin Sultan of Saudi Arabia were irrevocably shredded today, and now lie in tatters.

I attached the redacted 28 pages to my website.[37]

When the Boland Amendment went into effect in 1984, the secret agreement signed by President Nixon and King Faisal had been in effect ten years, but nobody knew about it except people very close to the Saudi king – such as Adnan Khashoggi, Kamal Adham, Prince Bandar – people who belonged to the five-nation Safari Club, none of whom gave a hoot about Nicaragua.

The only people who did care seemed to be retired American generals obsessed with an endemic fear of communism – who remembered stories about Cuba's takeover by a left-wing autocrat. They never seemed to figure out that autocrats from either direction – left or right – were not good for the people they tortured or slaughtered.

Singlaub as Cover Man

The CIA chose a bevy of retired generals and colonels to run cover to hide the billions of dollars flowing from the Saudis into the Swiss bank accounts. Major General John K. "Jack" Singlaub, who had served in the OSS in China with many of military and intelligence officials mentioned in other pages of this book, was tapped to be in charge of raising funds. Singlaub saw his commander in chief, President Jimmy Carter, much the same way that military brass of the '60s saw JFK.

When Singlaub told a reporter that President Jimmy Carter's "pledge to withdraw ground troops from South Korea was a mistake that would lead to war," he found himself summoned back to Washington to a meeting with the President.[38] Carter removed Singlaub from the No. 3 military post in Korea. He was being transferred to a new position at an equivalent degree of responsibility and stature," the President said.[39]

Singlaub retired instead and began speaking across the country, repeating his criticisms wherever he was invited to give a speech. As the new U.S. head of the World Anti-Communist League (WACL), he established a non-profit corporation in Arizona in 1981 – U.S. Council for World Freedom (USCWF) – granted tax-exempt status by the IRS so all donations would be tax deductible, and Singlaub was named president.

"The new American League chapter, the United States Council for World Freedom (USCWF), was born, facilitated by a loan of nearly twenty thousand dollars from Taiwan... Lieutenant General Daniel O. Graham, former director of the Defense Intelligence Agency, became its vice-chairman, while a retired Air Force lieutenant colonel, Albert [Thurmond] Koen, was treasurer."[40]

Koen was employed by Garrett Corporation, which had just built a new multi-million dollar manufacturing plant called AiResearch on Oracle Road in Tucson, conveniently located less than 20 miles from the CIA's airport at Marana, Arizona, where George Doole, Jr. hung out. Koen, however, died in 1985, as did Doole. So they didn't do much in the way of fund raising for contras.

Doole had created Pacific Corporation in Delaware in 1950, as we show elsewhere in this book, in order to shuffle aircraft continuously among various shell corporations and alter aircraft registration numbers. That practice has been recognized as a CIA tell since the days Gen. Claire Chennault worked with the Chinese air force fighting the Japanese.

It's a long sordid history. The China experience predated the military quagmire in Vietnam, and both wars were dependent upon covert funds gleaned from smuggling drugs for warlords.

Sadly, those same drugs which were smuggled into the United States addicted many former soldiers, who watched their own finances being drained away to fund yet another failed military operation against world communism

Endnotes

1   Jason Burke, "The making of Osama bin Laden," *Salon*, November 1, 2001. https://www.salon.com/2001/11/01/osama_profile/

2   Steve Coll, "The Fall of the bin Ladens," *The New Yorker*, September 11, 2021.

"Salem's home, near the decaying railroad town of Winter Garden, turned out to be an ochre-walled five-acre estate with horse stables, a tiled swimming pool, weeping willows, and palm trees. The main house, a Mediterranean Revival built during the 1920s, had russet Spanish-tile roofing, cupolas, and arched, shaded walkways; it rested on a knoll above a sparkling lake." Steve Coll, "The Bin Ladins," *New York Times*, March 31, 2008. Excerpted from *The Bin Ladens: An Arabian Family in the American Century* by Steve Coll. Reprinted by arrangement with The Penguin Press, a member of Penguin Group (USA), Inc. Copyright (c) April, 2008. https://www.nytimes.com/2008/03/31/books/20080401_COLL_EXCERPT.html

3   Salem was a pilot who bought a fixed-based services operation at San Antonio International Airport in 1973. The FBO was operated by Salem's deceased father's long-term pilot, Gerald L. Auerbach. Scott Stroud, "Did a 1988 death alter the course of history?" *San Antonio Express-News*, Sep 11, 2011. https://www.mysanantonio.com/news/news_columnists/scott_stroud/article/did-a-1988-death-alter-the-course-of-history-2165129.php

4   Mike Ward, "Bin Laden Relatives Have Ties to Texas," *Austin American Statesman*, November 9, 2001.

5   The 5-acre estate was on Lake Apopka (17812 W Colonial, Winter Garden, FL 34787) purchased in 1980.

6   William Van Wagenen, "How the Taliban crushed the CIA's heroin bonanza in Afghanistan," *The Cradle*, July 7, 2023. https://new.thecradle.co/articles/how-the-taliban-crushed-the-cias-heroin-in-bonanza-in-afghanistan.

7   Ibid.

8   Ibid.

9   Yogita Limaye, "Inside the Taliban's war on drugs - opium poppy crops slashed," BBC. https://www.bbc.com/news/world-asia-65787391

10   Dorothy Manners, "The Hollywood Scene," May 1966.

11   That same summer, however, his name was spelled right, when he hosted two California companies, Litton Industries and Western Bancorporation in his "plush penthouse office" in the IBM building in Beirut. Joe Alex Morris, Jr., "King Faisal Seen Key in Experiment in Free Enterprise," The Los Angeles Times, 25 Jul 1966, Page 54. Five years earlier this bank had changed its name from Firstamerica Corporation, but it's much more complicated than that. If it's something that interests you, the history is set out in Wikipedia under First Interstate Bancorp. https://en.wikipedia.org/wiki/First_Interstate_Bancorp

12   Kolb, Larry J., *Overworld* (p. 149). Penguin Publishing Group. Kindle Edition.

13   Kolb, Larry J., *Overworld* (pp. 150-151). Penguin Publishing Group. Kindle Edition.

14   https://www.aljazeera.com/program/riz-khan/2007/5/24/larry-kolb

15   Ronald Kessler, *The Richest Man in the World: The Story of Adnan Khashoggi*, 1986.

16   Bart Barnes, "Kermit Roosevelt, CIA Mideast Agent, Dies," *Washington Post*, June 10, 2000. https://www.washingtonpost.com/archive/local/2000/06/10/kermit-roosevelt-cia-mideast-agent-dies/37c280e2-c003-47a5-a864-cedd776867f8/

17   Text of President Kennedy's speech at a rally in front of the Texas Hotel, November 22, 1963. https://www.umsl.edu/~thomaskp/jfktfx.htm

18   A history of Chance Vought leading up to the LTV merger is set out at https://semspub.epa.gov/work/01/605966.pdf

19   "Air Force Plant 4 is a Government-Owned Contractor-Operated (GOCO) defense manufacturing facility. It is located in Tarrant County, Texas, 7 miles northwest of the City of Fort Worth. It occupies 605 acres and is bounded on the north by Lake Worth, on the east by Carswell Air Force Base (Carswell AFB), and on the south and west by the City of White Settlement." https://www.globalsecurity.org/military/facility/afp-4.htm

20   On April 18, 1948, the company announced that Chance Vought Aircraft would move its operations to Grand Prairie, Texas from Stratford, Connecticut. https://www.vought.org/special/html/smove3.html

21   *Pomona Progress Bulletin*, April 7, 1951.

22   https://quixoticjoust.blogspot.com/2016/03/permindex-and-double-chek-agents-and.html

23   Ibid.

24   "Senate Unit Probes TFX Contract Award." In CQ Almanac 1963, 19th ed., 1089-91. Washington, DC: *Congressional Quarterly*, 1964. http://library.cqpress.com/cqalmanac/cqal63-1315398.

25   In 2019 Associated Press dropped an intriguing aside to Korth's story by innocuously stating: "After ninth grade at El Paso High School, Beto O'Rourke told his parents he wanted to go away to school. He landed at Woodberry Forest, an all-male boarding academy in Virginia about 80 miles from Washington. His step-father, a Fort Worth bank president named Fred Korth who had been John F. Kennedy's Secretary of the Navy, was an alum." Will Weissert, "The Origin Story: A blind date, a border and Beto O'Rourke," Associated Press, March 29, 2019. https://apnews.com/article/964fda44687e4778a4c8ba3111d61f3c

26   We've recently learned that Fred Korth's second wife, Charlotte Korth of El Paso, is the mother of Beto O'Rorke, a perennial Democratic candidate in Texas elections. (See Korth's obit in   https://www.washingtonpost.com/archive/local/1998/09/16/lawyer-banker-frederick-korth-dies/3e1d4139-a181-4ec9-8c60-fdfb997a2fdb/). It would turn out that Fred Korth had ties to Lee Harvey Oswald, having handled a divorce for Oswald's mom against her second husband, Edwin Ekdahl. Conspiracy theories were rampant then and haven't diminished since. https://spartacus-educational.com/JFKkorth.htm; also see Linda Minor's research at her blog, https://quixotic-joust.blogspot.com/2012/05/colossal-failure-to-research-ekdahl.html.

27   Michael Ennis, "The Plane the Pentagon Couldn't Stop," *Texas Monthly*, June 1981. https://www.texasmonthly.com/news-politics/frustrating-development-f-16/

28   We found several coincidences intriguing here. Charles Manatt, the attorney who succeeded Robert Strauss as chief fundraiser at the Democratic National Committee in 1981, was attorney for developer and ex-banker Eugene Glick, who began developing in Palm Springs at the same time ex-president Gerald Ford decided to build a home there. Glick's company, Continental Desert Properties, once the Reagan-Bush Administration was in office, bought other properties in Arizona. Retired Gen. John K. Singlaub had been named the new chairman of the World Anti-Communist League at its meeting in Phoenix in 1985, which became a center of Contra fund-raising activities.

29   https://www.newspapers.com/article/evansville-courier-and-press-mt-kenya-s/133591504/

30   John Kamau, "Sex, gamblers and Mafia: The untold story of Nanyuki's Mt Kenya Safari Club," *The Citizen*, October 30, 2022. https://www.thecitizen.co.tz/tanzania/news/east-africa-news/sex-gamblers-and-mafia-the-untold-story-of-nanyuki-s-mt-kenya-safari-club-3801038

31   "Safari Club membership includes celebrities from around the world," *Arizona Republic*, 20 Sep 1978, Page 77. https://www.newspapers.com/article/arizona-republic-safari-clubed- ward-k-m/83242260/

32   Andrea Wong, Bloomberg, "The untold story behind Saudi Arabia's 41-year U.S. debt secret," *Chicago Tribune*, May 31, 2016. https://www.chicagotribune.com/business/ct-untold-story-saudi-arabia-us-debt-secret-20160531-story.html

33   https://www.law.virginia.edu/static/uvalawyer/html/alumni/uvalawyer/spr07/parsky.htm

34   Wong, Bloomberg, op. cit. https://www.chicagotribune.com/business/ct-untold-story-saudi-arabia-us-debt-secret-20160531-story.html

35   Ibid.

36   Mark Mazzetti and Matt Apuzzo, "U.S. Relies Heavily on Saudi Money to Support Syrian Rebels," *New York Times*, Jan. 23, 2016. https://www.nytimes.com/2016/01/24/world/middleeast/us-relies-heavily-on-saudi-money-to-support-syrian-rebels.html

37   https://www.madcowprod.com/wp-content/uploads/2016/07/declasspart4.pdf

38   Bernard Weinraub, "General Returns From South Korea to Face Carter," *New York Times*, May 21, 1977.

39   Edward Walsh and George C. Wilson, "President Defends His Korea Policy," *Washington Post*, May 27, 1977.

40   Scott Anderson and Jon Lee Anderson, *Inside the League*, out of print, 1986. https:// archive.org/details/inside-the-league-wacl/page/n3/mode/2up

CHAPTER TEN

IT'S ALL OVER NOW, DONNA BLUE

You must leave now, take what you need, you think will last
But whatever you wish to keep, you better grab it fast
Yonder stands your orphan with his gun
Crying like a fire in the sun
Look out the saints are comin' through,
And it's all over now, Baby Blue

– Bob Dylan

It began as a minor scandal with little fanfare on April 10, 2006 – a DC-9 from St. Petersburg, Florida caught carrying 5.5 tons of cocaine in Mexico's Yucatan peninsula.

Then – *drat the luck* – a *second* cocaine-laden plane – this one a Grumman American G-1159 Gulfstream II jet carrying registration N987SA – made an emergency crash landing eighteen months later, just 250 miles from where the first plane was busted. It, too, carried cocaine. Four tons of it. It turned into a major scandal.

The Gulfstream had been sold on August 30, 2007 out of a hangar at St. Pete-Clearwater Airport. Two weeks later, having been delivered to Fort Lauderdale to its alleged new owners, the jet flew from Fort Lauderdale to Miami, Florida, and then to Cancun, Mexico, then and on to the Medellin International Airport at Rio Negro, Colombia.

Before it took off on its return flight from in Rio Negro, late on September 23, the plane had been loaded with the cocaine, bound for the Cancun Airport in Yucatan, Mexico, where it was denied permission to land. One intrepid editor and publisher at *Por Esto!*, Mario Menendez Rodriguez, became everyone's on-the-ground source about the crash landing that followed.

Five years after the crash, Menendez was featured by Jonah Meadows of *Inside Out Radio*, who questioned Menendez about the reason the plane crashed.

"Menendez says the Air Traffic Controllers who were expecting the plane had gone home for the night, and the new shift denied permission to land."[1]

In response to Meadows' statement that "Newspapers wrote that Mexican military aircraft intercepted the plane," Menendez harrumphed: "That's bullshit! I think that's how you say it in English."[2]

After being denied landing in Cancun, the pilot was forced to employ Plan B, to fly on to the closest jet-equipped airport, which was in Merida. Approaching it in the earning morning hours, he got the same response, landing denied.

THERE WAS NO PLAN C.

The plane went into a holding pattern about 25 miles east of Merida, flying lazy circles above the mostly scrubby terrain near Tixkokob, a town whose Mayan name means "place of poisonous snakes." The mere thought of landing there evokes shivers.

"Should he contact the boss?" the pilot undoubtedly wondered. Would his juice extend this far?

If he was well-versed in Shakespeare, the phrase "*La discreción es la mejor parte del valor*," probably came to mind. Don't panic or do anything rash. Wait for instructions from the boss.

The unknown pilot, who had watched as at least 132 bags had been loaded aboard the plane, though there were no passengers, knew what could happen. If he lost the cargo, he would die. If caught with it, he would go to prison. What a choice.

He was a pilot in a pickle. Best thing to do was to do nothing.

The low-flying Gulfstream II circled for almost two hours. It was the middle of the night. The sound of its engines endlessly droning in the dark night sky would have been deafening, except there was nobody to hear. The plane was circling over the jungle. Then the sputtering started. An unmistakable clue that its fuel was all used up.

It was still dark, an hour or two before dawn with no lights below. The plane "skidded across the jungle floor."[3]

It was three miles from the whitewashed stone fences of Rancho San Francisco, an uninhabited area just north of Tixkokob.

GULFSTREAM SHISH KABOB IN TIXKOKOB

It was a hard landing which split the fuselage into three pieces, but there was no explosion or fire. Just a plane torn open like a Pez dispenser. The cargo – more than four tons of cocaine, as well as an undisclosed amount of heroin – spilled out across an area the length of three football fields.

First on the scene was *Por Esto!* (translates "For This!") editor/publisher Menendez, who watched the helicopters. But the military didn't allow the police, civil authorities, or newspapermen to enter.

They guarded it for the next 36 hours, repelling intrusions from other Mexican law enforcement agencies, as well as from the DEA, who had flown six agents in from Mexico City to reconnoiter.

Menendez brought in his own backup, in the form of his employee, Rafael Lores, to act as an "undercover reporter," without explaining how that worked. It was clear, however, they did not trust the guys in charge.

A couple days later Mexico's attorney general announced that authorities had apprehended one of the pilots. He was found about three miles from the site. Four days later, they apprehended a man alleged to be the copilot.

Por Esto! didn't buy it. None of the helicopters or other high-tech search equipment at the scene were mobilized to find the fleeing pilots. The paper doubted that the two men arrested had ever even been on the plane. Since, officially, nobody was found at the crash site, how would they even know who they were looking for?

The reporter added, "Those poor two guys didn't do anything."[4]

Lores researched the name of the alleged pilot and stated, "Nobody knows him. I called the pilots' association in Mexico City; they have a record of every single pilot and they don't know him."

"*Por Esto!* also claimed that the amount of cocaine at the crash site appeared to be much more than the 3.7 metric tons authorities reported."

That would explain why they wanted the area sealed.[5]

Menendez told Meadows, "We got close to the airplane and saw they were taking part of the cocaine." He claimed there was actually more drugs than the government admitted.

"*Six tons,* and they took *half* of it," Menendez shouted.[6]

"Narcoavion, That's How We Say It. Drug Planes."

Meadows did an excellent job in a radio broadcast five years after the Gulfstream crash. It was succinct and well documented with interviews of all the experts, including myself – noted expert that I am on the subject of drug planes – as well as Bob Norman of the *Broward Bulldog*, the local expert in Fort Lauderdale. Look for the link to the audio in endnotes.[7] Here's an excerpt:

> **JAY ROOT:** I mean, if you're flying to Guantanamo, it's government business.

JONAH MEADOWS: That was Jay Root, he reported on the plane for McClatchy Newspapers with his partner Kevin Hall.

KEVIN HALL: The CIA's confirmed it was used.... It was confirmed in earlier reports through the tail numbers.

JM: The plane shows up on the list of CIA planes compiled for the EU human rights investigation into the "extraordinary rendition" program. Still, just being used in the program doesn't mean it was ever used to transfer prisoners. Only 2% of its flights had prisoners on board ... the rest were logistical support.

ROOT: You know in some cases, soldiers literally, or, you know, CIA interrogators, missed Starbucks coffee, so they would fly in some Starbucks coffee.

JM: But even if the CIA was just using it for coffee runs...it was still a CIA jet. But the big question is: *Was it still a CIA jet at the time it crashed full of drugs?*

OFFICIAL: I can neither confirm nor deny...

JM: Tracing who the last owner was raises more questions than it answers. First: FAA records show the company that had the plane during its Guantanamo flights sold it on August 30.[8]

JM: The new owner? "Donna Blue Aircraft" a corporation recently registered in South Florida to two Brazilians.[9]

HALL: It's one of these mailboxes-R-us type of businesses.

JM: Donnablueaircraft dot com was registered just ten days before they bought the plane.[10] So is this just a Front Company?

Investigative journalist Daniel Hopsicker visited Donna Blue's listed address.... He found an empty office suite, a blank sign, and six unmarked police cruisers parked in front.[11]

DANIEL HOPSICKER: It's a phony front company. Exactly who these Brazilians are is a whole 'nuther story.

JM: Non-US citizens are not allowed to own N-Numbered Planes ... and ... neither one of these guys appears to be a US citizen.

HALL: He didn't check either box as to whether he was a US citizen.

JM: After just two weeks, the plane was sold again in another mysterious transaction. The only evidence for this is an anomalous bill of sale with the name of the new owner: Clyde O'Connor. He's a well-known guy around Fort Lauderdale Executive Airport [FLEA].

HALL: I had the sense they seemed to have known more about him than they were letting on, he seems to be a veteran around that area, who's got a bit of a checkered past.[12]

JM: O'Connor's been involved in at least two plane crashes, and he was cited for Criminal Air Safety violations in 2001.

BOB NORMAN: He'd gone through bankruptcies, a divorce, he's a chronic traffic offender.

JM: Florida reporter [and Blogger @ the *Broward Palm Beach New Times*] Bob Norman tried to track down O'Connor.

NORMAN: He's a slippery guy, … and where the money's coming from, I think that's a big question.

JM: Kevin Hall was wondering about O'Connor's money too.

HALL: …seems to own a $450,000 house, so he seems to be doin' pretty well, even though his businesses are going bad.

JM: He has two corporations registered in his name, but they're run out of Post Office Boxes and their phones are disconnected. Bob went looking for O'Connor at Fort Lauderdale Executive Airport. He just missed him.

NORMAN: I don't know why he was there, but it was the talk of the airport.

JM: So Bob reported he had been seen around the Fort Lauderdale airport days after the crash. The same day his story came out, O'Connor left the country in a hurry.[13] He flew to Canada and was arrested right away for lying about the guns in his bag.[14] He paid several thousand dollars to get his plane back and then flew it to the Azores. He still doesn't appear to be under investigation for any wrongdoing, despite being the cocaine plane's owner of record. This really gets Bob Norman's goat…

NORMAN: This is a trail that needs to be investigated. Clyde O'Connor needs to be investigated.

JM: And according to the bill of sale.… He was the lawful owner of the plane.

SLACK: Even though the paperwork may not be on record and filed, presumptive ownership transfers on the date of sale.

JM: There's another big question about Clyde…

ROOT: Who actually piloted the plane out of the US? Was it Mr. O'Connor, who wasn't certified?…

JM: So did he fly it illegally or did someone else fly it? And also, who gave O'Connor the money to buy the plane? According to the Brazilian owner, O'Connor was buying the plane on behalf of someone else. ... Then who's he buying it for? There was another name on the bill of Sale: Greg Smith, the only person involved in the deal not to have left the country.

JM: So Dan Hopsicker tried to get his side of the story.

HOPSICKER: The pilots aren't talking to the press, so I asked someone, who I know does business with the two pilots, to call, and Greg Smith blurted out *"it was Don's money"* ... [15]

JM: That's Don Whittington, a convicted drug smuggler, tax evader and champion race car driver.[16] Several of his planes were named in investigations of the CIA rendition program,[17] but we'll get back to him later.

So What do we know so far? ... We've got a crashed drug plane in Mexico. ... It's got a history of government use. ... It changes hands twice in a couple weeks before crashing...

And the people involved in the deal, Clyde O'Connor, Greg Smith, the Brazilian lawyer, Joao Luis Malago ... don't appear to have the means to throw down two million dollars of their own cash to buy a jet...

JM: South Florida has long been central to the drug war ... and the terror war. Especially Fort Lauderdale Executive Airport, says local reporter Bob Norman...

NORMAN: It [Fort Lauderdale Executive Airport used to be called FLEA, but because of the unfortunate connotation, changed the acronym to FXE[18]] has a reputation as a place where smuggling has occurred.

JM: South Florida, where the 9/11 pilots practiced on private planes,[19] has plenty of room for shady operators. ... Remember Don Whittington from earlier in the story? Alleged financier of the drug-plane and owner of several other rendition planes? He runs the largest operation at Fort Lauderdale Executive: World Jet International.

HOPSICKER: When Wally Hilliard, the owner of the flight school Mohammed Atta went to, bought a Lear jet that was busted with 43 pounds of heroin...

JM: Tail number N-351 WB...

HOPSICKER: He got his Lear Jet from Don Whittington too...

JM: I asked aviation attorney Michael Slack, "What's stopping someone from buying a private plane and then filling it up with drugs or explosives or guns?"

MICHAEL SLACK: Nothing. You know, you have various places where some- thing like that could be detected, but as long as the people doing it know how to make it look normal … then it's not gonna get detected.

JM: A good way to detect that sort of thing would be to check out the flight records. An FAA representative told me the rules were changed after 9/11. Record-keeping has been privatized to Lockheed Martin.[20] So now, flight records are private. And then there's the loopholes in outdated FAA rules and filing systems. Dan Hopsicker told me how you do it if you want to use a private plane for something shady…

HOPSICKER: You and I sign papers transferring the plane to me.

JM: But instead of sending them to the FAA...

HOPSICKER: You hold them...

JM: And if everything goes according to plan, as it normally does...

HOPSICKER: You tear up the documents. If, however, I get busted in Mexico with the plane...

JM: Then you send it in to FAA and there's a 30 day window after the sale to receive the paperwork… Then you've jumped the legal hurdles and muddied the waters for anyone trying to figure out what went down. And that's exactly what the evidence suggests these guys did.

ROOT: …they claim, 'hey we sold it, here's the bill of sale', and the FAA says 'no, we've never gotten that,' and it's sort of a he-said she-said.

JM: Unless there's a random "ramp check"[21] there's never anyone to check if the pilot is licensed, let alone to inspect *what's in those hundreds of black duffel bags you're carrying."*

Jonah Meadows ended the show with this comment: "Maybe the documented cases of protected drug smuggling in Laos, Afghanistan, Nicaragua and El Salvador weren't isolated incidents.

"Maybe this isn't either, but instead, more of the kind of corruption that's long been alleged, rarely admitted and sometimes proven."

He called it what it was: corruption. Thank you, Jonah Meadows.

St Pete-Clearwater International Airport Gets a Pass

Newspapers in Mexico joined the chorus of voices expressing indignation and began to examine the growing perception that owners of American-registered drug planes seemed to enjoy an immunity from prosecution envied by Mexican drug cartels.

Mainstream media in the U.S. ignored – with a vengeance – any implication that the governing elites in either Mexico or the U.S. were directly implicated in massive drug trafficking.

There were, however, a few surprising exceptions. Chief among them: local media – and local government officials – in St Petersburg and Clearwater, where outrage over the impunity of the drug trade was felt by many residents locally, as well as by newscasters on the local news.

The local FOX affiliate in Tampa, for example, aired a story that dripped with sarcasm over the seeming inability of aviation and law enforcement to deal with the problem.

Fox news anchor Kelly Ring was everything you'd expect: she was attractive and blond. But she was also no dummy. She even sounded impassioned as she began her report, saying "Right here in Pinellas County!"

Investigative reporter Craig Patrick, who today hosts his own show[22] sounded slightly more resigned to the situation.

> PATRICK: Well, Kelly, we all see the commercial airlines. They rent space right here at the terminal. But there are also private businesses that rent space on the other side of the tarmac. And Homeland Security does not keep track of what they sell or who buys it. Mexican soldiers found more than five tons of cocaine on a DC-9 jet. Then this Gulfstream jet crashed near Cancun … police found bag after bag of cocaine in the wreckage – another three and a half tons in all.
>
> Look at the bags… (Cut-away to the bags. There are many.)
>
> PATRICK: This flight too originated at the St Petersburg-Clearwater International Airport, flew to Colombia, and then on to Mexico, where it crash-landed in a field 45 kilometers outside of the Yucatan capital of Merida. Officials now say drug lords bought both planes from St. Pete-Clearwater Airport. Mexican police say drug lords have bought a number of cargo planes at the airport. Mexican police say members of their Sinaloa drug cartel showed up with money and made off with jets.
>
> But it turns out that the drug planes based here weren't even being investigated by local law enforcement authorities. Despite the

much-ballyhooed war on drugs, officials were falling all over themselves disclaiming any responsibility. The Airport director said it's
not his job to scrutinize his tenants. The FAA said it's not their job
either. Homeland Security also does not police who buys and sells
private jets at public airports. Neither does the Transportation Security Agency.

Private plane brokers rent space at the public airport and sell
jets for profit. Mexican police say members of the Sinaloa drug cartel showed up with money and made off with jets.… They screen
every passenger, but they don't screen smugglers who want to buy
entire jets.

The tone of citizen frustration was palpable. The massive seizures were
clearly adding to a litany of woes – busted-out banks, plundered public companies, and gutted savings and loans – which mere nation-states, even ones
as powerful as the United States, appeared powerless to prevent, or punish.

In "Circumstances Nebulae"

Less than two weeks after the crash, I paid a visit to the address in Coconut Beach, Florida, where FAA documents indicated the owner of
the plane, "Donna Blue Aircraft Inc.," had its place of business.

What I found was an empty office suite with a blank sign out front.
There was no sign of Donna Blue Aircraft. However, there were a half-doz-
en unmarked police cars parked directly in front of the empty suite.

It seemed too obvious that the cocaine-packed Gulfstream had again
been sheep-dipped. Donna Blue Aircraft – dba – as in CIA "doing business as" must have been a sick CIA joke.[24]

They love to use fake entities to throw trackers off the scent. We wondered, could initial DBA in this instance have been a clue that it was the
CIA doing business as an entity with those initials?

Only while editing *Gangster Planet* did we discover there was a real person named Donna Blue, who'd also filed corporate documents in Florida
shortly before the Gulfstream was publicly linked to CIA illegal renditions. Blue & Associates, Inc., like Donna Blue Aircraft, Inc., allegedly did
its business from a post office drop box – located in Tamarac, Florida – instead of at Coconut Creek, less than 10 miles away. And its incorporation
papers were signed by Donna B. Blue.

Small world.

We were slightly intrigued and dug deeper. It turned out Donna B.
Blue was the daughter of Marine corps Lt. Col. Donald Dexter Blue, a

graduate of the Naval Academy, and his wife Angeline Edith "Dorothy" Tassos, who had led fascinating, yet top secret covert lives before their respective deaths in 1989 and 1998.[25] Was there a possible connection between the two?

As I've said before, we're not cleared for that information.

The "Cliff Notes" definition for "covert" tells us only what we already knew: "As an adjective, covert means secret, concealed, or disguised – think of a spy who is under *cover*."[26]

WE COULD CALL IT "COCAINE TWO"

The Gulfstream II (N987SA), which crashed on September 23, 2007, with drugs aboard, had prompted media to turn the spotlight back on the DC-9 airliner busted in April 2006 at Ciudad del Carmen, also with drugs aboard.

Now they could disingenuously report that "only now" has it been learned that this flight also contained a number of comparable "anomalies."

One thing the two planes shared was the fact both had been sold out of the St. Petersburg-Clearwater Airport within two weeks of being caught flying with drugs on board.

According to reporting by the *Tampa Times*, whose reporter questioned why the Brazilian lawyer, Joao Luis Malago, chose this particular plane, he replied, "because I have a close friend who has a hangar, so this plane was just waiting for delivery.[27]

There were "wonderful similarities," reported *Por Esto!* drolly, "between the Gulfstream which crash-landed in the tiny hamlet of Tixkokob and the DC-9 busted in Ciudad del Carmen which help explain why – despite the fact that almost eighteen months has passed – the American owners of the DC-9 have not been charged with any crime."

The DC-9 had been painted to impersonate aircraft from the Department of Homeland Security, but the impounded Gulfstream II business jet (N987SA) – painted red, white and blue, like the American flag – didn't need to *impersonate* a U.S. government plane. It *was* a U.S. government plane.

Reporters in South America and Europe were focused on the Gulfstream's use by the CIA for "extraordinary renditions." That allowed the previously taboo subject of the CIA's worldwide involvement in drug trafficking to be implicitly raised – without really being confronted – the essence of diplomacy.

The Gulfstream, European officials coolly reported, before the sale to the Brazilians, had been used by the CIA in extraordinary renditions, and it had also been flown by the DEA for a half-dozen years. Documents proved it.

Jonah Meadows in his radio report had added his own analysis: "The reason this made the news is the history of the plane, tail number N987SA. Starting in 2003, the plane made several trips from Washington, D.C. and Connecticut to Guantanamo Bay. This led to questions of its use by military or intelligence agencies. Since," pausing for emphasis "... *how many people really fly from Connecticut to Guantanamo?*"

The Tixkokob crash had single-handedly ended a fifty-year old "official" narrative pushed inside the United States about the war on drugs. It shredded it.

Both planes had been purchased while located in hangars at St. Pete-Clearwater aircraft. *And* ... both had overt and suspicious connections with U.S. intelligence.

Before being sold to the non-existent Donna Blue, however, the Gulfstream was owned – for a long time – *by a Russian Mafia figure in Manhattan,* who claimed he'd leased it to others.

Were we about to find a link to RussiaGate?

Endnotes

1   Jonah Meadows had a PBS radio program in Chicago for WBEZ, entitled "Geo-politics of Drugs: Narcoavion de Guantanamo." Jonah Meadows, *Inside Out Radio*, "Geopolitics of Drugs: Narcoavion de Guantanamo," WBEZ Public Radio, 2-15-2012 Transcript: https://www.wbez.org/stories/geopolitics-of-drugs-narcoavian-de-guantanamo/faf9e583- 0598-4f39-b994-afdad0cca1a6.

2   Menendez has been boldly reporting about the abuse of America's war on drugs for decades and takes well-deserved pride in what he has uncovered. "His reward for reporting on high-level corruption? He gets grenades thrown in his offices," says radio narrator Meadows, mentioning also that in May 2000, Menendez was named 'Drug War Hero of the Month,' by NarcoNews. Meadows again quotes the *Por Esto!* publisher: "They tried to kill me they tried to kidnap me several times. I cannot go anywhere."

3   Associated Press, *USA Today*, 9-27-07. https://usatoday30.usatoday.com/news/world/2007-09-27-mexico-drug-plane_N.htm

4   Jonah Meadows, *Inside Out Radio*, "Geopolitics of Drugs: Narcoavion de Guantanamo," WBEZ Public Radio, 2-15-2012 Transcript: https://www.wbez.org/stories/geopolitics-of-drugs-narcoavian-de-guantanamo/faf9e583-0598-4f39-b994-afdad0cca1a6

5   Ibid.

6   The actual recorded program differs somewhat from the transcript of it. Listen here: https://soundcloud.com/jonah-meadows/worldview-geopolitics-of-drugs-guantanamo-drug-plane?si=2b86121a374c44bc89590ed0c9355546&utm_source=clipboard&utm_medium=text&utm_campaign=social_sharing.

7   https://soundcloud.com/jonah-meadows/worldview-geopolitics-of-drugs-guantanamo-drug-plane

8   Jay Root and Kevin G. Hall, "Who owned drug plane that crashed in Mexico?" McClatchy Newspapers, September 28, 2007. https://www.mcclatchydc.com/news/nation-world/world/article24470158.html#storylink=cpy

9   Sunbiz.org search for Donna Blue. http://search.sunbiz.org/Inquiry/CorporationSearch/ConvertTiffToPDF?storagePath=COR%5C2007%5C0402%5CH0080366.Tif&documentNumber=P07000039924.   Also   http://search.sunbiz.org/Inquiry/CorporationSearch/SearchResultDetail?inquirytype=EntityName&direction-Type=Initial&searchNameOrder=DONNABLUEAIRCRAFT%20P070000399240&ag-gregateId=domp-p07000039924--a65903e5-efd7-4374-a68f-9a17b59d9507&searchTerm=-donna%20blue&listNameOrder=DONNABLUEAIRCRAFT%20P070000399240.

10   According to Whosis, no longer extant.

11   https://www.madcowprod.com/2007/10/08/sloppy-tradecraft-exposes-cia-drug-plane/

12   In 2002 O'Connor was said to be Director of Operations at For Lauderdale Executive Airport when a pilot crashed there. Shannon O'Boye ,"PILOT SURVIVES AFTER PLANE CRASHES ON LANDING," *Sun Sentinel*, August 10, 2002. https://www.sun-sentinel.com/2002/08/10/pilot- survives-after-plane-crashes-on-landing/

13   Bob Norman, "Dogging a High-Flying Bird," Broward, *Palm Beach New Times*, October 11, 2007. https://www.browardpalmbeach.com/news/dogging-a-high-flying- bird-6310730

14   https://saltwire.pressreader.com/the-chronicle-herald.

15   I was on to the Whittingtons at least as far back as 2004, which I published a story called "The Secret History of Martha Stewart,"at my website. https://www.madcowprod.com/2004/03/08/the-secret-history-of-martha-stewart/

16   Gary Long, "Car-racing brothers went out limit of law," *Miami Herald*, 1616 Mar 1986, Page B-1. https://www.newspapers.com/clip/121278433/whittingtons-and-levitz-racing-and/

17   Although Jonah Meadows cited two sources for his statement, neither is extant now. We found nothing when we searched 'Whittington,' but searching his company, "World Jet," brought up an article written by Wayne Madsen. Wayne Madsen, "Is CIA Using Rendition Aircraft to Haul Drugs?" *OpEdNews*, 4/1/2008. https://www.opednews.com/articles/opedne_wayne_ma_080401_is_cia_using_renditi.htm

I also published an article at my website on Oct 18, 2007, though it's no longer found there, called, "'DON'S $2 MILLION BOUGHT THE PLANE'. Fortunately, the article was posted to an Internet group by one of my many fans. https://groups.google.com/g/misc.activism.progressive/c/QndXQ04-qfA

18   https://www.flyfxe.com/

19   Citing REPORT OF THE JOINT INQUIRY INTO THE TERRORIST ATTACKS OF SEPTEMBER 11, 2001 – BY THE HOUSE PERMANENT SELECT COMMITTEE ON INTELLIGENCE AND THE SENATE SELECT COMMITTEE ON INTELLIGENCE. https://irp.fas.org/congress/2002_rpt/911rept.pdf

20   https://www.aopa.org/advocacy/advocacy-briefs/air-traffic-services-brief-flight-   service-station-fss-modernization-lockheed-martin-to-provide-flight-services-for-the-21st

21   https://www.pilotmall.com/blogs/news/faa-ramp-check-the-10-things-you- should-do

22   https://www.fox13news.com/person/p/craig-patrick. See his channel: https://www.youtube.com/channel/UCEK4GhPj3t-6ksSg6bKkITg

23   https://www.tampabay.com/blogs/baybuzz/2018/05/21/longtime-pinellas-county-commissioner-john-morroni-loses-cancer-fight-at-63/

24   Jeremy R. Hammond began his article on September 13th, 2008, at *Dissident Voice* by saying the Gulfstream was "linked to the CIA through both its extraordinary rendition program and a supposed sting operation known as 'Mayan Express,'" though I kept wondering if he meant 'Mayan Jaguar.' [https://archivo.eluniversal.com.mx/nacion/162152. html]

He elaborated, "El Universal, in its initial report on the crash in 2007, stated that the cocaine was in 132 bags and noted the registration number of the wrecked plane. McClatchy Newspapers observed a few days after the crash that 'news reports have linked the plane to the transport of terrorist suspects to the U.S. Detention center at Guantanamo Bay, Cuba, but those reports cite logs that indicate only that the plane flew twice between Washington, D.C., and Guantanamo and once between Oxford, Conn., and Guantanamo.' https://dissidentvoice.org/2008/09/crashed-jet-carrying-cocaine-linked-to-cia/

McClatchy eventually closed down, and its domain went up for sale. Just in case the same thing happens to *Dissident Voice*, the evidence posted by Hammond is set out below.

McClatchy cited documents from the United States and the European Parliament which "show that that plane flew several times to Guantanamo, Cuba, presumably to transfer terrorism suspects." It said the European Parliament was investigating the jet for its possible use in "extraordinary rendition" flights, whereby prisoners are covertly transferred by the U.S. to a third country.

"In June, 2006, the British Department for Transport website published flight data on US aircraft into or out of the UK. According to the site, "This data had previously been released by Eurocontrol to the Parliamentary Assembly of the Council of Europe to assist with its enquiry into allegations of 'extraordinary rendition' flights operating in Europe." The jet that crashed in Mexico, with registration number N987SA, is listed in the data report.

"According to *El Universal*, FAA records show that the jet flew to Guantanamo on May 30, 2003. From June 23 to July 14, the jet flew from New York to Iceland, France, Italy, and Ireland. From July 16 to 20, it flew from the U.S. To Canada, the UK, Ireland, the UK, Canada, and back to the U.S. Again. From April 7 to 12, 2004, it went from New York to Canada, the UK, Canada, and again to the U.S. The jet then flew to Guantanamo again. On April 21, it flew from the U.S. To Canada, France, the UK, Canada, and back to the U.S. It left the U.S. For Guantanamo once more on January 21, 2005.

"The jet crashed on September 24, 2007. According to an Aviation Safety Network description of the accident, the Gulfstream [sic] Aerospace G-1159 Gulfstream II jet with registration N987SA crashed near Tixkokob in the northern part of the Yucatan Peninsula. ASN describes it as an 'Illegal Flight' and reports that 'When being chased by Mexican military helicopters, the crew carried out a crash-landing. No bodies were found in the wreckage, but soldiers found 132 bags containing about 3.6 tons (3.3. Metric tons) of cocaine.'...

"The Gulfstream II jet was one of two planes being used by the Mexican Sinaloa drug cartel, also known as the Pacific Cartel, to carry cocaine. The other jet, a DC-9, had been seized and was found to be carrying 5.5 tons of cocaine. Both aircraft were purchased by the cartel from St. Petersburg-Clearwater International Airport."

It wasn't just the Mad Cow News that linked the two planes together and to the CIA. *Dissident Voice* continued: "The DC-9 with tail number N00SA, was seized on April 11, 2006 carrying an amount of cocaine valued at an estimated $82,500,000, according to Airport-Dat.com. Reportedly sold in March, the jet was scheduled to depart for Simon Bolivar International airport in Venezuela on April 5. FAA records show that at the time of the seizure, it was still registered to Royal Sons Inc., which operates out of St. Petersburg-Clearwater International Airport. It was deregistered two days after the seizure and listed as exported to Venezuela.

"At the time of the crash, the Gulfstream II was registered to Donna Blue Aircraft Inc., owned by Joao Luiz Malago and Eduardo Dias Guimaraes, who had reportedly purchased the jet in July and then sold it to two Florida men on September 16. Two days later, the jet left Fort Lauderdale for Cancun. Then, according to Mexican authorities, it flew to Columbia [sic] to pick up the cocaine and was en route to deliver the drugs when it came to the attention of the military and crashed in the resulting chase.

"Some have speculated that Donna Blue Aircraft may have been a front company. The Florida Department of State Division of Corporations lists the "Date Filed" for the company as March 29, 2007. And from June 1, it was listed at an address in Coconut Creek, Florida. Then, on June 18, 2008, the company name was changed to North Atlantic Aircraft Services, Corp., listed at the same address, but with Malago as the sole owner.

"Journalist Daniel Hopsicker visited the Coconut Creek location and found no sign that such a business existed there. Hopsicker wrote, 'Moreover the brief description of Donna Blue on its Internet page, apparently designed to "flesh out the ghost a little," is such a clumsy half-hearted effort that it defeats the purpose of helping aid the construction of a plausible 'legend,' or cover, and ends up doing more harm than good… For example, the website features a quote from a satisfied Donna Blue Aircraft customer. Unfortunately, his name is 'John Doe.' And the listed phone number is right out of the movies: 415.555-5555.'"

Hammond then makes an intriguing statement: "According to Whois, the [Donna Blue] site was created on August 20, 2007, a month after the Gulfstream II was reportedly bought by the company and less than a month before it crashed carrying the cocaine. Once uploaded, the site was apparently never updated and seems to have gone offline sometime after February 2008. According to the site description still available on Alexa, the company opened in 1995 despite the fact, as noted above, that the date the company was filed with the Florida Department of State was in March 2007."

By 2023, all that was available was that the domain name belonged to godaddy.com in Tempe, AZ and all client information had been deleted. Not until 2013 was more information learned.

An affidavit revealed that "the aircraft had been confiscated during Operation 'MAYAN JAGUAR' carried out exercises with HL of the United States for eradication, interdiction, destruction and detection of illegal marihuana and poppy plantations in the border area of the Department of El Petén, Rio Dulce, Lago de Izabal, and Bahia Amatiques." https://www.google.com/url?sa=t&rct=-j&q=&esrc=s&source=web&cd=&ved=2ahUKEwiMprrb8Yj9AhVglmoFHZSiDro-QFnoECAkQA-Q&url=https%3A%2F%2Fwww.oas.org%2Fcsh%2Fenglish%2Fdocuments%2F-cp10115e08.doc&usg=AOvVaw1J9GfgTiuQXpJybUeoeuPR

25   Donald Dexter Blue was one of three sons born in Wichita Kansas in 1918 to John Emerson (Acy) Blue, who had risen in status from being an inspector at an oil refinery man- ager of the warehouse of an airplane factory in Wichita Kansas by 1929 – Stearman Aircraft – forerunner to Boeing. His father and two brothers all retired from Boeing, either in Kansas or in Seattle.

But Donald got a place at the Naval Academy in 1938 and graduated early because of Pearl Harbor being attacked late in 1941. He got his Navy commission in 1941, and it's possible he was stationed in San Antonio in 1942 (where all flight training for the military was done), and that he met his wife Angeline Edith "Dorothy" Tassos there. But they married in October 1944, at Ottumwa, Iowa, at the newest flight training base for the Navy.

Dorothy and her baby brother had been orphaned in 1922 when her mother died. Her Greek-born father operated restaurants in San Antonio, but remarried in 1929 and moved to Dallas. He died in 1941. Dorothy and her brother Billy were passed around, living with Greek families in San Antonio who claimed her as their niece. One was Andrew Nichols, and the other was Gus Tassos.

The names of Donald and Angeline Blue turned up in Florida not long after the war ended. While still in the Marines, he was shown in the Fort Lauderdale directory as the manager of the Pango Bar in 1946. Curiously, Kenneth Burnstine would be living a few miles from the bar fifteen years later.

Just a coincidence surely.

Don Blue retired from military and went to work for Boeing at Redstone Arsenal in Huntsville, Alabama, at a top-secret base. His obituary said he retired from Boeing and went into construction work but gave no details. He died in 1989. His wife died in 1998. Daughter Donna Blue married a Californian, Gerald Robert Beeson, who was in the Marine Corps before working for Raytheon in 1962. They divorced before his death in 1998. She also married a man named Martin L. Sewell, Jr., who had worked in Saudi Arabia for Aramco before moving back to Texas, where he was an artist in Kerrville. He was featured in the Kerrville Times in 1991 for smuggling art (his own) out of Saudi Arabia for fear it would be destroyed as "graven images." *Kerrville Times*, August 11, 1991.

26   https://www.cliffsnotes.com/cliffsnotes/subjects/literature/what-does-the-word-covert-mean

27   HOWARD ALTMAN and KAREN BRANCH-BRIOSO, "Financier's Arrest Ties Drug Jets Flown from St. Pete," *Tampa Tribune*, Nov. 27, 2007. https://www.aviationpros. com/home/news/10383896/financiers-arrest-ties-drug-jets-flown-from-st-pete

CHAPTER ELEVEN

TWO MIKES AND
THE "HOLLYWOOD THING"

*"I've got a Caribbean soul I can barely control, and some Texas hidden
deep in my heart!"*

– Jimmy Buffett

On a frigid February morning on in 2005, a Bombardier Challenger 600 luxury jet was struggling – and failing – to take off at Teterboro Airport in New Jersey, just outside New York City.

The plane hurtled off the end of a runway at nearly 200 miles an hour, swept across a ditch and plowed through a steel perimeter fence, before plunging across a major six-lane highway busy with morning rush hour traffic, the jet's wing sweeping like a scythe across the tops of cars.

The Challenger crashed through the airport fence, hurtled across the highway, and ultimately plunged its nose half in, half out of a clothing warehouse on the other side of the highway, where people were working. Then the warehouse burst into flames.

Dozens of gawking drivers and passengers on their way to work – almost like spectators at a drive-in movie – were paused in front of the jet's unscheduled morning matinee, waiting in line at a traffic signal. The spectators were saved from death by a red light. They are alive today – not because of the speedy action of the FAA or the NTSB, but simply because of the vagaries of a traffic signal.

According to the NTSB, neither the pilot nor co-pilot were rated to fly the plane they were flying. The flight attendant, Angelica Caled-Gomez, had no safety training. She was a dancer at the Voodoo Lounge in Miami.

"All I remember is we went straight through the airport perimeter fence and knowing we were going to crash into that building," the 22-year-old told reporters.[1]

"I hoped we would just stop and not blow up," she said. "I was praying to God. There was smoke in the cabin. It was not a pretty scene."[2]

The petite flight attendant said she was grateful some male passengers had the strength to pry open a stuck emergency door. Drenched in jet fuel and gagging from fumes, Caled-Gomez remembers crawling through snow, clutching her cell phone. Then, still dazed, she called her mother.

The worst two injuries on the plane were of the pilot and co-pilot, one with a broken leg. Those who were on the ground, however, suffered more. James Dinnall, a 66-year old New Jersey factory worker in a car on his way to work, was in the hospital with permanent brain damage after the Challenger jet ripped off the top of his Toyota Camry.

Dinnall had seen the plane coming as it hurtled towards them through an airport fence, after skidding off an airport runway. He shouted a desperate warning to the driver an instant before the corporate jet sheared off the roof of their car, and then paid for his heroic act by spending more than a month in a coma.[3]

The investigation of the crash uncovered abundant anomalies and evidence of a pattern of illegal activity by the charter company – so egregious, in fact, that the Federal Aviation Administration (FAA) came in for some rare criticism in 2006 from another Federal agency, the National Transportation Safety Board (NTSB) in its report.[4]

Michael Francis Brassington, a co-owner of Platinum Jet, also had a secret, maybe even classified, job. He was the personal pilot of the Premier of the Turk and Caicos Islands (TCI) Michael Misick.

A part of the United Kingdom's Jamaican colony until 1962, TCI became a separate Crown colony upon Jamaica's independence. The British governor of The Bahamas oversaw affairs from 1965 to 1973.

When the Bahamas gained independence in 1973, TCI got its own governor and also became a separate autonomous British Overseas Territory. The young country was as small as it was beautiful, and it was hoping to take advantage of whatever assets were available to it.

Michael F. Brassington had access to a small fleet of luxury jets held by corporations he and his Guyanese brother Paul had set up in Florida. In exchange Misick offered Brassington one particular asset he made full use of.

The Honourable Michael Misick – as head of a government recognized by the UN – enjoyed diplomatic immunity. He could claim a duffel-bag-sized pouch which Brassington was allowed to carry.

Co-Pilot of Orlando Heroin Jet Located at Last

The Bombardier Challenger 600 was flying for a rogue air charter operation called Platinum Jet Management, which we had not looked up at the time of the crash. The crash did not involve drugs, and we were already up to our eyeballs in other research at that time.

I'd been searching for him since the 2000 heroin bust in Orlando, when I knew him only as "the co-pilot," only to find he'd been openly flying under the radar for nine years – until a company he owned was caught flouting air safety standards.

But at the time, we didn't know Platinum Jet Management was owned and operated by none other than the drug pilot, Michael Francis Brassington, who was already well on his way toward becoming a career criminal.[5]

Brassington had survived previous scrapes with law enforcement, emerging curiously unscathed each time. He had suffered no ill effects from co-piloting drug flights with Diego Levine for Wally Hilliard's Plane 1 Leasing Co. – the same Wally Hilliard who owned the flight school where Mohamed Atta was learning to fly.

We knew nothing about Brassington's role at Teterboro either, in real time, because the only name mentioned was the front company name – Platinum Jet. The crash itself and Platinum did achieve notoriety. Mostly because the passengers whose lives the charter company had endangered weren't mere passengers. They were *celebrities.* The major offense: putting the priceless lives of celebrities in danger.

What led the "Evening News" that night on all three network newscasts was the spectacular crash of his jet. And the image, the plane sticking half out of the side of the building.

* * *

James Leif Sanders, discussed in the previous chapter, had told me about Brassington back in 2004, just after Sanders lost his job as a rookie Customs agent for not accepting the get-out-of-jail-free card Brassington had flashed in front of him.

But I must have been a little lax in failing to discover he'd owned his own charter company, or should I call it a proprietary? Or was it just a rogue enterprise working to raise campaign funds for whoever was providing cover for the drugs being smuggled into the U.S.?

The 39 weekly drug flights Brassington had co-piloted with Diego Levine, unlike this current imbroglio, were not celebrity enhanced, and therefore hadn't attracted anybody's attention. Nobody but me was looking for him. I knew he had to be "connected," the same way plane owner Wally Hilliard was.

The first time I wrote about the 2005 Teterboro crash was two weeks after the indictment finally was unsealed in February 2009.

"If fatalities had resulted from the accident, the US Attorney's office would have grounds for a negligent homicide indictment against Platinum Jet's executives and pilots." I wrote, quoting aviation attorney Mark Fava of Columbia, South Carolina.[6]

After finally linking up the two events, instead of being ecstatic, I was full of sardonic rage. Watching Brassington go down for endangering "celebrity" passengers was like watching a murderer being arrested for jaywalking, or Al Capone for not filing taxes.

My anger came from the fact that FBI agents had not swooped in to arrest Brassington in 2005. Why did it take four years for that to happen?

Do you remember the day Ronald Reagan was first inaugurated as President? News networks covered him taking the oath on a split screen – alongside pictures of the hostages from Lebanon returning home. The next day's *New York Times* had the picture of Reagan on page one and the hostages on page two. It was kinda like that.

It was not a subtle moment.

A CYNICISM-INSPIRING MOMENT

There are only so many coincidences an already cynical investigative reporter can pretend not to notice. The Brassington indictment was the same kind of cynicism-inspiring moment:

> "On January 23, 2009, a federal grand jury handed up a 23-Count Indictment," the appellate opinion in *U.S. versus Brassington* reads. "The first inauguration of Barack Obama as the 44th president of the United States took place on Tuesday, January 20, 2009," three days before a grand jury returned that indictment.

Just a coincidence? Not on your life.

Acting U.S. Attorney Ralph J. Marra, Jr.'s name appeared on the indictment.[7] The new Attorney General, Eric Holder, had allowed Marra to stay on until a new U.S. Attorney was named by President Barack Obama, even though Marra had been very close to Republican political appointee to the job, Chris Christie, who had helped raise $350,000 in 2000 for Bush – giving him status as a "Bush Pioneer."[8]

Christie resigned in December 2008 to run for governor against Jon Corzine, the Democratic incumbent. Christie beat Corzine, in spite of claims he was mob-connected. His aunt was married to the brother of a major figure in the Genovese crime family, its acting boss, no less – Tino Fiumara.[9]

Christie was barely out the door, when the indictment – already typed up and ready to go in 2005 – was delivered to the next grand jury. The case was tried in 2010 by Main Justice attorneys from the Government Fraud Unit and Criminal Division under Attorney General Eric Holder.

Michael Francis Brassington was convicted and finally sentenced in 2011 to prison.[10]

There had long been intense speculation about where Brassington got his juice. Platinum Jet Management had caused the injury of 20 people, including several maimed for life. Yet even the company (without the owner being named) had walked away with only a civil penalty of $150,000, half of which was suspended for two years, and then forgiven.

The NTSB had not withheld its withering criticism of his charter company for its role in the Teterboro crash, but then, there's a saying my mom taught me: "Sticks and stones will break your bones, but withering criticism will never hurt you." Something to that effect, at least.

Brassington's "luck" held from the date of the crash – a year, more or less, after his encounter with Leif Sanders in Fort Lauderdale – until January 23, 2009, when a federal grand jury handed up a 23-Count Indictment, in Criminal Case No. 09-45 (JAG).[11]

The indictment charging him with 23 counts comprising the violation of passenger safety would not have occurred but for enough voters going to the polls the previous November to elect a Democrat to run the White House. There is absolutely and unequivocally no other explanation for delaying his prosecution.

"Jet Company Allegedly Risked Celebrity Passengers' Lives for Cheap Fuel," an ABC headline read, after the indictment was unsealed.[12] New York's NBC 4 chief investigative reporter described Platinum Jet's luxury charter service as one which "catered to celebrities and ex-Presidents from Beyonce to Bill Clinton.

"Marquee names had dotted its passenger lists, sources said, including former president George H.W. Bush, basketball great Shaquille O'Neal, Hall of Fame quarterback Joe Montana, rappers Jay Z, Sean "Diddy" Combs, and Snoop Dogg, actor Burt Reynolds, and movie producer Harvey Weinstein," who later lost his celebrity status.[13] He replaced it with the title of rapist and convicted felon.

None of the mainstream news members asked what had given Platinum its apparent clout.[14] Endangering the lives of celebrities is no more serious a crime than endangering the lives of those unfortunates without prospect of fame. But well-known names did ensure Brassington's case got a lot of publicity. An additional two years passed, however, before Brassington marched off to prison.

Once we had Mike Brassington firmly in our sights, it wasn't hard to backtrack his activities during the decade after the 9/11 attack. In 2004 another private jet operated by Platinum out of Fort Lauderdale, for example, had run a jet off a runway at Peachtree-DeKalb Airport in Atlanta.[15]

THE SHARKS BEGIN TO CIRCLE

Michael Misick's "living large" lifestyle made him an attractive presence as he attended conferences on tourism and marketing in places like Atlanta and New York City.

Among those taking note was a voluptuous American woman, Omarosa, who was much classier than her association with Donald Trump would make her seem. She'd put herself through a small state university in Ohio by means of a volleyball scholarship and prizes in beauty contests.

Toughened by such competitive activities, Omarosa – veteran of the first season of NBC's top-rated reality show Trump hosted, *The Apprentice*, emerged as the contestant everyone loved to hate.

After being "fired" in the penultimate episode of the 2004 season, she kept returning to reprise her "mean girl" role in other Trump specials over the years, ending up with a job as a real-life aide in President Donald Trump's White House. The two *Apprentice* stars had one thing in common – huge narcissistic egos.

Like Trump, Omarosa sometimes had trouble separating reality-TV from real life. It was not by accident that Omarosa was one of only a few celebrities – like Oprah – known by their first names.

Before appearing on Trump's top-rated series, she had been hired in 1997 to work in Vice President Al Gore's office. A flop there, she was transferred three times before getting her final walking papers.

Like the proverbial bad penny, however, Omarosa just kept turning up. This time in the Trump White House, working with Trump staffers, Hope Hicks and Kellyanne Conway, more than a decade after her first appearance on *The Apprentice*.

Nothing had changed. She was still found lacking and canned. Trump's Chief of Staff, John Kelly, fired her in late 2017 for having "money and integrity issues," and for "inappropriate use of company vehicles."[16]

It was the height of irony, as the Trump White House would eventually play out – is still playing out *ad nauseum*. Of all the people with integrity issues, this woman was possibly the only one ever charged by prosecutors and ended up having to pay a $61,000 fine.[17]

Omarosa wrote a book detailing her tenure at the White House – becoming one of the first to slam Trump, calling him "unqualified" and racist." Published during the summer of 2018, it came out at the worst possible time – right in the middle of election season. It therefore got a lot of play on TV.

Days before it was released, she dropped the first of what she said were as many as 200 secret tapes she'd recorded during her White House tenure.

That certainly got attention.

It was the worst thing to happen to a Southern Strategy since Sherman's March to the Sea. Sherman's effort to prevent the South from rising again after the civil war had left the South with bitterness and a desire for revenge. In retrospect, considering the entire cast of characters, we found ourselves wondering whether any of them had met before.

We knew Brassington, according to an interview his dad gave in 1999, had been "stationed in the U.S.," and that the Guyana Defence Forces were overseen by Operation Tradewinds, based in Doral, Florida, where 4-Star Marine General John Kelly had headed the Southern Command before rising to head Homeland Security, and later Trump's Chief of Staff.[18]

Just so, Trump tried to derail Omarosa, who had recently married a Christian pastor – by releasing details of her secret dalliance with Michael Misick. There had been no photos at the time of the affair because no one knew or cared.

Michael Brassington, already an owner of Platinum Jet, was also the personal pilot of Michael Misick, Premier of the Turks and Caicos Islands. In an 'exclusive report' London's *Daily Mail* in August 2018 trumpeted in bold headlines details of a torrid six-month affair in 2005 between Omarosa and the shady Prime Minister of the Turks and Caicos Islands.[19]

**EXCLUSIVE: Omarosa's secret romance
with "corrupt" politician!**
**Fired Trump aide had six-month hook-up with Michael
Misick, former prime minister of Turks and Caicos!**

Dished the tabloid: "The duo stayed at five-star hotels around the world, enjoyed yacht parties, and spent time at Misick's home in the Turks & Caicos." Misick and Omarosa met at what the *Daily Mail* described as a "charity function" in New York City. Misick was described as "busily courting celebrities in a bid to bring wealth and glamour to his sun-drenched archipelago."[20]

Sparks had flown. That same night the duo checked in at the plush Four Seasons Hotel in Mid-Manhattan for an intimate tete-a-tete that stretched through the weekend.

"In New York they would dine at Sylvia's which was one of Mike's favorites and meet either at the Four Seasons or Mandarin Oriental where Mike usually stayed," gushed the tabloid.[21]

Misick flew back a week later to see her again. "'Omarosa clearly admired him," the paper reported. "And Misick was clearly aware of her ties with Trump.... Insiders say Omarosa also accompanied him to Dubai for an investment conference, where they stayed at the One and Only Royal Mirage Hotel, where suites cost up to $6,000 a night."[22]

The Backstory

Tracking Michael Brassington's activities quickly led to news of his prominent family in Guyana, and their relationship with a Russian oligarch (who became the first of many I would become acquainted with). Brassington's family – a mixture of blacks and Scottish whites – is one of the oldest in Guyana, stemming from when it was colonial British Guiana, attached to the eastern border of Venezuela.

A little research revealed that Russian oligarch Oleg Deripaska had done a billion-dollar deal with Michael Francis Brassington's equally-oligarchic family in Guyana.

Brassingtons had been in Guyana for almost two hundred years. They owned a sugar plantation located far from any road, deep in the jungle interior of the country, which – then and now – was about as deep as it got. Despite the fact that Guyana's mother country had outlawed slavery decades earlier, the plantation's remote location shielded from scrutiny the family's use of slaves well into the 1830's.

He was also descended from Jose Gomes D'Aguiar, whose son Peter was head of the Union Forces political party that supported Forbes Burnham – the candidate the CIA also supported.

Back before and after Kennedy was President, Guyana (British Guiana) was being closely watched by the Dulles faction who knew Guyana had "Communist" leanings. What the Dulles brothers and their corporate friends and clients most feared was expropriation – exemplified by Fidel Castro in Cuba.

A euphemistic synonym for expropriation is privatization, and Russia's example over the past thirty years has shown the world that "Minister for Privatization" is one of the planet's truly plum jobs.

Brassington's father, Michael A. Brassington, then his uncle, and still later his "Cousin Winston" each in turn had been Guyana's "Minister of Privatization."

A local subsidiary of U.S. aluminum giant Reynolds Company had been in Guyana for decades. Bauxite was one of the country's few exports, although there were traces also of oil and diamonds.

Yet when the time was ripe to divest Guyana's interest in its state-owned bauxite company, Cousin Winston summarily rejected Reynolds' bid. Winston turned around and sold the concession to Russian Aluminum (RusAl), controlled by Russian Mob Boss Oleg Deripaska. Winston Brassington and RusAl announced they had reached a billion-dollar deal.

Oleg Deripaska, one of the biggest Russian Oligarchs in the world, and his company, RUSAL, had fought for control of one of Russia's key industries, and became the world's largest aluminum producer. Deripaska had been the "last man standing" in what Russians call the "Aluminum Wars" during the 1990's. There were three of them, each more vicious than the last. It was like winning a UFC's death match, or a heavy-weight title back in the days of bareknuckle brawling.

"As Deripaska made his way up, 'protection' rackets run by organized crime groups were gradually taken over by law enforcement agencies," read a *New York Times* profile on him. "Aluminum is a very dangerous business in Russia."[23]

Deripaska turned out to be a Slavic Oliver North. Oleg was one of Putin's versatile go-to guys. Need somebody strong-armed or, alternatively, greased with bribes?

Deripaska organized the rapid rise of a drug gang in Kotor, Montenegro, turning men in wife-beater t-shirts and five o'clock shadows into Eurasia's tightest traffickers, even as he was building a billion-dollar resort in Kotor for his oligarch-pals and their hundred-foot yachts.

In his native land, Deripaska was a gangster's gangster. He seemed a fish out of water in Washington D.C., however, where he bought a mansion on Ambassador's Row right next to Trump advisor Kellyanne Conaway which he never moved into, as he was banned from entering the U.S., except to talk to the FBI.

So when Donald Trump made headlines in 2008 for peddling a rundown Palm Beach mansion to Russian oligarch Dmitry Rybolovlev for more money than ever, I paid attention, because the two of them ran with the same crowd in Moscow.

They were gangsters with all-day parking passes at every major Western bank's Moscow branch. I also tried to keep an eye on co-pilot Michael Francis Brassington's post-Hilliard career.

His was easily the most entertaining of anyone in what I began to call "The Shuffleboard Cartel," in honor of their home port's status as the world's top host for everything shuffleboard, from 24-hour courts to The International Shuffleboard Hall of Fame, which must be an inspiring attraction.

Winston Brassington also sold Deripaska land on which to build a vacation home in Guyana. The land was appraised at more than twice what Deripaska paid for it.

"Most disturbingly, the sales record indicates only partial payment even of that paltry sum," an anonymous official told a Guyana newspapers.

"It's vexatious."

Vexatious, indeed.

* * *

Back in 2008 or 2009, Michael Brassington's connection with Oleg Deripaska became my first introduction into the wonderful world of Russian oligarchs.

Then there was his job in the Turks & Caicos Islands. Michael Brassington, a short, squat, swarthy pilot with big ears. Yet here he was, finally achieving his own notoriety.

The massive corruption probe in the Turks & Caicos Islands (TCI) had heard testimony that placed Guyanese pilot Brassington – because of his close connection to the actual targets of the investigation – under intense scrutiny.[24]

Michael Francis Brassington had blown diplomatic cover. We suspected he had cover but, until he blew it, we didn't know where it came from. He acquired it by his association with another Mike.

Brassington became the personal pilot of Michael Misick, the 1st Premier of the Turks and Caicos, a tiny Caribbean nation of low-lying islands 600 miles southeast of Miami.

As scandal began to emerge, *The Independent* labeled Misick the "king of sleaze of the colonies," while adding that Sir Robin Auld's "incendiary interim report found 'information in abundance pointing to a high probability of systematic corruption or serious dishonesty' and concluded there were 'clear signs of political amorality and immaturity and of administrative incompetence.'"[25]

There's nothing like political amorality and immaturity to contribute color to a little administrative incompetence.

This is where the story begins to get colorful.

World-class Caribbean colorful.

The "LisaRaye" Years

However, within the first few months of their then-unpublicized fling, Omarosa soon had a rival for Misick's slavering affections, actress LisaRaye McCoy, a popular Hollywood hip-hop starlet with her own television series produced by Will Smith and his wife.

Soon after Misick began courting LisaRaye, she and her new Caribbean beau were becoming the stuff of legends. It was like Prince Charles and a hip-hop Diana, encircled by paparazzi.

Premier Michael Misick had been smitten. Again.

Michael Brassington – viewing both romances from the cockpit of the Turks & Caicos version of Air Force One – now began flying Misick back and forth to Hollywood, as well as between the Caribbean and all over the world.

But disaster struck.

No, the plane did not crash. Disaster is defined in this context as both babes showing up in the same place, at the same time.

"After a rumored blowout at an NAACP function at which LisaRaye confronted Omarosa about the affair, the two finally went their separate ways," reported *OK Magazine*.[23]

Another tabloid claimed Omarosa and Misick's tryst "fizzled out." Was LisaRaye a "fizzle block"?

Missing the Real Story

Omarosa and Misick stopped seeing each other years before Omarosa's tell-all book – it didn't refer to either Misick or LisaRaye – came out. According to the *Washington Post*, Donald Trump helped to make *Unhinged* a best-seller by calling the author "a crazed, crying low- life" and praising White House Chief of Staff John F. Kelly "for quickly firing that dog!"[24]

LisaRaye's romantic career was already being avidly, if not salaciously, chronicled in magazines and online publications. LisaRaye appeared in gossip magazines almost as often as Kim Kardashian, and the publicity experts from One TV network, like Britain's paparazzi, swooped in like vultures. But they all missed the real story.

I may have been the only reporter at the time who wasn't laughing, as I wrote in February 2009 on my website:

"Gulfstream jets were used by Misick to ferry Lisa Ray McCoy, the Hollywood TV actress and spokesmodel, back and forth between Los Angeles and the Caribbean.

"The duo also took side trips to Milan, Prague, Lausanne, Switzerland, Africa and Venezuela on the government Gulfstreams supplied by Brassington."[25]

In October 2005 Misick made a business trip to Bratislava, Slovenia, at the invitation of former Soviet Union oligarch Mario Hoffmann to discuss a land development on Salt Cay, one of TCI's islands Hoffmann had acquired in 2001. Once the glamor and glitz dissolves, something sinister remains. Just a few scant months after that trip, in 2006 LisaRaye, actually the 'other woman' in the Caribbean love triangle, became Premier Michael Misick's wife.

"It was a fairy tale come true," reported the April 13, 2006, *Miami Herald*. LisaRaye even wore a tiara, to complement her "backless Cinderella-inspired wedding dress."[26]

She spent a three-week honeymoon with her new hubby in such exotic locations as Jerusalem, Bali and Dubai – after no doubt verifying that their suite in Dubai was not the same one Michael had shared with Omarosa at the Royal Mirage.

HER MAJESTY'S GOVERNMENT "MANS UP"

Lest you get the idea the author of this book is one who drools at supermarket checkouts over David Pecker's *National Enquirer* headlines, I hasten to inform you my only interest was in trying to glean any tiny amount of information available on Misick's pilot.

As fascinating as the 2005 crash at Teterboro was, it had only become significant upon learning Brassington had been working for Misick at this crucial point in time.

Had I known about Michael Brassington's job as First Pilot in real time, keeping track of him would have involved nothing more strenuous than turning on "Entertainment Tonight".

Premier Mike's corruption grew so egregious – even by the Caribbean's less-than-rigid standards – that Great Britain was forced to man up and bite the bullet. The headline in the *Guardian* read:

"UK SEIZES CONTROL OF TURKS AND CAICOS OVER SLEAZE ALLEGATIONS."[27]

Her Majesty's government suffered a lot of bad publicity. Bad mojo was all around.

Mike Misick will be remembered as a man so corrupt that Great Britain resurrected the British Empire for a day. They took back a former colony – for the only time in history – that had already been granted independence.

Next, the British Government ordered a Commission of Inquiry into the breakdown of law and order in the Turks & Caicos, and the judges invited Ms McCoy to testify.

She did.

Boffo Box Office

For American tabloids and hip-hop blogs, it was like Christmas and Carnival all rolled into one.

LisaRaye had lots of fans, was on a hit ABC series, and had an uncanny knack of staying current, especially publicity-wise, and she burst onto the Turks & Caicos scene just as the Two Mikes – Misick and Brassington – were hellbent on getting richer than rich.

LisaRaye's testimony became the hot ticket in the Caribbean. It was strictly Standing Room Only. In a court filled with judges and lawyers in powdered wigs, the actress put on a dramatic and compelling performance.

One nugget from her testimony: When she married the boy, she told the judges, he owned only a small house and was worth $40,000.

Three years later, according to Ms McCoy, her former beau bragged to her that he was worth a cool $180 million dollars.

Rarely have the sex lives of the rich and famous intersected so directly with America's national security. This was one of those times.[28]

> **Sir Robin Auld:** Madam, what is the best way for us all to address you? Your name is double-barreled. Is it Mrs. McCoy – Misick, is that the right way to say it?[29]

She allowed it was. Sir Robin looked askance and began asking about expenses the two of them had incurred.

> **Q:** Is it true, you had gone to the trouble of having a family crest designed? It says "L and M" on it, I am going to guess that means LisaRaye and Michael? In the event, did you discuss this customizing, if I can call it that, with the Premier?

The notion that the Turks & Caicos had paid a fortune for LisaRaye McCoy-Misick to have a heraldic crest dreamed up left Sir Robin looking a bit gobsmacked. This was not – it was soon obvious – going to end well. Soon LisaRaye was talking about the $200,000 for clothes she was allotted each month from the government, and the $300,000 she'd been paid by the Tourism Board to pose in a swimsuit for an ad.

He decided to ask about the color swatches LisaRaye used to customize the interior of the plane.

> Q: I will pause you there for a second. You have referred to "Captain Mike," We see reference to a gentleman called Mike Brassington. Is that the man you knew as "Captain Mike"?
>
> Was it "Captain Mike" who sent them [the swatches] or did the Premier send you these? [30]

LisaRaye was only too happy to respond.

> A. Actually, we went through the plane with a fine toothcomb with our Captain – Captain Mike – and we pointed out everything we wanted, colors, fabrics, etc. He was actually sending me swatches, prices. We went through the whole thing.
>
> "Mike was like a kid in a candy store when he took over," his bodyguard, a burly former boxer, was quoted by *The Telegraph*. "He went through cash like he had a money tree."[31]

Meanwhile, in front of the Commission, Misick was evoking in his defense the words of assassinated American civil rights leader Martin Luther King.

"I echo the words of Dr King when he said, 'Injustice anywhere is a threat to justice everywhere.'"

Doing the "Hollywood Thing"

Motives are sometimes inscrutable. But one small disclosure seemed telling: Before she left Los Aangeles, Misick had the Turk & Caicos government pick up a $16,000 tab for LisaRaye's hairdresser.

> Q: Were all the payments made to her or were all the payments made to her in relation to work completed for you and you alone?
>
> LISA: No. She was also the stylist for him. We were doing the Hollywood thing. He wanted to change his look to complement mine. Also, I had to change my appearance for the First Lady thing. So, it was for both.

Premier Mike thought nothing of sticking the island's nearly-bankrupt government – which had just eliminated all student scholarships

– with the whopping $160,000 per month tab for the two Gulfstreams pilot Brassington was leasing. The split came – for Premier Mike – at the worst possible time. Just as he was being ousted from power and forced to resign.

London tabloids began referring to him as the "King of Sleaze in the Colonies."

Sniffed a British newspaper a few weeks before Christmas in 2012, "The former premier's rule was characterized by adultery, private jets and designer suits."[32]

They might have added "drug trafficking" to the litany of vices. Because unless "rampant drug trafficking" is added to the equation, it's almost impossible for Misick to be worth $180 million dollars.

CAPTAIN MIKE AND A BILL CLINTON STAFFER

A British Commission is a true spectacle. The Turks & Caicos Islands had never seen anything quite like it. The Judges wore powdered wigs and showed no understanding of hip-hop.

To people in the Turks & Caicos, it felt like they were living in a multiverse.

For his part, Chief Judge Sir Robin may have been wearing a powdered wig, but in other ways he sounded pretty up to date.

> **SIR ROBIN**: How often did you meet Jeffrey Watson?
>
> **LisaRaye**: Quite a bit. He would come to the island. He would stay with us at the house.
>
> **Q**: Was he a family friend?
>
> **A**: He was Michael's friend.

"WE AIN'T BROKE. WE RICH!"

As their marriage went south, LisaRaye was quick to release an account of their breakup which naturally painted her as a sympathetic figure. It was standard operating procedure, what press agents are paid to do.

The Turks & Caicos corruption inquiry was avidly followed by Caribbean newspapers, which reported details of venality and greed on such a massive scale that it appeared the Inquiry had been convened just in time to stop the plunderers from carting off all the sand.

> **SIR ROBIN**: Is that right, that what the Premier said to you constantly was, "We ain't broke" and that was about it?

A: He said, "We ain't broke, we rich." That was, you know, was our little slogan around the house.

Sir Robin moved on to ask about what he was most interested in – a shady bank in the Czech Republic that was claiming to hold the paper on a loan the bank made to the couple. The bank, we were later to learn, did not only have links to Mario Hoffmann, but also to Adnan Khashoggi, as we'll see in a later chapter.

The loan itself named both Michael E. Misick and LisaRaye McCoy Misick. But she couldn't recall it without prompting.

> **SIR ROBIN:** You touched on this in your evidence. I just want to make it clear. You never provided any financial information through a bank in the Czech Republic?
>
> **LISARAYE:** He did it through my company.
>
> **SIR ROBIN:** Yes, through "My Way's" bank account? Where you leased a Phantom Rolls Royce?

Wait. Leasing a Rolls Royce Phantom? Lisa thought the Phantom Rolls was hers.

MISICK AND THE CZECHS

Brassington figured prominently in the British Commission's report on Misick's corruption – not only as the personal pilot but as Misick's partner-in-crime as well.

"Bosses behind the massive Dellis Cay and Salt Cay schemes – accused of bullyboy tactics and bribery by Commission of Inquiry counsel – hope to prevent parts of the report alluding to misdeeds from being released," wrote the *Turks and Caicos Weekly News* on June 12, 2009. [33]

These "bosses" were Mario Hoffmann and Dr. Cem Kinay, wannabe oligarchs who were desperately trying to keep a low profile. Mario Hoffmann, a real estate developer from the former Czechoslovakia, was building a resort in the Turks and Caicos. [34]

Hoffmann and Kinay were two among many other former Soviet citizens who were busy looting the assets of the fallen USSR.

In a subsequent chapter we'll meet Arik Kislin, who joined with Michael Achenbaum of New York in reconstructing the ruins of the Third Turtle Inn – possibly the first luxury resort built in the Turks and Caicos Islands – into a branch of their Hotel Gansevoort chain. [35]

Misick's unredacted testimony revealed that he himself was also a shamelessly corrupt figure. He thought nothing of sticking his impoverished island nation with a whopping $160,000 per month tab for the two Gulfstream jets.

At the same time, his government was so broke classrooms went without roofs, communication systems at government offices were disconnected, and government employees were forced to bring their own rolls of toilet paper to work. The Commissioners asked him about it.

> **Q:** You understand that there have been allegations of excessive expenditure by the government in allegedly acquiring two jets. You are aware of that?
>
> **A:** I understand that that is the case.
>
> **Q:** Did in fact the government own either of the two jets, N165G and N25SV?
>
> **A:** No, the government owns no jets.

The Commission of Inquiry questioned him about people who had accompanied him on a flight by chartered jet to Portugal on April 18, 2007. Misick seemed eager to avoid specifics.

British MP Alex Milne asked specifically about Michael Brassington. "He was the pilot," replied Misick.

"Was Mr. Brassington someone who flew you on a regular basis?" Milne persisted. Pushing for specifics, he asked, "Is he a regular pilot for you though? Has he flown you on other occasions?"

"He has flown me on other occasions," conceded Misick. "Mr. Brassington is – while he is a pilot, he is also a broker – and also part owner of Aerojet," Misick responded.

Media reports weren't yet claiming that Michael Brassington had been *the* Michael Francis Brassington who was protected by a ring of corrupt Customs officials under investigation by the Department of Homeland Security.

Nor did they claim Brassington had been the co-pilot on a drug-running Lear jet (N351WB) caught by DEA agents at Orlando Executive Airport in July of 2000 with 43 pounds of heroin.

But the Guyanese pilot *was* called to task about reports in his native Guyana that he'd been named in a procurement scandal over the Guyana Defense Force's purchase from him of two antique 30-year-old helicopters from a "dummy" company in Delaware.

The owners of the two luxury Gulfstream jets Michael Brassington and Premier Michael Misick were using to advantage came as no huge surprise.

The intrigue surrounding Brassington may have been over his relationship with certain Russians. It suggests this is a far bigger scandal than a *"Tempest in the Turks & Caicos Teapot."*

The mask was slipping, if only a little bit.

Endnotes

1	Patrick McGeehan and Michelle O'Donnell, "First Findings See No Brakes Used in Most Of Jet's Path," *New York Times*, February 4, 2005. https://www.nytimes.com/2005/02/04/nyregion/first-findings-see-no-brakes-used-in-most-of-jets-path.html.

2	Mike Derer/The Associated Press, "Jet speeding down Teterboro Airport hits car, then crashes into warehouse," NJ.com, February 3, 2005. https://www.nj.com/ledgerarchives/2005/02/jet_speeding_down_teterboro_ai.html.

3	John Doyle, *New York Post*, February 3, 2005. https://nypost.com/2005/02/03/skidding-jet-in-hway-miracle-slides-off-n-j-runway-into-traffic-all-survive-fiery-warehouse-crash/

4	Doyle added, "The plane, owned by DDH Aviation of Fort Worth, Texas, was leased to Platinum Jet Management of Fort Lauderdale, Fla."

5	Runway Overrun and Collision, Platinum Jet Management, LLC, Bombardier Challenger CL-600-1A11, N370V, Teterboro, New Jersey, February 2, 2005. TSB/AAR-06/04 PB2007-910401 National Transportation Safety Board Notation 7715C, Adopted October 31, 2006. https://www.ntsb.gov/investigations/AccidentReports/Reports/AAR0604.pdf

6	*Aviation International News* (AINonline.com) on September 13, 2006, reported the flight was chartered by a New York investment firm, Kelso & Co. to take five employees from Teterboro to Chicago. They booked through a broker, Blue Star Jets, which arranged the flight through Platinum Jet Management. https://www.ainonline.com/aviation-news/aviation-international-news/2006-09-13/charter-under-microscope

7	Daniel Hopsicker, "Arrested Pilot Flew Private Jets Owned by Clinton White House Official," *MadCowNews*, February 19, 2009. https://www.madcowprod.com/2009/02/19/arrested-pilot-flew-private-jets-owned-by-clinton-white-house-official/.

8	Indictment at: http://a.abcnews.go.com/images/Blotter/Platinum%20Jet%20Indictment.pdf. Marra had been first assistant to Chris Christie and remained in his position until an ethics investigation was pursued against him for statements made when another indictment was announced the following summer. Katherine Santiago, "Acting U.S. Attorney Ralph Marra faces internal ethics probe," *Star Ledger*, Aug. 18, 2009. https://www.nj.com/news/2009/08/acting_us_attorney_ralph_marra.html

9	Political because Christie's law partner, William Palatucci, stupidly boasted he'd "selected" Christie, a corporate lawyer with little if any experience in criminal prosecution, as U.S. Attorney by simply forwarding his resume to Karl Rove, according to David D. Kirkpatrick and Jim Rutenberg, "E-Mail Shows Rove's Role in Fate of Prosecutors," *New York Times*, March 29, 2007. https://www.nytimes.com/2007/03/29/washington/29rove.html

10	"Fiumara's older brother, John, who lived in Livingston, a mile from the Christie home, was the second husband of Mr. Christie's aunt, Mr. Christie said. He said that he recalled seeing Tino Fiumara at large parties at his aunt's home when he was a boy." David M. Halbfinger and David Kocieniewski, "For Christie, Family Tie No Candidate Can Relish," *New York Times*, Sept. 23, 2009. https://www.nytimes.com/2009/09/24/nyregion/24christie.html?hp

11	Press Release, "Founders of luxury charter jet company sentenced to prison in illegal flight scheme," September 20, 2011. https://www.justice.gov/archive/usao/nj/Press/files/Brassington,%20Michael%20and%20Paul%20Sentencing%20News%20Release.html. Also published at https://www.oig.dot.gov/sites/default/files/Brassington%20et%20al%20%20Verdict%20PR.pdf

12	*U.S. v. Brassington*, United States District Court, D. New Jersey

13	Story by Richard Esposito, *ABC News*, February 4, 2009. https://abcnews.go.com/Blotter/story?id=6805353&page=1

14	Jonathan Dienst, WNBC at Channel 4 in New York, February 4, 2009. https://www.nbcnewyork.com/news/local/feds-fuel-scheme-led-to-nj-plane-crash/1907171/

15	The Associated Press reported at the time of the Teterboro crash that a Gulfstream 3 rolled off a runway into the mud at Atlanta's Peachtree-DeKalb Airport after a snowstorm. on Feb. 26, 2004, and according to the FAA website, was registered to a "company called 448 Alliance LLC, and gave an address in Dallas. Directory assistance has no company with that name but does show a DDH Aviation at the same address. No one answered the phone there." https://www.myplainview.com/news/article/Eleven-hurt-two-missing-in-N-J-jet-crash-8499896.php

16   *U.S. v. Omarosa Manigualt Newman*, Case No. 19-1868 (RGL), U.S.D.C. Washington, D.C. https://ecf.dcd.uscourts.gov/cgi-bin/show_public_doc?2019cv1868-51

17   Ryan King, Breaking Politics Reporter, *Washington Examiner*, March 16, 2022. https://www.washingtonexaminer.com/politics/omarosa-ordered-to-pay-61-000-fine-for-breach-of-financial-disclosure-rules

18   Spencer Ackerman, "Trump picks retired general John Kelly for homeland security," *The Guardian*, December 12, 2016. https://www.theguardian.com/us-news/2016/dec/12/trump-picks-retired-general-john-kly-for-homeland-security

19   Ben Ashford, "Exclusive: Omarosa's secret romance with 'corrupt' politi19cian with his own White House!" Dailymail.com, August 16, 2018. https://www.dailymail.co.uk/news/article-6067503/ Omarosa-six-month-affair-former-prime-minister-Turks-Caicos-Islands.html

20   Ibid.

21   Ibid.

22   Ibid.

23   "Everything You Need To Know About Omarosa and LisaRaye's Alleged Love Triangle," *OK Magazine*, published online August 16, 2018. https://okmagazine.com/photos/omarosa-lis-araye-michael-misick-love-triangle/

24   Ron Charles, "How Donald Trump turned Omarosa's 'Unhinged' tell-all into a bestseller," *Washington Post*, August 22, 2018. https://www.washingtonpost.com/entertainment/books/ how-donald-trump-turned-omarosas-unhinged-tell-all-into-a-bestseller/2018/08/22/89402bb4-a58a-11e8-97ce-cc9042272f07_story.html

25   "Corruption Probe," Madcowprod.com, February 17, 2009. https://www.madcowprod.com/2009/02/17/pilot-arrested-in-new-jersey-charter-crash-key-figure-in-caribbean-corruption-probe/#:~:text=The%20Gulf-stream%20jets%20were%20used%20by%20Misick%20to,Venezuela%20on%20the%20government%20Gulfstreams%20supplied%20by%20Brassington.

26   Jacqueline Charles, "Starry Wedding," *Miami Herald*, April 13, 2006.

27   Sam Jones, "UK seizes control of Turks and Caicos over sleaze allegations," *Guardian*, August 14, 2009.

28   https://assets.publishing.service.gov.uk/media/5a7cd53eed915d6b29fa8ef0/inquiry-report.pdf

29   Transcripts were accessed through Yumpu.com on November 24, 2023. Search for transcripts here: https://www.yumpu.com/user/tcinewsnow.com

30   Delana Isles, "LisaRaye testifies about private jets before SIPT," *Weekly News*, October 30, 2017. https://tcweeklynews.com/lisaraye-testifies-about-private-jets-before-sipt-p8252-127. htm

31   Philip Sherwell "Trouble in a British paradise," *The Telegraph*, April 18, 2009. https://www.telegraph.co.uk/news/worldnews/centralamericaandthecaribbean/turksandcaicosislands/5179010/Trouble-in-a-British-paradise.html

32   Lewis Smith, "Michael Misick: Turks and Caicos premier 'who left office with $180m fortune' arrested,"*The Independent*, December 8, 2012. https://www.independent.co.uk/news/world/americas/michael-misick-turks-and-caicos-premier-who-left-office-with-180m-fortune-arrest- ed-8393734.html

33   https://www.gov.uk/government/publications/turks-and-caicos-islands-commission-of-inquiry-2008-2009 and https://assets.publishing.service.gov.uk/government/uploads/system/uploads/attachment_data/file/268143/inquiry-report.pdf

34   The *TCI Weekly News* reported October 23, 2017, after the trial resumed: "Misick's involvement with the Czech billionaire has figured prominently in the trial which has been ongoing since December 2015. Back in August 2006, Salt Cay Golf Club was set up as the company that would own and operate the golf club. Fifty percent of the shares in that company were held by Hoffmann's Cyprus-based holding company and the other 50 percent was given to a holding company of which Michael Misick's brother, Chalmers 'Chal' Misick, was the owner. The transaction was allegedly concluded at a meeting between Misick and J&T Bank officials in Prague in 2005, which Hoffmann organised."

The *Guardian* didn't mince words in its criticism of Hoffman, saying that the Auld Inquiry "prompted accusations that the UK government failed in its duty to scrutinise a series of controversial property deals "Michael Misick has received more than $20m in loans from banks and businessmen but has yet to make any repayments on many of the advances "A plan to build a Dubai-style luxury island off the coast of the TCI – by dumping thousands of tons of sand into a maritime national park – was halted by the islands' planning board. Misick overturned the decision to block the development, leading to claims that he was encouraging environmental vandalism.

"The inquiry has heard how hundreds of thousands of dollars spent by Misick on his credit cards were paid off via a loan from a company called Arling Anstalt, based in Liechtenstein. Misick could not tell the inquiry who at Arling authorised the loan. He also obtained a loan from a Czech bank linked to his business developers in the TCI that allowed him to buy a Los Angeles house for himself and his second wife, LisaRaye McCoy, a former US soap star.

"The pair's lavish lifestyle has raised eyebrows on the island. It has emerged that Misick's ruling PNP party paid more than $100,000 for a hair stylist for McCoy. In addition, Misick is alleged to have claimed expenses during his honeymoon and for visits to the Funky Buddha nightclub in London. Hundreds of thousands of dollars were spent each month hiring a jet from a US lobbyist, Jeffrey Watson, a former aide to President Bill Clinton....

"It emerged during the inquiry that Misick's brother, Chal, and a Slovakian multi-millionaire developer, Mario Hoffman, bought a 99-year lease on 238 acres (96 hectares) they intend to turn into a luxury golf and hotel complex. The land was valued at nearly $8m a few years ago. Misick's cabinet allowed Hoffman to lease it for $238.72 a year – around £165.

"Hoffman, whose company, Istrokapital, is registered offshore in Cyprus, made his fortune buying up former Soviet Union-owned assets and privtising them. According to allegations submitted to the foreign affairs select committee, and denied by the company, Istrokapital 'is believed to have strong ties to the underworld.' The committee also heard allegations, again denied by the company, that it is a conduit 'for Russian money and used as a front for money-laundering.'"

Tomas Vasuta in his article, "A shark is just a small fish; Mario Hofmann's empire crumbled," IN-DEX, 19 Apr 2021, gave us an update on Hoffman's waning wealth: "Just a few years ago, the owner of the Istrokapitál group was in the first league of financiers. He worked his way to wealth thanks to his shark instinct and talent for being in the right place at the right time. However, times have changed, and the former financial shark has lost its teeth and power. It's hard to say which league Hoffmann belongs to at the moment. However, it seems that the best business years are behind him." Čítajte viac: https://index-sme-sk.translate.goog/c/22616059/ako-sa-rozpadlo-imperium-financnik-zralok-mario-hoffmann-istrokapital.html?ref=av-center&_x_tr_sl=auto&_x_tr_tl=en&_x_tr_hl=en&_x_tr_pto=wapp,. According to

The claims against Hoffmann and Kinay were subsequently settled by means of a confidential settlement agreement. Hayden Boyce, "Criminal Case against MARIO HOFFMAN Dropped with a CONFIDENTIAL SETTLEMENT," *Turks Journal*, 18/07/2012. https://turksjournal.wordpress.com/tag/providenciales-turks-and-caicos-islands/page/13/

35   The Third Turtle Inn was featured by James McLendon's article, "The Turkish Floridians," in the *Miami Herald*, May 25, 1975. The Turtle Inns were a project of Fritz Ludington and Benght Sodiqvest, whose most likely investor was the CIA-connected Richard Chichester du Pont, Jr. who used his Summit Aviation corporation like a CIA proprietary. Guillermo X. Garcia, "Evergreen denies CIA connection," The Arizona Daily Star, July 10, 1984.

Chapter Twelve

A Full Grasp Of The Big Picture

What turned me on then, and turns me on even today – and, when the time comes from me to retire from management, I think I'd still be interested in it – is that everything that happens in the world affects the price of securities.

– Sanford I. Weill

Heat is still coming off the hot asphalt in waves at 7 P.M. on July 25, 2000, when a luxury Lear 35 (tail# N351WB) lands at Orlando Executive Airport (OEA), located about 20 miles northeast of the entrance to Disney World. Everyone not at Disneyworld wishes they were somewhere else, somewhere other than in the middle of this steamy rainforest with a McDonald's on every corner.

If you've ever been there to see Mickey and Minnie, or gone to Epcot, you didn't land at this airport – unless you were flying a private corporate jet. On the tarmac, a cream-colored Learjet 35 rolls off the runway and pulls up to the Executive Air Center, the general aviation FBO (Fixed Base of Operations). Don't let the pilot talk fool you. It's a gas station with leather chairs in the lobby. FYI: There's another Executive Jet Center in Nassau in the Bahamas, that was owned by Wally Hilliard and an officer in the Jamaican Air Force, who's also a noted drug trafficker, named Alfonso Bowe. Surely just a coincidence.

Heavy Weight

The cockpit door opens, and two passengers – Edgar Javier Valles Diaz, and Neyra Rivas, both from Venezuela – gingerly step down, ready to begin wheeling their luggage towards the terminal. They won't make it.

A dozen armed DEA Agents emerge, armed with MAC-10 sub-machine guns. The first agent out the door motions with his gun for the couple to halt. Set down the suitcases. Agents move in. Some take the suitcases inside while others begin searching the Lear for other people or evidence. In an affidavit filed the next day at the Federal Court in Orlando, the Special Agent in charge describes what is found: "a white powdery substance which field-tests as heroin."

After searching hidden in nooks and crannies on the plane, authorities determine the Lear is carrying 43 lbs. of uncut heroin, which is known as "heavy weight." Each ounce when cut could bring in $5k-6k, or just under $4 million. You can do the math.

It took eight days for news of the bust to break in the local *Orlando Sentinel.* As far as we can tell, no other media picked up the story. Yet, according to the *Sentinel*, it is the biggest heroin bust in Central Florida history – even considering the fact they reported it as only as 30 pounds. [1]

Given the state's sordid past, this is no mean feat.

We didn't know it then, but what just happened would finally explain 9/11 – a huge chunk of it. At least, it did for me. It was also what ultimately would lead to the failure of America's 4th largest bank, Wachovia Corporation in Winston-Salem, North Carolina, of all places.

The heroin bust was described in my last chapter of *Welcome To Terror-Land*, so there's no real need to go into detail here. It's been more than two decades since 9/11. In the days that followed it, every outlandish 9/11 "truther" conspiracy theory would be widely publicized and discussed:

- No plane hit the Pentagon.
- There was thermite in the World Trade Center Towers.
- The collapse of WTC-7 was due to planted explosives.
- The Arab terrorists were "patsies," unaware of their fate.
- There weren't any planes: it was all a hologram.

The "9.11 Truth Movement" got lots of press in the years after the attack. It was stocked with true believers, in everything from Jesus to Urantia.

What I had discovered, however, would begin to be developed only after April 2006, once I found a connection back to the heroin bust – the only window into the 9/11 attack that went unexplained and unpublicized.

The drug connection to 9/11 was the only one that could be definitively proven: There was drug trafficking aboard a Learjet owned by secretive financier, Wally Hilliard, owner of Huffman Aviation, where terrorist pilot trainees Mohamed Atta and Marwan Al-Shehhi had enrolled the month before the Orlando bust. That made Venice, Florida the biggest 9/11 crime scene that wasn't reduced to rubble.

WALLY'S PLANE IMPOUNDED AND KEPT

We first learned of the heroin seizure on Hilliard's Learjet from an aviation executive in Naples. I might never have figured it out for myself. Why?

Because the FAA also listed the plane's owner as an unconnected dummy front company, without mentioning Wallace Hilliard's name. Fortunately, aviation executives who worked for any of his many companies were willing to talk, albeit with a nervous glance over their shoulder every so often. Several years after 9/11 they became a little more forthcoming.

One told me, "As far as intelligence or drugs, I am more willing to think this is drugs-related – but I am only looking at this differently *now*. When I worked for FLAIR (Hilliard's airline), I was threatened not to talk to anyone about FLAIR personnel. But now I don't have a job and they still owe me $8,000."[2]

Another of Hilliard's staff, John Villada, was a fiftyish pilot originally from Miami, who was the "jet manager" handling Hilliard's jets in Naples. There were 30-40 of them, I was to learn, in almost constant motion around the globe.

Villada had a beef with Hilliard. When federal officials from the FAA and DEA showed up at the aviation company – his facility – after the heroin bust, he was caught in the backwash and wasn't happy about it.

"After Wally's plane was impounded with the heroin, and the pilots had machine guns stuck in their faces, the DEA came to visit our maintenance facility," Villada said, indicating he was shocked and amazed at the casual arrogance Hilliard displayed when dealing with the DEA.

"Wally shouted to me – right in front of the DEA guy – 'Make sure all the heroin and cocaine is hidden!'

"That was in August of 2000. When I found out later that the DEA wouldn't let him have his plane back, I knew why."[3]

Hilliard's mock warning to hide the drugs, explained Villada, had been his way of telling the DEA how little he thought of them. The DEA hadn't forgotten.

"NEW IN TOWN?"

When I interviewed him, it was already a year since the 9/11 attack, and Villada seemed surprised I hadn't already learned about the heroin bust on Wally Hilliard's plane. He looked at me quizzically, as if to ask, "New in town?"

I realized – and not for the first time – how puny my investigative resources were, given the size of the story.

I had a firm grasp on the obvious, viewed up close, but at that time, I had nothing like an adequate grasp of the big picture.

It wasn't hard to confirm Villada's assertion. One good thing we can say for Florida is it has a simple way to check the corporate records filed with the Secretary of State's Office at Sunbiz.com.

Hilliard had owned Plane 1 Leasing, which owned the Learjet caught up in a major drug bust. Did I say "major?" Law enforcement authorities in 2000 had called it the biggest seizure of heroin *ever* in central Florida.

In 2002 I was still focused on tracking just *one* aspect of the case – what Mohamed Atta and his fellow terrorists had been doing in Florida – *the criminal conspiracy* – during the eighteen months *before* the attack.

Should anyone ever decide to investigate the FBI's non-performance after 9/11, they should begin on the date of the heroin bust – July 25, 2000 – when Atta and Marwan Al-Shehhi had already been training at Huffman Aviation for three weeks.

Was Wally Hilliard just an innocent elderly business owner victimized by unscrupulous clients? Was he an unwitting target of wily South American drug traffickers, in a world he never made?

* * *

As we were editing for publication, we happened upon an obituary for Wally, who died March 6, 2023, at the age of 90 after suffering for years with Alzheimer's. The glowing obit mentions his insurance career and sale of his company to American Express. That sale was followed by his forming a second insurance company, AMS, with a partner named Ron.

"AMS was sold in 1996. Ron and Wally are fondly remembered as the dynamic duo. Wally went on to start and fund numerous other businesses in Wisconsin and Florida," the obit said.

There are numerous comments, all calling him the salt of the earth, a great family man. One daughter wrote: "He got his pilots [sic] license and owned a flight school in Venice, Florida. He owned a private jet company 'Plane one Leasing' in Naples Florida (where we lived) and flew us everywhere. He lived a full and successful life. In my opinion he was extremely smart, even a genius."[4]

ASSISTANCE FROM LOIS BATTUELLO

"Is this the same man I had stalked for years?" I asked myself. Winston Churchill's often quoted phrase came to mind: "A riddle, wrapped in a mystery inside an enigma." So, I answered myself, "If Churchill could see a bigger picture, then so can I."

A year or two before Wally Hilliard's death, I'd received an email from a former associate, Lois Battuello, whom I mentioned in my second book, *Welcome to TerrorLand*, possibly without naming her. Because of her work with intelligence agencies, she didn't like her name freely scattered around.

Lois lived in California wine country, which has been the scene of substantial covert CIA activity for decades, and her family's winery had in fact been frequented by Kermit "Kim" Roosevelt and "the boys" of his day. During the 1960s, Kim Roosevelt, with his partner Miles Copeland, had mentored Adnan Khashoggi in his work for "the Company," possibly even assisting him in acquiring a controlling interest in one or more banks later rolled into California Bank, later United California Bank (UCB) and ultimately part of First Interstate bank conglomerate.[5]

Lois had a master's degree in finance from Stanford and "had cut her teeth at the United California Bank (UCB), right after former CIA director John McCone served as chairman," Sander Hicks wrote.[6]

Lois and her brother, as I recall, were fighting over her family's vineyard, which Kim Roosevelt liked to frequent, when she ran up against heavy-handed tactics used by Kim's 'boys'. I could be wrong. That was at least 25 years ago. Time moves in one direction, memory in another, as they say.

In 2000 Lois was anonymously writing a column called "Notes from the Waterfront," for a website created by disbarred attorney Kate Dixon of Oakland, who had set it up for another attorney, Virginia McCullough, a woman who had acquired Mae Brussell's archives. Linda Minor began her "publishing career" posting research at the website called "Newsmaking News."[7]

Author Sander Hicks, who later used Lois as a financial researcher, wrote in a 2012 book that Battuello often bragged that she had been trained inside a "CIA bank." Hicks wrote: "UCB had been known as John McCone's 'piggy bank,' and, with businessman Myron DuBain on the board, it allegedly 'attempted to recover monies looted and missing' by Saudi arms dealers, like Adnan Khashoggi and former CIA personnel."[80]

John McCone was a conservative Republican from California, whom President Kennedy appointed to head the CIA in 1962 when he fired Allen Dulles following the Bay of Pigs debacle. After the JFK assassination in 1963, newly named President Lyndon Johnson kept McCone in that role until 1965, even though, as Drew Pearson had disclosed in 1962, McCone had too many conflicts and should not have been confirmed.

Pearson was repeating many of the same conflicts of interest disclosed by the press in 1958 at the timePresident Dwight Eisenhower named McCone to head the Atomic Energy Commission (AEC), saying his shipping company, Joshua Hendry Ironworks, transported products of a plethora of contractors with the AEC.[9]

To resolve the conflict, Pearson said McCone simply transferred his corporate stock to United California Bank, as trustee. It wasn't a blind trust, since McCone was a stockholder and director of the bank.[11]

McCone returned to San Francisco in 1965 to oversee his businesses.

Lois' interest in United California Bank gave her an automatic curiosity about Wallace Hilliard, the owner of the Venice Flight School where Atta trained, since Wally had sold his insurance company to Myron DuBain's Fireman's Fund, and DuBain sat on the board of directors of United California Bank with McCone.

Though based in Los Angeles, UCB's territory also included counties adjacent to San Francisco, California – a playground of Adnan Khashoggi, the Sultan of Brunei, and others being groomed by the CIA. So, there's that.

Riggs Bank-Saudi Scandal and the Allbrittons

The Joint Terrorism Task Force (JTTF), with which Lois was connected, issued a "terror alert" for Wolfgang Bohringer, on November 16, 2006, based, Lois said, on my book, *Welcome to TerrorLand*. Lois claimed she had furnished a copy of *TerrorLand* to the JTTF.

Sander Hicks stated in his book that "Lois was a behind-the-scenes investigator who ended up helping to expose the Riggs Bank-Saudi scandal in 2003." Then he continued by saying:

> She taught Daniel Hopsicker and me a few techniques for real "gumshoe reporting": how to pull down publicly available corporate records.
>
> However, back in 2004, I trusted her too much. Under her influence, I placed too much blame for 9/11 on the Muslim Brotherhood and the international "far Right," when so much of 9/11 came from a pragmatic wing of the CIA/U.S. military.
>
> I see now there was a deliberate shifting of the blame on Lois's part, away from the CIA and onto an amorphous "international Reich movement" of Muslims and Nazis. We are no longer in touch.[12]

The Riggs Bank Scandal involved the venerable Washington, D.C. bank that a Houston, Texas businessman, Joe Lewis Allbritton bought in 1974. Joe was a 1949 graduate of Baylor Law School in Waco, Texas, and a long-time supporter of Lyndon Johnson. Joe had recruited Lloyd Nelson Hand, Senate Majority Leader Lyndon Johnson's aide since 1957, for his Houston law firm (Allbritton, McGee & Hand), to work in Los Angeles. When Johnson became JFK's vice president in 1961, Hand moved to California.[13]

We don't know if the Allbritton family was still in business with Lloyd Hand in 1974, though he would have been of great use in advising his former business and legal partner, given his previous role as Chief of Protocol, a large part of whose role is hobnobbing with foreign dignitaries. LBJ had died in February 1973, so the timing of the purchase seemed a bit suspicious.

LBJ's former best bud John Connally, who campaigned for Nixon in 1968 and became his Secretary of the Treasury, was indicted on August 1, 1974, in the Milk Fund Bribery Scandal. President Nixon had just signed a secret arrangement with Saudi Arabia (later known as the "28 Pages"), followed by Nixon's resignation a few days later on August 9th..

Gerald Ford ascended to power and named George H. W. Bush as Director of the CIA. The question then becomes who may have planted a bug in Allbritton's ear to buy Riggs Bank, which held deposits for not only many Congressmen and Senators, but for foreign ambassadors posted in the U.S. Capitol. There are a whole host of possibilities from both parties.

Riggs was investigated for not filing suspicious activity reports (SARs), as expanded by the Patriot Act, for Prince Bandar of the Saudi Embassy. The Joint House and Senate Committee on 9/11 had just published in December 2002 its report with 28 pages redacted.

The FBI cleared Prince Bandar, but in the process also learned of long-held accounts at the bank by Augusto Pinochet of Chile since he overthrew Allende in 1973.[14]

The *Washington Post* reported that the "FBI, bank regulators and three congressional committees continue to delve into Riggs's international banking relationships, particularly its two-decade role as chief banker for the Embassy of Saudi Arabia in Washington.

"Investigators are looking at the Saudi accounts for evidence of money laundering, which is the use of complex transactions to hide the origin or destination of funds related to illegal activities such as drug smuggling or terrorist acts. The investigators have reached no conclusions about the reasons for the transactions in the embassy accounts, including the personal accounts of the Saudi ambassador, Prince Bandar bin Sultan."[15]

Allbritton in 1975 bought the *Washington Star* in D.C., held by the same media company that owned media in Lynchburg, Virginia – all affiliated with ABC.

LOIS BATTUELLO AND OTHER LOOSE ENDS

When Linda Minor became involved with Gangster Planet, I hadn't spoken to Lois since the JTTF incident, so Linda reviewed Bohringer's old résume and looked at it from a different angle. She discovered Wolfgang was married to an Indian national, who had become an American citizen. Her name was Sujata, and they had been married with two children before Wolfgang underwent flight training a few miles inland from Satellite Beach, Florida, in 1995.[16]

Wolfgang reported to a job in Naples, Florida – a job with the Flying Club Munich of Naples, Inc. This Florida corporation was set up by an attorney for Hans and Lydia Forsbach, a German couple, who contracted with Centex, a Dallas-based multinational corporation, to build them a house in Naples. At the time of closing in 1991, the deed was granted to a German corporation – Olympia Taxi und Mietwagen, Gmbh (translated as 'taxi and car rental corporation') – then located at the Munich Airport.[17]

After suing Forsbach, Wolfgang formed a new company, Wolf Aero, Inc. – said to be a "Part 61" flight training school, chartered in Florida, giving as his address 6255 18th Avenue SW in Naples. This nonexistent address was also used when the business was transferred to Rex L. Gasteiger, who changed Wolf Aero to Rex Air, Inc. in April 1999.[18]

Wolfgang and Sujata bought the property as a vacant lot in 1996 and had a residence built that same year. It was sold – if you can believe it, on August 27, 2001 – exactly two weeks before 9/11!

The Bohringers were already living in Georgia by then. The first job shown on Sujata's résume was in August 2000 at Atlanta's Buckhead office of UBS, once known as Union Bank of Switzerland. A year and a half earlier UBS had settled a longstanding lawsuit filed by "heirs of those who deposited money in Swiss banks before World War II and later died in the Holocaust, as well as those whose looted assets may have passed through Swiss banks," according to the *New York Times*.[19]

Unlike Wolfgang, who did well to keep each of his jobs a whole year, Sujata was a compliance officer at UBS six and a half years, leaving in January 2007 to take a job at the Financial Industry Regulatory Authority (FINRA) as a "principal examiner" in the nongovernmental organization that writes and enforces the rules governing registered stockbrokers and securities dealers.

With her two jobs adding up to 17 years of experience, Sujata qualified as an examiner at the Securities and Exchange Commission (SEC) in Washington, D.C., in 2015, ten years after she divorced Wolfgang.

Wolfie spent more than a year at Harvard Capital & Investment of Nassau, Bahamas, as the personal pilot for Viktor Kozeny. According to the experience he listed online, however, he had left the "Pirate of Prague" to fly Mossimo Giannulli and Lauri Loughlin's private jet – long before that California power couple went to prison for buying their pampered daughters into Ivy League colleges.[20]

That gig was up in May 2000, just before Mohamed Atta was arriving at Huffman Aviation in Venice. Wolgang, while living in Naples with Sujata, still found time to party in Key West with his friends, or should I say Atta and his other "brothers" from Hamburg from time to time.

Things changed in February 2001. Now given the title of Senior Captain, Wolfgang was hired by HBO & Company (HBOC) of Alpharetta, Ga., which was in the process of being taken over by McKesson Corp. (the country's biggest wholesale prescription drug company), based in San Francisco – a job that lasted through 2003.

Most of McKesson-HBOC's top officials had already been sued and would soon be indicted for accounting fraud once FBI and SEC investigations concluded. According to the U.S. Attorney's office in 2010, investors had been defrauded in an amount in excess of $8.6 billion – billions with a capital B. Someone needed to pay.

One could predict a scandal in the making just from watching whom Wolfgang chose to work for. It wasn't long after their mid-2005 divorce that he was spotted at remote Fanning Island, where he told residents of the tiny island about his plans to create a flight school there.

That's what led up my own rift with Lois, which I kinda sorta described in a website article published February 4, 2015 – shortly after my return from open-heart surgery. I had reviewed my life up to that point, realizing I had a choice about what to do with the months or years I have left and wrote:

> Now I've been blessed with a choice: During the time remaining to me, do I want to continue? Or pursue something altogether different? (I don't know why, but sheep-ranching in the Australian Outback is the image which comes to mind.)

Didn't I realize the inherent absurdity of believing my feeble efforts would ever change anything? *Wasn't it childishly naive to think the truth will set you free?*

Did I really envision forcing the same Government that allows certain military-industrial complex-friendly figures to handle the import of cocaine and heroin turn around and legalize it, while freeing a million people in American penitentiaries for selling small amounts of what they're bringing into the U.S. by the ton?

Would my puny efforts ever get to the bottom of the collusion between corrupt Saudi-friendly officials in Florida and the 9/11 hijackers? Would they expose secret agreements whose beneficiaries most definitely did not include the American middle class taxpayers who fund their traveling circus?

Didn't I know that if demonstrations and protest marches accomplished anything, they'd have already been banned?[21]

That's when I mentioned Lois. I hadn't spoken to her at that point for several years. She and I did finally connect, however, sometime after I wrote the following:

> Nothing I've unearthed or exposed – from the CIA's continuing role in the international drug trade to the FBI terror alert in the Pacific for Wolfgang Bohringer, the German pilot who'd been Mohamed Atta's best buddy in Florida – has had the slightest impact.
>
> You might cite the FBI manhunt for Bohringer; however, after the first words out of his mouth when they caught up with him, they let him go.
>
> According to someone who happened to overhear a telephone conversation between an agent from the New York Joint Terrorism Task Force (JTTF) and the FBI agent who took him in, what Bohringer said was, "You can't arrest me. I'm with the CIA."

Lois had been that someone.

It was several years after I wrote about that incident that I received an email from Lois. It was incoherent, as most of her communication was. If she called, I had to record what she said. She talked so fast, I couldn't keep up. I'd listen to it several times just to get the jist of it. I think she was trying to apologize but did so in a way that made me feel I owed her for a huge favor she'd done me.

What she did say on that occasion, after the fact – years afterwards – was that Saudi banker, Khalid bin Mahfouz, had been suspected as being the man financing Bin Laden after BCCI collapsed in 1991. The Europeans had been after him for years. The EU set up European Union Agency for Criminal Justice Cooperation (Eurojust) in March 2002 to co-ordinate investigations into global terrorism.

But George W. Bush (43) wouldn't sign the agreement at the time, she said, because Condi Rice told him not to. Then at some point in 2006 – Lois said – he reversed himself. Why?

Lois' exact words were: "Bush was advised not to sign it by Condi Rice. Your research overcame this obstacle."[22]

Guess that makes me smarter than Condi. Not a big deal in my book. She then added:

> FBI and DEA began their joint investigations that took out Khalid bin Mahfouz who was in Ireland (why Stephan was in and out of Dublin flying for Khalid and hanging out there) in 2009 (extradited … to Saudi Arabia), and six months later, suddenly heart-attacked in Jeddah at age of 57. Took out the Uzbek heroin network/cocaine and designer drug network serving Al Qaeda and Hezbollah into US, and the drug dropping Hezbollah/Lebanese crowd.[23]

You get a sense of what I mean by incoherent.

Bin Mahfouz died in August 2009, and his obituary stated: "He rose to prominence through his 30 percent ownership in the Bank of Credit and Commerce International, which was shut down in 1991 after charges of financial chicanery and money laundering."[24]

Then she made a statement I don't know whether or not to believe. I mention it because someone else may be able to make some sense of it in the future. She wrote: "Wally's role was to put out Canadian Lebanese Bank (he was flown to Paris and Beirut to coordinate and serve Interpol warrants and get documents." [25]

The implication was that Wally was some type of intelligence official. Did that mean I was not to worry about the FACT that he had facilitated the distribution of heroin in the U.S. for at least 39 weeks and got away with it because he had connections?

Or the FACT that he provided cover for Saudi pilots who flew into the World Trade Center?

Thanks, but no thanks, Lois.

LOIS'S INSIGHT INTO HILLIARD'S CONNECTIONS

As I'd researched my way from the obvious to the big picture, I learned that financier Hilliard owned through legal entities three separate flight schools in Florida:

- Huffman Aviation in Venice,

- Ambassador Aviation in Naples, and

- Discover Air in Sanford, north of Orlando.

All three lost money. One even went bankrupt. Plus – as I was told repeatedly by flight school officials – as a rule of thumb, flight schools don't make money. Hilliard was already a multi-millionaire. So, this wasn't just a case of a retired guy in Florida looking to pick up a little money on the side.

Hilliard had run a mid-sized health insurance company out of Green Bay, Wisconsin, one of the largest employers in the town. He featured regularly in business news, which portrayed him as a pretty sober guy. About what you'd expect from an insurance executive.

Business reporters in Green Bay offered no hint that he had displayed any mad obsessions before moving to Florida.

Insurance sounds like a boring occupation. All those numbers and statistics. Of course, the dollar signs in front of the numbers aren't nearly as boring. Also, insurance companies are a popular way to launder money.

Hilliard cashed out of the insurance game after selling his company to a subsidiary of American Express Corporation (Amex), a company which keeps turning up in our story everywhere we look.

Another coincidence – what I like to call a CIA tell – is this: the man who presented him with his big check in 1982 was Myron DuBain, whose life-long ties to the CIA included two stints at the helm of the Stanford Research Institute (SRI) in Palo Alto, California. You know, the outfit where "remote viewing" experiments were paid for by CIA grant monies.

DuBain became chairman of SRI International in 1985, at a crucial time when the U.S. Defense Dept. was growing increasingly concerned with advances in psychic research behind what was then called the "Iron Curtain." That made him, in my mind, "the man who paid 'the Men Who Stare at Goats'," the title of a 2009 George Clooney film.[26]

A January 10, 1984, headline in the *New York Times* read "**Pentagon Is Said To Focus On ESP For Wartime Use.**"[27]

> The Pentagon has spent millions of dollars, according to three new reports, on secret projects to investigate extrasensory phenomena and to see if the sheer power of the human mind can be harnessed to perform various acts of espionage and war – penetrating secret files, for example, locating submarines or blowing up guided missiles in mid-flight.

177

DuBain was also president of SRI during the late 60's, and it was shortly afterward that the CIA began funding parapsychological experiments at SRI "by Russell Targ and Harold Puthoff, once with the NSA and at the time a Scientologist," continued the *Times* story.

> The effort initially focused on a few 'gifted individuals' such as New York artist Ingo Swann, an OT Level VII Scientologist. Many of the SRI 'empaths' were from the Church of Scientology. Individuals who appeared to show potential were trained and taught to use talents for 'psychic warfare'.

His time at SRI must have been appreciated, or perhaps there were other reasons he was in business in the exclusive Villa Taverna private club in San Francisco with Gordon Getty – son of uber-wealthy oilman J. Paul Getty – and former Reagan Secretary of State George Schultz. [28]

All this takes us to the reason for the quote at the beginning of the chapter by Sandy Weill.

FINANCIAL SERVICES – AN INDUSTRY LIKE NO OTHER

In the '70s and '80s a huge expansion occurred in the financial services industry beginning almost as soon as the New York Stock Exchange began to allow corporations to become members. Private partnerships one after another went public.[29]

The change allowed those making decisions to both decrease their potential liability and for the investment banking corporation to pass more money through the financial system.

Can you say "money laundering"?[30] That's the same time, incidentally, that the United States narcotics market switched its source of supply from Europe – as in The French Connection – to SE Asia and then South America.

There was, therefore, a huge need for money laundering services.

Example: The year before American Express bought Wally Hilliard's Wisconsin company, it acquired Shearson, Loeb Rhoades – which traced the Shearson in its name back to Shearson & Hammill & Co. with 63 offices in its heyday before the stock market crash of 1973-74 hit.

Time magazine reported in April 1973: "Such big houses as Loeb, Rhoades and Shearson, Hammill are cutting their staffs; others ... are being forced into mergers with stronger firms."[31]

Among the many staff members who lost jobs that year was a man whose son plays a larger than life role in a subsequent chapter of *Gang-*

ster Planet – Donald F. McClain, the Shearson, Hammill registered rep in smalltown Manchester, Connecticut, since 1961.

Shearson, Hammill merged with Hayden, Stone, Inc. in a 1974 deal managed by Sanford "Sandy" Weill. In 1981 Sandy Weill sold Shearson Loeb Rhoades (recently created by merger with the old Carl M. Loeb, Rhoades & Co. firm) to American Express Co. Weill was named Amex president two years later.

In 1984 Weill was elected chairman and CEO of American Express's insurance subsidiary, Fireman's Fund Insurance Company (DuBain's firm). So, Wally Hilliard's Wisconsin subsidiary fell under Weill's control. While at American Express, Weill began grooming as a protégé, Jamie Dimon, the future CEO of JPMorgan Chase.

Don't worry. We're not giving a test later. Believe it or not, however, some readers thrive on details like this.

Just one year after arriving in Naples, Florida, Hilliard found it necessary to purchase – not just the three flight schools – but a start-up airline, FLAIR, as well.

What was up with that? My parents retired to Florida in 1981. I remember one of my dad's first moves being the purchase of a new pastel golf wardrobe. I recall canary-yellow slacks, a wide white belt, and white golf shoes. He and my mom started playing doubles tennis.

Wally's choices in retirement didn't coincide with anything I'd ever seen before.

"I SUGGEST YOU BACK OUT OF THIS."

The *Orlando Sentinel* quoted an official who called the heroin bust "the largest find of its kind in the southeastern United States in recent years."[32] In Florida, every new bust seems to break all past records.

Only two categories of aviation "observers" would speak freely with me. Former business partners screwed on a deal, and bitter ex-wives and girlfriends. John Villada was in "Group A."

The FBI had been following him, Villada explained. He'd been shown photographs of himself and his family around Naples Airport. Rudi Dekkers, Hilliard's chief minion at the time, had forged his (Villada's) signature on aircraft repair orders.

"Rudi used my name illegally on a helicopter, telling the FAA the required repair work on the helicopter had been completed. Meaning if anything went wrong with the aircraft, it would be 'on' me."

He was legally compelled to report the violation to the FAA, Villada said, "After I reported Rudi for violations, an FAA guy came out. He sat me down and said: "I suggest you back out of this."

"I couldn't believe it." He shakes his head in disbelief. "I called the FAA to report a violation and was warned to leave him alone." John Villada was the kind of guy to respond to an insult by going out of his way to speak with a reporter. *Me.*

He said, "I know more about Wally Hilliard than I ever want to know. Why do you think the U.S. military didn't close the passes into Pakistan during the Tora Bora bombing? This all goes far deeper than you think."[32]

It was my turn to look surprised. Hand to heart, those were his exact words. You don't forget something like that.

I didn't, anyway.

"WHAT DOES IT TAKE TO QUALIFY AS "HEAVY WEIGHT?"

The *Orlando Sentinel* reported each flight aboard Hilliard's cream-colored Learjet originated in Caracas, Venezuela made a stop in Fort Lauderdale, then flew on to Orlando on its way to its ultimate destination across the river from New York, Teterboro Airport.

"It confirms the sad fact that a massive amount of heroin is coming through Central Florida," U.S. Drug Enforcement Administration special agent Brent Eaton told the paper when the arrests were announced. "It's very disturbing to the DEA that more and more high-quality heroin is coming from Colombia and at a cheaper price."[33]

The DEA was disturbed enough to look more closely at Hilliard's jet charter operation. The result was their firm opposition to returning the plane to Hilliard.

The passengers whose luggage contained heroin – Edgar Javier Valles Dias and Neyra Rivas, of Caracas, Venezuela – were immediately arrested. Most of the heroin was found hidden in the soles of tennis shoes stashed in their luggage. Eventually five people would be convicted, including the two Venezuelans.

Wally Hilliard desperately wanted his Learjet back. The Court routinely allows it, under the doctrine of "innocent owner." If the owner is not the one accused of importing the drugs, he's called "innocent," and typically gets his plane back.

That is, unless the DEA objects. The DEA did in this case, and so did the U.S. Attorney. Both opposed the plane's return, citing as the reason "because the property was used or acquired as a result of a violation of the Controlled Substances Act."

Boris From Uzbekistan

Here's the ultimate CIA tell: Venezuelan drug trafficker Edgar Valles-Diaz paid for each flight ... in *cash*.

"It was just blatant," said Hilliard's jet manager John Villada. "That same plane flew that same run thirty or forty times, ferrying the same people. And paid cash for each flight!"

Much later, an aviation insider in Fort Lauderdale with impeccable sources gave me the name of the man who met each flight at Teterboro Airport: Felix Borisevich Rabaev.

"Boris was from Uzbekistan, where he was – and maybe, who knows, still is – a prominent member of a Russian Mob family that operates a transshipment point for heroin from Afghanistan in the Uzbek capital of Tashkent."

"He escaped from Russia to Israel in the early Eighties by saying he was Jewish. Back then, that was the only way you could get out of the Soviet Union. But he's *not* Jewish.... He's Muslim, and he's got close ties with radical Muslim circles in the former Soviet republics between Russia and China – the 'Stans' – that are conduits for heroin coming out of Afghanistan."[34]

Non-Jewish Russian mobsters like Boris, he explained, used fraudulent claims of Jewish ancestry to gain easier movement in and out of Israel, where the Russian Mafia had a large operating base.

"It was a real scam of Russian organized crime. It was easier for lots of these people to say they were Jewish to get into Israel, become instant citizens, get Israeli passports, and off to the U.S."

The source in Fort Lauderdale demanded anonymity. He explained: "I've got a family." There were, indeed, Muslim Mobsters in Brighton Beach who got out of Russia by posing as Jews, I learned in *Red Mafiya*, by Robert I. Friedman, a terrific book from the '90s about Mobsters in the former USSR.[35] There were three or four major Russian crime families operating in Brighton Beach, the head of the New York FBI's Russian Mob unit told Friedman. The largest consisted primarily of Jewish émigrés from Odessa, followed by a second family from Tashkent, Uzbekistan that included Felix Rabaev that the FBI pegged as Muslim, although people in the Brighton Beach community insisted, they were Jewish. Brighton Beach, though we did not know it at the time, would play a big part in our story. That's because it's a big part of the big picture that included Wally Hilliard.

When You're Not Aware – You're Not Woke

Three weeks after the Lear was impounded by the DEA, Hilliard asked for it back. In a motion filed in the U.S. District Court in Orlando, he argued he was an "innocent owner" *unwittingly duped* by an *unknown individual.*

"Plane 1 and its officers, shareholders, and directors," his motion read, "were not aware of the identity of the passengers utilizing the Lear 35A on this trip other than Mr. Valles."

They were further not aware, it continued, that the "individuals chartering the plane were engaging in criminal conduct." Company executives were also: "not aware of any facts from which they should have been aware that individuals leasing the plane were engaging in criminal conduct."

Clearly, Plane 1 Leasing officials and employees, being so unaware, were not *woke*, which should have been a good thing in Florida. But it didn't convince the judge, even before Ron DeSantis was governor.

Finally, A Little Mainstream PR

After *Welcome to TerrorLand* came out three years after the attack, in 2004, the book caught the attention of Wally Hilliard's hometown newspaper, *Green Bay Press-Gazette.*

Jean Peerenboom at the Green Bay paper called me, asking for a phone interview. I remember thinking, *oh my god, Wally's hometown paper, here we go.*

Instead, refreshingly, she asked me what *she* should ask Wally. So, clearly, there were a few suspicions about Hilliard in his hometown of Green Bay. I told her to ask: Why did Wally buy a fleet of planes when he was supposed to be retired? Also, why was he in business with Dutch criminal Rudi Dekkers?

That story was probably the only mainstream media attention *Welcome to TerrorLand* received. Her story was splashed across the front page, on March 22, 2004 – *above the fold* – under a photo of my book.

The headlines and excerpts of the text follow:

Hilliard Bankrolled 9-11 Flight Academy
New book dramatizes mere coincidence AMS co-founder says

Terrorists, drug runners, cover-ups, the CIA the KGB, and shady characters are the cloak-and-dagger kind of elements that make for a riveting spy novel or action thriller. It's hardly the place you'd expect to find retired Green Bay businessman Wally J. Hilliard.

Hopsicker links Hilliard with Huffman Aviation. the flight school that trained Atta and the other hijackers who flew planes into the World Trade Center and the Pentagon on Sept 11, 2001.

The author implicates Hilliard in a complicated plot as the investor in the flight school in in Venice, Florida, and owner of a Learjet that was seized by Drug Enforcement Administration officials after it returned with a passenger who was jailed for possession of heroin.

Hilliard denies any wrongdoing, and no one in the story has been charged with anything. The material was posted on the Internet before being incorporated in the just-published book, so Hilliard has been aware of the claims for some time.

"Through a friend, I talked to an FBI Agent," Hilliard said during a visit to Green Bay last week. "He said freedom of speech laws protect the author. I could sue for libel, but even if I got a million dollars, that and fifty cents would get me a cup of coffee. And I'd have spent fifty thousand dollars in legal fees."[36]

His response recalled Carl Bernstein and Bob Woodward in *All the President's Men*. "That's a non-denial denial," I said when I read it.

The Venezuelan's Co-Pilot from Guyana

Diego Levine's co-pilot in the Plane 1 Leasing Learjet drug runs – the mysterious pilot never named in newspapers or court documents – was a former Guyanese military pilot named Michael Francis Brassington.

It took years after the 2000 bust for me to discover that detail, a discovery which in the telling earns Brassington a couple of chapters in this book.

Brassington thus becomes a key link to a Russian oligarch who is a primary Russian participant in the RussiaGate scandal – the same scandal pooh-poohed by Donald Trump and everyone who loved him.

His name is Oleg Deripaska, and he was Vladimir Putin's personal Swiss Army knife.

Endnotes

1   Pamela J. Johnson, "Record-Setting Heroin Seizure Nets 30 Pounds," *Orlando Sentinel*, August 2, 2000.

2   Author's Interview with source.

3   Author's interview with source.

4   "Wallace "Wally" J. Hilliard, May 23, 1932 ~ March 6, 2023 (age 90), Lyndahl Funeral Home & Cremation Services, https://www.lyndahl.com/obituary/WallaceWally-Hilliard.

5   McCone was CIA director under Democrats JFK and LBJ.

6   Sander Hicks, *Slingshot to the Juggernaut: Total Resistance to the Death Machine Means Complete Love of the Truth* (pp. 84-85). Catapult. Kindle Edition.

"7   Arab takeover: Banker with BG ties would let Arabs buy controlling interest," *The Park City Daily News* (Bowling Green, Kentucky), 27 Jan 1975, Page 12. Also see, "Arab banker battles bill to limit his investments," *Peninsula Times Tribune* (Palo Alto), 27 Jan 1975, Page 6.

8   Lois believed the CIA was working with organized crime elements in Sonoma County through front companies, saying: "The following CIA-related ('secret government') and organized crime fronts were plying San Francisco Bay waters and substantially controlled the docks during the Iran-Contra era. Were these fronts ever dismantled? They weren't prosecuted by local or federal authorities. Are they in place today? The names have deftly changed, but the players remain the same. The FBI in San Francisco, headed by US Attorney Mueller, a Bush factotum, has yet to prosecute any mob activity in Northern California. Mueller continues the tradition of former U.S. attorneys Joseph Russoniello (Rudi Guiliani's college roommate) and Michael Yamaguchi. Federal and State judges and local D.A.s take their cue from the local DOJ and FBI who all grease the way for drug, money laundering, kiddie porn and blackmail operations throughout the Bay Area. If anyone litigates against this low cabal or takes them on in any way, the low cabal arrogantly believes it can "destroy" that person or family. Such delusional and grandiose thinking is barely masked by the sickened faces of these federal and local judges and district attorneys who are so blackmailed by their pervert handlers that they dance for them like marionettes. And then there's the Bohemian Club, which is meeting this August near Santa Rosa, California...."

As for Kim Roosevelt, Lois wrote: "Buttes operated barges, tankers, and offshore rigs, headquartered in Oakland, CA. Buttes also operated citrus and other farms in Fresno and Napa counties. John Boreta was the President of Buttes. In other operations, Roosevelt was a partner with John B. Anderson in the ownership of 100,000 acres of land in Gila Bend, Arizona during the Iran-Contra period. Anderson in turn served as a front for Moe Shenker in the Nevada Dunes Resorts & Casino operations from 1983 and through its take-down of Eureka Federal Savings and Loan in the late 1980's, defaulting on $60 million in loans."

"Bank of American and BCCI engaged in the movement of money to support the crime syndicate and Iran Contra money/drug flow through tentacles in the Napa Valley Bank, Napa National Bank, and First Republic Thrift & Loan in Napa County. These banks set up huge money laundering mills into Napa County which included high-end real estate and businesses (wineries). All of the above-named business entities have various shells and subsidiaries, some with unrelated names which are retained despite later acquisitions. Almost all of the these entities have Canadian, Alaskan, Hawaiian subsidiaries and operate internationally."

Linda never met any of the other writers and had no real understanding of why the site was created. She was then assisting another CIA Drugs member, Catherine Austin Fitts, in her efforts to learn who had targeted Fitts' business. Newmaking News archive can be viewed at Wayback Machine, https://wayback.stanford.edu/was/20180311065725/http://www.newsmakingnews.com/#-SEARCH%20THE%20SITE!%C2%A0

9   Sander Hicks, *Slingshot to the Juggernaut: Total Resistance to the Death Machine Means Complete Love of the Truth* (pp. 84-85). Catapult. Kindle Edition.

10   Robert S. Allen, "McCone's 'Outside Interests,'" *San Bernardino County Sun*, San Bernardino, California, Sep 03, 1958, Page 26.

11   Drew Pearson's Washington Merry-Go-Round column. *Daily Times*, Salisbury, Maryland, Jan 17, 1962, Page 13.

12   Sander Hicks, *Slinghot to the Jugernaut*, op. cit.

13   George Reasons, "President's Call Sold Job to L.A. Attorney," *Los Angeles Times*, Jan 03,

1965, Page 39. Refer back to Footnote 16 in Chapter Eight, where we mentioned that Ling Electronics had been created in Anaheim, California in the 1950s, and Mac Wallace was hired there in a management position in 1961, the same year LBJ was inaugurated Vice President. Wallace held that job until he lost his security clearance in 1964 and left California. In 1958 Joe Allbritton, whose family owned a cafeteria in Houston on Waugh Drive, next door to LBJ pal Gus Wortham's big American General Insurance company, established a branch of his law firm in Burbank within the offices of Pierce Brothers Mortuaries and cemetery. (See *Van Nuys News* and *Valley Green Sheet*, Dec 25, 1958, Page 2). A partial history of this company is set out in a *Los Angeles Times* article, "Funeral Price Battle Looms," on May 24, 1950 at Page 2. Shortly after the inauguration in 1961, Lloyd Hand resigned his job as Johnson aide to work for Allbritton's law firm in California, where he remained as president of Pierce National Life Insurance Company until Johnson needed him again for his 1964 campaign. After the election he was named Chief of Protocol, replacing Angier Biddle Duke. Two years later he moved back to Los Angeles, possibly because Mac Wallace had just lost his security clearance and LBJ needed a spy in California to replace him. An article in the *L.A. Times* referred to his former position as one that entailed hobnobbing with kings and prime ministers. Hand could have given his partner, Joe Allbritton, insight into Riggs Bank's role in doing the same thing in 1974. The "Portal of the Folded Wings Shrine to Aviation," was located in one section of the cemetery, according to Cecilia Rasmussen, "Near the roar of jet engines, a shrine to early aviators," The *Los Angeles Times,* Aug 13, 2006, Page 230. Service Corp. International (SCI), a Houston funeral chain whose founder and chairman, Robert Waltrip, grew up in the same Houston neighborhood as Allbritton, bought Pierce Brothers in 1991.

14   Timothy L. O'Brien and Larry Rohter, "U.S. and Others Gave Millions to Pinochet," *New York Times*, December 7, 2004. https://www.nytimes.com/2004/12/07/business/us-and-others-gave-millions-to-pinochet.html

15   Kathleen Day and Terence O'Hara, "U.S. Ready To Fine Riggs Bank, Saudi Embassy Money Reports Scrutinized," *Washington Post*, April 17, 2004. https://www.washingtonpost.com/archive/politics/2004/04/18/us-ready-to-fine-riggs-bank/eb843382-229c-445f-a730-a284a4922890/

        The *Washington Star* followed up on the scandal, much as the corporate right-wing media does today, except back then there was more timidity about outright lying. See, for example, the correspondence between Joe Allbritton and his friend and then-Director of the CIA George Bush.   https://s3.documentcloud.org/documents/22831956/letter-to-honorable-george-bush-from-joe-l-albritton.pdf

16   Satellite Beach also happens to have been where Larry Kolb lived when he wrote his non-fiction spy books.

17   It's also mentioned in several articles at my website, such as "The Mystery of Fanning Island Was Mohamed Atta "Close associate" in Florida a CIA Pilot?" published on December 11, 2006. https://www.madcowprod.com/2006/12/11/the-mystery-of-fanning-island/

18   This corporation still shows up today as the owner of 5132 Lochwood Court, and it pays Collier County property taxes of over $4,000 a year promptly when billed.

19   Barry Meier, "Swiss Banks And Victims Of the Nazis Nearing Pact," *New York Times*, Jan. 23, 1999.

20   https://www.madcowprod.com/wolfgang-bohringer/

21   Daniel Hopsicker, "A Muckrakers Life, Interrupted," February 4, 2015. https://www.madcowprod.com/2015/02/04/a-muckraking-life-interrupted-2more-9705/

22   Anonymous email from associate dated Jun 30, 2021.

23   The Stephan she referred to was a Naples realtor and pilot who had sued me for mentioning his name at my website in 2003, so I'd removed his last name. https://www.madcowprod.com/2003/03/20/911-the-german-connection/

24   Douglas Martin, "Khalid bin Mahfouz, Saudi Banker, Dies at 60," *New York Times*, Aug. 27, 2009. https://www.nytimes.com/2009/08/28/world/middleeast/28mahfouz.html.

25   A press release about Lebanese Canadian Bank, "Treasury Identifies Lebanese Canadian Bank Sal as a 'Primary Money Laundering Concern,'" February 10, 2011. https://home.treasury.gov/news/press-releases/tg1057

26   The humorous movie was based on a documentary by Jon Ronson. https://www.slashfilm.com/588485/the-best-war-movies-on-netflix-right-now/ and also at https://www.youtube.com/ watch?v=ylV6fQVgLiQ.

27   William J. Broad, *New York Times*, January 10, 1984. https://www.nytimes.com/1984/01/10/science/pentagon-is-said-to-focus-on-esp-for-wartime-use.html

28   https://www.minardcapital.com/our-san-francisco/members-clubs. Also, according to the email I received from my former associate, soon after Mahfouz and his crew in Ireland were shut down, "their last stash at Gordon Getty and Bill Newsom's warehouse in Napa was fetched by a huge force of FBI, DEA, State Police, Napa Sheriff and Napa PD." But, of course, that coincidence doesn't really prove anything except, the richer you are, the more powerful and connected you become. And, if you're connected … you know the rest.

29   Carola Frydman and Eric Hilt, "Partnerships vs. Corporations in Investment Banking: Evidence From the Back Office Crisis in the 1960s," Yale Economic Growth Center, 2017. https://egc.yale.edu/sites/default/files/Economic%20History%20Conferences/2021-11/7%20Hilt%20ada-ns.pdf

30   Linda Minor, "Changing the Middleman," Commentary on *The Great Heroin Coup* by Quixotic Joust, 2014. https://quixoticjoust.blogspot.com/2014/01/the-great-heroin-coup-chapters-eighteen.html

31   "A Private Depression," Time, April 16, 1973. https://web.archive.org/web/20080206235057/http://www.time.com/time/magazine/article/0,9171,878565,00.html

32   *Orlando Sentinel*, August 2, 2000.

33   Daniel Hopsicker, *Welcome to TerrorLand*, 2004.

34   Anonymous source.

35   Robert I. Friedman, *Red Mafiya* (Boston, MA: Little, Brown & Co., 2000).

36   Jean Peerenboom, "Hilliard Bankrolled 911 Flight Academy," *Green Bay Press-Gazette*, March 22, 2004, Page 1.

CHAPTER THIRTEEN

STUART BURCHILL'S KARMA

You can't connect the dots looking forward. You can only connect them looking backward. So you have to trust that the dots will somehow connect in your future. You have to trust in something – your gut, destiny, life, karma, whatever.

— Steve Jobs, co-founder of Apple

The last time we saw Wally Hilliard's "accountant," Stuart Burchill, was in Chapter 20 of my last book, *Welcome to TerrorLand*. Eighteen or so years later, as we were in the middle of writing *Gangster Planet*, we looked deeper into his background. I was thinking of giving him another call.

By then, my doctors had already diagnosed me with stage-four prostate cancer. With a fall on top of that, I was also suffering from intense pain from a fractured hip. In the intervening years since *TerrorLand* was published, the world had changed significantly. So had I. But we gave it our best shot, just to see if anything had been overlooked.

We ended up playing the age-old conspiracy buffs' game of connect-a-dot, where, unfortunately, the dots have no numbers. As we drew lines from dot to dot, we had no idea what kind of image would emerge.

We'll leave it to the reader to judge.

Plane 1 Leasing Co., Inc. was a 1997 Wisconsin corporation, registered in Florida on October 30, 1999, by G. Stuart Burchill, its vice president and treasurer. Wallace J. Hilliard's name and address, without his signature, also appeared on the original filing, naming his as chairman, president and director. The two signatures on the Florida filing were those of Burchill and the registered agent, a woman of about 30, who lived in Connecticut.

G. Stuart Burchill, Jr. grew up in Tampa, Florida as the son of a Canadian-born headmaster at the Parish Day School at St. John's Episcopal Church in Tampa. Stuart's parents had met and become engaged in Halifax, Nova Scotia where Stu's maternal grandfather, fancily called "the Very Rev. Frederick Eveleigh Ellis" was "priest-vicar" of the All Saints' Cathedral there.[1]

George S. Burchill, Sr., Stu's dad, was from a rural farm community north of Halifax, who studied forestry at Dalhousie and King's College University in Halifax. Once he met the vicar's daughter, he soon "felt the call," and left his family's lumber business, following his fiancée, Anne Ellis, to The Bahamas. Rev. Ellis was appointed Dean, under supervision of Lord Bishop Spence Burton – rector there as far back as when the Duke of Windsor, formerly King Edward VIII, was in exile in Nassau.

Stuart's parents married at Christ Church in Nassau that same year. Anne's father and her husband seemingly took advantage of a powerful Anglican connection available to them to get George Burchill ordained in Florida. Even better, he got a job in Tampa, where the *Tampa Tribune* in May 1962 expounded fulsomely on his family background and career.[2] Stuart graduated from the elite St. Paul's School in New Hampshire in 1975, returned to Florida and eventually dropped out of the University of Florida, around 1979-80, ostensibly leaving Florida.

In 1985 Stuart reappeared in Tampa, where he married Barbara Marilyn Leonard in the fall of 1985. It was Barbara's third marriage. At the age of 24, she married her second husband, Alcide E. Leonard but divorced him just prior to marrying Stuart. They didn't have a big wedding at St. John's Cathedral like Stuart's siblings had done. That tells us something.

STUART'S WIFE'S OTHER HUSBANDS

Barbara's first husband was Dutch – a man named William van Lunteren – who brought her with him from Europe when he moved to Naples, Florida in the early '80s. Barbara Leonard in 1982 was managing an antique store located at 4526 North Tamiami Trail, a storefront site owned by her former husband, William Lunteren.[3]

Although no divorce shows up in Naples, Barbara Marilyn van Lunteren, at age 24, had remarried in June 1982. Her first husband had apparently evaporated.

There was a photo of Barbara's profile in the Naples newspaper, which could easily fit the description both Danielle Clarke and John Villada had given of Anna, the Russian amazon described in *Welcome to TerrorLand*.

Danielle Clarke, who had told me Stuart was "brought in" to look at Wally Hilliard's books for the businesses Rudi Dekkers managed, said she'd heard Stuart had found a new wife on the Internet through Russian-brides.com or the like. He went to Russia and came back with Anna. She described Anna as being "about 6'3" and looked like Bridget Nielson, Sly Stallone's ex-wife."[4]

John Villada had added: "a really tall blond woman got deported. Anna's parents were KGB. Stuart brought a Russian girl back from the KGB, married her, and brought her here." But he'd been warned not to let anything bad happen to Anna or he would be dead.[5]

Neither of them happened to mention what year all that took place.

We know Stuart had attended his brother as best man in his Tampa wedding in 1982 and married Barbara in October 1985. By 1987 Stuart was manager of a new branch of Smith & Associates Investments in Brandon, Florida, a Tampa suburb. As we now know, 1987 was not the best time to sell real estate. But bars and night clubs were doing great.

Stuart first incorporated a company with a generic corporate name, The International Real Estate Industries corporation (TIREC) in 1988 located at 707 N. Franklin in Tampa. Once he gave up on real estate, he changed the name from TIREC to The Principal Industries Corporation (TPIC), another generic name, at the same address.

Also doing business in Tampa in those years was a Texan named Lance McFaddin, who had entered the Tampa market as early as 1983. He was interviewed that year in connection with "Confetti," a night club "confronted with crowds" when it opened the Tampa branch. That might have meant anything.

A classic money-laundering scheme, night clubs generated tons of cash. But nowhere is that admitted in McFaddin's obituary or by the numerous charities he allegedly supported.[6] As Vespasian was known for saying in the days before the Roman Empire collapsed, "*Pecunia non olet.*"[7]

McFaddin Ventures, Inc. had been operating the Tampa Confetti in Tampa, just south of Tampa International Airport, for three years when it suddenly changed the name to The Ocean Club in June 1986. Stuart Burchill listed McFaddin on his CV, without giving specific information about the job.

From news reports we learned Burchill signed a contract in 1990 under his corporation's name TPIC to buy the Baja Beach Club at 901 N. Franklin in Tampa with big plans to renovate it. Wouldn't you know it? The project failed when a former employee of Baja then set up a makeshift bomb in an effort to burn out a cross-town competitor.[8] Was Burchill involved? No idea. We can make no sense of it. But it is a dot, should you wish to connect it.

Not long after this Tampa debacle, the Burchills moved to Naples, where Barbara had contacts. In 1993 a new Florida corporation was set up in Naples by "G. S. Burchill" called Pet Detective, Inc., which didn't last a full year.[9] We searched for a DBA in Florida's records, expecting to find a listing for Ace Ventura, but no such luck.

Barbara and Stuart Burchill had been married for eleven years when they divorced in November 1996 – three years before he set up Plane 1 Leasing for Wally, naming Elsa Balestrino as registered agent.

Elsa lived in Connecticut, but her father, Giustino C. "Giulio" Balestrino, had lived in Naples, Florida from September 2000 until November 2001, in the gated La Costa apartment complex. We couldn't call him; he'd died in 2014.

According to his obituary, Giulio had immigrated to North America in the 1960's, started a family and "enjoyed a long professional career in the manufacturing industry. At the outset, he obtained an MBA from the University of New Haven."[10]

Not Yale, but a university founded in 1920 on the Yale campus, which "also has campuses in Tuscany, Italy, and Orange, Conn."[11] Since Giulio was from Turin, Italy (born in 1939), had a degree in mechanical engineering, and had previously worked for Fiat in the 1960's, this college seemed tailor-made for him.

His daughter, Elsa, Wally's registered agent, worked as a paralegal. She also filed a trademark for a company called BACC, LLC, whose website gives its address in Abu Dhabi, UAE. BACC Oil and Gas Industrial Experts is a company that handles projects for the Adnoc Company Group. ADNOC stands for Abu Dhabi National Oil Company, which is wholly owned by the Abu Dhabi Government.[12]

We will discover more dots along the trail, linking back to Abu Dhabi and the UAE. They may or may not be relevant, but they are intriguing.

Barbara's Russian Hubby and Skorzeny

After the 1996 divorce, Barbara Burchill married again – this time a Russian named Michael Bondarenko, who had arrived as an infant from Bremerhaven, Germany on USS *General Langfitt*, a refugee ship bringing displaced persons to the U.S.[13] On that voyage, Michael and his father were listed as Russian, while his mother and older half-sister were born in Germany. The family's sponsor was the Tolstoy Foundation, which paid for their travel from Bremerhaven.[14]

The Tolstoy Foundation was described in Warren Commission hearings into the Kennedy Assassination as an anti-Communist organization which collected vast amounts of information on all persons it sponsored. We searched for the name "Tolstoy" within a 490-page file from the Warren Commission and found testimony from Paul Raigorodsky, which gave a very long-winded discussion about how displaced Russians were watched by the churches they joined.[15]

Richard Bartholomew's excellent work – "Possible Discovery of an Automobile Used in the JFK Conspiracy" – also documents the Russian emigres involved with the "CIA-funded St. Nicholas Parish" they founded.[16]

St Nicholas Parish of the Russian Orthodox Church Outside of Russia, located just outside the Tolstoy Farm in New Jersey, was three miles away from where the Bondarenko family had settled, and only five miles from where Michael attended high school at Montclair in 1972.

Peter Levenda has also written about his experience with this church in his series *Sinister Forces*, published by TrineDay.[17]

Other recent research directly connects the Tolstoy Foundation to the Nazi network of Otto Skorzeny:

> Here we find a decisive link to the Skorzeny network. In his capacity as member of the Tolstoy Foundation Board of Directors, Paul Raigorodsky would have worked directly with Colonel Herschel V. Williams, also a member of the board. Colonel Williams was the USAF intelligence officer and boss of Ilse Skorzeny's in the international division of Previews, Inc. in New York. He was in daily contact with Ilse and corresponded with Otto frequently.
>
> This is strong evidence that Colonel Williams was "in the know" concerning operations in Dallas. Also, Previews Inc. had an active office in Dallas at the time. The document that confirms beyond any doubt that Colonel Williams worked with Raigorodsky is found in the Appendix. Colonel Williams' name is second from the bottom on the list. The document is dated November 16, 1962. "In the brief review of the testimony before the Warren Commission by Raigorodsky, we found the name of his close friend and associate Dallas oil executive Jake Hamon ... who plays prominently in the background of George de Mohrenschildt, Paul Raigorodsky and the Skorzeny network as a whole....
>
> [I]t was Jake Hamon who recommended de Mohrenschildt for his position with the International Cooperation Administration (ICA) working in Yugoslavia in 1957. The ICA was already established in an earlier chapter as a cover organization for the CIA with imbedded Agency officers. Otto Skorzeny also worked with the ICA and is heavily documented in the Skorzeny papers for the period covering the 1950s.[18]

We only quote a small part of this book, which we highly recommend. As a followup, we suggest you also read the 2021 book, *Coup in Dallas*, by H. P. Albarelli Jr., and Leslie Sharp.[19]

The Jake Hamon mentioned above was actually Jake Hamon, Jr., whose father, because of his ties to circus owner John Ringling of Sarasota, appears in another chapter of our book. Small world.

STUART BURCHILL TODAY

Although Stuart Burchill was called an accountant by everyone in Naples who knew him, he was not a licensed CPA. He had left the University of Florida without graduating. The same year *TerrorLand* was published, Stuart applied for a patent for a product called "composition for thermal insulating layer."[20]

From 2004 forward, he's been working on marketing this, and possibly other, patents using a variety of company names – Industrial Nanotech, Nansulate, and Syneffex – often called scams by investment forums.

Since 2016 he's been prolifically posting at Twitter-X as @StuartBurchill, where recently critics have ridiculed his claims of getting rent-free offices in Dubai.[21]

When hounded by the SEC because the background he furnished was too sketchy and because he'd never submitted filings to them for review of his OTC traded penny stocks, he apparently responded by posting the following details, as recounted by his critics:

> After University, he left to travel Europe and then worked on a cattle ranch, from there he went on to work with Arabian horses for several years before beginning a professional career. [22]

Stuart omitted his work for Wally Hilliard in the bio he furnished for an interview with *Face2Face*, which stated:

> He began working with nanotechnology in 2002, after successfully managing a regional Florida medical journal. Prior to Industrial Nanotech, he worked extensively in real estate development, sales, and commercial property management.
>
> Mr Burchill's early business experience focused on marketing for a publicly held company, Mcfaddin Ventures, which maintained an extensive portfolio of hotels, restaurants, and nightclub properties.
>
> Mr Burchill has also served as a consultant to high net worth individuals in the area of mid-sized business acquisitions.[23]

Following that vague description of his job history, Stuart added an afterthought: "marketing for a publicly held company, Mcfaddin Ventures, the world's largest nightclub chain owner (Confetti, Todd's, Rialto, Ocean Club) with an additional portfolio of hotels and restaurants.[24]

CIA OR ORGANIZED CRIME – PERHAPS BOTH

Finally, something to follow up on – Lance McFaddin – a name that would take us down a Texas trail ride through through Houston, Austin, Dallas and Lufkin, where McFaddin's founders merged.

Lance McFaddin went to public grade school in Lufkin, Texas with the richest boy in town – Buddy Temple.[25] Buddy's dad was Arthur Temple, Jr., who'd turned his family's lumbermill in East Texas into a corporate conglomerate and became for a time the largest shareholder in Time, Inc.[26]

Lance was two years older than Buddy and went to Southern Methodist University (SMU) in Dallas, but Lance often returned to visit his family back in Lufkin in the mid '60s.

While at SMU, Lance married and got a job as the "resident innkeeper" at a newly built Holiday Inn in Dallas, where Lance continued to live after finishing at SMU. This hotel was owned by a family friend, a relative really, on his mother's side, who'd built the hotel himself with a franchise from the chain. Lots of older Holiday Inns in the Lufkin area, however, were for sale but needed fixin' up, as Texans like to say. All he needed was money.

Buddy had lots of money and was sold on the plan. They started with four Holiday Inns, all in East Texas, and set up a holding company called Lufkin Properties, Inc. (LPI) in 1967. In 1970 LPI made a deal to buy 12 more by merging with an existing company called Servico, Inc. which traded publicly over the counter. McFaddin became president of Servico and its subsidiary LPI.

Lance, however, wasn't satisfied. He saw another opportunity, which he talked up to a friend from SMU, Sammy K. Kendrick. They could start a business to revamp older hotels and another one to upgrade restaurants. That led eventually to starting nightclub chains, either in those restaurants or in other locations.

Buddy Temple, who had spent only a year at the University of Texas, had joined the Army in 1962 after getting married. His only other education consisted of a year or two at St. Stephen's Episcopal School in Austin, Texas (where his dad was a member of the board of Trustees with four Episcopal ministers, including Rt. Rev. John E. Hines, Bishop in Houston), and graduation from Lawrenceville Prep in New Jersey.

Buddy's father was "not your usual southern robber baron; he was a model of progressive liberalism," according to George Crile's 2003 book, *Charlie Wilson's War*. You may recall the movie where Charlie was played by Tom Hanks, fighting Communists with Joanne King Herring, played by Julia Roberts.[27]

In an oral interview Buddy Temple recalled that he first met fellow East Texas lawmaker, Rep. Charles Wilson in Austin at Governor John Connally's second inaugural ball in January 1963, two years after Charlie was first sworn in to his first term as state representative from the Lufkin district.

It was auspicious, occurring just ten months before Governor Connally was shot while riding in the same car with President Kennedy on November 22.

Naval Intelligence Career before Congress

Charlie, who was born in 1933 in Trinity, 50 miles southwest of Lufkin, graduated from the Naval Academy in Annapolis in 1956. His father was a bookkeeper and accountant for lumber mills, and even worked for a time with the state forestry agency in Marshall. By the time Charlie married in 1962, he was already serving in the Texas Legislature for the Trinity and Lufkin district.

According to Crile, before 1960 Charlie had been "assigned to a top secret post at the Pentagon, where he was part of an intelligence unit that evaluated the Soviet Union's nuclear forces ... rehearsing for all-out nuclear war."[28]

Records indicate Charlie was *still in the Navy* attached to the Pentagon in 1960, when he filed early in 1960 to run as state representative, defeating the incumbent in the May primary. He then won the general election that November and was sworn in for office in January 1961. He also campaigned for John F. Kennedy in Washington, D.C. while in Washington.

For some reason, however, July 1963 Navy Muster Roll shows Charles Nesbitt Wilson still listed as a lieutenant in the Navy. How is that possible? Charlie Wilson continued to be elected as a Democrat – a *liberal* Democrat – by his more conservative East Texas constituents for a total of twelve years in both the Texas House and Senate before running for U.S. Congress in 1972. In the meantime, all the conservative Democrats had seen the writing on the wall and started switching to the Republican party.

Often called "Good Time Charlie," when between wives, Charlie loved to party both before and after he met Houston's social butterfly Joanne Johnson King Herring.[29]

They first met after he was sworn in as a member of the U.S. House of Representatives in Washington, D.C. in 1973, according to Joanne's oral memoir of Charlie made after his death in 2010.[30] After graduation from Lamar High School in Houston, Joanne married Robert King and raised two children in River Oaks, where she knew everyone, including no doubt, the Allbritton family who bought Riggs Bank in Washington, D.C. in 1974.

Joanne's best friend from high school was busty Sandra Hovas, nick-named "Buckets," who married Baron Enrico "Ricky" di Portanova, earn-ing herself the overblown title of Baroness Alessandra.[31]

Ricky's mother, the black sheep daughter of one of Houston's richest oil men, Hugh Roy Cullen, had married an Italian man while in Califor-nia. Cullen had left her almost nothing when he died in 1957, but later little Ricky showed up from Italy and sued the estate. The court awarded him a monthly income in the millions.

That's dollars. Not lira, or even euros.

* * *

Ricky and Buckets then had enough money to party with her friend Jo-anne, whose second husband was possibly Houston's richest oil and gas ty-coon, Robert R. Herring, chairman of Houston Natural Gas – later Enron.[32]

It's the same Enron that collapsed overnight a few days before 9/11 – August 2001 – to be more exact.

Bob Herring got filthy rich by "doin' bidnes" – as Texans say – with Saudi Arabia and other Arab countries back in the '60s. He even took Joanne with him while he was negotiating with all the sheiks in Middle Eastern nations. This was years before President Nixon, on his way out the back door of the White House in 1974, signed a secret deal with Saudi King Faisal. [33]

Joanne King, then a brunette, had her own daytime talk show that aired on Houston's KHOU-TV and later KPRC-TV, which lasted twelve years.[34]

Joanne's connections and popularity paid off well for Robert Herring, who ferried his charismatic wife all over the world. She also became a fixture in Washington, D.C. society circles long before James A. Baker III was named President Reagan's chief of staff in 1981. The *New York Times* featured Joanne in a 1983 article which described a White House dinner she'd planned for 110 guests. All were amazed, but Baker just smiled, as he explained: "Joanne and I went to kindergarten together. We've known each other all our lives. She's a bright, imaginative, wonderful girl."[35]

The Times elaborated, "Joanne is Joanne King Herring, one of Hous-ton's seemingly endless supply of beautiful blonde heiresses, the honor-ary consul general of Morocco and Pakistan and a habitual visitor in the courts of the Middle East.

"Her friend Prince Bandar bin Sultan is Saudi Arabia's Ambassador to the United States. She wanted him to meet the right people. So, she borrowed the vast mezzanine of the Hay-Adams Hotel last week and threw him the sort of extravaganza most Americans know, if they know at all, only from fiction, the movies and television."[36]

In an oral memoir for Charlie Wilson, Joanne revealed:

> I was terrible when I first started in television. But the show ended up being the sixth highest-rated show in the United States. And so I had gotten a lot of national attention. And we became friends with the ambassador from Pakistan, who was a brilliant man, Yaqub Khan. You may have heard of him. Charlie became a very good friend of his...
>
> And he became a great friend of ours and he helped enormously in our ascension in Washington. And so they saw that we had political clout in Washington. And so they asked Bob if he would consider being the honorary consul of Pakistan.[37]

When she used the word "they," Joanne apparently meant Boris Karloff look-alike General Zia-Ul-Haq, Army Chief of Pakistan, whom one blogger calls the "Father of Taliban terrorism in Pakistan and Father of Drug smuggling Heroin and also Islamic Extremism and Terrorism known as Talibanisation and Saudisation and Wahabization of Pakistan."[38]

Phew, the blogger was as long-winded as Joanne herself.

Long story short. Joanne got the title of honorary consul because hubby was too busy. And she milked it to the hilt.

"I was appointed under Bhutto," she continues.

"But you see, he was the one cog in the way of the Russians. And if we had not had total cooperation from Zia, we couldn't have gotten anything [meaning weapons systems] into Afghanistan. And he risked everything to help us do that. And we know that he was killed by the Russians."[39]

By "we," she may have meant herself and Charlie, since investigations into the August 17, 1988, explosion of the C-130 plane, carrying Zia, two Americans, and an entourage of 27 Pakistani advisers, came up empty. Thirty years later, it's still murky, and "Gen Zia's death remains shrouded in mystery."[40]

STUART BURCHILL FINDS A JOB

McFaddin Ventures, which Stuart listed on his CV, had previously been known as McFaddin-Kendrick, and it built its first nightclubs in Dallas and Houston. Houston's club was next door to a 22-acre tract

Adnan Khashoggi's Triad Group owned. Located in the 5300 block of West Alabama, the club was variously called the Foxhunter, Confetti's and Cowboy and so on. Changing the theme and decor was part of the McFaddin trademark.

Adnan Khashoggi had been making his rounds in Houston society as early as 1969, mentioned alongside Joanne herself, who'd just gone blonde. Unfortunately, his name was misspelled.

Adnan appeared with Count Pierre de Mallarey in Houston in 1969, years before the Count bought a run-down White House replica – truly a "white elephant" – built by former Governor Ross Sterling on Galveston Bay some 30 miles east of Houston.[41]

By 2012, however, the Count was busily assisting Princess Gloria and her husband Johannes, heir to the fortune of the Thurn und Taxis family, in curating their voluminous art treasures that dated back a minimum of two centuries.[42]

Adnan collected wealthy contacts, like Sotheby's collects art connoisseurs. When he needed discrete assistance – totally hush hush – he had their numbers, and vice versa.[43]

PETE BREWTON EXPOSÉS

Pete Brewton made a valiant attempt before the 1992 election to explain what he'd been witnessing in Houston, Texas during the late '80s. Co-author Linda Minor had relocated from Austin to Houston in 1988 and began working for County Attorney Mike Driscoll the following year, just before the county judge of Harris County was named George H. W. Bush's campaign chairman for Houston.

Brewton, at the *Houston Post*, had been publishing a series of articles about financial fraud taking place in Texas, which inspired him to write a book, *The Mafia, CIA & George Bush*, which described some of the same events Minor was researching for Driscoll's Real Property Division during the same time, particularly regarding allegations made against Judge Jon Lindsay. Just so you know.[44]

One chapter of Brewton's book involved connections between James A. Baker III and various Texas savings and loan companies. Mainland Savings, for example, had purchased a series of by-then virtually worthless promissory notes from a New Yorker named Howard Pulver. Mainland paid $21 million for notes later sold by the receiver for $400,000.[45] Pulver and the group he worked with were engaged in turning apartment buildings in Houston into syndicated securities – at that time limited partnerships.

Brewton shared the *Post* byline with Gregory Seay on some of the stories that appeared in the *Post*. They speculated about where the money to buy the properties came from. Nobody knew for sure. The name Anthony Pedone – whose father was a big investor in racehorses and an agent for jockeys – was suggested as one possibility.[46]

Looking for Pedone and his partner Pulver, the *Post* journalists narrowed their search to one area at the northern tip of Great Neck, Long Island, where Pulver had acquired a mansion in the mid-'70s. It was within walking distance, they discovered, from Martin Schwimmer, a man who'd just been indicted with Mario Renda for racketeering and tax evasion. Prosecutors called their arrest – as they always do – "'the largest criminal union fraud scheme' ever prosecuted by the Justice Department."[47]

Brewton seems to have assumed at that point that the money Pulver's group was using came from the mob. Linda, however, kept searching through Pulver's projects in old deed records in Houston, and noticed something she didn't understand, but which stuck with her. She made notes about the transactions.

At least one of the limited partnerships was aimed at renovating an old office building in downtown Houston at 806 Main Street – the corner of Main and Rusk streets. South Coast Investment Co.'s entities operated their scams out of this building, which Pulver acquired. It is now the J. W. Marriott Hotel in downtown Houston.

HIDDEN ARAB INVESTORS?

Before relocating to Houston, Pulver had worked in Corpus Christi, where his primary clients wanted oil and gas properties (royalties, etc.) packaged as securities. Possibly the work was connected to the King Ranch and Kleberg family, who had a big presence there, but that's only a guess. The move to Houston focused on commercial buildings, which someone wanted to package and sell as limited partnerships.

A $1.6 million promissory note, secured by Pulver's building was executed by Munawar H. Hidayatallah, as president of Tark VI, Inc., a Texas corporation, as the sole general partner of Main/Rusk Associates, a Texas limited partnership. The note, guaranteed by another limited partnership in Manhattan called "Consolidated Holdings Limited" at 505 Park Avenue, NY, was transferred in April 1983 to Abu Dhabi Investment Co. (ADIC), and it was signed by Sultan Al-Suwaydi, whose signature was acknowledged by the U.S. Consul at the U.S. Embassy in the United Arab Emirates.[48]

As it turns out, Munawar H. "Micki" Hidayatallah, born in Pakistan in 1944, was an American citizen by 1979, attending hearings in Congress to discuss foreign investments in the U.S. His work history would eventually include various companies linked to the Bush family, such as Ideco, Bush's first employer in the 1950s. Ideco was a subsidiary of Dresser Industries.

Pulver and Pedone sold several of their projects, financed by a mobbed-up bank in New York, to a former Lufkin man, Joe A. McDermott, Jr., a developer of commercial projects, who'd worked for more than 20 years for Houston power developer Walter Mischer. We discovered he was also a friend of even higher powers like former Governor John Connally and Lt. Governor Ben Barnes.[49]

We found ourselves wondering if Lance McFaddin and Buddy Temple had known McDermott, but we never got around to doing further research.

HOUSTON'S SAUDI AFFAIR

B rewton called attention in his book to "the time in August 1985 when Mainland handed at least $12 million in cash to Adnan Khashoggi's company, just a week before Khashoggi paid over the initial $1 million of $5 million to Manucher Ghorbanifar to start a secret arms-for-hostages deal with Iran."[50]

Writing that Khashoggi first appeared in Houston in 1974 when one of his Triad subsidiaries "bought a 22-acre tract of vacant land in West Houston just southwest of the Galleria shopping center, Brewton indicated that Khashoggi purchased the land for a little more than $5 million from the Dallas financial conglomerate of Lomas & Nettleton," which had bought it at foreclosure of a John Jamail loan in default. The tract was said to be on West Alabama, at the intersection with Sage Blvd, a then-vacant corner that adjoined the Galleria shopping center west of Loop 610.

Triad claimed it was planning to build a $300 million commercial development with hotels, office buildings and retail shops – much like the Galleria that now exists. Then nothing happened. Part of Khashoggi's problem may have stemmed from John Connally's indictment in 1974 for bribery, perjury, and conspiracy to obstruct justice, just as Big John was planning to announce his run for President in 1976 – long before anyone had heard of Jimmy Carter. It may have been Connally's idea to pay for his campaign with money from his Saudi contacts.

After leaving the Governor's office in 1969, Connally joined one of Houston's oldest and largest law firms, Vinson and Elkins, whose senior partners were old friends of James A. Baker III.

Connally was also "named a member of President Richard M. Nixon's President's Intelligence Advisory Board (PIAB) and assumed a favored position among Nixon's advisors."[51] As Secretary of Treasury for Nixon, Connally was also privy to Nixon's secret 28-page agreement to allow Saudis to invest in banks and other businesses in the United States, though they had to do so through nominees.

Connally designated one of his attorneys, Frank Van Court, to be the nominee for Ghaith Pharaon and Khaled bin Mahfouz. The latter had founded the National Commercial Bank in 1953, which became the bank of the Saudi royal family at a time when oil revenues soared.

Khalid bin Mahfouz was named in Rachel Ehrenfeld's 2003 book, *Funding Evil: How Terrorism Is Financed and How to Stop It*, where she "alleged that Mahfouz and his two sons financed al-Qaida through the family's ownership of the National Commercial Bank of Saudi Arabia and through connections with Islamic charities," according to *The Guardian*.[52] Mahfouz sued in a British court and won a default defamation judgment in 2004 against her. Ehrenfeld then filed for an injunction from a federal court in New York.[53]

Republican legislators passed a bill in New York to prevent judgments from foreign libel suits to be collected against U.S. journalists, and Ehrenfeld's book soon became available again months before Mahfouz died, still fighting "a determined campaign against the international media to clear his name of any involvement in the financing of the September 11 attacks."[54]

An obituary in the *New York Times* related he'd lived in Houston during those active years just before Iran-Contra investigations spoiled the fun.[55] Had Khalid bin Mahfouz been the one behind the global financial network Tony Blair had talked about? If so, had he acted alone, or were there others?

Pharaon had also engaged in multiple deals in Texas, fronted by "James R. Bath, a deal broker whose alleged associations run from the CIA to a major shareholder and director of the Bank of Credit & Commerce International," according to *TIME* magazine.[56]

George W. Bush's "early 1980s tax records reviewed by *TIME* show that Bath invested $50,000 in Bush's energy ventures and remained a stockholder until Bush sold his company to Harken in 1986."[57]

It's indeed interesting that Time magazine broke the story, given the fact that two Democrats with LBJ connections – Joe Allbritton and Arthur Temple – sold their media empires to that magazine.

Did these two Saudis groomed by John Connally, join Adnan Khashoggi – who had worked with the "military-industrial complex" for years – transfer their allegiance in 1974 to the new Director of the CIA, George H. W. Bush?

From that point were the Saudis being protected by an unofficial – dare we call it "deep state" – committee headed by Bush and his banker friends in Texas?

The plans for the 22-acre tract sitting at the corner of Sage and West Alabama were revived again, Brewton wrote, when Khashoggi in 1979 came up with a new partner, Clint Murchison, Jr., who also owned the Dallas Cowboys. Together they borrowed $15 million from what was then called Texas Commerce Bank for a construction project to be headed by Richard "Dick" Knight, who had been brought into the project from New Orleans.

Dick Knight later worked with Harris County on its most secret deals without competitive bidding.[58] When County Attorney staff requested copies of documents showing names of those who held shares in his limited partnerships, Knight and his attorneys refused to furnish them.

Jon Lindsay, glaring at Driscoll's staff, his eyes filled with contempt, conveyed his message tersely, "The County has all it needs from Dick Knight," inferences about who held shares in the company be damned.

It would later be learned that Fayez Sarofim, at one time Houston's richest billionaire, managed the partnership. As the son-in-law of Herman Brown of Brown & Root – LBJ's biggest donor – Sarofim's political connections went very deep. All the future projects for modernizing downtown Houston were rumored to have been planned out for decades, and the land set aside with models created and set in place on a site plan hidden from view, except for the county judge and his cronies.[59]

McFaddin Ventures and CIA Links

While Khashoggi's land sat idle through the late '70s and early '80s, McFaddin Ventures kept building one new nightclub after another. There was one housed at 1301 Lavaca Street in Austin, right next door to the Texas Capitol. Charlie Wilson would have gone there during his last term as a state senator, if only to meet with a political friend, Glenn Kraege Polan, former aide to Governor Price Daniel, Jr. Polan was working in the Austin club in the early '70s before Charlie left Austin for Washington, D.C.

John Kelso, Austin's laid-back reporter in his "Bar Trail" column, wrote in 1980 about the bar McFaddin-Kendrick opened back in 1972 with help from Polan, after it changed its name to "Cowboy":

> Let's explain the existence of Cowboy, which used to be the Veranda, a Plastic fern bar. The Veranda was owned by the McFaddin-Kendrick Corp. out of Houston, which still owns various Verandas, elans, Todd's and Rodeos (all club) in other cities across the country. McFaddin-Kendrick also owns many, many Cowboys: in Houston, Dallas, St. Louis, Memphis, Tuscaloosa, Ala., St. Petersburg, Fla., and now here in Austin.[60]

It became clear in 1978 that Charlie Wilson knew both McFaddin and Kendrick and was an investor in their new nightclub in Washington, D.C. In her syndicated column about the Capital City, Betty Beale disclosed on July 9, 1978, that Congressman Charlie Wilson was an investor in Lance McFaddin's businesses.

> Those three young rich Texans – State Rep. Arthur Temple III [Buddy], hotel and restaurant owner Lance McFaddin and oil man Sam Kendrick – who founded the fabulously successful private Elan clubs in Houston, Dallas and Memphis, are about to open one here. U.S. Rep. Charlie Wilson, D-Tex., a friend of all three and a minor investor in the Washington Elan, said it won't be as luxurious as the Houston one.[61]

Charlie Wilson did like to party, but he had another side as well. Assigned in Congress to the all-important Appropriations Committee, with seats on the powerful national security and defense (which is responsible for funding CIA operations) subcommittees, Charlie had tremendous power.

> "I despise the Soviet Union, and I despise communism, and I despise bullies," Wilson said in a 2008 interview on U.S. public television. "And when the Soviet Union hurled the 40th Army on what they thought were helpless [Afghan] people – they hadn't read too much history – but what they thought were helpless people, it just totally outraged me, and I dedicated 10 years of my life to it."[62]

The protest at the U.S. Embassy in Pakistan came one day before student rebels in Iran seized hostages. It was Charlie Wilson who took Joanne Herring to meet President Carter, who "had his concerns about

Ziaul-Haq, and was upset Pakistan had begun a nuclear program and that former Prime Minister Zulfikar Ali Bhutto had been executed. With Iran becoming a major problem in the Middle East, however, Carter decided relations with Pakistan should be repaired."[63]

Margaret Thatcher got on board in January 1980.[64]

All that was a lead up to the October Surprise, the Boland Amendment and Iran Contra, mentioned elsewhere. Stuart Burchill had not yet returned to Tampa. We haven't been successful in learning his location from 1980 until 1985.

A THIRD MAGIC DUTCH BOY?

Stuart Burchill had met Barbara Marilyn van Lunteren Leonard while she worked for McFaddin Ventures' Confetti club, which opened in the West Shore area of Tampa in 1983. Two years later McFaddin Ventures went public and began selling stock on American Stock Exchange.

Barbara moved to a gated West Shore apartment in 1985 after divorcing Alcide Leonard.

Considering her Dutch background, it's possible she sought work at Ballast Nedam Construction Co., a new Florida corporation registered in 1985, affiliated with a Dutch engineering and construction conglomerate based in Nieuwegein, Utrecht, in the Netherlands.

The antique store in Naples which she had managed was built on land owned by Nedam, Inc., a Florida corporation set up by William van Lunteren, her first husband.

The Ballast Nedam Group arose in the Netherlands after Ballast and Nedam merged in 1969 to compete internationally. Their first big project – the King Fahd Bridge – was in Saudi Arabia in 1982, connecting the island nation of Bahrain to Al Khobar, Saudi Arabia.

Ballast Nedam was accused in 1980 by a Miami Beach company of being one-third owned by the family of a convicted Nazi collaborator in Holland, and another third of the stock by Saudis. Not long afterward, all the stock of Ballast Nedam was acquired by British Aerospace Engineering (BAe), caught up in yet another arms deal where weapons were being bartered.

An oil for stock deal in 1983 was allegedly arranged by the British Prime Minister's son, Mark Thatcher, that exhibited all the trappings of an intricate plan reminiscent of Adnan Khashoggi, the king of barter.[65] The Al Yamamah weapons sales occurred in September 1985, not only before Oliver North's Enterprise was arranging for delivery of its own weapons to Iran for the hostage release. According to a BBC probe in June 2007, "The UK's biggest arms dealer, BAE Systems, paid hundreds of millions of pounds to the ex-Saudi ambassador to the US, Prince Bandar bin Sultan."[66]

For the entire decade after her election in 1979, Ms. Thatcher was busy privatizing BAe and other formerly public-owned British companies. She tossed Ballast Nedam back and forth, until in 1993, Ballast Nedam was sold to a group of investors comprised of the German company Hochtief AG, Internationale Nederlanden Group, and the Ballast Nedam Pension Fund.[67]

Could that have been part of the nest from which sprang the magic Dutch boys who hooked up in southwest Florida with Wally Hilliard? The question is not rhetorical.

Back to the question posed earlier in this chapter: What happened to Anna, the Russian amazon described to me by Danielle Clarke?

* * *

Stuart Burchill married Laurie Ann Scherock Germain, ex-wife of a partner in one of the biggest car dealerships (Toyota, Honda and Lexus) in Naples. She grew up in Naples and had a degree from Stetson University, where she'd been an honor student in science. Allegedly, she helped Stuart invent Nansulate.

They married after he filed for divorce from the Russian wife Anna in 2002, who alleged in Collier County court documents he'd abused her. Although Anna was never served, a divorce was granted in 2003. The case still is not closed; it keeps being assigned to a new judge every year or so. Both Stuart and Laurie have since been arrested for fraud, among other crimes, and he's continually being evicted, according to online records in Collier County.

His only source of funds seems to be whatever he derives from those who fall for his penny stock scams, without filing any reports with the SEC. His involvement in Industrial Nanotech, Inc. continues to stir up angry comments. One irate poster at Investment Hub who connected the company to Stuart's job in 1999 as Treasurer at Huffman Aviation, wrote, "Not only has Stuart harmed countless gullible companies and individuals, he has also harmed this country with his involvement in Huffman Aviation, where Mohamed Atta and Marwan al-Shehhi learned to fly aircraft into the World Trade Center."

Stuart keeps making promises, however, and issues monthly press releases predicting millions will soon be seen by those who buy his stock.

Endnotes

1   "In the 1940s the Reverend Frederick Ellis, an Englishman of Anglo-Catholic inclination, was 'priest-vicar' of the Cathedral. I recall stories of parishioners pressing money into his hand at the church door with which to buy vestments; but he was never appointed dean, because, it was said, he lacked a university degree. The Bishop (later primate), George Frederick Kingston, was his own dean, in order to make sure, one suspects, that the Cathedral did not go too 'high'. Eventually, Father Ellis departed Nova Scotia to end his days as Dean of Nassau in the Bahamas. "The Impact of Tractarianism on the Maritimes," A paper delivered by Canon Robert C. Tuck, June 30, 1983 at The Atlantic Theological Conference, Charlottetown, Prince Edward Island, in marking the 150th anniversary of the Oxford Movement, 1833. (revised September 2002). http://anglicanhistory.org/essays/tuck_maritimes.pdf

2   Adiel J. Moncrief, "Faith that works," *Tampa Tribune*, 20 May 1962, Page 64. https:// I1Ni-IsInR5cCI6IkpXVCJ9.eyJmcmVlLXZpZXctaWQiOjMzMDUyODI1NiwiaWF0IjoxNzAxNzg5NDA5LC-JIeHAiOjE3MDE4NzU4MDI9.l4nRI9qOnVb50wQ9nvlaXWGc7SRdmyfqx5LnTlwty8s

3   *Naples Daily News*, October 3, 1982.

4   Daniel Hopsicker, *Welcome to Terrorland: Mohamed Atta & the 9-11 Cover-Up in Florida*, Madcow Press, 2004, p. 268.

5   *Terrorland*, p. 269.

6   https://www.legacy.com/us/obituaries/houstonchronicle/name/lance-mcfaddin-obituary?id=2081649

7   https://classicalassociationni.wordpress.com/2023/02/19/pecunia-non-olet-vespasian-and-the-smell-of-money/

8   Lisa Landers, "Bartender charged in attempt to bomb West Shore night club," *Tampa Tribune*, 26 Sep 1990, Page 60. https://www.newspapers.com/image/338026395/?clipping_id=136425884

9   Florida records can be searched at Sunbiz.com. Just put in the name Burchill and find all sorts of companies he and his family have filed over the years.

10   https://www.legacy.com/us/obituaries/nhregister/name/giulio-balestrino-obituary?id=17059078

11   https://www.newhaven.edu/about/index.php

12   https://bacc-llc.com/Services/

13   Ancestry.com records.

14   See document insert from Ancestry.com.

15   https://www.govinfo.gov/content/pkg/GPO-WARRENCOMMISSIONHEARINGS-9/pdf/GPO-WARRENCOMMISSIONHEARINGS-9.pdf

16   https://www.maryferrell.org/showDoc.html?docId=217852#relPageId=5&search=Tolstoy

17   See an article at Levenda's Substack to get a taste: Peter Levenda, "Unholy Communion," Sep 13, 2023. https://peterlevenda.substack.com/p/unholy-communion-0ab

18   Ganis, Major Ralph P., *The Skorzeny Papers: Evidence for the Plot to Kill JFK* (pp. 431-433). Hot Books. Kindle Edition.

19   H. P. Albarelli, Jr. and Leslie Sharp, *Coup in Dallas: The Decisive Investigation into Who Killed JFK*, Sky Horse Publishing, 2021.

20   US 7,144,522 B2; Dec. 5, 2006. https://patentimages.storage.googleapis.com/1a/5f/9d/98e1db419dbae5/US7144522.pdf

21   At twitter: "'Tomorrow we visit our free office space to be given to us by UAE for our contribution to their objectives.' Stuart Burchill." Poster "Demain," replies: "Stuart Burchill again provides evidence he is lying! Stuart is being careless in that he is providing solid evidence of his lies. If the free office space was not imaginary an address would be provided. Of course, the office space will either be in Stuart's wild imagination or in the virtual universe." *InvestorsHub*, Wednesday, July 13, 2022 10:56:55 AM, #41660 by Demain. https://investorshub.advfn.com/boards/read_msg.aspx-?message_id=169388158

22   *Post 41,636 by Demain: "Stuart Burchill worked as a self-employed handyman after he dropped out of college. In his fantasy biography, he imagines that he left to travel Europe and then*

worked on a cattle ranch, from there he went on to work with Arabian horses for several years and this is where he learned the art of bullsh-- and horsesh--. After his stint as a handyman he became Vice President of Huffman Aviation where Mohamed Atta and Marwan al-Shehhi had attended the school to learn how to fly small aircraft. Mohamed Atta crashed American Airlines Flight 11 into the North Tower, Marwan al-Shehhi crashed the Boeing 767 into the South Tower of the World Trade Center killing nearly 3,000 people on September 11, 2001."

23   Stuart submitted what one poster called a "fastasy biography submitted to OTC markets," at Post #41,636 by Demain, Investors Hub, 7-12-22. https://investorshub.advfn.com/boards/read_msg.aspx?message_id=169380417

24   If you are bored and need a laugh, subscribe free to Investors Hub and follow the posts under Industrial Nanotech (INTK). Through one post we learned of Stuart Burchill's arrest and mugshot at https://florida.arrests.org/Arrests/Stuart_Burchill_8376721/

25   https://www.sfasu.edu/heritagecenter/5385.asp

26   https://capitol.texas.gov/tlodocs/793/billtext/html/HR00268I.htm

27   George Crile, *Charlie Wilson's War: The Extraordinary Story of How the Wildest Man in Congress and a Rogue CIA Agent Changed the History of Our Times*, Grove Atlantic, 2003.

28   Ibid.

29   Annie Groer; Ann Gerhart, "The Reliable Source," *Washington Post*, February 12, 1999. https://www.washingtonpost.com/archive/lifestyle/1999/02/12/the-reliable-source/40702cda-d64e-408b-ba26-a0c28ef0282b/

30   https://www.sfasu.edu/heritagecenter/5377.asp

31   Barbara Kuntz, "River Oaks' Party Palace: Opulent mansion with a crazy history – and a baron past – hits the market," Aug 9, 2014. https://houston.culturemap.com/news/real-estate/0809-14-river-oaks-party-palace-opulent-mansion-with-a-crazy-history-and-a-baron-past-hits-themarket

32   "Robert D. Herring Dies at 60; Headed Houston Natural Gas," *New York Times*, October 13, 1981, Section B, Page 27. https://timesmachine.nytimes.com/timesmachine/1981/10/13/048737.html?pageNumber=49

33   The term "back door" was used by Andrea Wong in her article, "The untold story behind Saudi Arabia's 41-year secret debt," in *The Independent* (01 June 2016): "Treasury officials solved the dilemma by letting the Saudis in through the back door. In the first of many special arrangements, the US allowed Saudi Arabia to bypass the normal competitive bidding process for buying Treasuries by creating 'add-ons.' Those sales, which were excluded from the official auction totals, hid all traces of Saudi Arabia's presence in the US government debt market Instead of disclosing Saudi Arabia's holdings, the Treasury grouped them with 14 other nations, such as Kuwait, the United Arab Emirates and Nigeria, under the generic heading 'oil exporters' – a practice that continued for 41 years." harabia-s-41year-us-debt-secret-a7059041.html

Cited by Linda Minor in her blog, Quixotic Joust, "Within the Netherworld of International Currency Exchange Rates," August 22, 2018. https://quixoticjoust.blogspot.com/2018/08/within-netherworld-of-international.html?m=0

34   Outtakes from *The Joanne King Show* (1971). https://texasarchive.org/2012_00123. Affiliated with NBC, the channel had moved into modern studios in 1953 at 3014 Post Oak Road – back when television was in its infancy. She also wrote a society column for one of the Houston dailies, both of which were owned by Jesse Jones and his minions. Jones had been FDR's secretary of commerce but later set up a semi-secret group of cigar-smokers in his Lamar Hotel suite in Houston, known as the Suite 8F Crowd. They owned most of Houston as well as a big part of Texas itself. It was these bigwigs who financed Lyndon Johnson's Senate and White House campaigns. The studio was located a few blocks from where former "Suite 8F" members, their relatives and business partners planned to acquire land to build a super modern shopping mall (Galleria) in the late '60s, eventually getting Gerald D. Hines to build not only the mall but a dozen or so tall office buildings and hotels around it. The Transco Tower went up very close to where Joanne's studio had been. Images from the era appear at the *Houston Chronicle* website. If you look at snapshots of the KPR studios online, you'll note that the studio where Joanne went to work weekdays at noon was in the middle of nowhere, surrounded by wide open space, except for an adjacent drive-in movie theater that took up half the block. Both the studio and drive-in movie would be torn down in the late '60s to make room for Gerald Hines' South Post Oak developments. https://blog.chron.com/

bayoucityhistory/2012/02/batch-of-photos-shows-early-days-at-kprc/

35   Charlotte Curtis, "A Feast, Texas-Sized," *New York Times*, February 7, 1984, Section C, Page 12

36   Ibid.

37   https://www.sfasu.edu/heritagecenter/5377.asp

38   Blog called "Great Game Pashton's History; Great Game on Lands of Pashton and Af-ghans." https://drksy.wordpress.com/2019/03/17/joanne-king-herring/

39   Ibid., Zulfikar Ali Bhutto was Prime Minister of Pakistan from 1973 to 1977, and, prior to that, President of Pakistan from 1971 to 1973. We know Joanne wasn't a real blonde, and she was determined nobody would call her a dumb onr, so she talked non-stop at her interview, probably revealing more than she'd been cleared to say: "This is a very significant point. And the way we know, if you care, Alexandere de Marenches was a French… whose son had been killed. And so he devoted his life to the French CIA (France's external intelligence agency) from November 6, 1970 to June 12, 1981. And he was head of it through seven presidents He was called upon by the Pakistan government and a lot of the people to check into how Zia was killed, and it was the Russians. We know it was the Russians. Because it wasn't just Zia that was killed, but the most significant people that he had working in Pakistan. So, I became very significant in Pakistan. And so, Charlie also be-came a friend of Yaqub Khan and admired him very much and took an interest in Pakistan. But I was the one that introduced him to Zia."

40   Naziha Syed Ali, "Dawn investigations: Mystery still surrounds Gen Zia's death, 30 years on," *Dawn*, August 17, 2018. Scribe Publishing Platform. https://www.dawn.com/news/1427540

41   *Texas Monthly* described him thus: "An impetuous French count and oil trader, Pierre de Malleray de Barre, bought it around 1980 through Sotheby's International Realty and Houston realtor John Daugherty, but the count never moved to Texas." Patricia Sharpe, "Sold!" *Texas Monthly*, November 1987. In 1971 he wrote "The influence of taxation on the location and legal form of investments by United States companies in member countries of the European Economic Commu-nity," so appears to have been some kind of global tax expert as well as an oil trader.

42   *Connoisseur World*, January 1988, p. 38 and . See Wikipedia: https://en.wikipedia.org/wiki/Thurn_und_Taxis#Princes_of_Thurn_and_Taxis and for Princess Gloria, see https://en.wikipe-dia.org/wiki/Gloria_von_Thurn_und_Taxis

43   We learn a great deal about Gloria in one article by Christopher Bagley, "Gloria Takes Manhattan: Gloria von Thurn und Taxis," *W Magazine*, June 30, 2010. https://www.wmagazine.com/story/princess-gloria-tnt

"Freedom is a surprisingly new concept in the life of Princess Gloria, despite her well-known past as a madcap socialite. Married at age 20 to a distant cousin – the decadent, 53-year-old Prince Jo-hannes, scion of the family that founded Europe's postal system in the 15th century – Gloria spent much of the Eighties playing the frivolous, globe-trotting party girl, though many believe she was mostly living up to Johannes's rather peculiar idea of how a wife should behave.

"It was during this time that Gloria earned the nickname Princess TNT, with her multicolored hair, wacky couture outfits and outrageous antics, such as her barking-dog imitation, which she once performed on *Late Night With David Letterman*. But after Johannes's death in 1990, Gloria unexpectedly retreated to Regensburg and transformed herself into a disciplined hausfrau and es-tate manager, raising her three children and shoring up the family's billion-dollar fortune through astute sales of land, silver and other holdings.

"Her next surprise: becoming a devout Catholic and living part-time in Rome, where she could be closer to her friend Cardinal Ratzinger, now Pope Benedict XVI.

Today Princess Gloria is as religious as ever – she goes to Mass every day, even in Chelsea – but it's clear that New York is having a liberating effect, as it has on so many old-world aristocrats before her. She speaks of an "extreme widening of the horizons" in Manhattan, where she spends a couple of months every year….

"Gloria has no shortage of homes around the world – there's an apartment in Rome, a beach compound in Kenya and a sprawling lake house in Bavaria – but she says none of those locales offer anything close to the stimulation of New York, where she finds herself choosing among a half dozen invitations and events each day. During one typical stay last fall, in the hours when she wasn't going to Mass or seeing museum and gallery shows, she dressed up as a clown and partied at Allison Sarofim's raucous Halloween bash, and cooked dinner at home for 12, including artist Terence Koh and director Lee Daniels. [FYI: Allison Sarofim was the granddaughter of Herman Brown of Brown & Root of Houston, and her father was Houston's most secretive and wealthiest investment banker, Fayez Sarofim.]

"Gloria bought the Chelsea property in 2006, using some of the $8 million she'd received from auctioning off part of her contemporary art collection at Phillips de Pury. 'It's always dangerous to have some cash,' says Gloria, whose direct gaze, go-get-'em manner and short, simple haircut lend her the air of a particularly well-born soccer coach. She bought an entire floor, converting two apartments into an open-plan, 4,200-square-foot space....

"... She remarks that she was baptized and raised in the church, but admits there was a crucial turning point when she struck up a friendship with a high-ranking German cardinal, Joseph Alois Ratzinger, who'd been born not far from Regensburg. Gloria had her first sighting of Ratzinger almost three decades ago, when he preached at St. Emmeram Church. He was a saint, she decided, and she vowed to get close to him.... After Johannes died, however, Gloria began inviting the cardinal to say Mass in Regensburg, and by 2000 she'd bought a place in Rome, where, with her friend Alessandra Borghese, she started hosting exclusive religious salons and liturgical concerts. Five years later Ratzinger became pope, and Gloria had a friend in a very high place."

44   The Harris County archives reveal some of the detail of the County Attorney's investigation, including the name of Dick Knight, and the entity through which he worked, The City Partnership, Ltd. https://www.harriscountyarchives.com/Portals/1/Documents/Finding%20Aids/FA_CountyAttorney_TXvLindsayCR44.pdf?ver=2021-05-26-102317-453

45   Pete Brewton, *The Mafia, CIA and George Bush*, Spi Books Trade; First Edition (January 1, 1992), p. 42.

46   Ibid., p. 43.

47   Marilyn Berkery, "The president of a brokerage firm charged with stealing," UPI, May 26, 1988.   https://www.upi.com/Archives/1988/05/26/The-president-of-a-brokerage-firm-charged-with-stealing/1610580622400/

48   According to notes Linda had made, the promissory note dated March 31, 1980, was executed in New York by Munawar H. Hidayatallah, as president of Tark VI, Inc., a Texas corporation, as sole general partner of Main/Rusk Associates, a Texas limited partnership (guaranteed by Consolidated Holdings Limited, 505 Park Avenue, NY), and it was signed on behalf of ADIC by Sultan Al-Suwaydi and acknowledged by the U.S. Consul at the U.S. Embassy in the United Arab Emirates.

As it turns out, Munawar H. "Micki" Hidayatallah had direct connections to George H. W. Bush through a maze of corporations between 1985-88, such as Ideco, Bush's first employer in the 1950s. Ideco was a California subsidiary of Dresser Industries, owned by Brown Brothers Harriman. An astute financial writer should be able to trace the events connecting bush to Micki all those years ago. See, for example, "California firm acquires Allis-Chalmers," Milwaukee Business Journal, May 11, 2001. https://www.bizjournals.com/milwaukee/stories/2001/05/07/daily40.html

49   She made a note: " The real property was sold to Main/Rusk Associates on December 1, 1979, with a new deed of trust (wraparound) to Main, Ltd. [H431070]. A lien in the amount of $1.6 million to Development Services (CS), B.V. was made on March 31, 1980, modified on June 25, 1982, and assigned on April 1, 1983, to ADIC (Abu Dhabi Investment Company) Finance Company BV (Netherlands) c/o Pierson Trust BV in Rotterdam. The note was executed in New York by Munawar

H. Hidayatallah, president of Tark VI, Inc., a Texas corporation, as sole general partner of Main/Rusk Associates, a Texas limited partnership (guaranteed by Consolidated Holdings Limited, 505 Park Avenue, NY), and it was signed on behalf of ADIC by Sultan Al-Suwaydi and acknowledged by the U.S. Consul at the U.S. Embassy in the United Arab Emirates. In 1980 Pulver and Pedone executed collateral transfers of notes they received from the sale of shopping centers in Houston to Sterling National Bank at 540 Madison Ave. in New York [G504837-38]. In December of 1983 Sterling Bank released its lien when the centers were sold to Sultan Al-Suwaydi and acknowledged by the U.S. Consul at the U.S. Embassy in the United Arab Emirates [J351612-14]."

50   Pete Brewton, op cit., p. 53. You can read the document itself at https://www.cia.gov/readingroom/docs/CIA-RDP90-00552R000201260001-1.pdf

51   "John Connally," The Texas Politics Project: Governors of Texas. Reprinted with permission from the *Handbook of Texas Online*, a joint project of the Texas State Historical Association and the General Libraries at the University of Texas at Austin. © 2003, The Texas State Historical Association. https://texaspolitics.utexas.edu/archive/html/exec/governors/25.html

52   David Pallister, "US author mounts 'libel tourism' challenge," *The Guardian*, 15 Nov 2007. https://www.theguardian.com/world/2007/nov/15/books.usa

53   Ibid.

54   Frank Kane, "The eventful life of Khalid bin Mahfouz," *The National*, September 01, 2009. https://www.thenationalnews.com/business/the-eventful-life-of-khalid-bin-mahfouz-1.538872

55   Douglas Martin, "Khalid bin Mahfouz, Saudi Banker, Dies at 60," *New York Times*, Aug. 27, 2009. https://www.nytimes.com/2009/08/28/world/middleeast/28mahfouz.html

56   Jonathan Beaty, "A Mysterious Mover of Money and Planes," *Time*, Sunday, June 24, 2001. https://content.time.com/time/magazine/article/0,9171,155760,00.html

57   Ibid.

58   Harris County Archives, op. cit., https://www.harriscountyarchives.com/Portals/1/Documents/Finding%20Aids/FA_CountyAttorney_TXvLindsayCR44.pdf?ver=2021-05-26-102317-453

59   The hilarious tale, "Can't Buy Me Love," about Fayez Sarofim's affair, divorce and remarriage was told in Texas Monthly by Skip Hollandsworth, published October 2000. https://www.texasmonthly.com/articles/cant-buy-me-love/

60   John Kelso, "Go West, Young Man," *Austin American-Statesman*, 03 May 59, 1980, Page 74.

61   Betty Beale column, *News and Record*, Greensboro, N.C., 09 Jul 1978, Page 48.

62   Breffni O'Rourke, "Charlie Wilson, Congressman Who Helped Drive Soviets Out Of Afghanistan, Is Dead," Radio Free Europe, February 11, 2010. https://www.rferl.org/a/ExUS_Lawmaker_Wilson_Dead_At_76/1954654.html

63   https://www.warhistoryonline.com/history/true-story-charlie-wilsons-war.html

64   "Declassified files reveal Britain's secret support to Afghan Mujahideen," 30 Jan, 2018.   https://timesofislamabad.com/30-Jan-2018/declassified-files-reveal-britain-s-secret-support-to-afghan-mujahideen. Also see http://markcurtis.info/uk-declassified-documents/.

65   https://www.wikiwand.com/en/Al-Yamamah_arms_deal

66   "Saudi prince 'received arms cash'," BBC, 7 June 2007. http://news.bbc.co.uk/2/hi/business/6728773.stm

67   British Aerospace plc - Company Profile, Information, Business Description, History, Background Information on British Aerospace plc. https://www.referenceforbusiness.com/history2/5/British-Aerospace-plc.html

68   Daniel Hopsicker, *Welcome to Terrorland: Mohamed Atta & the 9-11 Cover-Up in Florida,"* Madcow Press, 2004, p. 268.

69   *Terrorland*, p. 269.

CHAPTER FOURTEEN

SPOOKS DON'T FLY SOUTHWEST

As the logistics man for Wexner, Epstein arranged the arrival of South-
ern Air Transport (SAT) to Rickenbacker Air Force Base in Columbus,
Ohio. The airline, formerly Air America, was infamous as an illegal
gun- and drug-running operation. SAT filed for bankruptcy in Colum-
bus on October 1, 1998, the same day the Central Intelligence Agency
Inspector General issued a report linking the cargo hauler to allegations
of drug-running in connection with U.S.-backed Contra rebels in Nica-
ragua in the 1980s.

– Bob Fitrakis, "Jeffrey Epstein:
There's Much More to the Story," 2020[1]

The first dozen or so chapters of *Gangster Planet* tell the story of CIA-pedigreed drug planes I spent a big chunk of my life researching. Telling that story was personal for me. Don't ask me why. I don't have an answer. It just was. My search gave me a reason to get up every day and at the same time, it kept me from sleeping.

Everyone who knows that feeling of obsession is blessed.

Simultaneously, it's a curse to find a question that nags you so much you can't move on until it's answered. People all around you don't see the world you live in. In Florida, life is about fun and sun. They don't get it. They don't even want to get it. They hate being woke to the world as it really is.

In 2005, it was estimated that the global trade of illegal drugs topped over $400 billion dollars, or roughly the same amount that is spent on food.

Drug trafficking is the most widespread and lucrative organized crime activity in the US, accounting for an estimated 40% of their business.

In 2006, the estimated street value of cocaine seized by the United States Coast Guard was estimated at $3.1 billion dollars. Who knows what it is today, with inflation and all?

"One Big Goddam Masked Ball"

General and business aviation – the method of choice for the transportation of illegal drugs – *should* mean that aircraft ownership, acquisition and registration records are the best means of identifying the traffickers. But, surprisingly, the government knows a lot more about who owns automobiles than it does about who owns multi-million-dollar aircraft that can transport multi-ton loads of cocaine.

Automobiles are registered within the county where the owner lives, but because airplanes can move around with such great speed, and possibly because there are fewer of them than there are cars, aircraft owned by U.S. residents and companies are all registered in one place – the Federal Aviation Administration.

The FAA's commitment to combating illegal activities is, however, often questioned. Its registration procedures are lax and riddled with loopholes that you could fly a DC-9 through. This is not by accident, but by design.

Meaning: the government wants things that way.

Why would that be? Perhaps because general aviation is crucial to the government's covert activities, most of which involve moving things in and out of countries without being detected. The best way to do that is by using planes. People, money, passports, weapons, drugs, and diamonds.

At the tiny Venice Airport, for example, there are no prying eyes in the control tower. Because there isn't a control tower. Jets fly in and out at all hours of the day and night, and there's nothing but 400 miles of water between Venice and Mexico's Yucatan peninsula.

A frustrated-beyond-disillusionment state cop in Arkansas once asked rhetorically, "What do you do when you find out that the biggest drug smuggler in the country… is the country?"

Even today, most Americans probably believe the Securities and Exchange Commission – to cite an example that bleeds untold billions from Americans through the simple expedient of looking the other way – referees the markets like a line judge in football, watching for a foot stepping out of bounds on a kick-off return.

A long-time pilot – let's call him Nick – in Florida said angrily, "The field of general aviation is one big goddamn masked ball. The FAA's job is to create doubt about the provenance of any American-registered airplane threatening to become a part of the current unpleasantness. Everybody knows the best way to be shady is in a plane. Not a commercial plane, though, right?"

Nick sneers. "Spooks don't fly Southwest."

211

The Whittingtons and World Jet

Start with World Jet, in Fort Lauderdale, once owned by the Whittington brothers – Don and Bill – notorious drug smugglers who in their heyday during the early '80s commanded fleets of fishing trawlers, sailboats, cigarette boats, and jets.

Tons of marijuana, and oceans of cash, flowed freely from the World Jet hangers at Fort Lauderdale Executive Airport through the streets and canals of Fort Lauderdale.

When federal indictments put the Whittington Brothers out of the game, their prized Learjet – at that time still something of a rarity – was "sold" to Barry Seal, soon to be the biggest drug smuggler in American history.

Was this just coincidence? Or was that one of a series of vital clues to a vast but hidden, and still-unnamed, global network? The global financial network Prime Minister Tony Blair said had financed terrorists who pulled off 9/11, perhaps?

* * *

Hilliard's Lear jet was carrying what is known in the drug trade as "heavy weight." In fact, it was the largest heroin seizure ever in Central Florida, said the *Orlando Sentinel*. And although Hilliard had purchased the Lear less than a year before, it had already made thirty-nine weekly runs down and back to Venezuela, the pilot admitted to the DEA. So even though Hilliard lost his plane through seizure, he undoubtedly got his use out of it.

While we're not experts on heroin trafficking, we figured that 43 pounds for one haul was a little steep for an individual. We figured that much dope no doubt belonged to an organization, a drug trafficking organization.

Wally Hilliard – Part of an Elite Network

We suspected, in fact, that the transfer to Hilliard of the Learjet before it was confiscated was not by accident. It was, instead, an exchange of assets within the organization.

And sure enough…when we looked up the previous owner of Hilliard's Lear jet, we discovered a name we had already run across during research for *Barry & 'the boys'* The man who owned the Learjet that ended up in Wally Hilliard's hands was an avid pilot and auto racer named Gary Levitz.

Old people still remember TV ads for a nationwide furniture chain from the 70s featuring a mindless jingle with a stupid but memorable chorus – "You'll Love It at Levitz" – that, once it got in your head, it seemed you could never get it out. You'd have to have that jingle surgically removed.

Wally Hilliard got Gary Levitz' Lear because Levitz didn't need it anymore. He was dead.

Levitz fatally flew into a pylon during the National Championship Air Races in Reno, Nevada in 1999, crashing his souped-up P-51 Mustang. It wasn't the first time such a thing had happened at Reno, as we'll see later.

CIA Tell #1 – Good PR

If you're taking notes, this is a "CIA tell." They are scattered throughout the book. Guys who are "connected" always get great PR. It must be a corporate benefit.

"Gary was a pretty amazing man," one of his managers told reporters. "He was a larger-than-life character. He would run the company day to day, and he flew warplanes and was a big-game hunter."

Big-game hunter. Flying warplanes. Guys like that used to be called – in more innocent times – "soldiers of fortune."

What Gary Levitz also was... was a big-time drug smuggler, at least by '70s standards. His brother, Mark Levitz, turned him in so he could get out of working for the Nicodemo D. "Little Nicky" Scarfo gang in 1986.[2] He'd already been convicted of money laundering, admitting in court to "helping the Whittingtons disguise narcotics profits by investing in legitimate business ventures." [3]

Twenty years later, the Whittington brothers will be selling a Learjet – which is soon busted – to Wally Hilliard. Is this the Great Circle of Life, or just another Day at the Office … if you need to work off a beef for the Feds?

Hilliard's purchase of Gary Levitz's Lear, after Levitz's death, from the Whittington Brothers – whose own Lear, when they went into "timeout" had been purchased two decades earlier by Barry Seal – can be seen as the work-a-day machinations of a secretive global organization at work… Perhaps unsurprisingly, Gary Levitz had also been in business with people at the Venice Airport.

"Ben Bradley's a DEA informant at the Venice Airport," said Coy Jacob, owner of a Mooney dealership there, and no friend of Bradley, who, he said, "set people up in Fort Lauderdale. Gary Levitz got into the drug trade, then rolled on the Whittingtons. So did Ben Bradley. When his life was threatened, he moved to Polk County, and moored his boat in Venice."[4]

And the man who *sold* Gary Levitz his P-51 warbird air-racer, which he crashed at the air races in Reno in 1976?

His name was Kenneth G. Burnstine from Fort Lauderdale, Florida, a city which is famous for a lot more than inventing Spring Break. By the time I'd learned about Kenny Burnstine, I then knew for a fact that the field of general aviation operates with no effective adult supervision.

After more than two decades of specializing in an arcane area – drug trafficking through Florida – I'd just realized there was a whole other drug kingpin I'd never heard of. Either that, or I'd forgotten everything I'd learned – which was even worse.

What I knew about my chosen subject still didn't amount to much. Maybe all the information keeps leaking out, or maybe they keep changing the rules without telling us. On any given day, there are dozens – hundreds? – of pilots flying drugs or laundered money around the world. We just can't seem to keep up.

OFFSHORE AVIATION TRUSTS

During the Iraq War under President George W. Bush, Houston was home to three general aviation charter companies flying extraordinary renditions for the CIA, a fact I only discovered while investigating the ownership of the luxury jets which ferried Saudi Royals out of Las Vegas and Lexington, Kentucky, six days after the 9/11 attack.

Houston is also home to another aviation company that has become crucial in keeping the names of plane owners secret – Aircraft Guaranty Holdings & Trust of Houston – founded in 1997 by a Lieutenant Colonel (retired) in the Army named Connie L. Wood, formerly a senior FAA official. Despite its tiny size, his company, Aircraft Guaranty, was the registered "owner" of more than six hundred American aircraft. "Offshore Aviation Trust" was his brainchild. The legality of getting around disguising a plane's ownership is set out in a brief history which rationalizes the act.[5]

According to the Transportation Code, "only aircraft owners who are citizens of the United States are permitted to register an aircraft," the writer tells us. The shareholders of a publicly traded entity (such as a U.S. airline) are constantly changing as its stock is traded. It's therefore impossible at any given moment to know if the shareholders are citizens, so the public airline corporation does not *technically* qualify to be registered. See the legal conundrum here?

The FAA made a decision in the '70s to allow a corporation to register if "non-US citizen beneficiaries [do] not have more than 25% interest in the aircraft." The FAA extended the regulations later to allow registration of aircraft owned by a trustee.

Lawyers do this type of thing all the time for clients with money and/or power, preferably both.

Aircraft Guaranty first achieved notoriety during the Iraq War when plane-spotters began noticing the company "owned" a large number of planes being used in CIA "extraordinary renditions." They also saw American Guaranty Holdings planes downed in Central and South America plane crashes or drug busts.... Or, more likely, plane crashes followed by drug busts.

The ownership became progressively less certain once Aircraft Guaranty took title to them.

> "According to the Federal Aviation Agency in the United States, the aircraft is owned by Aircraft Guaranty Holdings & Trust of Houston," The *Miami Herald* reported about a Venezuelan co-founder of Smartmatic voting systems based in Boca Raton, who died when his plane crashed into a house near Caracas airport in 2008.[6]

Well, not exactly. The downed plane was merely registered to Aircraft Guaranty, possibly a proprietary company whose job was to deliberately disguise ownership of planes into the wider world of general aviation – by holding title in trust for the real, unidentifiable, owner – often the CIA.

The process is called sheep dipping, after the practice of bathing sheep before they are sheared. This leaves unanswered the question, "Who's getting sheared in this process?"

The term is commonly used for disguising a spy's identity with a day job. The agent – or airplane – is cleaned up, and subtly altered, so that nobody knows where he's been.

Instead of laundering money, they're laundering protoplasm. The military even brags about it.[7] Plausible deniability (or lying) is considered a good thing.

It's "a boon for well-heeled U.S. owners seeking personal liability protection and ownership anonymity," Lt. Gen. Wood told "*Mooney Pilot,* an aviation magazine.[8]

"Soon," he predicted, "full FAA-approved and legal Off-Shore (as in the Cayman Islands) Aviation Trusts will be *the* way most liability conscious and financially established owner/pilots to take title to their aircraft... It promises to be far better than a typical corporate entity in protecting the beneficiary from personal liability exposure."[9]

He was touting "licenses to non-residents outside the U.S. without the applicant ever entering the U.S.," but claimed his "team of attorneys" were well-versed in all the U.S. laws to protect individuals behind the entities his company would set up.

Real world examples were strewn across the aviation landscape, not the least of which was the fact that Aircraft Guaranty "owned" a Lear Jet (N35NK) – that was previously registered to Huffman Aviation flight school owner Wally Hilliard's aviation charter company "Plane 1 Leasing." The Lear made frequent flights to Rum Cay in the Bahamas, a sleepy little isle which suddenly was drawn into Big-Time Drug Trafficking when work was completed on Rum Cay's new 5000-foot runway – that could take medium jets.[10]

After Hilliard was charged in 2004 for flying unauthorized flights for unspecified "Saudis," he sold the Lear to Aircraft Guaranty, which used it on flights into and out of Guantanamo. It became briefly famous after a plane-spotter snapped its picture during a rendition flight in Portugal.[11]

It also regularly flew into Caribbean hot spots that were known drug transfer points: Venice, Florida; Treasure Cay, San Salvador; Marsh Harbor in the Bahamas, St. Maarten, the Netherlands Antilles, and Toluca, Mexico. Toluca was the ultimate hot spot at that time because the Mexican government controlled the airport. Toluca was, you may recall, where the DC-9 in the Yucatan with 5.5 tons of coke was supposed to be off-loaded.

None of this is an accident.

BILL PAWLEY'S EXCELLENT ADVENTURE

William Douglas (Bill) Pawley, at 32 years of age, had already enjoyed more adventure than most men ever see.

Born in South Carolina in 1896 to an eighth-generation South Carolinian father, Pawley had few if any ancestors who'd ever lived anywhere else after arriving on colonial soil. Bill's dad, notwithstanding bankrupting his cotton business by short-selling cotton futures, moved his family to a small island near Guantánamo, Cuba in 1903, soon after the U.S. had signed a treaty with Spain that gave us the Spanish colonies of Cuba and the Philippines.

E.P.'s contract to supply the naval base with a variety of commodities came with his designation as consul at Guantánamo, but in 1910 his business license was revoked on a technicality. He had to move again – 200 miles southeast to Port-Au-Prince, Haiti.

Bill and his brother E.P., Jr., four years younger, were sent to Gordon Institute's military academy (equivalent to high school) in Barnesville, Georgia, but it's not clear whether he graduated. The highest level of education he received was the time he spent there. He seems instead to have dropped out in favor of forming a trading business in Venezuela.[12]

Nevertheless, he was in Georgia when he registered for WWI in 1918, claiming to be self-employed at age 22, but he did not enlist, nor was he drafted.

Pawley instead married Annie Dobbs from Marietta, Georgia a year later, and after living briefly in Quebec as a gold miner and in Delaware in the milk and tire business, he lived in Atlanta for a while before deciding to become a land developer in Florida during its big boom.

Hosting a huge party at Coral Gables Country Club in 1925 for his 29th birthday, according to his biographer, Anthony R. Carrozza: "He announced his retirement at the party, but 'they begged me to stay until January 1st.' His decision turned out to be costly because within four months the boom market bottomed out and Pawley lost $800,000."[13]

Three lean years from that point to the time he was hired by the "Glenn Curtiss interests" did not daunt his enthusiasm. He began promoting air races in Miami as a sideline to buying airfields and starting flying schools in 1928 for Clement Keys, who had bought out Glenn Curtiss in 1920.

After opening a municipal airport that would grow into Miami International, he flew to Washington D.C. to convince top military brass to send air race teams to the air show to dedicate the airport the following January.

Much of the story that follows alternates between sublime adventure and mundane and tedious recitation of detail. I caution the reader not to ignore the mundane. Therein lies the answer to the riddle of how things really work. Pay close attention to the math and the legalese.

It's the four-eyed accountants and lawyers who do the dirty work of hiding things in plain sight while all the spectators are watching flying trapezers and sexy pilots doing nose-dives.

ANNUAL AIR SHOW IN MIAMI

The first ever Miami Air Races were in January 1929 and became an annual event thereafter. Pawley, who tried to return to Miami for each race after the one he organized in 1929, had "missed the 1933 and 1934 shows," Carrozza wrote.

"At the January 1935 air show, however, when Capt. Claire Lee Chennault led his 'Men on a Flying Trapeze' trio of acrobatic fliers in a spectacular performance," Pawley had made a point to attend, bringing guests from China along.[14]

"Meeting the army aviator after the show, Pawley began a relationship with Chennault that lasted for years," Carrozza continued. "Stormy and contemptuous, they were often at odds with each other, but together they were to achieve a shining moment in U.S. military aviation history."[15]

Whether "shining" or not, it was indeed an historic moment. It was, in fact, that introduction which would rescue Chennault from an embarrassing early retirement two years later.

Intercontinent Aviation in Cuba and China

Before his auspicious meeting with Chennault, Pawley found himself in 1929 bidding against 27 others for the contract to carry mail between Havana and Santiago. Fulfilling the terms was less easy. Pawley moved back to Cuba where he had spent the first decade or so of his life, and he spent the next three years constructing an airport, expanding the airline from one route to eleven, and flying mail between fourteen airports – all by 1932.

Clement Keys had earned his first air-mail contract in 1925 (New York to Chicago), and, determined to build a worldwide mail distribution network, he hired Bill Pawley three years later to create mail routes inside Cuba. Keys had arranged $10 million in financing in 1928 through Dillon, Read & Co., whose attorneys set up Intercontinent Aviation, Inc. as a subsidiary under the Curtiss corporate umbrella[16].

Pawley's business in Cuba was a sub-subsidiary called Companie Nacional Cubana Curtiss. Like a game of hide-the-pea, the umbrella seemed to keep moving. Who knew where the pea would end up?

Keys had to build his own airfields in China and provide his own planes at great expense, but "on October 21 China Airways at last was able to open service. Three days later came Black Thursday. All stocks fell, but aircraft stocks nose-dived. Curtiss-Wright stock value dropped to $106 million.... Keys, his fortune nearly wiped out by the stock-market crash, relinquished control of Curtiss-Wright."[17]

When Pawley traveled to China in 1933 for the first time, negotiations were ongoing between North American and Juan Trippe of Pan Am, the proposed buyer of Curtiss-Wright stock. Once a price was agreed to, attorneys for the banker – Dillon, Read & Co. – drafted documents to give

SPOOKS DON'T FLY SOUTHWEST

Pan Am 50,000 shares of Intercontinent. CNAC, Intercontinent's new subsidiary, was paid 3,000 shares of Pan Am stock.

Intercontinent's Cuban subsidiary (Cubana Curtiss) had just been sold by Pawley's apparent boss when he returned from Cuba to Florida. In January 1933 he headed off to China to sell airplanes on commission to the Chinese government.

A small item on page four of the *Miami News* announced in September that in those nine months, he'd sold 36 planes. The next time he went to China he had a different mission. Not simply to sell existing American aircraft made in America, Pawley's task was to build and operate factories at the site of where Chinese pilots would be trained.

Under the name CAMCO – Central Aircraft Manufacturing Co. – Pawley and at least three of his brothers and one or more of his sons worked to establish these factories. Because China was at war with Japan all through the '30s, they had to keep moving the factory to safer locations. The last plant was built in India, close to the location where the Flying Tigers would take off to fly over the Hump to supply the Nationalist Chinese flyers.[18]

China National Aviation Corp.'s job was to carry mail, and initially its stock was wholly owned by the Nationalist Chinese government, according to Chinese law. Pawley's job was to provide an airport and planes for their operation and to supervise pilot training. That's what he'd brought Chennault in for, but the two men were often at odds because of their perspectives on how to do the work.

CHINA LOBBY'S FAVORED SOONG SISTERS

When Pawley arrived in China and met the finance minister, H.H. Kung, it was only the first of many introductions to members of the nepotistic Chinese government. The whole family was involved – as blatantly as Trump's kids and spouses would be in his administration.

Kung introduced him to Madame (Mei-ling) Chiang, wife of Generalissimo Chiang Kai-shek. Kung was married to Madame's sister. The sisters were daughters of Charlie Soong, the first of a long line of American-educated members of the Soong family.

Historian Sterling Seagrave, who grew up as the son of a missionary surgeon on the Burma Road, wrote several important books on China's history. *The Soong Dynasty* gives an inside peek at "Charlie" Soong, an 1885 graduate of then-Methodist-affiliated Vanderbilt in Tennessee.

Soong studied two years at Trinity College in North Carolina, living with the family of Julian Carr, the face of "Bull Durham" tobacco, sold in 1898 to the American Tobacco Company for a small fortune. A staunch Methodist, his money had helped found Duke University, and his network helped in bringing Charlie's six children to universities in the United States.

Seagrave's description of the grifting Soongs gives us insight into the reality of what was happening in those days as the Luce Press, a major part of the "China Lobby," perpetually whipped up anti-Japanese propaganda in support of trade with the Chinese, seen as more amenable to Christianity than their communist counterparts.

In 1938 Mei-ling Soong, a graduate of Wellesley, and her husband were announced as *Time's* Man & Wife of 1937: "Today Generalissimo & Mme Chiang have not conceded China's defeat, they long ago announced that their program for as many years as necessary will be to harass, exhaust and eventually ruin Japan by guerrilla warfare. If Generalissimo Chiang can achieve it, he may emerge Asia's Man of the Century...

> Her brother, Mr. T.V. Soong, today China's greatest financier, informed General Chiang as courteously as possible that a husband with concubines was scarcely acceptable as a suitor in the Chinese Christian family of Soong. Mei-ling's father, famed "Old Charlie" Soong, had made his fortune as a pioneer in printing and selling Bibles to Chinese as fast as the missionaries created a demand. Investing his profits at about 40% Chinese interest, he died a merchant prince.
>
> Old Mrs. Soong had not forgotten that her late husband had tumbled another of her daughters unceremoniously into the arms of old Dr. Sun Yat-sen (who also had another wife at the time) and that the marriage had been a master stroke for the House of Soong. Venerable Mother Soong therefore told General Chiang that if he would become a Christian, he could marry her attractive, Wellesley-graduated Mei-ling. The Conqueror replied that he would not adopt a new religion merely to win a bride, but that if Miss Soong would marry him, he would agree to study Christianity, and then do as he saw fit.
>
> No ordained Christian pastor could be found who thought General Chiang free to marry Miss Soong, so a lay Y.M.C.A. secretary united them in holy matrimony. From the day General Chiang thus took his No. 2 wife, both his character and his fortunes rapidly commenced to take on a certain grandeur. Eventually he also became a Christian.

Chiang Conquers All. The marriage of General Chiang was important because it made him the post-mortem brother-in-law of the Kuomintang's late sainted Sun; brother-in-law of Big Banker T.V. Soong; and brother-in-law of Dr. H.H. Kung, famed descendant of China's greatest sage Confucius, who also married a Soong girl.[19]

CHINESE AIR FORCE BEGINS AT MIAMI'S AIR RACES 1935

During Miami's seventh annual Air Races in January 1935, after their performance the three trapezers met with "Col. Mao Pang-chu, Chinese Air Force, along with several members of the Chinese Commission on Aeronautical Affairs, [who] attended the January show as Pawley's guests," according to Carrozza.[20]

> Pawley invited the trio to a party he hosted for the Chinese aboard his yacht in Miami harbor. Mao, impressed by their precision flying, offered all of them positions as flight instructors at the Hangchow aviation school. Williamson and McDonald declined because they hoped to receive U.S. Army Air Corps commissions, but after being passed over, both accepted and left for China in July 1936.[21]

When Chennault publicly applauded his "boys," in their endeavors in China, Army brass, not amused, transferred him from Alabama to Shreveport, Louisiana, in 1936, to await retirement. It didn't help that he was confined to a Louisiana hospital bed – suffering from low blood pressure, partial deafness, and chronic bronchitis.[22]

At the hospital Chennault received a letter from Lucius Roy Holbrook, Jr. offering him a three-month job – to evaluate, on behalf of the Chinese Commission of Aeronautical Affairs, the capabilities of the Chinese air force. Holbrook was then working for Pawley at CAMCO, as well as having a consulting contract with Kung, soon replaced by Madame Chiang.

CHENNAULT'S "RETIREMENT" OR NEW CAREER IN CHINA?

Chennault accepted the offer and immediately agreed to retire. In the meantime, a new offer came from Madame Chiang herself, who offered to put Chennault in charge of training Chinese pilots for the airline her husband had placed under her supervision.

Again, he did not hesitate. This was his big chance to rejoin Billy McDonald, one of the Trapezers from Maxwell Field, who had been hired in China two years earlier by William Pawley.

The two aviators arranged to meet at Chennault's last stop before reaching to take a quick tour around Japan, gathering whatever intelligence they could on the Japanese military, the KMT's enemy in the second Sino-Japanese war. McDonald, like Chennault, was understandably wary about entering Japan – essentially as a spy – and needed a cover story to prevent capture.[23]

What happened next is told in the book *Shadow Tigers* with a wideeyed innocence which subsequent events would seem to have made difficult to maintain. Their cover story was a version of the circus coming to town.

Drinking in a bar in Shanghai, McDonald had supposedly "ran into" an old fraternity brother, a guy who now was the manager of a circus troupe filled with Russian singers, Chinese jugglers, and from the Philippines, a trio called the Dixie Girls.[24]

And – what luck! The guy said the troupe was on its way to Japan for a few shows. And – way cooler even! – McDonald could come along, posing as the manager.

Chennault tagged along. After finishing up backstage, McDonald would slink away to meet with him, and pass along whatever intel he'd gathered. It was their idea of fun.

Holbrook met up with the men in Shanghai to escort Chennault to meet Madame Chiang at the French Concession in Shanghai, and from there to Hangchow. It was the summer of 1937, four and a half years before the United States was officially at war with Japan and bound by the Neutrality Act.

"While Chennault was evaluating the Chinese Air Force, Pawley was steadily becoming the main source of military aircraft for the Chinese," according to Carrozza. But Chennault was employed by the Chinese, and they were at war against what was then a superior power, Japan, with which we were legally neutral. Talk about sticky wickets!

Chennault's job was to train Chinese pilots in the 14th International Squadron all the tactics of flying he knew. That was as far as he could go. The problem was, according to Carrozza, that the "mercenaries channeled into the squadron seemed more interested in paychecks and the $1,000 bonus for every Japanese plane they downed than the honor of fighting for the defense of China."[25]

One would have thought if the Chinese really wanted capitalism to flourish in China, they would not have had to hire mercenaries, right? The truth was that only a small percentage of Chinese even considered economic systems at the time, and those were the ones who had been propagandized by Americans, either missionaries in China or in schools in the United States.

This mercenary Chinese squadron committed suicide in March 1938 when the idiots in charge left all their planes lined up, bomb-loaded the night before they were to make a raid. Before they could take off the next morning, there was a Japanese attack. It destroyed all their planes in one go. At that point, Pawley put his three brothers in charge of managing CAMCO.

The French, pressured by Japan, closed the Burma Road to war matériel, so Pawley hauled his shipments back to Haiphong and loaded it on ships to Rangoon, Burma. Factory crates were unloaded on the Burmese docks, reloaded onto railroad cars for a journey to Lashio. From there the crates were taken by barge and elephant to their final destination at CAMCO's new factory at Loiwing."[26]

Hundreds of Chinese workers at each factory site assembled each American plane from a kit Pawley purchased from American corporations with a 20% discount.

"In the three factories he operated in China, Pawley built and repaired $30 million worth of aircraft for the Chinese, resulting in profits as high as $1 million a year."[27]

AMERICAN FACTORIES IN CHINA

Pawley certainly didn't pass the discount on to the Chinese. That's true capitalism. Chennault and Pawley constantly argued over whether the planes his CAMCO factories put together met the manufacturer's specs. The State Department kept getting complaints that they hadn't been allowed to bid on the contract. Pawley's deal with Kung was called a "squeeze."

The solution to this problem wouldn't come for several years, as the U.S. inched closer to ending its neutrality with the Japanese. Chennault was getting letters and Christmas cards from pilots he'd worked with in the States. Elwyn Gibbon, "a former pilot with the Fourteenth International Squadron," sent him a card, to which Chennault replied: "write W.D. Pawley, Intercontinent Corporation, Hong Kong, for job as a pilot in a special squadron."[28]

The squadron began coming together as early as January 1940 by allowing the Chinese to purchase planes with credit established with American banks and obtain fifty Army and Navy pilots if the U.S. government allowed them to be recruited.

> Intercontinent would employ the pilots through a private contract with China "without any direct participation by the United States Government."[29]

CURRENCY STABILITY – AN ULTIMATE GOAL

It was not a simple negotiation process. China's finance minister, T. V. Soong, lobbied for *aid in a manner that wouldn't upset currency stability*, with help from FDR's assistants, Lauchlin Currie and Joe Alsop, a cousin in the press. Thomas "Tommy the Cork" Corcoran "would steer the Chinese minister through the quagmire of governmental policies...."[30]

> "Soong's initial request was for a $50 million credit against tungsten exports to purchase nonmilitary supplies and improve conditions along the Burma Road, a vital supply route to southwest China during the Japanese invasion. But when Soong met with Secretary Morgenthau on July 9, the ante was raised to $140 million in credit and Soong now wanted to purchase three hundred fighter planes and a hundred light bombers." By November Soong's request was upped to $200 million.[31]

The conduit for the money was Universal Trading Corporation, originally set up in 1938 to receive monies and credit from a loan processed between the RFC (Reconstruction Finance Corporation) and Soong's bank. It had been repaid by exports of metals from China to the U.S. Like Intercontinent Aviation, its headquarters was 30 Rockefeller Center. The president of Universal Trading was Archie Lochhead, the first head of the U.S. Exchange Stabilization Fund. Chennault's partner Whiting Willauer was secretary.[32]

* * *

By the time the terms of the contract were finalized, CAMCO had moved its plant from Yunnan to Rangoon in Burma. On April 15, 1941, Roosevelt signed a "secret, unlisted executive order" authorizing a private corporation holding a contract with a foreign government to hire U.S. military officers.[33] The contract was between the Chinese and CAMCO, and the officers they hired became the American Volunteer Group (AVG), better known as the Flying Tigers.

Whatever the source of the symbol – perhaps a Chinese proverb about "giving wings to the tiger" has been suggested – Disney Studio in Hollywood designed a logo of a winged Bengal tiger with outstretched claws which got promoted in *Time* magazine three weeks after the Pearl Harbor attack. That was when the United States went to war for real against Japan. After that there was no further need to worry about violating the Neutrality Act.

STICKY WICKETS AREN'T CRICKET

Juan Trippe himself answered only to his board of directors, chairman of which was Cornelius Vanderbilt "Sonny" Whitney, the largest investor from the time it was founded, who'd always been a director, along with America's other wealthiest men like William Rockefeller and William H. Vanderbilt – his first cousins.

Sonny's palatial home on Long Island, was at Old Westbury, almost next door to Poppy Bush's maternal grandfather, Bert Walker, a close friend of Sonny's dad, Harry Payne Whitney, and a banking partner of Democrat, Averell Harriman, and his Republican brother Roland Harriman.

When Sonny Whitney was 26, his father named him as his replacement director on numerous boards, including the Guaranty Trust. He did very little actual business, though he did play lot of polo, got married and divorced a few times. Things like that. Even got into the movie business with his cousin Jock.

Unfortunately for Juan Trippe and his fellow Pan Am board members – cousins Sonny and Jock Whitney, Sloan Colt, Bobby Lehman, E.O. McDonnell, FDR's first cousin Lyman Delano, and Sherman Fairchild, for example – on October 1, 1949, the Central People's Government of China proclaimed itself the *real* Chinese Government. To get Pan Am's investment back required a lawsuit and an appeal.

CNAC's Chinese president had absconded, quickly transferring his allegiance to the new Communist Government in Peking. He'd abandoned the Nationalist government of Chiang, which was even then being forced onto the most southern Chinese island of Formosa (Taiwan).

Chiang's government announced its new name and, at the same time, claimed to own the aircraft CNAC's president had handed over to the Reds. A tug of war ensued.

The cricket term "sticky wicket" indeed fit the situation. If you've ever watched a cricket match, you know the two plus years it took to reach a result was about average. The Supreme Court of Hong Kong, still a British colony at that time, in 1951 decided in favor of the Red Chinese.

CIVIL AIR TRANSPORT IN A PICKLE

Pan American Airways found itself temporarily in partnership with the Reds! While the appeal was pending, title to the aircraft was in limbo. A number of the aircraft had to be "pickled" in Hong Kong, placing CAT (Civil Air Transport) itself in a bit of a pickle. They couldn't use the pickled planes to deliver mail under the contract, and they were in desperate need of money. Truman's new CIA came to the rescue.

Documents transferring the ownership of CAT and its assets to the Central Intelligence Agency were drafted – but classified as secret – and not disclosed until after Watergate in the Church hearings of 1975. The first step, however, was in figuring out the value of the two Chinese squadrons, while factoring in the 20% interest Pan Am acquired in 1943 when it bought out the Curtiss-Wright interest in China Airways.

The negotiation process was discussed in Robert Daley's book about Juan Trippe:

> There was only one way for the Nationalist [Chinese] government, as majority stockholder, to unblock the airline's frozen dollar assets, and that was to buy out Pan American's 20 percent share. Negotiations began in November 1949 and lasted most of the month. T. V. Soong represented China; [William Langhorne] Bond and a company lawyer spoke for Pan American. Most negotiating sessions took place in Soong's luxuriously appointed apartment on Fifth Avenue overlooking Central Park.
>
> Bond had his instructions from Trippe. CNAC's assets had recently been appraised, and 20 percent of these assets came to just under $2 million. This was to be Bond's asking price. Soong's first firm offer was $1 million. Bond said he could not even take such an offer back to Trippe. After much haggling, Soong agreed on a purchase price of $1.25 million, adding, "Tell Mr. Trippe I wouldn't give that to him – not to anybody else in the world, Bondy, but you."[34]

The CIA officially took over the airline as a proprietary in a document signed November 1, 1949, agreeing to pay $1,200,000 each year to maintain it. Thomas G. "Tommy the Cork" Corcoran, who had been involved in all sorts of legal sleightof-hand since Franklin Roosevelt's first days in office, now got help in doing the legal work from Paul Helliwell, a Florida lawyer then in the OSS.[35]

The Miami lawyer would later go on to set up Southern Air Transport (SAT) and Air Asia as CIA proprietaries.

George Doole's Spook Airline

George Doole, who had been a civilian employee of PanAm for years, transferred over to CAT, which later became known as "Air America, Inc." In the aftermath of Church Committee revelations about the CIA's assassination and mind control programs, the Agency was under strong pressure to sell off the front companies used to hide their fleet of planes.

George Doole was just your average farm-bred boy in western Illinois until he graduated from the University of Illinois in Urbana. Born in 1909, a year already ushering in a new age of transportation technology – airways – he dreamed of making a new niche for air transport.

He received his sheepskin in general agricultural in 1932, at the same time he was awarded a commission in the Army Reserves, having been in ROTC. Though his dad's middle name was "Andrew," and George had a different middle name – Arntzen, his mother's maiden name – shown in his military records and on his gravestone, he was often known simply as G. A. Doole, Jr.

Eight months of regular pilot training during his senior year of college (likely at Randolph Field in San Antonio, Texas) qualified him for an additional four months of advanced pilot training at Kelly Army Air Corps base in San Antonio.

Designated as a flight cadet, Doole was technically a civilian when hired by Pan American Airways Corporation at the end of his advanced training, and he shipped off to Honolulu in October 1932. Pan Am was a private corporation, cooperating with the federal government toward a dual purpose – building a commercial transnational airline service that could be converted to military purposes in the event of war.

For income in the meantime, Pan Am's corporate directors would use contacts within the political power structure to gain concessions and contracts with the federal government – to ferry mail, materiel or even to transport charter passengers if needed. They agreed to convert to military use in event of war, a provision of the contract that enabled the company to be subsidized by the feds.

Doole was a mere grunt in the operation in those days, with assignments in Panama and Brownsville, Texas in addition to Hawaii. Pan Am flew only to certain countries in South America at first, leading up to its goal of expanding to China and the Far East.

Most of us never heard of Doole at all until 1975, when his name came up in Congressional House and Senate Reports after hearings had been held to investigate the CIA's aviation activities – and abuses – worldwide. By that time, Doole was the head of Air America, known by some as "Spook Air." How did Lt. George Doole rise to the top?

GEORGE DOOLE'S SECRET HISTORY

We've tracked his life to Hawaii in 1933, where generals, colonels and majors in the Army Air Corps got to spend their peacetime years right alongside admirals, captains, and commanders in the Navy. They all preferred to keep military use of airplanes within their own branch's control, though there was another more powerful force that wanted to create a separate air force with a separate leadership, which finally won out.

What the directors of Pan Am wanted was to use every funding stream possible to build up their commercial enterprise – including whatever income they could finagle from military connections. Between 1932 and 1936 a great many of those connections were enjoying life in the middle of the Pacific Ocean, building up Pearl Harbor and the Hickham air base, initially under Army control.

While making jaunts between San Francisco, Panama, and Honolulu, Doole found his way to Brownsville, Texas, where one of his Pan Am colleagues with a slightly higher rank than his was Henry C. Kristofferson – the father of later Rhodes Scholar and country pop musician, Kris – cohort of the legendary Willie Nelson and the Highwaymen.

In mid-November 1936 Doole was a member of a reserve unit designated as the 42nd Reserve Bombardment, which was being given $30,000 from the federal government to build a new hangar adjacent to an unused municipal airport in Brownsville, near the border with Mexico. Doole was then the communications officer, while Kristofferson was assistant engineering officer. Later that month both men were transferred to Panama.

From Panama their paths would separate. During war years Doole's status changed from reserve to active, as he served in the Air Force Transport Service in the India-China-Burma Theater. For several years Kristofferson would ferry executives of Saudi Aramco from place to place on Pan American Airways planes, even living in Saudi Arabia himself in 1962. We see his service as a model of how the plan's design worked for Doole as well.

In 1943-45 Doole was captain of a Pan Am plane, busily transporting Naval Air troops between New York and Ireland, Portugal, Bermuda, and Brazil. Brazil was a fueling stop on the way to the Far East Theater – Philippines, Kunming and Indochina – dominated by Claire Chennault's Flying Tigers and the OSS forces there.

There were many characters in our book who found themselves in that area during those same years, and we'll introduce them in subsequent chapters. Men like David Breed Lindsay, Sr. and Jr., Lucien Conein, Mitchell Livingston WerBell III. There may be others.

SLITHERING SNAKES HIDE IN PROPRIETARIES

Claire Chennault's CAT may have been the first CIA proprietary created, but it was far from the last one. Air America itself actually started
as two private companies founded by pilots trained to fight in World War
II and the Korean War. One of those pilots headed back home after the
war to McMinnville, Oregon, the home base for Evergreen Helicopters,
Inc. founded in 1959. It sustained its existence by doing contracts with
the U.S. Forest Service and Bureau of Land Management – fighting fires
and reseeding forests using helicopters.

Similarly, Intermountain Aviation leased space at a county-owned airport in Pinal County, Arizona, also contracting with federal agencies in
need of helicopters, in a desert area 90 miles southeast of Phoenix.

Marana, Arizona was a remote airbase which seemed to appear out
of an unbroken vista of cactus and tumbleweed. One journalist trying to
unravel the mystery of how the Agency hid, or "sheep-dipped," planes acquired by the CIA from early days through the Vietnam War thought he
found the key there in the desert.

The Watergate scandal opened up a Pandora's Box of covert activities
that had been going on for decades, so secret it shocked even hardened
members of Congress. Nixon's "smoking gun" tape – reminding the CIA
about the "whole Bay of Pigs thing," released shortly before he resigned in
1974 – gave Congress an excuse to investigate all sorts of covert intelligence
activities, just as the snakes began to slither into the brush for deeper cover.

So the CIA's new director told the public that, since there was no further
need for Air America, Southern Air Transport, Air Asia, and other CIA-
owned airlines, they would sell them off. What they didn't say is that they
would just modify the form of ownership and not disclose how it was done.

A decade later we got a closer look at that new form of sheep-dipping
when Eugene Hasenfus appeared out of nowhere in Nicaragua, claiming
to be working for the CIA. One more Congressional Report revealed not
only the new ways to hide intelligence agency ownership, but also how
funds can be disguised through Swiss banks and Caribbean entities.

William J. Casey, Stanley Sporkin, and William P. Barr, to name only three
lawyers, were there to give the Agency, as well as that era's Republican Administration, tips on how to extort funds from foreign nationals to fund an
illegal war. Barr has since stepped up to the plate every time the CIA needs
to have its man in place within a Republican White House. If you've read the
proceeding pages, however, you know it all began under Democrats.

The CIA is no respecter of parties.

When the Marana base was privatized in 1975, around the same time President Gerald Ford began building his retirement home in the same general area, top CIA aviation officers, including the Agency's legendary George A. Doole, Jr., "retired" and went to work there for the now-private Evergreen International – the company resulting from the merger of Evergreen Helicopters and Intermountain Aviation.

The CIA's far-flung aviation operations, which span the globe, would continue to be run from there. Thousands of airplanes sitting parked, waiting to be reactivated. Inside the largest hanger hangs a plaque dedicated to Doole, who died in 1985.

The subsequent privatization of government assets into private hands had the same result as it did when Russia began to privatize 15 years later. The aviation wing of American crony capitalism was born.

Soon retired Generals, like Richard Secord and John Singlaub, became instant corporate CEO's, running aircraft charter and aviation companies that continued doing the CIA's bidding.

Who's been doing their bidding ever since? Suffice it to say it's a bit murky at this time. As you read this, my work is done. I have, as Shakespeare said, "shuffled off this mortal coil."

The next generation must pick up where the boomers leave off.

All I have to leave you with is a clue. Reread the excerpt at the beginning of this chapter. Then start digging.

Hasta la vista, Baby.

Endnotes

1	Bob Fitrakis, "Jeffrey Epstein: There's Much More to the Story," *Columbus Free Press*, June 18, 2020. https://columbusfreepress.com/article/jeffrey-epstein-there%E2%80%99s-muchmore-story-2

2	Believe it or not, "Little Nicky" will be mentioned again later in connection with Donald Trump's associate, Leslie Greyling.

3	"WHITTINGTONS, LEVITZ PLEAD GUILTY, FORFEIT MILLIONS IN SMUG-GLING CASE," *South Florida Sun Sentinel*, March 15, 1986. https://www.sun-sentinel.com/1986/03/15/whittingtons-levitz-plead-guilty-forfeit-millions-in-smuggling-case/

4	Interview with author.

5	Tracey Cheek, "The History of Aircraft Trusts," March 28, 2018. https://agcorp.com/2018/03/the-history-of-aircraft-trusts/

6	Smartmatic had earlier merged with Sequoia Voting Systems, and it was regularly accused by the CIA of rigging elections. "Venezuela election bets on Florida voting machine," Tampa Bay Times, 20 Jul 2004, Page 31. Also see crash report in the *Miami Herald*, 01 May 2008, Page 29.

7	Blake Stilwell, "'Sheep Dipping' is the worst name for the military's best job," *We Are The Mighty Military News*, December 29, 2022. https://www.wearethemighty.com/mighty-culture/sheep-dipping/

8	Volume I Issue III December 2000 *Mooney Pilot* 39.

9	Ibid.

10	Daniel Hopsicker, "Terror Flight School Owner's Lear Flew Saudis on Unsupervised Flights, May 4, 2004. hlear-flew-saudis-on-unsupervised-flights/htion-flights

11	Anthony R. Carrozza, *William D. Pawley: The Extraordinary Life of the Adventurer, Entrepreneur, and Diplomat Who Cofounded the Flying Tigers* (Potomac Books 2012).

12	Ibid.

13	Ibid., (p. 14). Potomac Books. Kindle Edition.

14	Ibid.

15	Daley, Robert. *An American Saga Juan Trippe and his Pan Am Empire*. Riviera Productions Ltd.. Kindle Edition.

16	Ibid.

17	Carrozza, Anthony R. (p. 53). Potomac Books. Kindle Edition.

18	"Man & Wife of the Year," *Time* magazine, Monday, Jan. 03, 1938. https://content.time.com/time/subscriber/article/0,33009,847922-5,00.html

19	Carrozza, Anthony R. (p. 39). Potomac Books. Kindle Edition.

20	Carrozza, Anthony R. (p. 40). Potomac Books. Kindle Edition.

21	Carrozza, Anthony R (p. 38). Potomac Books. Kindle Edition.

22	Carrozza, Anthony R. (p. 42). Potomac Books. Kindle Edition.

23	William C McDonald III and Barbara L Evenson, *The Shadow Tiger: Billy McDonald, Wingman to Chennault* (July 24, 2016).

24	Carrozza, Anthony R. (p. 53). Potomac Books. Kindle Edition.

25	Carrozza, Anthony R. (p. 53). Potomac Books. Kindle Edition.

26	Carrozza, Anthony R (p. 54). Potomac Books. Kindle Edition.

27	Carrozza, Anthony R. (p. 61). Potomac Books. Kindle Edition.

28	Carrozza, Anthony R. (p. 62). Potomac Books. Kindle Edition.

29	Carrozza, Anthony R. (p. 64). Potomac Books. Kindle Edition.

30	Carrozza, Anthony R. (p. 64). Potomac Books. Kindle Edition.

31	Carrozza, Anthony R. (p. 70). Potomac Books. Kindle Edition.

32	Carrozza, Anthony R. (p. 81). Potomac Books. Kindle Edition.

33	Daley, Robert. *An American Saga Juan Trippe and his Pan Am Empire*. Riviera Productions Ltd. Kindle Edition.

34	Alfred T. Cox, "CIVIL AIR TRANSPORT (CAT): A PROPRIETARY AIRLINE," *Clandestine Services History*, April 1969. https://www.cia.gov/readingroom/docs/%28est%20pub%20 date%29%20 civil%20air%20%5B15503623%5D.pdf

CHAPTER FIFTEEN

THE BOSS HOGS OF SARASOTA COUNTY

> *I'm tired of being an object of the power-mad desire of David Lindsay. He controls this community.... He controls both political parties. He elects five out of five city commissioners and five out of five county commissioners. He affects 95 percent of the appointments. The reason he can't control this airport is simple. We don't run this airport the way we want to. We are controlled by state and federal governments.*
> – SRQ Airport Manager Richard Wolf (1978)

W hy Donald Trump's alt-right insurgency set up shop in Sarasota, Florida, may ultimately be unknowable. But there is at least one previous precedent for the operation: Arkansas, while Bill Clinton was Governor.

Sarasota County gave the alt-right what Mena, Arkansas gave to Clinton-era Democrats: total control, and the ability to enforce the level of secrecy needed to allow drug trafficking and money laundering operations to flourish.

It's all about one-party rule.

Under Steve Bannon, Trump's alt-right team was able to slip into a Republican stronghold and get down to the business of the accumulation of capital.

One of America's finest financial journalists, Christopher Byron, called the series of blatant and brazen stock frauds executed in Sarasota a "swindle-romp." Byron died several years ago; I don't know what he would have called the blatant drug trafficking.

THE PLAYERS ALL KNOW EACH OTHER

I t's been twenty years since a retired US Customs Agent who tracked Barry Seal from Customs' Intelligence Center in El Paso gave me a "heads up" about something that's resonated ever since with facts on the ground as I've found them.

During a long lunch over crawfish etouffee in Abbeville, Louisiana, he gave me a short course on arcane relationships – those which are mysterious or secret, known, or knowable to only a few.

How had CIA pilot Barry Seal from Baton Rouge, I asked him, come to know rancher Richmond Harper from tiny Eagle Pass, Texas, hundreds of miles away?

See, Harper had supplied Seal with seven tons of plastic explosives that he'd flown to Mexico on a U.S. government surplus DC-4 and delivered to certain Mexican Generals, in exchange for heroin Seal then flew back to the States.

With a tight smile, the Customs Agent replied, "There aren't that many players out there. They all pretty much know each other."

There's no place in the world where those words ring truer than Sarasota, Florida. There's always been something slightly weird about Sarasota, in a different sense than Austin and Portland are weird.

In all the world, there's only one Sarasota. Nobody knows where the word came from, or even what it's supposed to mean. There aren't many places like that.

Still, there are any number of red state strongholds that Trump's minions could have chosen. Is it mere coincidence they picked Sarasota because it was where the long and influential careers of two men crossed, like Longfellow's two ships passing in the night? Two men whose actions have shaped – or warped – the area to this day.

One of them, General Claire Chennault, led the swashbuckling Flying Tigers in World War II, trying to keep China from being swallowed up by the Japanese.

The second man – actually, it isn't one man, but a father-son team – was David Breed Lindsay Sr. and his son, David Breed Lindsay Jr., successive publishers of the *Sarasota Herald-Tribune*. The name Lindsay was a dynasty that ruled Sarasota County with an iron fist for decades.

The Lindsays were the "Boss Hogs" of Sarasota County.

At first, all I knew about the Lindsays was what I read in the newspapers. Correction: in his newspaper. It includes doing unique service during WWII.

David Senior's interest in Asia never diminished. After WWII, he and his third wife took a private plane from Sarasota to San Francisco to begin a month-long cruise to the Far East aboard the USS *President Cleveland*. The former Isabel Dickinson Maltby, like David Sr., had been married twice before. Her previous husband, John L. Tallman, headed Curtis Publishing's advertising department, more commonly recognized as the *Saturday Evening Post*.

Lindsay's first marriage to Helen Carter Dodson, David Jr.'s mother, had taken place in North Carolina in December 1921, seven months after he'd bought the *Fayetteville Observer*, his first newspaper. That's where he settled first after being a pilot in World War I, not that far from Morris Field.

Lindsay's son, David B. Lindsay Jr., became unofficially known as the "Godfather of Sarasota County." He created a key component – a docile local press – that covert operations need to run smoothly and without friction with the local populace. Or rather, he maintained it. The previous publisher and owner, his father, David Breed Lindsay, Sr., should probably be credited with creating it.

They were accused of controlling the entire county – both political parties. Not many bosses can make a claim to such a broad reach.

Lindsay Senior first came to Florida as a pilot in World War I, but he married a North Carolina native while stationed there, only later convincing her to move to Sarasota. According to the December 18, 1942, *Sarasota Herald-Tribune*, Major David Lindsay Sr. had been "assigned to duties abroad" and would be "debarking soon, before the end of the year."

I don't recall ever seeing someone "debark." Being "assigned to duties abroad" also seems a tad vague. It had a "you're not cleared for that information" kind of vibe.

After we did some digging, the picture began to clear up. The David Lindsays – both father and son – spent World War II serving in the same place. Where was that place? The same place that the OSS and General Claire Chennault and his Flying Tigers were based: Kunming, China.

Kunming was the center of opium and heroin trafficking for the Nationalist Chinese, which was how Chiang Kai-shek financed his war with the Japanese before the Communists took over the mainland. Then it financed the Nationalists' war against the Red Chinese.

As it happens, in China David Lindsay Sr. was a top aide to General Claire Chennault of the famous Flying Tigers, according to the obituary that appeared in the *Bradenton Herald* without a byline.

> At the outbreak of World War II, Lindsay, although in his 50s, again volunteered for active duty as a major in aviation. He served two years with Maj. Claire L. Chennault's Eighth Air Force in China, returning with the rank of lieutenant colonel. His last assignment was as base commander at Kunwing [sic] Air Base at the terminus of the "Hump" supply route from India.[1]

Chenault has, as we wrote elsewhere, also been repeatedly identified as the man responsible for America's first big leap into the illegal drug trade, by creating the country's first officially sanctioned drug trafficking pipeline at Kunming.

And David Lindsay, Sr., from little ol' Sarasota, Florida, ran the base.

THE LINDSAYS OF KUNMING

In a travel essay called "China Sojourn," Christopher Ryan wrote about Kunming, where David Lindsay Sr. had once commanded base operations without any mention that his boss had been involved.[2]

> Surrounded by scenic mountains, Kunming, at 6,200 feet, is nick-named 'the city of eternal spring' for its almost year-round pleasant weather. In World War II this intriguing city was headquarters for Gen. Claire Chennault's Flying Tigers.
>
> It is a city of contrasts, with a dark side, where illegal drugs stain the memory of the folklore hero.[3]

Robert Schriebman described Kunming less poetically: "The covert U.S. effort in China 'makes the Iran-Contra affair look like a small-scale operation.'"[4]

Chinese fliers even trained at the airport in Sarasota, at the airport thirty miles south in Venice, FL, then known as Venice Army Airfield, and at the airport in St. Petersburg, Florida, known as Pinellas Army Airfield, which today is the Clearwater-St Petersburg International Airport. The same one where the drug-carrying planes described in the first part of this book originated.

Was it just coincidental that Morris Field in North Carolina, 130 miles from Fayetteville, would be selected in 1942 as the first location for the 337th Air Fighter Group?

The group's second home would be Drew Field (now St. Pete-Clearwater or PIE) before the 337th moved to the airport north of Sarasota (now called SRQ). It was announced the group would be moving to Venice, but seems to have been mysteriously terminated.

When the 337th ended its service in Portland, Oregon in 1966, was it secretly rolled into the newly formed Portland-based Pacific Corporation, a holding company for CIA drug running proprietaries? We have not been able to confirm that. Such information remains classified. It cannot be just a coincidence that all three airports have extensive subsequent histories of involvement in drug trafficking. Also, at all three air bases, there was much talk of the war in Asia.

"Venice Soldiers to Hear of War in China" was the *Herald-Tribune* headline on November 5, 1944, where a veteran of the "China-Burma-India theater" spoke about "knocking out Jap shipping and locomotives and harassing Jap convoys on the Burma Road."

I came across that newsclip because I had been investigating the year-long activities in Florida of the terrorist hijackers for my book *Welcome to TerrorLand*. Mohamed Atta learned to fly in Venice, and I eventually discovered a pattern of covert activity at the Venice Municipal Airport that remained remarkably consistent over six decades. It also has ties to the airports where the 337th was stationed.

CHINESE PILOTS AT DREW FIELD

General Chennault's ghost-like presence seemed especially strong at Clearwater-St. Pete-International Airport, formerly Drew Field. Because that airport had been mentioned repeatedly in the news as the origin of drug smuggling, I wanted to view the location with my own eyes.

What I saw was a glorification of an army aviator who had been on the ground floor of a habit that seemed impossible to end.

It was well worth the trip. Once I found myself inside the terminal and on the second floor, I immediately saw a wall devoted to celebrating the airport's roots, as far back as when it was known as Drew Field.

I've since looked for a reference online to the exhibit with no success, so it's fortuitous I went when I did. Someone seems to have since tossed the exhibit into Orwell's "memory hole."

Bold professional graphics heralded the Flying Tigers of the American Volunteer Group (AVG), "a band of American pilots who literally built an air force from scratch," while training in St Petersburg.[5]

There were other news reports saying much the same thing about the presence in SW Florida of Chennault's Flying Tigers. One, datelined "Tampa," with the headline "**CHINESE MEMBERS OF FLYING TIGERS ARE NATURALIZED**," reported that, as the war ended, nineteen Chinese members of the Flying Tigers were supposed to take part in a naturalization ceremony in Venice, until it was called off at the last minute because the Chinese pilots couldn't prove they'd legally entered the U.S.

> Officials at the Venice Air Base planned to send the group to Cuba, the shortest distance to a foreign country, before they could re-enter, but when they arrived in Miami a hurricane sweeping up the Atlantic grounded planes, and they returned to Venice, where they were packed into planes and flown to Windsor, Ontario, across from Detroit, then brought back to apply for legal entry in Detroit.[6]

OPEN SECRETS

After my visit to the Clearwater -St Pete International Airport, where the Skyway planes and Donna Blue had once been parked inside hangars, I knew more about the scandal I was investigating. No wonder that airport had been chosen to fly drugs.

The Mexican Attorney General's Office in 2007 had traced drug money used to purchase Cocaine One to a major money laundering conduit between Mexican drug traffickers and American banks – notably Wachovia, then America's fourth largest bank, headquartered in North Carolina, of all places.[7]

The *Guardian* claimed they had found something new when they reported the same information in 2011.

> Mexican soldiers, waiting to intercept it, found 128 cases packed with 5.7 tons of cocaine, valued at $100m. But something else – more important and far-reaching – was discovered in the paper trail behind the purchase of the plane by the Sinaloa narco-trafficking cartel.
>
> During a 22-month investigation by agents from the US Drug Enforcement Administration, the Internal Revenue Service and others, it emerged that the cocaine smugglers had bought the plane with money they had laundered through one of the biggest banks in the United States: Wachovia, now part of the giant Wells Fargo. "The authorities uncovered billions of dollars in wire transfers, traveller's cheques and cash shipments through Mexican exchanges into Wachovia accounts. Wachovia was put under immediate investigation for failing to maintain an effective anti-money laundering programme. Of special significance was that the period concerned began in 2004, which coincided with the first escalation of violence along the US-Mexico border that ignited the current drugs war...
>
> José Luis Marmolejo, who prosecuted those running one of the casas de cambio at the Mexican end, said: "Wachovia handled all the transfers. They never reported any as suspicious. [8]
>
> Investigators settled on Wachovia – located in Charlotte, North Carolina – because much of the information the bank had reported about large volume customers was deficient. Martin Woods worked at the London office of Wachovia Bank in February 2005, hired as a senior anti-money laundering officer, and he began to notice and report the abnormalities of the deposits from Mexico.
>
> Woods identified a number of suspicious transactions relating to *casas de cambio* [CDC] customers in Mexico by August 2006,

237

six months or so after the DC-9 was seized in Ciudad del Carmen. According to Woods, the deposits primarily involved "traveller's cheques in euros. They had sequential numbers and deposited larger amounts of money than any innocent travelling person would need, with inadequate or no KYC [know your customer] information on them and what seemed to a trained eye to be dubious signatures.[9]

Woods sent the information from London back to Wachovia headquarters in Charlotte, N.C., and, as a result, almost lost his job and his mind. But he didn't quit. He had fortuitously shared the information with American drug enforcement personnel at a conference, and they also began investigating the bank as early as 2005.

"Through CDCs," said the court document, "persons in Mexico can use hard currency and … wire transfer the value of that currency to US bank accounts to purchase items in the United States or other countries. The nature of the CDC business allows money launderers the opportunity to move drug dollars that are in Mexico into CDCs and ultimately into the US banking system."[10]

"On numerous occasions," say the court papers, "monies were deposited into a CDC by a drug-trafficking organisation. Using false identities, the CDC then wired that money through its Wachovia correspondent bank accounts for the purchase of airplanes for drug-trafficking organisations." The court settlement of 2010 would detail that "nearly $13m went through correspondent bank accounts at Wachovia for the purchase of aircraft to be used in the illegal narcotics trade. From these aircraft, more than 20,000kg of cocaine were seized…"

Antonio Maria Costa, who was executive director of the UN's office on drugs and crime from May 2002 to August 2010, charts the history of the contamination of the global banking industry by drug and criminal money since his first initiatives to try to curb it from the European commission during the 1990s. "The connection between organised crime and financial institutions started in the late 1970s, early 1980s," he says, "when the mafia became globalised."

Until then, criminal money had circulated largely in cash, with the authorities making the occasional, spectacular "sting" or haul. During Costa's time as director for economics and finance at the EC in Brussels, from 1987, inroads were made against penetration of banks by criminal laundering, and "criminal money started moving back to cash, out of the financial institutions and banks."

Then two things happened: the financial crisis in Russia, after the emergence of the Russian mafia, and the crises of 2003 and 2007-08.

"With these crises," says Costa, "the banking sector was short of liquidity, the banks exposed themselves to the criminal syndicates, who had cash in hand."[11]

DANNY'S DICTUM

American drug plane scandals always manage to make sure that the only place where heads roll is on Mexico's mean streets. Wachovia Bank is dead. Long live Wells Fargo.

The discovery was part of a major breakthrough in unmasking the identities of people who, the DEA strenuously insisted, didn't even exist: *American Drug Lords.*

In many ways the American banking connection had long been an "open secret," at least to those on the inside of the drug trade. That secret, which is worth repeating for emphasis, is a corollary to what I've labeled "Danny's Dictum":

> *In every country on this Gangster Planet that hosts a significant local market, the people who control the market are the same people who control the country.*

Transnational organized crime has gained an upper hand over legitimate business enterprise during the decades since WWII. It has been assisted by our own military, as well as a select group of public officials, to whom intelligence agencies have funneled money for political campaigns.

"I STARTED A JOKE"

Even if they're from long ago, the U.S. Government doesn't give up its secrets easily. Ironically, it was precisely the elaborate cover-up at the Venice Airport – clearly designed to prevent the Venice Airport's clandestine role from becoming public knowledge – that gave up the game. It's always the cover-up rather than the crime itself. The attempt to conceal the airport's original mission remained visible directly across from the Venice Airport, where an historical plaque commemorated the airport's beginnings as a U.S. Army Air Base, which it called the "337th Army Air Field Base."[12]

> Venice Army Air Field opened during WWII on July 7, 1942. By March 1944, the Base was moved to this location. In all, nine groups were trained, with the 337th being the permanent party.

Airplanes filled the skies, as hundreds of pilots were trained
in P38's, 40's, and 51's. The Base was officially designated Venice
Army Air Field in 1945.

But, guess what? There was no 337th Army Airfield, and there never
had been. What was going on? The Venice Historical Archives explained,
"The designation was meant as a "'joke.'"

"The plaque commemorates the 337th Army Air Field Base and was
erected by the Venice Aviation Society Inc. in October 1992," they told me.

It turns out, the society had been incorporated in 1991 by attorney
Steve Boone of the tri-Boone firm near the old airfield.

"The plaque has numerous errors including referring to the Base as the
337th and the entire second sentence. The caricatured mosquito, symbolic of the striking power of the P-51, was designed by Capt. James H. Archibald as the 'official' insignia of the '337th AAF Base Unit' known as the
VAAF's permanent 'Party' outfit. Both the insignia and unit designation
were intended as a joke!"[13]

An official historical plaque "intended as a joke" was a new one to me.
I doubt anyone at the Venice Archives and Area Historical Collection had
ever heard of one either. Even if there was, the point of the "joke" – why it
should be considered funny – went unexplained.

I decided to look up the commander of the base named on the plaque
– Col. Vincent B. Dixon, who had been in charge of pursuit training at
Craig Field in Selma, Alabama before being named in charge at Venice in
February 1943.

Rumors were reported in the late summer of 1944 that Venice Air
Field was closing. Colonel Dixon stated he had been getting reports from
his men that they couldn't find affordable housing in the area due to the
fact that landlords were jacking up the rent as winter approached. He dis-
pelled rumors of the base closure, but before long, Dixon was replaced by
Col. Von R. Shores, who was stationed in Venice until the war ended.[14]

I knew all too well how "mean" landlords in Venice can be. I was evicted from where I had lived in Nokomis for several years, after being diagnosed with prostate cancer. I couldn't find a new place to live anywhere
in Sarasota County. It was a nightmare. Even the price of Motel 6 had
doubled overnight!

It appeared clear that the 337th Army Air Field plaque in Venice had
been a cryptic reference to the fact that Flying Tigers from China had
been trained in both St. Petersburg and Venice. It was that fact which the

Venice Historical Society had been tap-dancing to avoid. Or, maybe to heap praise on, like "Skull and Bones" at Yale honoring the 322 group of Illuminati that got the whole ball rolling.

After finding news reports about Venice Air Field, it hit me. The joke was not about there being a base there; it was about calling it the 337th!

I remembered something I'd seen on the wall at Clearwater-St Pete Airport, stating, "One of the units training in St Petersburg was *the 337th Fighter Group.*"

The "Incident of the Plaque" also illustrated that the faction responsible for sixty years of covert ops run through the Venice Airport still retained a tight grip on power.

Because otherwise, why was the Venice Historical Society lying?

CHENNAULT'S YOUTHFUL SHENANIGANS

There is no doubt Claire Chennault was an American hero during World War II. But he was a hero with – shall we say – certain *pecca-dillos.*

There's no easy way to say this: Decades before Chennault became famous, he was arrested for white slavery, a heinous crime from which few ever recover their reputation.

Here's what happened: In 1914, Claire Chennault had been the principal of a school in Franklin Parish, Louisiana when he left town in a hurry. Months later he was busted in Wisconsin, on September 4, 1914, along with one of his 16-year-old students, Annie Mae Griffin of Delhi, Louisiana, where her father was the mayor. Both were summarily extradited to Louisiana, where Chennault faced a charge of violating the Mann "White Slavery" Act.

We don't see that term much anymore, so I looked it up. A white slaver was defined as "a person who procures or forces women to become prostitutes."

SOCIETY COUPLE FACE ARREST AS WHITE SLAVES, reported one headline.[15] Claire Chennault's well-known family in rural Gilbert, in North Louisi-ana, were not quite what we think of as High Society, but at least it sounded good.

The damsel in distress, Anna, was reported by another newspaper to be "a handsome girl, the daughter of Delhi's mayor [sic], where her family stands high socially."[16] Anna "has a bright face and appears little more than a child," but still she was "being treated as a material witness."[17]

The story's coast-to-coast notoriety was assured once details of a dramatic twist were added. Claire Chennault's young student, it turned out, was *already married, to Chennault's brother, William.* Both brothers were charged as white slavers.

Amazingly, Claire Chennault's sticky wicket – already as sticky as "Gorilla Glue" – soon got even stickier. Chennault, it turned out, was also already married, and had a child, both of whom he abandoned for Miss Anna.

"The accused, a married man, eloped with Anna Mae Griffin Chennault, his young brother's wife."[18]

Before long came the trial. The Alexandria, Louisiana *Weekly Town Talk* reported the sordid tale, with Anna as the prosecution's chief witness. Sobbing and scared by the crowded courtroom, the poor little country girl told her story. Chennault was the principal of the school she attended, Delhi Consolidated, and he boarded at her home.

It's easy to picture him sneaking into her bedroom in the middle of night, seducing her, and later, her panic at learning she was having a baby. The judge recessed the court to allow Anna to compose herself. When court resumed, she testified, "Claire promised me that if anything happened, he would take me away from home," even though she knew he was both a husband and father.

After he'd left for LSU in Baton Rouge, she wrote him to say "she was in a delicate condition." Claire did nothing until Anna's brother entered the picture. He too wrote to Claire, telling him he knew all about his improper relations with his sister, who he said was threatening suicide.

That's when Claire prevailed on his younger brother William to marry her. William testified he'd married her only "to shield Claire, because he didn't want to spoil his brother's future."[19]

To hell with poor Anna.

"William, the husband, had even purchased the tickets which allowed Claire and Anna to elope to Chicago," said federal prosecutors.

Anxious for weeks because of the double elopement, the girl's father and brothers arrived by train to escort her home. For his part, Claire averred that once he got her out of Louisiana, he had no intention of living with her as his wife, which would have violated the Mann Act.

Yeah, right.

William Chennault was eventually acquitted of white slavery, while Claire Chennault was convicted on three counts. But he didn't end up breaking rocks at Angola State Prison. A year later, the January 27, 1916, *Shreveport Times* reported that Chennault had been granted a new trial.

But what really saved him was that the United States declared war on Germany. He had been saved in the nick of time.

"Three Men on a Flying Trapeze"

In between wars Chennault was stationed in such places as El Paso, Hawaii and San Antonio, the latter where all flight training for the Army Air Corps was done. Claire taught many pilots during that assignment.

Then he was transferred to Maxfield Air Force Base in Alabama.

There he led a troupe of aeronautical artists called "Three Men on a Flying Trapeze," formed in 1932 and lasting into 1936. The fliers were all based at the time at the Air Corps Tactical School at Maxwell AFB in Birmingham. It was like their own flying circus for several years. They soon learned, however, flying was more than just fun. For the wizards of Wall Street, who financed the industry, it was serious business.

Chennault retired from the U.S. military, more than two years before war in Europe would be declared in September 1939, after receiving an offer to work in China for the Nationalist Chinese Air Force. During that time Nationalist China ruled the entire mainland, in addition to the offshore islands to which it was confined by 1949. For years China had been defending itself from the much smaller Japanese empire.

There was no declared war at the time, except between China and Japan. The U.S. was officially neutral, so the pilots had to be very careful to avoid the Neutrality Act. But then, all spies have to be careful, just to remain alive. Chennault and his old flying pal, Bill McDonald, while making their way to China, were also gathering intelligence along the way.[20]

"Stooge of Chiang Kai-shek"

Once the U.S. declared war against Japan in 1941, there were no holds barred. No need for subterfuge or pretense about neutrality. As China's war against Japan morphed into our own war, the Chinese we had been assisting for years continued to lose ground to other forces inside China – the Reds.

More than a decade later, just after Christmas in 1950, Drew Pearson wrote a column headlined "**General Chennault Fights Communism**," which began:

> Claire Chennault, a big leathery man with a gruff intensity, has a plan for starting fires in Asia against Stalinism.
>
> "The famous Flying Tiger General who fought with the nationalist Chinese," he wrote, had been "pounding on doors in Washington, saying "Let's arm the hatred against Russia which is speeding across China. The greatest fear of the Communists is of the guerrillas – a million of whom hold great pockets on the mainland. We should drop weapons to them and smuggle munitions across the borders."

By this time, Claire Chennault had been in China for more than a decade and was running Civil Air Transport, the CIA's first full-fledged airline. (It later became Air America.) The secret financing mechanism was not disclosed until years later, as well as the meaning of repayment.

"The spirit of revolt is so strong in China today," claimed Chennault, "that Communist members don't dare go out alone for fear of being ambushed."

Coming just a few years after Mao's total victory over Chiang Kai-shek, these were bold words bordering on a falsehood. Maybe that's just hindsight. But Pearson, a propagandist himself, enthusiastically endorsed the sentiment.

Pearson spread the rumors of what he called "intelligence shipped out of China to Chennault," giving the "picture on the Chinese mainland" as teeming with three groups of anti-communist guerilla forces not attached to Chiang, and "available to foment revolt" against the Reds.[21]

Unfortunately, all the leaders of these mostly Muslim groups soon fled China for the U.S., Hong Kong, and even Mexico.

"Here in Asia is where the Communist conspirators have elected to make their play for global conquest," General Douglas MacArthur told reporters, indicating his belief in the domino theory so prominent during the Cold War.[22]

President Truman's forceful response came the following April when he relieved MacArthur of command. The action echoed what one British official had said, according to a Drew Pearson column of December 1950:

> I have no intention of backing the befuddled dangerous policies of General MacArthur. We have no intention of losing thousands of troops on Chinese soil. We consider MacArthur a stooge of Chiang Kai-shek.[23]

Brits' Wars on Opium

The British had been calling the shots in China since they won two Opium Wars there in the mid-19th century, gaining Hong Kong in the process. FDR well understood their power, to which his Delano wealth from "the China trade" attested.

American profits from the trade had long been laundered through Boston and New York bank accounts in the names of Forbes, Delano, Russell, Low, Perkins, Cushing, Coolidge and the like. The money made its way into politics – Republican and Democratic alike.

General Claire Chennault was widely disliked by his peers. According to newspaper reports at the time, his military career was sidetracked by his superiors.

He was one of the most controversial American military figures in U.S. history and was at the forefront of American military and intelligence efforts to fund anti-communist endeavors through heroin trafficking during and after World War II. Many writers from Alfred McCoy to Peter Dale Scott have written tirelessly about the drug menace created in that exact area of the world and about its effect on American life since World War II.

Excerpts help to make our point:

Joseph Trento wrote in *The Secret History of the CIA*:

> General Claire Chennault, organizer of the Flying Tigers during World War II, was put in charge of Civil Air Transport (which later became Air America), while his wife Anna spent her time lobbying in Washington for more aid to help her husband's effort against the Communist Chinese.
>
> Chiang Kai-shek's men, funded by the CIA, became the foot soldiers of Asia's drug armies.... Hundreds of tons of opium and heroin ... were carried on these CIA flights. [24]

Douglas Valentine, author of the history the Federal Bureau of Narcotics and its offshoots, added:

> Despite the July 1949 seizure in Hong Kong reported by the *New York Times* of 22 pounds of heroin emanating from a CIA-supplied outpost in Kunming ... the China Lobby launched a massive propaganda campaign based on the allegation by the head of the Federal Bureau of Narcotics that the Red Chinese were the source of all the illicit dope reaching Japan....
>
> The China Lobby raised $5 million which the CIA used to purchase General Claire Chennault's fleet of planes and convert them into the CIA's first proprietary Air Force.[25]

Edwin Clausen noted:

> No one could have foreseen that one legacy of the Flying Tigers would become Air America. Claire Chennault and the Flying Tigers symbolize the ... failure of American foreign policy in the region.[26]

Dan Russell's essay then boiled it all down succinctly:

> The practical effect of all of this was to turn Claire Chennault's Flying Tigers into flying dope peddlers.[27]

245

Who Managed Their Pub?

Today, according to Wikipedia, Gilbert, Louisiana, has a population of 510, and boasts on its welcome sign that it is the home of Lt. General Claire Chennault. In 2017, his granddaughter spoke at the town's 13th annual Armed Forces Day ceremony.

After his death in 1958, his widow Anna Chen Chennault, with whom he had two children, enjoyed an influential career as a Washington insider and Republican member of the China Lobby.[28]

After Chennault's conviction for "white slavery," he appealed and was released to await the outcome. Anna Griffin had a baby boy and moved to Texas, cutting off all contact. Claire moved his wife and children to Akron, Ohio and was working at a Goodyear Rubber factory in April 1917 when the United States entered World War I.

The *Akron Beacon* reported he had been given a commission as a lieutenant in the reserves in field artillery, with full pay until he was called up to active duty.

See, that's the thing about good publicity. If you're lucky enough to be "tapped" to receive it, you can receive full pay with no questions asked, even if you've been previously charged with white slavery.

You see how that works?

Endnotes

1   "David B. Lindsay, Sr. Found Dead," *Bradenton Herald*, May 5, 1968, pp. 1, 3. h t t p s : / / www.newspapers.com/article/the-bradenton-herald-david-lindsay-found/140235886/

2   Christopher Ryan wrote for the *St. Petersburg Times* (now *Tampa Bay Times*). Lindsay Sr. worked for Paul Poynter in the 1920s and later with Nelson Poynter, who founded the Poynter Institute. For – don't you know – journalistic integrity. After Poynter Institute was ridiculed by right-wing media for blacklisting 515 media sources in need of fact-checking, it removed its list. Joe Concha, "Poynter pulls blacklist of 'unreliable' news websites after backlash," *The Hill*, May 3, 2019. https://thehill.com/homenews/media/441959-poynter-pulls-blacklist-of-unreliable-news-web-sites-after-backlash/

3   Christopher Ryan, *Tampa Bay Times*, Nov. 7, 1993. https://www.newspapers. com/article/tampa-bay-times-christopher-ryanchina-s/132129197/

4   Quoted by Ralph Vartabedian, syndicated writer for *Los Angeles Times-Washington Post* Service, appearing in a variety of papers in July 1991.

5   I posted about my visit in 2010 at my website. https://www.madcowprod.com/2010/03/08/60-years-of-drug-trafficking-at-the-venice-municipal-airport/

6   The story was written by Associated Press and carried by numerous newspapers, including the *Miami Herald*, 24 Sep 1944. It also said the Chinese airmen from various parts of China were trained at Venice as "the 14th service group, part of the Flying Tigers." https://www.newspapers.com/article/the-tampa-tribune-chinese-fly-to-cana- da/140108749/

7   "Mexico Atty General: Busted American Drug Planes Flown by Same Opera-tion,"   https://www.madcowprod.com/2007/11/12/mexico-atty-general-busted-ameri-can-drug-planes-flown-by-same-operation/

LaJornada also covered the story in an article by Gustavo Castillo Garcia (as translated into En-glish) on Dec. 27, 2007, at https://www-jornada-com-mx.translate.goog/2007/12/27/ index.php?-section=politica&article=014n2pol&_x_tr_sl=es&_x_tr_tl=en&_x_tr_ hl=en&_x_tr_pto=wapp:

"The Attorney General's Office (PGR) is investigating the acquisition of 50 aircraft that Pedro Alfonso Alatorre Damy, manager of the Puebla exchange house, paid for the Joaquín El Chapo Guz-mán Loera cartel. Alatorre was detained last November by federal agents, agency officials revealed.

"Among the aircraft that Alatorre Damy would have acquired for the Sinaloa cartel are a DC-9 seized in 2006, in Ciudad del Carmen, Campeche, with almost six tons of cocaine and a small plane seized last October, in Tixkokob, Yucatán, with almost four tons of the same drug....

"According to records of the Attorney General's Office, among the planes acquired by the Sinaloa cartel through the intervention of El Piri are a DC-9 registration N900SA, located in Campeche on April 10, 2006, in which 5,000 were found."

8   Ed Vulliamy, "How a big US bank laundered billions from Mexico's murderous drug gangs," The *Guardian*, Sat 2 Apr 2011. In addition to this excerpt, the article continues at length. https://www.theguardian.com/world/2011/apr/03/us-bank-mexico-drug-gangs (accessed Jan 13, 2023). Investigators settled on Wachovia – located in Charlotte, North Carolina – because much of the information it reported about large volume customers was deficient. Martin Woods was at the London office of Wachovia Bank in February 2005, hired as a senior anti-money laundering officer and began to notice and report the abnormalities of the deposits from Mexico.

"By August 2006, Woods had identified a number of suspicious transactions relating to casas de cambio [CDC] customers in Mexico. Primarily, these involved deposits of traveller's cheques in euros. They had sequential numbers and deposited larger amounts of money than any innocent travelling person would need, with inadequate or no KYC [know your customer] information on them and what seemed to a trained eye to be dubious signatures."

Woods sent the information from London back to Wachovia headquarters in Charlotte, N.C., and, as a result, almost lost his job and his mind. But he didn't quit. He had fortuitously shared the information with American drug enforcement personnel at a conference, and they also began investigating the bank as early as 2005.

"'Through CDCs,' said the court document, 'persons in Mexico can use hard currency and ... wire transfer the value of that currency to US bank accounts to purchase items in the United States or other countries. The nature of the CDC business allows money launderers the opportunity to move drug dollars that are in Mexico into CDCs and ultimately into the US banking system.'

"'On numerous occasions,' say the court papers, 'monies were deposited into a CDC by a drug-trafficking organisation. Using false identities, the CDC then wired that money through its Wachovia correspondent bank accounts for the purchase of airplanes for drug-trafficking organisations.'The court settlement of 2010 would detail that 'nearly $13m went through correspondent bank accounts at Wachovia for the purchase of aircraft to be used in the illegal narcotics trade. From these aircraft, more than 20,000kg of cocaine were seized.'...

"Antonio Maria Costa, who was executive director of the UN's office on drugs and crime from May 2002 to August 2010, charts the history of the contamination of the global banking industry by drug and criminal money since his first initiatives to try to curb it from the European commission during the 1990s. 'The connection between organised crime and financial institutions started in the late 1970s, early 1980s,' he says, 'when the mafia became globalised.'

"Until then, criminal money had circulated largely in cash, with the authorities making the occasional, spectacular 'sting' or haul. During Costa's time as director for economics and finance at the EC in Brussels, from 1987, inroads were made against penetration of banks by criminal laundering, and 'criminal money started moving back to cash, out of the financial institutions and banks.

'Then two things happened: the financial crisis in Russia, after the emergence of the Russian mafia, and the crises of 2003 and 2007-08.'

" 'With these crises,' says Costa, 'the banking sector was short of liquidity, the banks exposed themselves to the criminal syndicates, who had cash in hand.'"

9   Ibid.

10   Ibid.

11   Ibid.

12   https://www.hmdb.org/Photos1/116/Photo116100o.jpg?11252005

13   We did, however, locate the man the Venice Aviation Society, Inc. referred to as Capt. James H. Archibald, Jr. who designed the mosquito mascot for the 337th. Born in New York in 1918, he obtained a college degree in art, and then had joined the Army as a 1st Lt., but was soon promoted to captain. The Florida census in 1945 showed him living in Venice with wife Grace and baby daughter Lynn, while serving out his enlistment in the Army. After the war he returned to New York for a while, to a job of designing packages, but they eventually moved back to Florida. He set up an antique business at 4155 S. Tamiami in Sarasota but moved to Bradenton near a mobile home village – keeping the business alive by advertising Caban-a-Room Sales as an attachment to mobile homes. Retirement enabled him to return to his first love of art and design. His name never appeared on legal documents for VASI, but someone obviously knew him and his connection to the Venice Airport. But we located him too late. He is now deceased.

14   Major General Von R. Shores today is director, Secretary of the Air Force Personnel Council, Headquarters U.S. Air Force. "He returned from North Africa in February 1943 and was again transferred to the Panama Canal Zone. He served as deputy commander and executive officer of the XXVI Fighter Command until May 1945. During this period, he was associated with the Brazilian Air Force in the initial organization and training of a fighter squadron which later participated in active operations against Axis powers. General Shores returned to the United States and was assigned as commander of the Fighter Combat Crew Training Center at Venice, Fla. When that center was closed at the end of World War II, he was assigned as base commander at Will Rogers Field, Okla." https://www.af.mil/About-Us/Biographies/Display/Article/105539/major-general-   von-r-shores/

15   Society Couple Face Arrest as White Slaves," *Wilkes-Barre Times Leader*, the Evening News, 05 Sep 1914, Page 9. https://www.newspapers.com/clip/122142997/society-couple-face- arrest-as-white/

16   "Let Wife Elope with Brother," *Blackwell Daily News*, Blackwell, Oklahoma, September 19, 1914. https://www.newspapers.com/image/582610687/?match=1&clipping_id=131953146

17   Ibid

18   Ibid.

19   "Claire Chennault Convicted," *The Town Talk*, Alexandria, Louisiana, 17 Dec 1914, Page 7. https://www.newspapers.com/clip/116526758/chennault-mistrial-for-white-slavery/

20   Several books have been written about those days America's heroic pilots spent in China, training Chinese volunteers to be pilots. One was *The Shadow Tiger: Billy McDonald, Wingman to Chennault*, written by the aviator's son in 2016. Another was Sam Kleiner's *The Flying Tigers: The Untold Story of the American Pilots Who Waged a Secret War Against Japan*, published two years later. War enthusiasts can learn a lot from both.

21   The Pearson column appeared, for example, in the Sioux Falls, S.D., *Daily Argus-Leader*, 28 Dec 1950, Page 6. https://www.newspapers.com/article/argus-leader-drew-pearson-column/141702553/

22   "MacArthur's stand on war is disputed by Democrats," *Spokane Chronicle*, 06 Apr 1951, Page 2. https://www.newspapers.com/article/spokane-chronicle-gen-macarthur-letter/141702914/

23   Drew Pearson op ed, Paris, TX *Evening Standard*, 28 Dec 1950, Page 4. https://www.newspapers.com/article/the-paris-news-drew-pearson-quoting-kenn/141703740/

24   Joseph John Trento, *The Secret History of the CIA* (Roseville, CA: Prima Publishing, 2001), p. 384.

25   Douglas Valentine, *Strength of the Wolf: The Secret History of America's War on Drugs* (London, New York: Verso, 2004), p. 77.

26   Ke-wen Wang and CRSN Staff, *Modern China: An Encyclopedia of History, Culture, and Nationalism*, (Abingdon, UK: Routledge Press, 1997).

27   Dan Russell, "Prohibition Is Treason," an essay in *Under the Influence: The Disinformation Guide to Drugs*, edited by Preston Peet (New York, NY: Disinformation Co.), p. 55.

28   Chennault also had eight children born during his marriage to his first wife, Nell, who had forgiven his 1914 indiscretion, but eventually divorced him in 1946.

CHAPTER SIXTEEN

"TUESDAY IS
THE DRUG DOG'S NIGHT OFF"

Dogs have always been man's best friend. In the past couple of decades, their incredible olfactory sense has found a new use: keeping the friendly skies safe for us all. Dogs at airports are a common sight these days, and TSA implemented canines into its cargo screening protocols in 2008. A dog can be trained to recognize a wide range of different scents. This makes them an incredible security asset, as they can identify threats before humans can.
–3dk9detection Website

Today he's a lawyer in Kentucky. But when James Leif Sanders had an unforgettable encounter with Guyanese military drug pilot Michael Francis Brassington on a quiet Tuesday night in April of 2004, instead of a budding barrister, Sanders was a rookie US Customs Agent, and he'll never forget their encounter at Fort Lauderdale International Airport.

Although he was a newbie, Sanders somehow had been left in charge of the late shift at the airport, when a "very special" private plane from the Bahamas landed and taxied over to the general aviation terminal.

Customs Agent Sanders' job that night was examining everyone coming through the general aviation terminal before allowing them to enter the U.S. You know the drill if you've flown internationally on a commercial flight.

So, when Brassington's Challenger luxury jet with two people aboard rolled to a stop, Sanders was there to check them in.

What happened next was not only the most memorable – it was almost the last – event to occur during his abbreviated Customs career. Years later, the encounter was still vivid in his mind. He got in touch with me after reading about Brassington on my website, madcowprod.com, which had a dozen stories about him.

The first thing the lanky reddish-blond Sanders said when we met was "You were right about Brassington."[1]

"There Was A Red Flag By His Name"

Leif first examined Brassington's passport, he said, and lo and behold: "There was a notation following his name in my Customs computer, containing information on Brassington's DEA narcotics record."[2]

"Brassington went through Immigration first," explained Sanders. "The Immigration Inspector had 'top-stamped' his Customs declaration, which means he needed to be 'secondary-ed.' That meant giving him a closer inspection. Search his luggage, at the very least, and ask him more questions."

Sanders grimaced.

"The INS Agent came over and whispered to me that Brassington had a narcotics 'lookout,' plus he was flying in on a Challenger jet (N600S) suspected of being used for money laundering. And if that wasn't enough, his passenger, Anthony Cirillo, was also flagged in the computer for having been on suspicious flights!"[3]

"So, I scrutinized him a little more closely," Sanders told me, looking around him as he spoke. "And he had a 'lookout' from the DEA for heroin smuggling, for having copiloted a Lear jet (N351WB), it said, on the 25th of July, 2000, into Executive Airport in Orlando."[4]

"Come to find out later, Brassington had been working for 9/11 flight school owner Wallace J. Hilliard. But I only found that out much later, after I discovered your website!

"What was really strange was that the subject never came up. So, at time I couldn't have imagined what happened to me could in any way be connected to 9/11."[5]

According to the lookout, Brassington had flown "thirty-nine weekly drug flights" on a Learjet belonging to the owner of the flight school Mohamed Atta began attending three weeks before this Orlando bust.

Sanders shook his head sadly while uttering, "This information was somehow deemed irrelevant to the 9/11 attack."

The response to the revelation? Official silence. And it has been completely ignored in the mainstream media since. First for years, and now decades.

Ice De-Activates DEA "Look Out"

What happened next remains for Sanders – even a decade later – unpleasant to talk about. He grimaced at the memory.

"Brassington immediately became belligerent," he said, speaking slowly, "and he brandished a letter in my face, even as I was looking at his own narcotics record on the Customs computer," Sanders, still incredulous at the memory, exclaimed.

251

"This is what the Department of Homeland Security has to say about someone caught smuggling drugs for a 9/11 flight school owner," Sanders said, unable to keep his voice from rising in indignation as he read the letter to me.

> This is in reference to your letter of September 23, 2003, when you expressed concerns you were having trouble clearing Customs when returning to the United States from foreign travel.
>
> Please let us apologize for any inconvenience or unpleasantness you may have experienced. On behalf of the Border and Transportation security directorate, let me assure you it is not our intent to subject the traveling public to unwarranted scrutiny.
>
> The traveling public is entitled to and is accorded the utmost courtesy and facilitation we can offer within the limits of our enforcement responsibilities. Regrettably our efforts can occasionally cause inconvenience.
>
> We have reviewed our records and taken action so you will no longer encounter any automatic special attention beyond normal probabilities upon future return to the United States or territories thereof."

They were saying they were going to de-activate his lookout. But the lookout was placed there by the DEA. It was a DEA record.[6]

So, U.S. Customs is countermanding a record placed by another Federal Agency, which is illegal.

"DEA be damned! De-activate his lookout!" Sanders shouted, shaking his head.

"It was signed by Gloria Marshall, head of something called the 'Information Disclosure Unit' of the 'Mission Support Division' of the Department of Homeland Security."[7]

The letter seemed clearly designed to smooth Brassington's entry into the U.S. But Rookie Customs Agent Sanders didn't take the hint.

"I felt like a deer in the headlights," he recalled. "It was a strange occurrence. He has this official-looking letter that says they're going to take care of his record. Yet he still has an active record."

"So, I hesitated. I said, 'wait a second.'"

A "GRAVE THREAT TO NATIONAL SECURITY"

Unsure what to do – he was still a rookie, after all – Leif Sanders called a Supervisor of Immigration and Customs Enforcement (ICE) for guidance, a man said to be in charge of Brassington's file.

Leif shrugs as relates the story. "I didn't know what to do. But I *did* have just enough presence of mind to call Special Agent Norm Bright, the man listed as Brassington's 'point of contact.'"[8]

"Point of contact," he explained, "is U.S. Customs jargon for an Agent who's been assigned particular responsibility for someone whose movements are being tracked."

"Special Agent Bright was a local ICE Agent assigned to tracking Brassington," Sanders said. "I told him about the letter. He said 'you can disregard the letter.' He told me to ignore it."

Then Special Agent Norm Bright said something curious. He ordered Sanders to treat Brassington – who was standing right in front of him – as a *"grave threat to national security."*

Sanders said those were the Supervisor's exact words: "*A grave threat to national security.*"

Sanders' face reflected his disgust. "I had no idea of the shitstorm I was about to ignite." He continued, "Then he told me that I needed to check him, search him, and search all his passengers. And that's what I did."

"I searched the luggage of his passengers, and then I searched his plane. I needed to check him really close. Understand, I wasn't thinking of him as a terrorist suspect. I just thought he was really into drugs."

Supervisor Norm Bright also told him to try to get a drug dog.

"The problem with that," Sanders said, "is that on Tuesday nights at Fort Lauderdale International Airport, there aren't any drug dogs available."

He shrugged. "Tuesday night is the drug dog's night off."

THE ALFONSO BOWE SMUGGLING GROUP

Customs Agent Leif Sanders had *confirmed* that Brassington had been the co-pilot when Wally Hilliard's Learjet was busted in Orlando.

That was big news, at least to me. Sanders ticked off the numerous red flags.

- The pilot had a "lookout" for heroin smuggling.

- His name was Mike Brassington.

- He had in his possession a letter from the Bureau of Immigration and Customs Enforcement stating Brassington's record was being modified so he would no longer receive close scrutiny from Customs.

- *However,* he still had an active drug record in the system.

- The letter he had was from U.S. Customs, but the notation on his passport was from the DEA.

253

Had U.S. Customs been moved from the Treasury Department into the newly created Department of Homeland Security for a reason? Had this move made it easier to override a narcotics "lookout" placed by the DEA? Sanders said he had no idea. But those were not the only red flags concerning Brassington.

"In the 'active lookout' it stated Brassington was known for bringing in suspect passengers," Sanders told me.

"Then he handed me the manifest for his flight. He'd flown that Tuesday from *Executive Flight Support in the Bahamas* into general aviation at Fort Lauderdale Executive Airport. I found out later [Nassau's] Executive was managed by Alfonso (aka Alphonso aka Alfonzo) Bowe but owned by Wally Hilliard.

Sanders then stated, "So, Brassington apparently still had some kind of financial relationship with Hilliard several years after the Orlando bust."

"In the Customs computer system, Executive Flight Support is described as a criminal organization associated with the 'Alfonso Bowe Smuggling Group'!"

This was the first I'd heard that Huffman Aviation flight school owner Wally Hilliard was also the owner of the FBO (fixed base of operations) in Nassau, and also that someone named "Alfonso Bowe" managed the facility. When I searched the Internet, what I did find was that a "prominent Bahamian lawyer [named] F. Nigel Bowe, accused of helping the Medellin cartel run cocaine to the United States through the island chain" had been convicted in federal court.[9]

The Drug Enforcement Administration's Miami office hailed that verdict as a "momentous occasion" because of the years of effort to bring Bowe to justice. Nigel Bowe had been indicted as far back as 1985, charged with helping Colombia's Medellin cocaine cartel ship drugs through the Bahamas to the United States. Extradition to the U.S. for trial was stalled until 1992. The trial led to his ultimate conviction.[10]

Was Nigel related to Alfonso Bowe, we wondered.

DEATH SQUADS, DRUG TRAFFICKING, AND THE CIA

I was also learning new things about Guyana, Brassington's home country, previously best-known for the Rev. Jim Jones' Jonestown cult's suicides, in which more than 900 people perished.

The current Guyanese government, I discovered, had a reputation for "playing ball" with major drug traffickers.

Recently, Guyana achieved a certain infamy as a regional distribution hub for narcotics shipments that made their way across that country's easily crossed borders with Brazil, Venezuela and French Guiana, bound for the wider world outside South America.

A high-level DEA source in Miami brusquely confirmed to me that Brassington had been fingered for involvement in a secret internal investigation at the Department of Homeland Security.

"It's an ICE operation, out of Miami," stated the Miami DEA official. "It has nothing whatsoever to do with the DEA. You want more information, check with the OIG (Office of inspector General) in the Department of Homeland Security in Washington."

The Department of Homeland Security – created after the 9/11 attack – had taken over U.S. Customs and inherited all of that Agency's dirty secrets.

U.S. Customs corruption in Mexico and Latin America was one of America's open secrets: known by many, talked about by few. It was a well ingrained, decades-old practice, used by political leaders in both parties for personal purposes and to pay off political debts.

As it happened, the *Miami Herald* had published specific allegations against Miami's much-celebrated Contraband Enforcement Team (CET). The paper confirmed the allegations through documents in investigative files. "They were out of control, and everyone knew it," said a Customs investigator involved. "Out of control. No question about it."[11]

A later internal investigation by the Homeland Security Department's OIG into the "Contraband Enforcement Team" had been thwarted, a source in Fort Lauderdale told me grimly. "The Special Agent in charge was re-assigned."[12]

During the '80s and '90s, the program had been used to stem the flow of marijuana and cocaine heading into Florida. It was then beginning to fade out, until it got a new lease on life after the 9/11 attack.

"That CET group had a lot of power, and Customs did everything it could to make the case go away – the merits of the complaint be damned," an investigator said. "Truth was not a concern. Everyone in Customs knew the truth. The concern was for saving face."[13]

"Operation Blue Lightning"

Mike Brassington's extensive history of brushes with U.S. law enforcement was still mostly unknown. I learned he was suspected of trafficking drugs, passports, people, currency, and diamonds into the U.S., using two airports in Fort Lauderdale, Florida, and that was the subject of a Multi-Agency Federal Task Force called "Operation Blue Lightning."[14] It was a Customs Supervisor in Miami – tasked with tracking Brassington's movements during Operation Blue Lightning – who had first warned rookie Agent Leif Sanders at Fort Lauderdale International Airport to treat him as a "grave threat to national security."

Predictably, the investigation went nowhere. According to a Customs Agent in Fort Lauderdale, who regularly examined Brassington as he passed through U.S. Customs, both while entering and leaving the U.S., informed me that the lead FAA investigator on the case – under extremely suspicious circumstances – had been called off and reassigned.

An internal investigation by the Homeland Security Department's Office of the Inspector General was *also* thwarted, and its Special Agent in Charge re-assigned.

In the DEA (which fell under the Justice Department's supervision, they were discreetly passing-the-buck. This took the form of repeated denials by DEA officials of any DEA investigation or involvement in the case. Indeed, the top DEA official in Miami told me firmly that there was no ongoing DEA investigation.

"The case involves corruption in a U.S. Custom's 'rogue operation,'" he asserted gruffly, "which is properly investigated *internally* by the Inspector General's Office in the Department of Homeland Security."[15]

End of story?

"THEY ALL KNOW EACH OTHER"

More research turned up the very first newspaper mentions of Operation Blue Lightning: during the spring of 1985, United Press International called it "an unprecedented assault that rousted drug smugglers from island sanctuaries in the Bahamas and into a massive military trap that netted $100 million in drugs, boats and planes."[16]

A familiar government figure was on hand in 1985 to praise Operation Blue Lightning's inception: Vice President George Herbert Walker Bush, who reportedly had implemented the South Florida Task Force on Drugs.[17]

Bush had been in charge of a similar undercover operation called "Operation Screamer," in which the DEA busted Barry Seal on April 26, 1983, for importing methaqualone (200,000 Quaaludes) into Fort Lauderdale.

From *Barry and 'the boys'*: "Seal was said to have been angry over what he considered Vice President George Bush's shabby treatment of him. In the deal the two had cut, Seal felt Bush was to take care of his legal difficulties. He hadn't."

For Seal to agree to go into business with the guys in Mena he would have insisted on "protection."[4]

After he and members of his crew were separately arrested in 1981 and then indicted in March 1983, Barry Seal hired a lawyer who had connections to Bill and Hillary Clinton – Richard Ben-Veniste – who got Barry an appointment in Washington, D.C. in March 1984 to meet with Vice President George Bush.[18]

All top investigators agreed Bush as Vice President had for years been involved with then-Arkansas-Governor Bill Clinton in the top-secret weapons-for-drugs CIA operation ongoing at isolated airports at Mena and Nella, Arkansas.

Drug smuggler Barry Seal's movements were overseen by a CIA agent code-named Robert Johnson (actually a younger and thinner William P. Barr), whose cover was his job as general counsel for Southern Air Transport in Miami, the "former" CIA proprietary airline.

Barr joined the CIA in 1973, working for them during the day, while they paid for his night classes at George Washington Law School. Once he had his law degree, he worked for George H.W. Bush, Director of the CIA under President Gerald Ford after Nixon resigned in 1974.[19]

Barr was rewarded by Vice President Bush with such sensitive appointments as making sure Bush's Democratic partners in the Mena drug operation did not make off with more money than the Bush team collected. Later Barr went to the Justice Department after Bush became President and became Attorney General.

Barr later became infamous as Donald Trump's notorious AG who, a man who lied about almost everything, especially what the Mueller Report found about Russian involvement in Trump's 2016 election.[20]

Barry Seal's Turks and Caicos Interlude

Back in November 1985 Barry Seal was testifying – to work off his 10-year sentence in a court in Fort Lauderdale – against the second defendant he'd helped the DEA set up.

Norman Saunders, Sr. was a former chief minister of the Turks & Caicos Islands. Working undercover, Seal secretly videoed Saunders accepting stacks of cash while promising Seal he could refuel his drug plane at the Esso facility Saunders owned.[21] Norman Saunders got an eight-year sentence in a Florida prison. He and his son would later resurface in a new scandal – their names appearing in the TCI Inquiry into Mike Misick's indiscretions.

Seal's cooperation with the DEA was supposed to buy Seal his freedom. Instead, it resulted in his death. The Louisiana judge who sentenced him refused to let him off for time served, it was said, ordering him to be hung out to dry at a halfway house, where he was an easy target.

Was the hit ordered by the cartel's Jorge Ochoa, as the U.S. insisted? Or did Bush order the hit because of persistent rumors that Seal had a videotape of the Bush boys – George Jr and Jeb?

Oddly enough, twenty-something years later Bill Clinton's name also surfaced again in the same Turks & Caicos' drug scandal.

You'd have thought the years in prison might teach Saunders and his family a lesson. There's an old saying that's been around awhile: "Opportunity may knock only once, but temptation leans on the doorbell."

There's just no way to dismantle that doorbell. Mike Misick got caught by the same temptations that took down his predecessor Norman Saunders.

In 2008, a new British Commission of Inquiry into Misick's corruption began hearing testimony. It explored Misick's extensive travel expenses. In July or August 2005, he'd decided to save money:

Instead of flying LisaRaye back and forth between Los Angeles and the Islands using a charter service (in which she made "two or three round trips per month, up to and beyond their marriage in April 2006"). The Court took out its calculator. "This represents expenditure of between $4 million and $6 million," it concluded, based on LisaRaye's testimony about the frequency of flights that ended only after she thought they bought their own plane in 2007.[22]

However, instead of purchasing a luxury jet outright for $6.25 million, Misick contacted a friend of his in Washington, D.C. Miami native Jeffrey Watson a former Clinton' White House aide.

Watson agreed to buy the plane in the name of Indigo Transportation Partners LLC (which he formed in April 2007) and then to lease it back to the TCI Government for $165,000 per month.

However, LisaRaye assumed it was *their* plane. She thought former Clinton aide Jeffrey Watson was just the *decorator*. After all, he was bringing her books of swatches to pick colors to turn the interior into LisaRaye's own personal global taxi, all paid from the coffers of the Turks & Caicos' nearly bankrupt government.

Jeffrey Watson had been a Clinton transition team political aide in Little Rock during the election year when Clinton defeated the elder Bush. Of course, by then Barry Seal was dead, having been removed from the Mena airport operation he had helmed.

Seal had flown drugs from Nicaragua to the U.S, and returned with weapons for Reagan and Bush's Contras, in an operation overseen by William P. Barr, working undercover for the CIA (as Robert Johnson).

Barr was also supposed to be making sure Governor Bill Clinton of Arkansas – and his money-launderer buddy Dan Lasater – didn't steal Bush's share of the loot. Author Terry Reed published the offending documents in his book, "*Compromised*."[23]

Though the Iran Contra scandal was over by 1992, back in the mid-'80s the Whitewater investigation was still in the future, and Monica was around 12 years old.

After Clinton left office, Watson became a self-employed Washington D.C. lobbyist. Watson had earlier been a housing official in Miami – called "a Florida insider in the White House." He doled out $75 million in Federal government largesse after Hurricane Andrew.[24]

WALLY & THE "ALFONSO BOWE SMUGGLING GROUP"

When Brassington's trial on his 27-count indictment began, there was absolutely no testimony about Brassington's involvement with Wally Hilliard or the "Alfonso Bowe Smuggling Group."

There was, however, quite a bit about how he had recklessly endangered the lives of passengers, among whose number included ex-Presidents George Herbert Walker Bush and Bill Clinton, as well as numerous celebrities.

It doesn't take elaborate radar detection and counter-surveillance electronic gear to become a successful drug trafficker.

Anyone – like Michael Brassington – with an "in" at U.S. Customs, could be clued-in about the best time of the week to enter the U.S. through Fort Lauderdale.

On Tuesday night.

While a rookie Agent was in charge.

While the drug dogs were out bowling.

"Whenever Brassington entered the U.S. a special team from Miami was supposed to come up," former Fort Lauderdale Customs Agent James Leif Sanders had told us. "Brassington was supposed to be met by Customs Agents from Operation Blue Lightning."

This occurred in 2004, while the kinks were still being worked out over who was responsible for what after Homeland Security had just merged about eight agencies into its department.

Rookie Customs Agent James Sanders said he only "found out later, from a chief inspector on the team, that I wasn't supposed to inspect him."

But he was still fired.

Sanders' encounter with Guyanese drug pilot Michael Brassington ended up costing him his job.

INAUGURATION YEAR SHIFT CHANGE

Before he was indicted in 2008 – just two weeks after the George W. Bush Administration left office – Brassington had regularly flouted U.S. and international law with impunity.

One of the many agencies involved in Operation Blue Lightning clearly seemed intent on making sure Brassington received "special handling." When I asked a top DEA official in Miami which agency gave Brassington his protection, he had informed me that the DEA had not mounted an investigation into the owners of two planes caught carrying over 10 tons of cocaine in Mexico's Yucatan, because the two planes belonged to a "rogue" operation of U.S. Customs, otherwise known as ICE.

Explained the DEA official, "So the investigation properly belonged to the Office of Inspector General in the Department of Homeland Security."

An official in the Department of Homeland Security's Inspector General's office said the Department's practice is to neither confirm nor deny the existence of any internal investigation conducted by the Inspector General's office.

Later, I discovered the lead FAA investigator on the case had also been called off and reassigned, under suspicious circumstances.

To this day Brassington has never been charged with drug trafficking. As rookie Customs Agent James Sanders learned the hard way, Brassington was protected by top figures in the Department of Homeland Security. The government – when they want to protect or cover something up – has a neat trick. They "investigate" it.

Despite incriminating facts, two career Customs officials with checkered histories in Miami, Thomas Winkowski and Jayson Ahern, had intervened on Brassington's behalf, after he had written a letter of complaint to Ahern, then the third highest ranking official in U.S. Customs.Rookie Customs Agent James Sanders' encounter with Guyanese drug pilot Michael Brassington cost him his job, but he won my undying admiration.

It was a strange pass to come to. It was about to get even stranger.

Endnotes

1   Quotes which follow resulted from interviews and correspondence between author and James Leif Sanders.

2   Interview with James Leif Sanders.

3   Anthony Cirillo may well be a common name among Italians. But when I looked the name up, I found an article by Larry McShane in the *New York Daily News*, April 30, 2017. Because Cirillo's name had been flagged in 2004 as 'suspicious', it seemed possible the following report referred to him: "Reputed Philadelphia Mafia boss Joseph (Skinny Joey) Merlino and his racketeering co-defendant Anthony Cirillo were approved to attend the Sunday nuptials in Florida – just not at the same time. Under the terms of their release pending trial, the 55-year-old Merlino and alleged Gambino family associate Cirillo, 51, of

Englewood Cliffs, N.J., are barred from contact. 'Mr. Merlino will attend the wedding ceremony ONLY, which is scheduled to begin at 9:30 A.M.,' suggested Jacobs in a letter to the judge. 'Mr. Merlino will then leave immediately following the wedding ceremony in order to allow Mr. Cirillo to attend the remaining reception/luncheon.' Sullivan showed some love to both defendants and signed off on the deal, with his 'no contact' caveat. Merlino, a convicted felon, was arrested in Florida last August for conspiring with members of the city's Genovese, Gambino, Lucchese and Bonanno families in a wide-ranging racketeering operation."

4   Information from author's interview with James Leif Sanders. Also shown in article by Pamela J. Johnson, "Record-setting heroin seizure nets 30 pounds," *The Orlando Sentinel*, 02 Aug 2000, Page 35. https://www.newspapers.com/article/the-orlando-sentinel-orlando-executive-a/55224650/

5   Ibid.

6   DEA falls under supervision of the Department of Justice.

7   This unit was mentioned in a government document dated October 13, 2006, concerning the Electronic Travel Document System. https://www.dhs.gov/xlibrary/assets/privacy/ privacy_pia_ice_etd.pdf;

While George W. Bush was President, 9/11 occurred, resulting in a complete overhaul of Immigration, Customs and Border Patrol into one agency. Traditional ways of handling cases were revamped by regulations written in federal government jargon that can only be translated, of course, by higher-ups with political appointments from the Executive Branch of the government. See "Name Change of Two DHS Components," dated 03/16/2010, which states: "On March 31, 2007, the name of the Bureau of Customs and Border Protection changed to U.S. Customs and Border Protection (CBP) and the name of the Bureau of Immigration and Customs Enforcement changed to U.S. Immigration and Customs Enforcement (ICE). This final rule revises two chapter headings in title 19 of the Code of Federal Regulations to reflect the name changes for those two Department of Homeland Security (DHS) components." https://www.federalregister. gov/documents/2010/03/16/2010-5639/name-change-of-two-dhs-components

8   Sadly, this patriotic American, Norman Bright, passed away on October 4th, 2021, with a memorial service held in Freehold, NJ. https://claytonfuneralhome.com/tribute/details/4314/Norman-Bright/obituary.html

9   "Bahamian lawyer guilty of drug charge,"*Tampa Bay Times*, published Dec. 18, 1993 (updated Oct. 10, 2005). hof-drug-charge/

10   Ibid.

11   "Special Report: U.S. Customs," *Miami Herald*, December 13, 1998.

12   Anonymous source interview.

13   "Special Report: U.S. Customs," *Miami Herald*, December 13, 1998.

14   Operation Blue Lighting had been initiated in 1985 as a two-week operation by U.S. Customs, which boasted so much success that it made a recommendation: "Joint Federal-State-local interdiction operations, such as Operation Blue Lightning, should be refined and *used wherever feasible and desirable.*" Thereafter, numerous operations began to appear almost everywhere even after Customs had been rolled into Homeland Security. https://druglibrary.net/schaffer/GovPubs/ amhab/amhabc8.htm President's Commission on Organized Crime, 1986.

15   Keep in mind that 9/11 occurred eight months after George W. Bush was inaugurated as President. The Homeland Security Act was enacted November 25, 2002, in the wake of the

9/11 attacks and subsequent mailing of anthrax spores to Democrats in Congress. The first person appointed under the law to serve as Inspector General over the Department of Homeland Security was named Clark Kent Ervin, a graduate of Houston's elite, then almost-entirely-white Kincaid School, attended by the children of wealthy Houstonians with political clout. Ervin seems to have been the only black face in his 1977 class. Samantha Levine dug deeper into Ervin's background for "A job for Superman," in *Money & Business*, June 20, 2004, revealing: "Ervin was pushed by two elementary school teachers to apply to the city's elite Kinkaid School, George W. Bush's alma mater; he became the first African American male ever to attend the school. When Ervin started as a seventh grader there in 1971, most classmates were accepting. But one boy called Ervin a n r every day until they graduated more than five years later. 'Clark never once broke,' recalls his friend Allison Marich. An accomplished classical pianist and a political junkie, Ervin became one of the nation's top high school debaters Ervin attended Harvard University for college and law school, separated by stint as a Rhodes scholar at Oxford University." Archived at http://www.usnews.com/usnews/news/articles/040628/28ervin.htm

16   Mark Schwed, "Massive Drug Bust Nets $100 Million," United Press International, *Tampa Tribune*, April 20, 1985. One of its biggest goals seems to have been acquiring smugglers' assets by the process of forfeiture. Barry Seal had been arrested in New Orleans, LA a year before Operation Blue Lightning was implemented. Tom Aswell in "Barry Seal murder in Baton Rouge 25 years ago helped expose Iran-Contra debacle," at *Louisiana Voice* (February 14, 2011) gave us the 'official' account of Seal's arrest and its aftermath, which differs in significant aspects with what I wrote in the last ten or so chapters of my first book, Barry and 'the boys'.

17   "The raids were planned after a February White House meeting attended by Vice President Bush and two Bahamian ministers. Officials said relations between the two countries had been cool since news accounts of some Bahamian officials acquiescing in the drug trade. Bush, who heads a federal task force on drug-trafficking in South Florida, praised the operation as 'an unprecedented effort to seal off the Florida coast to smugglers.' He called the drug seizure 'a significant achievement.'" Howard Kurtz, "2 Nations Stage Huge Drug Raid," *Washington Post*, April 20, 1985.

"Operation Blue Lightning then became the permanent Blue Lightning Strike Force, which uses the well known U.S. Customs Cigarette boats touted by Vice President George Bush, who heads a task force against drugs in South Florida." Also listen to audio: "Drug Fight Unleashes New Weapon," *Orlando Sentinel*, February 12, 1986. https://www.orlandosentinel. com/1986/02/12/drug-fight-unleashes-new-weapon/

18   Ben-Veniste rose to prominence after President Nixon fired Archibald Cox as special prosecutor, and Attorney General Elliott Richardson and his deputy resigned. That left then-youthful attorneys Ben-Veniste and Jill Wine (now Banks), sometimes seen as a consultant on MSNBC, in charge of prosecuting the Watergate defendants. I wrote in my first book that, after the Watergate prosecutions, "he will be Democratic co-counsel for the Congressional Whitewater committee. Ben-Veniste reportedly proved helpful in steering the Committee away from the rocky shoals of Clinton's possible involvement in the drug smuggling through Mena into the calmer waters of Presidential blow-jobs." Daniel Hopsicker, *Barry and 'the boys': The CIA, the Mob and America's Secret History* (Noti, OR: Madcow Press, 2001), chapter 38.

Terry Reed's book, *Compromised*, exposes what was happening in Arkansas at the time through the eyes of the author, Reed, who in the fall of 1985 had just moved his family to Arkansas to set up a CIA proprietary business with Seth Ward's company. He also had contact with "Robert Johnson," who, he was informed, was "SAT's General Counsel, but also 'a stockholder' in SAT, and one of those 'Yale lawyer types' who had lately started running the Agency."

Terry Reed and John Cummings, *Compromised: Clinton, Bush and The CIA* (New York, NY: S.P.I. Books, /Shapolsky Publishers, Inc, 1994), p. 195.

19   From AP and *Washington Post* Dispatches, "Popular deputy chosen to be attorney general," *Courier-Journal*, Louisville, KY, 17 Oct 1991, p. 3 https://www.newspapers. com/clip/30222602/barr-was-cia1991/#

20   We're still not quite sure what to make of the fact that his father, Donald Barr, who was headmaster at the Dalton School, may have been the first to recognize the 'value' of Jeffrey Epstein and reward him with a job for which he did not qualify, lacking any college degree or teaching credential. Mike Baker and Amy Julia Harris, "Jeffrey Epstein Taught at Dalton. His Behavior Was Noticed." *New York Times*, July 12, 2019. hfrey-epstein-dalton-teacher.html

21   A member of Norman Saunders' government in 1985 when Barry Seal set him up was a man named Ariel Misick, an older brother of Premier Mike. He and two other brothers seemed to be engaged in deals to sell or lease valuable TCI properties, with funds going to their political party to ensure their future elections. Power everywhere has become not only a means to an end but an end in itself.

"Turks & Caicos Islands government reached an agreement with the Sandals Group in relation to investigations by the special investigation and prosecution team (SIPT) that involves a payment by Sandals of US$12 million to the government, reports *Caribbean News Now* (Jan. 23, 2013):

"The agreement is said to be without any admission of liability by the company, its directors and/or officers. In Nov. 2011, *The Tribune* newspaper in The Bahamas revealed the existence of an investigation conducted by US government officials into the wire transfer of funds totaling $1.65 million from accounts belonging to Sandals/Beaches resorts into the hands of the Progressive National Party (PNP) and former TCI premier Michael Misick, *using his brothers' firms*.

The funds were divided between Misick and Stanbrook, headed by Ariel Misick; Chalmers & Co., headed by Chalmers *Chal* Misick; and Prestigious Properties headed by Washington Misick; One million dollars of the funds from Sandals to pay debts and obligations of Michael Misick himself. In the case of Prestigious Properties, an examination of its files reportedly revealed notes redirecting the funds to the accounts of Michael Misick, now under arrest in Brazil pending extradition to the TCI. Washington Misick, former TCI chief minister for the PNP in the early 1990s, is the territory's minister of finance. He also headed the TCI Bank as chairman of the board of directors. TCI Bank has been in liquidation since April 2010 when it failed, taking down with it 4,000 personal accounts of islanders and $22.9 million in islanders' pension funds."

The Free Library. "$12 million from Sandals." Retrieved Jan 21, 2023, https://www.thefreelibrary.com/%2412+million+from+Sandals.-a0320848195

22   Delana Isles, "LisaRaye testifies about private jets before SIPT," *Weekly News* reporter, October 30, 2017. https://tcweeklynews.com/lisaraye-testifies-about-private-jetsbe-fore-sipt-p8252-127.htm

23   Terry Reed and John Cummings, *Compromised.*

24   The April 29, 1993, *Fort Lauderdale Sun-Sentinel* reported, "The hurricane plan was shaped in part by Florida's insider in the White House: Jeffrey Watson."

Chapter Seventeen

Argyll Biotech and Goat's Blood

Oh yeah. That's part of why this story is still so interesting is that people are still promoting it for all sorts of things. I talked to a few people for the podcast series who continue to push versions of this serum to this day. One of those people is someone named Douglas Arthur McClain Sr.
                                                   – Grant Hill, podcast producer[1]

Successful scam artists are craftsmen in their world – producers, performers, promoters – who leap from one role to another, changing costumes, dialects and set backgrounds. Getting a picture of who they really are seems an impossible task.

We watched Douglas McClain, Sr. "mature," after being born in a cult, into serial fraud at International Profit Associates (IPA), and while working in the hyena pack controlled by Robert Colgin Wilson.

In 1998 Wilson, McClain's friend and mentor, had just been sentenced to a total of 8 years and 7 months, if served consecutively, on two criminal counts, while also consenting to a civil judgment in Florida. His pack of hyenas had bled Sarasota-based U.S. Employer Consumer Self-Insurance Fund Inc. (USEC) dry – to the tune of $3.9 million. [2]

It was time for Wilson's henchmen to go into business on their own. Jim Miceli and the younger McClain at first remained in the Chicago area. Jim had grown up there, working with his dad in the construction business. The *Chicago Tribune* once reported there were 50 civil suits filed against the Miceli father-son team before someone thought to prosecute them criminally in 1998.[3]

Miceli's parents split, and his mother returned to her roots in southern California. Jim followed her and turned up in Poway, California, near La Jolla.

They created in 2003 the Argyll Group, LLC in Delaware as a holding company with two subsidiaries – a new Nevada entity based in La Jolla, and the original one, based in Boerne, TX. The holding company was to be "capitalized with funds borrowed from Director's Performance Fund

[DPF]," a hedge fund owned by Sharon (Shea) Vaughn in Lake Forest, Illinois.[4]

How they heard about Vaughn, we aren't sure, though she was operating from her home in Lake Forest, Illinois, and they were in Schaumburg, Illinois – each suburb about 30 miles northwest of Chicago.

Shea and her then-husband, Stephen Ferrone, lived in a multi-million-dollar mansion in Lake Forest, where Chicago's millionaire families for more than a century have socialized together in the summer. Many Lake Forest homes were still owned by descendants of wealthy Gilded Age tycoons – several generations down from those who made the fortune – such as the son of Cyrus McCormick (Harold Fowler McCormick), who married a daughter of John D. Rockefeller, and built the first magnificent mansion on the north shore of Lake Michigan.

Lake Forest epitomized ostentatious wealth – the same way Sarasota, Florida, would do, after it was "discovered" by a few rich retail magnates from the same Chicago suburb.

The SEC was able to trace Shea Vaughn's investors' money into Argyll Equities. The loan from her was Argyll's original capital – the $9.6 million "loan" from Director's Performance Fund (DPF), Sharon Vaughn's hedge fund.[5]

But Shea Vaughn's loan wasn't the only capital Argyll Equities started with, according to a lawsuit filed by a Boca Raton, Florida, realtor named Eleanor Z. Rabin.[6]

Allegations in Rabin's lawsuit furnish particulars of the money trail. Beginning during the time that the McClains and Miceli worked together at International Profit Associates (IPA) in Illinois, according to the lawsuit, McClain Sr. became involved with a "public entity known as Nextpath Technologies [formed in January 1999] and began selling large volumes of stock to investors based on false information for approximately $6,000,000."[7]

"McClain Jr., and Miceli left IPA and used money from the sale of Nextpath stock to finance the start of a new entity, FIT Management," which then "financed the start of an entity known as Argyll Equities, which had the appearance of a legitimate financial/stock lender 'but operated more akin to a Ponzi scheme.'... Plaintiff also alleged Argyll Equities financed the start up of Argyll Biotechnologies, and that Argyll Equities and/or Argyll Biotechnologies financed the start up of Immunosyn."[8]

Eleanor Rabin had purchased shares in Immunosyn, which she asserted was under the financial control of Miceli and McClain Jr.[9]

The Securities and Exchange Commission had been kept busy investigating the three men's activities for years. I myself first caught up with them in 2006, just after "Cocaine One," owned by Skyway was busted.[10]

We will give full details soon about how Skyway was created.

Before creating her hedge fund with money from 22 investors, Shea Vaughn had been ranked on Bloomberg Wealth Manager's annual list of high-end personal money managers. Her hedge fund was a different story. It became a magnet for fraudsters.

Argyll applied for the loan from her DPF hedge fund shortly before Shea Vaughn, DPF's manager, found herself in a bit of hot water.

A WOLF PACK WORKS OVER SHEA VAUGHN

On October 5, 2005, Vaughn was terrified. She had bet the ranch, more than $24 million – almost every penny in her hedge fund – on "a sham company at the center of a scheme in which promoters promised extravagant returns from a government-backed group," as securities regulators later called it. $25 million disappeared down a black hole, and she was having trouble explaining to Argyll why she couldn't fund their loan.

The previous March of 2005, she'd begun dealing with some men who had promised her 10% in profit per week. Expecting to make a quick $60 million in three weeks, Shea planned to get in and out fast. But things hadn't gone according to plan.

Ten percent per week! Could anyone fall for such an obvious lie? What was it P. T. Barnum once said, "There's a sucker born every minute"? Shea Vaughn was one of those suckers.

One Forbes pundit put it this way: "In consent decrees, Vaughn neither admitted nor denied being the dumbest money manager out there."[11]

Panic caused her to contact appropriate authorities, who, mark my words, never do anything out of the goodness of their hearts. They wanted something in exchange for helping her.

When an indictment was unsealed on Tuesday, November 16, 2005, the *Chicago Tribune,* Sharon Vaughn's local paper, reported the story, omitting her name: "Three businessmen, including a director of a Virginia bank, swindled a Lake Forest investment fund out of $25 million in a fraudulent deal that promised profits of 10 percent per week, prosecutors said Tuesday."[12]

They spelled out the name of individuals who had been arrested as "Frank Cowles, a member of the board of Virginia Commerce Bank in Arlington and two co-defendants."

Cowles seemed to be the big fish they had caught.[13]

Cowles' hometown paper, the *Washington Post,* had waited five days to report the story under a headline subtle enough to omit his name, although it was clearly spelled out in the first paragraph. [14]

The Post said Cowles was arrested at his Scottsville horse farm the previous week and released on $1 million bail, making his appearance in U.S. District Court in Chicago on Thursday.

He had resigned from Virginia Commerce Bank – which he had co-founded in 1988. The *Post* added that Cowles owned about 4 percent of the bank's stock and also owned Nissan and Chrysler dealerships in Woodbridge, Virginia, as well as a large Arabian horse farm in central Virginia. Then they quoted from a criminal complaint unsealed in the Chicago federal court:

> According to the criminal complaint, Cowles is the secretary of American Trade Industries Inc. Richard E. Warren, 63, of Fredericksburg, identified as the president of American Trade, and "associate" David L. Myatt, 41, of Los Banos, Calif., were implicated with Cowles in the alleged conspiracy.[15]
>
> The government alleged that beginning in March, Myatt and Warren pitched the Illinois hedge fund manager [unnamed Individual-1] on an investment program in which American Trade Industries would use the money to trade bonds, promising a 10 percent profit each week.
>
> While Myatt and Warren returned $3.4 million to the hedge fund, the hedge fund manager could not get the two men to provide a written accounting of where the $25 million investment was being held, the complaint said.[16]

The *Post*, citing the complaint, also revealed what Vaughn had done after contacting the Justice Department and Secret Service. She "flew to Washington to meet with Warren and Cowles on Oct. 21." When she had conversations with the men later, she tape-recorded them for the Secret Service. According to the complaint, "Cowles allegedly described how the hedge fund manager's money was tied up *in foreign bank accounts* and said that the 'Fed administrator' was tying up the funds."

In their last conversation on November 10, prior to the indictment, the taped conversation had Cowles saying Vaughn "would have to pay Myatt an additional $500,000 for the 'Fed administrator' to return the funds."[17]

They had him dead to rights. Only… they didn't, as we'll see later.

Working Off a Beef

At the time McClain and Miceli (as Argyll Equities) approached Sharon Vaughn for the loan, they had no way of knowing she was caught in the Cowles trap, since her license wouldn't be revoked until after the Argyll deal was in play. She had agreed to work off her beef with the SEC by cooperating with the feds in catching anybody who thereafter approached her for a loan, as well as to pay a 10% fine to the SEC based on the transactional amount.

Shea Vaughn signed the "consent decree," saying she did not admit any wrongdoing, while the SEC said she was an "unwitting victim" of the Cowles scam, but she had committed several other no-no's. The securities regulator accused her of promising her investors she'd invest only in low-risk stocks and bonds, then failing to tell them when she handed $25 million – their money – over to the Cowles team.

The SEC may have known she had been about to fund a loan to Argyll. They most certainly knew about the $17 million Argyll "loaned" to Grupo TMM's drug-smuggling subsidiary, in which the Segovias were the major shareholders.

Argyll's principals – the McClains and Miceli – were still on the loose, and the SEC wanted Vaughn to help the Feds put the three men away. Once she – miraculously? – had the $25 million back from the Cowles group, she funded the $9.6 million loan to the Argyll Group, which held the stock of two branches of Argyll Equities LLC.

Offshore Trusts Hide a Multitude of Crimes

The only principal of Argyll who lived in Boerne, Texas, was Douglas A. McClain, Sr. – former cult member and minion of the Robert Colgin Wilson hyena pack. But, as it turned out, he also had friends there. Could it be that those friends were the reason he'd moved from Florida to Texas?

The Boerne law firm he went to for help was owned by J. Ken Nunley, who had a connection to another Texas attorney named Samuel Lane Boyd of Dallas.

When Linda researched their names, she was awestruck. Nunley, for example, had been born in her own birthplace – San Angelo, Texas – just two years before her own birth. Boyd had graduated from the same law school – Texas Tech – two years after she did, though he was a few years older.[18]

Pure coincidence. Linda never crossed paths with either of them to her knowledge. Nevertheless, she was intrigued.

The first link between the two Texas lawyers and McClain we discovered stemmed from actions that occurred in central Long Island, Suffolk County, New York in the late '90s when a target of the scam (called the "mark") had unfortunately consulted Robert Colgin Wilson, the head of a vicious "hyena pack" McClain was part of. The mark was seeking a loan for $18 million to expand its software business.

"Euro Scotia Group Limited" – described by the court as Wilson's "interconnected web of transnational corporations," was promising Appgen/Codapro (the mark) financing in the form of EuroBonds.[19]

There was a whole plethora of fake interrelated corporations making up the Euro Scotia group – all named as co-defendants in the case.[20] Individuals (including Douglas, Sr. and his wife, Deborah McClain) were also named, though their roles were not explained in the filing we had access to.[21]

Sam L. Boyd, the Texas lawyer, however, had a prominent role. He "participated in the deal by transferring funds from his law firm trust account to Codapro on behalf of the Euro Scotia Group."[22]

Boyd claimed to be acting on behalf of all the other defendants when he filed a motion to have the case, originally filed in a New York state court, "removed" to the Eastern District of New York – a federal court.

Boyd's opponent, being savvier, quickly objected, demanding that Boyd present evidence that he actually represented the others. Without that proof, they were all subject to a default judgment for not answering the lawsuit in time.

Boyd offered as evidence a "letter that he wrote to 'Ken Nunley, Esq.,' which states, 'Thank you for your kind assistance in connection with our removal of the Suffolk County state court case to the United States District Court.'"[23]

The letter gave the plaintiff even more ammunition, since Nunley was nowhere named in the litigation, either as a party or as official counsel for a party. Boyd lost his motion, and the case went back to state court.

In a different case, Boyd had been named as a participant with McClain in a scam played on a non-profit charity called Cleft of the Rock Foundation, located on Long Island's north shore. Here the same hyena pack was "alleged to have laundered some proceeds of this fraud through his attorney trust account," according to the judge.[24]

It appears Doug McClain, Sr. went to Ken Nunley's Boerne office at some point before the end of 2007 to talk to him about putting his percentage of the Argyll business into an offshore corporation. Nunley's CPA, Lynn Booker, in San Antonio took care of that detail. There were three BVI corporations created – Padmore Holdings, Ltd., Clairsvelle Holdings, Ltd., and Cuxhaven Holdings, Ltd. [25]

A subpoena was issued on January 20, 2006, by the SEC pursuant to proceedings captioned "In the Matter of Directors Financial Group, Ltd." (Shea Vaughn's hedge fund) and "In the Matter of Prime Bank Securities," so it looks as though Doug was planning to hide his assets. The SEC had also sent two other subpoenas "to affiliates of Argyll Biotech" on March 30, 2006, in a case called "In the Matter of The Argyll Group, LLC," seeking production of documents concerning such subjects as the prior licensee of SF-1019 and Nurovysn Merger Corporation. A third subpoena, dated December 15, 2006, was issued to Immunosyn.

Before it reached its denouement, the dirty duo had taken on a third partner, Jeffrey R. Spanier, former owner of Amerifund Capital Finance LLC. As the *San Diego Union Tribune* reported:

> The scheme preyed on wealthy stockholders from the U.S., Canada, Mexico, Panama, China, England and Belgium. McClain and Miceli, owners of Poway-based Argyll Equities, partnered with Spanier's firm to offer loans to corporate executives.
>
> The executives put up millions of dollars of stock in publicly-traded companies as collateral, and were promised that nothing would happen to the stock as long as there were no defaults on the loan, court records show…
>
> Rather than hang onto the stock, the men sold it immediately, using the cash to fund the loans. The unsuspecting borrowers also paid monthly interest payments on their loans."[26]

Miceli and Doug Jr. and Spanier were indicted in 2012 and tried a year later. Miceli was saved from being humiliated by committing suicide. The other two men were convicted of multiple counts of conspiracy, mail fraud, wire fraud, securities fraud, and money laundering and sentenced in 2014 to multiple years in prison.[27] For selling goat's blood as a cancer cure, among other crimes, Douglas McClain Jr, was sentenced to 14 years in prison in federal court in San Diego.

One Link after Another

In addition to being involved with Argyll, Miceli also worked on another scam in the San Diego area – M3 Energy Resources in Kentucky – which seems to have picked up where one of Robert Colgin Wilson's scams from decades earlier left off.

A CPA named Gregory Witz was named in this project. His LinkedIn account mentioned his work history: "M3 Management Resources, LLC & Affilated [sic] Companies, 2005 – 2011. 6 years. Rancho Bernardo, CA – Directed Finance and Accounting department for this San Diego based private equity firm and its 200+ employee-based Kentucky affiliate M3 Energy Resources. Managed preparation of annual budgets, forecasts, consolidated financial statements. Provided oversight of HR department, treasury management activities, and risk management activities."

Doug McClain, Sr. had also used this same company in his sales pitch to elderly "investors" lured into his web, saying he had a coal mine he owned in Kentucky, as surety that he would return investor money. Only, McClain didn't own a coal mine in Kentucky. He did, however, have a mail drop at 10531 4S Commons Drive, Ste 473, San Diego, in the name of a Delaware entity called M3 Energy Resources, LLC, which was registered in Kentucky.

At the time Argyll Equities in La Jolla was created in 2002, Greg Witz was living there and had a side business selling a product called Pyruvate. He sold this through an entity called Grelor Enterprises, advertised in 1997 to lose fat, enhance endurance, and prevent muscle loss – all at a wholesale price of $39.95.

Pyrovate sounded an awful lot like the products Immunosyn's scientific director, Dr. Myron Wentz, had been marketing in Utah through USANA – an antioxidant nutrient compound sold using the "multi-level marketing" technique often called simply an "illegal pyramid scheme."

In 2008 Wentz was named a director of Immunosyn Corporation, which had "exclusive worldwide rights from its largest shareholder, Argyll Biotechnologies, LLC, to market, sell and distribute SF-1019."[28]

GOAT'S BLOOD TONIC, ANYONE?

"At one point," the *San Diego Union Tribune* reporter had added, "in an effort to legitimize themselves, McClain and Miceli launched a shell biotech company, Immunosyn Corporation, that was purportedly developing goat blood into a new wonder drug to cure multiple sclerosis and other terminal illnesses. The men raised more than $20 million from investors between 2006 and 2010, prosecutors said."[29]

We hadn't considered Immunosyn – an even worse fraud – as a means of "sanitizing" their image. If that was their intent, it was a massive failure.

Argyll had branched out into biotech, managing to suck even Shea Vaughn's husband Stephen Ferrone into a scheme involving a corporation it planned to take public.

Argyll Biotechnology had first been created in the UK, with a branch in San Diego, managing to acquire the patent (Patent No. 7,358,044 B2) for a drug called SF-1019.[30]

When Argyll Biotech began touting a serum made from goat's blood that could cure multiple schlerosis (MS) and AIDS, the claims triggered such a powerful resonance with CIA projects of the '70s, it was almost impossible to ignore the CIA's old connections to SRI, chaired a couple of times by Myron DuBain, mentioned previously.

WHO CREATED SF-1019?

Three scientific men had been collaborating on research on various animals before 2003. I must confess the fact that I'm not a chemist, though I did experiment with a few chemicals back in the day. Realizing that my experimentation does not qualify me as an expert, I'll just leave it at that. So don't ask me what the words in the goat's blood patent mean.

Patent US7358044B2 was a drug labeled "PROPHYLACTIC AND THERAPEUTIC BENEFITS OF A NEW CLASS OF IMMUNE STIMULATING PEPTIDES," filed in April 2004. It was later assigned to Argyll Biotechnologies, LLC., an entity registered to Doug McClain, Jr. and James Miceli.

Argyll owned more than 10% – 28 million of the 280 million shares – of Immunosyn (IMYN), while Sharon Vaughn and Stephen Ferrone, her husband, owned a mere 1.75 million shares. Nevertheless, the IMYN board voted to make Ferrone president in 2007. According to the SEC, his actions helped "goose the stock price" of the company, resulting in other investors being scammed to the tune of $20 million.[31]

Ferrone's trial did not occur until 2016, when he testified he'd been introduced to Immunosyn and its goat blood drug by his wife's former business partner, Miceli, and that he believed that the drug "had the potential to be used in so many different ways."[32]

A SINGING OSMOND BROTHER

Alan Osmond, Donny and Marie's older brother, was interviewed by Sherri Snelling in 2012. "'I was given a cortisone shot when I was first diagnosed [with multiple sclerosis] in 1987,' Alan says, 'and it just about killed me. It was right then that I decided there has to be a better way and I started investigating alternative medicines.'"

Snelling described Alan's nutritional regime without mentioning his support for Dr. Myron Wentz, who had a treatment center for MS patients in Rosarita, Mexico, in Baja, just south of Tijuana. To be close to his "alternative medical" clinic, Wentz relocated from Utah (where the Osmonds originated) to National City, California, where he likely first met Jim Miceli or Gregory Witz.

Argyll Equities LLC was being sued at one time by garbage king Lou Paolino, CEO of Mace International, who had obtained a $4 million loan from Argyll Equities, brokered by a Boca Raton company called Ameri-Fund Capital Finance – Spanier's little investment company. The lawyer who defended Argyll was Chicago attorney John A. Franczyk, who was also helpful in setting up Argyll Biotech UK, created in October 2005.

Argyll Biotech bought the exclusive right to market the patented drug SF-1019 and created Immunosyn Corporation allegedly to complete the required clinical trials necessary to bring the drug to market. They took Immunosyn Corporation public and made its first SEC filing on February 16, 2007, with shares of OTC penny stock.

Once the lawsuits began, Dr. Wentz turned on everyone who'd been hired to set up the companies, suing them for breach of contract.[33]

Part of his complaint stated that Alan Osmond was being paid to promote SF-1019 as a treatment for MS. Osmond had created a website (now defunct) on which he began touting the wonders of Immunosyn as early as July 5, 2008, almost two weeks before Immunosyn made any public announcement – seemingly indicating some insider trading was going on, when he said:

"NOW, you can see a doctor for treatment of SF-1019. Argyll has been given permission to open the 'Renewed Hope Clinic in Beaver, Utah.'"[34]

TULSA'S DR. GARY DAVIS – THE GOAT DOCTOR

SF-1019 had been patented by three researchers who adapted a goat serum first used by Dr. Gary Davis in a failed clinical trial (BB7075). Dr. Davis, called "the Goat Doctor," in a *Washington Post* article in June 2000, had been working through the National Institutes of Health (NIH) to become approved for clinical trials on humans since 1994. His antibody approach to a "cure" for AIDS and the HIV virus was looked at with skepticism by Dr. Anthony Fauci at the CDC but allowed to continue.

Something had happened around 2007, the year of Dr Davis' mysterious death. Dr. Myron Wentz, formerly of Utah, Osmond's home state, was named a director of Immunosyn in March 2008. His website in Africa stated that in 2005 Wentz donated funds to establish a medical clinic in Uganda through an existing mission.

When J. Ken Nunley, the Boerne lawyer friend of Doug McClain, Sr., died in 2013, his hagiographic obituary revealed that he and his wife had gone on a mission trip to Uganda in 2010.

Call me cynical. I'm not buying this as just a coincidence. It doesn't pass the smell test.

In 1974, Dr. Wentz had founded Gull Laboratories and, as President and Chairman from 1974 to 1994, he "developed, manufactured, and marketed medical diagnostic test kits designed to detect infectious diseases, particularly those caused by viruses, and used in private and hospital laboratories around the world. Gull was sold to Fresenius, a German medical products company, in 1994 although Dr. Wentz continued as Chairman until 1998."[35]

Today Fresenius has clinics nationwide for dialysis patients. Wentz also founded Sanoviv Medical Institute in 1998, a holistic medical facility located on the Pacific Coast near Rosarito Beach, Mexico after leaving Fresenius. It was situated just south of the U.S. mainland at San Diego, and Wentz actually lived at National City, California.

Was Wentz part of the hyena pack, or was he an innocent victim of the fraud because of his desire to do good deeds? We are left wondering.

According to an email furnished to me by Dennis Delaney after he saw my April 2, 2009, story entitled "Art Nadel 'Ponzi Pal' linked to 5-ton coke bust," Doug McClain, Jr. had written a brief bio of himself that was available for a time online. He claimed he graduated in 1996 "with a BBA in finance from Mercer University's Stetson School of Business and Economics in Georgia. During that time, Mr. McClain completed internships in Asia, Australia and throughout Europe. After which, he became a financial advisor with American Express Financial Advisors/IDS Life (AEFA)."

In several other places in this book we've identified a pattern that keeps reappearing. American Express and IDS (short for Investors Diversified Services). American Express acquired IDS in 1983, and the very next acquisition it made was – drum roll, please – the Wisconsin Employers Casualty Company of Green Bay, Wisconsin, founded by Wally Hilliard.

Connection? Or coincidence?

After Hilliard sold WECC to the American Express Fireman's Fund, Hilliard moved to Naples, Florida, to "retire." Instead, as I've reported in my website for years, he "accidentally" began laundering drug money, using at least two airplanes he leased or chartered to South Americans involved in smuggling heroin and cocaine into Florida.

Tracking activities of a criminal organization is somewhat like watching two stones being dropped into a body of water. Each causes waves of concentric circles to ripple out, intersecting with the other. The ripples make it appear that the two stones are connected. Unfortunately, we cannot know for certain they were dropped by the same person.

SWITCHEROO – FROM PREY TO PREDATOR?

On a similar note, it's also hard to tell when a person is a true *victim* of the con or also a *participant* in the scheme. There's a part of our mind that really likes to believe we can get something for nothing. Conmen, like spiders, know this and use it to their advantage to lure insects into their webs.

Let's look back briefly at Shea Vaughn who wanted to make 10% return per WEEK on her $25 million. She was conned, but it was no excuse, the SEC told her, because she violated her oath, as it were, to act as a fiduciary for the funds entrusted to her.

"Thank God I went to the Department of Justice and the Secret Service," Shea was quoted as saying when she got back the millions she'd wired to a bank in Italy.[36]

It was four months after the three men who had targeted her had been indicted. But then, suddenly, all charges against Frank Cowles, the one who had appeared to have been the mastermind, were dismissed. The person who had appeared to be the victim, Shea Vaughn, was now fined over $800,000 and lost her ability to handle hedge funds in the future.

"The person that was thought to be the predator was actually the prey," the attorney, who represented an "ebullient" Frank L. Cowles Jr., told the *Washington Post* when his client was released.

When I wrote my three-part mini-series called "True Detective" at my website, I knew something hinky was going on. It was mentioned in the affidavit of the Secret Service agent who filed the criminal complaint. I obtained a copy of it at the time and posted a link at my website.[37]

Shea was in a panic, desperate to get a copy of the Italian bank's statement that reflected her account's status. She wasn't authorized, they said. Still, she gave them an additional $5 million, persuaded by their assurances that it was easier to make this kind of profit in Europe where they aren't regulated. She requested J.P. Morgan twice to wire funds directly to Meliorbanca in Milan.

Something Hinky This Way Comes

A red flag went up when I read that. That name sounded so familiar. My old, dog-eared copy of Penny Lernoux's book, *In Banks We Trust*, however, was in storage somewhere. Before long I'd forgotten all about it.

Still, I knew things weren't quite right.

When we were reviewing the files for the book, the name of the Italian bank where the funds were wired leapt out again. Meliorbanca, *not Mediobanca*, was the Italian bank I was thinking of. My Italian is as lacking as it ever was. The similar-sounding name of a second Milanese private bank had sent shivers up my spine.

I'd read about Sicilian gangsters and political fascists during the so-called "Years of Lead," reminiscent of the Al Capone era in our own country – from the late 1960s to the early 1980s, a period marked "by thousands of terrorist attacks and over twelve hundred casualties among Italian citizens."[38]

In Italy the *Propaganda Due* (P-2) masonic lodge was central to the story of Roberto Calvi, hanging from Blackfriar's Bridge in London.[39]

At long last we found our copy of the Lernoux book and began re-reading about how Michele Sindona had threatened Enrico Cuccia, the president of *Mediobanca* S.p.A, which "controlled important parts of the Italian economy for decades."

Cuccia used the Mediobanca investment funds to "broker mergers and buy shares in a vast web of industrial groups known as the 'Mediobanca galaxy,' and including Fiat, Pirelli and Olivetti," according to his obituary in 2000.[40]

"What Cuccia wants, God wants, too," investor Leopoldo Pirelli once joked. But he wasn't really amused.

Cuccia "worked closely with the Fiat chairman Gianni Agnelli," helping the Agnellis "get rid of the Libyan leader Col. Muammar el-Qaddafi as a shareholder in Fiat by buying back shares of the automotive empire worth $3.1 billion," the *Times* obituary continued. Although the deal was good for the Agnelli family, the downside was it "cost an international group of banks $600 million in losses."[41]

While reading about the "Years of Lead," we also dived deeper into the Cowles Identity.

You Can't Overlook the Exes

Cowles' arrest had been a "mistake," causing him to resign "as a director of Virginia Commerce Bank," Cowles' spokesman told the public, averring Cowles had an unblemished background and no reason to be involved in hedge fund stealing. He was already rich. He owned Greenfield Farm and Hidden Hill Arabians in Virginia where he raised thoroughbred horses.[42]

Cowles, we learned by checking his background, was a man who enjoyed getting married. He did it often. The first time was in 1950, to Nancy O'Meara, who in 1953 divorced him for desertion. The second marriage occurred in 1956 when he married Hazel Scott, an airline stewardess. During that marriage two sons were born.

He also got a law degree from Clark Hall Law School at the University of Virginia in Charlottesville, becoming the last student to enter the law school without a college degree. It sounds like the all-too-common occurrence when a wife puts her husband through law school, and then gets dumped.

In 1979 Frank married Susan Lynn Cancilla, a daughter of a former chief of the weapons and fire control of the Army Materiel Command. Natale Cancilla was a naturalized American citizen, born in Sicily, who retired in Alexandria, Virginia, before his death in 2002.[43]

Twenty years later, just a month before he married Teresa Leila Rachid Lichi from Paraguay, his divorce from Susan became final.

BRIEF HISTORY OF PARAGUAY – 1998-2006

The well-educated and accomplished Paraguayan beauty had a doctorate from Complutense, the largest university in Spain. She began her career in 1982, working within government agencies in Paraguay.[44] Paraguay at that time gives us a perfect picture of what some people fear could happen in the United States in the event Donald Trump is elected again in November 2024.

Leila Rachid de Cowles was working smack dab in the center of what resembled a return to Italy's "Years of Lead," beginning in 1998. An Army general (Oviedo) who had come to power through a coup in 1996 was running for reelection in 1998, for which he is sentenced to prison for 10 years. His running mate (Cubas) runs in his place and wins with the slogan, "Cubas in government, Oviedo in power." A month later the Paraguayan Congress passes a law saying the president cannot pardon anyone who has not served at least half of his or her prison term.

Thumbing his nose at the law, three days after Cubas' inauguration, he reduces Oviedo's sentence to time served and releases him from jail.

The Paraguayan Supreme Court in December 1998 orders Oviedo back to jail. President Cubas defies the Order. The Chamber of Deputies votes to charge Cubas with abuse of power in February 1999 – two votes shy of formal impeachment. Cubas' vice-president, Argaña, who had been named as Cubas' running mate, leading the anti-Oviedo bloc, is brutally murdered on March 23, 1999, and Cubas is implicated. Protests break out with thousands participating in public demonstrations led by striking workers who demand that Cubas resign. Security forces are called out and seven people are shot to death with dozens more injured.

March 24, 1999, the Chamber of Deputies votes overwhelmingly to impeach Cubas. Facing certain conviction and removal from office by the Senate, Cubas resigns on March 28, 1999, and flees to Brazil.

A court orders Oviedo back to prison. He finally returns to Paraguay in 2002 and is immediately arrested and tried for conspiracy to murder Argaña.

On August 2, 2000, Macchi becomes President and appoints Leila Rachid de Cowles to the post of Ambassador of Paraguay to the United States, and she is confirmed a month later. Macchi serves until 2003.

Duarte succeeds Macchi and appoints Leila Rachid to be Minister of Foreign Affairs of Paraguay until his term ends in 2006. Leila is poised to become Paraguay's Ambassador to the United Nations when her husband is indicted in Chicago by a grand jury called by U.S. Attorney Patrick Fitzgerald.

She has missed her opportunity, even though her husband is, by all accounts, cleared of wrongdoing. The evidence against Cowles could not have been stronger. Could he – like Vaughn – have been working off a beef of his own that we didn't know about, just to get his "co-conspirators" put away?

As for why Cowles ventured into Paraguay and met the love of his life, we also can't say. But we're glad to have been reminded to reread "*In Banks We Trust*," which has this to say about Paraguay:

"Paraguay has traditionally been the last refuge in Latin America for right-wing villains on the run, a haven for German Nazis as well as for former Nicaraguan dictator Anastacio Somoza, General Alfredo Stroessner, the region's longest ruling dictator, has also given sanctuary to drug traffickers and neofascist terrorists."[45]

Endnotes

1	"A Miracle Cure for AIDS or Snake Oil?" Reveal, © 2023 The Center for Investigative Reporting. https://revealnews.org/podcast/a-miracle-cure-for-aids-or-snake-oil/

2	Remaining perps in that civil action brought by Florida Insurance Department were John J. Kenny, with offices in Boca Raton and St. Louis; Steven Signer, a stockbroker with Denver-based Cohig & Associates, which also has an office in Boca Raton; and Gary L. Long, a real estate investor and business consultant from Knoxville, Tenn. Some of these names appear in other chapters. 921 F. Supp. 750 (M.D. Fla. 1996), FLA. DEPT. INSURANCE, As Receiver of United States Employer Consumer Self-Insurance Fund of Florida, Plaintiff v. DEBENTURE GUARANTY; Robert Colgin Wilson; Gary L. Long; C. Beverly Lance; Thomas Bertram Lance; James E. Carter, III; John J. Kenny; Nicholson/Kenny Capital Management, Inc.; Pauli & Company, Inc.; Steven Signer; Cohig & Associates; George R. Johnston; Johnston & Kent Securities, Inc.; John Balazovic; and Jeffrey L. Crowley, Defendants. Case No. 95-1826-CIV-T-17E. (United States of America, M.D. Florida, Tampa Division), April 8, 1996. https://law.justia.com/cases/federal/district-courts/FSupp/921/750/1988180/

3	Carolyn Starks and Douglas Holt, "Developer faces probe for string of unfinished homes," *Chicago Tribune* (Chicago, Illinois), Feb 26, 1998, Page 16.

4	Originally filed by Miceli and McClain against Scott, it backfired when Scott filed a counterclaim against them. https://www.madcowprod.com/wp-content/uploads/2015/07/cross_complaint_scott_v._miceli.pdf

5	Kim Janssen, "Jury: Movie star's stepdad misled investors," *Chicago Tribune*, 03 May 2016, Page 1-7. https://www.newspapers.com/article/chicago-tribune-stephen-ferrone-vaughnm/11080493/

6	Civil Action No. SA–10–CV–981–XR. Rabin v. McClain, United States District Court, W.D. Texas, San Antonio Division, 881 F. Supp. 2d 758 (W.D. Tex. 2012). https://casetext.com/case/rabin-v-mcclain-2

7	Doug McClain Sr. was sued in the United States District Court for Massachusetts, resulting in a judgment against him for $4,500,000. And Miceli was convicted of felony laundering, forgery, perjury, and theft over $100,000 in the State of Illinois" Rabin v. McClain, 881 F. Supp. 2d 758, 761 n.2 (W.D. Tex. 2012).

8	"Plaintiff asserts that because of numerous civil judgments against Argyll Equities and FIT Management, McClain Sr. did not publically [sic] own Argyll Equities, but instead operated the company as a consultant and secret owner. Id. at ¶ 35." Rabin v. McClain, 881 F. Supp. 2d 758, 761 n.4 (W.D. Tex. 2012).

9	"Plaintiff alleges that Argyll Biotechnologies was formed because numerous persons brought civil suits against Argyll Equities, and that as a result Argyll Equities' reputation as a reputable and financially stable company deteriorated. Id. at ¶ 39." Rabin v. McClain, 881 F. Supp. 2d 758, 761 n.5 (W.D. Tex. 2012).

10	https://www.madcowprod.com/2006/08/07/cocaine-one-bust-lifts-veil-on-global-narcotics-cartel/

11	Carrie Coolidge, "Option This Case," *Forbes*, Jul 3, 2006. https://www.forbes.com/forbes/2006/0703/042.html?sh=19e71a6c69a8

12	Michael Higgins, "3 face charges in Lake Forest fund scheme," *Chicago Tribune*, 16 Nov 2005, Pages 2-4. https://www.newspapers.com/article/chicago-tribune-frank-cowleslake-forest/136273473/

13	Ibid.

14	Terence O'Hara, *Washington Post* Staff Writer, "U.S. Arrests Three In Hedge Fund Case," *Washington Post*, Monday, November 21, 2005.

15	Richard Warren would later be convicted and sentenced to a total of 200 months in prison. The appellate court later wrote that, "Warren, who is pro se, argues in this direct appeal that the district court lacked both personal and subject-matter jurisdiction because he is a 'citizen of GOD's Kingdom and not of Earth.'" David L. Myatt pled guilty with Warren in 2007. The two men had much in common. Myatt was born in Southern Oregon, but grew up in Ukiah, California where his father was an Assembly of God minister. Their church was located less than ten miles from where Rev. Jim Jones had built the Peoples Temple in 1969, but that does not imply it was also a cult.

16   Terence O'Hara, *Washington Post* Staff Writer, "U.S. Arrests Three In Hedge Fund Case," *Washington Post*, Monday, November 21, 2005.

17   Ibid.

18   Boyd's office at #600 at 6440 N. Central Expy in Dallas is between E. University and Fondren, and his residence on Binkley in University Park is a large valuable lot with an old home. He and his wife have owned both since before 1999.

19   *Codapro Corp. v. Wilson*, 997 F. Supp. 322, 323 (E.D.N.Y. 1998). https://casetext.com/ case/codapro-corp-v-wilson

20   Euro Scotia Funding Limited, Euro Scotia Group Limited, Euro Scotia Funding (U.S.A.), Inc., Euro Scotia Funding (Barbados) Ltd., Euro American Insurance Co. Ltd., and Debenture Guaranty Corporation.

21   Veronica Canino Wilson, Douglas McClain, Deborah McClain, Donald Edel, Edward Nicholas Canino, Gary Long, Robert Carter Dye, Peter Dale, Dieter Wicki, and James Garro – as either directors, employees, or representatives of the various Euro Scotia Group companies.

22   *Codapro Corp. v. Wilson*, 997 F. Supp. 322, 323 (E.D.N.Y. 1998). https://casetext.com/ case/codapro-corp-v-wilson

23   *Codapro Corp. v. Wilson*, 997 F. Supp. 322, 323 (E.D.N.Y. 1998), p. 326.

24   *Cleft of the Rock Foundation v. WILSON, 992 F. Supp. 574 (1998) E.D. New York: January 30, 1998. https://www.anylaw.com/case/cleft-of-the-rock-found-v-wilson/e-d-new-york/01-30-1998/15W2Q2YBTlTomsSBFXnf*

25   Civil Action No. SA-10-CV-981-XR, USDC for Western Division, San Antonio. https://cv-00981-1.pdf

26   https://www.madcowprod.com/wp-content/uploads/2015/07/cross_complaint_scott_v._miceli.pdf

27   Kristina Davis, "Prison for duo behind $100M stock fraud," *San Diego Union Tribune*, June 23, 2013. https://www.sandiegouniontribune.com/sdut-spanier-mcclain-stock-fraud-sentence-argyll-2014jun24-story.html

28   https://www.justice.gov/usao-sdca/pr/owner-florida-stock-lending-firm-sentenced-10-years-prison-his-part-100-million-fraud

29   https://www.sec.gov/Archives/edgar/data/1375623/000095012008000097/exh_99-1. htm

30   Ibid.

31   https://patentimages.storage.googleapis.com/54/9a/14/dd73421191f5fd/US7358044. pdf

32   Kim Janssen, "Jury: Movie star's stepdad misled investors," *Chicago Tribune,* 03 May 2016, Page 1-7. https://www.newspapers.com/article/chicago-tribune-stephen-ferrone-vaughnm/11080493/

33   Ibid.

34   10-Q2010 Q1 Quarterly report Immunosyn. 24 May 2010. https://capedge.com/filing/1375623/0001437749-10-001689/IMYN-10Q-2010Q1

35   https://immunosyn.wordpress.com/tag/alan-osmond/

36   Dr. Myron Wentz, PhD website. http://drwentz.com.s3-website-us-east-1.amazonaws.com/scientist.html

37   "SEC Sues Hedge Fund for Investment in Another Fund," ALM Think Advisor, March 13, 2006. Copyright © 2023 ALM Global, LLC. https://www.thinkadvisor.com/2006/03/13/sec-sues-hedge-fund-for-investment-in-another-fund/

38   https://www.madcowprod.com/wp-content/uploads/2015/07/sawant-argyllbeef.pdf

39   Center on Terrorism, Extremism, and Counterterrorism, "Lead: A Closer Look at the Nuclei Armati Rivoluzionari," Middlebury College, March 4, 2022. https://www.middlebury.edu/institute/academics/centers-initiatives/ctec/publications/italian-neofascism-and-yearslead-closer-look

40   https://www.italyonthisday.com/2017/03/michele-sindona-fraudster-and-killer.html

41   Alessandra Stanley, "Enrico Cuccia Is Dead at 92; Key Figure in Italian Banking," *New York Times*, June 24, 2000. https://www.nytimes.com/2000/06/24/business/enrico-cuccia-is-dead-at-92-key-figure-in-italian-banking.html

42   Ibid.

43   Cecilia King, "Charges Against Cowles Dropped U.S. Court Clears Local Executive," *Washington Post*, March 18, 2006. The attorney was Robert D. Luskin of the law firm Patton Boggs. https://www.washingtonpost.com/archive/business/2006/03/18/charges-against-cowles- dropped-span-classbankheadus-court-clears-local-executivespan/06f185b8-99b0-42ca-8c7d- d11c349eb0f5/

44   Born in Isnello, Palermo, Sicily, Italy, he was the son of Mariano and Angela Mazzola Cancilla and spent much of his childhood in Pittsfield, Massachusetts, graduating from Pittsfield High School in 1927. He graduated from the University of Michigan in 1934 with a bachelor's degree in mechanical engineering and a bachelor's degree in aeronautical engineering. He was appointed cadet commandant of the ROTC unit and commissioned a second lieutenant in the infantry in 1933. In 1960, he became chief of the weapons and fire control of the Army Materiel Command. At AMC, he was involved with many weapon systems including the production of the M-14 and M-16 rifles. He retired from federal service in January 1979. He had lived in Alexandria since 1960. He lived in Arlington, Va., in the 1940s during World War II. He leaves his wife, the former Helen Taylor, whom he married Feb. 10, 1947; three daughters, Judith Cancilla McCarthy of Alexandria, Susan Cancilla Cowles of Mineral Wells, Texas, and Ellen Cancilla Richardson of Huntsville, Ala. https://www.iberkshires.com/community/printerFriendly.php?ob_id=1984

45   https://www.itaipu.gov.br/sites/default/files/u8/CV/Lelia%20Rachid%20Lichi.pdf. Penny Lernoux, *In Banks We Trust* (Garden City, NY: Anchor Press/Doubleday, 1984), p. 208

CHAPTER EIGHTEEN

CHRISTIAN INTELLIGENCE ASSETS (CIA)

*In many countries, clergy, both indigenous and American, CIA Director
William Colby told Senator Frank Church, "play a significant role and
can be of assistance to the United States through CIA with no reflection
upon their integrity nor their mission."*

– Matthew Avery Sutton, *Double Crossed* (2019)[1]

Donna Blue Aircraft, Inc. was a curious phenomenon that arose
in late 2007. Two Brazilians showed up owning the plane but
claimed they'd sold it several weeks earlier to two Americans.

The Mexican press expressed doubt that all the facts regarding the
ownership of the plane had been furnished, but not quite saying out loud
that the owners of American-registered drug planes seem to enjoy an apparent immunity from prosecution. It's one of those too-obvious facts the
press has been bred to ignore.

"The proprietary company of the unit, Donna Blue Inc. Aircraft
(DBA), is another mystery and probably it is a ghost company," reported
Mexico City's *La Reforma*.[2]

The skepticism was justified. Increasing my own suspicion was the sug-
gestion, in a report of a committee of the European Parliament, that in
addition to having been used in drug trafficking, the Gulfstream II had
flown CIA rendition flights to Guantanamo.[3]

Unnamed authorities quoted in some Associated Press accounts dismissed that report. "Where's the evidence?" the AP's unnamed military
authority sources asked, while ignoring the fact that Guantanamo is highly restricted airspace, and any plane landing there can be *presumed to be
working for the U.S. Government.*[4]

The presumption that Donna Blue was a front company, unfortunately, would not be confirmed until years later – by mistake. Somehow an
affidavit intended to be filed under seal in a court proceeding would be
captured by an eagle-eyed reporter.

If McClatchy News Service writers Jay Root and Kevin G. Hall didn't get a Pulitzer for their investigation, they certainly should have. Shortly after the September 2007 crash of the Gulfstream, they obtained a copy of a bill of sale for the aircraft sometimes dubbed Cocaine II. We wrote about it in Part One. We repeat here only to emphasize how much time had passed before the whole truth leaked out.

Most of what we knew in 2007 began with what Root and Hall exposed about Donna Blue. What we were to learn six years after the crash would be the proof of what McClatchy had alleged about Donna Blue – the ghost company acquired the plane from Russians who, during their ownership, made trips in 2003, 2004 and 2005 to the U.S. military base in Guantanamo Bay in Cuba:

> The company had itself acquired the Gulfstream II at the end of August from *Air Rutter International, which leased the plane between 2001 and August 2007.*
>
> Air Rutter is controlled by two New York businessmen, William Achenbaum and Arik Kislin, who also manage the highly fashionable Hotel Gansevoort in the Meatpacking district of New York. Kislin has interests in a series of companies active in air transportation, notably SA Holdings, Bon Voyage and C/K Air.
>
> Kislin is associated in C/K Air with Rina Chernaya, daughter of the former Russian aluminium king Mikhail Chernoy (who recently took the name of Michael Cherney). The Kislin and Cherney families have long-standing ties: Seymon Kislin, the uncle of Arik, employed Cherney for years as manager of his firm Trans Commodities, Inc.
>
> A house belonging to Cherney at Boca Raton in Florida is partly owned by Hudson International, a firm chaired by Arik Kislin. Even though the American authorities have refused Cherney a visa since 1999 because of his suspected links with organized crime, he has sponsored a conference devoted to intelligence, *The Intelligence Summit,* chaired by John Loftus, for the past two years.[5]
>
> When Air Rutter leased the Gulfstream II, it carried out several flights between the United States and the American base at Guantanamo Bay. Although Air Rutter states it has never worked for the American government, private aircraft are often used by the U.S. to carry suspected terrorists to Guantanamo for interrogation."[6]

Before I began the *Gangster Planet* project – God, it's been at least four years ago, maybe five! – I outlined, not long after Donald Trump's election in 2016, a book to be called *American Krysha*. I'd gone so far as to write a chapter or two and submit it to a writer I admired, for his honest opinion.

He never wrote me back. Linda Minor, who has since become the coauthor of this book, looked at it and announced it was all Greek (actually Russian) to her. So, I gave up on that title. The idea persisted but with a bigger focus on the late Adnan Khashoggi and his henchman, Ramy El-Batrawi.

I had been right the first time. Life moves so fast today that when you mention the name "Khashoggi," everyone, including google, thinks you're referring to the nephew who was dismembered by the guys taking orders from Saudi prince, MBS.

Call it information overload. As Ferris Bueller said, "Life moves pretty fast. If you don't stop and look around once in a while, you could miss it." We were sidetracked at the time by two guys the Brazilians sold the plane to Clyde O'Connor and Greg Smith – who, between them, we were crudely told, didn't have a pot to piss in – much less $2 million in cash to pay the Brazilians for the airplane.

It was a dead-end until the DEA decided they needed to collect some money from the brokers of planes housed at hangars at the St. Pete-Clearwater Airport, the same guys it seemed we'd been looking for since April of 2006. The DEA had decided to investigate – again – the car racing family named Whittington, who had very secretly brokered some very secret transactions.

Somehow, while based in Fort Lauderdale, these unnamed brokers had been shuffling planes between the CIA – when it needed to transport Colombians to trial or alleged terrorists to a variety of secret prisons worldwide – and, when the CIA didn't need them for such National Security Emergencies, felt free to earn money off the planes in other ways we won't mention.

The Whittingtons' extended family owned a ranch in southern Colorado in a lovely town called Pagosa Springs. We've been there. Dipped our toes in the pools of hot springs located on the side of the San Juan River, wending its way through the center of town. There's a Mexican restaurant overlooking the resort that serves delicious margaritas you can sip while watching kayakers and tubers waft down the river.

It's colorful. Picturesque even.

The first ghastly news that the DEA wanted to search the emails of the Whittingtons' accounts from a local Internet service provider appeared in the *Pagosa Springs Sun* around Thanksgiving 2013. The article appeared under a shocking headline:

DEA EXECUTES SEARCH WARRANT
RESORT FAMILY IMPLICATED IN ALLEGED MONEY LAUNDERING, DRUG TRAFFICKING.[7]

The 35-page affidavit had been filed in the Federal Court in Denver and was attached to a story by *The Durango Herald*, which stated that DEA agents "had Don Whittington under surveillance when he flew into Pagosa Springs on April 19, according to the affidavit. The pilot of that flight was Gregory Dean Smith, who the DEA says is a World Jet contract employee and a 'pilot of interest' in investigations of Latin American drug smuggling."[8]

I had called the Americans who bought from Donna Blue Aircraft "hapless," only to learn that, all along, they'd worked for the Whittington family!

The *Miami New Times* mentioned the same search warrant affidavit a few months later, calling it "a damning search warrant application accusing the Whittingtons of helming an international ring that sells planes at inflated costs to drug smugglers in Mexico, Venezuela, Colombia, and Congo."[9]

The *New Times* authors admitted ruefully that it was hard to hope Bill Whittington's drug smuggling days were over when evidence appeared that his wealth from an "account with LGT Bank in Vaduz, Liechtenstein – 'a preferred financial location for narcotics traffickers' – has grown from $1 million to nearly $11 million."[10]

The reporters recounted the history of the brothers' exploits from the '80s to recent times, including their stints in prison. But they saved the explosive news about the Gulfstream II (N9875A) for last.

> Then, on September 24, 2007, a turbo jet laden with nearly four tons of cocaine crashed in the Yucatán. Flight logs reportedly showed the plane had flown years earlier from Washington, D.C., to Guantánamo...
>
> The aircraft's owner was a shell company called Donna Blue. According to the recent Miami DEA affidavit targeting the Whittington brothers, the firm was *being used for 'Operation Mayan Jaguar,'* a clandestine program run by U.S. Immigration and Customs Enforcement....
>
> One of the jet's pilots was Gregory Dean Smith, a Fort Lauderdale man who today is a "target for trafficking cocaine from South America to Central America," the Miami DEA affidavit alleges. Stranger still, the investigative website *Narco News* alleges Smith, who today pilots for the Whittingtons, has worked for numerous U.S. intelligence operations."[11]

Because they were "connected," the Whittingtons mistakenly thought they'd always be protected. They ignored the caveat to that arrangement, which is, um, best I can figure, is: "Running drugs and laundering CIA profits are OK, but don't tell anyone AND report all your income to the IRS."

Bill Whittington lived to the ripe old age of 72, dying in 2021. You can almost hear a choir of angels singing in the background of the obituary that appeared in the *Pagosa Springs Sun*, celebrating his life and all his good deeds, but omitting any tales about helping South American cartels deliver drugs into the country or US Intelligence agents kidnapping innocent citizens with foreign names.[12]

Nothing can ever atone for his ghost life, lived on Gangster Planet.

DRUG SMUGGLERS WORKING FOR ICE?

Mayan Jaguar was a long-running joint operation with Guatemala overseen in the U.S. by Marine General John Kelly at the US Southern Command.

General Kelly would later ascend – or descend, according to your perspective – to be named Donald Trump's Chief of Staff. Presumably, Kelly's superiors thought Trump could be controlled.

One of Kelly's most virulent critics, Jean Guy Allard, on April 1, 2014, accused Kelly of attacking the "nation of Hugo Chávez by rudely contributing to the international campaign of disinformation against Venezuela with lies among the most violent heard in this alleged 'crisis.'"[13]

It was no April Fool's Day joke. Allard, admittedly a left-wing propagandist, doubled down on Kelly:

> In his numerous tours – widely publicized by the different Yankee embassies – in Latin America, John Kelly does not stop praising the supposed "mission" of the Southern Command that he directs. He constantly repeats to the press that "the main priority" of his troops is "the fight against drug trafficking," a task that over the years has turned out to be a huge failure on a continent where criminal activity continues to spread.
>
> In several countries, it subsidizes repressive police forces under humanitarian pretexts of aiding social reintegration, distributing equipment, vehicles of all kinds, and powerful weapons…
>
> Kelly was a combat officer in Baghdad and Tikrit in 2003 and then in Fallujah in 2004 where he "distinguished" himself for his lethal efficiency.[14]

Prior to this kill piece against the Southern Command's tactics, Evan Munsing,[15] teamed up with Christopher J. Lamb[16] – the two men had crossed paths at the National Defense University at Georgetown in Washington, D.C. – to do what public relations experts do. They touted the Southern Command in its most favorable light in their "Joint Interagency Task Force– South: The Best Known, Least Understood Interagency Success."[17]

Having two teams of equally biased public relations writers working against each other makes finding the truth as difficult as finding the proverbial needle in a haystack. That's what real reporters and historians are for, winnowing through to the straw and coming up with a needle.

But people hate history, we've been told.

Actually, it's school kids who hate history, just like they hate taking bad-tasting medicine. History and medicine, though, can be good for you. Ask Mary Poppins. But expect her to sugarcoat it.

What is real? What is true? Since the age of Donald Trump, questions like that have become almost impossible to answer.

LOOKING FOR A NEEDLE

Take Gregory Dean Smith, for example. Was he a contract drug smuggler for the Whittingtons? Or were both he and the Whittingtons involved in some kind of undercover work with an unknown government agency?

If the last question is answered yes, then which agency? Was it ICE? DEA? Southern Command's joint taskforce?

When I published "Feds raid CIA-connected air charter in Fort Lauderdale," on December 12, 2013, I had recently interviewed the No 2 DEA official in Miami, who insisted on anonymity for reasons which will soon become obvious.[18]

In my whiniest citizen-journalist voice, I asked him plaintively, "How come you guys aren't investigating the planes out of St Petersburg busted with 10 tons of cocaine?"

He calmly replied that one Federal Agency does not, as a matter of course, investigate the operations of another Federal Agency. What had been exposed by the DC-9 and Gulfstream II seizures, he said, was a "rogue" U.S. Customs operation (ICE is part of Customs, which in turn is part of Homeland Security).

For further answers, he pointed me to the Homeland Security's Office of Professional Responsibility, charged with investigating internal misconduct. Ten years later, I'm still waiting to hear back from them.

I was left with only another question: Now that the notorious Whittington brothers are – once again – the target of a major DEA investigation, the real question is: Why now?

SHOCKED, SHOCKED

Douglas McClain's arrest in 2014 at about the same time the 35-page affidavit showed up, had been obstructed for as many years as Whittington's arrest, if not longer.

His crime spree would have been brought to an end six years earlier, one retired detective from the San Antonio police force said sadly, if it weren't for seeming deliberate obstruction from the San Antonio office of the FBI.

"We were ready to charge him back in 2008," said the retired detective in a recent phone interview. "Then the local office of the FBI got involved. Everything we had, the Feds just kind of adopted as their own, and then took it over.

"And when we'd ask what they were doing with it, they'd say, oh, we still have it.' But that would be it. If I pressed them, they'd get sort of deliberately vague. We worked a lot of cases with the Feds. I knew these guys personally, but they would not talk about it.

"It wasn't normal. It was just very surprising to me," he stated. "I'm shocked that it's taken so long to bring criminal charges against this guy."[19]

It was McClain's arrest in 2014 that prompted us to dig deeper into his background, as well as into the death of Sam Fife and three of his American followers on April 26, 1979. Despite claiming he would never die, Fife was "killed" when the private airplane he was piloting encountered heavy fog and crashed into a mountainside in Guatemala. They buried him nearby in Quetzaltenango.

Co-founder of the cult with Fife, and the cult's second most powerful man, was Carrel Erastmus "Buddy" Cobb, Jr., a former airline pilot and the pastor of the Word Mission in Hollywood, Florida. Cobb, who preferred being called Buddy for obvious reasons, had enlisted in 1944 in the Army Air Corps during World War II at Fort McPherson in Atlanta, Georgia. After his discharge, he worked for National Air Lines in Jacksonville, Florida.

Cobb's connection to airplanes led us to his son Darryl Cobb, who was in charge of what was in 2014 the Bowen's Mill Christian Center Airport near Fitzgerald, Georgia. At that time you could still view the airport's profile at a website that showed a satellite photo of its runway and pictures of nine planes said to belong to Presidential Aviation of 105 Gathering Place Road in Fitzgerald, Georgia, that called the airport home.

All that fancy infrastructure disappeared in the blink of an eye, almost as soon as our first story on the cult appeared. Presidential Airways International, we learned, was one of those ghost companies, a "shell company,"[20] that flew extraordinary renditions. Like the one that carried Maher Arar from the US to Jordan in October 2002. That excursion would change European attitudes about the way the U.S. was conducting the war on terror.[21]

TERRORS OF THE WAR ON TERROR

It was thirteen months after 9/11. On a warm October evening in 2002, in the skies over Rome, Italy, an executive jet radioed ahead that it would be landing shortly at Ciampino Airport, a small military field near Italy's ancient Via Appia. On board were five CIA agents, two pilots... and Maher Arar, a tall, Canadian man wearing a green sweater, a pair of jeans, and metal shackles.

The plane was a Gulfstream III (N829MG), owned by Presidential Aviation International, Inc., involved in flying "extraordinary renditions," a phrase and concept not then widely known.[22] After touching down on European soil just long enough to refuel – 37 minutes – the Gulfstream III took off for Amman, Jordan, where Maher Arar was carried off the plane, beaten, and loaded into a van headed to Damascus.

Arar, born in Syria, was a Canadian citizen and computer programmer with no relationship with terrorism, yet he endured 10 months of torture based on completely false evidence. The investigations and recriminations which followed provoked a deep sense of alarm across Europe. The use of Italian airports to transport Arar led to the collapse of Italy's government.

A European Union report spoke uneasily of similar cases beginning to emerge. Relations between the U.S. and European allies soured, as the allies began facing outrage from their own people.

In Canada, Maher Arar's case led to the resignation of the head of the Royal Canadian Mounted Police, an apology from the Canadian Prime Minister, payment of $11.5-million in damages. It also raised a remarkable level of tension between ideological bedfellows – the Republican Administration in the U.S. and the Conservative Party in Canada. I was hot on the trail of any connection between the airplane that ferried Arar and a cult in which one of our Skyway-linked characters (Doug McClain of Argyll) grew up, nagged by the question of why nine planes owned by this CIA-linked shell company listed this tiny airport – with no tower, no amenities, and a dirt and grass runway – as its home?

Did those untethered links provide possible evidence that Doug Mc-Clain was working for, even protected by, the same organization involved in the rendition of alleged terrorists to "black sites" – defined by Wikipedia as "clandestine detention centres operated by a state where prisoners who have not been charged with a crime are incarcerated without due process or court order."[23]

"The End Is Near."

"Your reporting was totally bogus," Darryl Cobb asserted a few days after my story went up. "There's no way anything like that ever happened here, all those planes landing here."

The allegation was absurd, Cobb said. The airport was only used by "a bunch of ministers that had their own airplanes," he said. It was a grass field, completely unsuitable for Presidential Aviation's high-end Gulfstream III's and IV's – known as "heavy iron."

"I never reported the planes *landed* at your airport," I retorted snarkily.

"Well, then what are you saying?" he challenged.

"I'm saying," I replied in an even more acidic tone, "a CIA-connected aviation charter company called Presidential Aviation *listed* your airport as its home base for nine very expensive airplanes, and you can't, or won't, tell me why."

I wanted to add, "So there!" but I restrained myself.

Before locating Darryl, I had tried to call the phone number that was listed at Presidential Aviation's website. You guessed it. No longer in service. Calling Presidential's headquarters at the notorious Fort Lauderdale Executive Airport earned me a big laugh at the flight room on the other end, but not much else.

So I had to settle for one more run at Darryl Cobb, simply out of frustration. I asked him, "How did the group acquire so many airplanes?"

"The church never owned any planes," Cobb replied. "Local churches registered the planes. It was like a network, but there was no official organization." Each minister owned his own plane, but there was no central authority or company involved.

"We don't have any *membership*. Every group is autonomous," he continued. "They're only affiliated through like-beliefs, and through their understanding of 'the Word.' They are all independent ministries."

Right, I thought. And John Gotti and his buddies at the Ravenite Social Club in New York just got together to play cards. I moved on. "So, um, in the early '80's, how did your group end up with communes in Colombia, Peru, and Guatemala?"

Cobb matched my stammer with one of his own. "That was due to, ah, the fact that we had a minister who felt the world economic system wasn't in such great shape," he replied, without much conviction.

"Sam Fife had an understanding that there could be a possible collapse of the economic system of the world," he continued, recovering quickly. "Same as what everyone's taking about today, you know? Sam said we had only five years. And for him, he did have five years … till he crashed a plane down in Guatemala."

I reminded Darryl that people have been saying "the end is near" since well before Jesus walked the earth. He merely grunted.

Fortunately, I had the presence of mind before slamming down my landline phone, to say, "Yeah, well, today we just call it 'grifting.'"

"GOD'S ARMY" OF AVIATORS

On May 30, 2007, I had written a piece at my website about a Christian missionary group, this one flying out of an airport I knew all too well.

"A mysterious missionary support organization flying weekly 'relief flights' to Haiti from the Airport in Venice, FL. may be providing 'cover' for CIA covert operations in the Caribbean, the *Mad Cow Morning News* has learned," I wrote in an article cutely dubbed "Pirates of the Caribbean."

Run by an ordained Southern Baptist minister, AGAPE Flights is a fundamentalist Christian operation which has been involved in some highly *un*-Christian activities, like flying shipments of food and "religious supplies" on a regular basis to a man accused of plotting a coup in Haiti after being caught importing an M-16, a Beretta, and a camouflage uniform emblazoned with the words *"God's Army."*

Coming on the heels of revelations about an unpaid million dollar loan made to recently-deceased televangelist Jerry Falwell by Wally Hilliard – owner of terror flight school Huffman Aviation – the news marked the second time fundamentalist Christian groups had surfaced in unexplained operations at the Venice Airport.

AN AGENDA OTHER THAN THAT OF THE ALMIGHTY?

"What is there that suggests U.S. covert intelligence involvement in AGAPE Flights?" I had to ask myself.

Absent a CIA parking pass on the dashboard of one of the SUV's in AGAPE's parking lot, a web of connections offered clues that AGAPE may be serving agendas other than that of the Almighty:

First, the group had links to the controversial *Summer Institute of Linguistics (SIL)*, accused in the Latin American press of being funded by American intelligence to export a virulent brand of Christian fundamentalism to undermine the social cohesion of aboriginal communities and eliminate obstacles to natural resource exploitation. The SIL was also covered voluminously in a 1995 Gerard Colby book about Nelson Rockefeller's role in intelligence in South America – *Thy Will Be Done: The Conquest of the Amazon: Nelson Rockefeller and Evangelism in the Age of Oil.* [24]

Rockefeller was appointed in 1940 to a position called Coordinator of Inter-American Affairs (sort of like a CIA just for South and Central America) that lasted until President Truman abolished the agency at the close of the war.

AGAPE was also suspected of involvement in the aforementioned CIA-backed coup in Haiti. Also, the U. S. Treasury Dept. gave its permission for AGAPE to fly regularly to Cuba.

Oddly enough, we discovered Mohamed Atta's flight instructor at Huffman Aviation, Mark Mikarts, was a volunteer pilot for AGAPE. Even odder, Mikarts had previously gone by the surname of Wierdak. [25]

Spies often use aliases, don't they? That's not to say Mikarts was one. He was still hanging out in Sarasota when the *Port Charlotte Sun* found him after he crash-landed a single-engine plane near North Port in 2015, working as a flight instructor for Arne Kruithof. Only the reporter, no doubt a newbie, misspelled Arne's name as Kauithof.

TANGLED WEBS, WELL-WOVEN

Back in June 2006, two months after the drug plane's seizure in Mexico, Tropical Storm Alberto was lashing Florida's west coast with rain and wind while bearing down on Tampa, Florida. As the storm reached peak intensity, on June 12, forecasters at the National Hurricane Center predicted Alberto would soon attain hurricane status.

It was raining so hard that Cynthia Tate, a Tampa homeowner, was watching the Doppler radar on TV to see how bad things might get. Then she heard a strange sound. "It sounded like a missile," she would tell the *Tampa Tribune* nine months later, after their house had been rebuilt by a television show called *Extreme Makeover.* [26]

INTO THE TEETH OF A HURRICANE...

"It was gone for a split second, and then it was twice as loud. All of a sudden, in my window, in my view, was the airplane. It was coming right at me," Cynthia recalled.

As she watched in horror through her living room window, a small plane, later identified as a twin-engine Beechcraft King Air 90, headed straight for her, crashing into her yellow wood-frame house between the sunroom and a bedroom and then exploding in a blast of fire.

"You could smell and taste the fuel," Tate said.

The pilot, Steve Huisman, who also worked for AGAPE Flights, died instantly. "This has been a pretty overwhelming time," AGAPE's Charlie Gardner said, adding that staff members at AGAPE Flights were visiting with Huisman's wife Sonja and his four children, all younger than the age of 10."[27]

SPRAYING FOR MED-FLIES... IN A HURRICANE?

The men had been flying a mission from Sarasota, newspapers reported, to release sterilized Mediterranean fruit flies. But because there was no flight plan filed for the flight, investigators said it wasn't clear where they'd flown before the crash.

The explanation for why the plane was flying in the first place sounded a little thin. We could, if given time, come up with good reasons to take off in near-hurricane conditions...

But spraying for Med flies isn't one of them. Nor were we alone in our suspicions...

"Many people are asking why a small plane that crashed while attempting an emergency landing near Tampa was flying on a day when a hurricane churned in the gulf," reported the *Tampa Tribune*.

Witness "Bill Povey told police he heard the plane just before the crash, and thought it was flying low, and wondered: 'Who is flying in this weather?'"

SHARING CHRISTIAN FAITH IN AFGHANISTAN

At the time of the crash Steve Huisman was flying for a company called Dynamic Aviation based in Connecticut, while still flying for Venice, Florida's AGAPE. If we are correct in our hypothesis, both companies work for THE Company, making them virtually interchangeable. But it's just a theory, you realize. I'm not stating it's a fact.

Huisman was "a tall, straight-shooting, family man with four kids, a hearty appetite and a faith that literally motivated him to fly." He had an "infectious smile and a life-long desire to share his Christian faith.... Huisman, 41, grew up in Papua New Guinea, the son of missionary Wycliffe Bible Translators. He trained to become a missionary pilot at Moody Bible Institute... He had moved to Florida five years ago to work for AGAPE Flights in Sarasota, where his work brought him to Haiti and the Dominican Republic, the *Tampa Tribune* revealed."[28]

"Part of what attracted Huisman to Dynamic was the *opportunity to fly to Afghanistan* for the company," the reporter added, seemingly awestruck by that fact. "On those flights, he carried supplies as well as passengers. And *while the Middle East trips did not have a religious function*, friends said Huisman always found ways to minister to those around him."[29]

SECRET HISTORY WEATHER-WATCH

Strangely, the plane that crashed was photographed by one of the ubiquitous plane-spotters, who wrote:

> *"Call me paranoid, but I think someone or something is staring back at me from the last window,"* I quoted one plane-spotter at my website.
>
> Huisman's non-religious trips to Afghanistan would be something of a red flag, CIA-wise. Then, at Dynamic Aviation's company website we found their rather grandiloquent and very Homeland Security-ish motto, which has since been changed: "PARTNERS SAFEGUARD-ING EARTH." No wonder they took that motto down.
>
> Does Pilot Huisman's involvement with Dynamic Aviation, of Bridgewater, Virginia, help us penetrate the façade to the real secret history?
>
> Well, consider this little tidbit: In 1996, the company "purchased the U.S. Army's fleet of 124 non-pressurized BE-90s, enabling the company to significantly broaden its scope" of operations, to include fire management and airborne data acquisition.[30]

The Pentagon had outsourced its airline of small planes to Dynamic Aviation.
If that's not persuasive enough, we've got more. In 2008, Dynamic Aviation lost a twin turboprop Beechcraft King, with two of its employees from Harrisburg, while it was flying Patrick Murphy, a "specialist from Terraquest, Ltd. under contract with U308 Corp. of Toronto, doing a survey in Guyana, "searching for uranium in the rainforest."[31] The following year, U308 was named in an investigation with Ontario securities regulators for illegal practices.[32]

Then in 2016, when the very first Air Force One – known as "Columbine II," a 1948 C-121 Constellation flown in by President Eisenhower – was about to be consigned to the scrap heap, it was flown to Bridgewater, Virginia's Dynamic Aviation.[33]

Can you venture a guess about where it was being stored before that? It was just sitting out in the open at – where else? – Marana, Arizona, at the same airport George Doole had once called home.

No, we don't make this stuff up.

WHITE MAN'S BURDEN, 2007

Steve Husiman's biography also offers clues to the hidden history of covert activities engaged in by American intelligence groups in South America.

"Huisman, 41, grew up in Papua New Guinea, the son of missionary Wycliffe Bible Translators."

Sounds innocuous enough to those who do not already know that "Wycliffe Bible Translators" is the polite name for a notorious organization known as the Summer Institute of Linguistics (SIL) which numerous articles in the Latin American press have accused of being funded by American intelligence.

SIL is, according to the book, *Thy Will Be Done,* the vanguard of the destruction of the rainforests and – even worse – their native inhabitants, in military fashion.

A SWEETHEART OF A SWEETHEART DEAL

Another significant sign that something is being concealed from view is the fact that AGAPE has had its path smoothed regularly by the government.

According to aviation observers quoted in local newspapers, for example, AGAPE got a real sweetheart deal at the Venice Airport, paying *significantly less* than the fair market rate.

From the Sarasota *Herald Tribune:*

> When the City Council agreed in December to lease AGAPE Flights a hangar and office space at the Venice airport for $2,114 per month, the humanitarian relief organization heaped on the praise.
>
> "Venice is really the right place for us," said Charlie Gardner, AGAPE's executive director. "The community is very supportive."
>
> Supportive may be an understatement. Under the approved deal, the city allowed AGAPE to sublease some of its office space

to two other companies, who pay a total of $5,000 per month. Before the doors are unlocked on the first of each month, AGAPE has already netted a profit of $2,886.[34]

Though practically unheard of at other general aviation airports in the state, deals such as these aren't unusual at Venice Municipal Airport.

"PRAISE THE LORD. AND GIMME A CUBA LIBRE.

Ask yourself: When was the last time the government offered *you* a deal that cleared you *$3000 a month for doing nothing?*

At their former home base at the Sarasota Airport, AGAPE had also been the grateful beneficiary of unexplained largesse, this time from the Florida State University (FSU) Foundation, from whom they subleased land for a song.

Wait a minute, we asked? How did FSU get control of New College, located between John and Mable Ringling's classic Italianate mansion and the Bradenton-Sarasota Airport? New College had been locally funded for years by David B. Lindsay (both of them, as well as Sr.'s parents, the George D. Lindsays). As a matter of fact, New College had leased the land on which it was built "for decades as part of a 100-year agreement that expires in 2056," according to an article by Kerry Sheridan.[35]

We decided it was worth looking into. It would give us a chance to learn a little more about Sarasota and Venice in their glory days.

Endnotes

1   Sutton, Matthew Avery, *Double Crossed* (p. 342). Basic Books. Kindle Edition.

2   Quoting Reforma by Vanguard online news site. https://vanguardia.com.mx/no-ticias/nacional/3083215-arrestan-supuesto-tripulante-de-avion-caido-con-droga-en-yucat-an-FYVG3083215

3   https://www.europarl.europa.eu/RegData/presse/pr_info/2007/EN/03A-DV-PRESSE_IPR(2007)02-09(02947)_EN.pdf

4   AP sources, cited by Amnesty International. https://www.amnesty.org/es/wp-content/uploads/2021/06/eur010272010en.pdf

5   https://www.europarl.europa.eu/doceo/document/TA-6-2007-0032_EN.html John Loftus, former high level U.S. government prosecutor and former Army intelligence officer, is a published author, whose books include *The Secret War Against the Jews* (1994) and *America's Nazi Secret* (2010).

6   Jay Root and Kevin G. Hall, "Drugs on crashed jet belong to drug kingpin," McClatchy News Service, *Miami Herald*, October 01, 2007. https://www.newspapers.com/clip/52092852/ yucatanel-chapomystery2007/

7   Staff Writer, "DEA executes search warrant Resort, family implicated in alleged money laundering, drug trafficking," *Pagosa Sun*, November 21, 2013. https://pagosasun. com/2013/11/21/dea-executes-search-warrant-resort-family-implicated-in-alleged-money-laundering-drug-trafficking/

8   The affidavit was leaked by the *Durango Herald*, whose reporter, Joe Hanel, obtained a copy from the federal court before it was sealed. https://dur-duweb.newscyclecloud.com/assets/pdf/DU1460241118.pdf Entire affidavit can be viewed at our website. https://www.madcowprod.com/wp-content/uploads/2013/12/whittington.pdf

9   Terrence McCoy and Penn Bullock, "Racecar Drivers Don and Bill Whittington: Drug Smugglers and CIA Helpers?" *Miami New Times*, February 6, 2014. https://www.miaminewtimes.com/news/racecar-drivers-don-and-bill-whittington-drug-smugglers-and-cia-helpers-6394730

10   Ibid.

11   McCoy and Bullock, *Miami New Times*, February 6, 2014. They quoted a source in their article. Bill Conroy at Narco News via The Narcosphere, "Second Informant Surfaces in ICE's Mayan Jaguar Cocaine-Plane Op," June 2, 2014. hond-informant-surfaces-ice%E2%80%99s-mayan-jaguar-cocaine-plane-op. https://wayback.stanford.edu/was/20180311065725/http://narconews.com/ Robert Wilonsky at the *Dallas Observer* wrote "Kicking Down the Door at the 'House of Death,'" March 8, 2007,which partially explains the work Conroy had done to expose the abuses of the "War on Drugs" by U.S. agencies. https://www.dallasobserver.com/news/kicking-down-the-door-at-the-house-of-death-7143732

12   "William Marvin Whittington," *Pagosa Sun*, April 29, 2021. https://www.pagosasun. com/stories/william-marvin-whittington,15567

13   Jean Guy Allard, "John Kelly: Assassin in Iraq, executioner in Guantánamo and slanderer of Venezuela," *Latin American Summary*, April 1, 2014. https://rebelion-org.translate. goog/john-kelly-asesino-en-irak-verdugo-en-guantanamo-y-difamador-de-venezuela/?_x_tr_sl=es&_x_tr_tl=en&_x_tr_hl=en&_x_tr_pto=wapp. Source: http://www.resumenlatinoamericano.org/?p=2757

14   Ibid.

15   LinkedIn page for Evan Munsing III: https://www.linkedin.com/in/evan-munsing-7bbb4911/ So proud was Munsing of his writing, he set up his own website to promote it at https://smallwarsjournal.com/author/evan-munsing.

16   Dr. Christopher J. Lamb at Center for Strategic Research, Institute for National Strategic Studies, curriculum vitae. https://docs.house.gov/meetings/AS/AS00/20140624/102377/HHRG113-AS00-Bio-LambC-20140624.pdf

17   "What does seem quite clear is that JIATF–South deserves its accolade as the gold standard for interagency collaboration; it has proven its model and staying power as a high-performing interagency organization. It can be and often is argued that the implicit metric for JIATF– South's operational success – metric tons seized – is inferior to other measures of success such as profits seized or damage to the narcotrafficking organization." https://www.files.ethz.ch/ isn/133749/SP_TaskForceSouth.pdf

18   Daniel Hopsicker, "Feds raid CIA-connected air charter in Fort Lauderdale," December 12, 2013. https://www.madcowprod.com/2013/12/12/fort-lauderdale- florida-is-a-protestant-palermo/

19   Interview with anonymous source.

20   https://www.therenditionproject.org.uk/flights/companies/index.html#Presidential

21   https://www.therenditionproject.org.uk/flights/aircraft/N829MG.html

Presidential Aviation also operated a Gulfstream IV (tail number N841PA), owned by S/A Holdings LLC (Achenbaum) before it went through multiple changes. Eurocontrol UK indicated N800BQ was CIA-linked when it was operated by Presidential while owned by Mark J. Gordon (G IV Leasing, LLC). It was placed into a trust held by Wells Fargo Bank, Trustee and changed to N388CA. S/A also owned the Gulfstream II (N987SA) up until two weeks before it was sold to Donna Blue Aircraft.

22   https://en.wikipedia.org/wiki/Black_site

23   Gerard Colby and Charlotte Dennett, *Thy Will Be Done: The Conquest of the Amazon: Nelson Rockefeller and Evangelism in the Age of Oil*, Open Road Media (November 21, 2017).

24   Daniel Hopsicker, "Pirates of the Caribbean," *MadCow News*, May 30, 2007. https://www.madcowprod.com/2007/05/30/pirates-of-the-caribbean/

25   B. C. Manion, "Starting Over," *Tampa Tribune*, March 05, 2007, Page 57.

26   Rebecca Catalanello, "Pilot love faith, flying, and family," *Tampa Bay Times*, June 22, 2006, Page 22.

27   Ibid.

28   "Rescue Plan, Toronto, Ont. National Post, Nov 04, 2008, Page 9; "Aviation company says plane is missing," *Roanoke Times*, Nov 04, 2008, Page 11.

29   https://www.capitalmarketstribunal.ca/sites/default/files/pdfs/proceedings/set_20101004_uranium308_0.pdf

30   Vice Bradshaw, "Rare Bird," *Rocky Mount Telegram*, April 10, 2016, Page 7

31   Paul Quinlan, " Venice airport's low leases are letting revenues fly away," *Sarasota Herald Tribune*, March 24, 2006. https://www.heraldtribune.com/story/news/2006/03/25/venice-airports-low-leases-are-letting-revenue-fly-away/28468594007/ and https://www.heraldtribune.com/story/news/local/venice/2018/05/21/venice-and-agape-at-loggerheads-over-lease-extension/12169514007/

32   Dynamic Aviation website (accessed 4/28/2024). https://www.dynamicaviation.com/1-company-history/

33   Daniel Routh, "The Camera Never Blinks or Weeps," *Tampa Tribune*, Jan 16, 2007 ·Page 17.

34   Kerry Sheridan, "The FAA blocks Sarasota airport's land sale to New College," Station WUSF, April 12, 2024. https://www.wusf.org/education/2024-04-12/sarasota-airport-new-college-land-deal-blocked-faa

Chapter Nineteen

Art and Circuses

Now that no one buys our votes, the public has long since cast off its cares; the people that once bestowed commands, consulships, legions and all else, now meddles no more and longs eagerly for just two things, bread and circuses.

–Juvenal, *Satire X*

For almost a century – from Civil War days through the Great Depression of the 1930's – according to Time Magazine, "the circus reigned as far and away America's premier form of popular entertainment."[1]

It was a once-a-year event, "an opportunity to see the impossible made real: aerialists, tightrope walkers, and equestrians performed superhuman feats; lion 'tamers' turned their charges into obliging pussycats; elephants performed ballets by Balanchine; and the clowns were there to elicit laughter and compassion, bridging the gap between the incredible feats taking place in the rings and the awed onlookers in the stands."[2]

By 1959, however, the dozens of circuses that had existed across America a century earlier had been whittled down to just one – Ringling Bros., Barnum & Bailey's Greatest Show on Earth. That very year the circus moved its winter quarters from Sarasota, Florida, to tiny Venice, Florida, only 25 miles south down the Tamiami Trail.[3]

The first winter I visited my parents after they'd retired to Venice in the early '80s, they told stories about cries in the dark when the circus train arrived at the downtown depot for the winter. Sounds of trumpeting elephants and roaring lions could be heard for miles, as the trains unloaded a menagerie of exotic animals. I can attest to hearing the cacophony myself before the circus closed down.

Little did I know at the time how Venice's history with the Ringling Bros. Circus would dovetail into my own research involving the CIA.

As Mark Twain may have said, history never repeats itself, but it sure do rhyme.

SARASOTA – WINTER HOME OF CHICAGOANS

In the early days of the twentieth century, Southwest Florida caught the eye of men and women who'd already spent years inheriting and adding to business fortunes in midwestern cities like Pittsburgh and Chicago. Folks who should have been thinking about retirement now heard voices telling them instead to invest their fortunes in raw land – beautiful, exotic land.

We've heard all the official stories about how Bertha Honore Palmer, wife of Chicago hotel magnate, Potter Palmer, "discovered" Sarasota and built a second fortune in land development. Seven years after Potter died in 1902, Bertha was just getting started. In 1910 Bertha converged on the area alongside several other people she had been acquainted with back in Chicago.

John and Mable Ringling had lived at the Palmer House in Chicago for several years before Bertha announced that Sarasota was to become her new winter home. Bertha Honore's wealth came from a father who had helped develop Chicago's suburbs, and he and his sons saw a similar opportunity in Florida.

Another associate from Chicago, Owen Burns, arrived in Sarasota at almost the same time. A mere coincidence? Perhaps. Jessi Smith's online tale at the *Visit Sarasota* website mentions all of them, without noting they had been acquainted previously.[4]

We were intrigued by our research into the background of Owen Burns, one of many brothers whose father had been a decorated member of the U.S. Navy before the Civil War, shortly before his death left his wife to raise their large family in Baltimore.[5]

Owen Burns had become quite notorious among members of the Calumet Club in Chicago when, in a 1908 divorce, he named the club, of which Bertha's sons – Potter, Jr. and Honore Palmer – were members, as co-respondent in a divorce.[6]

That affront was forgiven, however, a year or so later when the wealthy Palmers, the Ringlings (former residents of Palmer House in Chicago), and Owen Burns met up only two years later in Sarasota, Florida.

Small world? Why am I always so suspicious?

Bertha built her winter home at Osprey, a few miles south of Sarasota, just north of what was to become Venice, whose history is rife with activities that, in my mind at least, don't quite pass the "coincidence" test.

BUILDING A TEMPLATE IN VENICE ... WITH A LITTLE HELP FROM THE BLE

D r. Fred H. Albee, a bone surgeon from Harvard, who had perfected the surgical procedure of grafting bones during World War I – the Hawkeye Pierce of his day – acquired land south of Bertha Palmer's residence near Osprey. His name was associated with the founding of Venice Bay Country Club in 1918 even before he purchased land around Venice Beach in 1925 and selected John Nolen, a pioneer city planner from Harvard, to draw up a plat of the City of Venice.

Almost immediately – like magic – Albee suddenly was presented with an offer from the Brotherhood of Locomotive Engineers (BLE) to sell his land at a profit of 540% in just nine weeks!

BLE's officials were also buying thousands of acres of land all around Albee's tract. The union leaders had no problem dispensing funds to lay out the new city according to Nolen's plans, as Dr. Albee had recommended. In fact, they proceeded to pour at least $16 million of their members' retirement funds into clearing, constructing drainage works, building streets, and creating lighting for the city of Venice, Florida.

Though union bosses claimed the city would be a great "investment" for BLE pensioners, it was designed for more upscale tastes – like an acquired taste for caviar – for which railroad workers never had the time or money to develop.

There were 54 eastern railroads, including the New York Central, the Pennsylvania, Erie and the Baltimore & Ohio Railroad, whose unionized employees made up the Brotherhood of Locomotive Engineers membership. The corporate stock of those railroads was controlled by the richest robber barons of that day, whose sons and daughters, with names like Whitney, Vanderbilt and Harriman, would wield great influence a few years later when the U.S. government set up the CIA. Hell, they were the U.S. government.

It goes without saying that the railroads' management hated unions as much as they hated strikes, raises, and benefits to railroad employees. That's why God's nemesis – whoever that selfish rascal was – invented financial fraud and designed a template that would be copied later by Jimmy Hoffa, who loaned funds to cohorts at low interest rates to build hotels and gambling casinos, racetracks and other businesses linked to organized crime.

NETWORKS OF EXPERTS

It's no surprise that BLE president Warren Stone was a believer in the dream of Harvard Professor T. N. Carver.[7] Carver was a colleague of John Nolen, who had been designing plans in Tampa and St. Petersburg when Dr. Albee enticed him to come farther south.[8]

High praise was bestowed on Nolen's work in a 1922 editorial in the *St. Petersburg* (now *Tampa Bay*) *Times*, owned at the time by Paul Poynter, a friend and colleague of Sarasota's own David Breed Lindsay, Sr. and his father George D. Lindsay.[9] Before meeting up in Tampa, they'd lived thirty miles apart in Kokomo and Marion, Indiana.

I became familiar with the Poynter Institute when, shortly after "Welcome to TerrorLand" was published, one of its "ethics group leaders" pointed a finger at *moi*, my ownself.

A reporter for the *Sarasota Herald-Tribune*, which the Lindsays sold to the New York Times Co. in 1982 for a cool $30 million, wrote on July 11, 2005:

> Why should they believe him when he writes that Mohamed Atta, the terrorist who flew the first plane into the World Trade Center on Sept. 11, 2001, and one of three hijackers who lived in Venice, was a cocaine-bingeing sex fiend?
>
> Why should they believe that the whole ordeal – everything from the flight school where the hijackers trained until the day they crashed commercial airliners into the Twin Towers and Pentagon – was a CIA conspiracy?[10]

Not knowing who "they" were – these readers of mine she was so interested in protecting from me – I had sardonically replied with my own probing question, "Why should I believe anything *you* write?"[11]

Clearly not fazed by my touché rejoinder, she cited statistics equally as credible as the voluminous works of the Warren Commission's own disreputable coverup. Whether or not she saw the humor in my next comment I can't say, but she didn't laugh, or even smile.

> "Hopsicker says he's heard no complaints about the book.
>
> "'Except for the guy who's suing me over it,' he said."[12]

Then she talked about a lawsuit filed by an unnamed plaintiff suing me over *Barry and 'the boys,'* which she said was about "Barry Seals." Jeez, couldn't she at least spell his name right?

Moving on to another unprincipled source, Rudi Dekkers, she quoted the S.O.B. calling me an S.O.B.:

> "This S.O.B., he doesn't realize he destroys families and people," Dekkers said in a telephone interview Thursday. "I have seen nothing that's the truth. He fantasizes. He fantasizes stories, and names."
>
> "If I had the money, would I sue him? Into hell," added Dekkers, a Dutch immigrant who now charters airplanes from Naples. "I would sue him into hell."
>
> With so many books published about Sept. 11, Hopsicker's tome may have gone unnoticed were it not for the Internet.
>
> Typing his name into Google brings up 13,200 results, several of which also mention Dekkers... Most of the results are conspiracy-theory Web sites, such as SanderHicks.com and OnlineJournal.com.
>
> Hopsicker's Web site is a mix of press releases, conspiracy theories, news stories and sales pitches. He sells his books online, along with several documentaries that he produced and funded himself.[13]

I could feel the vacuous hauteur dripping off her words. That's when I realized "somethin' wasn't jes' quite right," as an old mentor of mine used to say. In her snobbishness, she felt inclined to quote the expert in ethics from the Poynter Institute:

> "The problem with the Internet now is it's a kind of anything-goes, Wild West frontier, and there's not a lot of accountability," said Kelly McBride, ethics group leader at journalism's Poynter Institute in St. Petersburg.
>
> _Only i6d then, it will_ be interesting to watch and see what the courts do to it."[14]

WHERE BODIES WERE BURIED

As we show elsewhere in this book, the Lindsays had close connections for decades to airplanes, airports, and aircraft companies in Sarasota County, and their role in publishing seemed to keep knowledge about such activities cloistered within a small network of their friends and associates. George D. Lindsay had been editor and general manager of the _Herald_ as early as 1927, and he would have known where all the bodies were buried, information he shared with his son and grandson.

The same year George Lindsay arrived in Sarasota to live, 1927, a scathing indictment of Venice's swindlers was published by an organization called the Trade Union Educational League – a faction within the Communist Party USA (CPUSA) controlled by William Z. Foster – began proclaiming that BLE Grand Chief Engineer Warren Stone had wrecked the union whose funds he had been entrusted to manage.

Foster mocked Stone, who allegedly had said "it's as easy to operate a bank as to run a peanut stand," and he was suspicious when Stone had "proceeded to establish labor banks all over the country. All that was necessary was money to float them, then riches would come."[15]

Nevertheless, members of Stone's union, the Brotherhood, believed their leader. Foster said that, as a consequence of their faith in him, they "scraped together their savings and, trusting their officials implicitly, poured their money into the various financial schemes one after the other."[16]

Building the city of Venice was only one of Stone's "schemes," but it was a huge one, which alone used up $16 million in pension funds. Even more money in 1923 from the BLE funds had purchased less than a controlling share in the Empire Trust Company and in New York City's Equitable Building at 120 Broadway.

If we want to know who was ultimately behind the scheme – the wizard behind the curtain, as it were – the best tool for finding out is to use Cicero's classic query in accusing Mark Antony of murdering Caesar: "*Cui bono – To whose advantage was it?*"[17]

William Z. Foster believed the labor movement had been infiltrated after World War I, when he said, "the United States became the most powerful capitalist country in the world. It passed from the status of debtor to a creditor nation, exporting capital from 1920 to 1929 to the then unheard-of total of $20 billion. All over the world it conducted an active campaign to capture markets, as against other big countries which were weakened by the war."[18]

"Super-heated soothsayers," Foster said, proclaimed, "There would be no more economic crises or mass unemployment....The 'New Capitalism' was ... [an] American miracle."[19]

That's when trade unions were profoundly affected, and "Labor officialdom, including the progressives, listened open-mouthed when [Harvard's] Professor Carver explained how the workers through their savings were buying control of the great industries....They declared that the path of progress for labor lay through cooperation with the employers to increase production. The class struggle was ended, strikes were a thing of the past, Socialism was an outworn dogma. The big thing was the "Higher

Strategy of Labor" (no-strike, *speed-up*, policy), labor banks, and class collaboration on every front."[20] (emphasis added)

Foster's accusation was leveled primarily at Jay Lovestone, a secretive man who was ousted from the Communist Party for his pro-capitalist stance, by spouting what Foster called "the poison of American imperialist propaganda," which had infiltrated labor unions.[21]

After Lovestone was ousted from the Communist Party by Stalin himself, he continued to lead what biographer Ted Morgan called "a covert life."[22] It was so covert, in fact, it's hard to tell whether he was working for the labor movement or was in fact a card-carrying member of the Central Intelligence Agency, and little was known about what he was up to until Frances Stonor Saunders published her work about the Congress of Cultural Freedom in 2000.[23]

Lovestone was, however, on friendly terms with James Jesus Angleton, the CIA's "paranoid" Chief of counterintelligence,[24] and, according to Ted Morgan, it was Allen Dulles who transferred Lovestone over to Angleton's supervision in 1954.[25] Readers who are interested in the CIA's role in the labor movement, including who benefited from building Venice, are encouraged to read the sources named above.

EMPIRE TRUST'S INTELLIGENCE CONNECTIONS

"Sarasota History Alive!" website tells us that the city of Venice "dedicated the Fred Albee Municipal Airport in January 1939. A private pilot, Albee had given land for the airport."[26] The website adds that the "Army Air Corps used the municipal airport while it built the Venice Army Air Base [VAAB] during World War II.

After the war, the VAAB property was turned over to the city and became a civilian airport in 1946. The two airports co-existed until the 1950s, when the School Board acquired the Albee Airport land and began construction of an educational complex on it."[27]

Shortly after WWI, however, Albee had just made a huge windfall by buying land in a vacant patch of land to become Venice, by selling it less than three months later to the Brotherhood of Locomotive Engineers.[28] Before Venice Army Air Base was built for WWII, Albee is said to have acquired the land for the city airport from the Palmer Estate, which bought it up cheaply after the BLE lands were foreclosed on.

In 1939 Leroy W. Baldwin, who had been president and a director of Empire Trust when it was owned by the BLE in 1923, and was replaced as president by Henry C. "Harry" Brunie, who had been best man in John

J. McCloy's 1930 wedding. F. Trubee Davidson, a close Yale (Skull and Bones) friend of Prescott Bush, also attended McCloy's wedding.[29]

In 1942 Prescott was rescued from the ignominy of being linked to Nazi, Fritz Thyssen, whose German funds were moved by Prescott's father-in-law, G. H. Walker, into a bank set up by the Harriman 15 Corporation through a duplicitous scheme.[30] An excellent source showing the Bush and Walker connection to Thyssen and Hitler is Ben Aris and Duncan Campbell's article in *The Guardian*, "How Bush's grandfather helped Hitler's rise to power" published in 2004.[31]

Brunie could have been more famous in his day had he followed his dream of being a professional tennis player. Instead, as president of the Empire Trust, he worked more covertly with the highest officials in the federal government.[32] It was Jack McCloy's old tennis friend, Harry Brunie that Assistant Secretary of War McCloy chose to initiate Prescott Bush into the United Service Organizations (USO) office, and thus shield him from accusations about the work Prescott did for Fritz Thyssen.[33]

In 1963 Brunie was named chairman of Empire Trust as it merged into the Bank of New York (BNY), some of whose officers would be indicted in 1999 for illegally running a money transfer business for Russian mobsters.[34] The bank itself would be called a laundromat for Russian oligarchs like Semyon Mogilevich.[35]

Throughout most of the '50s, Brunie's vice president in charge of oil and gas properties, was a man whose name JFK researchers will easily recognize: John Alston "Jack" Crichton.[36] Crichton had been the negotiator of a "pioneer oil concession in the 'forbidden kingdom' of Yemen" in 1955.[37]

Decades later Crichton's Dallas, Texas companies, Arabian Shield Development and Dorchester Master Limited Partnership, in which hidden partners included BCCI Saudi banker Kamal Adham, filed a billion-dollar lawsuit against Ray Hunt, youngest son of Texas wildcatter H. L. Hunt, taking it to the U.S. Supreme Court only to lose. Citing a cause of action that amounted to "alienation of business affections," he claimed that Hunt, during a period of turmoil in Yemen in the early days of the Reagan-Bush administration, sneaked in and absconded with Crichton's proprietary documents. All appeals said Crichton had been too late in filing his complaint in 1987.[38]

We have shown elsewhere in these pages how wealthy businessmen from Dallas were involved in top-secret missile-testing at the airport in Venice. We sometimes wonder whether "national security" is to protect our nation's secrets or whether our representatives tend to confuse their own business interests with those that would benefit the nation as a whole.

PALACE FIT FOR A CIRCUS KING

John and Mable Ringling did not begin building their palatial mansion named Cà d'Zan (Italian patois for House of John) which sits on Sarasota Bay, four miles north of Bayfront Park in downtown Sarasota, until they had wintered there for 15 or more years. The other months they lived either in the Ritz-Carlton Hotel in New York or were traveling to Europe or wherever else the circus was booked.

Since their only "children" were the animals they had traveled the world with – gorillas, elephants, lions, and the like – it's no wonder they decided to build a Venetian palace, if only to separate themselves from the noisy, smelly menagerie.

Across the street from their winter palace, they also built a museum to display art works collected primarily in Europe. The plan was to make the area into "a splendid resort community for society, captains of industry, bluebloods, and the moneyed class," hoping to attract such people to buy land around them.[39] In short, it was designed to fit in for those who might be attracted to sojourn in the City of Venice, being built at almost the same time.

John Ringling North and Henry W. Ringling North were brothers born six years apart to Ida Ringling North, John's only sister. Their father was an engineer for Chicago and Northwestern Railroad, and at times the boys lived in Chicago and at other times in tiny Baraboo, Wisconsin, in a red brick Victorian mansion, which Ida Ringling North had inherited from her father.

John Ringling North entered Yale University in the Class of 1924. His brother Henry would follow in the Class of 1933. They had no pedigree that guaranteed their entry, nor any family tradition that enabled them to be tapped for a secret society.

The only apparent claim to fame either lad accomplished while at Yale was that Henry roomed in the Harkness Memorial Quad dormitory in 1932 with the estranged son of a French-American named Charles Bedaux, an efficiency expert despised by unions for his "speed-up" system of labor. Just the sort of thing that would attract the admiration of the millionaires who owned railroads in that day.

As it happened, Bedaux also attracted Baltimore's wannabe-Queen Wallis Simpson, who married abdicated King Edward VIII in Bedaux's villa in France in 1938.

Surely that fact emerged when Henry North was being vetted for OSS. In 1943 the elder Bedaux and his son would be arrested by Americans in

North Africa, the same location Henry North's "MacGregor Mission" had found itself at the same time. The charge was collaboration with fascists. Though arrested, it took some doing to get him indicted for treason and returned to Miami, in transit to Washington, D. C.

Alas. Bedaux committed suicide in Miami's border patrol building on Biscayne Avenue before a trial could be arranged. No word of the where-abouts of Charles, Jr., Henry's roommate, ever leaked out. Neither did evidence of how Bedaux acquired the drugs he used to kill himself. It's simply one of those mysteries which remain forever murky.

You can visit Cà d'Zan today, if you're inclined to pay the entry fee. It was willed by John Ringling to the State of Florida in a Codicil, subject to terms of the will to which it was annexed, that gave the North family the right to administer the estate. A gross legal oversight that couldn't be undone after Ringling's death in 1936.

The museum and art gallery are now either part of or in the vicinity of Sarasota's New College, which recent news reported that Governor Ron DeSantis was unilaterally changing its curriculum from the study of liberal arts to, well, whatever it is the governor calls education.

RINGLING'S MILLIONS

When the Florida Land Boom crashed in 1926, John Ringling sold hisrailroad to the Santa Fe system and poured the proceeds into building the art museum. Oil royalties from the Oklahoma wells kept paying for a few more years.

In the months before the October 1929 stock market crash, John Ringling watched his wife Mable wither away before his eyes, losing her in June. At the same time Mable took to her death bed, "in the spring of 1929, it was time to negotiate the usual circus contract with Madison Square Garden for the season of 1930. A date was set for a meeting with the officials of the Garden. Uncle John did not show up."[40]

John gave no explanation, and "a violent scene" ensued with the owners of Madison Square Garden [MSG], after which "Uncle John told them with anatomical exactitude precisely where they could put their contract," and he then moved the circus to a different location.[41]

When MSG signed a new contract with American Circus Corporation to appear that year, Ringling then bought that circus for $2,000,000, paying a small down payment and giving a note for $1,700,000 to the Prudence Bond and Mortgage Company.

No one at the time predicted the stock market would crash a few months later.

American Circus Corporation was a circus based in Peru, Indiana, only 30 miles from Marion, the former home of George D. Lindsay. Included in the sale were 1,000 acres, as well as numerous other circuses and wild west shows and their menageries and equipment.[42]

Prudence Bond and Mortgage was headed by William M. Greve, who was one of an extremely powerful group of Brooklyn men, who in 1927 bought five lots in Ringling Estates at Lido Beach to build a club. Notable among them was William J. Burns, the famous international detective. Also in the group were two New York judges and a couple of state officials. Then there was Samuel W. Gumpertz, who turns out, according to Henry Ringling North's version of the story, to be the villain in this conspiracy.[43]

Gumpertz was actually working behind Ringling's back to take over the circus and had set up "two groups of businessmen, who, under the corporate titles of Allied Owners and New York Investors, bought the note from the Prudence Company."[44]

PREDATORS AT THE GATE

William Greve had shape-shifted to become Allied Owners, which demanded payment of the note in full because one installment's interest payment was late. But there was a way out, Greve told Ringling, limping from a blood clot from which he had been recuperating at Gumpertz's hotel on Coney Island. If he wanted to avoid involuntary bankruptcy, Greve said at a meeting held in July 1932, Ringling could set up a new corporation with shares divided three ways – one third each to Charles Ringling's widow and son, and one third to John Ringling – after subtracting a ten-percent fee in stock for Allied Owners, of course.

But here's the kicker. New York Investors, Inc, the second group of conspirators, demanded to hold collateral for the note assumed by the new corporation, in the form of all of Ringling's art works collected over the years throughout his travels, until the remaining $1 million note was paid off.

John Ringling caved to all the demands. The new company was, of course, incorporated in Delaware, and title to the entire art collection was transferred to Rembrandt Corporation, subject to a lien securing the Prudence Bond note.

A few months later, John Ringling "suffered a paralytic stroke."[45]

The stroke was disabling but not fatal. He had four years yet to live. Henry North was at the time in his last year at Yale. At this point in Henry North's memoire, he suddenly shifted focus, to mention that in 1926 Owen Burns had just opened his famed Vernona Hotel on which the same Prudence Bond and Mortgage foreclosed. John Ringling bought the hotel from the mortgage company, and six years later, renamed the Ringling Hotel, it became part of the collateral demanded by Allied Owners and New York Investors.

HENRY RINGLING NORTH AND THE LINDSAYS

In another section of his book, North happened to mention his wife, Ada Thornburg, whose name was "inadvertently" misspelled:

> After the break with Uncle John in 1936, I went to work for the Chronicle Publishing Company in Marion, Indiana, under my friend David Lindsay. There I met Ada Mae Thornburgh, a lovely petite blonde. We were married in the autumn of 1936. Ada Mae and I were very happy together until the circus recalled me to her exacting service.[46]

Ada was the daughter of Alfred and Golda Thornburg, managers of the Hotel Spencer in Marion, Indiana, and she had been in her junior year at the University of Michigan in Ann Arbor when she returned home to Marion, shortly after her mother's remarriage.

Ada's new stepfather, Carlton Lane Houston, was her new husband's competitor. As editor of the *Marion Leader-Tribune*, he only supported Democrats and their local candidates.

Henry, however, had been sent to Marion to work for the *Chronicle*, whose editor was George D. Lindsay, the father of David Breed Lindsay, Sr. The *Chronicle* had traditionally been the official mouthpiece of Republicans. The exception was in 1922 when George got into a notorious feud with Grant County's Republican chairman, a man named Jones, who declared by resolution that the *Marion Chronicle* would "no longer be the official organ of the Republican party in Grant County."

George Lindsay then called the Republican district and county chairman a "predatory machine politician."[47] Closer to the election, Lindsay was so actively inserting himself into the news that three counties away the *Indianapolis Star* accused him of writing editorials "with a pen dipped in vitriol," when he called the county "boss" a "representative of 'invisible government.'"[48]

The feud between the "boss politician," and Lindsay occurred the same year David B. Lindsay married and settled down in North Carolina – 1922. After the election, the Marion County press club – whose head was none other than Carlton Houston – threw a banquet to honor George on the occasion of his imminent departure for a "European trip."[49]

The trip included a visit to Lindsay's son in North Carolina, as well as his future home in Florida, previously visited when his son had been stationed there during the war. To document the trip, George began a series of articles for the *Marion Chronicle* – one of which, "Hoosier Editor Tours Florida," was reprinted in the *Tampa Times*.[50]

Spies R Us

We already introduced you to James Nolen, who drew up the city plan for Venice, Florida. If you want to know anything about Sarasota, you also need to meet Dwight James Baum, a New York architect, whose name became synonymous with Sarasota architecture.

Even before they hired Baum to design Cà d'Zan, John and Mable had been buying artworks throughout the world, but mostly in Italy. According to Henry North's account: "John Ringling bought [art] literally by the shipload. On one occasion at least, he chartered a freighter to bring his purchases directly from Genoa [Italy] to Port Tampa. The lesser statuary he scattered among his keys to add a touch of ancient grace to his real-estate development…. The best pieces were reserved for the future John and Mable Ringling Museum of Art."[51]

After Uncle John's death in 1936, the estate was tied up in litigation for years, with John North as executor. Henry North was back in Sarasota by 1940, when he registered for the draft, eventually joining the Navy, and remaining on active duty until January 1946. He retired from the Naval Reserve in 1954 as a Commander, promoted because of a combat citation.[52]

We know he was in the Office of Strategic Services in the mid-40s, however, because of a Memo Henry wrote to Allen Dulles, to report that a prisoner of war had informed him that German art dealer Julius Bohler had a definite affinity for doing business with Nazis. The blurb merely states:

Memoranda to Allen Dulles regarding one Julius Bohler, a German art dealer, December 20, 1944, 3 pp. Lt. Henry R. North wrote the original memo after talking to a POW who knew Bohler. North identifies Bohler as having amassed a fortune by "acting as art agent for many high placed

Nazis." North felt that Bohler would be interested in swapping immunity in exchange for information on the "actions and whereabouts" of those high placed Nazis. North also mentions a list of Swiss art dealers known to have dealt extensively with the Nazis which was kept at the Arts and Monuments Section, G-5 Division, SHAEF. According to that list, the Fischer Galleries "are reputed to have had the largest dealings with Nazi purchasers."[53]

It's commonly known that at the same time he had "started building his Ritz Carlton hotel on Longboat Key," starting buying "ornaments and art for the hotel. Albert Keller, the president of the Ritz Hotel Corporation in America, introduced John to his friend Julius Bohler, a well-know and trusted art dealer in Munich,"[54] but whose invoices were submitted with a Lucerne, Switzerland, letterhead.[55]

From Rubens' cartoons and paintings to Renaissance art, John Ringling was mentored by Julius Bohler – the man in Munich who would be dubbed after Ringling's death, "Hitler's art dealer."[56]

The entire history is laid out at the Cà d'Zan Mansion, now the Ringling Museum, and the art gallery next door. John Ringling's Last Will bequeathed these two buildings and contents to the state of Florida upon his demise. The North boys spent six years fighting the state over what was by then a $23 million estate, including the rare art works, only to lose in court.

John North signed up for the draft in 1942 while he lived in the only house on Bird Key in Sarasota with his mother, Ida North, brother Henry, and Henry's wife Ada.

John had been in the brokerage business from at least 1929 before rising to the top of the big top, as it were. As a broker he had assisted his uncle with circus business interests, as well as his remaining oil properties.

It was rumored that clowns detested John Ringling North, referring to him as "the fop of the big top." His two ex-wives would have agreed. His first marriage lasted less than a year, and his second to a French actress, made him a laughingstock when she talked to the press:

> "Our home was more of a circus than a home. We never sat down
> to dinner with fewer than seven people. More often there were 20.
> It is not always fun to live with a genius – or a man who thinks he's
> a genius."[57]

Nevertheless, nobody could say that John Ringling North failed in putting his own stamp on his uncle's circus. He replaced traditional acts with thematic programs, hiring George Balanchine to choreograph a ballet using the circus's elephants, with music by Igor Stravinsky, who composed the Circus Polka for the elephant dance.

North traveled with the circus around the world in a luxurious Pullman train car built by his uncle, attended by a chef, a chauffeur, and a valet. As his uncle had done, John also toured Europe seeking gargantuan circus talent. His greatest discovery was a giant 6-foot, 6-inch gorilla named – what else? – Gargantua the Great. Treated to an air-conditioned cage, the prodigious primate quickly became the biggest draw in circus history.

Gargantua expressed his gratitude by grabbing North as he passed his cage one day, biting his arm. Feeling Gargantua must be lonely, John went on a second tour to find him a gorilla bride.

John's wife, feeling somewhat lonely herself, divorced him in 1945.

* * *

While John was scrounging Europe for circus talent, Henry joined the Navy as a lieutenant and, probably because of his rich source of contacts, was seconded to OSS. As part of the "MacGregor Mission" he sometimes worked directly under William "Wild Bill" Donovan, at times doing assignments others had turned down.

In 1932 Donovan ran an unsuccessful race for Governor of New York, with financial help from the wife of utilities tycoon Harrison Williams, his second biggest donor in that campaign. A few years later, as Wild Bill set out for Europe in charge of the Office of Strategic Services, Mrs. Williams (Mona) asked him to make sure the Brits or OSS boys who camped out in her Villa Fortino on Capri did no damage to it. Thinking he might need to hit her up for another campaign contribution after the war, Donovan humbly agreed.

When he reached the Italian section, Donovan first assigned the task of overseeing the villa to OSS Colonel Donald Downes, whose terse response was that he did not choose to fight a war "protecting Mrs. Williams' pleasure dome."

Equally terse, Donovan ordered Downes to get out of Italy and not to return, according to Stephen E. Ambrose, in *Ike's Spies: Eisenhower and the Espionage Establishment*.[58]

Donovan then gave that duty to Henry Ringling North, who had just arrived from Ponza after rescuing three ardent anti-fascists, including Tito Zaniboni, the man who had been imprisoned since 1926 for attempting to assassinate Mussolini.[59]

North was also responsible for securing the release from other Italian prisons of key mafia figures, who repaid his kindness by assisting in the Allied invasion of Sicily in 1944.

Formerly classified documents indicate that the OSS had turned over control of the New York docks in New York to the Office of Naval Intelligence (ONI), which had a greater interest in protecting shipping than did the OSS. Supplementing these files with interviews, Alexander Cockburn and Jeffrey St. Clair set out the full unvarnished truth about how the ONI had worked out a deal with the civilian establishment.[60]

Initially, the government's intelligence connection with the Mafia had been arranged by George Hunter White, counterintelligence head within OSS, whose primary interest was in developing a truth serum made of concentrated cannabis (THC). Believing he had perfected the serum by 1943, White strongly urged OSS head Bill Donovan to distance itself from the criminal gangs.

Donovan concurred, and the OSS then ceded most of its intelligence operations in Italy and Sicily to the ONI, which had been making its own overtures to the Mafia as part of its efforts to prevent sabotage in New York.[61]

John Foster Dulles and Allen Dulles, along with James Forrestal, a partner in Dillon Read & Co. – Clarence Dillon's investment banking firm – guaranteed that Lucky Luciano could uninterruptedly pursue his global heroin business by working from Naples, Italy, monitored by ONI. To make it even easier, they had him deported to that very location.

George Hunter White would go on to an equally reprehensible career with drug enforcement work thereafter for the American government, his exploits detailed by several authors including Douglas Valentine.[62]

MONEY ONLY THE SECOND REASON

I found myself wondering where all that money came from to build such a luxurious palace, not to mention all the famous works of art. Surely there wasn't that much wealth to be made in a circus.

Col. John Ringling, as I learned, was a railroad builder in Montana when he first met the father of a man mentioned in chapter 13. Jake Louis Hamon, Sr. in 1912 was an Oklahoma entrepreneur, whose son – I'm not making this up – ended up as a Dallas oil executive with close ties to the group of Russians who surrounded Lee Harvey Oswald's wife, Marina, and his "handler," George de Mohrenschildt.

Hamon managed to team up with John Ringling in 1912 to build a railroad in southern Oklahoma. They struck oil on Ringling's railroad land – the Healdton Field – the biggest boom of those years.[63]

Less than eight years after the oil gusher, reporters were on the scene in Ardmore, Oklahoma one day after Jake Hamon walked two blocks to the hospital, bleeding from a bullet wound.

"Jake L. Hamon, Ardmore millionaire … wounded Republican national committeeman" he was called repeatedly.[64] Although he claimed to have shot himself accidentally, the United Press wire service was quick to add that police had charged his long-time steno, Clara Barton Smith, of Ringling, Oklahoma, with attempted murder. UP then added succinctly, "and an information charging the couple with a 'statutory' offense."[65]

Several years earlier, Clara had married Jake's nephew – who received money every month for the honor of covering Jake's infidelity. Marrying someone with the same last name as her lover made it much easier for Clara to share hotel rooms with Jake – you know, Mr. and Mrs. Hamon – even though it was a fraud.

It took less time for the sleazy gossip to emerge than it did to count ballots in the election held three weeks earlier, in which Jake Hamon had a vested interest. His friend, Warren Harding, was declared the victor on November 6 after the November 2 election. Hamon's death on November 26, if all the details had emerged, would have become the first scandal of the Harding Presidency, even though he had not yet been inaugurated.

Jake's Republican cronies had been trying all month to convince him to force his mistress Clara to leave his hotel in Ardmore. They were counting on his being named Secretary of the Interior, and they did not want a personal scandal to interfere.

No witnesses were present when the deed was done, thus making the real story a bit clouded to this day. All we can factually say is Jake Hamon was shot on November 21, and he died in the hospital five days later. Clara escaped to Mexico, but she voluntarily returned to Oklahoma for Christmas. In the short interim, the wannabe actress practiced her courtroom performance.

A speedy trial that took place less than three months later. Reports of Clara's harrowing ordeal kept readers buying papers that told the sordid details. Clara cried a lot during her first-person testimony, the trial's denouement.

"He bent my fingers back and tried to break them, then he said, 'I will cut your throat.'"[66]

Her histrionics convinced the jury she deserved an acquittal. Afterwards, she became determined to reprise her talents through a movie.

"But not alone for moral uplift am I to place my life's story in photoplay form," she declared. "Frankly, I will state that my entering into film production is for a two-fold purpose. Money is the second reason."[67]

You gotta love Clara's unblemished honesty.

FIRST IMPRISONMENT OF U.S. CABINET OFFICIAL

Warren Harding's illustrious time in office, alas, ended in the late summer of 1923 when he died while on an Alaskan cruise. Although some folks gossiped he'd been poisoned, he'd actually committed the ultimate faux pas – consuming bad crab in August.

The position of Secretary of the Interior that had been promised to Jake had to be revoked because of his unexpected and scandalous demise. As a result, we read about Albert B. Fall's becoming the eponymous fall guy, instead of Jake Hamon.

Harding was, nevertheless, as Wikipedia informs us, one of the most popular Presidents in history, and his election occurred – give or take a day or two – exactly one hundred years before that of Donald J. Trump's. As we know all too well, to Trump popularity was, and still is, everything.[68]

It is perhaps that popularity among the electorate that reminds us of what accelerated the decline of the Roman and Greek republics – bread and of circuses – keeping the populace distracted. Full bellies, fun, games, and amusements. That was certainly true of those in the Harding Administration, just as it seems to be the case for some among us today.

U.S. Senate hearings on the Teapot Dome Scandal in 1924 delved into Jake Hamon's successor's political, rather than romantic, affairs, but the headlines were equally sensational.

"Fall was convicted of accepting a $100,000 bribe from oil magnate Edward Doheny. The court imposed a $100,000 fine and a one-year prison sentence. He was the first cabinet member in American history to be convicted of committing a crime while in office."[69]

Fall and Harry Sinclair were also tried on charges of conspiracy to defraud the United States, which "ended in mistrial when it was discovered that Mr. Sinclair had jury members followed by private detectives. Mr. Sinclair was later found guilty of criminal contempt of court and jury tampering and, in addition to the three-month sentence he'd received for contempt of Congress, he was sentenced to six months in prison."[70]

Ringling friend, William J. Burns – famous international detective – was the boss of the gumshoes who were following the jurors. Before and after his own trial for spying on jurors during Harry Sinclair's trial, Burns was found to be hiding out in Ringling's Sarasota mansion.[71] The date tells us it was before Cà d'Zan was built and was, therefore, the less glamorous Palms Elysian residence, which he bought from the wealthy general agent of the New York Central Railroad, Ralph Caples.

John Ringling fortuitously escaped any mention of his involvement with Hamon, who had allegedly schemed to bribe Republican politicians to get Harding elected so they could get access to the oil reserves.

Al Jennings, a train robber-turned evangelist and Oklahoma politician, told Senate questioners in 1924 of his intimate conversations, saying Jake told him he spent a million dollars getting Warren Harding elected, by bribing delegates to the convention.[72]

Hamon had asserted, "I'm going to be the biggest man in the United States before I close my career."[73]

Hamon's death in 1920 gave his fellow Republican cronies cause to celebrate not having to reward him with oil land contracts at Elk Hills or Teapot Dome. A century later, almost to the day, reporters look back and compare the Harding scandals to the Trump ones.

The *Washington Post* said the Senate's investigation into secret drilling in the Teapot Dome naval oil reserve field in Wyoming "revealed another type of attack on democracy: the greasing of the wheels of government to benefit rich and powerful interests. The hearings uncovered brazen bribery in arguably the country's biggest political scandal until Watergate, resulting in the first imprisonment of a former Cabinet member."[74]

That scandal in the 1920s was the biggest corruption in government since Ulysses Grant's administration a half century earlier. President Grant had, of course, been the father-in-law of Bertha Palmer's sister, Ida Honore Palmer Grant. [75]

It's a small, but very corrupt, world – with much of the corruption linked to Sarasota County.

Ringling's Friend in Brighton Beach

John Ringling's role in the circus, while his older brothers lived, had been to travel abroad, ostensibly in search of new circus acts. One of his companions on those trips was a "showman," Sam Gumpertz, who managed Dreamland Amusements at Coney Island and Brighton Beach for years, until Dreamland went down in flames in 1911.[76]

Arson investigations revealed rich, powerful and criminal men in New York had been investors who'd groused they'd never seen one red cent of Dreamland's profits. These men included the *Brooklyn Daily Eagle*'s managing editor, William Engeman, who coincidentally owned Brighton Beach racetrack. The name Arnold Rothstein was also listed in 1911, as one Dreamland investor who may have had a motive for arson.[77]

Rothstein, after the 1911 fire, went on to bigger, if not better, things – like fixing the 1919 World Series. Dead by 1928 in a drive-by shooting, Rothstein left documents that Feds declared proved he had financed the nationwide "dope racket."

Gumpertz also went on to bigger things after 1911. At the site of the burned-out business, he assembled all the now-unemployed midgets and freaks he'd managed for the former owner, creating Dreamland Circus Sideshow in a tent on Surf Avenue, also booking them on tours to country fairs throughout the country.[78]

When Gumpertz sailed to Europe to search out new acts, he was sometimes accompanied by John Ringling, and both names were listed together on the manifest of an eleven-day ocean voyage aboard the Italian *S.S. Duilio* bound for New York, which had set out from Naples, Italy, on November 26, 1925.[79] The ornate ship suited the baroque taste of both men.

Gumpertz also constructed a new building to house his own amusement companies, as well as the Half Moon Hotel at the end of West 28th Street, where he hosted his friend John Ringling while he recuperated from a stroke in 1932.

I call it forgotten history. The kind of history, that if seen in real time, before being hidden behind a curtain, would reveal how it all came to be.

When Ringling and Gumpertz met up in Sarasota, they tinkered just a little with what Juvenal said about the public's cravings. The poor might want bread, but the wealthy class, which Ringling wanted to attract, already had bread. What they really needed, he decided, was art.

Sarasota was to become a center for art and circuses – and, in the process, gave the public a shit show of corruption, "the likes of which the world has never known," as Donald Trump might say.

PROHIBITION GREAT FOR CRIMINALS

The Half Moon was "a huge sixteen story, 400 room hotel [that] rose on the beach," and managed to survive a foreclosure attempt during the Depression, remaining open through Prohibition.[80]

"Prohibition had been great for one group of people–criminals," wrote Suzanne Spellen. "By the late 1930s the newspapers were filled with lurid tales of gangsters who were filling their pockets with bootleg booze money and filling their criminal competitors with holes."[81]

Coney Island and Brighton Beach as early as 1932, were already descending into the hands of criminals, many of whom had emigrated from foreign countries a few years earlier.[82]

Russian gangsters who began arriving decades later often found family members living in tenements there – tenements by then owned by none other than Fred Trump, now better known as father of The Donald.

Fred purchased "Steeplechase Park, the longest surviving of Coney Island's great amusement parks," where he built more housing for new immigrants.[83]

Was it an accident that Donald would eventually buy out James Crosby's interest in Atlantic City's Resorts International and build a casino destined for bankruptcy?

What about his friendship with Russian gangsters who began settling in Brighton Beach at about the same time?

Endnotes

1   Les Standiford, "The Circus Was Once America's Top Entertainment. Here's Why Its Golden Age Began to Fade," Time, June 15, 2021. https://time.com/6073381/circus-history/

2   Ibid.

3   There is an amazing history of the Ringling family and their visible connection to Sarasota written by Marissa Perino, "The rise and fall of the 'Greatest Show on Earth' and the Ringling family's circus empire," at Business Insider, Dec 6, 2019. The copyrighted photos should be viewed there to get a better idea of the people discussed in this chapter and others throughout Gangster Planet. https://www.businessinsider.com/ringling-bros-circus-empire-family-history-2019-12

4   Jessi Smith, "Time-Traveler's Guide: A Brief History of Sarasota County ," *Visit Sarasota*. https://www.visitsarasota.com/article/time-travelers-guide-brief-history-sarasota-county

5   The sons soon left Baltimore to seek their fortunes in business all across the nation and even the entire globe.

6   The Chicago judge ordered Burns to give the actual name of the man involved, to remove suspicion from every male Calumet Club member. The divorce scandal in 1908 had not been Owen's first brush with public impropriety, however. Six years earlier Owen was visiting in San Francisco, California – several of his older brothers were engaged in business there – when his name made headlines in conjunction with Juliette Cornelia Morris Smith, "a strikingly beautiful woman of the blond type," as well as a very wealthy widow. "Demanded Money at Point of Pistol," read a headline (Oakland Tribune, on March 17, 1903, at Page 7), followed by a story revealing how Mrs. Morris Smith had met Owen in London in 1899, not long after she inherited an interest in a large estate in Virginia from her deceased husband only to watch Owen abscond with thousands of her inherited dollars.

She reported him tearfully sometime after the incident to an unnamed reporter with a Chicago dateline. Newspapers nationwide then raked up old gossip about Owen's much-besmirched family, which included Owen's brother and employer Walter F. Burns, of New York. Walter himself had been previously involved in a scandalous affair in New Jersey when at the age of 35 he'd married then 18-year-old "Alice Gladys Castleman Downs Braeumlich Burns Brooks," according to The Brooklyn Daily Eagle's May 23, 1901, edition, when she was already married. The Sunday Examiner Magazine made a mockery of Walter in its feature called "A Bigamous Bride, a Bogus Baby and a Man Who Was Fooled." (San Francisco Examiner, May 25, 1902, Page 48). Walter had been rescued from the void marriage by his sister, Mrs. J. Anthony Wilkins and her husband.

But that wasn't the end of Burns family skeletons. Rollo (Ignatius Raleigh) Burns had fled lawsuits and eventual bankruptcy in San Francisco, leaving behind his wife, Harriet "Hattie" Whitney, and daughter, whom he'd abandoned in Santa Cruz, California, while he became quickly engaged to Bessie Afong, daughter of a millionaire Chinese man in Honolulu. To avoid bigamy charges, Rollo had to return to California to beg Hattie to give him a divorce. Rollo and Bessie settled in – where else? – Sarasota, Florida where they lived out their lives in close proximity to Owen Burns.

Yet another brother, Xavier Eugene Burns, had married a daughter of Thomas Fallon, an Irish national in the U.S. Army who helped John C. Fremont raise the flag that claimed the California territory for the United States in 1846. Fallon had remained in Santa Cruz, California and married Maria del Carmen Juana Josefa "Carmelita" Cota, whose mother (Maria Martina Castro) was one of the area's largest landowners. She owned the Rancho Soquel and Rancho Augmentation grants from the Mexican government before the land was claimed by Fremont, and courts found her title superior to that of the U.S.

Owen Burns, the Chicago laughingstock, several years later became John Ringling's partner in building Sarasota, Florida's roads and bridges, hotels and museums. His erstwhile fellow Calumet Club members – the Palmer boys – held most of the land around them. Fortunately for Owen, he'd met a New York girl, nineteen-year-old Vernona Hall Freeman in 1912. By then, Owen was 43. In Sarasota he built a hotel named for his child bride, the Venona Hotel, which eventually was rescued from bankruptcy by John Ringling. The Burns family are worthy of real biography, and we have only exposed the tip of a salacious and somewhat mysterious family that can be traced back to Baltimore, MD and to Amelia Island in Florida where their father, Captain Owen Burns, Sr. was a member of the U.S. Navy before the Civil War.

7   *Manual of Planning Information, 1923.* Harvard University Press, 1928. https://ia801501.us.archive.org/19/items/in.ernet.dli.2015.210/2015.210.Manual-Of-Planning-Informa-

tion.pdf

8   "Tampa and City Planning," *The Tampa Tribune*, August 25, 1924, Page 6.

9   *Tampa Bay Times*, St. Petersburg, Florida, August 3, 1922, Page 4. See also endnote 2 after chapter 15.

10   Lauren Glenn, "Venice author questions 9/11 findings in controversial book," *Sarasota Herald-Tribune*, July 11, 2005, Page E1. https://www.heraldtribune.com/story/news/2005/07/11/venice-author-questions-911-findings-in-controversial-book/28853117007/

11   Ibid.

12   Ibid.

13   Ibid.

14   Ibid.

15   William Z. Foster, *Wrecking the Labor Banks, The Collapse of the Labor Banks and Investment Companies of the Brotherhood of Locomotive Engineers* (New York: Trade Union Educational League, 1927), p. 10. https://play.google.com/books/reader?id=sEGOwGfxbAcC&p-g=GBS.PA11&hl=en

16   Ibid.

17   Cicero, Philippic 2 (14)(35), 44 & 43 B.C. "And yet, if to have wished for Caesar's slaying is a crime, consider, I pray, Antonius, what will be your position, who, it is well known, entered into this scheme ....But if any one were to drag you into court, and were to adopt that maxim of Cassius, *'To whose advantage was it?'* take care, I pray, you are not embarrassed. Although that deed was in fact, as you said, a gain for all men who repudiated slavery, yet for you it was especially so, who not only are not a slave, but even a king, who have at the Temple of Ops delivered yourself from a load of debt; who by means of those same documents have squandered moneys innumerable; you, to whom so much was brought out of Caesar's house; you, at whose house is a most lucrative factory of forged note-books and signatures, a most outrageous market for lands, towns, exemptions from taxation, revenues. [36] For what could have alleviated your need and your debt save the death of Caesar? You seem to me somewhat disturbed: have you some secret fear this charge may seem to attach to you? I free you from apprehension: no one will ever believe it; it is not your nature to deserve well of the State: as authors of that most glorious deed the State possesses most illustrious men: I only say you are glad of it, I do not contend you did it." http://attalus.org/cicero/philippic2.html#35

18   William Z. Foster, "On the question of revisionism," *Report to the National Committee meeting of the C.P.A.*, June 18-20, 1945. New York: New Century Publishers, February 1946. https://www.marxists.org/archive/foster/1945/05/20.htm#

19   Ibid.

20   Ibid. Note that the phrase "speed-up" is italicized in the quotation. That concept was connected with management consultant and efficiency expert Charles Bedaux, mentioned elsewhere in this book as being the father of Henry Ringling North's roommate at Yale.

21   William Z. Foster, "On the Question of Revisionism," *Report to the National Committee meeting of the C.P.A., June 18-20, 1945*. https://www.marxists.org/archive/foster/1945/05/20.htm

22   Ted Morgan, *A Covert Life: Jay Lovestone: Communist, Anti-Communist, and Spymaster*, Random House; First Edition (March 16, 1999).

23   Frances Stonor Saunders, *Who Paid the Piper: The CIA And The Cultural Cold War,* Granta Books (January 1, 2000).

24   Frances Stonor Saunders, *The Cultural Cold War: The CIA and the World of Arts and Letters*, The New Press, 2001. See shorter blurb at Spartacus website, https://spartacus-educational.com/USAlovestoneJ.htm

25   Ted Morgan, op cit.

26   "Fred Albee Municipal Airport," Sarasota History Alive! website, http://www.sarasota-historyalive.com/index.php?src=directory&view=history&srctype=detail&refno=836&category=Markers.

27   Ibid. A map at the link indicates that the Albee Airport was a mile north of what became today's Venice Airport. Albee's airport lay between the Intracoastal Waterway on the east and Bahama Street as its west border and including the land that became the winter quarters of the circus in 1959. See also "Wings over Venice," Port Charlotte Sun, Oct 23, 2019, Page V5.

28   Shortly before buying tens of thousands of acres of land comprising the town of Venice, the Brotherhood of Locomotive Engineers had acquired the Hudson Trust, merging it into the Empire Trust in June 1924. Located at 120 Broadway in New York, the Empire Trust chairman was Coleman du Pont, and its directors included president Leroy Baldwin, Jules S. Bache, an art collector and broker; F. Donaldson Brown, an official in DuPont Powder Co.; Minor Cooper Keith, founder of United Fruit Co. and Costa Rican Railways, companies known to have ties to Central Intelligence Agency in the 1950s; Alfred P. Sloan, Jr., an executive of General Motors, then controlled by the Du Pont family; Percy R. Pyne II, connected to Citigroup; and Harry P. Daugherty, a vice president of the Brotherhood of Locomotive Engineers (who would be found guilty in 1927 of negligence in office. Wilmington, DE *Morning News*, "Empire Trust Company," November 17, 1925.

29   "Ellen Zinsser Hastings Bride," Yonkers, NY, *Statesman*, April 26, 1930, Page 8.

30   Webster Griffin Tarpley and Anton Chaitkin, *George Bush: The Unauthorized Biography*, Progressive Press; Reprint edition (October 7, 2004). See https://ia800902.us.archive.org/7/items/pdfy-asES-WBBT_9-wRIF/George%20Bush%20The%20Unauthorized%20Biography.pdf

31   Ben Aris in Berlin and Duncan Campbell in Washington, "How Bush's grandfather helped Hitler's rise to power," *The Guardian*, 25 Sep 2004. https://www.theguardian.com/world/2004/sep/25/usa.secondworldwar

32   Henry C. Brunie obituary, *New York Times*, April 13, 1985.

33   Brunie and Bush worked together at USO, as is documented in *Diary of John J. McCloy*, 1942 in John J. McCloy Papers (Box DY1, folders 47), Archives and Special Collections, Amherst College Library. https://www.amherst.edu/system/files/McCloy_diary_1942_1.pdf

34   Press Release, "The Bank of New York Resolves Parallel Criminal Investigations Through Non-prosecution Agreement with the United States," US Attorney, Eastern District of New York, November 08, 2005. https://www.justice.gov/archive/usao/nye/pr/2005/2005nov08.html

35   Liz Moyer, "Bank Of New York's Bad Russian Suit," *Forbes*, June 19, 2013. https://www.forbes.com/2007/05/17/bony-russia-lawsuit-biz-services-cx_lm_0517suit.html

36   Mary Dejevsky, "Russian mafia `laundered $10bn at Bank of New York,'" *Independent*, 20 August 1999. https://www.independent.co.uk/news/world/russian-mafia-laundered-10bn-at-bank-of-new-york-p-1113796.html

"Crichton makes offer to buy Pure Oil, *The Shreveport Journal*, July 2, 1964, Page 7.

37   The Kilgore *News Herald*, September 25, 1956, Page 8.

38   Rob Wells, "Sheik Key BCCI Figure, *Johnson City (Tennessee) Press*, September 15, 1991.

39   Gregg M. Turner, *The Florida Land Boom of the 1920s* (McFarland, Oct 14, 2015), p. 129.

40   Henry Ringling North with Alden Hatch, *Circus Kings, Our Ringling Family Story*, Doubleday: 1960, p. 163. Red Kestrel Books. Kindle Edition.

41   Ibid.

42   "Ringling buys five circuses," and "Sparks circus visits Bedford," *The Bedford [IN] Times-Mail*, 10 Sep 1929, Page 1. See other details online at https://circushistory.org/sparks-circus/

43   "New Yorkers Pick Lots at Sarasota for Beach Casino," *The Tampa Tribune*, 15 Mar 1927, Page 3. John Ringling North with Alden Hatch, *Circus Kings, Our Ringling Family Story*, Doubleday, 1960.

44   North and Hatch, *Circus Kings*, p. 166.

45   Ibid., p. 168.

46   Ibid., p. 184.

47   *Chronicle Tribune*, May 6, 1922, Page 1.

48   Everett C. Watkins, "Grant County Vote Is Vital for Kraus," *The Indianapolis Star*, 26 Oct 1922, Page 5. This article appeared years before the Star was acquired by Eugene Pulliam, Dan Quayle's grandfather.

49   "Lindsay Says Election Means Press Freedom," *The Indianapolis News*, February 7, 1923, Page 17.

50   The Tampa Times, April 9, 1923, Page 4. An interesting tidbit in this article revealed

Lindsay had been in southwest Florida five years earlier, where he reeled in a tarpon at Punta Gorda, while visiting Lt. David B. Lindsay, who was stationed at Carlstrom Aviation field. (The Tampa Tribune, 26 May 1918, Page 26. https://www.newspapers.com/article/the-tampa-tribune-editor-george-d-linds/56188314/)

51   Henry Ringling North with Alden Hatch, *Circus Kings, Our Ringling Family Story,* Doubleday: 1960, p. 148.]

52   U.S., Select Military Registers, 1862-1985 (Ancestry.com)

53   Records of the Office of Strategic Services (RG 226): Entry 211, WN#23987. https://www.archives.gov/iwg/declassified-records/rg-226-oss/entry-211.html

54   Virtual Library on the Ringling Museum. http://ringlingdocents.org/johns-art.htm

55   Virtual Library on the Ringling Museum. Invoice from The Lucerne Fine Art Co., Ltd. http://ringlingdocents.org/graphics/cartoons-invoice.jpg

56   Dalya Alberge, "A Renaissance masterpiece, Nazi looters, a double murder … and a happy ending," *The Guardian,* 26 Jul 2020. https://www.theguardian.com/artanddesign/2020/jul/26/a-renaissance-masterpiece-nazi-looters-a-double-and-a-happy-ending; Jonathan Petropoulos, *Goering's Man in Paris: The Story of a Nazi Art Plunderer and His World,* Yale University Press, 2021.

57   Jess Stearn, "Henry's with the Circus, Too," *New York Daily News,* April 5, 1953, Page 63.

58   Stephen E. Ambrose, *Ike's Spies: Eisenhower and the Espionage Establishment,* University Press of Mississippi; Reprint edition (November 1, 1999).

59   Don Whitehead, *Beachhead Don: Reporting the War from the European Theater: 1942-1945,* Fordham University Press; Illustrated edition (October 1, 2004).

60   Alexander Cockburn and Jeffrey St. Clair, *Whiteout: The CIA, Drugs and the Press,* Verso (December 16, 2014).

61   Cockburn, Alexander. *Whiteout* (p. 118). Verso Books. Kindle Edition.

62   Douglas Valentine, *The Strength of the Wolf: The Secret History of America's War on Drugs,* Douglas Valentine (September 10, 2019).

63   See Sam Henderson, "Circus King Tied to State's Past," *The Oklahoman,* June 17, 1984. https://www.oklahoman.com/story/news/1984/06/17/circus-king-tied-to-states-past/62799871007/

64   "Wound May Be Fatal to Hamon," United Press, Enid, OK Daily News, November 24, 1920.

65   Ibid.

66   "Clara Hamon Tells of Fatal Shot," Lafayette, Indiana Journal and Courier, March 15, 1921. https://www.newspapers.com/image/261860678/?match=1&clipping_id=130056752

67   "Clara Hamon's Here To Fight; Wishes To Make Good Says Jake Hamon's Slayer," *The Los Angeles Times,* 23 Apr 1921, Sat · Page 17. https://www.newspapers.com/article/the-los-angeles-times-clara-hamon-smith/130052698/ The trial began in Ardmore, Oklahoma in mid-March 1921 and was reported widely in various newspapers, including Selma, Alabama's *Times-Journal.* https://www.newspapers.com/image/571398851/?match=1&clipping_id=130055238. It was also read with great interest in Muncie, Indiana. https://www.newspapers.com/image/254196208/?-match=1&clipping_id=130055623.

68   Most people have no idea who Harding's opponent was – James Middleton Cox – whose grandson in 2004 married Nabila, the divorced daughter of Adnan Khashoggi. She appears in a subsequent chapter of this book. https://marriedceleb.com/nabila-khashoggi

69   "Portraits in Oversight: Thomas Walsh and the Teapot Dome Investigation." Levin Center website. https://levin-center.org/thomas-walsh-and-the-teapot-dome-investigation/

70   Ibid.

71   William R. Hunt, *Front-page Detective: William J. Burns and the Detective Profession, 1880-1930* (Bowling Green State University Popular Press, 1990), pp. 187-192.

72   Alphonso J. Jennings had a colorful background that left him open to a great deal of ridicule and allowed his credibility to be easily attacked. *The Encyclopedia of Oklahoma History and Culture* https://www.okhistory.org/publications/enc/entry?entry=JE006

73   Associated Press, "Former Bandit Insists Hamon Spent Million," *The Miami News,* 27

Mar 1924, Page 1.

74   Ronald G. Shafer, "A century before Jan. 6, bombshell hearings on another assault on democracy," Washington Post, January 15, 2022. https://www.washingtonpost.com/history/2022/01/09/teapot-dome-hearings/

75   The Honore and Palmer families were closely bound up with the Republican President, Ulysses S. Grant since Ida Honore had married his son, Frederick Dent Grant, in 1874 before Grant left office, and Ida lived in the White House while her husband was away on military assignments.

76   Sam spent his younger years working as a circus acrobat and a cowboy in wild west shows, maturing into a role as manager of highbrow stage productions. See "The People of Coney Island," *American Experience on PBS*, https://www.pbs.org/wgbh/americanexperience/features/coney-people/

       After meeting actress, Evie Stetson of St. Louis, he married her in 1892. Evie and Sam's sister, Janet Melville, teamed up as Melville & Stetson, a famous vaudeville act for many years, traveling widely with Sam as their manager. At the World's Fair in St. Louis in 1904, Sam met William H. Reynolds, who was there buying an attraction called Creation from the Fair's owners, according to Suzanne Spellen, who also tells us that Reynolds hired Sam as the new manager of Dreamland, to "travel to World Fairs and other exhibitions to bring back the best to Coney Island." See Suzanne Spellen, "Walkabout: William H. Reynolds, Parts 1-3, *The Brownstoner*, https://www.brownstoner.com/brooklyn-life/walkabout-trump/

77   Copyright © 2015 David A. Sullivan | WWW.HEARTOFCONEYISLAND.COM https://www.heartofconeyisland.com/dreamland-coney-island.html

78   Jeffrey Stanton, "Coney Island - Freaks & Shows," at Coney Island History Site. https://www.westland.net/coneyisland/articles/freaks.htm See also "The People of Coney Island," American Experience on PBS, https://www.pbs.org/wgbh/americanexperience/features/coney-people/

79   New York, U.S., Arriving Passenger and Crew Lists (including Castle Garden and Ellis Island), 1820-1957, Ancestry.com. https://www.ancestry.com/imageviewer/collections/7488/images/NYT715_3768-0493?pId=2001787341

80   Suzanne Spellen, "Past and Present: The Half Moon Hotel, Coney Island," *The Brownstoner*, Jun 14, 2013. https://www.brownstoner.com/history/past-and-present-the-half-moon-hotel-coney-island/

81   Ibid.

82   When Gumpertz applied for his passport in 1921, his address was at Parkway Baths Apartments at Brighton Beach. His neighbors, as shown in the 1920 census, reveal a plethora of Russian names at that time.

83   "Coney Island History: The Story of George Tilyou and Steeplechase Park," https://www.heartofconeyisland.com/steeplechase-park-coney-island.html

CHAPTER TWENTY

WELCOME TO BRIGHTON BEACH

Russian emigre communities in New York's Brighton Beach district, in Israel, Paris and London were seeded with mafia spawn."
— BBC News, 21 November, 1998

In the spring of 2001, William S. "Bill" Achenbaum (through his company, S/A Holdings LLC) found himself in need of a jet. He didn't have to explain why, after he'd been in business 30 years or more, he *suddenly* needed to own an airplane. He wasn't a pilot.

Neither was his son, Michael, who was set to go into business with his dad. They had a new project for which a plane would come in handy, and a new partner with business in Israel and in Russia that courts would later declare a money-laundering business.

Arik Kislin owned Air Rutter International, which managed charter contracts for the Achenbaums' jet.[1] Alas, during the time Achenbaum and Kislin were in possession (2001-2007) their plane was doing favors for the CIA, which used it for extraordinary renditions of possible terrorists. This was unsurprising. The plane they'd bought was well-known in Colombia as a long-time CIA plane, which they occasionally loaned out to the DEA.

COLLAPSE OF SOVIET SAFETY NET

Arik's uncle, Semyon (Sam) Kislin had been known for several decades as the Russian Mob's "man on the ground" in New York, going back since the old days of the Soviet Union.

A BBC special report gave details:

> The downfall of communism left an economic, moral and social vacuum which the mafia has been only too happy to fill. Hundreds of ex-KGB men and veterans of the Afghan war offered their skills to the crime bosses. The mafia also provided money and jobs to young men in Moscow, St Petersburg and Kiev who were struggling to cope following the collapse of the communist safety net.

> Early on, in 1989, the octopus began reaching its tentacles out-
> wards across Europe and America. Russian emigre communities
> in New York's Brighton Beach district, in Israel, Paris and London
> were seeded with mafia spawn.[2]

The verbiage could have come straight out of a Minecraft game. All that was missing was the Kraken.

It is well-known, even before Vladimir Putin was elected first President of the Russian Federation in 1991, Russian gangsters had begun arriving in Brighton Beach.

Craig Unger in his book *American Kompromat*, revealed that by the early '80s some Russians had already begun establishing a beachhead for the Russian government's intelligence agencies.

> Yuri Shvets, posted to Washington by the Soviet Union in the
> 1980s, compares the former US president [Trump] to "the Cam-
> bridge five," the British spy ring that passed secrets to Moscow
> during the second world war and early cold war," reported David
> Smith for *The Guardian* in his review of *American Kompromat*.[3]
>
> Unger describes how Trump first appeared on the Russians' radar
> in 1977 when he married his first wife, Ivana Zelnickova, a Czech
> model. Trump became the target of a spying operation overseen by
> Czechoslovakia's intelligence service in cooperation with the KGB.
>
> Three years later Trump opened his first big property development,
> the Grand Hyatt New York hotel near Grand Central station. Trump
> bought 200 television sets for the hotel from Semyon "Sam'" Kislin,
> a Soviet émigré who co-owned Joy-Lud electronics on Fifth Avenue."
>
> According to Shvets, Joy-Lud was controlled by the KGB and
> Kislin worked as a so-called "'potter agent" who identified Trump,
> a young businessman on the rise, as a potential asset. [4]

Probably Sam Kislin was influential in convincing Donald and Ivana Trump to visit Moscow and St Petersburg for the first time. "The Donald" was a sap for sweet deals like those at Joy Lud, where he bought 500 cutrate TV's for his hotels, and contributed to his first hotel success. On the make for more deals, Trump became the proverbial fly in the spider web.

Easy money was his brand.

"Vacuum Cleaners and Juice Squeezers"

Sam Kislin's partner in Joy Lud was Tamir Sapir, who gave a fake name (Temur Joseb) to reporter Celestine Bohlen when she interviewed him for a *New York Times* piece in January 1989:

Temur Joseb, a Soviet Georgian who emigrated 14 years ago, owns Joy Lud Electronics Inc. at 200 Fifth Avenue, near 23d Street, a store that has come to be a first stop for many Soviet visitors.

"Mostly they know what they want," he said. "They have all the information, the model numbers, the prices."

For those who didn't have all the information, Mr. Joseb had a new Soviet cooperative in Moscow give out his address to prospective New York-bound tourists, for a fee of 20 rubles."

The Joy Lud customers visiting from the USSR, Bohlen wrote sardonically, were called "vacuum cleaners," or "juice squeezers," or later, "Gorbachev's avengers."[5]

"Like flies to honey, these vacuum cleaners descend upon us, and drive us to the brink. What they want, they buy right up. But hey – they got here, and we have to treat them right," the *Times* reporter had written in 1989, long before Trump even thought about becoming the U.S. President 20 years later. It was still two years before the Soviet Union would collapse.

The store was highly trusted by the most discerning of its foreign customers, who included "Soviet bigwigs," like foreign ministers Eduard Shevardnadze and Andre Gromyko, and others who bought products that made them fortunes on the Russian black market.

Deprived of ordinary capitalism all their lives, these Soviet citizens had no notion how "free enterprise" worked. What they *did* know was the black market – illegal capitalism.

Craig Unger called Sam Kislin a "spotter" for the KGB's Odessa branch, possibly from as early as 1974, the same year he emigrated on the condition he act as recruiter for potential undercover spies.

In 1972, Sam's brother left the USSR, moving first to Israel for a year, then to the west coast of Italy until 1973, where his family – including four-year-old Arik, Sam's nephew – waited to emigrate to the United States. Arik later told a journalist that his family settled near Boston, before their move to New Jersey.

Arik's name appeared in Asbury and Central New Jersey newspapers in 1986 as a high school senior at Madison Central High School. On the baseball team, Arik played first base and earned fame as the team's power-hitter. After graduation, Arik went to work for his father's "jewelry/pawn shop in Atlantic City," according to an interview with him in 2016. "The very nature of that business forced him to work 'fireman' hours there, as the customers would come in at the oddest times."[6]

Why would "customers" need to visit a pawn shop at odd hours? Well, duh. Arik's daddy was a "*fence*," a fact Arik left out, along with a few other juicy tales about the pawn shop industry.

While working at the pawn shop one day, Arik just happened to meet "someone who was looking for a watch, and after talking to him, offered him a new opportunity. After a few years at the shop, Arik was off to Moscow to utilize his language skills and Russian culture, and there he met people who would become industry leaders in Russia. Although his job was more of an assistant's role, he took it in stride and watched and absorbed the information."[7]

WHO CHARTERED THE GULFSTREAM (N987SA)?

So now we have two possibilities about who was using the Gulfstream for rendition of the unproven "terrorists."

Take your pick: The CIA? Or the KGB? Or, perhaps it was a combination of the two, all rolled into what we now call trans-national organized crime?

As Arik Kislin flew back and forth from New York to Russia and Ukraine during the '90s, what else was he engaged in?

Hooking up – for starters – with famous Russian Mobster Mikhail Chernoy (sometimes Chernoi),who was fighting to capture a larger stake of the metals market, even as the Russian government was disintegrating. As chaos reigned amidst government corruption and the absence of viable capitalism, the Soviet economy fell apart in 1991 and Mikhail and his brother Lev became part of a particular Russian brand of crime arising from the longstanding black market.

In 1996, according to Knut Royce of the Center for Public Integrity, Interpol revealed that Semyon "Kislin's firm, Trans Commodities, Inc., was used by Lev and Mikhail Chernoy, two reputed mobsters from Uzbekistan, for fraud and embezzlement.

"A confidential 1994 FBI intelligence report on the Brooklyn, N.Y., mob organization headed by Vyacheslav Ivankov, the imprisoned godfather of Russian organized crime in the United States, lists Kislin as a 'member/associate' of Ivankov's gang," Royce reported. The 1994 report also claimed that Sam Kislin's company co-sponsored a Russian crime boss and contract killer for a US visa and asserted that he was a close associate of the late notorious German arms dealer Babeck Seroush, who settled in Russia before his death in 1992.[8]

As all this happened, Sam Kislin was one of the biggest donors to Rudy Giuliani (first as U.S. Attorney for the Southern District of New York), who campaigned both for Governor of New York state and for the U.S. Senate. As U.S. Attorney, however, Giuliani had indicted Seroush in 1984 for conspiring to smuggle communications systems equipment to Austria for export to the USSR.[9]

Sam and Rudy remained close for years afterwards with Kislin's companies also hosting fundraisers for Rudy in his losing campaign for the U.S. Senate.[10]

FROM COOKIE FACTORIES TO CHELSEA MARKET

When Arik moved to New York, he worked with Irwin Cohen, owner of Around-the-Clock Management, who had formed a syndicate of investors, on a project to acquire and renovate the area just north of the Meatpacking District on Manhattan's West side – the old Nabisco "biscuit factory," where Oreo cookies were first made.

By the time the factory closed in 1958, the area "could show some of New York City's seediest, most violent, or most disreputable scenes, from men in blood-spattered jackets carting meat carcasses, to sex workers plying their trade, often playing out right next to each other."[11]

Cohen had the ideas and the contacts but needed money. Kislin had nothing *but* money – derived from the Chernoy brothers' Izmailovskaya criminal network – which needed to launder its vice proceeds and profit from them.

It was the best of all possible worlds.

The *New York Post* interviewed Cohen after he'd finished: "'It was a very tough neighborhood,' Cohen said. 'Going to work every day was a little dangerous. In fact, my Russian investors had to send over retired KGB agents.'

"But flush with the Russian cash, Cohen and his daughter Cheryl implemented their idea of 'having only wholesale food suppliers who would also then go into a small part' of the retail business."[12]

Unfortunately, Cohen neglected to name his Russian investors.

"LOOSE LIPS SINK SHIPS."

Chelsea Market opened in November 1997. By this time, William Achenbaum and his son Michael were interested in "investing" in the next phase of the West Side development. The Achenbaums and Arik Kislin (who, coincidentally, were close neighbors in King's Point, Long Island on Manhasset Bay) were set to build Manhattan's Hotel Gansevoort in New York's Meatpacking District.

This district, fronting the Hudson River, adjacent to the south side of the old cookie factory (now renamed Chelsea Market), was comprised of historic slaughterhouses and butcher shops, being converted into highly lucrative properties. The hotel, begun some months after 9/11, was completed in 2004.

The date they began constructing the Hotel Gansevoort coincides with March 2001 – he date Mikhail Chernoy had lunch with Oleg Deripaska at the Landsborough Hotel in London. [13] It was one of those *"he said-he said"* kinds of meetings that ended up with both sides suing each other. All that both men agreed on later was that they first met at a dinner in 1993.

The lawsuits, which began in 2006, have been flying back and forth ever since. Each was about to be forced to tell his side of the story – *under oath!* – in a London court in July 2012 a process so horrifying that they settled the following March.

Naturally, the terms were undisclosed.

Oligarchs are reluctant to be forced to reveal their secrets under oath. Ask Rupert Murdoch about the reason he settled the Dominion Voting case.

Oleg Deripaska was apparently in some despair. As author and columnist John Helmer phrased it, "his line of defense [was] falling apart. His PR people commissioned an article that shot him in the foot. Or maybe higher up." Helmer, a Harvard-educated Australian freelance journalist living in Moscow, attributed his insight into Oleg's state of mind to a "source close to the Deripaska defense team in London."[14]

TEARING DOWN THE ROOF

As Deripaska made his way up, "protection" rackets run by organized crime groups were gradually taken over by law enforcement agencies," wrote Catherine Belton.[15]

Belton airily explained Deripaska's rise in the aluminum industry. "Mr. Deripaska sided with them as he strengthened his ties with the country's ruling elite, marrying Yeltsin's step-granddaughter Polina in 2001 and creating a powerful security service of his own." Oleg's wife, Polina, was the daughter of President Boris Yeltsin's loyal chief of staff, Valentin Yumashev, and his first wife. When Yumashev later married Yeltsin's daughter, Yeltsin considered Polina as if she were his own granddaughter.

So trusted was his new son-in-law, Yeltsin felt, that he depended on him to find his replacement, and he's given credit for grooming Vladimir Putin for that role – bringing him from the KGB to the Kremlin in 1997.[16] Deripaska's marriage to Polina Yumashev in 2001 cemented his leap, making him the financial representative of the Yeltsin family, according to a banker with knowledge of the matter who was interviewed by Belton for the Financial Times. "It's a family partnership. You don't mess with ex-presidents or their families."[17]

After sixteen years of marriage and two children, plus Oleg having a mistress or two on the side, Polina decided enough was enough. In October 2017 she received 6.9 percent of shares in the Deripaska company, En+ Group, said to be "worth $440 million after the company's IPO in London."[18]

A review by Luke Harding of Catherine Belton's book appeared in *The Guardian* on April 12, 2020. He called her book "relentless and convincing."[19] Not long after publication, however, Roman Abramovich sued Belton and her publisher for libel over certain claims made in the book.

Despite revisions she agreed to make, the settlement agreement, according to Harding, "is being seen overall as a victory for Belton, who has come under unprecedented legal assault from billionaires with Kremlin ties. Abramovich served for eight years as governor of Chukotka, a region in Russia's far east. He has consistently denied being under the Russian government's control."[20]

Another lawsuit, brought by Michael Cherney (same as Mikhail Chernoy) in July 2012 sought to collect a billion pounds from Oleg Deripaska, but it too settled out of court without disclosing terms.

Cherney had admitted receiving a quarter of a billion dollars in 2001 – remember the lunch meeting in March 2001 – but he claimed the money was a partial payment for his "partnership" with Deripaska, who continued to insist the payment was illegally extorted from him and he'd never been part of the criminal network.

NATION OF LAWS – NOT MEN?

Although we don't know the terms of their 2012 settlement, documents in a case filed in New York – leaked to the public after the court issued a gag order – revealed exactly the opposite of what Deripaska asserted.

The "rule of law" – the political philosophy that all citizens and institutions (including lawmakers and leaders) within a country, state, or community are accountable to the same laws – is the model Western nations long ago adopted to handle disputes.

The decade after the collapse of the Soviet Union began seeing one civil lawsuit after another filed – in Germany, Switzerland, the United Kingdom, and New York – seeking to prove their claims, since the Russian courts cannot be trusted.[21]

Ironically, as oligarchs have increasingly found themselves at odds with other oligarchs over who has the best claim over certain assets, they have turned to Western courts to resolve the right to possession.

Former Soviet spy Yuri Shvets, mentioned earlier, was Craig Unger's primary source for stating that Donald Trump had been recruited as a Kremlin asset somewhere back in the mists of time.

In late 1994 Shvets published a memoir with Simon & Schuster – *Washington Station: My Life as a KGB Spy in America* – which asserted "he recruited as a Soviet agent a former Carter White House adviser, code-named "*Socrates*" in the late '80s.[22]

Some claimed John Helmer was Socrates.

Helmer has collected his articles into a blog called *Dances With Bears.*[23]

There he posted on March 28, 2012:

> After years of telling the press and signing affidavits to his bank lenders that his business relationship with Cherney wasn't what evidence now proves it to have been – and after experts found Deripaska's signature on Cherney's primary evidence is genuine – Deripaska's last defense is that he signed under duress. [24]

The use of that defense could only imply that Deripaska had been a total victim of a Russian gangland conspiracy to extort protection money from him. Given Deripaska's own power, it was a dubious claim, at best.

It's no wonder the court rejected it. Anton Malevsky was closer to Deripaska than he was to Cherney, after all.

Deripaska's London lawyers hired a New York lawyer to file a lawsuit in US District Court for the Eastern District of New York (Brooklyn) – alleging that Arik Kislin and by-then-deceased Malevsky had been in a "gangland conspiracy," in connection with metal trading business with Cherney. The London attorney wanted the New York court to compel "discovery from Arik Kislin for use in an action pending in the [UK] High Court of Justice."[25]

Kislin replied through an attorney, who threatened to countersue. The action was soon dropped.

ORGANIZED CRIME VS. TRANSNTIONAL ORGANIZED CRIME

Bill Achenbaum started out in the construction business in New York with his wife's brother, Terry Bernstein. When Terry got his law degree and settled into a real estate practice in Garden City, New York, Achenbaum formed other entities to combine his construction skills with other lucrative opportunities.

S/A Enterprises was created when he partnered with Donald O. Stein, who had found himself in the spotlight in 1976, accused of bilking the city in a scheme that involved a variety of Democratic politicians and high-profile law firms.

It was a feeding frenzy. They were chumming already shark-infested waters. All of them wanted a piece of the more than $14 million a year of public funds."[26]

Achenbaum was mentioned prominently in news reports. But it was a politician he paid off – caught wiping the blood off his mouth – who was charged with the crime. Achenbaum already had a history of paying bribes going back before Russian Jews even began washing ashore along the New York waterfront. They'd clustered in Brighton Beach – the gooey part between two halves of an Oreo – smooshed between Coney Island and Manhattan Beach.

Less than a week after the Gulfstream II jet's crash in September 2007 Achenbaum was identified as the plane's "previous" owner.

The *New York Post* reported, "When Achenbaum owned it, the plane was managed by a Long Beach, California company, Air Rutter International, which offered it for charter. Air Rutter was owned by Arik Kislin of Long Island.

Kislin's previous company (Blonde Management) sponsored a U.S. visa sought in the early 1990s for Anton Malevsky, said to be a notorious hitman for the Russian mob, just a few years before Achenbaum bought the Gulfstream.

So, Arik Kislin and his family – and their Russian connections – seemed to be a subject worth pursuing in re global drug trafficking. During the time William Achenbaum's company (S/A Holdings) owned the plane, it made trips in 2003, 2004 and 2005 to the U.S. military base in Guantanamo Bay in Cuba, McClatchy Newspapers group reported.[27]

RUSSIAN MAFIA? FAKE NEWS! MEDIA HYSTERICS!

Ivankov was identified as a "*Vory y Zakone*," or thief in law (meaning "legalized thief" or "thief who is the Law"), in a *New York Times* article in 1994.[28] He thought he was invincible.

It was almost impossible at the time to convict members of the Russian gangs who had taken over Brighton Beach. They had family back in

Russia who might be killed if relatives in New York gave evidence. Said one DEA agent, "Russians are into narcotics for the long haul. They do not just have a foot in the door; they are in the house."[29]

Ivankov himself was quoted saying, "There is no myth about organized crime in Russia. Everyone there knows that 'Russia is one uninterrupted criminal swamp.' The criminals are in the Kremlin and the Duma (the legislature). Anyone who thinks that someone is the head of all these 'bandits' is delirious."[30]

But that was quoted in 1998. Today everyone knows who's in charge.

Vladimir Putin.

Sam Kislin seemed part of Ivankov's operation; his donations to Rudolph Giuliani's campaigns for mayor in 1993 and 1997 and the U.S. Senate in 2000 – estimated at over $64,000 – may have been an attempt to turn the United States into the same type of criminal swamp he had known in the Soviet Union.

The FBI thought so, too. An FBI report on Ivanhov in 1994 said Kislin's company, Trans Commodities, "was known to have laundered millions of dollars from Russia to New York."

Asked about that statement, Sam Kislin demurred. "There's no such thing as the Russian mafia.... It's media hysteria." [31]

He could have called it a hoax or a witch hunt. Just saying.

More than a decade later, a German court issued a ruling in a 2010 money laundering trial which declared that the "war chest of the [mob] organization was the Trenton Business Corporation. Today, the gang is engaged in robberies, extortion shakedowns, drug and weapons dealing, as well as illegal prostitution and money laundering."[32]

Following this German ruling, other details about Kislin emerged in a massive civil suit in London pitting Russian metals oligarch Oleg Deripaska against Cherney. It was an ownership struggle over the world's largest aluminum producer, Rusal, in which it was alleged that London lawyers were demanding documents that "they claimed would prove Cherney's involvement in Russian organized crime."[33]

"Krysha" and the New York Investments

As the London trial opened in mid-summer 2012, Obama's first term was ending, and the re-election campaign was ramping up. There was as yet no hint that Donald Trump would become a candidate three years later.

Reuters reported that Cherney was accusing Deripaska of trying to "rewrite history," and attempting to erase him from their partnership. Cherney's statement said he first met Deripaska "at a dinner in 1993, spotted his acumen, and entrusted him with business interests," though their oral agreement was not put in writing until 2001.[34]

Deripaska characterized their relationship, Reuter's reported, as an "old fashioned protection racket," saying the "papers signed were a sham agreement."[35]

The $250 million Deripaska admitted to giving Cherney in London in March 2001 was made "to end a complex protection arrangement – known in Russian as *krysha*, or roof – which also included Anton Malevsky, named in court papers as the head of a criminal network."[36]

But Chernoi (aka Chernoy aka Cherney aka Cherny) had made new investment commitments based on anticipated payments to be made to him. He needed the money badly, so he filed a lawsuit against Deripaska in 2006.

Meanwhile, the Gansevoort Hotel Group was expanding. A resort was being built in the Turks and Caicos, as well as in Miami Beach and Las Vegas. Fronting for Gansevoort Group were Kislin and Achenbaum. Because of our previous chapter about drug smuggling connections to the Turks and Caicos, I checked into this resort.

Not literally, of course.

I just checked it out online.

Endnotes

1   Dan Mangan, "Crash Jet Had Air of Mystery," *New York Post*, October 1, 2007. https://nypost.com/2007/10/01/crash-jet-had-air-of-mystery/

2   "The rise and rise of the Russian mafia," *BBC Special Report*, November 21, 1998. http://news.bbc.co.uk/2/hi/special_report/1998/03/98/russian_mafia/70095.stm

3   David Smith, "'The perfect target': Russia cultivated Trump as asset for 40 years – ex-KGB spy," The *Guardian*, January 29, 2021. https://www.theguardian.com/usnews/2021/jan/29/trump-russia-asset-claims-former-kgb-spy-new-book

4   Ibid.

5   Celestine Bohlen, "From Russia, With Love for U.S. Goods," *New York Times*, Jan. 10, 1989. https://www.nytimes.com/1989/01/10/nyregion/from-russia-with-love-for-usgoods.html

6   Michael Micucci-Kosowski, "Arik Kislin: An Immigrant's Story from Modest Means to Quiet Philanthropy," *The Times of Israel*, December 2, 2016. (Accessed 4/29/2024) https://blogs.timesofisrael.com/arik-kislin-an-immigrants-story-from-modest-means-to-quiet-philanthropy/. These details are according to a blog written by a New Yorker with a degree in Art History and Russian Studies from Binghamton who writes at an Israeli website called "*The Times of Israel*," as well as for the *Jerusalem Post*.

7   Michael Micucci-Kosowski, *The Times of Israel*. https://blogs.timesofisrael.com/arikkislin-an-immigrants-story-from-modest-means-to-quiet-philanthropy/

8   Knut Royce, "FBI tracked alleged Russian mob ties of Giuliani campaign supporter," The Center for Public Integrity, December 14, 1999. https://publicintegrity.org/politics/elections/fbi-tracked-alleged-russian-mob-ties-of-giuliani-campaign-supporter/. Also see Pete Cobus, "Inside Giuliani's Ukrainian Network," *VOA News*, undated, https://projects.voanews.com/impeachment/giuliani.html

9   United Press International, "W. German Indicted for Smuggling," *Pacific Daily News*, May 30, 1985.

10   https://publicintegrity.org/politics/elections/fbi-tracked-alleged-russian-mob-ties-of-giuliani-campaign-supporter/ . Excerpt from Knut Royce article: "According to New York corporate records, Arik Kislin is chairman of Blonde Management Corp., 459 W. 15th St. in Manhattan [a Chelsea Market address]. In the early 1990s, Blonde shared space with Trans Commodities and co-sponsored the person alleged by law enforcement agencies to be a hit man, Anton Malevskiy, for the US visa, according to the 1994 FBI report. Malevskiy, an acknowledged friend of the Chernoys, also is reputed to be the head of one of Russia's top mob families, Moscow's Izmaylovo gang. A 1996 Interpol report based on several ongoing investigations of the Chernoys at the time claimed that Blonde Management also was controlled by the Chernoy brothers and that this company, too, is "a money laundering company target of US law enforcement." Citing the Russian national police, Interpol said that the brothers, natives of Uzbekistan and now Israeli citizens, are "suspected of money laundering, embezzlement of funds, contract killing." Arik Kislin, in a telephone interview, would say only that he owns Blonde Management. Asked to discuss what role, if any, the Chernoys have had with the company, he said, "Any involvement with any people that I know is not something I'm willing to discuss."

    "Asked whether Blonde Management co-sponsored Malevskiy for a U.S. visa, he initially said, "That I have no clue about." Later, he added, "During the course of doing business over the years a lot of names have come to this office, so I don't know." Semyon Kislin told the Center that Blonde Management is owned by Mikhail Chernoy, and that Arik Kislin is the salaried manager of the firm."

11   https://www.smithsonianmag.com/history/factory-oreos-built-180969121/

12   Jennifer Gould, "Murder, the KGB and 9/11: Inside the weird, secret history of Chelsea Market," *New York Post*, November 17, 2022. https://nypost.com/2022/11/17/inside-theweird-secret-history-of-chelsea-market/

13   Nick Kochan, "The deal that made a Russian oligarch," The *Guardian*, July 5, 2003.

14   John Helmer, "Deripaska Tries Desperation Measures, Suckering Murdoch's Post, Triggering Contempt Of Court Investigation In New York, *Dances with Bears*, a blog, March 28, 2012. https://johnhelmer.net/deripaska-tries-desperation-measures-suckering-murdoch%e2%80%99s-post-triggering-contempt-of-court-investigation-in-new-york/.

15   Catherine Belton, "'I don't need to defend myself.' An old dispute returns to haunt Rusal's

Deripaska," *London Financial Times*, July 13, 2007, p. 9. The article was excerpted from Belton's book, *Putin's People: How the KGB Took Back Russia and Then Took On the West*, (Glasgow: HarperCollins Publishers Ltd, 2020).

16 Andrew E. Kamer, "Out of Siberia, a Russian Way to Wealth," The *New York Times*, August 6, 2006.

17 Catherine Belton,"'I don't need to defend myself.' An old dispute returns to haunt Rusal's Deripaska," *London Financial Times*, July 13, 2007, p. 9.

18 Ksenia Zubacheva, "Millions for freedom: The 5 most expensive Russian oligarch divorces," Russia Beyond, September 3, 2019. https://www.rbth.com/business/330918-most-expensive-divorces

19 Luke Harding, "Putin's People by Catherine Belton review – relentless and convincing," The *Guardian*, April 12, 2020. https://www.theguardian.com/books/2020/apr/12/putins-people-by-catherine-belton-review-relentless-and-convincing . The review states: "Putin was a senior liaison officer with the Stasi, East Germany's secret police, she suggests. And Dresden was a key base for KGB operations, including murderous ones, in which Putin allegedly played a direct part.... Moscow's goal was to disrupt and to 'sow chaos in the west,' the ex-terrorist tells Belton, a mission Putin would continue energetically from within the Kremlin, as prime minister and president."

20 Luke Harding,"Roman Abramovich settles libel claim over Putin biography," The *Guardian*, December 22, 2021. https://www.theguardian.com/world/2021/dec/22/roman-abramovich-settles-libel-claim-over-putin-biography

21 Oleg Deripaska prevailed in London's High Court against former Russian finance minister Vladimir Chernukhin over a real estate development joint venture in Moscow, and Reuters reported that Deripaska's spokesman claimed gleefully that "Chernukhin's case collapsed like a house of cards under the scrutiny of the trial. The ridiculous accusations raised by Mr Chernukhin were nothing but shameless lies driven by animosity, gall, and petty grudges. Mr Deripaska is glad to see that this time, despite the ongoing frenzy, the UK courts demonstrate independence and choose to rule cases on their merits." Sam Tobin, "Russian tycoon Deripaska cleared of contempt of court in London," Reuters, April 5, 2023. https://www.reuters.com/world/europe/russian-tycoon-deripaska-cleared-contempt-court-london-2023-04-05/

22 Daniel L. Wick, "Another Ex-KGB Spy Spills the Beans / Yuri B. Shvets claims he recruited a former Carter adviser," *SF Gate*, March 12, 1995. In his review, Wick, while following clues left in Shvets' book, also noted: "Socrates was identified by Shvets on '60 Minutes' March 5 as John Helmer, a minor White House aide in the Carter administration who is currently lecturing in Moscow. Helmer denies being Socrates." Wick also analyzes the truth and accuracy of his writings, saying: "But the spy stories that Shvets relates should be taken with a grain of salt and a shot of pepper vodka." https://www.sfgate.com/books/article/Another-Ex-KGB-Spy-Spills-the-Beans-Yuri-B-3041643.php

23 https://johnhelmer.net/. He also posts on Twitter – as @bears_with.

24 Ibid.

25 John Helmer, "DERIPASKA TRIES DESPERATION MEASURES, SUCKERING MURDOCH'S POST, TRIGGERING CONTEMPT OF COURT INVESTIGATION IN NEW YORK, Dances with Bears, March 28, 2012. https://johnhelmer.net/deripaska-tries-desperation-measures-suckering-murdoch%e2%80%99s-post-triggering-contempt-of-court-investigation-in-new-york/

26 John L. Hess, "Hidden Ownerships Found by Day Care Center Audit," *New York Times*, August 3, 1976. https://www.nytimes.com/1976/08/03/archives/hidden-ownerships-found-by-daycare-center-audit-center-owners-found.html

District Attorney Robert Morgenthau (an Alvin Bragg predecessor) charged a City employee with accepting a $3,000 bribe from a broker who represented Achenbaum and Bernstein in a deal to lease land for day care centers to New York City. Robert Crane, "Indict City Big for Taking 3G in Lease Deal," *New York Daily News*, August 19, 1976.

27 See previous chapter.

28 "The Vory was born of Stalin's prison camps and grew into a group of criminal barons who kept order in the gulags and governed the dark gaps in Soviet life beyond the reach of the KGB. While the Communist Party had a steadfast grip on government and soci-ety, the Vory had something of a monopoly on crime." Michael Schwirtz, "Russian criminal lore, *New York Times*, July 29, 2008. https://www.nytimes.com/2008/07/29/world/europe/29iht-moscow.4.14865004.html?pagewanted=all&_r=0

29   Selwyn Raab, "Influx of Russian Gangsters Troubles F.B.I. in Brooklyn," *New York Times*, August 23, 1994. https://www.nytimes.com/1994/08/23/nyregion/influx-ofrussian-gangsters-troubles-fbi-in-brooklyn.html

30   PBS: *Frontline*, 1998. https://www.pbs.org/wgbh/pages/frontline/shows/hockey/etc/yap.html

31   Timothy Williams, "Giuliani contributor denies mob ties," *The Record*, Hackensack, New Jersey, 30 Dec 1999.

32   Mitchel Maddux, "'Russian mob' ties revealed," *New York Post*, March 26, 2012. https://www.madcowprod.com/new-york-post-russian-mob-ties-revealed/

33   Mitchel Maddux, *New York Post*.

34   Clara Ferreira-Marques, "Metals magnates trade blows as London case opens," Reuters, July 9, 2012. https://www.reuters.com/article/britain-oligarchs-court/metals-magnates-trade-blows-as-london-case-opens-idUKL6E8I9BK520120709

35   Ibid., Reuters.

36   Ibid., Reuters.

CHAPTER TWENTY-ONE

MYSTERY OF THE THIRD TURTLE INN

Developed by Fritz Ludington in 1969, the Third Turtle Inn was the first hotel in Turks and Caicos. The historic hotel prospered for 20 years before ceasing operations in 1989.
–Ad for Loren at Turtle Cove © 2024

Kathy Borsuk wrote an article in 2018 about the history of the area where Arik Kislin decided to build a new resort after he'd finished construction of his newest Hotel Gansevoort.[1]

"Turks Cay Resort & Marina plans to introduce a luxury experience in beachfront resort living that will usher in a new era in TCI accommodations. In a befitting twist of fate, it is located on the site of Providenciales' first hotel – the Third Turtle Inn – and flanks the birthplace of tourism at Turtle Cove."[2]

The fact that the Third Turtle Inn was being replaced by an Arik Kislin resort is more than a mere "twist of fate." It's one of those coincidences that's not a coincidence – the epitome of "being connected."

> Turks Cay construction is not contingent on pre-sales; all the financing is already in place. The original Third Turtle Inn was built in the late 1960s to accommodate luxury travelers of the day. It stood on the bluff, which will be part of Turks Cay Resort's future development.
>
> It's interesting that Providenciales' first visionaries were the wealthy Du Ponts and Ludingtons, who arrived in Turtle Cove in the 1960s and set off to create an idyllic island hideaway, which was once a haunt of celebrities...[3]

"Did the CIA already own the Third Turtle Inn?" I asked myself. "Does its ghost haunt the Islands to this day?"

SUMMIT AVIATION'S CIA TIES

The clunky inn, once occupied by descendants of politically connected bankers, Presidents and CIA planners, had been idly sitting in the

Turks and Caicos Islands for decades, waiting to be used for whatever purpose its erstwhile owners or their scions would later decide. Featured by James McLendon in a 1975 article published in the *Miami Herald*, the Third Turtle was said to be a project of Fritz Ludington and Benght Sodiqvest – two men whose most likely investor was the CIA-connected Richard Chichester du Pont, Jr., whose father had died in a glider crash in 1943.

Richard C. du Pont, Sr. at the time of his death was director of the Army's glider program under General Henry H. "Hap" Arnold. A. Felix du Pont, Sr., who died five years later, was Richard, Jr.'s grandfather. A. Felix du Pont, Jr. and his nephew, Richard C. du Pont, Jr. then set up Summit Aviation Corporation, which, it has been said, was operated like a CIA proprietary.[4]

Ever since Ronald Reagan's inauguration as President in January 1981, while Americans watched hostages being freed on split-screen television, the Republican administration was determined to rid our hemisphere of anyone who even thought about the USSR (now Russia) or communism.

As the CIA saw it, nation building was not an option for the people anywhere south of the U.S. southern border. The Reagan and Bush regime's foreign policy was to root out all traces of self-help that emitted even a whiff of socialism. The result has been what we have been seeing since – hordes of Central and South Americans emigrating their war-torn countries where democracy has not been allowed to flourish.

Congressman Edward P. Boland's sources told him that the CIA "was mining Nicaraguan harbors and promoting methods to 'neutralize' the Sandinista leadership" when he offered up an amendment in 1984 ending all aid to the contras, the rebels the U.S. supported in trying to overthrow the Sandinista National Liberation Front (FSLN), which came to power in 1979 after overthrowing dictator Anastasio Somoza.

"The secret war hasn't brought Central America closer to peace or Nicaragua closer to democracy," he said on the House floor. "What it does is provide the Sandinistas with the perfect excuse to foist unfair elections, a huge army, censorship and the draft on the Nicaraguan people," the *Washington Post* wrote as a tribute to Boland shortly after his death in 2001.[5]

In 1983 Senator Joe Biden (now U.S. President) was a member of the Senate Intelligence Committee when he received an inquiry from a constituent about secret aviation work being done by "a Delaware aircraft outfitting company," called Summit Aviation. According to FAA records, Summit had transferred title to a Cessna 404 that crashed in June 1983 in Nicaragua while bombing the airport in Managua.

Amid claims that the plane was an asset of the CIA, Biden voiced concern publicly. Reporter Phil Milford of the *Wilmington, Delaware News Journal,* then did his own digging. He made calls to Richard C. du Pont III, known as "Kip," but couldn't contact him at any of his phone numbers. Other key officials at Summit refused either to comment or to speak to news media.

FAA documents revealed Summit acquired the Cessna 404 from Trager Aviation Center in Lima, Ohio, another Cessna dealer. The plane was modified by adding "unspecified equipment," before Summit then resold it to another "Delaware corporation based in McLean, Virginia."

Need I say more?

Milford called what he had discovered "a shadowy network of companies involved in Summit's refurbishing program under a government contract about which Summit officials won't comment."[6]

Milford said he'd found during the previous twelve months Summit had "equipped" ten civilian multi-engine planes, some "with highly sophisticated military electronics and surveillance equipment." Six planes it dealt with were, however, unable to be traced through FAA records, while others were leased from Virginia and North Carolina companies. Another plane Summit, modified and sold to Investair Leasing Corp., crashed in Managua in September.

Robert Parry wrote a story, picked up by Associated Press, and published widely on October 7, 1983, stating that Investair's manager had been a "top official at Intermountain Aviation, Inc., a now defunct company that was owned by the CIA."[7] Reporter Jeff Gerth had broken the story the previous day for the *New York Times* with essentially the same information.[8]

Everyone seems to agree that the CIA had used the du Pont-owned company, Summit Aviation, as a propriety. Was the Third Turtle Inn in the Turks and Caicos Islands simply a proprietary of the real estate variety?

The Third Turtle Inn – formerly the exclusive Caribbean hangout of Kip du Pont and his friends and family – would be developed many years later by Arik Kislin. Was this Russian-born man being handled by the same government agency the former owners were connected to?

IS THE DU PONT FUND A SICK CIA JOKE?

Skyway Communications by 2006 had what someone believed gave them a license to traffic cocaine. All they needed were the planes.

Jonathan Curshen was a Sarasota, Florida resident, a U.S.-UK dual national who controlled a money-laundering company in Costa Rica called Red Sea Management, which became the means of providing Skyway with the McDonnell-Douglas DC-9 (N900SA) that ended up busted in Mexico in April 2006 – carrying 5.5 tons of cocaine.

Skyway officials transferred 28,000,000 shares of common stock to Red Sea Management as part of the deal to buy the plane. It didn't matter that the stock was worthless. Curshen's Costa Rica brokerage Red Sea Management Co., the transferee, was in on the fraud. Red Sea's role was to launder the funds used to purchase the DC-9. Red Sea (Curshen) get 25 percent of the profits the plane brought in.

Skyway's next move was to hide the transaction in plain sight. The public corporation simply issued a press release in August 2004. It had a catchy headline: "*The Du Pont Investment Fund 57289, Inc. Satisfies $7 Million Funding Agreement with Sky Way Communications Holding Corp.*" The *Tampa Business Journal* took the bait and republished it. "SkyWay Communications Holding Corp. (OTCBB: SWYC) in Clearwater and its subsidiary, SkyWay Aircraft Inc., announced Tuesday a funding commitment of $7 million from the du Pont Investment Fund 57289 Inc. The $7 million was to be paid in seven payments of $1 million, at a cost to Skyway of 4,545,454 shares per million," it read.[9]

The stock was to be paid for on the installment plan. As each load of smuggled drugs was delivered, the company would presumably have money to pay for the next installment. But the press release didn't say that. Instead, it delivered a false message that the Du Pont Fund funds (held by Curshen in Costa Rica) would actually be used to develop the product SkyWay was promising to build.

"The funds will provide financial support for SkyWay to continue the build-out phase of its ground tower network to support Southeast Airlines, the company reported."

Southeast Airlines in Largo, Florida, had been founded in 1992 and was said to be "classified as a charter airline" in accordance with Federal Regulations. Southeast's website explained that "simply means that we must escrow each passenger's funds paid in advance of travel dates in a federally approved depository bank until that passenger has traveled. This provides the maximum consumer protection possible."[10]

A former Sky Way executive to me explained later: "They wrote it up in a press release, touting how they'd just received a big investment from the Du Pont Foundation, but it turned out to be bogus. It was just some guy (Curshen) at a desk in Costa Rica."

The DC-9 was said to be worth $7 million, the same value as the 28 million shares of Skyway stock. Both titles were to be placed in escrow until the deal was complete, which it never was.

After the plane was busted in Mexico in 2006, other reporters besides me had been eager to follow up on the story. Bill Conroy, for example, wrote:

> Skyway Communications, the parent company of Skyway Aircraft in Clearwater, arranged to purchase the DC-9 (tail number N900SA) via a stock swap with a Costa Rica-based firm called Dupont Investment Fund #57289, in November 2004, according to a filing with the U.S. Securities and Exchange Commission (SEC). However, the jet was ultimately registered with the FAA in August 2005 by a company called Royal Sons Inc. prior to being sold to an unknown Venezuelan buyer only days before it was apprehended in Mexico on April 10, 2006, with 5.5 tons of cocaine onboard.
>
> Royal Sons President Frederick J. Geffon is a shareholder in Skyway Communications and his company is a major creditor in the Skyway Communications bankruptcy.[11]

Fred Geffon, whom we met in an earlier chapter, had allegedly been duped into buying Skyway shares at a presentation Brent Kovar had made. They agreed to a swap. Since Geffon's business – Royal Sons Motor Yacht Sales, Inc. DBA Royal Sons – owned a DC-9, he would trade it for the stock. The plane wasn't owned outright. It was subject to a loan from a bank in St. Petersburg, and guaranteed by Brent Kovar for the corporation, as was shown in the 10QSB report Skyway filed with the SEC in 2004.[12]

It was a highly complicated transaction.

On the same date, an escrow agreement was signed between Du Pont Investment Fund #57289, with a principal place of business located at Apartado 10455-1000, San Jose, Costa Rica – the address of Curshen's Red Sea Management – and Skyway at 6021-142nd Avenue North, Clearwater, Florida. The escrow agent, Carl Dilley, President of Island Stock Transfer Co. in St. Pete, would hold the title until the swap occurred to the parties' satisfaction.[13]

Brent Kovar did not sign this document. Instead, it was executed by James S. Kent, while the form was prepared for Richard du Pont to sign on behalf of the investment fund. We never saw a signed copy.

Was this company a real one, or perhaps made up by someone at the CIA in charge of laundering Company profits? Perhaps it was someone else entirely.

Will the real Richard du Pont please stand up?

Since we know that there had been three men named Richard C. du Pont – with at least two of them connected to the CIA – we leaned toward the second option before we realized that the "Dick du Pont," referenced by one source, was more definitively identified as Richard S. du Pont by another. Richard S. "Dick" du Pont was the only one of the four Richard du Ponts still alive during the Skyway operation.

Here's what we know about Richard C. du Pont: "Richard du Pont [born immersed himself in the Central Intelligence Agency's (CIA) clandestine operation and reaped another megamillion-dollar windfall in the process," Michael Newton's *Encyclopedia of Conspiracies and Conspiracy Theories* tells us. [14]

"Du Pont's Summit Aviation company, founded shortly after the CIA's Bay of Pigs invasion in Cuba, was organized with assistance from CIA operative Patrick Foley. During the next decade, Summit furnished 'civic action' aircraft for the CIA's Air America network and sold converted warplanes to right-wing dictators in Guatemala, Haiti, Honduras, Nicaragua, and Vietnam. The conversion process from civilian aircraft to gunship boosted the sales price of an average Cessna 500 percent." [15]

We also found the name "Richard du Pont" in Whitney Webb's recent book, where she also described Patrick Foley as "a CIA operative," who had "flown 747s on behalf of Flying Tiger Lines, the aviation company set up by the Chennaults." [16]

Richard Chichester du Pont Jr. founded Summit Aviation and also was a "director at Edward [Bradford] du Pont's Atlantic Aviation, where the aforementioned CIA asset and Bush ally, James R. Bath, had served as vice president," Webb wrote. [17]

You can't get much more CIA than that. Only problem was all our Richard C. du Ponts were deceased by 1988. Only a cousin called Dick du Pont would have been alive when Skyway was getting money from the du Pont Investment Fund. Was Richard S. involved? Or was it some kind of sick joke?

Another du Pont, Edward Bradford du Pont, also an aviation-addict, was a cousin who lived until 2017. [18] These men were born into what is possibly the biggest and tightest – and definitely the most powerful – American family of their day. The Dick du Pont, possibly the one mentioned above, Richard Simmons du Pont, had two important connections to the Bush family. His mother was Virginia Simmons, a granddaughter of the Simmons Hardware Co. founder in St. Louis, where Prescott Bush was employed when he met his wife, Dotty Walker. The Simmons and Walker families were close. Numerous Simmons sons were members of the same secret society at Yale which tapped Prescott and both George Bushes in their years there – Skull and Bones.

The second connection was through Dick du Pont's grandfather, William Kemble du Pont, a brother of Mrs. Hugh Rodney Sharp. The Sharps' son Bayard, retired with a high rank in the Naval Reserve, ran the Boca Grande Inn in southwest Florida, frequented by the Bush family as well as Bayard's son-in-law, William Stamps Farish III. The Sharps have long been close to the Bush family ever since the first George Bush arrived in Houston in the late '50s. Bush made friends with Will Farish, heir to Exxon fortune, who married Sarah McClellan Sharp. Farish would be the investment banker Bush chose to manage his blind trust when he was elected to Congress. We'll also cover him in more detail later.

THIRD TURTLE INN BUILT BY 7 MILLIONAIRES

Richard Simmons "Dick" du Pont was in his early 20s when his cousins began visiting the Turks and Caicos Islands (TCI), where the Third Turtle Inn was being built.

The timing was interesting, being in the mid-'70s, just as George H. W. Bush became head of the CIA. James McLendon published a couple of references in Miami to du Pont involvement in TCI.[19]

The story – awash with photos of a hippie-like community of "wealthy ex-patriots" hidden away from civilization in an undeveloped tropical paradise – seemed almost too bizarre. The story has been verified by other sources in the islands.[20]

Bush was heavily involved at the time with covering up the murder of Orlando Letelier, a Chilean economist and refugee from the military dictatorship of General Augusto Pinochet. The CIA files remained classified for years, unsealed only after Bush's death. They show Letelier had been assassinated on the order of General Pinochet.[21]

Robert Parry was bold enough to report at the time:

> The Bush Family's role in the Pinochet cover-up began in 1976 when then-CIA Director George H.W. Bush diverted investigators away from Pinochet's guilt in a car bombing in Washington that killed political rival Orlando Letelier and an American, Ronni Moffitt. The cover-up stretched into the presidency of George W. Bush when he sidetracked an FBI recommendation to indict Pinochet in the Letelier-Moffitt murders.
>
> Over those intervening 30 years, Pinochet allegedly engaged in a variety of illicit operations, including terrorism, torture, murder,

drug trafficking, money-laundering and illicit arms shipments – sometimes with the official collusion of the U.S. government. In the 1980s, when George H.W. Bush was Vice President, Pinochet's regime helped funnel weapons to the Nicaraguan contra rebels and to Saddam Hussein's Iraq, an operation that also implicated then-CIA official Robert M. Gates, who will be the next U.S. Secretary of Defense.[24]

DU PONTS, ROOSEVELTS, AND BUSHES – OH MY!

Providenciales (often just Provo), is the third largest island in the TCI chain and was rumored to be the "full-time or part-time home for the likes of Kip and Dick du Pont, Teddy Roosevelt III, and Secretary of Commerce Rogers Morton."[25]

Kip was the son of Richard C. du Pont, Jr. and was three or four years older than his cousin Dick.

Like the du Ponts, the late President Theodore Roosevelt, Jr.'s descendants were also very powerful, though not nearly as numerous as the du Ponts. Theodore Roosevelt IV called himself Teddy III (counting down from the President) and lived during the same time as his cousin, Kermit Roosevelt Jr. (called Kim), who spent his life in the CIA's covert operations branch.

Teddy III's brother, Quentin Roosevelt II, had been Director of the China National Aviation Corporation, but was killed in a plane crash in Hong Kong on December 21, 1948, at the age of 29.

Teddy had worked for the DuPont corporation before World War II and had settled in Bryn Mawr, Pennsylvania. After the war, he was an investment banker in Philadelphia, only 30 miles northeast of Wilmington, Delaware. Kip du Pont co-founded Summit Aviation at Middleton, a few miles further south of Philly, as a fixed base of operations (FBO) which offered charter flights and services for general aviation. In 1961 Summit became a Cessna dealer and later added Lear Jet and Enstrom Helicopter dealerships.[26]

In the late 1960s Kip joined with Joseph Walker Wear II – called Joey in his days at Andover in the early '50s – in creating a freight-cargo carrier called Del-Air, which would later be called Summit Airlines. Kip's father had died in a gliding accident in 1943.

This turns out to be yet another Bush family connection to the du Ponts. Joey Wear was born in 1934 to William Potter and (Doris L. Stewart) Wear, and his paternal grandfather (the first Joseph Walker Wear) was the brother of Mrs. George Herbert Walker, Poppy Bush's namesake. The families were involved in very incestuous business relationship – with most of the men being stockbrokers promoting the stock of those actually involved in business.

Poppy's dad, for example, Prescott Bush – whose wife was a Walker and first cousin of the Wears – was a business partner of the Harriman brothers, whose sister Carol nee Harriman was the second wife of a man named W. Plunket Stewart. His first wife had been a daughter of the head of the Pennsylvania Railroad, A. J. Cassatt. They were horsey folk who took fox hunts seriously.

The Pennsylvania brokers and businessmen were also linked to the Bullitts, the Biddles, the Drexels – all those "old money" families that trace back to the First Bank of the U.S., not to mention to Wharton and perhaps even to Michael Milken.

The Harrimans, after their merger with Alexander Brown's sons in the New York Brown Brothers firm, trace back to the opium smuggling families in the China trade.

In the mid-1960s the people running the major railroads wanted to merge the Pennsylvania Railroad and the New York Central (whose major shareholders were Vanderbilts, Whitneys and Harrimans by then). President Kennedy hadn't decided if he would oppose or approve it before his death. Not long after LBJ was sworn in, he quickly approved the merger.

When the railroad assets were looted afterwards, the Penn Central ended up being lumped into Carl Lindner's grab bag called American Financial Corporation – along with the old United Fruit company, Great Southwest Corp., Six Flags, and several others. Linda Minor was writing about these scandals while I was focusing on Barry Seal. Who knew then it was all about the same thing?

BARRY SEAL AND SUMMIT AVIATION

I was curious why these young scions of such notable families were lazing in the sun at the Third Turtle Inn with Fritz Ludington. My first thought was drug smuggling, natch.

In my book about Barry Seal, I wrote: "Summit Aviation, was doing business with Barry Seal, proved by records in his widow's possession. According to congressional sources, Summit did 'contract' work for the CIA, had former CIA personnel on the payroll, and had been linked through ownership records to the Cessna that crashed while bombing Managua."[27]

347

All the foregoing links between the name du Pont and the CIA now lead us to only one question – whether the Richard du Pont, allegedly the principal in the du Pont Investment Fund was a real person whose money was being washed through Jonathan Curshen's Du Pont Investment Fund 57289, Inc. or just a fake name, made up to honor a CIA hero.

It's not unlike the question about Donna Blue Aviation. As I thought at that time, the biggest clue of the true identity of the individuals or organization operating behind the dummy front of "Donna Blue Aircraft" was in its initials, "DBA," for "doing business as." It was the kind of cute nomenclature for which "the boys" are known to be fond.

The boys like to play games. It amuses them to use the names of their heroes as a ploy to throw the uninitiated off the track.

Then they watch confused mortals run around in circles in an attempt to decipher their poor excuse for tradecraft.

The CIA and RussiaGate

Arik met William Achenbaum (owner of the Gulfstream II) and his son Michael, possibly as a result of being neighbors in Great Neck, Long Island.[28]

Was it an abandoned building in search of funding or dirty money in search of a project that got the ball rolling? At any rate, the two came together and became quite a hit.[29]

"By 2001, Arik Kislin was prepared for his next venture, partnering with the Achenbaum family to form the Gansevoort Hotel Group (GHG)."[30]

Had the Gulfstream II drug plane – also implicated in CIA covert ops like illegal kidnapping and transportation of suspected terrorists never formally charged or tried – also been used to accommodate *Russian* intel? It's a legitimate question which remains – like so much else touching on drug trafficking and transnational organized crime – unasked and unanswered. It smells of cover-up.

Sam Kislin was instrumental in creating the scenario for which Trump was impeached – trying to bribe acting Ambassador Gordon Sondland into extorting from President Zelensky a promise to dig up dirt on the Biden family. Does anyone remember that big highlight of Trump Impeachment I: *"I want you to do me a favor though."*

Before Zelensky was elected as Ukraine's President, Sam Kislin had bought a Cypress-based shell company called Opalcore Ltd., which consisted of some of the assets President Viktor Yanukovych had stolen from the Ukrainian government – one of 400 such shells listed in a secret law-suit leaked in 2018 to the public by *Al Jazeera*.[31]

Yanukovych put his deputy, Viktor Yushchenko, in charge of these assets and then fled to Russia in 2014, just as Putin began his invasion of Crimea, which was part of Ukraine. It was like Mexico deciding to take Texas back. Except most Americans today might thank Mexico for doing them a favor.

Yushchenko in turn redelegated the task to Arkady Kashkin, and then promptly fled for Russia, leaving poor Arkady, the last man standing. Kashkin was getting threats from Ukrainian prosecutor Yuri Lutsenko. "Hand over the stolen property, or else!"

Naturally he caves. What has Putin done for him? So Lutsenko takes the money out of the bank and puts it back in Ukraine's state treasury. Kislin, who had bought a small fraction of the $1.5 billion in stolen government bonds, believed his share was enough for him to exert pressure on everyone he knew in the United States to get it back for him.

It had been a great deal he'd made, he screamed, even if it was stolen when he bought it from a bank acting as a fence for stolen goods. As we know, that was also the Kislins' modus operandi. Kislin never thought the government would declare the purchase illegal and resteal his stolen bonds. He *knew* people!

He started with Rudy Giuliani, then moved on to Donald Trump. From there he went to U.S. Ambassador Marie Yovanovitch in Ukraine. Trump fired her in May 2019, leaving State Department personnel William Taylor and Fiona Hill in place to answer to the new acting Ambassador Sondland, who had no experience in such matters.

Taylor and Hill became cautious when they saw Sam Kislin's messages addressed to the ex-Ambassador, in which he claimed to be "an informal adviser to US President Donald Trump on Eastern Europe."[32]

John Bolton's words were some of the most memorable. He told Fiona Hill, "I want no part of whatever drug deal Sondland and Mulvaney are cooking up," and predicted Giuliani could become "a hand grenade who's going to blow everybody up."[33]

John Bolton must have known about the billions in stolen assets from Ukraine the absconded president had sold off, with the proceeds going – not to the citizens of Ukraine – but to accounts set aside for Putin and his oligarchs.

PROJECTION PERSONIFIED

Sam Kislin and his lawyers argued that poor Sam was the helpless "victim of Ukrainian 'corruption,'" and they urged the staff of fired U.S. Ambassador Marie Yovanovitch "to intercede with Ukrainian officials on Kislin's behalf."[34]

Sam Kislin took his wife and an American attorney, Jeffrey Dannenbaum, to Ukraine, where they met with a Ukrainian attorney and reporters in December 2017. He was there, he said, because he "wanted to get his $20.9 million and invest it in the Ukrainian economy."[35]

Trans Commodities, the firm Sam Kislin owned with Mikhail Chernoi – who doesn't know how to spell his own name – had bought Opalcore Ltd. from a British firm known as Exbridge Properties LP, which Ukraine's official investigation found was "associated with companies that ... belong to the 'money laundry' of the fugitive oligarch Sergei Kurchenko and Deputy Prime Minister of Yanukovych, Sergei Arbuzov."[36]

These money laundering whiz kids are impossible to trace, according to experts.[37] While researching the many companies involved in the hiding of these stolen funds, we ran into the name Hunter Biden, the man the alt-right love to blame without an inkling of understanding about what they accuse him of.

Mykola Zlochevsky, the ecology minister who headed Burisma Holdings and named Hunter Biden to its board, was part of Yanukovych's administration. He fled Ukraine in 2016. It was almost as though Hunter was sheep-dipped to work undercover. He should write a tell-all book once it's all said and done.

Another Ukrainian newspaper caught Sam Kislin in a lie when he said he didn't know the former president who looted the state treasury. *Forum Daily* wrote in broken English:

> "It is also known that the company Kislin Trans commodities at one time she worked with Viktor Yanukovych. In 2002-year, Trans commodities invested $13million in Makeevsky metallurgical plant. Yanukovych, the then governor of the Donetsk region, boasted about attracting an American investor to the region. But the American company in a few months left the enterprise."[38]

PAUL MANAFORT'S POLITICAL STRATAGEMS

Pro-Putin Yanukovych would never have been elected president of Ukraine without the highly paid political strategy services of Paul

Manafort, former partner of Republican dirty trickster Roger Stone. The two Republican political operatives first became acquainted in 1972 as members of the College Republican organization, along with Karl Rove, Terry Dolan and Lee Atwater, to mention a few.[39]

Before 1980, when Manafort and Stone set up their own lobbying office with Charles Black, they had been introduced to Roy Cohn and Donald Trump through Tom Barrack. According to *Vanity Fair*:

> "Their first client, Stone recalled, was none other than Donald Trump, who retained him, irrespective of any role Manafort might have had in the firm, for help with federal issues such as obtaining a permit from the Army Corps of Engineers to dredge the channel to the Atlantic City marina to accommodate his yacht, the *Trump Princess*."[40]

Manafort was also paid millions of dollars by Putin's friend Oleg Deripaska to teach the candidate Yanukovych to lie with a straight face. Republicans are experts at that.

Manafort's new-found wealth would later be exposed during his uncontested trial when he refused to drop a dime on Trump for his role in the Putin-backed scheme of destroying Ukraine's economy. Without Manafort's treason against the United States Donald Trump, also a traitor, would never have been elected.

ELECTION FRAUD IS LIKE HERPES. IT'S BEEN AROUND A LONG TIME.

Allegations of election fraud have been around forever. Election rigging is an open secret: Everybody knows about it. Donald Trump has been holding it as a trump card since 2015.

Election companies like Dominion Voting Systems have been steeped in graft, scandal and corruption since Dwight David Eisenhower was in knee pants. They have the potential of corrupting the vote, if the people in charge allow them to do it.

Most people like to think their sacred vote is being cast and tabulated under the watchful eye of guys in white lab coats with pocket protectors. Nerds. All that changed once Trump lost in 2020. He already had his trump card ready to play. If he had won, well, the same election would have been squeaky clean.

When it comes to election fraud, I have the same goal Gary Webb did about CIA drug trafficking. He told me that he just wanted to able to say that he'd helped to drag the dead body out from underneath the bed just a few more inches.

There's no such thing as *voter* fraud except maybe for a handful of amateurs. That's because the retail worth of voter fraud, with 150 million people casting ballots is *NADA*. But don't be discouraged. Because there is plenty of *election* fraud, which is a whole different animal.

Wholesale fraud is pretty lucrative.

THE BIG FIX 2000: WATCH IT ON AMAZON PRIME

Twenty something years ago I did a documentary called *The Big Fix 2000* on a subject that had never been covered before. Instead of profiling ways election machines can be hacked – there were already plenty of documentaries about that – I decided to investigate the ownership of the two companies that – then and now – dominate the American election industry.

I traveled to Ireland to find the man whose election company made George W. Bush America's president. His name was Dr. Michael Smurfit, Ireland's richest multimillionaire. He got his start as a bagman for David Rockefeller, an Irish private detective told me. And he hung out at racetracks in Switzerland with Zurich currency speculators.

Election companies are owned by New Jersey Mobsters, by international gamblers, Zurich currency manipulators, Bahamian resort owners, and supra-national financiers. Their companies have untraceable shareholders, and numbered bank accounts in Switzerland and the Channel Islands. Their corporate documents are often signed by fictitious nominees. And they are routinely involved in systemic bribery of public officials, like the Prime Minister of Ireland.

You've probably figured out that this is a "problem" that won't get fixed anytime soon. And you'd be right.

Back in 2006, the U.S. government began an investigation of Smartmatic – which had been linked to the leftist government of Venezuelan President Hugo Chavez – because they'd just bought Sequoia Pacific, a company which moves around a lot.

An American Congresswoman called into question the national security implications involved in the sale of an American election services company to a Venezuelan software firm, Smartmatic.

Of course, it wasn't *really* Venezuelan. Not exactly, anyway…. Smartmatic was actually owned by a trust in Amsterdam. Not exactly, though …

Because the trust in Amsterdam was itself owned...by a company in the Netherlands Antilles, but not exactly...

Because the company in the Netherland Antilles was owned by a private foundation in Geneva, Switzerland.

In America's hugely compromised election industry, this is business as usual. Yet somehow this fact completely escapes scrutiny every four years. In the mainstream media, except for that brief brouhaha, because of the dread specter of Venezuelan leftist Hugo Chavez.

But here's the beauty part.... And forgive me for waiting till the end to tell you: It was a Democrat who first blew the whistle on Smartmatic.

"The government should know who owns our voting machines," harrumphed Carolyn B. Maloney, Democrat of New York, as she asked the Bush administration to review Smartmatic's takeover of Sequoia Voting Systems, "an industry leader which counts one of every three American votes."[41]

"There seems to have been an obvious effort to obscure the ownership of the company," Rep. Maloney said.

Good for her. An investigation into corruption in the election services industry is so long overdue that, in gratitude, FOX should set aside a pair of tickets to the World Series every year to Hugo Chavez' next of kin.

Because even communists like baseball. And phony outrage is fake news.

Endnotes

1   Kathy Bordsuk, "The Islands' New Cay," *Times of the Islands*, Summer 2018. https:// www. timespub.tc/2018/07/the-islands-new-cay/

2   Ibid.

3   Ibid.

4   Guillermo X. Garcia, "Evergreen denies CIA connection," *Arizona Daily Star*, July 10, 1984.

5   Adam Bernstein, "Mass. Representative Edward Boland, 90, Dies," *Washington Post*, November 5, 2001. https://www.washingtonpost.com/archive/local/2001/11/06/mass-representative-edward-boland-90-dies/7b72cf4e-433f-467b-805f-ddddaa09e3da/

6   Phil Milford, "Mystery plane tied to Delaware firm," *Willmington News Journal*, October 7, 1983. https://www.newspapers.com/article/the-news-journal-myster-plane-summit-avi/146303516/

7   Robert Parry, Associated Press, "CIA reportedly aiding guerillas," https://www.newspapers.com/article/the-buffalo-news-robert-parry-cia-plane/146306769/

8   Jeff Gerth, "On Trail of a Latin Mystery, CIA Footprints," *New York Times*, October 6, 1983. https://www.nytimes.com/1983/10/06/world/on-trail-of-a-latin-mystery-cia-footprints.html

9   "SkyWay lands investment funding," *Tampa Business Journal*, Aug 24, 2004. https:// www.bizjournals.com/tampabay/stories/2004/08/23/daily12.html

10   Ibid.

11   Bill Conroy, "Third Cocaine Plane Surfaces and is Tied to Web of Government Connections," *The Narco News Bulletin*, Issue49/article2989, January 29, 2008. https://www.narconews.com/print4e224e22.html?ArticleID=2989&lang=en

12   Skyway Communications Holding Corp. '10QSB' for 1/31/04 – EX-10.2. https://www.secinfo.com/d11Q1u.12p.c.htm#1stPage

13   https://www.secinfo.com/d1zWxj.16r.d.htm

14   Michael Newton, *Encyclopedia of Conspiracies and Conspiracy Theories*, 2006, page 103.

15   Ibid.

16   Whitney Webb, *One Nation under Blackmail, Vol. 1*, Trine Day, 2022, p 291.

17   Ibid.

18   https://www.chandlerfuneralhome.com/obituaries/edward-b-du-pont/

19   James McClendon, "The Turkish Floridians," *Tropic*, an insert in *Miami Herald*, 25 May 1975, Sun ·Page 241.

20   History Turks and Caicos Information TCI Mall. https://tcimall.tc/history/

21   Jonathan Franklin, "Pinochet directly ordered killing on US soil of Chilean diplomat, papers reveal," 8 Oct 2015. https://www.theguardian.com/world/2015/oct/08/pinochet-directly-ordered-washington-killing-diplomat-documents-orlando-letelier-declassified

        Also see CIA: "Pinochet personally ordered" Letelier bombing. https://nsarchive.gwu.edu/briefing-book/chile/2016-09-23/cia-pinochet-personally-ordered-letelier-bombing

22   Robert Parry, "Pinochet's Death Spares Bush Family," *Consortium News*, Decmber 12, 2006. Archived: https://archive.globalpolicy.org/intljustice/wanted/2006/1212bushfamily.htm

23   https://www.dahf.org/KipDu Pont.html

24   Ibid.

25   Matt Smith and Lance Williams, "Russian-American business exec with ties to Trump is drawn into impeachment inquiry, *Reveal*, October 5, 2019. U.S. Department of State Case No. F-2019-06295 Doc No. C06804813 Date: 09/27/2019.

26   The law firm representing Kislin's company in the matter of Opalcore bonds purchased from Oshchadbank was Kestenbaum, Dannenberg & Klein.The heavily redacted files, released in response to a FOIA lawsuit filed by Reveal, indicate that Kislin claimed he was Trump's financial adviser. https://www.documentcloud.org/documents/6454510-Claims-Presidents-Advisor.html#document/p1/a528886; also see https://s3.documentcloud.org/documents/6454510/Claims-Presidents-Advisor.pdf.

27   Daniel Hopsicker, *Barry & 'the boys,'* 2000, p. 319.

28   Their mansions backed up to Manhasset Bay. Achenbaum's house at 4 Turtle Cove sat

next-door to his previous partner, Terry S. Bernstein – his wife's brother – who was also an attorney with a real estate practice in Garden City, New York. Arik lived at 570 E. Shore Road, just ten water-front houses away, not counting the Broadlawn Harbour Yacht Club. He'd first rented next door to Achenbaum until a suitable house came available to buy.

29   Intriguingly, the investment bank which bought them out – Angelo, Gordon & Co. – was founded by two men who had met during their long careers at L.F. Rothschild, according to James Nash of Bloomberg News, "Investment firm CEO was art collector too," *Honolulu Star-Adver-tiser*, Honolulu, Hawaii, January 04, 2016. Jacob Rothschild acquired a large percentage of stock in L.F. Rothschild, though it's said there's no familial relationship between L.F. and Jacob, according to Kurt Eichenwald, "Jacob Rothschild: a maverick deal maker defies tradition," *New York Times*, re-printed in the Chapel Hill Newspaper, July 16, 1989. Eichenwald quotes John Angelo, who in that article called himself Jacob's "longtime friend." There are so many Rothschilds, in fact, it's hard to keep them all straight. For example, Sir Evelyn Robert Adrian de Rothschild married American Lynn Forester and became Hillary Clinton's close friend and donor in her 2016 Presidential election cam-paign against Donald Trump. Vanessa Williams, "They were Hillary Clinton's die-hard loyalists. Here's where they are now," *Washington Post*, May 2, 2015. https://www.washingtonpost.com/politics/they-were-hillary-clintons-die-hard-loyalists-heres-where-they-are-now/2015/05/02/82025cf2-e92a-11e4-aae1-d642717d8afa_story.html . Co-author Linda Minor wrote a background study of Lady Lynn Forester de Rothschild in 2015, finding some astounding information. Linda Minor, "Tale about a Tail Number (Part II)," QuixoticJoust blog, March 19, 2015. https://quixoticjoust.blogspot.com/2015/03/tale-about-tail-number-part-ii.html

30   Lisa Mascaro, Mary Clare Jalonick, and Eric Tucker, Associated Press, "Aide says Ambassa-dor did 'political errand' for Trump," *Miami Herald*, November 22, 2019.

31   Will Thorne, "Secret court document exposes state looting in Ukraine," *Aljazeera*, January 10, 2018. The link to the list of companies is embedded in article link: listhttps://www.aljazeera.com/news/2018/1/10/secret-court-document-exposes-state-looting-in-ukraine. List: https://www.alja-zeera.com/mritems/Documents/2018/1/10/f33608170ade4b18a32e023b62a11663_100.pdf.

32   Chris Summerfeldt, "Bolton: I'll talk to air Ukraine 'drug deal' if Senate allows it," *New York Daily News*, 07 Jan 2020, Page 8.

33   Matt Smith and Lance Williams, *Reveal*, October 5, 2019. https://www.document-cloud.org/documents/6454510-Claims-Presidents-Advisor.html#document/p1/a528886; also see https://s3.documentcloud.org/documents/6454510/Claims-Presidents-Advisor.pdf.

34   Anna Babinets and Olena Loginova, "Yanukovych's billions: will the money return to the Ukrainian budget for a long time?" Slidstvo.Info, January 19, 2018.

35   Copy of letter written by Kislin's attorney is embedded within article: https://www-slid-stvo-info.translate.goog/articles/kislin/?_x_tr_sl=uk&_x_tr_tl=en&_x_tr_hl=en-US..

36   Anna Babinets and Olena Loginova, "Yanukovych's billions: will the money return to the Ukrainian budget for a long time?" Slidstvo.Info, January 19, 2018.

37   Two examples from those who've tried are articles by 1) Stephen Grey, Tom Bergin, Sevgil Musaieva and Jack Stubbs in "Special Report: How a 29-year-old Ukrainian made a killing on Russian gas," Reuters, December 11, 2014. https://www.reuters.com/article/idUSKBN0JP1KM/; and 2) Graham Barrow, "Corporate registers and the veneer of transparency," https://grahambarrow.com/corporate-registers-and-the-veneer-of-transparency/

38   Lyuba Petrushko, "Associated with Trump Ukrainian American will sue Ukraine for the money Yanukovych," *Forum Daily*, January 1, 2018. https://www.forumdaily.com/en/svyazan-nyj-s-trampom-ukrainskij-amerikanec-budet-suditsya-s-ukrainoj-iz-za-deneg-yanukovicha/

39   Kate Brannen, "A Timeline of Paul Manafort's Relationship with the Trump World," Just Security website, October 30, 2017. https://web.archive.org/web/20210808024709/https://www.justsecurity.org/46464/timeline-paul-manaforts-relationship-trump-world/. Also see the Mueller Report, "Report On The Investigation Into Russian Interference In The 2016 Presidential Election," U.S. Department of Justice (Washington, D.C.: March 2019), p. 134. https://www.justice.gov/ar-chives/sco/file/1373816/download

40   Marie Brenner, "Deal with the Devil," *Vanity Fair*, August 2017. https://archive.vanityfair.com/article/share/5baf1e07-19a9-4617-977d-55a24497704e

41   Tim Golden, "U.S. Investigates Voting Machines' Venezuela Ties," *New York Times*,   Oct. 29, 2006. https://www.nytimes.com/2006/10/29/washington/29ballot.html

CHAPTER TWENTY-TWO

HOW TO DO THE SNITCH AND ROLL

The so-called "political process" is a fraud: Our elected officials, like our bureaucratic functionaries, like even our judges, are largely the indentured servants of the commercial interests.

– Edward Abbey

The Renewable Corporation winked into existence like an afterthought during the presidential campaign of 2008. Its birth came shortly after John McCain's loss in the Iowa Caucuses. He had campaigned to end subsidies paid to corn growers in the Midwest. What sane Iowa farmer would vote for a candidate who wants to cut off a major source of his cash flow?

As late as October 15, 2008, Republican presidential candidate John McCain said in a televised debate with Democratic rival Barack Obama, "I would eliminate the tariff on imported sugar cane-based ethanol from Brazil," adding that "he opposed subsidies for ethanol because they distort the market and could lead to inflation."[1]

IBC's subsidiary, Renewable Fuels of America, Inc., was already in a joint venture in Brazil producing ethanol. Joey Barquin told me that he'd been to Brazil twice with Curshen and Badolato after he'd invested in what he thought at the time was legitimate – a company that would be ready to deliver on McCain's promise if he became President.

When McCain had opposed the popular "bipartisan" $300 billion farm bill, however, calling it "bloated," Republicans had about as much chance of winning Iowa's seven electoral votes as Iowa had of winning the Super Bowl without a pro football team.

"AN HISTORIC CRISIS IN OUR FINANCIAL SYSTEM"

McCain was scheduled to debate Barack Obama on September 26, 2008. Two days before the debate, however, McCain made a dramatic, almost-insane announcement.

"The sound of jaws hitting the floor reverberated in Washington this afternoon when Republican presidential nominee John McCain announced that he would suspend his campaign and asked that Friday's debate be postponed. Why? Because of the 'historic crisis in our financial system,' said McCain, who intends to return to Washington tomorrow to participate in Wall Street bailout negotiations on the Hill," reported the conservative US News and World Report.[2]

He didn't get the reaction he'd hoped for. Yelling, like Henny Penny in the child's folktale, "The sky is falling!" may have fooled a couple of voters, but his opponent, Barack Obama, didn't fall for the ruse.

Obama, astounded, claimed there was no need to cancel the debate. But McCain insisted he must get to Washington immediately to meet with fellow Republicans and stick his thumb in the failing dam.

Laughed Representative Barney Frank, "It's the longest Hail Mary pass in the history of either football or Mary's."

"I wish McCain had shown the same concern when he didn't show up in the Senate to vote on the extension of the renewable energy tax credit," Governor Ed Rendell of Pennsylvania told the *New York Times*. [3]

McCain's suspension was not an astute political move. A few days later he resumed the campaign.

BADOLATO AT THE HELM OF IBC

What had put John McCain into a sudden frenzy the day before his announcement was news that a big part of his campaign financing mechanism was tanking.

Only two weeks prior to September 24, visualize this scene: September 9, 2008, Andrew Badolato, CEO of Industrial Biotechnology (IBOT), issues a press release, announcing "plans for its operating subsidiary, Renewable Fuels of America Inc., to import and distribute Brazilian sugarcane ethanol into US and coastal markets."[4]

On September 10, one day later, Jonathan Curshen is arrested in New York six days after a criminal complaint was filed under seal.[5] The charges remain sealed until October 23, the date Curshen is schedule to plead guilty in open court. Curshen pays a bond of $2 million for his release, telling Badolato he has a very limited window of time to keep the crime from being connected to McCain's campaign promise. Badolato has to find a very large broom in order to sweep this crisis under the rug so reporters won't sense that a big chunk of the illegal profits Curshen was making, by pumping up the share price of IBC stock, would be going into Republican campaign coffers.

Curshen had been promised 25% of his take for flogging IBC stock, which traded as IBOT on the Vancouver Stock Exchange. Reporter David Baines had been watching as a colorful cast of international fraudsters, including Sarasota-based Curshen and Vancouver-based Aarif Jamani, who were busted as part of the same investigation.[6]

As early as the summer of 2007, a Vancouver police officer went undercover, posing as a drug trafficker who wanted to build up a brokerage business to launder drug money. We'll call him UCV. He made contact first with Aarif Jamani, as a potential client. The next step was for the UCV to introduce the targeted criminal to a "friend," who happened to be a New York FBI undercover officer (NYUC). NYUC was using the alias "Charlie Moore," and pretending to be a New York broker with a roster of amenable and wealthy client-investors.

Jamani had been hooked in October 2007. That's about the same time Curshen was assigned to go to Vancouver to flog Badolato's IBOT stock. Badolato had almost outed himself at that same time by attracting the attention of a reporter in Sarasota. On June 8, 2007, Michael Pollick's interview of the IBC president appeared in the *Sarasota Herald Tribune* to get his take on why IBC had filed a lawsuit against its former vice president for production and marketing, Yung Huoy "Mark" Truei, a chemist from Taiwan.

"The company's founders now say in a civil lawsuit filed against it in Sarasota County that they were taken for a ride," Pollick wrote.[7]

> The Taiwanese entrepreneur [Truei] was pitching them the 'Super Bug,' a supposed bacteria developed in China that would speed up the production of ethanol from plants. It would make growing a crop for ethanol into a cheaper source for both fuel and plastics than paying Big Oil for its expensive and dwindling reserves.
>
> Truei claimed he had his own tightly held sources within the Chinese government, its secret service and its military, people who could pry the genie out of the bottle.

Had Andy at first thought he'd bought himself a Chinese spy with connections to the inner workings of the Chinese Government? Had he reported that to President George W. Bush or anyone in charge of foreign relations? We don't know the answer, unfortunately.

By all appearances, the potential "Chinese spy," educated in the U.S., was simply trying to bring a useful product to market with technology discovered in China. But, as I said, we don't really know.

Pollick, for one, wasn't buying Andy's optimism, though his hints were subtle. "Truei told managers they needed to make him a top executive of their *little publicly traded company,* living hand-to-mouth through small secondary offerings," he wrote with a twinge of irony.[8]

Mark Truei, according to a press release issued by himself a year before, had hired "Dr. Kung-Ta Lee as a member of IBC's highly qualified and respected team of Scientific Advisors ... Dr. Lee possesses the knowledge and experience necessary to execute the optimization, scale-up and commercialization of the numerous compounds in IBC's pipeline scheduled for roll-out."[9]

The PR sounded so legit it probably was. If he used the lawsuit as a scare tactic to get rid of Truei and Dr. Lee, it backfired when the press came calling.

Pollick allowed Andy one last self-serving quote: "We are very much actively pursuing this, with no guarantee of success, but we are highly confident that we possess both the economics and the technology to deliver a bio-renewable feedstock compound at or below the current petrochemical price."

But then he countered with a big slap, saying, "Wall Street appears to have its doubts. After trading as high as $3 in early 2006, Industrial Biotech's shares now change hands for a few thousandths of a cent. Badolato said the company has raised about $600,000 since December, just to pay for current operations."

The SEC had also been watching Jonathan Curshen's trading practices for years by this time. *Silicon Investor,* an online forum for investors had posted:

> SEC targets tout CURSHEN, a YBM post-promo alumnus
> 2003-04-25 20:15 ET *Street Wire*
> Ontario Securities Commission
>
> by Brent Mudry
>
> The United States Securities and Exchange Commission has launched a pump-and-dump prosecution of *Freedom Golf Corp.* figures, including self-styled Florida investment banker JONATHAN CURSHEN. Mr. CURSHEN is best known in Canadian financial circles for his previous role in a bizarre 1998 takeover bid for YBM Magnex International seven months after the Toronto Stock Exchange-listed company collapsed amid U.S.-led revelations it was an apparent money laundering vehicle for respected Russian mobster Semion Mogilevitch.[10]

The blowback to McCain's run for President would have been devastating if Badolato's company had been tied to Curshen's shenanigans. McCain must have known, or else he would not have been so desperate to suspend his campaign as he did.

In retrospect, we may have become aware of a Russia connection to influence American political campaigns even earlier if all the connections had not remained hidden. For that reason, we'll spell them out in detail for you here.

THE CORPORATE-POLITICAL COMPLEX

John McCain had announced his run for the Republican Presidential primary on April 25, 2007, and appointed strategist John Weaver as chief fundraiser. On July 6, less than three months later, "McCain parted ways with his longtime aide and engineered a dramatic shake-up of his presidential campaign team as he sought to reverse a months-long downward spiral that has left him short of cash and struggling for support," the *Washington Post* reported.[11]

> Rick Davis, who took Weaver's place, was intent on calming members of the campaign staff and reassuring donors and fundraisers, the Post continued, adding that it was expected by McCain's staff that "veteran GOP strategist Charlie Black" would also play a larger role in campaign strategy.[12] But Black never showed up.
>
> Charlie Black had been a partner of Roger Stone and Paul Manafort in the early days but left them in the mid-1990s. Rick Davis then founded a new firm with Manafort, which Rick Gates joined in 2006. Rick Davis claimed to have left the firm when hired by McCain, though it was revealed that "when Davis joined the campaign in January 2007, he asked that his $20,000-a-month salary be paid directly to Davis Manafort," according to two *Newsweek* sources who asked not to be identified.
>
> *Newsweek* reviewed Federal campaign records, which brought to light that Davis Manafort received $90,000 from the McCain campaign through July 2007, the date Davis allegedly began to work as an unpaid volunteer. In fact, however, Davis's firm secretly created an entity called 3eDC with the same address as the Davis Manafort firm. An internet search gave only one hit for 3eDC – a voting lawsuit involving Sidney Powell and others.
>
> John McCain's campaign assisted in FUNDING the development of GEMS web monitoring via WEB Services with 3EDC and Dynology," we read from a Sidney Powell exhibit in a lawsuit filed against

her and others involved in Trump's campaign. She had submitted the affidavit with the name of the expert omitted in Case Number 2020CV34319, styled "Eric Coomer, Ph.D., Plaintiff, vs. Donald J. Trump for President, Inc. et al, Defendants" on December 2, 2020.[13]

The quoted statement was Item 121 in an affidavit we've since discovered was sworn to by Terpsehore P. "Tore" Maras, who thereafter ran for secretary of state in Ohio.[14]

She also filed a lawsuit in 2021 against Dominion in Nashville, Tennessee, for defamation, alleging in Paragraph 21 that "Dominion falsely stated that "wholly unreliable sources" put forward by [Sidney] Powell and [Lin] Wood in that case (whose declarations were posted on Powell's fundraising website) included Terpsichore [sic] Maras-Lindeman [sic], Russell Ramsland, William Briggs, and Josh Merritt a.k.a. 'Spyder.'" [15]

She had also been all over the country, including North Dakota and Kansas, where Dion Lefler reported that a woman named Tore Maras, "a QAnon podcaster who ran as an independent for Ohio secretary of state in 2022....The court ruled Maras' candidacy could go forward and she got 1% of the vote."[16]

The following week he said that when he'd mentioned the previous week that the Kansas legislative hearing on election security was giving 'a platform to QAnon supporters and other "Stop the Steal" fringie flakes' ... he didn't understand the overwhelming brilliance of Ms. Maras, who has at various times claimed to have been a Naval Intelligence officer, international intelligence contractor, a cryptolinguist, a medical researcher and a physician, among other things."[17]

The latter column is a must-read but can't be quoted in full here. The essential part, however, notes:

> Defendant, using various social media websites, created an entirely fake online persona," the judgment said. ... Maras or Lindeman, or whatever her name is this week, was outed on Christmas Eve 2020 by The *Washington Post* as one of the supposed secret expert witnesses cited by lawyer Sidney Powell – a onetime President Donald Trump adviser – who filed lawsuits in multiple states seeking to overturn the 2020 election. Powell was more recently seen having her mug shot taken in jail, one of Trump's co-defendants in a criminal racketeering case over efforts to overthrow the will of the voters in Georgia.[18]

But we still had one question for Maras Lindeman: Who told her how McCain paid Rick Davis?

That bit of knowledge alone leaves us wondering what her real credentials were. Unfortunately, our deadline loomed ages ago, and we'll have to trust readers to continue this research. Our republic is at stake. If we can't trust our ability to vote universally, safely and securely, what's the point of elections?

McCain's campaign manager, Rick Davis, was being paid through an entity that existed in 2007-2008, tasked with developing GEMS – Global Electronic Monitoring System, described in a book by Jim Marrs, published in 2010.[19]

GEMS, originally created by Premier Election Solutions, a subsidiary of Diebold, was already "developed," as Marrs revealed in his book:

> At the conclusion of the investigation in 2009, Secretary of State Debra Bowen decertified Diebold's Global Election Management System (GEMS) version 1.18.10 software program and three other electronic voting systems, meaning they cannot be used in California.
>
> In March 2009, Diebold/PES's problems became much larger when the firm admitted in a Sacramento hearing that audit logs produced by its tabulation software could miss significant events such as the deletion of votes. The company acknowledged that the problem existed with every version of its tabulation software, even those used in other states. Vote-counting GEMS software is used to tabulate votes cast on every Premier/Diebold touch-screen or optical-scan machine in more than fourteen hundred election districts in thirty-one states.
>
> "Today's hearing confirmed one of my worst fears," said Kim Alexander, founder and president of the nonprofit California Voter Foundation. Alexander noted, "The audit logs [a program that monitors additions and deletions to the operating program] have been the top selling point for vendors hawking paperless voting systems. They and the jurisdictions that have used paperless voting machines have repeatedly pointed to the audit logs as the primary security mechanism and 'fail-safe' for any glitch that might occur on machines. To discover that the fail-safe itself is unreliable eliminates one of the key selling points for electronic voting security."
>
> In 2007, the Maryland General Assembly voted for paper ballots counted by optical scanners to replace paperless touch-screen voting machines. But the plan fell apart in 2008 when a vote in the U.S. House of Representatives didn't approve an Election Assistance Commission program to provide the necessary states funds for the purchase of paper ballots as a backup to voting machines.

In other words, efforts to return to paper ballots have been blocked at the federal level. Could this be because the New World Order socialists (sometimes National Socialists, sometimes Marxist Socialists) have gained control over the federal apparatus? Wits have said that if God intended for us to vote, he would have given us candidates. It can likewise be said that if we were intended to have fair voting, we would have hard-copy paper ballots that could remain for years in case of the need for a recount.[20]

According to research by *PC Magazine*, "Roughly 25% of votes cast in the U.S. employ this system, and there has been a lot of controversy over its use. GEMS was found to be easily compromised if election officials were not extremely careful."[21]

This entity "received payments from the McCain campaign for Web services, collecting $971,860 through March 2008."[22]

McCain's spokesman, Brian Jones, told a reporter from *US News* in 2007 that Davis "did not disclose his interest in 3eDC to Senator McCain. 3eDC helped build the campaign's website and maintains its infrastructure," but Davis refused to describe the contract between the campaign and 3edc LLC," whose other owner was Paul Manafort, Steve Bannon's predecessor at the helm of Donald Trump's campaign.[23]

Brett Kavanaugh Likes Beer and Politics

When Brett Kavanaugh's name came up for the next Supreme Court seat in 2018, Wayne Madsen reminded us how political Brett was, having worked closely with Karl Rove in coordinating operations with "Rick Davis, who was John McCain's campaign manager in his failed 2000 presidential bid, and Davis's partner, Paul Manafort, who was campaign chairman for Donald Trump's 2016 campaign."[23]

Madsen said Manafort and Davis had worked together in 2004 for Viktor Yanukovych in Ukraine, getting paid through Davis Manafort International LLC, incorporated in Delaware and headquartered Alexandria, Virginia.

"In 2006, Davis Manafort International acquired as a client the Russian oligarch Oleg Deripaska, who is believed to have been a major cog in the illegalities surrounding the Trump election victory in 2016. Another Davis, Manafort client was Ukrainian oligarch Dmitry Firtash, who is currently living in Austria, but is the subject of a U.S. extradition request not, specifically, involving the Mueller investigation," Madsen wrote.[24]

Turning back to Kavanaugh, he reminded us he was "one of the infamous 'Brooks Brothers Brigade' members who descended upon Florida to demand a stop to the Florida Supreme Court-ordered hand recount of votes in the contested 2000 election."[25]

At that point he also brought up the fact that "Manafort and Davis also established 3EDC, LLC, a firm dedicated to leveraging social media on the Internet on behalf of their candidates. Manafort and Davis worked closely with Connell and Averbeck, as well as Ohio's corrupt GOP Secretary of State, Ken Blackwell, on the Bush 2004 campaign.... Another firm connected to Connell's and Averbeck's operations was Dynology Corporation of Vienna, Virginia. Dynology was founded in 1999 and has contracts with several U.S. defense and intelligence agencies."[26]

THE BEGINNING OF THE GREAT RECESSION

Rick Davis' firm, as the *New York Times* wrote, "specialized in covering over the bloody records of dictators like Mobutu Sese Seko of Zaire and Ferdinand Marcos of the Philippines with copious coats of high-gloss spin, presenting them as freedom-loving democrats."[27] It was for that specialization that Davis partner, Paul Manafort had been tapped to work for pro-Russian Ukrainian candidate Viktor Yanukovych" in 2006, while concealing the nature of that work, as they routed millions of dollars through foreign accounts to evade reporting requirements and the IRS."[28]

Madsen had previously posted at his website an article by Bob Fitrakis and Harvey Wasserman entitled "Convicted Trumputin consigliere Paul Manafort linked to Ohio's stolen 2004 election," discussing the role of Republican operatives Michael Connell (New Media Communications) and Jeff Averbeck (Airnet Group, the parent company of SmarTech), once referred to as two of the five "strategic partners" of 3EDC, LLC.[29]

As these events were occurring, Badolato's eagerness to make fast money made us think someone, perhaps linked to the Trump campaign, was tightening the screws on him to deliver more funds for Republicans. We know it was not Andy Badolato's top priority for IBC to create a real product because the company he acquired came with the patents, which he never bothered to renew. IBC was acquired to be used simply as a pump and dump operation – to make a fast buck, much of which he'd just hand over to Republican fund raisers. Was he working on behalf of Rick Davis, we wondered?

CHARLIE DON'T SURF ... OR EVEN EXIST

"Charlie Moore" wasn't his real name, of course. But when Jonathan Curshen was released on bond on September 10, 2008, that was the name he relayed to Andy Badolato and disillusioned investor Joey Barquin. Years later, after Joey contacted me, he insisted I find an FBI agent named Charlie Moore. It turned out to be something easier said than done, since an agent with that name did not exist. It was his undercover name.

David Baines explained in a November 2008 article how Curshen was drawn into what he termed an intricate "police spider web." Jamani, a fellow criminal, had introduced Curshen to the Vancouver undercover cop posing as a wannabe money launderer (UCV), who in turn introduced him to "Charlie Moore," the undercover New York FBI agent (NYUC) posing as a "broker."[30]

They met, cloak and dagger style, on an FBI boat on a foggy night in New York Harbor in October 2007, almost a year before the arrest occurred. For Jonathan Curshen and Andy Badolato, business went on as usual in Sarasota. In 2008 Curshen went back to New York, where the Feds finally busted him as the sting operation was winding down. The arrest occurred on September 10, 2008, six days after a federal criminal complaint was filed under seal in the Southern District (SDNY).

TIMING IS EVERYTHING

As we said, all during September 2008 McCain was campaigning on his plan to switch from Iowa corn to Brazilian sugar cane to make ethanol, while Andy Badolato was CEO of a public corporation telling potential investors IBC was ready to profit from that switch in national priorities.

Precisely one day after Jonathan Curshen pled guilty to conspiracy to commit securities fraud and commercial bribery of an undercover FBI agent to buy the stock of Industrial Biotechnology Corporation, IBC instantly disappeared. It became a ghost, absorbed into The Renewable Corporation (TRC), which rose from IBC's ashes under a new name on October 24, 2008.

The boys in Sarasota weren't wasting any time. When it was next reported to the SEC, it was buried within the filing of UTEK's December 31, 2008, 10-K, all of which is totally above my pay grade to decipher.[31]

Maybe Badolato thought the name change would divert attention. Maybe he still owed money to his seller and simply gave it back. At any rate, it had worked like a charm. Suspicion never fell on him or McCain.

There were still some immediate consequences of Curshen's arrest. For one, the "Government of Costa Rica withdrew the credentials of Jonathan Curshen as honorary consul of San Cristobal and Nevis, an Antillean federation. Curshen, a renowned stock exchange promoter with offices at the Columbus Center in San Jose, Costa Rica, was arrested by agents of the Federal Bureau of Investigation (FBI) in September," a Costa Rican newspaper reported on October 21, 2008.[32]

The same paper had previously reported Curshen's arrest in September. Costa Rican authorities were promptly notified by the SEC that Curshen had been charged with bribery, and that notice was the only information necessary for Costa Rica's President Escar Arias and Foreign Minister Bruno Stagno to "revoke the exequatátur (credential) given to Jonathan Randall Curshen, honorary consul of San Cristobal y Nieves in Costa Rica," *La Nacion* reported.[33]

WHY IT'S CALLED "TRANSNATIONAL ORGANIZED CRIME"

Badolato started his career as a stockbroker in 1996, setting up I.M.O.A., Inc., in Florida as an offshoot of Investment Managementof America, Inc. of Delaware. His first office was rented inside the Sarasota Square shopping mall at 8201 S. Tamiami Trail in southwest Sarasota but within a year or so he'd moved to an out-of-the-way building west of the mall.

By 1997 Badolato moved to 7820 S. Holiday Drive, the same address he used to incorporate Biznet Solutions, Inc. and AB Banyan Holdings LLC a year later. Business must have been slow.

Then in 2003 he hooked up with Steve Bannon – their names first appearing together on a document filed by Michael W. Hawkins of Melbourne, Florida, which registered a Delaware corporation called Donna Messenger Corporation to do business in Florida. There would also be a related DM-Sargon LLC, which later changed to Sargon Holdings II, LLC. This connection to Bannon and the other men named on the document made Andy optimistic enough to move up to the high-rent district in downtown Sarasota. From his new 4th floor office at 2033 Main Street, he could look out the window to view the iconic county courthouse built by Dwight James Baum.

Badolato became chairman and CEO of Industrial Biotechnology Corporation (IBC) in 2004. It was a spinoff of a company called UTEK, operated by Dr. Clifford M. Gross, a seemingly legitimate educator and author of *Technology Transfer for Entrepreneurs*.[34]

As the buyer of UTEK's company, Badolato's name saw print in – of all places – the tony *Oxford Mail,* which quoted him saying: "We now have a core of intellectual property and patents that can be applied to successfully develop and commercialize biologically derived compounds," and, as the *Mail* reported, they would also "sell chemicals for the flavors and fragrances industries, as well as bio-fuels, pharmaceuticals, agricultural and bio-pesticides."[35]

Many companies Badolato was linked with appear to have been spun off from UTEK. Some of them even seemed to rise from the dead, resurrected *again and again,* like corporate zombies, given a new name, a new corporate mission, and shoved back out into the fray. That was the value of the shells. Trading rights lived on. *The grifting could continue.*

CORPORATE GRAVEYARD OF SHELLS

Jonathan Curshen's brother-in-law, Michael G. Brown also got involved, as their Sarasota attorney. Brown got Advanced Bioscience, Inc. (ABI) – originally filed in Florida by UTEK's general counsel on May 31, 2005 – and had it reinstated in October 2006 under new ownership. Since Andy still hadn't learned by then to file annual reports, his charters kept being revoked, with large fines having to be paid to get them reinstated.[36]

ABI spun off a new trading subsidiary – Industrial Biotechnology Corporation (IBC), using a shell Badolato's team had acquired in order to use its ability to trade on a variety of stock exchanges. It didn't have anything as retro as a product or innovation.[37]

Strewn behind this shell, IBC's past reveals the components of a graveyard *filled with dead bodies built out of old body parts,* easily traced back through SEC filings.

Newtrack Mining – the remaining shell of a company which already had a sordid history of pump and dump – was IBC's last prior existence, created in 2004 for resale to a Las Vegas buyer who wanted to sell stock over the counter in the unregulated "pink sheets."

Before that, it was named Track II Industries, Inc. and registered in the state of Washington, which permanently revoked its charter in July 1999 because of its use in financial fraud.

But here's the beauty of shells: the trading rights live on. A savvy buyer can pick it up, refile it somewhere else and give it a new name and stock ticker.

"SCAM CAPITAL OF THE WORLD"

Before being moved to the U.S., Track II had first opened its eyes, so to speak, on February 26, 1992 in Vancouver, B.C. as Bare Track Industries, Inc.[38] Of all its later incarnations, this is the strangest. It gives us a glimpse back to the early days of the Russian mob's attempt to take over North American stock exchanges.

Vancouver was "a stronghold for the last of the Wild West stock exchanges, where penny stocks glitter brighter than Miss Kitty's rhinestones and flimflam artists have long found a home," wrote Harriet King in 1977.[39]

By the early Nineties, the Vancouver Stock Exchange (VSE) was known as the "scam capital of the world," primarily because it was cheap to list a stock on the exchange. It was flooded with what are called "junior" companies just starting out with stock valued in the pennies – thus, *"penny stock."*[40]

Assume that back then you owned 100,000 shares of a stock called Mad Cow Dung, worth $0.0001 per share. Those shares are worth all of $10 when acquired. You move to Florida, say, and find a legitimate company with a patent for weight loss and buy it through a reverse merger with Mad Cow Dung, but you then change the name to Shrinking Cow, Inc. (NYSE: SHIT).

You're in business. You hire a telemarketer to begin talking about the miracles that can be expected once the patent completes its trials and goes on the market. The stock price slowly climbs higher and higher, reaching $2.57 a share. You sell, making $257,000. Less the initial $10 investment, of course. Warning: The foregoing anecdote may contain forward-looking statements, and should not be taken as reality...

Vancouver had a very serious problem with money laundering in the late 1980s. Criminals discovered the lax restrictions for entry into the Vancouver Stock Exchange made it easy to invest dirty cash from drugs, for example by purchasing stocks, "in order to make the funds seem legitimate. The more layers of legitimate purchases in a laundering scheme, the more difficult it is for authorities to trace the original criminal source."[41]

Nik Markovina was an immigrant to Canada from Croatia, who had recently taken up with a long-time Vancouver fraudster, Beverlee Claydon Kamerling. She left Canada for Bellevue, Washington because she had been banned from Canadian stock markets in 1989.

The duo were stock promoters working stocks called United Fire Technology, and International Indigo Industries – under the guise of a Canadian investment company called Bare Track Investments, Inc. – which promised returns up to 25% on the stocks.

When the SEC began investigating Nik and Beverlee's ongoing scams, Nik got nervous, and began providing ever more lucrative incentives to potential customers. That's a story in itself we won't go into here.

What made him nervous? He was also tangled up in one of the many scandals afflicting a Vancouver attorney named Martin Chambers, who had friends in both the Hell's Angels and the Russian Mob.

After a conviction for laundering millions of dollars for a Colombian drug cartel, Chambers was dubbed by the Vancouver press as "B.C.'s Lex Luthor," Batman's nemesis. Chambers ended up spending thirteen years in a U.S. federal prison in Arkansas.

The western Balkans, where Nik came from, had a well-established history of drug trafficking in Europe since at least the '80s. Its location on the route from Afghanistan – where poppies were grown, before being eradicated by the Taliban – to Iran, then passing through Turkey into the Balkans, was the shortest and most direct land route to European consumer markets.[42] More direct cocaine trafficking routes from South and Central America have departed from the land routes in collaboration with South American cartels.[43]

Montenegro and its neighboring state Croatia both became new nations when Yugoslavia, one of the Soviet Republics, was dissolved along with the USSR in 1991. Nik Markovina provides evidence of a drug cartel that existed in Montenegro and Croatia. Shortly after the Soviet Union broke apart a segment of the Balkan cartel relocated to Vancouver – the dirtiest stock exchange in North America – as the ideal place to launder criminal profits.

Was it this same Montenegro cartel which smuggled cocaine into Philadelphia aboard a container ship? We'll examine that question soon.

No matter how drugs are moved – by land, sea or air – criminals will find a way to move them. As legitimate businessmen try their own hands at either transport or distribution of illegal drugs, they never seem to escape the spider web which traps them.

They may try to keep their white collars clean by engaging only in the money laundering end of the game, but they soon find themselves encased in a game of corruption that expands into every corner of their lives. When enough people have dirtied their hands, and their white collars, by handling the drugs, the distinct line between good and evil turns gray and eventually simply disappears altogether.

Corruption oozes into every crevice of our society.

Endnotes

1   Liz Halloran, "McCain Suspends Campaign, Shocks Republicans," US News & World Report, September 24, 2008. https://www.usnews.com/news/campaign-2008/articles/2008/09/24/mccain-suspends-campaign-shocks-republicans

2   Elisabeth Bumiller and Michael Cooper, "Obama Rebuffs McCain on Debate Delay," *New York Times*, Sept. 24, 2008. https://www.nytimes.com/2008/09/25/us/politics/25mccain.html

3   Press release, Marketwire September 9, 2008. https://www.globenewswire.com/news-release/2008/09/09/1353824/0/en/Controversy-Benefits-of-Brazilian-Sugarcane-Based-Ethanol-Chemicals-and-Fuels.html

4   "La Nacion" Costa Rica, September 24, 2008. https://www.nacion.com/ sucesos/pais-retira-credencial-a-consul-de-san-cristobal-y-nieves/5UYIC2NP3VCFZBPCNWO5VTS5WA/story/

5   David Baines,"Stock promoters, broker busted in cross-border sting," *Investment Executive*, December 1, 2008. https://www.investmentexecutive.com/newspaper_/news-newspaper/news-47221/

6   Ibid.

7   Michael Pollick, "Business in Sarasota says it was taken in by a promised breakthrough," *Sarasota Herald Tribune*, June 8, 2007. https://www.heraldtribune.com/story/news/2007/06/08/business-in-sarasota-says-it-was-taken-in-by-a-promised-breakthrough/28552622007/

8   Ibid.

9   Press Release, "Industrial Biotechnology Corporation Appoints National Taiwan University Professor, Dr. Kung-Ta Lee, To Scientific Advisory Board," *Biospace*, May 25, 2006. https://www.biospace.com/article/releases/industrial-biotechnology-corporation-appoints-b-national-taiwan-university-b-professor-b-dr-kung-ta-lee-b-to-scientific-advisory-board-/

10   https://www.siliconinvestor.com/readmsg.aspx?msgid=23855230&srchtxt=curshen

11   Dan Balz and Anne E. Kornblut, "Top Aides Leave McCain Camp," *Washington Post*, July 11, 2007. https://www.washingtonpost.com/wp-dyn/content/article/2007/07/10/AR2007071000759.html

12   Ibid.

13   Other defendants are Sidney Powell; Sidney Powell, P.C.; Rudolph Giuliani; Joseph Oltmann; FEC United; Shuffling Madness Media, Inc. dba Conservative Daily; James Hoft; TGP Communications LLC dba The Gateway Pundit; Michelle Malkin; Eric Metaxas; Chanel Rion; Herring Networks, Inc. dba One America News Network; and Newsmax Media, Inc.

14   "Podcaster ruled ineligible in race for Ohio elections chief," *The Lima News*, 01 Sep 2022, Page 2.

15   Terpsehore Maras, Plaintiff, v. US DOMINION, INC. et al, Defendants. https://storage.courtlistener.com/recap/gov.uscourts.tnmd.87372/gov.uscourts.tnmd.87372.1.0.pdf

16   Dion Lefler, "KS election committee spends thousands to hear QAnon wackos, billionaires' wish list," *The Wichita Eagle*, September 15, 2023. hcolumns-blogs/dion-lefler/article279223379.html

17   Dion Lefler, "Election security 'expert' scammed fire victims, Christians; fans still bought her a Tesla," *The Wichita Eagle,* September 20, 2023. https://www.kansas.com/opinion/opn-columns-blogs/dion-lefler/article279474549.html

18   Liz Dye, "Kraken Witness Files Defamation Suit Against Dominion For ... Oh, Who The Hell Even Knows?" *Above the Law*, August 18, 2021. Case 3:21-cv-00636. https://abovethelaw.com/2021/08/kraken-witness-files-defamation-suit-against-dominion-for-oh-who-the-hell-even-knows/

19   Jim   Marrs,   *Trillion   Dollar   Conspiracy*.   https://files.secure.website/wscfus/10348600/28684043/trillion-dollar-conspiracy-the-how-the-new-world-order-man-made-diseases-zombie-banks-are-destroying-america.pdf

20   Ibid.

21   Copyright © 19812024. https://www.pcmag.com/encyclopedia/term/gems

22   Hilzoy, "Rick Davis, Yet Again" *Washington Monthly*, quoted and attributed to Newsweek.

https://washingtonmonthly.com/2008/09/28/rick-davis-yet-again/

23   Jim Geraghty "Who's left on Team McCain?" *National Review*, July 10, 2007. https://www.nationalreview.com/the-campaign-spot/whos-left-team-mccain-five-departures-today-updated-jim-geraghty/

24   Wayne Madsen, "Bush backed Kavanaugh to keep election thefts of 2000 and 2004 a secret," *Intrepid Reporter*, October 15, 2018. http://www.intrepidreport.com/archives/25312

25   Ibid.

26   Ibid.

27   Ibid.

28   Jim Rutenberg, "The Untold Story of 'Russiagate' and the Road to War in Ukraine," *New York Times*, Nov. 2, 2022. https://www.nytimes.com/2022/11/02/magazine/russiagate-paul- manafort-ukraine-war.html

29   Reid Pillifant of *Slate*, Oct 30, 2017. https://slate.com/news-and-politics/2017/10/rickgates-relationship-to-manafort-and-trump-explained.html

30   Bob Fitrakis and Harvey Wasserman, "Convicted Trumputin Consigliere Paul Manafort Linked to Ohio's Stolen 2004 Election," *Free Press*, September 6, 2018. https://freepress.org/article/convicted-trumputin-consigliere-paul-manafort-linked-ohios-stolen-2004-election

31   David Baines, "Geologist suspended for six months," *Vancouver Sun*, 05 Nov 2008, Page 33. In a previous article in which he reported the arrest, Baines called the action "extensive cross-border stock bribery sting operation." David Baines, "Promoters, broker implicated in alleged bribery scheme," The Vancouver Sun, 22 Oct 2008, Page 1. https://www.investmentexecutive.com/newspaper_/news-newspaper/news-47221/hm#toc21853_11

32   Otto Vargas M, "Country credential from consul of St Kitts and Nevis," *La Nacion*, October 21, 2008. https://www-nacion-com.translate.goog/sucesos/pais-retira-credencial-a-consul-de-san-cristobal-y-nieves/5UYIC2NP3VCFZBPCNWO5VTS5WA/story/?_x_tr_sl=es&_x_tr_tl=en&_x_tr_hl=en&_x_tr_pto=sc

33   Ibid.

34   https://www.twst.com/bio/clifford-m-gross/

35   https://www.oxfordmail.co.uk/business/news/882243.sticky-plastic-receives-500-000-boost/

36   Sam I. Reiber: https://www.newspapers.com/article/the-tampa-tribune-sam-i-reiber/125845242/ See also http://search.sunbiz.org/Inquiry/CorporationSearch/ConvertTiffToPDF?storagePath=COR%5C2006%5C1017%5C36080120.tif&documentNumber=P05000078105.   A Utek SEC filing shows the purchase price of Industrial Biotechnology Corporation. https://www.sec.gov/Archives/edgar/data/1098482/000119312509049301/d10k.htm

37   The news was published in the *Tampa Bay Business Journal* on November 11, 2005. https://www.bizjournals.com/tampabay/stories/2005/11/14/daily32.html

38   I originally found the history online with the SEC, but the link has since been changed. See https://www.madcowprod.com/2021/01/17/sarasota-fbi-protected-decade-long-maga-mega-fraud//

39   Harriet King, "Vancouver's Penny Stocks: You Takes Your Chances," *New York Times*, November 13, 1977. https://www.nytimes.com/1977/11/13/archives/vancouvers-penny-stocks-you-takes-your-chances.html

40   Ibid.

41   Matteo Miceli, "The Vancouver Stock Exchange: A Legacy of Fraud and Money Laundering Part I, Vancouver Police Museum, Jan 18, 2020. https://www.vancouverpolicemuseum.ca/post/the-vancouver-stock-exchange-a-legacy-of-fraud-and-money-laundering-part-i

42   "Opioid trafficking routes from Asia to Europe," European Monitoring Centre for Drugs and Drug Addiction, Updated April 6, 2015. https://www.emcdda.europa.eu/system/files/publications/2747/att_239691_EN_Opioid%20trafficking%20routes_POD2015.pdf

43   "The illicit trade of cocaine from Latin America to Europe from oligopolies to free-for-all?" UNODC, undated. https://www.unodc.org/documents/data-and-analysis/cocaine/Cocaine_ Insights_2021.pdf

44.

CHAPTER TWENTY-THREE

ADNAN THE BAGMAN

The 9/11 terror plot intersected with the activities of a drug trafficking network of international scope, in ways that form a "crystal clear" picture of what was going on.

                            –Sibel Edmonds.

G angsters and racketeers ran loose through Sarasota's well-swept streets for the first two decades of the 21st century. None of them, unfortunately, having the élan or the *je ne sais quoi* of Saudi CIA fixer Adnan Khashoggi. It therefore came as quite a shock to me when I began picking up traces – almost invisible fingerprints – of his presence all around what had been my turf during those twenty years.

Was a be-robed Saudi prince, directing alt-right riffraff in SW Florida, just one more thing I'd missed? Well, why not? The men in Sarasota were, after all, engaged in transnational organized crime. Adnan Khashoggi, middleman between Saudi princes and kings and the American military-industrial complex, had practically invented transnational organized crime in the mid-1960s.

An example of an invisible fingerprint popped up in the spring of 2004 – almost three years after 9/11. I took notice of it without identifying Khashoggi's involvement:

> A federal complaint filed April 5 [2004] in Ft. Myers, FL. accusing flight school owners Wally Hilliard and Rudi Dekkers of flying numerous "unauthorized and unsupervised flights" during April and May of 1999 makes no mention of the clients on the illegal flights, who the *MadCowMorningNews* has learned were Saudi nationals.
>
> Federal officials declined to discuss the case, other than to say it was a civil matter unrelated to 9/11.[1]

But was it, in fact, "unrelated"?

Mr. Plausible Deniability

That was a huge clue connecting Khashoggi to both Wally Hilliard and Rudi Dekkers – two of the main subjects in my previous book, *Welcome To Terrorland* – that I failed to follow up on at the time. Years later I realized Khashoggi had all along been deeply implicated in those 1999 flights, as well as some of the other big capers I was investigating. He was the throughline.

"They were flying for the Saudis," said an aviation executive I spoke to, who was familiar with the operation. "You can go to jail for the kind of things they're charged with. They were ferrying Saudi princes all over the U.S."

"What they were doing was blatantly illegal. But all they got was a slap on the wrist. The Government had little or no idea where those Saudi charters flew, or who was on board. Whoever they were flying around didn't want anyone to know."

So after hiding the ferrying activities for five years after the flights began in April 1999, they just decided now to do a little house-keeping? Surprise! The cow is out of the barn. Or is it the horse? Whatever.

Let's be crystal clear here. In 1999 – at least two years before 9/11 – the flight school where two or more 9/11 terrorist pilots took flying lessons – had been engaged in illegally flying charters containing unnamed Saudis – gallivanting all over the Caribbean Basin, with no adult supervision whatsoever. And it took almost three whole years after those trainee Saudi pilots crashed into buildings on September 11 for the FAA to decide, "Hey, maybe we should cite these guys for a parking ticket or something."

It was way too late for the FAA to start curbing suspicious aviation activity in Florida by Wally Hilliard or Rudi Dekkers. More than 3,000 people were already dead.

I asked one of my sources, a pilot at the Naples Airport, "Why start now?"

"Because they're back in business," hissed the source. "This could become a major embarrassment."

The news should have kicked up some dust. It didn't.

As Lily Tomlin famously said, "No matter how cynical I get, I just can't keep up."

"A Loose Affiliation of Millionaires and Billionaires"

The *Miami Herald* on June 10, 1985, carried a story in its "international trade" section entitled "Chinese bargain tough on five used planes."[2] Jetborne had a starring role in the feature, though no details about its owners were given. But there was a large photo of two smiling Chinese engineers looking at the underbelly of a Boeing 707 aircraft, one of five they'd just agreed to buy for the People's Republic of China.

The seller was Batchelor Enterprises, whose marketing agent, Boyd D. Mesecher, helped the reporter with the story. Mesecher, we found, was an old military hand who'd worked for Air Asia Co. – a proprietary set up by Claire Chennault for the CIA. He was also known as "B.D. Mesecher, Director of Technical Services for Air America, Inc."[3]

He later ended up in Miami, associated with George E. Batchelor in eighteen companies in Florida. He had even brought a Chinese wife, the former Carol Wei, back to the States.

The Chinese government had been introduced to Batchelor by Jet-borne, Inc., the broker of the deal, through a subsidiary, Tradewinds International, located on the west side of the Miami airport. Jetborne vice president Gary Girard boasted 100 employees available to negotiate all the details with sellers of products desired by its customers. We'll see Girard again in the next chapter.

Jetborne even had numerous subsidiaries throughout the world, we discovered, including Garrick Overseas International, set up by Ramy El-Batrawi in Panama on April 8, 1985 – according to an "unrecoverable document" leaked from Mossack Fonseca in the Panama Papers.[4]

The 1985 *Miami Herald* article was published at the exact time the Reagan White House's National Security guys were getting ready to fly missiles (with financing á la Adnan) to Iran by way of Israel, in exchange for hostages held by Hezbollah in Lebanon.

Sending TOW missiles to Iran itself was on the borderline of illegal for Oliver North, but then when he added a side venture – diverting part of the funds raised from weapons sales to send to the anti-Sandinista Contras – there should have been no question a new federal law called the "Boland Amendment" had been violated.

Most of the "disappeared" several hundred million was never recovered or accounted for. Republicans only groused about the money spent investigating.

El-Batrawi was no mere flash in the pan. Fifteen years later he attends as many D-list celebrity parties as he can, with pals like disgraced NBA Clippers' owner Donald Sterling, corporate raider Carl Icahn, and Ivanka Trump. In his recent autobiography, he refers to these parties as "my appearance on the charity circuit,"[5] but what he does not reveal is how that so-called "charity" network is only part of the scam he practices.

El Batrawi's most recent business venture was a company called "Yayyo," what the kids call cocaine these days. Just a coincidence, I'm sure.

WHAT TRUMP AND KHASHOGGI SHARED

Donald Trump and Adnan the Bagman had a surprising amount in common. An easy relationship with the mainstream media, for example. Both regularly made news without even trying. So their schemes never lacked publicity. It was free advertising.

Nor did Adnan and Donald's similarities end there. Both were involved in money laundering – at the same time – with the same financial institution – Germany's Deutsche Bank. No one in the mainstream media appeared to notice, though it would become increasingly obvious that they were part of the same operation.

And there was one other "tell." When "AK" was on the lam avoiding an Interpol arrest warrant, a reliable source informed me, Trump hid him out in one of the cottages at Mar a Lago.

According to the 2006 federal complaint, "Mr. Khashoggi's whereabouts are unknown, and Mr. El-Batrawi has no listed telephone number in Los Angeles," and the *New York Times* reported, "Lawyers for Mr. El-Batrawi and Mr. Khashoggi could not be immediately located for comment."[6]

When even your lawyers go on the lam, with seeming impunity, the conclusion is unavoidable that something fishy was going on.

Despite his loud protestations to the contrary, Donald Trump had not been *victimized* by the deep state.

Donald Trump *was* the deep state.

COOKIES & MILK, KHASHOGGI & TRUMP

The first time I saw Donald Trump's name linked with Adnan Khashoggi's was in a wickedly funny article from the early 90's in *Spy Magazine* called "Who is America's cheapest zillionaire?"[7]

The satirical magazine went looking for the cheapest mega-rich person in New York. They created a phony business, then sent "refund checks" to 58 rich New Yorkers … for $1.11.

Twenty-six frugal people, dubbed "The Bargain-Basement 26," cashed their $1.11 checks, including Cher, Harry Helmsley, Michael Douglas, Shirley MacLaine, Kurt Vonnegut, Donald Trump and Adnan Khashoggi. Then they sent a second check to those who'd cashed the $1.11 check, only for half as much. Donald Trump, Adnan Khashoggi, and eleven other extraordinarily cheap people – who shall remain nameless – each cashed a check for 64 cents.

They were "The Chintzy 13." Each now received a final check… for just 13 cents. Surely the prank was over. Who would go to thew trouble to cash a check for 13 cents?

Two men: Donald Trump and Adnan Khashoggi.

Back to The Future of Iran Contra

This was shortly after the Iran Contra scandal reached its not-with-a-bang-but-a-whimper conclusion.

Clues remained, however. One of the covert operatives who had been involved, retired Navy Lt. Commander Al Martin, later told me, "Iran Contra went far beyond a simple operation to finance the 50,000-man Contra army." He said, "It created an intricate web of state-sponsored crime."[8]

The operation spearheaded by Ollie North was very successful – until they got caught. Then, as now, however, they rationalized their actions. Nobody took responsibility for making an end run around the law.

According to Republican philosophy, they were engaged in enforcing the executive's foreign policy. Later, they added the section of the Constitution which sets out the President's powers, leading Trump to claim he had the Article II. Republicans claim only the President can make policy, so duly enacted and signed legislation can "technically" be avoided.

The Boland Amendment, they said, was a nothing burger.

The "intricate web of state-sponsored crime," which Al Martin spoke of, was familiar to attorneys working for intelligence agencies at the time. William J. Casey, Stanley Sporkin, William P. Barr, and numerous others had for years seen how easy it was to hide state-sponsored crime behind claims of "executive privilege" and "national security."[9]

There were even legal models for them to use – like an attorney uses form books – to set up proprietary corporations which could be "plausibly denied." Secret schemes to avoid following the law, as we showed previously in connection with Claire Chennault and William Pawley's attorneys who did the legal work for the Flying Tigers and Civil Air Transport and other proprietaries financed by illicit activities.

The use of crime sponsored by the state did not end when Iran-Contra perpetrators were convicted. If anything, it only got worse. Most of those convicted in Iran Contra, called patriots and heroes, got pardons on Christmas Eve 1992 from their former boss, the vice-president, who ultimately became the 41st President, George H. W. Bush.[10]

EVERY BAGMAN NEEDS MINIONS

In all this, "AK" was ably assisted by his chief lieutenant and loyal henchman Ramy El-Batrawi, who was by his side from the beginning, or at
least since around 1985.

Soon, Khashoggi – working with El-Batrawi – was taking down, in a
good year, billions of dollars. Billions with a 'B'.

They helped engineer the SkyWay financial fraud deal with huge defense contractor Titan. In a dramatic press release, Titan trumpeted the
news that it was spending a half-billion dollars – that's 500 million dollars
– for SkyWay software which didn't exist. SkyWay's "invention" was too
ephemeral to even be considered vapor ware.

The Sarasota-based hyena pack came into being in the days after Adnan Khashoggi was prosecuted and acquitted of the massive fraud known
as the MJK Clearing/Stockwalk Scandal which caused more than a $100
million loss to brokerages. "AK" was the group's linchpin. Personnel included Sarasota-based Jonathan Curshen, who was typical of the group's
transnational ambitions.

A dual-UK-US citizen, Curshen created a base in Vancouver, which
boasted a Wild West-style stock market. He later moved to Costa Rica,
with a diplomatic passport from Caribbean islands St. Kitts-Nevis. His
ambition spanned the globe, however. Example: Curshen was laundering
money through South Asia's Seychelle Islands, for infamous mercenary
Erik Prince, according to the Seychelle's financial commission and documents discovered by ICIJ.[11]

The well-traveled Curshen exemplified the truly global trend towards,
well, towards globalization. He was a new breed of Global Gangster, at
home everywhere from Tel Aviv in the Middle East to the Seychelle Islands in the Indian Ocean, to St Kitts and Nevis in the Caribbean.

Khashoggi himself had been one of the masterminds of financial crime
allowed to run their scams and attend each other's parties while "winter-
ing" in Palm Beach – as long as they also did the bidding of the CIA, which
issued them a hall pass marked "national security." From Palm Beach they
could freely move on to the South of France or Marbella, Spain, where
Khashoggi had his biggest mansion.

As transnational organized crime was becoming the economic story of the 21st century, Adnan Khashoggi smoothly transitioned. He
began using thinly traded public companies which were basically unknown, then ran their stock up in classic pump-and-dump schemes,

snookering unsophisticated investors. Khashoggi was a prodigiously gifted financial fraudster who escalated his game from the simple to truly ingenious swindles.

Skyway's sole reason for existence, as near as anyone could tell, was to offer mini-cap stock enthusiasts shares in a company which owned two identical McDonnell Douglas DC-9's, used to smuggle drugs. One of those planes, N900SA, was busted in Mexico in April 2006.

GenesisIntermedia Scheme

The list of professional financial criminals he assembled indicates why Khashoggi was so successful. Adnan's Gangster Planet All Stars included Kenneth D'Angelo, a New Jersey investment manager, who colluded with El-Batrawi and Khashoggi in the scheme.[12]

Paul Waldie in the *Toronto Globe and Mail* described it perfectly:

> Wayne Breedon must have been intrigued when he got a call from his old colleague Kenneth D'Angelo in the summer of 1999.
>
> Mr. Breedon was managing the stock loan department at the Deutsche Bank Securities Ltd. office in Toronto at the time and Mr. D'Angelo ran a New Jersey investment company called RBF International Inc. The two knew each other well and had worked together before.
>
> Mr. D'Angelo needed Mr. Breedon's help. He had just been hired by Ramy el-Batrawi, chief executive officer and majority shareholder of GenesisIntermedia Inc., a California-based company that specialized in infomercials for gizmos such as the Ab Twister and audiotapes based on the book *Men are from Mars, Women are from Venus*. Genesis had just gone public on the Nasdaq Stock Market and Mr. D'Angelo had been retained to carry out a novel plan.
>
> Over the next two years, according to allegations filed recently in court by the U.S. Securities and Exchange Commission, the three men embarked on a sophisticated stock scam that netted more than $130 million (U.S.) and crippled several brokerage firms. According to the SEC, the financial devastation was so severe that the Securities Investor Protection Corp., a U.S. federal agency that insures brokerage accounts, "had to conduct the largest bailout in its history."
>
> The SEC alleges the scam also involved a CNBC television commentator and Saudi financier Adnan Khashoggi, best known for his role in the 1980s Iran-contra arms sales.[13]

BOARD MEETINGS AT THE SPEARMINT RHINO?

Richard J. Evangelista was the former senior vice president at Native Nations, the company owned by Valerie Red-Horse, and was fired in September 2001 for falsifying Native Nations' accounts in connection with certain securities loan transactions. He was also president of Local 18 of the International Brotherhood of Teamsters, the same union controlled by mafia associates decades ago. Does the name Jimmy Hoffa ring a bell?

Las Vegas Strip club entrepreneur Bradford Keiller, who owned "Spearmint Rhino" strip clubs in London, Moscow, Las Vegas and Los Angeles, even wormed his way into the group. His name is listed in the same lawsuits as Evangelista's.[15] There are as many descripttions of what the perpetrators did as there are prosecutions against them.

For example: "Defendant Bradford Keiller is a resident of Texas and Nevada A lawyer and former strip club owner, the Complaints assert that he engaged in active day trading in order to artificially maintain the price of GENI stock Between February and September 2001, Keiller bought and sold more than $22 million worth of GENI stock and sent millions of dollars to Ultimate Holdings [Khashoggi's offshore corporation]." [14]

Is business news too boring for your taste? Maybe Brad's other sideline is more appealing. A New York writer for London's Mirror Group wrote in 2002 about Keiller's Las Vegas strip club:

> Brad Keiller, a partner at Spearmint Rhino, an upscale strip joint that caters to conventioneers, says: 'My top girls might make $1,000 or even $2,000 a night in tips. I'm sure casinos are losing some of the discretionary spending,' but Keiller said he's not worried about the new competition from the topless casino shows. He added: "It's the difference between watching the Playboy channel and having the Playboy girl come over and rub you down."[15]

EQUAL OPPORTUNITY SCAM

Then there's America's first brokerage owned by Native Americans – naturally called Native Nations Securities. It was left holding the bag on the $300 million dollar clearance scandal.

Native Nations was the brainchild of an attractive Hollywood actress named Valerie Red-Horse. The first Native American to control a securities firm, Ms. Red-Horse had learned financial fraud at the feet of the master. As a theater student at my own alma mater, UCLA, Valerie "went looking for part-time work and was referred through the school's placement office to the Beverly Hills office of Drexel Burnham Lambert, where she landed a job as an assistant to junk-bond king Michael Milken."[16]

She combined her financial career with acting. One movie was called "Naturally Native," followed by guest-starring on *Babylon 5*, then in ABC's made-for-television movie called "The Secret of Lizard Woman."

You missed those? Well, Valerie was best known for serving as the model for Mattel's "Pocahontas" doll, but I'd bet her name wasn't on the packaging.

Native Nations' rapid descent came after the shares of Khashoggi's company, GenesisIntermedia, plunged 65 percent in the seven trading days following the 9/11 terrorist attack.

Last, but certainly not least, is a Brooklyn attorney who left his family's law firm and moved to Miami. Michael D. Farkas, created the shell company that Sky Way Aircraft of St. Petersburg, Florida used to go public through what was then called a "reverse merger." Maybe the boys thought you wouldn't notice that it was the same maneuver they now call a SPAC – special purpose acquisition company.

Merge a dog company (Sky Way Aircraft) into a pre-fab shell that can trade publicly. Voila! You have a new corporation (Skyway Communications Holding Corp.) that can now make money in two ways: first, through financial fraud since the shell it merged into had ability to be traded on stock exchanges, and second, by chartering its planes to drug traffickers.

Farkas was American sales agent for anti-missile technology of Israel Aircraft Industries, and even the Director of CCS, a spy technology store in Miami. He also founded a company called Blink, which makes charging stations for electric vehicles. So he seemed legit, notwithstanding a plethora of intel connections with Israel.

The problem with prolific scam artists is that there was a finite number of them and – for lack of enough bodies to fill all the slots – they ended up serving in interlocking directorships with other scam artists, thus exposing their hidden associations.

Members of Adnan's crime ring shared other characteristics. Bankruptcy, for example, haunted the companies they controlled like the Grim Reaper haunts hobos.

ADNAN'S BIG "SWINDLE ROMP"

New York Post business writer Christopher Byron, my favorite business writer, because he was never boring, described what Adnan the Bagman had been doing while at the same time coining the phrase "swindle-romp."

With whatever grace we can muster, we must face the humiliating fact that we live today in a country where "swindle-romp" is a common thing.

Khashoggi orchestrated in 1999 a price-rigging scheme that was successful in pumping up worthless Genesis shares by 1,400 percent in just two years using accounts in Bermuda. We have to wonder whose drug money he was laundering. It could have been for almost anyone, since he knew all the prime ministers, presidents, princes and kings. He was useful. So he was protected.

But only until he was no longer useful.

Endnotes

1   Daniel Hopsicker, "Terror Flight School Owner's Lear Flew Saudis on Unsupervised Flights," May 4, 2004. https://www.madcowprod.com/2004/05/04/terror-flight-school-owners-lear-flew-saudis-on-unsupervised-flights/

2   Andres Oppenheimer, "Chinese bargain tough on 5 used planes," *Miami Herald*, June 10, 1985, Page 67. https://offshoreleaks.icij.org/nodes/10166923

3   Air America: Upholding the Airmen's Bond. CIA download. https://www.cia.gov/static/Air-America-Upholding-the-Airmens-Bond.pdf

4   https://offshoreleaks.icij.org/nodes/10166923

5   El-Batrawi, Ramy. *Can You Really Think and Grow Rich?: Keys to Unlock an Extraordinary Life* (p. 150). Kindle Edition.

6   Bloomberg News, "S.E.C. Accuses Saudi Financier and Executive of Stock Fraud," *New York Times*, April 14, 2006 . https://www.nytimes.com/2006/04/14/business/sec-accuses-saudi-financier-and-executive-of-stock-fraud.html

7   The following were found at the Ronald Reagan Presidential Library, Digital Library Collections: Collection: Culvahouse, Arthur B.: Files; Folder Title: Iran/Arms Transaction: Legal Memoranda Nicaraguan Contra Aid [Boland Amendment] (4); Box: CFOA 1131. https://www. reaganlibrary.gov/public/digitallibrary/smof/counsel/culvahouse/cfoa1131/40-123-12011812CFOA1131-049-2018.pdf

In Proclamation 6518 – Grant of Executive Clemency – Bush declared: "As Secretary of Defense throughout most of the Reagan Presidency, Caspar Weinberger was one of the principal architects of the downfall of the Berlin Wall and the Soviet Union. He directed the military renaissance in this country that led to the breakup of the communist bloc and a new birth of freedom and democracy As Secretary Weinberger's pardon request noted, it is a bitter irony that on the day the first charges against Secretary Weinberger were filed, Russian President

Boris Yeltsin arrived in the United States to celebrate the end of the Cold War I have also decided to pardon five other individuals for their conduct related to the Iran-Contra affair: Elliott Abrams, Duane Clarridge, Alan Fiers, Clair George, and Robert McFarlane. First, the common denominator of their motivation – whether their actions were right or wrong – was patriotism. Second, they did not profit or seek to profit from their conduct. Third, each has a record of long and distinguished service to this country. And finally, all five have already paid a price – in depleted savings, lost careers, anguished families – grossly disproportionate to any misdeeds or errors of judgment they may have committed."

"The prosecutions of the individuals I am pardoning represent what I believe is a profoundly troubling development in the political and legal climate of our country: the criminalization of policy differences. These differences should be addressed in the political arena, without the Damocles sword of criminality hanging over the heads of some of the combatants. The proper target is the President, not his subordinates; the proper forum is the voting booth, not the courtroom." December 24, 1992. https://www.presidency.ucsb.edu/documents/proclamation-6518-grant-executive-clemency.

8   Al Martin, *The Conspirators: Secrets of an Iran-Contra Insider*, National Liberty Press; 2nd edition (February 17, 2020)

9   Ibid.

10   Hacker News website forum. https://news.ycombinator.com/item?id=22987742

11   https://media.seylii.org/files/judgments/scca/2012/27/2012-scca-27.pdf   Blackwater Initiatives LLC had an account with Red Sea Management, set up in the Seychelle Islands, according to documents filed in Seychelles Court of Appeal.

12   Securities and Exchange Commission v. Kenneth P. D'Angelo and RBF International, Inc., United States District Court for the Central District of California, Case No. LACV 03-6499 CAS (VBKx) (September 11, 2003). SEC FILES FRAUD CHARGES ARISING OUT OF $130 MILLION STOCK LENDING AND MANIPULATION SCHEME. https://www.sec.gov/litigation/litreleases/lr-18344

13   Paul Waldie, Europe Correspondent, "Banker, buddy, scam," *The Globe and Mail* (Toronto, Canada, April 21, 2006). https://www.theglobeandmail.com/report-on-business/banker-buddy-scam/article1098193/

14   Evangelista's name came up in Stephenson v. DEUTSCHE BANK AG, Civil File No. 02-4845 (MJD/AJB) (D. Minn. Mar. 9, 2007). Previous case before appeal: 282 F.Supp.2d 1032 (2003). One

filed in Canada was shown here: https://www.govinfo.gov/app/details/USCOURTS- mnd-0_04-cv-01469/USCOURTS-mnd-0_04-cv-01469-0   and in an Excerpt from 282 F.Supp.2d 1032 (2003). https://scholar.google.com/scholar_case?-case=13516904850459950813&q=Stephenson+v.+-Deutsche+Bank+AG&hl=en&as_sdt=6,44&as_ vis=1

15   "Drew MacKenzie, "Viva Lust Vegas; FULL FRONTAL BATTLE OF THE BOOBS AS THE WORLD'S GAMBLING CAPITAL GOES BACK TO SLEAZE."The Free Library. 2002 MGN LTD, 27 Sep. 2023. https://www.thefreelibrary.com/Viva+Lust+Vegas%3B+FULL+FRONTAL+BAT- TLE+OF+THE+BOO BS+AS+THE+WORLD%27S...-a083782821

16   Ianthe Jeanne Dugan, Staff Reporter of the *Wall Street Journal*, Sept. 6, 2001.

Chapter Twenty-four

Jetborne and The Gurus

People had come to view Rennie Davis as better, more dedicated than the rest of us, and now, suddenly, he was telling us to surrender our hearts and minds to a barely pubescent self-proclaimed Perfect Master from India and waltz into Nirvana. It was as if Che Guevara had returned to recruit for the Campfire Girls: the anomaly was as profound as the amazement.
– Ken Kelley, Ramparts magazine, July 1973

W hile Adnan and wife, Soraya, were in Central Africa in the early '70s, Soraya and Sudan's President engaged in a little hanky panky. MI5 (the Brits' FBI, sort of) tattled on her to Adnan, and he instantly divorced her – in a fashion similar to the way Donald Trump would later claim to be able to de-classify secret government documents.[1]

Poof, we're divorced.

Less than a year after the "divorce," Khashoggi and "former CIA" covert operative Kim Roosevelt had their names blasted across the news. They were being investigated for taking bribes paid by American multi-national corporations to brokers who arranged contracts with foreign governments.

> Some of the country's flagship corporations – Exxon, Lockheed, Northrop, Gulf, United Brands – have admitted funneling massive amounts of cash to officials of foreign governments and hiding the transactions from their shareholders and directors. With their ethics as well as their profits under attack, many businessmen view themselves as Job beset by a plague of boils.
>
> Of all the tribulations, the exposure of shady foreign business practices was the most unexpected, concerning as it does a practice that has existed at least since the 1600's, when the British East India Company [BEIC] won duty-free treatment for its exports by giving Mogul rulers "rare treasures," including paintings, carvings and "costly objects made of copper, brass and stone."[2]

Not to mention, of course, the British East India Company's most lucrative commodity – opium to China.

THEY CALLED HIM MR. X

A year or so after the bribery scandal Khashoggi decided to buy the Mt. Kenya Safari Club in East Africa – which happens to border South Sudan. It's possible there were powerful Brits in control of MI5 – also members of the Safari Club – who forced Khashoggi to buy their shares, but that's only speculation. It's the timing that's so suspicious.

But not just that. A couple years after he acquired Mt. Kenya Safari Club, Adnan was sued by his ex-wife for cheating her out of her rightful share of his assets. The suit, filed by famed palimony lawyer Marvin Mitchelson of California, was still pending when Soraya returned to London and was almost immediately set upon by three Scotland Yard detectives attempting to blackmail her about a particular affair she'd had soon after the 1974 divorce.

She refused to pay them and instead had them arrested. Their trial was held just before Christmas in 1979 at the Old Bailey, and – no, they weren't represented by Rumpole as their Barrister.

Soraya – the 'witness for the prosecution' – had to testify. The defence – when in England, use British spelling – took the position that Scotland Yard detectives had a duty to investigate her as a security risk because of an affair she was having with a prominent British politician. They demanded that "Mr. X" be named.

Not until the judge told her to write the name on a slip of paper for only the eyes of the judge and jury, did Soraya agree to disclose the identity of the man, whom she called "more than a friend."

The paparazzi called him "Mr. X."

The *Daily Mail* couldn't get enough of Soraya's sex life and published a chronology of her affairs and one or two other marriages in late 1979. It was a salacious tabloid's wet dream, especially when Mr. X came forward.

Winston Churchill, Member of Parliament, grandson of the famous wartime Prime Minister, soon admitted publicly that he was the guilty party who'd cheated on his wife several years earlier.

Soraya's billion-dollar trial against Adnan was still pending until 1982, when they reached an out of court settlement. [3]

Sir Winston, the war-time Prime Minister who'd died in 1965, had been one of the founding members of the Safari Club, but whether he ever introduced his grandson and namesake to the scene is unknown.

For those wishing to map the family tree, MP Winston's father was Randolph, the only son of Sir Winston, who had died three years after his famous father. Randolph's wife was Pamela Digby – the mother of Soraya's

385

Mr. X – who was married to Prescott Bush's banking partner, Averell Harriman from 1971 until his death in 1986.

THE MINI GURU AND THE GODMAN

In 1957 Randolph Churchill, also the father of Arabella, a daughter born to his second wife, hired a researcher named Andrew Kerr (a descendant of Lord Lothian) to help Randolph Churchill write a biography of Sir Anthony Eden. While working at Randolph's Suffolk mansion, the two men became fast friends until Randolph's death in June 1968.

Kerr met Arabella during that time, and in 1971 planned the first Glastonbury Festival. All this seemingly irrelevant information is actually a prelude to introduce you to the 13-year-old guru who made his debut at that same Glastonbury festival in 1971, shortly before he left the UK for his first tour in America.[4]

Andrew Kerr became a worker for the Divine Light Mission of Guru Maharaji (another name for Premie Rawat) a few years later.[5]

"ARCHETYPAL UNCTUOUS FIXER"

Larry Kolb wrote in his book *Overworld*, about Khashoggi's favorite swami, Chandraswamy (or Swamiji), who died in 2017. Swamiji had first entered the political scene back in 1971, when he at 22 years of age, was introduced to India's future prime minister, P. V. Narasimha Rao.

Four years later, while in London, he was presented to Margaret Thatcher, whose attention he reputedly captured by predicting she would become prime minister within 3 or 4 years and would serve for either 9, 11 or 13 years in that role – both of which forecasts proved true. Sounds as if the boys in the back room – whoever they are – were making their plans.

Maggie applauded Swamiji's prediction and thereafter kept him close. Maggie was no dummy and clearly recognized the swami as a tool of the boys. It was a mutual benefit society that would provide the exact opposite of the peace promised by popular Indian gurus of those years.

The *Mumbai Mirror*, in its 2017 obituary of Swamiji, called him the "archetypal unctuous fixer," before asking: "But just who was he? How did he acquire influential followers and travel on their private jets and fancy yachts? And why was he so important to politicians and dictators across the world?"[6]

The *Mirror* never came even close to offering the answer, of course. It was classified. The godman, prince of peace, was a go-between for dirty weapons deals.

BARTER AS A FINANCING SCHEME

D irty weapons deals had a lot in common with my main interest that stemmed from the same era: drug smuggling by the CIA. In fact, there were times the drugs were swapped for weapons, as we all know. That's exactly what was going on in Mena, Arkansas – why Barry Seal was recruited to work for Bush and Clinton's team. Read my first book for the evidence.

Just as Republican Bush teamed up with Democrat Clinton – each with his own ties to CIA – in the mid-'80s, British politicians were working toward a similar goal. All of them needed a cover – just in case something went wrong.

Adnan Khashoggi, as a CIA asset, engaged with both parties in the U.S. government while he also dealt with the Conservative and Labor governments in the UK. Both MI6 and the CIA used him to their advantage – while he had millions of Pounds and Dollars wired to his accounts in Liechtenstein. Other clients paid in other currencies from every end of the earth. It's the magic of currency exchange.

The fact that both gurus came from India to the UK before flying to the United States may have some significance. A Houston, Texas, man who later became close to Khashoggi and Ramy El-Batrawi – John Gray – claims to have studied under a third famous guru, Maharishi Mahesh Yogi of the Transcendental Meditation program, from 1969 through 1978, before becoming a self-help writer in California in the mid-'80s.

We knew nothing about any connection to any gurus other than John Gray's nebulous link to the Maharishi when we started our search for the CIA's weapons dealing proprietary airline.

MY YEARS AS A NON-SLAVE

T here are many sides to the following story, mostly gleaned from a website called Ex-premi.org – presented by "ex-followers of Prem Rawat, a.k.a. Maharaji, the ex-'Lord of the Universe.'"[7] Anyone reading this who's remotely curious should spend some time perusing the site. There are too many facets to the story of this cult to be written about in this book – too incredible to be believed without seeing their evidence. While reviewing a chat forum at the site, I learned about what appeared to be an intelligence proprietary known simply as DECA.[8]

Michael Dettmers was one former Premie, as they called themselves, and he wrote of his experience:

> I, and others, created DECA in the late 70s to refurbish a used
> Boeing 707 to provide transportation for Maharaji and Élan Vital

personnel. It is true that many premies from around the world gave of their time and skills on this project for very little money and/or modest support.

However, nobody was a slave laborer. Slaves do not have the power to choose their situation. When the project was completed in 1980, DECA evolved into an aircraft completion center, fabricating and installing interiors for corporate jets.

This endeavor proved to be commercially unviable and, within a year or so, the company was sold to an independent (i.e. non-premie) buyer [Roger Koch, also a premie] who was primarily interested in the aircraft seating products DECA had designed and certified.

Shortly thereafter, the company was re-named Aircraft Modular Products (AMP) and some of the premies that worked at DECA, including my brother, chose to remain as paid employees of AMP. I am not qualified, nor is it my business, to comment on what became of AMP after the sale. In 1984, my brother left AMP to start Dettmers Precision Crafting, a sole proprietorship... [9]

The mini guru had by then moved to Malibu from Denver, where the headquarters of Divine Light Mission remained. Yet the Boeing makeover was happening in Miami, a city that had been the center of mob activity and anti-Communist intrigue for decades.

The Central Intelligence Agency hid a multitude of sins behind anti-Communism. Many of those sins will never be known, and some are only being disclosed 60 or 70 years later.

What the boys were doing in Guatemala and Nicaragua in the '60s and '70s still haunts us today as migrants flee the drug culture and terror that exists south of our own border. But there were too many exploitative North American corporate shareholders who feared losing, not so much their "investments," but the profits on those investments in South and Central America. They believed then and now it was their right to protect them at the expense of democratic ideals.

We reap what we sow.

Iran-Contra in the '80s was about not only protecting those investments, but also about profits that could be derived from selling weapons systems, airplanes, parts and ammunition to autocratic governments. Anything to even out the US balance of payments at the Bank for International Settlements, while rooting out any trace of anti-capitalist sentiment.

The same was also true of Margaret Thatcher's Conservatives who rose to power in 1979. India had a long history as a member of the British Commonwealth and some of those in India stood ready to help the Royalty and landed class whose family investment in the colonies went back centuries by then. The French and Dutch could say the same about territory in Africa and Asia where they still had influence.

The United States did not develop its own colonial aspirations until Teddy Roosevelt's splendid little war in Cuba and the Philippines – a war fought to acquire territories from Spain. Subsequent Roosevelt generations did not shy away from making use of colonial territories by the Central Intelligence Agency, which always welcomes elite deviants with open arms into its fold. The Roosevelt family had its share of family members represented within CIA ranks.

SWAMI MAGIC IN INDIA

Rajiv Gandhi, assassinated in 1991, became prime minister of India in 1984 – the year his mother, Indira Nehru Gandhi, was assassinated. Mrs. Gandhi became prime minister in 1966, almost 20 years after India gained independence.

P.V. Narasimha Rao, mentioned earlier as Swamijji's first prominent follower, was named to replace Rajiv.

In 1995 the *New York Times* wrote: "For days, Indian newspapers have concentrated on events surrounding Mr. Rao's spiritual adviser, Chandraswamy, a 46-year-old faith healer, self-professed psychic, and rags-to-riches millionaire, whom Mr. Rao brought to the capital from obscurity in southern India a quarter of a century ago."[10]

Chandraswamy had been controversial in India for years, while being admired by Adnan Khashoggi, Elizabeth Taylor and the Sultan of Brunei – three people who had at least two things in common: super wealth and being "connected".

In 1995 *The Independent* reported, "The guru was known in Britain for meddling in the Harrods takeover battle between the Fayed brothers and Lonrho's chief, Tiny Rowland, and he was often seen on the yacht of Mr Khashoggi the Saudi entrepreneur."[11]

The *Times* article hawked us back to '60s and '70s – to the Beatles' idol, Maharish Mahesh Yogi in Northern India – seemingly unaware of the covert operation in Florida in which the mini guru Prem Rawat was used as cover for the proprietary selected to deliver missiles from Israel to Iran in 1985 in a scheme designed by Adnan Khashoggi.

Chandraswamy (called simply Swamiji in Larry Kolb's book) was at that same time transferring funds from the Sultan of Brunei into Khashoggi's bank account. Those funds amounted to $11 million!

Donald Trump also came into focus in the aftermath of a deal between Khashoggi and the Sultan.

> Khashoggi once persuaded the sultan to guarantee a $50 million Swiss bank loan, with the Saudi putting up as collateral an ornate, gadget-filled 282-foot yacht featuring suites with private entertainment centers and gold-plated fittings.... When Khashoggi defaulted on the loan, it said, Hassanal [the Sultan of Brunei] was stuck with the debt and the yacht. By this account, the sultan eventually sold the boat at a $20 million loss, and it wound up in the hands of Donald Trump.[12]

The CIA has a long history of intrigue involving swamis. When something seems too impossible to be true but is, I usually start with the C.I.A. – the guys who can, like a magician pulling a rabbit out of a hat, make what you see with your own eyes seem like something else entirely. Swamis are the proverbial wolves in sheep's clothing. They seem so peaceful and gentle. That's by design. It puts you off the scent of an evil intent lurking underneath.

THE MINI GURU

It's early September 1971, four years after the Summer of Love blossomed in California. Like a mob of sex-crazed groupies at a Beatles concert, those gathered outside LAX are jumping up and down as Guru Maharaj Ji, a young teenager – only 13 years of age – lands on a TWA flight from England.

Shortly before shuffling off his mortal coil in 1966, Hans Maharaj had named his youngest son as his successor; the young guru was only eight years old. Their home was in the Himalayan Mountains, northeast of New Delhi and northwest of Nepal.

"It was as far north as one could go without entering China," according to Joan Apter, National Promotions Director for the Divine Light Mission, the religion the boy represented.[13]

The *London Evening Standard* reported three months earlier, on June 17 that the "Mini Guru" flew into Heathrow to begin a two-week tour that would include an appearance at the Glastonbury Festival on Mid-Summer's Day, better known as the summer solstice. It turned out to be England's version of our own Woodstock, arranged by an heir of Sir Winston Churchill – his granddaughter Arabella – whose brother, Winston, was a newly installed MP.

Not far away from the village where the young guru was born and had been giving incoherent talks was New Delhi, the home of Subramanian Swamy, who received his education in America, thanks to a full Rockefeller scholarship to Harvard. This swami got his PhD there at the age of 24 and stayed, teaching economics in 1962-69, before returning to New Delhi to teach at the India Institute of Technology, while working as a visiting professor at Harvard during the summers of 1971 and 1973.

In 1974 he took a seat in the upper house of the Indian Parliament. The Associated Press in 1976 reported claims by various groups that Dr. Subramanian Swamy was an active agent of the CIA.

In 1970 Subramanian Swamy had been a member of a group that recommended that Prime Minister Indira Gandhi manufacture nuclear weapons. She had taken his advice, So, in case you're counting, besides the U.S. and USSR, the UK, then France and China, India was the sixth country to announce it had nukes, in May 1974 – the first after the non-proliferation treaty was signed.

That fact alone would have perked up the ears of the CIA. And anyone else who happened to be listening.

• • •

Rising from the ashes of the OSS in 1947, the CIA was officially born by a law passed by Congress and signed by President Harry Truman, the malleable former Democratic Senator from Missouri.

America's most experienced Arabist spies during World War II were officially assigned in 1947 to operate in the Middle East. Kermit "Kim" Roosevelt, Jr. was sent to Beirut, Lebanon as head of the CIA's Near East and Africa division, and his pal, Miles Axe Copeland, Jr., ended up in Damascus, Syria. They quickly put their heads together with British Arabists like Kim Philby, who had long been tasked with saving oil for the white western world.

Although the spies warned elected leaders against setting up a divided state in Palestine and of recognizing the demands of Zionists in Israel, higher-ups in the chain ignored the warning – as political hacks often do.

As the world was still staggering from the horrors of Auschwitz and Dachau, President Truman ignored the Arabists' wise advice and quickly recognized the new national Jewish State of Israel, created within Palestinian territory.

Today the region is an absolute hellhole where genocide committed by both sides reigns supreme.

Once the State of Israel was declared – as the OSS Arabists had predicted – a war quickly ensued among the new nation of Israel and existing Arab countries.

Israel's war chest was financed by criminal and terrorist elements such as Irgun, Haganah and the Stern Gang, whose members had joined with the Italian mafia in taking over organized crime in the United States. Meyer Lansky's men were some of Israel's biggest donors, but when Lansky sought refuge there to flee prosecution in the United States, he was ordered to be expelled. [14]

CIA men, however, are anything but inflexible. They quickly justified the politicians' ill-advised decisions – in order to keep American Zionist donors mollified.

The CIA, equally convinced by their Wall Street friends, knew instinctively that, when allowed free elections, "the people" would decide in their own interest – which is almost never the same as Wall Street's. An American puppet leader was much preferable, even an autocratic one.

"He Didn't Talk Spooks To Me"

What the spooks did has been recounted in books about coups in Syria in 1949 and in Iran in 1953, though government documents may remain classified seven decades later. The spooks never even told their wives or children. They were having too much fun to talk about what they were doing behind the scenes.

Kim Roosevelt's wife admitted in his obituary in the *New York Times* in June 2000:

> "That was spook talk," she said. "He didn't talk spooks to me." Mrs. Roosevelt added that her husband never told her what he had done during World War II, when he was in the Office of Strategic Services, the forerunner to the C.I.A.[15]

The Arabists had been right about what would happen if the new state of Israel was given territory inside Palestinian boundaries, but no one had listened. Consequently, the Arabists in 1949 became part of what historian Hugh Wilford calls "America's Great Game," in redesigning Syria. It was a game – a "test case," replacing the elected leader with a military dictator. From that point forward, the CIA engaged in covert operations in other countries at least 20 more times in the next 30 years leading up to 1979.

Covert ops require deniability. That alone makes financing them a big challenge, since everything they do is classified.

National Security Directive 10/2, as Wilford explains, in 1948 entrusted to the CIA "covert operations, that is, 'all activities' carried out against 'hostile foreign states or groups' in such a way 'that, if uncovered, the U.S. Government can plausibly disclaim any responsibility for them.'"[16]

Anti-Zionist groups fell under Kim Roosevelt's domain, but his first two attempts attracted few members and insignificant financial backing. The third iteration was called "American Friends of the Middle East [AFME], which the CIA secretly funded and to some extent managed as well. And it was very pro-Arab and quite critical of U.S. support for Israel," according to an interview Hugh Wilford did with *U.S. News & World Report*, found online.[17]

Friends' groups were the CIA's favorite covers for covert ops, as well as groups like the "East West Contacts Committee" set up within the State Department, which was used for the fake defector program to put Americans (like Marina Oswald's "friend," Ruth Paine) in touch with people in the Soviet Union. Any time a group uses the word "friends" in its title, you can almost be assured, the CIA is involved. It's a tell.

"The Entire Enterprise Was a CIA Plot."

That's where Rennie Davis comes into our story. *Ramparts* magazine in March 1967 blew the cover off the CIA's covert funding operations, including primarily the National Student Association (NSA). Even more significant, *Ramparts*, in regard to Rennie Davis' "incredible story of his conversion to the divine prodigy, Satguru Maharaj Ji," that Paul Krassner knew of what he spoke when he insisted "the entire enterprise was a CIA plot."[18]

The NSA was founded in 1947 at a time that the CIA was swimming in money resulting from the Marshall Fund's so-called "counterpart funds," handled by the CIA's Irving Brown and Jay Lovestone.[19]

One of NSA's major goals was to spread propaganda around about the superiority of capital enterprise system over communism, at the same time the Soviets were expanding their empire.

Czechoslovakia was a battleground for young minds in Europe, just as Korea became a literal battleground for armed soldiers in the same war against Communism. The NSA was ripe for true believers in capitalism throughout those years and was used as a CIA conduit as early as 1950.

Some of NSA's members founded Students for a Democratic Society (SDS) at Port Huron, Michigan, in 1962. Rennie Davis, a political science graduate of Oberlin College, who was working on a PhD at the University of Illinois, was one of those SDS founders.

His father, John Cordon Davis, had been a teacher at Ohio State University in 1930, but moved on to Michigan State, where he taught Economics. During WWII, John C. Davis served on the Ship-Building Commission and was a member of the Council of Economic Advisers in Washington, D.C. during the Truman Administration. His son Rennie was supposedly the level-headed member of the Chicago Seven, brought to trial after violence erupted at the Democratic National Convention in Chicago in 1968.

RENNIE DAVIS ON THE PAYROLL

But Rennie, alas, was already on the payroll of the CIA, or at least of a domestic organization that was given illegal funds by the CIA – one of the many organizations whose cover was blown by *Ramparts* in 1967. His brother, John Willard Davis, was also active in SDS, and still another brother, Robert Dean Davis, was alleged to have been living in Miami with his wife, Lynne Davis, and participating in the project that supported the guru Rennie had helped bring to the U.S.[20]

It was, of course, just a coincidence, right?

Every report about the "roly poly boy god," was politically incorrect by today's standards. Columnist Lester Kinsolving, for example, said "the boy God looks as if he is either a prepubescent Gautama suited up for Pop Warner football – or else the world's best fed midget."[21]

Robert Scheer gave us some insight into Rennie Davis, "whom one had thought to be an eminently sensible and serious type," as he recounted his career highlights. How could Rennie "have arrived at this bizarre place," he wondered, and what did it say "about the history we shared." When he heard "Rennie's all-too-familiar voice urging us to 'join me in crawling on my belly, if necessary, across the surface of this earth to kiss the lotus feet of the Guru Maharaj Ji,'" well, that was way too much.[22]

Larry Canada was once married to Kathy Noyes, an heiress to the Eli Lilly drug fortune. Rennie worked with Larry on the May Day demonstrations in Washington, D.C. in 1971. In March, while they were there, the Capitol was bombed. Canada was arrested but later freed.

Linda Minor was down in Texas, protesting the opening of the LBJ Library in Austin. I myself was at UCLA gearing up with my mates for May Day.

Where were you?

The *Indianapolis Star* reported in November 1973 that both men had been in Santa Barbara, California, "last spring," working to build a church for their guru, who had recently moved to Los Angeles. The Santa Barbara church was not far from the half-million-dollar residence the Premies, as followers of Prem Rawat were called, bought for him in the far west part of Los Angeles County.

The boy first came to California in the summer of 1971, stayed only a short time, but returned again in 1972. The first year his handlers arranged a charter flight, packing a Boeing 727 with hippies willing to take a free trip to India. In November 1972 there were seven chartered plane-loads of cultists bound for India's Holi Festival in the Himalayas. Clearly the movement had grown.

Predicting a new millennium long before the century's end, Rennie Davis was placed in charge of "Millennium '73," a convention of Premies held in Houston's still iconic Astrodome in November 1973. It is indeed strange how quickly Rennie's focus on protesting war to promoting peace changed, even though the war continued unabated long after Nixon left office.

But things changed when the young guru at 16 decided to marry his 23-year-old secretary, Marolyn Lois Johnson, from San Diego. A Denver juvenile court judge agreed to let the minor marry in May 1974. By year's end he was fighting with his family in India over control of the Mission (and the money). The cult began its decline as true believers dropped away.

In addition to his Los Angeles County mansion, the boy guru also acquired a home in Colorado, and the headquarters of the DLM moved into four floors of offices in Denver's Kitteridge Building. Rennie lived not far away in Boulder, and his brother Bob moved to Evergreen, Colorado, with his wife Lynne, with whom Roger Koch had lodged when he first moved to Miami. All this is hidden within the trove of memories at the Prem-Rawat website cited earlier.

Rennie Davis and Larry Canada, who, people said, still had access to an Eli Lilly trust's funds, were responsible for setting the guru up in a half-million-dollar Malibu mansion – located at 31334 Anacapa View Drive off Trancas Canyon Road, where he was still living in 1980. The guru soon requested a permit from the City of Malibu to allow him to build a helipad near his mansion. The city granted him six landings and later approved twelve, but a new request in 1985 for 36, was too much. Permit denied.

By 1994, a new multi-million-dollar home had been built around the original structure, which was then demolished. It was revealed that title to the residence was held in the name of Seva Corp., a Nevada corporation.

Seva's attorney, Robert A. Jacobs, was employed by the firm of Manatt & Phelps, whose senior partner, Charles Manatt, replaced Robert Strauss as head of the Democratic National Committee in 1981 through 1985. It's often called "controlling the opposition." In this case, it's called money laundering.

Manatt also was vice chair of the National Endowment for Democracy (NED) – funded by Congress with tax dollars largely channeled through the U.S. Information Agency (USIA) and the Agency for International Development (AID).

Oliver North was raising funds for the Nicaraguan Contras while he was financed by the NED, which makes "hundreds of grants each year to support pro-democracy groups in Africa, Asia, Central and Eastern Europe, Eurasia, Latin America, and the Middle East."[23]

Who else did Charles Manatt represent? Well, in 1982 he was attorney for real estate developer Eugene Glick. I looked through documents shown me by Barry Seal's wife, Debbie Seal, who allowed me to make copies of some of them for my first book.

Continental Desert Properties, Inc. was a real estate development company which Eugene Glick started in Palm Springs in early 1976. He also bought at the same time 54 lots on the fairway of Rancho Mirage's Thunderbird Palm Estates, where former President Gerald Ford began building a new home after vacating the White House in January 1977. Ford moved into the Thunderbird house in 1978 and lived there until he died in 2006.[24]

Soon after buying the Thunderbird lots, Glick also acquired real property in Tucson that once housed a bank computer center. By then he lived in Woodland Hills, California, a neighborhood bordering the Santa Monica Mountains in the San Fernando Valley, just north of the guru's mountaintop mansion when Manatt was Seva's attorney.

Glick also acquired a Beechcraft King Airplane 200, tail number N6308F, once owned by Systems Marketing, Inc. (SMI), a computer leasing company founded in Phoenix in 1971 by Robert R. Russell.

SMI was sold to Omaha-based Commercial Federal Corporation, parent of Commercial Federal Savings and Loan, between 1984 and 1987. A news article in the *Albuquerque Journal* at that time revealed that El Paso Electric was "diversifying" its utility business by spending $60 million to buy preferred stock of Commercial Federal.

El Paso Electric was also planning to provide $2.5 million in "debt financing" to America West Airlines and $1.5 million to Dallas-based LTV.

"Both loans would be guaranteed by Systems Marketing, Inc., a Phoenix-based leasing company, whose majority owner is Commercial Federal, [B.E.] Bostic said."[25]

Systems Marketing, Inc., which later showed up as owner of the Beechcraft King 200, was bleeding out to the tune of $1 million per month in 1989, according to William A. Fitzgerald, president and CEO of Commercial Federal Corporation, which sold SMI earlier that year.[26] When he was asked by a reporter of the *Des Moines Register* in October 1989 who bought SMI, Commercial Federal Corp., he "wouldn't identify the buyer or disclose the sale price."[27]

Glick through one of these companies leased Barry Seal the airplane, which could be directly connected to a CIA "front" company through a series of fraudulent financial transactions. After Seal was murdered in 1986, the plane was bought by the State of Texas for the use of Governor George W. Bush. The "boys" call it an inside joke. Over time, they've developed quite a warped sense of humor.

WHAT IS IT ABOUT WOODLAND HILLS?

Also living in Woodland Hills at that time was another attorney – Asher M. Leids – a tax attorney mentioned in Chapter Four. Leids worked with Michael Roy Fugler, who had moved up from the Baton Rouge swamp to Manhattan and at that time was operating the North American branch of a firm called Millennium Financial Group. Both Leids and Fugler handled different aspects of the initial public offering (IPO) for GenesisIntermedia, the company Ramy El-Batrawi took public for Adnan Khashoggi.

Ramy had been setting up corporations in Florida since 1987, first working with Fugler on Sunray (later Nationwide) Vans – a company that did conversions and modifications of different van types. That's described in Chapter Three..

SECRET GURU BUSINESS

That the young guru was being used for secret government operations was confirmed by Roger Koch, who posted at a website set up by Divine Light Mission (DLM) critics. Koch wrote that he first became involved with DLM in the fall of 1972 after his future wife's brother made a trip to India. Roger and his wife became serious devotees of the boy guru for five years while Roger studied agriculture and engineering in Iowa. He graduated from college in 1977 and was assigned by the DLM to work first in Chicago for two years, he claimed.

After the Chicago stint, Koch wrote, "I was called to Miami to work at DECA, and specifically to work on redesigning the Holi Gun [a water sprinkler invention]. I think this was Feb. 79. At this time, DECA was pretty much a secret. I did not know what went on there until I arrived. ... When I got to DECA, the aircraft project was in full swing, as were several other projects for Maharaj Ji."[28]

In Miami for almost four years, Roger lived with Rennie Davis' brother, Bob Davis and his wife, Lynne, who worked, respectively, in the DLM's construction arm (CRA) and in finance (DECA). When DECA closed in October 1983, the Davis family moved to Denver.

Roger's online essay is filled with hints about what this mysterious religious group was actually doing. For example, he says, "The name DECA stayed with the aviation business and the construction business became known as CRA. ... Upon my return from India, there was work to be done to make money. The first few jobs at DECA included Resorts International and the Leona Helmsley BAC-111."

Harry and Leona Helmsley bought the British-made BAC-111 in 1981, according to a to gossip in the *New York Daily News*, boasting the jet cost about $5 million, plus another $1 million or so every year to house and maintain.[29] This information came from "a Helmsley spokesman," who told her they'd spent $300,000 to completely redesign the plane's interior. The plane would be mentioned several more times over the years until 1988 when the Helmsleys were hit by the IRS for tax problems, forcing them to sell the plane, which was leased to the Portland Trail Blazers. It had to have another "massive renovation" to remove the round king-size bed, among other changes.[30]

Leona Helmsley, in case you're too young to remember, was once known as the "Queen of Mean," and the archrival of the man we wish we could forget, Donald J. Trump. *Variety's* writer, Matt Donnelly purports to offer "'smoking gun' evidence that will question the tax evasion case brought on her by Rudy Giuliani in 1988."[31]

Leona thought she was above the law and fought against going to prison until 1992, when she had a different jet fly her to Kentucky to serve her time.[32] She was released after eleven months for good behavior.

DECA's OTHER CLIENTS

Roger Koch said the DLM also worked an account for Resorts International Inc. (RII), but without his giving the year, we don't know whether it was for the James M. Crosby family or for Donald

Trump, who acquired a 73 percent voting stake in Resorts International Inc. in 1987.[33]

RII under Crosby opened the first casino in Atlantic City in 1978, after
gambling was legalized there in 1976, and he also owned a 9-percent stake
in troubled Pan Am Airways, said to be worth about $56 million. Resorts
also owned three Sikorsky S-61 helicopters that Resorts International
Airlines (RIA) used to shuttle high rollers to the Resorts Casino Hotel in
Atlantic City.

Koch added, somewhat disjointedly, that "Several other customers ma-
terialized including Air Florida and Pan Aviation…. Pan Aviation was the
corporate arm of Sarkis Soghanalian, a reputed weapons dealer. DECA
was doing maintenance on the Pan Aviation 727."[34]

There's no way to comprehend how an authentic guru advocating
peace and justice would act as cover for the likes of Soghanalian. Apparently, Koch spent some time with Soghanalian's company because the
arms merchant took a fancy to his work and "considered me to be a genius," transporting him to Europe to fix a Cessna, without taking his passport along. This event turned into a joke that Koch *"had been kidnapped
and taken to Bahgdad."*[35]

As Koch tells his stories from memory years later, we learn the kidnapping flight had begun well enough with inflight service of Caviar and
Dom Perignon and a pretty waitress," then off to Europe, stopping "in excellent quarters in Basil Switzerland. After a couple nights of revelrie [sic],
we headed for Frankfort, supposedly to fix said Cessna. However, we did
not end up going to Frankfurt. Instead, we ended up heading for Baghdad,
Iraq. This is too weird to process, just suffice it to say that after a horren-
dous set of flight circumstances, we survived and ended up in *Baghdad,
right in the middle of the Iran Iraq war."*[36]

Long story, short: When they finally got down to business, Soganhalian "explained to me that when I fixed his airplane air conditioning,
that he had told Sadaam that he had found a genius engineer to solve his
aircraft A/C problem. So we set out for an Iraqi Air Force aircraft hangar.
I was convinced that I was a dead man. We arrived at the hangar filled with
Russian MiG fighters and Russians as well. The Russians were pissed and
put up a fight but were escorted out. I didn't know what to do."

Then he offers a few more clues as he finishes this part of the story:

> Sarkis asked me to take a look at the aircraft and figure out how to
> A/C the plane. This was important because the pilots were over-

heating and passing out on the runway. Now at this point, I didn't care about the Iraqi pilots, I just wanted to get home alive. So, I used my American ingenuity and lied. I said that I thought that I could fit an air cycle machine in the fuel tank behind the cockpit. We removed the tank, took it to the 727 and loaded it in the cargo hold. I explained that I needed to get back to Miami to work out the details, and off we went. It worked and I made it back to Miami safely. Should I say by the grace. I am sure I did then.[37]

Pan Aviation didn't pay it's [sic] bills. Another customer, Nigerians I think, didn't pay, and suddenly it was all over. Everyone dispersed so quickly it was hard to keep track of what was happening.

We know the CIA is not legally allowed to operate on U.S. soil. So who was in charge of the guru op? Documents have since been released from the Soghanalian files that led Lauren Harper to write:

> What remains unclear is who Soghanalian's primary government contacts were, aside from the FBI's Miami bureau. Most believe he was a CIA informant, although others argue that Soghanalian's handlers were primarily from the *Defense Intelligence Agency and the White House,* in part because Sarkis found the CIA "largely incompetent… [and] he repeatedly ran into their less than stellar arms buying operations and exposed and embarrassed them."[38]

She quotes from one document in which Soghanalian claimed: "The Americans knew what I was doing, every minute, every hour. If I drank a glass of water, they were aware of it and what kind of water it was."[39]

In a 2001 interview by *Frontline,* she writes, Soghanalian said, "when the U.S. approached him about selling weapons to Iran during the Iran-Iraq War he refused, saying arming 'Iran is like riding two horses in a horse race. You can't do that.'" That was clearly a lie, given Roger Koch's experience. Unfortunately, he did not reveal which agency. Then Koch drops the big bomb about Jetborne:

> One of the DECA customers, Jetborne, ended up buying DECA. Jetborne was an Israeli company with no ties to DECA. The Jetborne management asked me to stay and run the remainder of DECA. I was also asked by the DECA management to stay on with the Jetborne acquisition, so I did. This was in the fall of 1983. Jetborne changed the company name to AMP.
>
> … Jetborne owned AMP until they sold it for $10.7 Million to a group led by myself 7 years later in Dec, 1990…

> The group led by myself made AMP very successful. We sold it
> to BE Aerospace in 1998 for $106 Million. At this time we had over
> 300 employees. I did not own it all, only about 51 percent. [40]

DECA Group's aviation business consisted of converting interiors of ordinary used aircraft into luxury private jets. Could displaced DECA workers have decided to do the same type of modification to vans? That would explain how Ramy El-Batrawi could have become involved with Sunray. Only Ramy knows for sure, and he ain't sayin'.

Moving from Miami to Clearwater, Florida in 1987 would have been the first step, then branching out to Tampa and New Port Richey. It is interesting to note that the location in Clearwater put the company quite close to the college which Michael Farkas used as the address for his internet-based company that would morph Sky Way Aircraft into Skyway Communications.

DECA's former Miami location – a pink building now called M3 Studios is a hodgepodge of offices that have used other addresses, primarily the same one Jetborne International, Inc. began using – 4010 NW 36th Avenue – as its address when it was first incorporated in Delaware in 1987.

HIDING JETBORNE IN PLAIN SIGHT

So what was AMP, we wondered. We found it in Jetborne International's SEC filings for 1996 and 1997:

> Jetborne International, Inc. (the 'Company') was incorporated in the State of Delaware on January 30, 1987. The Company was organized for the purpose of capital formation through an initial public offering to develop and expand the business of Jetborne, Inc., a Florida corporation incorporated on or about April 24, 1980 and generally engaged in the sale of aircraft parts and aircraft components.
>
> On February 2, 1987, shortly after the Company's inception, the stockholders of Jetborne, Inc. transferred all of its issued and outstanding common stock to the Registrant, Jetborne International, Inc....
>
> On December 10, 1991, the Company was placed in an involuntary, Chapter 11 Federal Bankruptcy proceeding, and on December 16, 1991, Jetborne, Inc., the Company's only significant remaining subsidiary at the time, filed a voluntary petition in the same Bankruptcy Court.[41]

The filing made no mention of alleged former shareholder Roger Koch. Instead, it states that the largest shareholders in 1997 (after the reporting period) were RADA Electronic Industries Ltd. and Bodstray Company Limited. It also recited the following:

> Until approximately October 31, 1997, the Company's principal offices were located at 4010 N.W. 36th Avenue, Miami, Florida 33142. The Company had been leasing offices and facilities from its former subsidiary, *Aircraft Modular Products, Inc.* (AMP). The Company now occupies its new leased premises at 8361 N.W. 64th Street, Miami, Florida 33166 pursuant to a lease.[42]

Aircraft Modular Products, Inc. was chartered in Florida in May 1981 by Roger Koch, according to Sunbiz. Four years later he incorporated National Airspace Media Corporation with the Israeli men whose names were connected to the original Jetborne, Inc. of Florida – Allen Blattner, Michael Lefkowitz and Amos Alouf. In 1990 he incorporated RTE Acquisition with Anthony J. Tripodo, the same man who name was connected with AMP earlier. Tripodo also incorporated DECA Flying Club in 1983. In 1991 the Israelis involved in Jetborne International (Allen and David Blattner and their brother-in-law Michael Levkowitz) were suspended after Jetborne International was indicted for selling airplane parts to Iran.

The *Miami Herald* then reported:

> The officers were replaced by a newly elected board of directors controlled by a British group named Finstock, Ltd. that recently gained control of the company.[43]

Finstock was, of course, the offshore entity controlled by Adnan Khashoggi.

Another news story identified Allen Blattner as "an Israeli born in Egypt [who] came to America from London in 1979."[44] The story said that Blattner created Jetborne.

"There was not much money. The warehouse sat on a grubby dead-end street in Northwest Miami. Then Blattner bought a hangar at Miami International Airport; later, a boat dealership. Next he grabbed off an airplane-seat manufacturer."[45]

FRAMING ROGER RABBIT?

There had been a Roger Koch working for Boeing in 1977, quoted as a spokesman about Boeing being awarded a contract with NASA for the space shuttle. So the timing seems off if they are the same man. A different news service (UPI) that year quoted Roger Koch of Boeing talking about medical services at NASA's JSC in Houston. But our Roger claims he only got his degree in chemical engineering in 1977, so it can't be the same person. Nevertheless, I did manage to verify certain claims.

Another page of the ex-premie website declares:

> A 1961 vintage aircraft was acquired for US$1 million from an American Football Team. A business operation called the DECA Project and based in Florida was set up and ashram residents were drafted in [sic] provide Prem Rawat with a customized Boeing 707 for his personal use.
>
> The headquarters of DLM was moved to Miami and large numbers of the most skilled and dedicated ashram premies were moved to Miami and run-down hotels were rented to accommodate them. This had a significant effect on communities throughout the USA, and to a certain extent, other countries, as many of the most committed devotees were taken to Miami to do unskilled labour....
>
> DECA did provide a model for income generation which was free of the costs and other considerations of the ashram system. Although dependent on the ashrams for its existence, DECA, or at least the funding expertise that it generated, can be seen as the development which allowed Rawat to dissolve the costly ashram system in 1982 and 1983, and to still maintain an income flow to his organizations.[46]

In November 1987, Jetborne International, Inc. announced it had formed a new subsidiary at a hangar at the Miami international airport called Jet Engineering & Technical Services, Inc., a Florida corporation filed the previous month. It gave an address for its president, Allen Blattner, at 4010 NW 36th Avenue in Miami.

Another director was Robert Kurau, who a few years earlier had been a vice president at Walter E. Heller & Co., Southeast and officer at three branches of Sun Banks. Walter E. Heller had been a major lender to drug smuggler Kenneth Burnstine in the 70's.

Learning about Burnstine was a big surprise for me. I'd long thought Barry Seal was the first of America's drug lords. Turns out Kenny Burnstine preceded Barry by at least a decade.

As a man whose flamboyant style, wild life, and addiction to deals made him notorious – like Barry, he also had connections.

Endnotes

1   A few years after Nimeri took office in 1969, Khashoggi convinced him, as a fellow Muslim, to assist Israel's Ariel Sharon with a secret scheme of using Sudan as an arms cache for Israelis to use against Iran and Libya. When Nimeri then agreed to allow Jews to escape Ethiopia on their path to Israel by way of Sudan, the news leaked out to other Arab countries, and Nimeri was overthrown.

2   Milton S. Gwirtzman, "IS BRIBERY DEFENSIBLE?," the *New York Times*, October 5, 1975, page 245. https://www.nytimes.com/1975/10/05/archives/is-bribery-defensible-bribery.html

3   "A $2.5 billion divorce suit filed by Saroya [sic] Khashoggi...," UPI Archives, Jan. 20, 1982. https://gi/4002380350800/

4   "Hallelujah! The mini guru, aged 13, cometh," *Evening Standard*, 17 Jun 1971, Page 11. https://www.newspapers.com/image/721559653/?terms=glastonbury%20guru&match=1

5   Jonathan Sale, "Andrew Kerr obituary," The *Guardian*, 13 Oct 2014. https://www.theguardian.com/music/2014/oct/13/andrew-kerr

6   "The ungodly life and high flying times of Chandra Swami," *Mumbai Mirror, India Times* May 28, 2017. https://bangaloremirror.indiatimes.com/opinion/sunday-read/the-ungodlylife-and-high-flying-times-of-chandra-swami/articleshow/58875558.cms

7   http://www.ex-premie.org/

8   See site map: http://www.ex-premie.org/pages/sitemap.htm

9   Michael Dettmers posts: http://www.ex-premie.org/pages/best.htm#MD

10   John F. Burns, "Indian Premier's Swami Has a Run of Bad Karma, New York Times, Sept. 21, 1995. https://www.nytimes.com/1995/09/21/world/indian-premier-s-swami-has-a-run-of-bad-karma.html

11   Tim McGirk, "Net Closes on Rao's own `Rasputin'," *Independent*, 20 September 1995. https://www.independent.co.uk/news/world/net-closes-on-rao-s-own-rasputin-1602139.html

12   Citing the Ron Kessler book, The Richest Man in the World, by William Branigin, "Churchill Pushed Aside For Museum Celebrating Brunei's Wealthy Sultan, *Washington Post*, October 13, 1992.

13   https://www.prem-rawat-bio.org/newspapers/CC/r73_blissed.html

14   "Lansky Ordered Expelled from Israel," Jewish Telegraphic Agency Archives, September 12, 1972. https://www.jta.org/archive/lansky-ordered-expelled-from-israel See also an Arab written policy paper called "The Roots of Zionist Terrorism,"
https://www.palestine-studies.org/en/ node/1654849

15   We don't really need Kermit's version of events, however, since many of the documents have since been declassified. The CIA has even said it's sorry, an almost unheard of response to its actions. They always wait for the operatives to die of course. "CIA Confirms Role in 1953 Iran Coup," *National Security Archive Electronic Briefing Book No. 435*, August 19, 2013, Edited by Malcolm Byrne https://nsarchive2.gwu.edu/NSAEBB/NSAEBB435/#_ftn1

16   Hugh Wilford, *America's Great Game: The CIA's Secret Arabists and the Shaping of the Modern Middle East* (Basic Books; 1st edition, January 3, 2017). See NSC 10/2 at https:// history.state.gov/historicaldocuments/frus1945-50Intel/d292

17   Kira Zalan, "How the CIA Shaped the Modern Middle East," Interview with History Professor Hugh Wilford. Jan. 16, 2014. Copyright 2023 ©U.S. *News & World Report* L.P. https://www.usnews.com/opinion/articles/2014/01/16/the-great-game-and-the-cia-shaped-the-modern-middle-east

18   Ken Kelley, "Blissed Out With The Perfect Master," *Ramparts Magazine*, July 1973, Pages 32-34. https://www.prem-rawat-bio.org/newspapers/CC/r73_blissed.html

19   See Frances Stonor Saunders, *The Cultural Cold War: The Cia and The World Of Arts and Letters*. The New Press (April 1, 2001)

20   Posted by Roger Koch on January 29, 2012 :"Bob D. was Rennie D.'s brother and Bob's wife Lynne is one of the best cooks ever. Bob worked for CRA, the construction arm of DECA, and Lynne worked in finance at DECA. They had 2 beautiful boys, one who was born in the apartment while I was living there. We lived together until DECA closed in Oct. 83, and they moved to Denver. I have not seen them for several years, but think of them often." http://ex-premie.org/pages/journs/ koch.htm

21   Lester Kinsolving, "India's Rich, Roly Poly Boy God," *Capital Times*, Madison, Wisconsin, January 6, 1973.

22   Robert Scheer, "Death of the Salesman," *Playboy*, June 1974, pages 107-108, 112, 236, 238-240. https://www.prem-rawat-bio.org/magazines/1974/plboy0674.html

23   The source for this quote is an article published March 2, 2012, by the Militarist Monitor, which seems to have links back to the Institute of Policy Studies (IPS), co-founded by the father of Congressman Jamie Raskin – Marcus Raskin. https://militarist-monitor.org/profile/national_endowment_for_democracy/

24   Though Ford was from Michigan, he first moved to Palm Springs when he left the Presidency, while the home in Rancho Mirage was being built. Steven Stolman, "Inside President Gerald Ford's Distinguished Desert Getaway," *Town & Country*, Jun 02, 2019. ©2023 Hearst Magazine Media, Inc. hford-betty-ford-house/

25   A. C. Etheridge, "Utility Plan Could Benefit Southern N.M.," *Albuquerque Journal*, February 22, 1987. https://www.newspapers.com/image/157908509/

26   John Taylor, "New S&L Rules Called Bad Deal," *Omaha World Herald*, November 2, 1989.

27   "Commercial Federal sells Systems Marketing unit," *Des Moines Register*, 06 Oct 1989, Fri ·Page 19.

28   http://ex-premie.org/pages/journs/koch.htm

29   Claudia Cohen, "Helmsley buys giant jet; wife made him do it," *New York Daily News*, 26 Mar 1981, Page 67.

30   Terry Foster, *Detroit Free Press*, 25 Mar 1990, Page 56.

31   Matt Donnelly, "Trump Nemesis and 'Queen of Mean' Leona Helmsley Subject of Juicy New Documentary (EXCLUSIVE), *Variety*, May 25, 2022. The documentary promises to be a blockbuster with this: "We received a tip from an insider about the Leona prosecution. Then I discovered the 'Leona is a bitch' narrative was started by none other than Donald Trump, when he was competing against her and Harry. That immediately intrigued me. When we started chipping away at that 1989 narrative, we were shocked – I mean, jaw on the floor – with what we uncovered. We have unprecedented access to those close to what happened and who want to set the record straight to be on the right side of history. We can't give that much away, but you will be shocked. I promise. This is "The Jinx"-level stuff."

32   "Helmsley Takes Company Jet to Kentucky, Goes to Prison in Limo," *L.A. Times* Archives, April 16, 1992. https://www.latimes.com/archives/la-xpm-1992-04-16-mn-906-story.html

33   John Crudele, *New York Times*, March 10, 1987, Section D, Page 5 Trump agreed to pay $79 million ($135 per share for 585,000 shares) from the estate and family of James M. Crosby, who died in April 1986.

34   Journeys: Roger Koch. January 29, 2012. http://ex-premie.org/pages/journs/koch.htm

35   Ibid. For more on Soganhalian, see Lauren Harper, "The Merchant of Death's Account Book," National Security Archive Electronic Briefing Book No. 502, February 23, 2015. https:// nsarchive2.gwu.edu/NSAEBB/NSAEBB502/

36   Journeys: Roger Koch. January 29, 2012. http://ex-premie.org/pages/journs/koch.htm.

37   Ibid.

38   Lauren Harper, "The Merchant of Death's Account Book," op cit. https://nsarchive2.gwu.edu/NSAEBB/NSAEBB502/

39   Ibid.

40   Crudele, *New York Times*, March 10, 1987.

41   "After the Company converted the original proceeding from an involuntary to a voluntary bankruptcy, the bankruptcy cases were consolidated. The Company emerged from bankruptcy protection on September 17, 1993 by entry of the Bankruptcy Court's order confirming its third amended plan of reorganization. From late 1991 until September 17, 1993, the Company operated as Debtor-In-Possession under Chapter 11 Bankruptcy protection, Case No. 91-16169-BKC-AJC, U.S. Bankruptcy Court Southern District of Florida. See Item 3., 'Legal Proceedings' and Item 8., 'Financial Statements'." https://www.sec.gov/Archives/edgar/data/811786/0000943440-97-000070.txt

42   Ibid.

43   *Miami Herald*, 16 May 1991, Page 32.

44   Gregg Fields, "Aircraft firm's fast rise cut short," *Miami Herald*, 08 Apr 1991, Page 129.

45   Ibid.

46   https://www.prem-rawat-bio.org/deca.html

Chapter Twenty-five

Wiretappers and Soldiers of Fortune

They were rogue cops and shakedown artists. They were wiretappers and soldiers of fortune and faggot lounge entertainers. Had one second of their lives deviated off course, American History would not exist as we know it.

— James Ellroy, *American Tabloid*

Friday, the 11th of January 1974 is an unusual day in aviation in Charlotte County, Florida. Bordering Sarasota County's south line, the county was still a largely rural swatch of humidity and palmetto groves – as much of Florida started out.

Noted in those days for bankrupt land projects planned by developers who had given up before their goldmine produced a single gold nugget, all that was left for their effort was a maze of paved roads, sprouting weeds within their cracks. That was how West Rotonda looked from a low-flying propeller plane flying above.

The twin-engine Lockheed Lodestar, a workhorse cargo plane from World War II, rumbled above the circular land development with the appearance below of a giant ferris wheel smashed onto the ground. Developers had built streets and canals, but sold almost no homesites, thus debunking the adage, "If you build it, they will come."

Smuggler's Paradise

Placida and its surrounding area, including nearby North Port, in 1974 contains dozens of miles of crisscrossing roads without a car in sight, and with no lights visible in any direction at night.

It's a perfect description of a smuggler's paradise.

The pilot of the Lodestar, as he begins his descent without lights, doesn't see the power lines running alongside Gasparilla Road, which he uses as his landing strip. The propellers become entangled in the power lines. Only a quarter-mile short of the runway, the pilot crash-lands. Two men free themselves from the plane and take off willy-nilly on foot.

Nineteen US Customs Agents called to the scene – an extraordinary number in one area at that time – flood into Charlotte County, assisted by other law enforcement teams. The police dragnet trudges through the woods and wetlands of the peninsula created by the Myakka River to the east, as it flows into Gasparilla Sound, a sheltered body of water wrapping itself around the land from its western border.

Mosquitoes buzz around the search teams for almost six hours. Then, at last, in a palmetto field six miles north of the wreck, an excited searcher cries out for assistance.

One man, at first suspected of being the downed pilot, is spotted at around eleven A.M., crouched, well hidden inside the scrawny brush. He gives his name as William E. "Billy" Klein, Jr., originally from Darien, Connecticut, currently living in Miami Beach.

"What about my partner?" Billy asks officers. "Have you found the pilot? Is he okay?"

The Sheriff's Office deputies have seen no sign of another man, especially one described as a "dead ringer for LBJ," the former President who'd died less than a year earlier.

A massive search – the largest in county history anyway – continues until nightfall without success.

LYNDON LOOKALIKE

"He is believed to be about six feet tall, 55-60 years of age, and he resembles [smiling widely now and clearing his throat] ... ahem ... former President Lyndon Baines Johnson."[1]

Reporters will try to keep the hint of a smirk from leaking into their stories, but it is hard not to believe that Billy Klein, even as he is being handcuffed and stuffed into the sheriff's vehicle, isn't somehow making fun of the Charlotte County Sheriff's Department's Southern Sheriff. Many officials are still a mite touchy and self-conscious about, maybe, coming off too much like Andy of Mayberry.

Texas-born Capt. James Horace Chance, who learned to fly in the U.S. Air Force, is soon identified as the missing pilot. Once caught, he tells authorities he managed to get a ride after fleeing the plane and made his way home.

As the pilot, he would have known who would be picking up the load. Whoever it was – most likely from Boca Grande or Englewood – must have observed the crash from the agreed point of delivery.

Deputies clamber inside the downed plane. Instead of the pilot's body they find 38 burlap bags, each containing what will weigh in as 60 pounds of marijuana – more than a ton in all of what the Sheriff tells reporters is "the illegal weed."[2]

It is estimated the cargo has a street value of over $1 million dollars, huge for those days. Investigators also find the Lodestar's registration records on board, noting that the plane belongs to Florida Airways International – known by the acronym FLAIR – already a familiar name to reporters.

The missing pilot, Captain J.H. Chance, had flown for both Florida Atlantic and Florida Airways for at least ten years. It was a no-brainer for the Charlotte County Sheriff to issue an all points bulletin for, not only Chance, but also for Kenneth G. Burnstine – the Big Kahuna of America's first big national drug ring.

Kenneth Burnstine may have been America's first truly international drug trafficker, who, until his death in 1976 was a linchpin of clandestine activity, organized crime, and financial fraud from Sarasota to Fort Lauderdale, Florida and even farther south. But he was much more than that.

Sunday's newspapers make the connection between the plane that crashed on Florida's southwest coast and Kenneth G. Burnstine of Fort Lauderdale – on the state's southeastern coast. Burnstine, back home, was having a different kind of crisis that weekend, as we will see.

"Trespassers Will Be Eaten"

Three-year-old Ryan Murphy was playing peacefully on the lawn of his parents' home in Fort Lauderdale on Saturday, January 12. It was near dusk, and fashionable Middle Road Drive was enjoying the cocktail hour. The street was empty.

Across the street sits Kenneth Burnstine's estate, surrounded by a five-foot wall, resembling a fortress. Inside the fortification lives Sonia, a lioness, who has also been playfully romping around in the Burnstine back yard with 17-year-old Gary Pearce, Burnstine's stepson.

Gary made a huge mistake. He went inside the house for only a minute, but it was long enough. Sonia found herself alone, and bored. Observing the wall, she takes a long, effortless leap, and she's over it. Swiftly, silently, the lioness crosses the street. Glimpsing young Ryan, she pounces, clamping her jaws around his delicate young neck, holding him in a vise-like grip.[3]

Todd Murphy, Ryan's seven-year-old brother, seeing a lion, begins to scream, and the boys' father, Terry Murphy, hears the shouts from within the house and comes running.

By the time Terry arrived, Sonia, the 130-pound lioness, was shaking her victim. Blood was flowing from the neck wounds caused by her long, sharp teeth. Desperately, the father grabbed the animal by the jaws, trying to pull them apart, no thought at all for his own safety.

The screams reverberated back to the Burnstine home, where Gary Pearce heard the calls for help and came running with Sonia's leash in one hand and a whip in the other. As Gary beat the lioness across the body, she was distracted long enough for Terry Murphy to pull her jaws apart.

Ryan was freed and soon transported to nearby Holy Cross Hospital, where a doctor said the lion's teeth missed his carotid artery by only a couple of millimeters.

"If the animal had struck there, the child would be dead," the doctor told the distraught Murphy family. He was fortunate to have only a 6-inch scar.[4]

Later that evening, as curious neighbors rubbernecked back and forth down Middle River Drive, they undoubtedly noticed the electronically operated gates, spotlights, and attack dogs within the compound, and a prominently displayed sign: *TRESPASSERS WILL BE EATEN.*

Kenneth Burnstine was then America's premier drug smuggler, making millions by illegally smuggling drugs into Florida. At the same time, he was trying to build Florida Airways International, Inc. (called FLAIR for short). He had already failed by then to get Florida Atlantic Airways (also called FLAIR) the contract to fly from Fort Lauderdale to the Bahamas. Trying to bribe a lame duck Congressman from Coney Island hadn't been much use.[5]

Only three days earlier, a FLAIR-owned plane had crashed near Placida on Florida's West Coast with 2,300 lbs. of marijuana on board, and a pilot employed by Burnstine had been arrested.

When finally contacted, Burnstine, like any other narcissist would do, blamed the victim.

"Apparently, what happened – and this happens with any kind of wild animal – something upset her [Sonia, the lioness]. She may have heard the boy's tricycle clanking, and that may have upset her, and she went after it."[6]

SURVEILLANCE AFTER THE CHARLOTTE COUNTY CRASH

Less than two weeks after the sheriff had put out his APB for pilot Chance and plane-owner Burnstine, Detective Lenny Olivieri of Fort Lauderdale's organized crime division began monitoring Burnstine's frequent haunts, places like the Banana Boat Lounge and Sneaky Pete's Restaurant, also known to be LCN (La Cosa Nostra) hangouts, Olivieri noted.

When I contacted him many years later, Lenny, as he asked me to call him, didn't recall Burnstine. "There had been so many of those guys…," he told me, trailing off while trying to bring the past back to his aging brain. His notes, however, were preserved and described Burnstine's network in detail.[6]

Photos of Burnstine didn't resemble my image of a drug lord. But there were plenty of other hints. For one thing, he owned an 18-carat gold diamond-studded cocaine sniffer in the voluptuous shape of a naked woman. "The precious gems are in the appropriate places, anatomically-speaking," he was quoted by "true"-crime writer Ron Peterson Jr., author of a book about drug smuggler Wally Thrasher.[7]

Peterson, not one to cite sources, also described the inside of the mansion, from which Sonia the lioness had escaped:

> Burnstine's ostentatious taste was also on display at his castle-like 7,000 square foot mansion on the Intracoastal Waterway, at 2101 Middle River Drive, in Lauderdale. In his oak-paneled library, a button slid a wall of books away – James Bond style – to reveal a fully-equipped shooting range and an assortment of pistols, rifles and other weapons hanging on the wall, ready to shoot.[8]

Kenny had joined the Marine Corps after finishing college, the same month the Korean War ended. The cold war, however, was still ongoing. After a year of high-level intelligence training in California and Quantico, he shipped out to Atsugi's Mag-11 top-secret base in Japan in September 1955. He remained there until only weeks before another Marine, Lee Harvey Oswald, showed up in his place.

He returned from Japan to marry Ann Mitchell from a wealthy Jewish family in Mobile, Alabama, where he began his post-Marines career working for an affiliate of his wife's family's company, the Mitchell Corp.

The couple moved to Fort Lauderdale before 1961 to combine the real estate expertise he'd learned from Ann's brothers with a nonstop social life, filled with airplanes, boats and his local temple where Meyer Lansky's henchmen attended their own grandsons' bar mitzvahs.

As a Marine reservist with a specialty in counterfeit currency, Kenny was called up for a special and very secret assignment only a year after the move. Mario Garcia Kohly, a Cuban who had fled after Castro's takeover, claimed he would be the next leader of Cuba once a highly classified operation to flood Cuba with $50 million in counterfeit 50-peso notes was implemented.[9]

What Kohly didn't know was that the plan would be scrapped because the Bay of Pigs operation was pulled, and Allen Dulles fired. Robert D. Morrow spearheaded the destabilization effort and later wrote a book about it, claiming to have been assisted by an unnamed CIA agent.[10]

That agent may well have been Kenny Burnstine. The CIA, of course, denied any involvement in the failed attempt to bankrupt Cuba's economy or in fomenting the insurrection itself.

Plausible deniability is a euphemism for lying. When the government lies to the people it represents, it effectively renders truth obsolete.

Kenny returned to Fort Lauderdale from that adventure with his reputation still intact. But within a couple of years things gradually began to change quite drastically.

TRAINED IN COUNTERFEIT CURRENCY AT ATSUGI

Kenneth Gordon Burnstine grew up in Chicago, and he already had two degrees, including an MBA from Northwestern, before he joined the Marine Corps in July 1953 during the Korean War. His duty assignments record indicates that a year after entering basic training, he was sent to Quantico, Virginia, for six months. From Virginia, he went to California's El Toro for three months, then was based in San Francisco for various types of intelligence training for six months. He was also in MAG 11, a Marine aviation unit sent to Atsugi, Japan in September 1955, where elements of MAG 11 actively participated in air operations against North Korean and Chinese Communist forces.

Author Jack Swike was at Marine Base Atsugi in Japan the same year, where he knew two Marines, Lee Harvey Oswald and Kenneth G. Burnstine, during his tour. He wrote, however, that he was sandwiched in between the two, and they could not have run into each other there. But it was obvious each was being groomed by someone for something big.

Burnstine returned to the States in April 1956, assigned to Glenview, Illinois, MCRRD – 9th Marine Corps District, based out of Naval Station Great Lakes, Illinois – the same base where George H. W. Bush had qualified for aircraft carrier landings. As WWII closed, Glenview changed from the primary air training base to the Naval Air Reserve Training Command, including Marine Corps reservists, until 1973.[11]

Kenneth married Ann Mitchell, daughter of Joseph and Rebecca Mitchell, and settled for a time in Mobile, Alabama, working at their family business.

KENANN GRAND OPENING IN 1964

Kenny and Ann attained immortality of a sort by naming the first-round office building in Florida the Kenann Building using the first letters of their first names. The building's occupants laughingly boasted they could never be cornered there. The grand opening in 1964 of the Jetson-style office building was a social event in itself and led to bigger and ever more dangerous enterprises for Kenny.

Starting with the affair he had in 1965 with his secretary, Sue Guilbert Pearce, Gary's mom, who in 1954 had been one of the first Rockettes (then called Roxyettes) at Rockefeller Center in Manhattan.[11]

A year after Kenny and Sue, or Suzy, as he called her, were married, Puerto Rico tried to extradite Kenny for grand larceny – alleging he'd stolen a check amounting to $156,000 payable to Talcott InterAmerican Corp. The details were murky.

A few months later Kenny found himself standing trial in Florida for firing gunshots into a car and wounding a man named Thomas Russo. After that everything went silent for a while.

HAD PROTECTION BEEN ARRANGED?

Burnstine became a partner in a company called Karol Investments with Michael J. Zorovich, who had set the company up in 1969. But there a number of other companies as well. Karol owned the plane that crashed in Charlotte County, subject to a long-term lease to FLAIR. But Zorovich had left the scene in the summer of 1973 while taking off from Chubb Cay in the Bahamas. The body of his young copilot, Quentin Bunn, was found.[12] Zorovich was still missing.

By 1974 almost everyone in law enforcement – to say nothing of the press and public – knew Burnside was bringing in marijuana on a regular basis but could do nothing about it. Even when his planes crashed, there was no proof the jaunty little man with the straight back and furrowed brow had anything to do with it. People were always renting, or stealing, his planes for unlawful purposes, he insisted.

> "I liken it to Hertz renting a car to a bank robber," he said when questioned about his application to operate Florida Airways International – a charter and leasing firm at Fort Lauderdale's Executive Airport. In an interview with the *Miami Herald,* he asked a reporter: "Do you think I am going to run a smuggling operation with planes registered to companies of which I am the president? What Am I? Stupid?"[12]

It was a game that Burnstine enjoyed. "It's sort of funny," he admitted to the reporter. "I can just see these cats in the tower jumping around and running to the telephone every time I climb into a plane."[13]

DISAPPEARED WITHOUT A TRACE

Legally speaking, the actual owner of the plane is Karol Investment Corporation, created in Florida in 1969 by Michael J. Zorovich, its first president. Karol owned a number of World War II Lodestar planes which it "leased" to Florida Airways International (FLAIR), a chartering airline.

Zorovich himself had disappeared the previous summer in Chub Cay in the Bahamas, an incident which did not make the front page of American papers. Watergate hearings were distracting the nation from the new drug smuggling phenomenon. But Burnstine, pictured standing proudly in front of his twin prop plane, got a big spread in the *Miami Herald* on July 2, 1973 more than a month following his partner's crash.

The body found at Chub Cay – floating near the crashed plane – was that of a man recently hired as a copilot for Zorovich, and it was ringed by 240 pounds of marijuana. Strangely, it was only a fraction of the ton and a half of weed that had been loaded aboard the modified Lockheed Lodestar N620S when it took off.

Zorovich was declared dead though no trace of his body was ever found. There were, of course, lots of questions, especially from insurance investigators.

Whoever did the paperwork for Karol Investments soon amended its corporate documents, replacing Zorovich's name with that of Kenneth G. Burnstine as the top officer. George J. Schirrman, a Fort Lauderdale real estate broker who was also an officer of Armament Leasing Corporation of America with Burnstine beginning late in 1970, was also added to Karol documents.

The leasing arrangement allowed the company's officials to stay out of jail for years, the same way my old "friend" Wally Hilliard managed to do, by simply giving one of three unprovable excuses for why he was not responsible for the plane's illegal cargo.

I can remember them by using the acronym LBS for "lying bull shit."

L – smugglers LEASED the plane.

B – smugglers BORROWED the plane.

S – smugglers STOLE the plane. In each instance the plane they owned wasn't responsible for what the smugglers did.

See how easy that is.

I don't know nuthin' 'bout nuthin', man!

PUBLIC RELATIONS COUP AND *THE FRENCH CONNECTION*

None of what was happening was an accident. Just as Barry Seal would later be merely a small cog in a much bigger strategy, so was legitimate businessman Kenny Burnstine coopted into something larger than himself.

It was a public relations operation staged from the get-go, most likely by Burnstine's superiors in the Marine Corps. But that's just a wild guess.

Another PR coup, staged back in 1961, was dredged up by the CIA, which wanted to control the new drugs policy being planned after Dick Nixon's election in 1968. The plan included Harvard grad and Air Force veteran Robert (Robin) L. Moore, Jr., whose father was part owner of the Sheraton Hotel chain. Robin was hired by his dad to handle the hotel's PR. Sheraton Hotels had also been involved a conspiracy of sorts to host the Republican convention in 1972 during the time the CIA was planning to support Augusto Pinochet's 1973 coup in Chile. Records can now be viewed at the Nixon Presidential Library's website.

From one tiny arrest reported in the *New York Daily News*' March 1961 edition – designed to hype the careers of Harry J. Anslinger, Deputy Chief Inspector Edward F. Carey, and George Gaffney – Robin Moore helped create a national media uproar against French drug smugglers.

Back in 1961 the three narcotics agents were praised for cracking down on heroin supply to such an extent that it "ruptured the heroin pipeline all the way back to the Orient."[14]

Crediting "wolfpack" teams like the "international ten-strike scored by national and local narcotics agents, cooperating with French police last October," the Daily News, explained that New York's heroin supply had dried up because of the bust of "a gigantic ring that used diplomatic couriers to smuggle heroin into the country."[15]

On the same inside page of the *Daily News*, in a separate story, appeared the names of two detectives, Edward Egan and Salvatore Grosso, who'd managed to arrest one "dope-starved addict," almost by accident.[16]

Moore blew the story up in 1969 into a "non-fiction" novel called *The French Connection*, made into a 1971 movie, just in time to assist the White House with the smoke and mirrors needed to hide the new government policy in the works – creation of the Drug Enforcement Agency (DEA).

In 2013 co-author Linda Minor read Henrik Kruger's book, *The Great Heroin Coup*, then made a clumsy attempt at her blog to reveal how Nixon's team accomplished their plan.[17]

Publisher, Trine Day, also realized the importance of the book and reprinted the Danish author's translated book in the U.S. in 2015.[18]

The history of the DEA that today appears online at its website is spelled out for us, while purposefully omitting to mention some essential facts, as follows:

> By the early 1970s, drug use had not yet reached its all-time peak, but the problem was sufficiently serious to warrant a serious response. Consequently, the Drug Enforcement Administration (DEA) was created in 1973 to deal with America's growing drug problem.
>
> At that time, the well-organized international drug trafficking syndicates headquartered in Colombia and Mexico had not yet assumed their place on the world stage as the preeminent drug suppliers. All of the heroin and cocaine, and most of the marijuana that entered the U.S. was being trafficked by lesser international drug dealers who had targeted cities and towns within the nation.[19]

This historian is simply saying: Once the DEA was created in 1973, the U.S. drug problem escalated from a minor one to a well-organized one. Right?

Remember the pilot who started off our chapter with the crash in Charlotte County? Well, the Sheriff became one of the first locals to call in Nixon's newly created Drug Enforcement Administration (DEA) for a more extensive investigation.

Only one year prior to the Charlotte County crash, the airline FLAIR had been profiled in the *Miami Herald*, complete with a three-column-wide picture of Burnstine lighting a cigar. His story at the time was the same one that would soon become all too familiar – the airports where he kept his planes were often stolen by crackers who wanted to get into smuggling, and though he complained to airport owners, they had never upped their security.

Five years before Barry Seal got caught in Honduras smuggling 40 kilos of cocaine – an unheard-of amount in late 1979 – Burnstine was already famous. Burnstine had already negotiated a deal committing him to import just under a billion-dollars-worth ($900 million!) of cocaine over the length of his contract.

For me it was like knowing Apple helped create the market for personal computers, but not knowing about Steve Wozniak or Steve Jobs.

SEEING THE WRITING ON THE WALL

Late in 1974, Burnstine decided he was becoming too famous. His marriage to Sue, whom he had called Suzy Q and named his favorite plane after, was starting to break up after five years. He sent her ahead of him with a million dollars to find them a new home in California, an island in Newport Beach.

Meanwhile his pilots began to fly in marijuana from Colombia. The markets in Jamaica and the Bahamas had been largely closed by authorities. A group of New Yorkers contracted to take all he could deliver, and they added a new gimmick to the transportation machinery. The planes would land near Sanford in central Florida, the southern terminus of the Auto-Train, which carries tourists and their cars to Florida from the eastern seaboard.

Instead of making the long haul north by truck, the New Yorkers merely loaded it in cars and put the cars on the train. Everything went north together: smugglers, cars, and marijuana, with no likelihood of inspection. No need to smear the cars with crushed pineapple to kill the odor of the pungent weed. It was fast and convenient, but Burnstine felt the buyers tried to take advantage of his absence while he lived in California. After only a few months, he terminated that deal.

THINGS GO BETTER WITH COKE, HE DECIDED

The market for cocaine had grown tremendously; the profit margin was much greater; the risk potential much less. One could make fewer trips and not have to worry about an overloaded plane. The advantages were obvious. The only problem was to make connection!

And now Burnstine's luck deserted him.

Billy Klein, the Charlotte County copilot busted in January 1974, contacted a well-known drug smuggler who'd been turned into "a confidential informant (CI)." A snitch. After talking with Klein, the CI reported to authorities that Burnstine's organization was moving into cocaine.

Who would be the Mexican connection? The snitch was told to pass on a name to Burnstine in Mexico. Special Agent Arthur Sedillo was dispatched to Vera Cruz to play the part. Klein also showed up at the meet where Sedillo convinced him that he had access to unlimited supplies of cocaine. More coke than Scarface.

Excited when Billy Klein gave him the false skinny, Burnstine decided to investigate personally. He showed up in Vera Cruz, walked into Sedillo's hotel room, and introduced himself as the "big boss."

Perfect! Could you smile for this camera over here?

All went well. When Burnstine told him what he wanted, Sedillo didn't blink. The meeting ended with hearty good-byes; everybody was happy. Sedillo said he liked Burnstine's Guayabera shirt. Burnstine peeled it off and said, "it's yours." It was later introduced into evidence at Burnstine's trial.

A federal grand jury in Miami secretly indicted Burnstine and Klein for conspiracy in December 1974. Burnstine was arrested at his new home on Balboa Island in Newport Beach. Luckily, although his wife Susie had just left him, his millionaire lifestyle had attracted an even younger babe.

The trial was set in Miami for February 1975. The Assistant U.S. Attorney was Karen L. Atkinson, who during her career would deal with many CIA-connected drug smugglers – including the notorious Gerald Patrick Hemming.

Burnstine was convicted and sentenced to seven years in prison. Trial over, he told everyone he was talking to prosecutors. He wouldn't go into witness protection. No living under another name. He already had a name.

"He was the most optimistic man I ever met," said the smuggler.

THE BIGGEST SNITCH SINCE JOE VALACHI"

Among those Burnstine was fingering to "work off his beef," was everyone from Mitch WerBell III, the notorious arms dealer, Cleveland Mob boss John Nardi, a beat cop in Deerfield Beach, Florida, and an insurance company executive in Ohio. All were soon charged with trading MAC-10 weapon's for marijuana.

The close associates and business partners of Ken Burnstine almost scream "Secret Team," as L. Fletcher Prouty called it. Later they would just be called "the boys."

Mitchell Livingston WerBell III was a genius in explosives. He invented some strange devices and manufactured them in Powder Springs, Georgia, a name that makes you think there's probably a story there.

Like Barry Seal, he was described as a "a soldier of fortune," as if that meant anything. And because some of his tales of high adventure seemed almost intended as jokes, investigators found it difficult to separate fact from fiction.

But Mitch wasn't hard to suss out.

He served in the old OSS in World War II. That was where he met "Three-fingered Louie," as he dubbed Lucien Conein, an association which continued after the war, when WerBell, who'd grown up in Philadelphia, moved to Georgia. It picked up again as WerBell became an arms dealer of renown.

Conein had been picked as early as 1970 to run the new Special Operations Branch of the DEA – as part of Nixon's "War on Drugs."

Bernie Spindel and the Safe House

Once chosen, Conein set up a "safe house" for his crew in a two-story apartment at 1028 Connecticut Avenue N.W. in Washington, provided by his buddy Mitch WerBell who'd recently bought the B.R. Fox Company that leased the facilities.

B.R. Fox specialized in manufacturing exotic assassination devices: exploding telephones, flashlights, and cameras, all with triggering mechanisms set to time, movement, light, or sound.

Senator Lowell Weicker created a small sensation when he asked, in a public hearing, if Conein was offered B.R. Fox's unusual inventory of devices to use against drug smugglers. Conein admitted he'd been tempted. But his real interest was in eavesdropping devices the company also produced. In a word, bugs.

Spindel had been featured in *Life* magazine in 1966, following his acquittal with Jimmy Hoffa for illegal wiretapping, and before his conviction in 1969 of spying on the wife of Meyer Lansky's unsuccessful competitor, Huntington Hartford in the Bahamas. Poor Bernie Fox died at only 48 after suffering a heart attack.

It was the stress that did him in. He left his wife, formerly Barbara Fox, with seven children to support. Fortunately for her, everyone knew Bernie. All his old associates were bidding for the business. She sold the whole business, including equipment, to WerBell, as a subsidiary to his own company that made gun silencers.

WerBell was also tight with Robert Vesco, a fugitive financier. But it was his association with Kenny Burnstine that was his immediate problem.

Burnstine, while wearing a hidden wire, had introduced WerBell to DEA undercover agents and also to Cleveland Mob Boss John Nardi. Indictments soon followed.

Big Ball's in Cowtown

The trial was set for August 25, 1976, with Burnstine to be the star witness for the prosecution. Pre-trial matters began months earlier, with WerBell hiring Edwin Marger, a criminal attorney from Miami who'd specialized in drug cases long before he relocated to Atlanta around 1968.

Marger owned Haiti Airlines and had often flown Burnstine to Haiti. They were friends, but, despite that fact, WerBell wanted Marger to be his attorney. He waived the conflict of interest.

Marger was also known for having *grandes cojones*, his ability to subpoena as witnesses the likes of U.S. Presidents and Directors of the CIA. He had done that previously in 1966 as attorney for an international group of pilots who'd formed a CIA proprietary in Buffalo, New York.

They bought refurbished war planes and resold them to countries engaged in "nation building," i.e., fighting "communism" and other enemies of the western democracies. In that case it was Portugal, where Marger subpoenaed Richard Helms and Richard Bissell, the two top men in the CIA, for whom the defendants claimed to have been authorized to sell the planes without export licenses approved through the Department of State.

If the truth be known, it was that delicate portion of Marger's anatomy that WerBell believed could be useful to him should the CIA ever use and try to disavow him. He'd been right to be suspicious. But he didn't stop with suspicion. He took action.

Despite his new-found reputation as a dangerous snitch, Burnstine decided to race his P-51 at the Mojave Air Races, in Antelope Valley north of Los Angeles. In mid-June, he had a couple of months before his scheduled testimony as star witness.

Burnstine was not only an avid air racer, but a successful one. He won the Reno Air Race in 1974 in Suzy Q. Now, he wanted to add the cup at Mojave. Or maybe, what he really wanted was to take his mind off the upcoming trial.

He flew one of his two P-51 Mustangs into Mojave. Each plane had set him back almost $100,000. Maybe flying the Suzy Q, named after the wife who had so recently left him, created bad mojo.

He had flown it when he won Reno, and he trusted the plane. Burnstine told the tower he was going to take a spin around the course, usual practice for arriving pilots. He dropped down from eight thousand feet and went around the first pylon, and then went into a "split S" roll, a beautiful maneuver supposed to terminate at three thousand feet. Something went wrong.

When Burnstine kicked the rudder to bring the plane out of the roll, it didn't respond. The plane rolled into a forty-five-degree angle while heading straight down into the Mojave Desert two miles from the airport, where it blew apart and disintegrated.

Had the plane malfunctioned? Been sabotaged? Witnesses on the scene ruled out pilot error. An FBI Special Agent said suicide was "unthinkable."

One rumor persisted – that all they found of Burnstine was a thumb. A right thumb. "There was speculation that Kenny cut off his thumb and then bailed out before the crash," said the Special Agent. "But there was no evidence whatsoever to support the theory. Besides, he wasn't the type to cut off his thumb."

Gaeton Fonzi only trusted one thing. Evidence. So he flew out west and looked at the file

"Kenneth Burnstine is Still Dead."

Gaeton Fonzi at the time was a journalist who worked at a magazine called *Gold Coast* and, after investigating, concluded Burnstine had been murdered to prevent his testimony to validate the recording he had made.

"Burnstine was known to indulge his show-off tendencies upon takeoff by rolling his plane as soon as he gained enough altitude. When he did so that day, he cried out suddenly and his plane plunged out of control into the ground," writes Bernard McCormick, a blogger, who was once Fonzi's partner at the magazine.[20]

"One theory was that a motion-activated bomb went off as soon as he started his maneuver. That bomb would burn out and leave no trace behind. His plane had been untended the night before and someone could have planted the bomb without being seen."

Now in August, all hope of convicting WerBell and his Mafia friends died in the wreckage of Burnstine's P-51 Mustang.

Tape recordings and video of meetings between Burnstine and the defendants could no longer be introduced, the Justice Department admitted. But the trial would be held on schedule notwithstanding the absence of the chief witness.

WerBell's defense was simple, if not quite accurate: He claimed to be a government agent working for Conein. All his contacts with drug smugglers were attempts to entrap them. Marger backed up the defense by asking the judge to issue a subpoena to Richard Nixon to testify on his behalf.

The judge's gaze moved down Marger's visage – from head, chest, waist, and below – confirming his reputation. *Grandes cojones* indeed. Then he set the subpoena aside, just in case, suggesting perhaps Egil Krogh and Lucien Conein might suffice. He postponed his ruling about calling the disgraced former President until later in the trial.

It would depend on how dynamic a case the prosecution could present now that Burnstine was dead.

Egil "Bud" Krogh testified that to his knowledge WerBell had not been employed by any federal agency. But he admitted he didn't know all of Conein's people.

On the stand, WerBell cheerfully admitted that, if Conein was asked to testify – which he never was – he would deny their relationship.

"Some things have to be denied," he said later.

Odd fact: the Asst. U.S. Attorney prosecuting was the same Karen Atkinson that Burnstine had flirted with throughout his own trial. But this time she lost. All the defendants were guilty, but these were acquitted.

The next day Conein suffered a stroke but lived.

Defendant John Nardi returned to Cleveland, only to be blown up during "a struggle for control of the rackets." His associate Henry Grecco, gunned down in a "gangland slaying," was scheduled to be a defendant in another smuggling case made by Burnstine the following month.

WerBell returned to Atlanta and got into far-right politics. The country wasn't being run properly, he ranted. Something needed to be done! Maybe Major General John K. Singlaub – reprimanded twice and then fired for criticizing President Jimmy Carter – could help remedy the situation.

In an after-operation critique, a U.S. Customs agent in Tampa named John L. Warr wrote: "The operation confirmed that Air Defense radar coverage of the approaches to Florida is a disgrace."

He stated emphatically, "This situation must be corrected for the purpose of national security, if for no other reason."[21]

In retrospect, the fact that Air Defense radar did not provide coverage of the approaches into Florida, we now know, was not by accident.

But by design.

Endnotes

1 "Authorities Call Off Hunt for Pilot of Pot Laden Plane," *Miami Herald*, 13 Jan 1974, Page 101.

2 Mike Fuery, "Bail Raised to $200,000 in Narcotics Case," *Charlotte News-Press*, Jan 13, 1974, Page 1

3 Barbara Greenberg, "Pet Lioness leaps wall, mauls Lauderdale boy," *Fort Lauderdale News*, Jan 13, 1974 Page 6

4 Karen Heller, "Even Without the Caged Pet Lioness, Kenneth Burnstine Home a Curiosity," *Miami Herald*, Jan 13, 1974, Page 132. Also see AP, the *Edwardsville Intelligencer*, Jan 14, 1974, Page 2.

5 "U.S. Indicts Representative for bribery," *Pensacola News Journal*, Jul 13, 1973, Page 20.

6 Jim Trotter, "3-year-old boy mauled by neighbor's pet lion," *Miami Herald*, Jan 13, 1974, Page 132NARA Record Number: 180-10112-10049. Released in 1992 under "John F. Kennedy Assassination Review Act." https://www.maryferrell.org/showDoc.html?docId=197073#relPageId=1&search=olivieri

7 Ron Peterson, Jr., *Chasing the Squirrel,* iUniverse (May 27, 2020)

8 Ibid.

9 Mario Kohly worked with CIA on the counterfeiting: https://spartacus-educational.com/JFKkohly.htm. Robert D. Morrow was also involved with the CIA operation: https://spartacus-educational.com/JFKmorrow.htm. See also declassified files at https://www.fordlibrarymuseum.gov/library/document/0014/1075850.pdf

10 Robert D. Morrow, *First Hand Knowledge: How I Participated in the Cia-Mafia Murder of President Kennedy*, S.P.I. Books (August 1, 1992).

11 Military information obtained through Ancestry.com records.

12 "Romance at the Fair," Picture of Sue Guilbert and Marcus Pearce. https://www.newspapers.com/article/the-oneonta-star-sue-guilbert-pearce-1/146597113/

12 Wayne Thomis, "Crash Victim Promised Large Sum, Kin Reports," *Fort Lauderdale News*, May 23, 1973 Page 21. https://www.newspapers.com/article/fort-lauderdale-news-chubb-key-crashbur/146599154/

13 Ibid.

14 William Federici and Loren Craft, "There's a Panic on Junkie St.," *New York Daily News*, Mar 20, 1961, Page 2.

15 Ibid. p. 24.

16 Leeds Moberley, "Dope-Starved, He Battles Cops; Shot," *New York Daily News*, March 20, p. 24.

17 https://quixoticjoust.blogspot.com/2013/12/the-great-heroin-coup-chapter-13.html

18 Henrik Krüger, Jerry Meldon, *The Great Heroin Coup: Drugs, Intelligence & International Fascism*, Trine Day LLC Copyright © 2015

19 https://www.dea.gov/sites/default/files/2018-07/1970-1975%20p%2030-39.pdf

20 https://www.mccormick-place.com/

21 Penny Lernoux, *In Banks We Trust*.

CHAPTER TWENTY-SIX

A SWANK RESORT FOR "SWELLS"

A nob can be a swell if he chooses, i.e., if he will spend the money; but for his social existence this is unnecessary. A nob is like a poet – nascitur non fit; not so a swell – he creates himself.
—Ward McAllister, *Society As I Have Found It*

T he swank Boca Grande Resort on Gasparilla Island, 30 miles south of Sarasota, has long been a haunt of what used to be called "the swells," a term created by Ward McAllister, the Gilded Age purveyor of such jargon. The "nobs," he said are made up of old (inherited) money and the swells of the new vintage. Combining the two wealthy classes gives us the "snobs," who look down their noses at the rest of us.

Charlotte County takes in the north half of Gasparilla Island, which includes a quaint village called Boca Grande. Punta Gorda on the mainland, just across the bay, is the only incorporated city in the county and is the county seat where the Sheriff's Office is located. There are several larger unincorporated communities also, but half or more of the land within the county is composed of swamp – the Babcock Ranch – preserved by a Pittsburgh millionaire's descendants.

Midway between Fort Myers and Sarasota, lies an island on which is situated the Gasparilla Inn, which "played host to a who's who of early 20th century American wealth and power, including J.P. Morgan, Henry du Pont (whose heirs now own the resort), Henry Ford and others," according to one travel website.

J. P. Morgan had, in fact, died at the inn in 1913. Among those "unnamed heirs" of du Ponts were Henry F. du Pont, his sister Louise du Pont Crowninshield and a cousin, Isabella Mathieu du Pont Sharp, owners of the first winter residences at Boca Grande in the 1920s. It was their winter getaway from the Brandywine in Delaware – a quiet haven where they met with Morgan's other banking clients for decades. By 1961, they'd mostly died away. Their kids were grown – with minds still preoccupied with war and communism – looking for a base perhaps from which to spy on Fidel Castro's Cuba.

HAVEN FOR J.P. MORGAN INTERESTS

Isabella du Pont Sharp's sons Bayard and H. Rodney Sharp, Jr. bought the Gasparilla Inn in 1961 as part of an investment group, which also acquired hundreds of acres surrounding the island. The seller was the Barron G. Collier Estate, which had owned virtually all of Collier County for decades by then.

Bayard Sharp had been a squash champ during college in 1930, became a lieutenant commander in the Navy during World War II, and a Republican political activist his remaining years. The obit issued by the Associated Press says he "donated 113 acres and a mile of beachfront property to create a state park in Florida, where he lived part time and owned the Gasparilla Inn and Cottages, a resort on Gasparilla Island."[1]

"The inn and its cottages became a familiar gathering place for Sharp's family. Bayard and Mary Sharp's daughter, Sarah, and her husband, William S. Farish, often stayed at one of the cottages with their four children – Hillary, Mary, Laura and Bill – during spring breaks and for Christmas and Thanksgiving holidays. It was through William Farish, once ambassador to Great Britain, that Sharp met George H.W. Bush, who would soon join the Sharp family in vacationing at Boca Grande," wrote the Sarasota Herald-Tribune after Sharp's death.[2]

When Sarah married William Stamps "Will" Farish III in 1956, Texas oil wealth was combined with the Du Pont Chemical fortune – leading the way for what we were warned about by "Mr. Robinson," Dustin Hoffman's mentor in *The Graduate* – "Plastics!"

Will shared his oil fortune with his late father's sister – Martha Farish, who married Edward Harriman Gerry of New York. W. S. Farish, Sr., was a co-founder of Humble Oil in Houston, the company which began as Humble Oil, then became Standard Oil of New Jersey – and in 1972 – Exxon.

Everyone knows Du Pont began with dynamite, expanded into other chemicals and then created plastic from petroleum. Oil and plastic go together like cookies and milk, a metaphor I never tire of. Or is it a simile?

The Farish oil wealth was not a fortune any snob worthy of his genes would turn up his nose at. Except maybe Democrats in the U.S. Senate's Patent Committee, who accused Standard Oil in 1942 of "trading with the enemy."

Standard Oil back as early as 1927 entered into a partnership with the German I.G. Farben company. During the '30s, as the Nazis gained control of the German government, the agreement was modified to make it easier for control of certain patents covered to be in the hands of the German company. [3]

The patents covered things like synthetic rubber, a process invented in American labs but transferred to I.G. Farben's control.[4]

The Securities and Exchange Commission (SEC) had begun investigating early in 1942 before the U.S. Senate's Patents Committee held hearings the following August to get to the bottom of things.[5]

Standard Oil officials were called as witnesses and tried to say their company had helped the American side. By the end of August, it was clear that was a lie. The SEC completed its case with a consent decree, requiring the patents and other intangibles be turned over in exchange for the SEC dropping its case.

DISGRACE AND DEATH

Farish was devastated and embarrassed. He died within months of his disgrace. Only later would it be revealed that Exxon's partner Farben also manufactured Zyklon-B cyanide tablets, used to gas millions of Jews.

But, as the famous Republican President Calvin Coolidge loved to say, the business of America is, well, business. So, the faux pas was overlooked and quickly forgotten – until it was dredged up again in 1983 by Charles Higham, whose book *Trading with the Enemy*, was excerpted in the *Indianapolis Star*.

ISOLATIONISM – EXCUSE FOR EXCLUDING INFERIOR BLOOD?

Four years earlier had been a much happier time for William Stamps Farish. The oil baron and his wife traveled to Lake Forest, Illinois to watch their only son marry a daughter of the man, Robert E. Wood, who was in the process of creating the first America First Committee – whose members included Henry Ford and Charles Lindbergh.[6]

The Farish-Wood marriage in 1938 added part of Chicago's old retail power to Houston's new oil wealth. As Hitler's forces in Europe were threatening to change the face of Europe, Wood struggled to keep the country out of war while Farish and friends tried to throw their weight on the side of the enemy, Germany.

As Farish's face was spread across newspapers as an example of "trading with the enemy," many in Wood's committee were busy spreading vile anti-Semitic and racist statements.

> It is time to ... build our White ramparts again. This alliance with foreign races means nothing but death to us. It is our turn to guard our heritage from Mongol and Persian and Moor, before we be-

come engulfed in a limitless foreign sea. Our civilization depends on a united strength among ourselves; on strength too great for foreign enemies to challenge; on a Western Wall of race and arms which can hold back either a Genghis Khan or the infiltration of inferior blood; on an English fleet, a German air force, a French army, an American nation, standing together as guardians of our common heritage, sharing strength, dividing influence.[7]

Mary Wood Farish had lived with her husband in Houston since 1938 and had already settled into a new home by the time her husband died in an airplane crash in 1943.

Her son's grandmother, Libbie Rice Farish, was a descendant of the brother of William Marsh Rice – whose death gave life to Rice University. The Rice family has always been synonymous with "Houston Society." It still is.

Mary's second husband, an architect, was the son of investment banker, Hugo V. and Kate Rice Neuhaus. His brothers Joseph Rice and Philip Ross Neuhaus managed the banking firm while Hugo Jr. was busy designing homes for Houston's millionaires.

In 1948 Neuhaus & Co. merged with an investment company founded by Milton R. Underwood, son-in-law of Walter W. Fondren, Sr., one of the nine founders of Humble Oil.[8] With just their familial contacts, this merger pretty much had all of Houston's wealth covered.

HOUSTON ADOPTS POPPY BUSH

Not only did Underwood, Neuhaus manage young Will Farish III's trust estate left by his grandfather and father, but either it or a successor bank, would have a hand in advising George H. W. Bush once he moved from the Permian Basin in West Texas to Houston.

In 1956 it seemed fitting for horse-breeder/capitalist/banker Will Farish III in 1956 to combine his family's assets with those of his bride's mother's inheritance from the du Pont family. The du Ponts had always been encouraged, according to biographer Leonard Mosley, to marry cousins to ensure "honesty of soul and purity of blood."[9]

A reviewer of Mosley's book reported, however, somewhat ironically: "Several generations later, the reigning patriarch was grumbling that 'the thinning' of that pure blood by inbreeding was producing freaks. But the intermarrying cousins," kept marrying each other and "by the 1920's, the close Delaware clan was the richest family in America."[10]

Riches were amassed from two world wars, for which Du Pont factories supplied explosives and gunpowder, thus increasing the family fortune to $250 million by the end of World War I.

What had brought the du Ponts to Boca Grande initially had not been the great tarpon fishing, but the phosphate discovered there. Sarah Sharp's mother, Isabella M. du Pont, a daughter of Lammot du Pont I, was a sister of Pierre Samuel du Pont and Lammot II.

Even after three or four generations in America, the du Ponts still name their sons French names like Pierre, Lammot, and Irénée, so it's almost impossible to keep them all straight.

The Lammot du Pont born in 1831, blasted himself into the next world in a nitroglycerine explosion in 1884. He had eleven children in all, Isabella being the second youngest. She married H. Rodney Sharp, whose family also lived in Delaware.

A decade after her cousin Ethel du Pont married President Roosevelt's son, Franklin Jr. in 1936, however, Isabella died. She only experienced being related to the most powerful man in the country ten years.

Franklin Roosevelt, Jr. divorced cousin Ethel a few months after FDR's death, and Ethel died by suicide a few years later. Wealth is not always what it's cracked up to be.

The du Ponts had spent much of their time and money buying themselves a U.S. President, a Democrat, who had willingly taken their money. But FDR followed his own policies instead of theirs. They felt betrayed, calling him a "traitor to his class." Isabella's sons – H. Rodney, Jr. and Bayard – no doubt still felt the sting years later.

MIXING GENES FOR FUN AND PROFIT

Ethel's cousins and their children – the next generation of du Ponts – would thereafter look in another direction for a President. They did, in fact, make such a discreet transaction that nobody suspected anything for years. But there were clues, visible clues hidden in plain sight, in southwestern Florida.

Will's mother was from Chicago, where her father, retired General Robert Elkington Wood, ran Sears, Roebuck & Co., the retail catalog company.

His first job after leaving the military, however, was as the assistant to the vice president of E. I. du Pont de Nemours Co. Mary Stovall Wood was born in Delaware in 1917, so she already had a connection to the du Pont family.[11] During the construction of the Panama Canal, General

Wood was chief quartermaster – a position often turned into a trope for people who sell goods that "fall off the back of a truck."[12]

We like to think Joseph Heller had General Wood in mind when he created the character, Milo Minderbinder, in *Catch-22*, though others who served as quartermasters fit the bill as well.

Other members of Mary Wood's family had equally impressive marriages. One sister married Calvin H. Fentress, head of the insurance company subsidiary of Sears.

Another sister was the second wife of William H. Mitchell, Sr., the man who actually married Ginevra King – "Daisy Buchanan" in F. Scott Fitzgerald's novel. Mitchell's brother, John J. Mitchell, Jr. was married to Lolita Armour, heir to J. Ogden Armour, Chicago meatpacker.

The year Will Farish married Sarah Sharp – 1956 – was the same year George H. W. Bush arrived in Odessa, Texas to begin his career in oil. Having been through that desolate city, I can only admire George and Barb for lasting as long as they did there.

Bush soon moved to Houston where they hooked up with people closer to their own – I hesitate to say "class" – level of education and status. Coincidentally, around the same time Sarah Sharp Farish's father acquired the Gasparilla Inn, George Bush broke off from his Oklahoma partners (the Liedtke brothers – and set up Zapata Offshore, just after Fidel Castro took over Cuba.

Some have said, without much evidence, that he formed the "offshore" drilling company and operated it as a CIA proprietary, working undercover for Allen Dulles, Director of the CIA. That doesn't say evidence didn't exist, just that they hid it well.

Bush located the Zapata Offshore, Inc. offices in the same Houston building with the Underwood, Neuhaus investment bank, which managed the fortune Will Farish III inherited from his Nazi-leaning grandpa.

Zapata Offshore, as it happens, owned a substantial amount of stock in International Mining & Chemical (IMC) when Bush sold his stock to run for Congress. We were puzzled until we discovered that much of Gasparilla Island after 1913 had been owned by Peter and Robert Bradley, who built the inn and operated it in connection with American Agricultural Chemical Company, the phosphate company they controlled, later acquired by IMC.

Charlotte Harbor Railroad was constructed to transport the mined phosphate from the island to central Florida for processing. In 1930 Barron Gift Collier's corporation bought out the Bradleys. Collier owned over a million acres of land in Charlotte and Lee Counties, and in 1928 he made a deal with the State of Florida. He would complete the Tamiami Trail if his acreage could be cut out of Charlotte County to make a new county. That's how Collier County got its name.

His land included the future city of Naples at that time. Of course, it's only a coincidence Wallace J. Hilliard chose Naples as the place to build his retirement home in 1995, even though the Colliers were known to have allowed Useppa Island, which they owned, to be used by the CIA as a staging ground for the Bay of Pigs.

So much of history can be explained by simply describing how rich people handle their business interests. Would you dare call that a conspiracy?

Bush's Political Donors

By 1966 George Bush had been talked into changing careers – entering politics – to manipulate government oil policy from the inside. After serving two terms as a Congressman from Houston's wealthiest district, in 1970 he risked running for the U.S. Senate seat long held by Texas populist Democrat Ralph Yarborough.

It's possible he made a deal with Texas insurance executive Lloyd Bentsen to run in the Democratic primary, just to make sure, whoever won, big business would be rid of the popular Senator. After Bentsen won in the primary, Bush lost to him in the general election, but Bush soon wormed his way into national politics through his closeness to Richard Nixon and Gerald Ford.

In 1970 by far the largest Bush donor was W. S. Farish III with a $12,000 donation; another $7,000 was coughed up by Robert L. Gerry, Jr., his aunt's brother-in-law. The Gerrys had several marital connections to the family of Averell Harriman – an old Skull and Bones banking partner of Prescott Bush, George's dad. Another Brown Brother Harriman banker, Richard Fisher, would be cast as a fake Democrat in 1993 when Bentsen left his Senate seat to be Bill Clinton's Secretary of the Treasury.

In the special election held to replace Bentsen, Bush's people managed to pick all the candidates who ran. It was revealed during the campaign Fisher had never even voted in a Texas election prior to running.

Shenanigans like that help explain how Republicans turned Texas into a Red State. These were George's money men whom most of us knew nothing about. In his biography, *Looking Forward*, George claimed his investors in Zapata were dredged up by Uncle Herbie Walker, but not once did he mention Exxon's Farish and Gerry families or the du Pont Sharp family – who really owned his soul.

By the time George was Ronald Reagan's vice president in 1981, he was in need of a private place to relax with his handlers, away from prying eyes. Florida became that place – exclusive Jupiter Island's Hobe Sound on the eastern shore, where his parents had retired, Will Farish's Gulf Stream mansion in Palm Beach County, and Bayard Sharp's Boca Grande in southwest Florida.

Three points of a golden triangle where tons of drugs a year were entering the USA, protected by someone with power.

Southwest Florida – A CIA Drug Base

Harper Sibley, Jr. stepped into the development of the island in 1978, announcing his plan to open the Boca Grande Club. One of his partners was Lou Chesler's successor in the General Development Corporation, which had acquired thousands of acres around Murdock, Florida, in the 1950s – just before Chesler bowed out to develop a gambling resort in the Bahamas.

Meyer Lansky had been kicked out of Cuba and was planning to move his gambling interests to The Bahamas, so that was where the new action was. The Bahamian Islands became a way point between the source of the drugs and Miami.

In the 1960s we first started seeing P-51's carrying marijuana from the Bahamas, crashing in central and western Florida – places where General Development had been pouring hundreds of thousands of investment dollars.

Just a coincidence, surely.

Carl Lindner, Jr., a Cincinnati developer friend of George Bush, who'd built the Ocean Reef Club at Key Largo, was another of Sibley's partners in Boca Grande Club in 1981, buying out the rest of the stock a decade later.

Pete Brewton, in my opinion, is the best source of information about both Lindner and Sibley, having written about their links to Bush in his classic *The Mafia, CIA and George Bush*.[13]

Like me, Brewton was fascinated by the plethora of drug pilots in Florida, and he paid special attention to a pilot named Jack Raymond DeVoe. What caused DeVoe to stand out was that he "used Miami attorney Lawrence Freeman to launder some of his drug money."[14]

Freeman associated with "CIA operatives and mob figures" Brewton wrote, adding that in 1980 the pilot bought a condo at Lindner's Ocean Reef Club at Key Largo and used the landing strip there "to fly in much of his cocaine from Colombia."[15]

DeVoe was incarcerated in a Memphis federal prison in November 1985 when Florida Department of Law Enforcement (FDLE) interviewed him about his smuggling of cocaine into Lindner's Ocean Reef Club. "DeVoe stated that the majority of the hangars at Ocean Reef were used for drug smuggling for many years and a lot of people knew about it," according to the report they wrote.[16]

Brewton added that "Harper Sibley, the chairman of the board of Ocean Reef Club for Lindner, 'just seemed to tolerate anything that went on at Ocean Reef, legal or illegal.'"[17]

As a result of this investigation, Ocean Reef Club agreed in 1988 to transfer title to 31 acres of land valued at almost a half million dollars to the state of Florida in lieu of having to fight a RICO forfeiture action.

"The probe showed that DeVoe had used about $411,000 in drug profits as a down payment on five lots in the Ocean Reef complex," the Associated Press reported on July 9, 1988, while adding that DeVoe later defaulted on the mortgage and lost the property.[18] Guess it was hard to make the payments when he couldn't use dirty money.

Lawrence Freeman had served as a Judge Advocate General (JAG) in the Air Force for five years before joining Paul Helliwell's law firm in Miami in 1970 – six years before Paul Helliwell's death from emphysema complications.[19] Nixon's pal, Bebe Rebozo, had vouched for him, according to Brewton's research.

While working at Helliwell's firm, Freeman also became a witness in the Bahamian Castle Bank & Trust tax avoidance litigation described in Alan A. Block's 1991 book, *Masters of Paradise*. Jim Drinkhall of the *Wall Street Journal* also wrote about the bank, which had been the target of investigations in 1977 by both the IRS (Project Haven) and the Justice Department.

Drinkhall surmised that the reason the Justice Department backed off from further investigation was "the CIA's argument that pursuit of the Castle Bank would endanger 'national security.' This was involved because that bank, besides its possible use as a haven for tax evaders, was the conduit for millions of dollars earmarked by the CIA for the funding of clandestine operations against Cuba and for other covert intelligence operations directed at countries in Latin America and the Far East. A major tax evasion investigation of the bank probably would have endangered these CIA operations."[20]

Block presumed otherwise. Too many organized crime figures were involved with the offshore banks Helliwell and his associates had set up. Pressure wasn't being applied strictly by intelligence sources. Republican politicians also had their fingers in the pie. In those days income tax rates were still at 70% for income in excess of $200,000, and some wealthy taxpayers were willing to do almost anything to avoid paying that high premium.[21]

HELLIWELL'S BACKGROUND WITH CIA

Paul Helliwell began his life in Brooklyn as the son of an English textile worker from Yorkshire, who came to America in 1904, settling near Pascoag, Rhode Island. He married Nola Harless in 1910. As a school superintendent at Hampton Sydney in Tennessee, Nola left her state for Massachusetts when a man was brought in to replace her.

Lionel Helliwell became a U.S. citizen in 1911, and the couple moved to Brooklyn to be close to the Port where commission merchants and brokers operated. Paul was born in 1914, and Lionel moved his family to an upscale neighborhood in New Jersey.

After WWI, Paul's dad and uncle, and a few other family members moved to Tampa, Florida, where Lionel was hired at the Tampa Port as a Customs inspector. A few years later they moved again to Miami, where the elder Helliwell was promoted to the position of examiner for Customs. Paul had completed an undergraduate degree and was a licensed attorney by 1940.

When the war came, Paul enlisted and quickly rose to the rank of colonel in the U.S. Army's G-2 Intelligence units in Cairo and Bahgdad – the same area where Kermit (Kim) Roosevelt, Jr. was chief of the Office of Strategic Services (OSS). Kim and his friend, Miles Copeland, stationed in Egypt, orchestrated Project FF – the official name for what Miles jokingly dubbed "Fat Fucker," which is what he called King Farouk to his CIA pals. They'd apparently decided duly elected guys in charge of the country constituted a "corrupt political system in Egypt," and that Farouk's "progressive dictatorship" would be "more amenable to American control."[22]

After transferring from G-2 to OSS., Helliwell ended up being Chief of Intelligence in China, with a reputation, according to reporter Jim Drinkhall, for buying information with bars of opium.[23]

Helliwell reputedly met with North Vietnamese leader Ho Chi Minh three times in 1945. The U.S. wanted to provide Ho with weapons to use against Japan, but Ho wouldn't swear he wouldn't use them against the French as well.[24] Consequently, almost 30 years later, the U.S. was still bogged down in fighting Ho's armies.

When the O.S.S. was disbanded, Helliwell was part of the War Department's intelligence unit, from which he retired around 1947.

At that point he set up a Miami law office called Bouvier, Helliwell & Clarke. With a top-secret security clearance, as well as connections to Frank Wisner, Sr., Kim Roosevelt, and Miles Copeland, he was often called upon to do contract work for the Central Intelligence Agency after its formation the same year he "retired."

His first major assignment after the war was to find a way for the CIA to subsidize Claire Chennault's Civil Air Transport, in litigation limbo after a Hong Kong court ruled in 1950 in favor of giving the airline to the Chinese Government. Since the Red Chinese had defeated the U.S.-supported Nationalists, there was a dispute over which China owned the government's assets. The case was decided in favor of the Reds, and then quickly appealed to a British court. CAT's assets were frozen pending reversal of the case, which would not come until late 1952.

Helliwell filed incorporation documents for Sea Supply Corp., the CIA's first proprietary company in December 1950. Within months he would be appointed Thai Consul for the Miami, Florida region.

HELLIWELL'S ROLE AS CHIEF MONEY LAUNDERER

Before the 1952 election, Helliwell hired a young attorney named James Guilmartin to work with him. The red-headed Guilmartin, though previously a Democrat, formed a group of Democrats for Eisenhower. Recently married to the daughter of a Miami insurance man – Kirk Alfred Landon – Guilmartin joined with Helliwell in criss-crossing the state to elect the new Republican President.

Helliwell also became associated with his partner's father-in-law in the insurance business. Helliwell was secretary for American Bankers Insurance Group and American Bankers Life Insurance – both located in the Landon Building at 600 Brickell in Miami. An attorney associated with his law firm, Mary Jane Melrose, was assistant secretary of both, while Helliwell was a director of both.

With Helliwell on the boards sat a man from Utah named George S. Eccles, brother and banking partner of Marriner S. Eccles, who practically ran the Federal Reserve Board from 1934 until 1951.[25]

George ran the brothers' banking empire of "seventeen banks in Utah, Idaho, and Wyoming, and organized the First Security Corporation, believed to be the first multibank holding company, to manage the fifteen banks and a savings and loan institution."[26]

Helliwell was a frequent witness before U.S. Congressional Committees, where we learned American Bankers Insurance used the First Security Corporation, owned by Marriner and George Eccles, for its offshore reinsurance.[27]

It's not surprising Liechtenstein was both Eccles' and Helliwell's preferred jurisdiction. Adnan Khashoggi also based his Triad corporations in Salt Lake City, home to the Morman Eccles brothers, and Khashoggi was early on advised to go to Liechtenstein for his banking.

Coincidence? I wouldn't bet on it.

Money Laundering – From Analog to Digital

It seems almost ironic that Helliwell, while he was so dependent upon the brother of the man given the greatest power over setting up the New Deal's monetary policy, and while he partnered with FDR's "fixer, Tommy "the Cork" Corcoran, he was so adamant about electing a Republican.

Landon, Helliwell, and Guilmartin were the three men given the most credit for Florida's switching from a blue to a red state, years before election returns were broadcast in color.

When Landon died soon after Eisenhower became President, Helliwell continued his work in insurance at American Bankers, which soon merged with other financial services companies.

We would discover decades later, just before American International Group (AIG) imploded in 2008, that, at least a decade prior to its collapse, AIG desperately wanted to acquire AmBank, the nickname of Landon's insurance company. Why?

For What It's Worth, Here's My Take

Let's call pre-2000 finance the Analog Age of Money Laundering. The last 25 years of the 20th century was a transition period, ushering us into a new digital age of technology. Symbolic of that is Hong Kong, which has always been the drugs clearing house, so to speak, for Gangster Planet, starting with the days of the Opium Wars.

When Hong Kong's 99-year lease to Britain ended in July 1997, it marked the end of the British Empire – the end of the treaty that followed the Opium Wars. A treaty negotiated in 1984, however, provided that Hong Kong would continue operating in a capitalist economy, and residents would continue to have rights to speech, press, assembly and religious belief, among others – at least until 2047.[28]

In 1990 a research article published by the U.S. Department of Justice reported that "billions of dollars are being washed in Hong Kong by both local and overseas drug traffickers, to be reinvested eventually throughout the world."[29]

Money launderers were scrambling to take over for whoever was exiting Hong Kong. According to the *New York Times* in 1998:

> The new offer by American International Group [AIG], one of the country's largest insurers, matches the amount offered in a hostile bid by the Cendant Corporation, a leading discount shopping and franchising company – $58 a share, or a total of about $2.7 billion…
>
> Henry R. Silverman, the chief executive of Cendant, said he was still determined to buy American Bankers, which sells credit-related insurance. He said he expected to make his next move in a few days after further evaluating American Bankers.[30]

Cendant came to life only weeks after the British bankers lost their favored role in Hong Kong. Talcott, Inc. was a textile "factor," an industry that "evolved in the U. S. from the old time commission merchants" into a cross between financing companies and service organizations." It grew out of the textile trade, in which Paul Helliwell's British-born father had spent his career.[31]

Textiles was only one big international business, but it was possibly the largest one in the 19th century. Consider the fact that the well-connected Brown Bros. & Co. also began in textiles in Liverpool. It was the training ground for international commerce in those days.

Talcott National Corporation came to be controlled by Herbert R. Silverman after its founder died.[32] Silverman also chaired the finance committee of Helmsley-Spear Inc. – Leona Helmsley's real estate firm – from 1974 until 1990.[33]

Talcott's name changed to Leucadia, a company once linked to Finova Capital, which handled airplane financing for drug pilots like Barry Seal.[34]

The small world of money laundering! Analog style.

Consider this fact: Between 1996 and 2000, almost half the Helmsley properties, for which Silverman had worked, were sold for about $2.5 billion.[35]

Silverman, like Fred Trump, had sent his son to U Penn, but, unlike young Donald J. Trump, Henry R. Silverman went into law instead of finance.[36] He created Cendant in 1998 to acquire Resort Condominiums International (RCI), the first time share business we know of. It began small in 1975 for individual owners of vacation condos to sell segments of time to others.[37]

RCI has dominated the time-share market ever since. It quickly became the ultimate way to launder money through real estate throughout the world. Cendant early on had its eye on Helliwell's AmBank but failed to acquire it when a scandal unraveled in the middle of the bidding war. If you're my age, the scandals of the 1980-2008 era tend to run together like the colors in a tie-dyed shirt. But, as my hippie generation has matured, we've come to realize something pretty profound.

Even if a new industry is not *all* about drugs, it's clearly about *washing the proceeds* derived from illegal drug trafficking.

Finance is the sexier end of the drug trafficking stick, and usually less deadly. Still, we can sympathize with Jason Bateman's "Marty Byrne" character in the Netflix thriller series *Ozark*. The enormous profits made by just one drug lord are so humongous, it seems impossible to cram all the money invested into "legitimate" business, especially with all the competitors trying to take you out.

"Being Connected Means…" – *You Know the Rest*

Paul Helliwell was a model for modern day money launderers who have since WWII operated with government protection. The drugs transported by CIA proprietaries resulted in revenue that had to be laundered, and Helliwell was the lawyer who figured out how to do it. His associates in Sea Supply, and later in the Caribbean area planning the overthrow of President Jacobo Arbenz of Guatemala, included New York attorney Thomas G. Corcoran (one of FDR's "Brain Trust") and the CIA's Frank Wisner.

Paul Helliwell, as everybody should know, was Chief of Special Intelligence in China for OSS during World War II, afterward representing opium-dealing leaders of Thailand. As a Miami lawyer, he also served as counsel for Castle Bank & Trust in The Bahamas, incorporated by associates in his law firm.

Associate, Lawrence Freeman, got indicted for laundering drug money for Jack DeVoe in 1985. "The indictment against Mr. Freeman alleges that he laundered $1.7 million in drug smuggling proceeds from a major drug smuggling organization first broken up by cocaine smuggling arrests in 1984," wrote the *Sun Sentinel* in South Florida. "The organization, we alleged at that time, was headed by Jack DeVoe, who has since been convicted."[38]

A law clerk working for Lawrence Freeman had been named president of a somewhat ephemeral corporation called "Panhandle Coast," which had contracted to purchase land owned by St. Joe Paper Co. (owned by a du Pont foundation) and sell to a joint venture composed of a Houston developer, Mike Adkinson, and Southmark, the Gene Phillips company discussed in another chapter. The timing of that transaction became suspect when an indictment was handed down a week later charging Freeman with laundering drug money for a pilot named Jack DeVoe, whom U.S. Customs accused of smuggling Colombian cocaine into the landing strip at Opa-Locka Airport in Miami. [39]

DeVoe's name again came up in a 2000 trial of a co-conspirator – a Bahamian lawyer named F. Nigel Bowe. The Eleventh Circuit's opinion in *United States v. Bowe* states:

> Bowe flew to Cartagena [Colombia] in a leased Lear jet with Jack Devoe, a pilot who flew drugs into the United States, and two Miami lawyers. In Cartagena, Bowe introduced Devoe to Pepe Cabrera, a major drug supplier. Law enforcement had seized two of Cabrera's drug-smuggling planes in the United States, and Cabrera was looking for pilots with their own aircraft to transport his cocaine.
>
> After discussing the logistics of the proposed operation, Cabrera, Devoe, and Bowe allegedly reached an agreement. Devoe would be responsible for picking up Cabrera's cocaine in Colombia and flying it in large shipments to the Bahamas. Devoe would then break down the shipment into smaller quantities and move the cocaine into Florida in a series of flights. Bowe would protect the operation from law enforcement in the Bahamas. Under the terms of this agreement, Devoe was to keep ten percent of the cocaine he transported. Devoe, in turn, would pass ten percent of the money he earned from his sale of that cocaine on to Bowe.[40]

F. Nigel Bowe was a partner in the law firm of Cash, Fountain & Bowe, which represented the late Congressman Adam Clayton Powell, Jr.'s mistress after 1972.

Over a decade later, Bowe was charged with 20 counts in an indictment by Federal and Florida law enforcement officials. Bowe was said to be a "bagman for Bahamian police, who they say allowed Colombian drug traffickers to ship drugs through remote Bahamian islands to Florida."[41]

In addition, the indictment accused him of helping smugglers, including Jose "Pepe" Cabrera-Sarmiento, a man convicted on drug charges, who later testified against Panamanian dictator Manuel Noriega.[42]

Bowe fought extradition to the United States for seven years, while being held in Fox Hill prison near Nassau, but was finally tried in 1992. Because of his closeness to Prime Minister Lynden O. Pindling, Nigel Bowe was related to the Bowe brothers – Charles, Alfonso, and Franz – who ran the FBO called Executive Flight Services at Pindling Airport in Nassau, Bahamas some years later.[43] Their sister, Diane Bowe, an accountant and banker, married Sir Lynden Pindling's eldest son, Obie Pindling in 1990.[44]

BROTHER, CAN YOU SPARE A GUILDER?

Wally Hilliard also had an interest in Executive Flight Services with Alfonso Bowe, created one year prior to 9/11, only two months after the Orlando heroin bust. We found online an ad for the brand, Bowe Joubert Winery, written in a flowery style:

> Alphonso was already the proud owner of another Boland wine farm near Worcester, which he bought in 1996, having fallen in love with the splendour of the Cape on his first visit to South Africa. One of Alphonso's friends and business partners, Andrew Hilliard [Wally's son and heir], an investment capitalist from Green Bay, Wisconsin, became the third partner in the new venture. The new company took the names of the major players to become known as the Bowe-Joubert Vineyards & Winery.[45]

Another advertising piece, purporting to explain what convinced him to buy in South Africa, tells a strange tale: "Bowe and [Nelson] Mandela met early one morning in the men's toilet at Amsterdam's Schiphol Airport when the elder statesman turned to the Bahamian for assistance, not having the necessary toilet requisites with him. At a subsequent meeting Mandela persuaded Bowe to shelve the plan to buy a wine farm in Chile."[46]

No shit, Sherlock, no pun intended.

Endnotes

1   "Du Pont heir and political activist, Bayard Sharp, 89, dies at home," Easton, *Maryland Star-Democrat*, August 12, 2002.

2   "The End of an Era," *Sarasota Herald-Tribune*, Aug 18, 2002.

3   The various agreements were reviewed in court cases brought against the Alien Property Custodian, who seized properties for use by the U.S. Government during World War II. STANDARD OIL CO. et al. v. CLARK, Atty. Gen., 163 F.2d 917 (2d Cir. 1947). https://casetext.com/case/standard-oil-co-v-clark

4   United Press, "Standard Chief insists cartel helped U.S.," *St. Louis Star and Times*, Mar 31, 1942. Page 1 hish/140728611/

5   Joseph A. Fox, "Standard Oil, Rubber and the Cartel Question," Washington, District of Columbia, *Evening Star*, April 05, 1942.

6   https://en.wikipedia.org/wiki/America_First_Committee

7   Charles Lindbergh published these words in an essay entitled "Geography, Aviation, and Race" in *Reader's Digest* in 1939. Quoted by Jason Stanley, "Tucker Carlson is not an anti-war populist rebel. He is a fascist," The *Guardian*, 28 April 2023. https://www.theguardian.com/commentisfree/2023/apr/28/tucker-carlson-politics-fascism

8   Obituaries: Philip Ross Neuhaus (1919-2013); Walter W. Fondren, Sr. https://www.legacy.com/us/obituaries/houstonchronicle/name/philip-neuhaus-obituary?id=8580306   https://www.findagrave.com/memorial/76711443/walter_william_fondren

9   Leonard Mosley, *Blood Relations: The Rise and Fall of the du Ponts of Delaware* (Atheneum), 1980. See quote at hdu-ponts-delaware

10   Barbara Klaw, "Blood Relations: The Rise and Fall of the Du Ponts of Delaware," *American Heritage*, Volume 31, Issue 4, June/July 1980. hrelations-rise-and-fall-du-ponts-delaware

11   Youngstown Vindicator, Mar 10, 1940, Page 5. https://news.google.com/newspapers?id=Mo5cAAAAIBAJ&sjid=uVcNAAAAIBAJ&pg=5404%2C2773221

12   https://official-tropes.fandom.com/wiki/Honest_John%27s_Dealership

13   Pete Brewton, *The Mafia, CIA and George Bush*, (Shapolsky Publishers 1992).

14   Ibid.

15   Ibid.

16   https://alt.sports.baseball.cinci-reds.narkive.com/Inavvqjw/the-lindner-file-corruption-dope-dealing-looting-cia

17   Quoted by Pete Brewton, Mafia, CIA and George Bush, at p. 287. See https://dokumen.pub/the-mafia-cia-amp-george-bush-1561712035-9781561712038.html

18   Ibid, at p. 291.

19   Jim Drinkhall, "CIA Helped Quash Major, Star-Studded Tax Evasion Case: CIA Tie to Nassau Bank Led to End of Tax Case," *The Wall Street Journal* (Copyright 1980), reprinted by the Washington Post, April 23, 1980. https://www.washingtonpost.com/archive/politics/1980/04/24/cia- helped-quash-major-star-studded-tax-evasion-case/a55ddf06-2a3f-4e04-a687-a3dd87c32b82/

20   Ibid.

21   https://files.taxfoundation.org/legacy/docs/fed_individual_rate_history_nominal.pdf

22   Matthew F. Holland, *America and Egypt: From Roosevelt to Eisenhower*, Praeger 1996.

23   Jim Drinkhall, "IRS vs. CIA: Big Tax Investigation Was Quietly Scuttled by Intelligence Agency," *Wall Street Journal,* April 18, 1980. https://www.cia.gov/readingroom/docs/CIA- RDP90-01208R000100100061-5.pdf   Also see sources listed by John Simkin in Spartacus Education- al. https://spartacus-educational.com/JFKhelliwell.htm

24   Sterling Seagrave, *The Marcos Dynasty* (Harper and Row, Inc) ©1988. "Vietnam: The OSS and Ho Chi Minh, 1945," author unknown. https://parallelnarratives.com/vietnam-vignette-the-oss-and-ho-chi-minh-1945/?preview=true&preview_id=4203&preview_nonce=c40ec7aeae

https://quixoticjoust.blogspot.com/2013/05/an-off-books-private-war.html

25   https://www.federalreservehistory.org/people/marriner-s-eccles

26   Ibid.

27   The Insurance Industry: Hearings, Eighty-fifth Congress, Second Session ... By United

States. Congress. Senate. Committee on the Judiciary. Subcommittee on Antitrust and Monopoly (1960). https://books.google.com/books?id=dIgbEVBsYwQC&pg=PA5927&lpg=PA5927&dq=helli-well+mchugh+%22first+security%22&source=bl&ots=-_d7Eb9tgl&sig=ACfU3U0cLtpQuxx-OunRFvl1GU1l-CGHEIw&hl=en&sa=X&ved=2ahUKEwjniKW7ubWEAxVOnGoFHZmOAKIQ6AF-6BAgKEAM#v=onepage&q=helliwell%20mchugh%20%22first%20security%22&f=false

28   Becky Little, "How Hong Kong Came Under 'One Country, Two Systems' Rule, History Channel, September 3, 2019. https://www.history.com/news/hong-kong-china-great-britain

29   *Contemporary Crises Journal, Volume: 14 Issue: 1,* (March 1990), Pages: 23-37. https://www.ojp.gov/ncjrs/virtual-library/abstracts/chinese-laundry-international-drug-trafficking-and-hong-kongs

30   "Cendant wins dual with cash," *South Florida Sun Sentinel,* 24 Mar 1998, Pages 39-40. President's Commission on Organized Crime, 1986.

31   Time, Monday, Nov. 30, 1936https://content.time.com/time/subscriber/article/0,33009,757049,00.html

32   Maurice Carroll, "SILVERMAN HEADS CENTER PROJECT," *New York Times,* March 13, 1974. https://www.nytimes.com/1974/03/13/archives/silverman-heads-center-project-realestate-executive-gets-west-side.html

33   Wolfgang Saxon, "H. Silverman, 91, Innovator In Financing," *New York Times,* Aug. 23, 2003. https://www.nytimes.com/2003/08/23/business/h-silverman-91-innovator-in-financing.html

34   John R. Emshwiller, "Finova Group Inc., in another setback, announced termination of an investment agreement with Leucadia National Corp." *Wall Street Journal,* Jan. 25, 2001. See also https://www.berkshirehathaway.com/news/feb2701.html and https://www.deseret.com/2000/11/14/19538953/finova-tentatively-agrees-to-buy-control-of-leucadia-for-350-million

35   Helmsley-Spear history. https://www.zippia.com/helmsley-spear-careers-59754/history/#

36   https://en.wikipedia.org/wiki/Henry_Silverman

37   Sue Napier,"Share your vacation apartment," *Lexington Herald,* 20 Apr 1975, Page 111.

38   https://www.sun-sentinel.com/1985/11/08/miami-lawyer-accused-in-drug-racketeering/

39   https://www.druglibrary.org/schaffer/govpubs/amhab/amhabc3.htm

40   *UNITED STATES of America, Plaintiff-Appellee, v. Frederick Nigel BOWE,* 221 F.3d 1183 (11th Cir. 2000). https://casetext.com/case/us-v-bowe

41   David Lyons, "Bahamian attorney to face smuggling charges," *Miami Herald,* 25 Jul 1992, Page 144.

42   "Nassau attorney to face charges," UPI Archives, July 25, 1992. https://www.upi.com/Archives/1992/07/25/Nassau-attorney-to-face-charges/4376712036800/

43   "Pindling Family Relative Jailed For Drugs In US.," Copyright © 2024 BahamasB2B.com, August 18, 2005. hfor-drugs-in-us

44   Ibid.

"45   The BoweJoubert story," WineNet (PTY) Ltd., *Southern Africa's Freight News,* by FLW, 29 October, 2001. https://news.wine.co.za/news.aspx?NEWSID=1650

46   Ray Smuts, "Mandela attracts investment from Bahamas in SA wine farm," 12 Oct 2001

CHAPTER TWENTY-SEVEN

TRUMP DESCENDS INTO THE ABYSS

He who fights with monsters might take care lest he thereby become a monster. And if you gaze for long into an abyss, the abyss gazes also into you.
— Nietzsche, *Beyond Good and Evil*

It's now an empty lot on the beach in Sarasota, where a house used to be. The house was where Steve Bannon lieutenant, Andy Badolato, once lived. That's where a small part of this story begins.

Two major events in the alt-right financial ring helmed by Steve Bannon came as huge shocks to those following the scandal, mostly me and a few other similarly deluded souls.

First, as the scandal kept slowly growing, Badolato's house disappeared. Then, now more than a year ago, Steve Bannon and Andy Badolato were indicted in New York. As the trial date kept getting moved forward, Bannon pulled out his "Pardon My Foe Paw" card, changing the whole dynamic of what I'd thought at the time promised to be dynamite.

Steve Bannon had been a political strategist for the President of the United States. Some say Trump would not have been elected but for Bannon. Paul Manafort had been chief strategist for the Trump campaign from June 20 to August 19, 2016. His previous big job had been in Ukraine as strategist for Viktor Yanukovych, a pro-Russian politician with strong ties to Russian president Vladimir Putin. Manafort had been advising him since 2004.

FBI reportedly began a criminal investigation into Manafort in 2014 as hints of a possible RussiaGate scandal pervaded the air. Jim Rutenberg would describe how it happened in his analysis for the *New York Times* called "The Untold Story of 'Russiagate' and the Road to War in Ukraine" years after the fact.

He wrote: "On the night of July 28, 2016, as Hillary Clinton was accepting the Democratic presidential nomination in Philadelphia, Donald J. Trump's campaign chairman, Paul Manafort, received an urgent email from Moscow.

"The sender was a friend and business associate named Konstantin Kilimnik. A Russian citizen born in Soviet Ukraine, Kilimnik ran the Kyiv office of Manafort's international consulting firm, known for bringing cutting-edge American campaign techniques to clients seeking to have their way with fragile democracies around the world."[1]

Manafort and Kilimnik had plans to meet at the top of Jared Kushner's demonic-symbol-addressed building – 666 Fifth Avenue – shortly after the Russian arrived at JFK Airport on August 2, 2016.

Rutenburg described the scene as:

> ... a perfectly put-up stage set for a caricature drama of furtive figures hatching covert schemes with questionable intent – a dark-lit cigar bar with mahogany-paneled walls and floor-to-ceiling windows columned in thick velvet drapes, its leather club chairs typically filled by large men with open collars sipping Scotch and drawing on *parejos* and *figurados*.
>
> Men, that is, like Paul Manafort, with his dyed-black pompadour and penchant for pinstripes. There, with the skyline shimmering through the cigar-smoke haze, Kilimnik shared a secret plan whose significance would only become clear six years later, as Vladimir V. Putin's invading Russian Army pushed into Ukraine.[2]

Oleg Deripaska first entered my own radar around 2008 after I discovered he'd bought a state-owned bauxite plant in Guyana with help from Michael Francis Brassington's dad, Mike Brassington of the Ministry of Privatization in charge of selling off assets of the formerly communist-leaning country in South America, which the CIA had been monitoring for years.

The younger Brassington, you may recall, had been the unnamed copilot ignored when Wally Hilliard's Learjet was busted in Orlando in July 2000 – 13½ months prior to 9/11 – with heroin on board. The Feds had permanently seized the plane held by Plane 1 Leasing, in which Hilliard was the major shareholder.

Bauxite, I learned, was an essential ingredient in the making of aluminum, and Russian Oleg Deripaska by 2004, when he hooked up with Paul Manafort, was richer, and doing more deals, than anyone alive.

UKRAINE'S OIL AND GAS

Ukraine, Russia's next-door neighbor, had new elections in 2004 and the two candidates were beginning campaigns in September when the pro-Western opposition candidate, Viktor Yushchenko, fell ill. He'd been poisoned "(allegedly carried out by the Ukrainian State Security Service), which left his face disfigured."[3]

"Yushchenko's supporters charged fraud and staged mass protests that came to be known as the Orange Revolution. Protestors clad in orange, Yushchenko's campaign colour, took to the streets, and the country endured nearly two weeks of demonstrations. Yanukovych's supporters in the east threatened to secede from Ukraine if the results were annulled. Nevertheless, on December 3 the Supreme Court ruled the election invalid and ordered a new runoff for December 26."[4]

Yushchenko defeated Yanukovych by garnering some 52 percent of the vote. Although Yanukovych challenged the validity of the results, Yushchenko was inaugurated on January 23, 2005. But it was not the kind of government the U.S. is used to. Instead of Congress, Ukraine's constitution calls for both an elected President and an elected Parliament, which chooses its leader (the Prime Minister) like in Great Britain. If no party wins a majority, the elected ministers can form a coalition to choose the leader.

In this case, Yushchenko was President and – horror of horrors – the Prime Minister chosen in 2006 was his opponent from the last election, Yanukovych! Fortunately, it lasted only a year, but parliament continued to bounce around until the Presidential election of 2010 when Yanukovych won and began creeping ever closer into Russia's sphere of influence and away from a decision to join the European Union.

The climax occurred with the Maidan Riots in Kiev in January 2014, followed by clashes that went on until the end of February.

On February 6 that year, Reuters had reported that Russia and the U.S. had taken opposite positions about how to end "a violent standoff in the streets." Russia blamed the U.S. for arming the radical protesters.

Washington urged the President to "share power with a unity government," accusing Russia of pressuring Kiev officials not to join a trade pact with the European Union. On the other hand, they blamed Yanukovich for "protests in November when he turned down the EU accord and took financial aid instead from Moscow."[5]

Almost immediately after the resolution of the conflict, Yanukovych and many of his ministers fled the capital on February 22, and Russia began sending troops to Crimea. Putin announced the region was being annexed by the Russian Federation.

Each side tried to rationalize its position based on democratic ideals of the people, but few said much about oil and gas, which was what the spat was really about. The situation was the equivalent of Mexico deciding to annex Texas, claiming the Texan heritage was more aligned with Mexico than with the U.S. – when what they craved was the income from the Texas oil and gas industry, which they took over for the country of Mexico to operate.

Some experts, like Dr. Frank Umbach, who wrote in the *NATO Review*, did emphasize how strategic Crimea was to Russia, saying, "It has vast offshore oil and gas resources in the Black Sea, estimated between 4-13 trillion cm of natural gas." Umbach added that "Ukraine is now concerned about losing one of the two largest shale gas fields … in the Donetsk and Kharkiv 'oblasts' or regions. Ukraine holds Europe's third largest shale gas reserves."[6]

Once Crimea was annexed, Putin nationalized the Ukrainian oil and gas business, placing it under management of his two close friends, Arkavy and Boris Rotenberg of Gazprom. They became two of the biggest targets for sanctions by the Obama Administration. But they were so adept at evading sanctions that "*Forbes* magazine estimated their combined wealth at $4.9 billion this year."[7]

PAUL MANAFORT'S CAREER

Growing up in New Britain, Connecticut, Paul was the son of a proud vet who instilled in him Republican values. Paul Manafort Sr.'s obituary was two 9-inch columns in the *Hartford Courant*, listing every lodge and fraternal society he'd ever attended, and there were many, perhaps most of the Italian brotherhood persuasion, with Armenian and Polish thrown into the mix.[8]

The junior Manafort worked in his first presidential campaign in 1976 for Gerald Ford and every Republican candidate who followed. He didn't confine himself to American politics either – working for foreign dictators as well, such as Ferdinand Marcos in the Philippines (1985), Zaire's Mobutu Sese Seko (1989), and Angolan guerrilla leader Jonas Savimbi (1985-89), among others.[9]

After assisting what the *Daily Beast* called "the torturers' lobby," Manafort's work as Trump's unpaid campaign chairman must have seemed like a piece of cake, at least until Trump asked him to resign after the press revealed Manafort had lobbied on behalf of Ukraine's ruling *pro-Russian* political party for a decade.

"In his deal with Deripaska," NPR reported, "Manafort promised to *counter anti-Russian sentiment*, according to Day and his AP colleague Jeff Horwitz. Citing a strategy memo from 2005, they say Manafort told Deripaska that he would advocate a pro-Russian agenda both in former republics and 'at the highest levels of the U.S. government – the White House, Capitol Hill and the State Department.'"[10]

It was a $10 million deal, but he never registered as a foreign lobbyist, until after the story broke, by which time he'd been paid a total of $12.7 million.

The Associated Press revealed Manafort had been indirectly working for Putin, with Deripaska as the man paying him, adding that "federal criminal prosecutors became interested in Manafort's activities years ago as part of a broad investigation to recover stolen Ukraine assets after the ouster of pro-Russian President Viktor Yanukovych there in early 2014. No U.S. criminal charges have ever been filed in the case."[11]

We talk about those assets in a separate chapter of the book.

A SECRET PLAN – THE MARIUPOL PLAN

Manafort pled guilty and was imprisoned for months, completing his sentence at home. He had Covid to thank for getting out of jail early. He had Trump to thank for rewarding him with a pardon for refusing to talk. It was what any good mob boss would have done, and it also served as a carrot for Bannon to follow suit.

Bannon successfully completed his role within the campaign by getting Trump elected. Then he worked on the transition team, as a member of the National Security Council's top committee and part of the Trump Administration. Nevertheless, huge egos were involved. Matthew Lysiak wrote in the July 27, 2020, edition of *Vanity Fair*:

> "Trump had long fumed over the public perception that Bannon was responsible for the president's shocking electoral victory. The February 2017 *Time* cover featuring Bannon above the headline "THE GREAT MANIPULATOR" had further soured their relationship.
>
> By the time an interview appeared showing Bannon contradicting Trump on North Korea, Trump had had enough. On Friday, August 18, 2017, seven months into Trump's term, Bannon was fired."[12]

Bannon left the White House in January 2018. Matt Drudge, who was possibly jealous of Bannon's competition, was the first to announce his departure, but he couldn't have welcomed the news announced by Breitbart that Bannon would be returning as its executive chairman.

And, of course, Bannon brought back his buddy Badolato to Breitbart. Who knows what they saw in each other? The years each man spent subjected to Jesuit indoctrination must have made them comfortably simpatico – like wafers and wine – or even old dirty shoes or beer bellies.

Both Bannon and Badolato would later be criminally charged with setting up shell corporations to launder money from the "Build the Wall" fund. We waited several months after January 2021 to see what the Court would do about Bannon's pardon by Trump.

The Court dismissed the indictment of Bannon, leaving Badolato and the others with nobody to rat on to save themselves.

"Badolato-Involved"

Badolato was the subject of a September 2016 article at my website, called "*Trump campaign chief's hidden ties to Sarasota grifter*." It may have been the first time his name appeared there, though I subsequently found it necessary to mention his name before the indictment a futher eleven times – including one entitled "*From Barry Seal to Donald Trump*."

I even set him up with a webpage, titled "Andrew Badolato Bookmarks," consisting of links to his various financial crimes, for which, before the indictment, he'd been charged with precisely none.

In network demographics, they call people who watch The Weather Channel for more than three hours a day "weather-involved."

I guess you could call me "Badolato-involved."

In the days following the indictment, I was about as optimistic as I allow my cynical self to be, while thinking there was much they weren't telling us. What should have had tongues wagging, I thought, was that "certain something" Bannon and Badolato brought to the party – the French call it *je ne sais quoi*. That phrase sounds too chic. Their aura was more shabby chic minus the chic.

I excitedly thought at the time that getting the press interested in Bannon's and Badolato's shared activities might make Trump's "*descending into the abyss of politics*" a complete failure. That descent, which Trump friend, Michael Caputo, called "a symbol of how much he was giving up in order to do this," I saw in a completely different light.[13] How our collective sanity had been forfeited by having him take over our day-to-day lives.

But then my hopes and daydreams were dashed while I waited for the trial. There were several postponements, Bannon's pardon upheld, and much later Badolato's guilty plea. The story just died without, as I had hoped, bringing down the big megillah.[14]

CHINA SYNDROME

Only hours before Bannon's August 2020 arrest for ripping off hundreds of thousands of donors in the "We Build the Wall" fundraiser scam, an enterprising photographer caught a pic of Steve relaxing aboard a fugitive Chinese billionaire's 150-foot superyacht, on which, the *Washington Post* reported, he'd then been living for several months.

The yacht Bannon was draping himself all over back in 2020 was owned by a fugitive Chinese billionaire named Guo Wengui, a man quick "to cast himself as an anti-communist dissident."

What's ironic, however, is how much like Andy Badolato Guo was – just Bannon's type, apparently.

According to a David Ignatius op-ed in April 2016, Guo had close ties to Ma Jian, counterespionage specialist in the Ministry of State Security (MSS), who went to prison for taking bribes. Many of the bribes had been paid by Guo, who was arrested in January 2015. A search of his home turned up "transcripts of wiretaps made secretly of Xi and other party leaders."[15]

Guo, it would seem, like Badolato, had been wearing a wire. Either that, or he obtained the transcripts from whoever bugged members of the CCP.

Then there was Guo's penchant for rape, also reminiscent of Bannon's friend Andy. Not long after arriving in New York, Guo, an asylum seeker holding passports from eleven countries, allegedly lured Rui Ma from China to work as his personal assistant, then took control of her passport, overworked her, even raped her on two occasions, she claimed in the September 2017 lawsuit she filed in a lower New York court.

Guo had conveniently ended up in Manhattan just in time to have witnessed Trump's escalator descent into the political abyss in 2015. He would immediately be drawn to members of the campaign. And they to him.

Referred to in news clippings as a "billionaire," Guo was once the No. 2 man at China's HNA Group – diversely involved in aviation, real estate, financial services, tourism, logistics – which, alas, was staring at bankruptcy. Moreover, there were, in *New York Times*-speak, "deepened uncertainties surrounding the debt-laden Chinese conglomerate's restructuring."[16]

Bannon's new buddy had got out of China just in time. Guo's former boss, Wang Jian, co-chairman and a co-founder of HNA Group of China, would, in July 2018, snap the most expensive selfie ever taken. While on a business-pleasure trip to the South of France, according to local police who investigated, he was leaning way out over an embankment to get a good shot of himself when he took a 50-foot plunge to the base of a picturesque hilltop village in Provence.

The key headline: "Shares of HNA Group's listed entities dropped on news of the abrupt death of its key deal-maker Wang Jian."[17]

Even locally, where they have no rooting interest in corporate wars in China, there was considerable dissension with the police account. Even among French police, who doubted he'd committed suicide.

Guys worth $50 billion, one would think, have people who take their selfies for them. More importantly, a lot of people in Provence were convinced he was murdered.

The previous year HNA's stock had toppled. Guo, by then a fugitive who had taken up residence in New York, had begun spreading rumors about corruption in the Chinese Communist business world, i.e., about the bribes he'd paid.

"Interpol on Tuesday evening issued a red notice for Chinese tycoon Guo Wengui at China's request, sources who were briefed on the notice told the *South China Morning Post*," as reported April 19, 2017 – just eight days after Rui Ma filed her rape lawsuit against Guo.[18]

Hainan Airlines began life as an on-demand charter service, the first private airline in China in 1992. Capitalized by a $300 million securities offering on the Beijing Stock Exchange, it grew quickly and made a $72 million profit in the first year.

By 2006 Hainan had greatly expanded its operations headed by Chen Feng as chairman. Wang Jian was rarely mentioned, let alone pictured, in the public press, allowing Chen to be its public face. Maybe Jian's last selfie had also been his first.

The *New York Times*, however, did verify that his name appeared in company documents dating back to the founding of Hainan Airlines in the mid-1990s and HNA Group, which became its parent corporation about ten years later.

Various sources have referred to these filings as "opaque," meaning they don't reveal much, if anything about shareholders. According to a *New York Times* article dated March 27, 2018, Wang Jian's brother, Wang Wei, and other insiders of Hainan Airlines "restructured the state-backed airline into a privately held parent company called the HNA Group. A large portion of HNA's shares were then shifted offshore, to Pan American Aviation, a company registered in the Cayman Islands, according to a review of corporate filings in China and Hong Kong.

In a subsequent chapter in this book appears a tale about a huge drug bust aboard the MSC *Gayane*, a container ship at the Port of Philadelphia. By "huge," I mean 20 tons of cocaine. And change. Worth $1.3 billion dollars.

I suspected the 20 tons of narcotics were being moved by Russian Mob allies of Donald Trump, and because of that, the poor mentally challenged Republican U.S. Attorney in Philadelphia didn't know whether to shit or go blind. He'd just seized something someone needed BAD … and FAST. I had boiled the heist down to two suspects. According to my calculations, the first suspect, Mediterranean Shipping (MSC), owned by Italy's biggest Mafia clan, was closely linked to the Russian Mob in Montenegro.

That was also the culprit all the arrested crew members on the MSC Gayane pointed to.

There was only one other suspect besides the Russian Mob, and that was the company I'd tracked down to HNA Group – which, at the time, owned a staggering $35 billion worth of investments in the U.S.

In Hainan Airlines' earliest days, George Soros, the man the alt-right loves to hate, was said to have been the biggest outside investor.

Now, HNA was down by two of its top executives, 20 tons of cocaine, and still hadn't been bailed out. As bankruptcy loomed, a massive amount of seized cocaine was still in the hands of the Philly port authorities.

The question that's never been satisfactorily answered is "In whose hands was that cocaine intended to end up?"

When Bannon was escorted by Federal agents of the U.S. Postal Service from a 151-foot silver and glass superyacht anchored off the coast of Westbrook, Connecticut, well, that yacht was owned by the man who'd fled China after being at the second rung from the top of the ladder of HNA Group.

That man, Guo Wengui, once seemed to be Bannon's best hope for replacing Facebook, Twitter and all other forms of social media with a new brand geared to capture all those advertising dollars liberals and Democrats have "canceled" for being politically incorrect. The *Washington Post* described Bannon's brand as a "potent platform for disinformation."[19]

At least, that *was* true before September 2021, when the SEC charged New York City-based GTV Media Group and Saraca Media Group, as well as Phoenix, Arizona-based Voice of Guo Media, with "conducting illegal securities offerings." They had together raised $487 million from securities sales but agreed to settle by disgorging profits and paying interest and fines totaling $539 million.

But that wouldn't be the last we'd see of HO WAN KWOK, a/k/a "Miles Guo," a/k/a "Miles Kwok," a/k/a "Guo Wengui," a/k/a "Brother Seven," a/k/a "The Principal," who was arrested on March 15, 2023. The indictment alleged that Guo and his financial adviser, Kin Ming Je, "were behind an elaborate scheme that defrauded thousands of individuals of over one billion dollars." [20]

Judge Analisa Torres said in a written order that she didn't trust that Guo Wengui would obey court orders if released, even with strict bail conditions including GPS monitoring and a 24-hour guard.[21]

The Guo Wengui trial ran from April 8, 2024 through July, during which time he remained in jail. At its conclusion, he was founf guilty of nine out of 13 counts with sentencing set for November 2024. Guo's pal Steve Bannon, also lost all appeals on his Contempt of Congress conviction and marched into a cell July 1, 2024.

The world will be a little safer with two less scoundrels preying on mankind.

Endnotes

1   Jim Rutenberg, "The Untold Story of 'Russiagate' and the Road to War in Ukraine," *New York Times*, Nov. 2, 2022. hpaul-manafort-ukraine-war.html

2   Ibid.

3   "The Orange Revolution and the Yushchenko presidency," *Britannica*. https://www.britannica.com/place/Ukraine/The-crisis-in-Crimea-and-eastern-Ukraine

4   Ibid.

5   Alastair Macdonald, "Putin aide warns U.S. on Ukraine, says Russia could act," Reuters, February 6, 2014. hBREA150X720140206/

6   Dr. Frank Umbach, "The energy dimensions of Russia's annexation of Crimea," *NATO Review*, May 27, 2014. https://www.nato.int/docu/review/articles/2014/05/27/the-energy-dimensions-of-russias-annexation-of-crimea/index.html

7   "Leaked Emails Reveal How Putin's Friends Dodged Sanctions With Help of Western Enablers," Organized Crime and Corruption Reporting Project (OCCRP). https://www.occrp. org/en/rotenberg-files/leaked-emails-reveal-how-putins-friends-dodged-sanctions-with-help-ofwestern-enablers

8   Obituary of Paul J. Manafort, *Hartford Courant*, 25 Jan 2013, Page B8.

9   Betsy Swan and Tim Mark,"Top Trump Aide Led the'Torturers' Lobby'" *Daily Beast*, Nov. 06, 2017. https://www.thedailybeast.com/top-trump-aide-led-the-torturers-lobby

10   Bill Chappell,"Former Trump Campaign Head Manafort Was Paid Millions By A Putin Ally, AP Says,"*NPR*, March 22, 2017. https://www.npr.org/sections/thetwo-way/2017/03/22/521088772/former-trump-campaign-head-manafort-was-paid-millions-by-a-putin-ally-ap-says

11   Associated Press writers Jack Gillum, Eric Tucker, Julie Pace, Ted Bridis, Stephen Braun, Julie Bykowicz and Monika Mathur contributed to this report in Washington; Nataliya Vasilyeva contributed from Moscow and Kiev, Ukraine; and Jake Pearson contributed from New York. https://apnews.com/article/122ae0b5848345faa88108a03de40c5a

12   Matthew Lysiak, "'Fuck the Corporate Media': How Matt Drudge Wields Power Inside Trumpworld," *Vanity Fair*, July 27, 2020. https://www.vanityfair.com/news/2020/07/how-matt-drudge-wields-power-inside-trumpworld

13   hnouncement-tower-escalator-oral-history-227148/

14   Press release from U.S. Attorney's Office, Southern District of New York. https://www.justice.gov/usao-sdny/pr/two-sentenced-prison-we-build-wall-online-fundraising-fraud-scheme

15   David Ignatius, "China's intelligence shake-up mirrors its political tumult," *Washington Post*, March 31, 2016. https://www.washingtonpost.com/opinions/chinas-intelli- gence-shake-up-mirrors-its-political-tumult/2016/03/31/bb62d77c-f78b-11e5-9804-537defc- c3cf6_story.html

16   Nikki Sun, "HNA deal-maker's death rocks shares and group's future," *Nikkei Asia*, July 6, 2018. https://asia.nikkei.com/Business/Companies/HNA-deal-maker-s-death-rocks-shares-and-group-s-future

17   Ibid.

18   Nectar Gan and Jun Mai in Beijing, "Interpol issues red notice for Chinese tycoon Guo Wengui 'at Beijing's request' after corruption claim report," *South China Morning Post*, 19 Apr, 2017. htice-chinese-tycoon-guo-wengui

19   Jeanne Whalen, Craig Timberg and Eva Dou, "Bannon is driving force 1for a sprawling disinformation network, researchers say,"*Washington Post*, May 17, 2021. https://www.washingtonpost.com/technology/2021/05/17/guo-wengui-disinformation-steve-bannon/

20   Press Release: " Ho Wan Kwok, A/K/A "Miles Guo," Arrested For Orchestrating Over $1 Bil- lion Dollar Fraud Conspiracy," U.S. Attorney's Office, Southern District of New York, March 15, 2023. https://www.justice.gov/usao-sdny/pr/ho-wan-kwok-aka-miles-guo-arrested-orchestrating-over- 1-billion-dollar-fraud-conspiracy

21   Larry Neumeister, "Judge nixes bail for Chinese businessman in $1B fraud case," Associated Press, April 20, 2023. https://apnews.com/article/guo-wengui-chinese-businessman-fraud-31583ef5cd3ec16b9ff92e6fc7cb8a43

CHAPTER TWENTY-EIGHT

HAVE YOU SEEN THIS HOUSE?

The secret we should never let the gamemasters know is that they don't need any rules.
— Gary Gygax, creator of Dungeons and Dragons game

Something really strange just happened to me, in the middle of an otherwise unremarkable gorgeous spring day in Florida. Remember that guy on *Game of Thrones* – the bastard son of one of the warlords – who was nonetheless lucky enough to score a fiercely loyal red-haired girlfriend? Who, when he needed to hear it, would tell him, eyeball to eyeball: "You know nothing, Jon Snow."

That's me.

Standing in the middle of the road on two-lane Casey Key Road, which snakes up the narrow eight-mile-long island. Gazing in slack-jawed wonder at what lay across the street.

What was shocking wasn't what was in front of me, but what wasn't. A character and storyline I'd been writing about was no longer there. It had disappeared.

Why *"vanished without a trace"* is such a cliché, I suddenly realized, was because it's exactly what springs to mind when you're left fumbling for words.

"Dude. I'm telling you: It was gone. Vanished without a trace."

It wasn't a person that was missing. It was a house. A famous house. A 15-year-old yellow McMansion with a circular driveway, worth $1.8 million, on Casey Key, happy to be known as "an exclusive enclave" of Sarasota, Florida.

NO APB'S ON FLEEING REAL ESTATE

I was there on a tip from a reliable source, though one I had not spoken with in a while. He had been a goldmine of information about the infiltration of organized crime into already shady Sarasota brokerage firms, and their subsequent participation in an amazing number and variety of penny stock promotions pumping up the stock of companies that in many cases didn't even exist.

Joey Barquin is as close to a hipster as white bread Sarasota, Florida will probably ever see. Even though he's spent 30 years living on Florida's Sun Coast, his skin has a nighttime pallor. He wears a fedora, with a brim pulled down over his eyes. It's a Rat Pack ready look. He's Runyon-esque. Joey was an investor who had been defrauded in a deal with a man he'd known for 25 years. Confidential sources are usually either bitter exwives, or pissed-off former business partners, or both. Joey falls into the latter category.

There was something I had to see, he told me over the phone. I needed to take a drive and look at the beach house of his fraudster ex-partner.

Joey said, "Don't ask questions. Just go there and you'll see."

It had been almost four years since the beach house had its brush with fame, and the story felt like an old postcard worn around the edges.

What could be new in a four-year-old scandal? Still, I went. I wanted to know more about the connection between Sarasota and transnational organized crime.

NIGHTTIME BONFIRES & DRUM CIRCLES

Everybody had wanted a piece of the story in 2016 when it first came out, starting with the local *Sarasota Herald Tribune*, which had been controlled for 75 years by a father-son team, David Breed Lindsay Sr., David Breed Lindsay Jr.

Both men had spent World War II in Kunming, China, with the OSS and General Claire Chennault's Flying Tigers, supporting General Chiang Kai Shek's nationalists, a grouping which represented America's first big leap into the illegal drug trade. The Flying Tigers also play a role in this story, in another chapter.

Unusual for a newspaper publisher, the younger David Breed Lindsay pursued a second career as a weapons manufacturer. He took WWII surplus P-51 fighters and upgraded them for the rigors of 60's-era warfare. He called them "Cavaliers." And they were a popular item, from Guatemala on down, with some of the most repressive regimes on the planet.

They were strafing machines. They sold well. Because, unlike jets – which were all arms suppliers like the U.S. sold anymore – Lindsay's propeller-driven Cavaliers were able to fly slowly enough to bring the full power of their upgraded twin machine guns to bear on crowds of peasants, or insurgents, or hopefully both.

Having your local newspaper publisher running a sideline peddling weapons to almost-exclusively fascist regimes might pose a bit of a public relations hurdle in most cities.

But not in Sarasota. The meanest city in America. At least, that's what *USA Today* called it, after civic leaders decided to rip out all park benches to keep homeless people from sitting on them or getting them dirty.

Casey Key Mystery

It was a beautiful cloudless March morning, with a fresh breeze blowing off the Gulf. Not too hot, not too humid. Florida has three or four days like this – every other leap year.

When I arrived at the address, 3108 Casey Key Road, I could not see the house. It wasn't hidden by a wall, or tall shrubbery. It wasn't there.

It was gone. Where a house once stood, there was now nothing but bare earth, and a couple of pick-up trucks parked haphazardly near the back of a vacant lot. My conclusion was that somebody deliberately tore it down.

Rule of thumb: Houses in beachfront transactions account for half the sale price. The beachfront lot is the other half. So, someone tore down a home worth roughly $900,000. Who does things like that?

A few orange traffic cones anchored a chain running about a foot off the ground across the front of the lot.

There was a sign on the chain, hanging limply in the dirt. It read "Private Property No Trespassing." There was also a phone number, but no indication of why anyone would call it. To report a trespasser? With no hint of a reward? It hardly seemed likely.

I hesitated for a moment, then did what I often do in similar circumstances: blundered ahead. I stepped over the chain, stopping to examine the sign. The phone number had a 312 prefix.

That's Chicago's area code, and Chicago has always been the home of serious organized crime. Maybe I was in the right place after all.

Along with a score of other publications, the *Sarasota Herald Tribune*, under new ownership, had begun to investigate Andrew Badolato. The paper seemed perfectly positioned to turn the heat up on what was also a local scandal.

"Andrew Badolato has had a relationship with former presidential adviser Steve Bannon that goes back for decades," wrote reporter Chris Anderson.

"Questions raised about President Trump's association with former adviser Stephen K. Bannon mirror those raised about Bannon's relationship with Andrew Badolato. Experts question whether he should have disclosed this relationship before joining the White House team."

Good question. Did Bannon "disclose this relationship" to the FBI? If he did, and if Badolato was already an FBI informant, what would the FBI have done? What happens when the FBI has mixed feelings?

PROPERTY IS THEFT

I thought maybe Andy Badolato's beach house would someday be recognized as a world-historical site, like Al Capone's mansion in Miami Beach, as the place where Trump's alt-right comrades and shady business partners in organized crime mingled with their Russian counterparts. You know, transnational organized crime.

Had it been moved? A house that big would seem to be too wide for a narrow two-lane road. I tried to picture it moving, like it was on some mythical Discovery Channel-like series called "Big Movers, Big Moves."

It didn't compute. The house wasn't gargantuan by any means. But it was only 15 years old, and statement-level big, at least for a mini-mansion.

Was. That was now the operative word.

Until he sold it to Badolato in 1997, the house at 3108 Casey Key Road had been owned by a certain Bradford Baker, once known as a boy wonder in Sarasota. At the other end of its life, Andy's beach house closed out its nasty brutish and short life in the hands of Dean LeBaron, a wealthy retired hedge fund operator from Boston, who happened to own the house next door. Efforts to reach Baker and LeBaron received no response. My name has always – for wholly admirable reasons – been "mud" in Sarasota, Florida.

Sarasota had also been home to Arthur C. Nadel, called the "Mini-Madoff," who ran a Ponzi scheme that stole $300 million from local investors, numerous charities, and the public at large. Even though he looked like Wally Cox, Art Nadel was a player. We can all agree $300 million is a "big boy" score.

Plus, several years earlier, Nadel had gotten the nod to take over Huffman Aviation in Venice from Wally Hilliard, who was tired of getting bad press, even in his hometown Green Bay, Wisconsin.

Another poignant story about one of Sarasota's former denizens involves *Pee-Wee's Playhouse* star Paul Reubens, who grew up in Sarasota. In 1991 during a visit home, he was arrested for indecent exposure at the XXX South Trail Cinema during its triple bill that night – *Catalina Five-O Tiger Shark, Nurse Nancy,* and *Turn Up the Heat.*

When arrested by Detective William Walters who caught him "masterbating" in public. Peewee offered to perform a children's benefit for the sheriff's office if the charges were dropped. Luckily, they didn't add bribery to the charge.[1]

It destroyed Rubens' career. Comparing Pee-Wee jerking off in a dark theater watching porn to Andy Badolato's far more serious sexual peccadillos – multiple allegations of rape, covered up by the Sarasota Sheriff's Department – one has to wonder if politics plays a big role in who gets arrested in Sarasota.

A Grifter's Greatest Gift

I investigate the drug trade in Florida, where it is the major industry. Drugs are to Florida what corn is to Iowa.

And since three of the four pilots in the 9/11 attack were revealed to have learned to fly at the tiny Venice Florida Airport in Sarasota County, I have also been tracking spooks and mil-intel involvement in Southwest Florida. In many ways, the two stories are one.

But even so, there was much more going on here than I had known about, and connections to transnational organized crime are far stronger here than I ever thought possible.

Sarasota's connections with organized crime before 2016 weren't known to extend much farther than the compound on Casey Key once owned by John Gotti, which later served as a set on his daughter's TV show about Mob Wives.

That began to change as Sarasota's involvement in what became known as Russiagate slowly became visible.

When Steve Bannon's Cambridge Analytica declared bankruptcy in the U.K., its creditor matrix listed the name of a "Sarasota-based company called *The USA Exchange*," just one of Andrew Badolato's companies.[2] He had set it up in March 2015 while officing at 2033 Main Street in a Fifth Floor office, perhaps the third office he'd occupied in that building, then known as the Infinium Building.

Badolato's LinkedIn page listed him as CEO of the company called USAX for short, saying the idea "originated from an economic theory and white paper created in 2009 by the company's co-founder Andy Badolato." It's all about supply chains that seek to market products either to consumers or to businesses. That's BS jargon for grift. It has no product and offers no real service. It just full of baloney, or BS – take your pick.

Cambridge Analytica's representative in the U.S. was a man who is not a character in our book but does deserve mention here. Brad Parscale was digital media director for two and a half years for Donald Trump's 2016 campaign.

"Parscale's firm [based in San Antonio, Texas] had been designing websites for Trump since 2011 and had proven its worth and value. Parscale not only provided quality work, but he did it at a price that firms in New York City couldn't match."[3]

Cambridge Analytica's 2018 contract with Andy Badolato spelled out what USA Exchange was expected to do: "We will utilize our databases and proprietary qualitative market research to provide data analytics services, messaging guidance and digital targeting."[4]

It was the same thing Brad Parscale did for the Trump campaign. Fortunately, Parscale later regretted what he'd done. When contacted by text by reporter Katrina Pierson on January 6, 2021, as the U.S. Capitol was being overrun, Brad told her, "This is about Trump pushing for uncertainty in this country. A sitting president asking for civil war. This week I feel guilty for helping him win."[5]

Parscale was quoted by Joel Winston at the *Startup Grind* in 2016. "I always wonder why people in politics act like this stuff is so mystical," he said. "It's the same shit we use in commercials, just has fancier names."[6]

"On the strength of Parscale's ability to generate campaign donations using Facebook and e-mail, the digital operations division was the Trump campaign's largest source of cash," Winston reported.[7]

He also quoted Steve Bannon: "'I wouldn't have come aboard, even for Trump, if I hadn't known they were building this massive Facebook and data engine,' says the Trump campaign Chairman Steve Bannon. (Bannon is also a Board Member of Cambridge Analytica.) 'Facebook is what propelled Breitbart to a massive audience. We know its power.'"[8]

Facebook's revenue from advertising in 2015 alone was $17.9 billion dollars. Its annual report filed with the SEC for year 2015 said that Facebook "generates substantially all of our revenue from advertising."[9]

What exactly are "messaging guidance" and "digital targeting," though? It was like the wet dream of every con artist who ever picked the pockets of the most gullible mark. Like leading sheep to slaughter.

It's the grifter's greatest gift.

Can you say that phrase three times real fast?

RUSSIAN TROLLS AND WORLD OF WARCRAFT

Congress wanted to know if Facebook had helped swing the election to Trump. Mark Zuckerberg was politely invited to testify. He had a lot to explain.

Zuckerberg appeared before a "blockbuster joint hearing of the US Senate's commerce and judiciary committees on Capitol Hill" for two days after Facebook had admitted personal information of up to 87 million users had been "harvested" without their permission. It sounded like a science fiction movie about human organ trafficking.

In answer to a question whether he could guarantee that Russian trolls wouldn't do again what they'd done in 2016, Zuckerberg answered, "Senator, no, I can't guarantee that because this is an ongoing arms race. As long as there are people sitting in Russia whose job it is to try and interfere with elections around the world, this is going to be an ongoing conflict."

"Earlier in the hearing, Zuckerberg acknowledged that 'one of my greatest regrets in running the company' was being slow to uncover and act against disinformation campaigns by Russian trolls during the election."[10]

Robert Mueller's report about Russian interference in the 2016 election and the Trump campaign seemed to take forever to come out, but when it did, Buzzfeed said the report provided "one of the most detailed looks at how Russia's Internet Research Agency [IRA] – the infamous Kremlin-linked troll farm – tried to hijack the 2016 election and swing the vote in favor of Donald Trump."[11]

IRA, BuzzFeed said, "learned how to use platforms like Facebook and Twitter over the span of four years. By the end, it used analytical tools and the built-in network effect of massive social media platforms to create large artificial grassroots political organizations that were aggressively targeting both Republicans and Democrats."[12]

It reached almost 130 million Americans before the election by using fraudulent accounts, groups and ads, and it misused Twitter with similar faked accounts that organized rallies and mobilized political action on behalf of Trump's campaign.

All of this tied in with what Steve Bannon and Andy Badolato had been doing since taking over the Breitbart website after the creator, Andrew Breitbart, died in 2012.

Jane Coaston said it well at Vox. "The conservative movement is no longer represented by submissive, bow-tied conservative nerds."[13] In her article, she voiced her opinion that "Bannon didn't want to start fights with MoveOn.org or MSNBC.

BANNON THE BARBARIAN

Bannon wanted to win in DC. The shift within Breitbart from a website for the "happy warrior" to a site that viewed itself as a political action committee for the far right was a gradual one. By 2014, Bannon was telling staff that he wanted to destroy the Republican establishment, one wild-card candidate and angry rant at a time."[14]

What was going on with Bannon in the years prior to 2012, before any-one really heard of him? How Bannon traveled from being the suit and tie clad banker at Goldman Sachs to being in the center of Trump's inner circle is explained by Joshua Green, a *Bloomberg Businessweek* reporter whose book about Bannon came out in the summer before the 2018 mid-terms.[15] It has been said that the book is what led to Bannon's exit from Trump's inner circle in August that year.

Bannon, whose ego is second only to Trump's, believed the election would not have been won without his team of mind manipulators trolling on Facebook and Twitter. Trump, being Trump, bows to no one and did not hesitate to make Bannon pay.

"Mr. Trump had also reportedly grown weary of press leaks and of Mr. Bannon taking credit for his election victory.

"Mr. Bannon headed back to Breitbart, vowing to wage war on the president's opponents. 'I've got my hands back on my weapons.... It's Bannon the Barbarian,' he said at the time."[16]

VIRTUAL GOLD IN A VIRTUAL WORLD

The reference escaped some of us at the time, not knowing he had been sucked for a few years into the virtual World of Warcraft gaming in 2004 and beyond. Joshua Green wrote that Bannon "left Hollywood for the other side of the globe, Hong Kong, where [by 2005] he became involved in what was undoubtedly the strangest business of any in his ka-leidoscopic career – one that introduced him to a hidden world, burrowed deep into his psyche, and provided a kind of conceptual framework that he would later draw on to build up the audience for Breitbart News, and then to help marshal the online armies of trolls and activists that overran national politics and helped give rise to Donald Trump."[17]

It was called Internet Gaming Entertainment (IGE), which traded in virtual currency. Wikipedia will give you the basics about how it worked by using gaming software like the video game called *World of Warcraft*, created by other companies and played on the internet. All one needed was a subscription to enter the "massively multiplayer online role-playing game (MMO)".

Ten million subscribers could compete against each other in a fantasy world made of elves, dwarfs, trolls, goblins, and dragons.

Not weird enough for your taste? Then how about this?

"Skilled players can win weapons, armor, and gold. These are, of course, virtual items acquired and used within the game. Yet ardent enthusiasts were willing to buy them for real money, in the real world, to help them conquer World of Warcraft and other MMOs – a practice known as 're-al-money trading.'" They called it "gold farming."[18]

It's possible Bannon met his friend Guo Wengui while he was working in Hong Kong. The world is full of such weird humanoid characters who meet up for a time, hang out and then disappear. Narcissists don't really seem to form friendships.

Bannon and Brock Pierce had that same type of quasi-relationship. Child movie star Brock Pierce had founded IGE in 2001 and gave Bannon a seat on the company's board for his efforts in raising startup funding. There was a merger before 2008 with Affinity Media, formed as a startup in 1998 to create software to allow "sharing information between comput-er systems."[19]

The Guardian took notice of this not-quite-real world of virtual gold farmers, made up of men locked up in Chinese prisons. One inmate told reporter Danny Vincent in Beijing he'd been "forced to play online games to build up credits that prison guards would then trade for real money... Millions of gamers around the world are prepared to pay real money for such online credits, which they can use to progress in the online games."[20] Brock Pierce later went on to create Bitfinex and Tether, which would be shut down by a New York prosecutor Latitia James, who has since become famous for prosecuting the Trump Organization and asking for millions of dollars in fines against Trump businesses.[21]

The *Washington Post* explained how the company Bannon was a direc-tor of, Internet Gaming Entertainment (IGE), from its offices on "the 19th floor of a skyscraper in Hong Kong" made millions of dollars a month by selling "virtual goods for real money – magical swords and capes and oth-er accoutrements that granted video-game players power and access in more than a dozen popular online role-playing games."[22]

I had to wonder. Is that like forcing someone else to go to jail to earn a getout-of-jail-free Monopoly card to sell to drug smugglers?

I'll take three of them. You never know when one will come in handy.

Endnotes

1   Mark Harris and Ty Burr, "The Pee-wee Herman scandal," *Entertainment Weekly*, August 16, 1991. https://ew.com/article/1991/08/16/pee-wee-herman-scandal/

2   Chris Anderson, "Cambridge Analytica scandal has Sarasota ties," *Sarasota Herald Tribune*, June 10, 2018. hca-scandal-has-sarasota-ties/12004509007/

3   *San Antonio Business Journal*, July 2015.

4   Ibid.

5   https://en.wikipedia.org/wiki/Brad_Parscale

6   Joel Winston, "How the Trump Campaign Built an Identity Database and Used Facebook Ads to Win the Election," *Start Up Grind*, Nov 18, 2016. Reprinted in *Medium*. https://medium.com/startup-grind/how-the-trump-campaign-built-an-identity-database-and-used-facebook-ads-tow-in-the-election-4ff7d24269ac

7   Joel Winston, *Start Up Grind*, Nov 18, 2016. Reprinted in *Medium*.

8   Ibid.

9   Ibid.

10   David Smith, "Mark Zuckerberg vows to fight election meddling in marathon Senate grilling," The *Guardian*, April 10, 2018. https://www.theguardian.com/technology/2018/apr/10/zuckerberg-facebook-testimony-latest-news-regulation-congress

11   Ryan Broderick, "Here's Everything The Mueller Report Says About How Russian Trolls Used Social Media," *BuzzFeed News*, April 18, 2019. https://www.buzzfeednews.com/article/ryan-hatesthis/mueller-report-internet-research-agency-detailed-2016

12   Ryan Broderick, "Here's Everything The Mueller Report Says About How Russian Trolls Used Social Media," *BuzzFeed News Reporter*, April 18, 2019.

13   Jane Coaston, "Bannon's Breitbart is dead. But Breitbart will live on," Vox, Jan 14, 2018. https://www.vox.com/2018/1/14/16875288/bannon-breitbart-conservative-media

14   Ibid., https://www.vox.com/2018/1/14/16875288/bannon-breitbart-conservative-media

15   Joshua Green, *Devil's Bargain: Steve Bannon, Donald Trump, and the Storming of the Presidency*, Penguin Press, 2017. https://www.usatoday.com/story/tech/talkingtech/2017/07/18/steve-bannon-learned-harness-troll-army-world-warcraft/489713001/

16   "The Downfall of Steve Bannon," *BBC*, 21 October 2022. https://www.bbc.com/news/election-us-2016-37971742

17   Joshua Green. *Devil's Bargain* (p. 80). Penguin Publishing Group. Kindle Edition.

18   Joshua Green. *Devil's Bargain* (pp. 81-82). In Green's words: "The Hong Kong company Bannon joined, Internet Gaming Entertainment, sought to take gold farming to industrial scale by building out a supply chain of low-wage Chinese workers who played World of Warcraft in continuous, rotating shifts, battling monsters and dragons to produce a steady stream of virtual goods that IGE sold to gold-hungry gamers in the West.

Founded by a former child actor, Brock Pierce, who starred in Disney's *Mighty Ducks* movies, IGE proved that real-money trading was a sizable market, one the company claimed was worth nearly $1 billion. Whether it was a legal market was less clear. World of Warcraft's publisher, Blizzard Entertainment, frowned on real-money trading. Many gamers hated the practice and considered it a form of cheating. They flooded gaming boards with anti-Chinese vitriol to protest farmers and their sponsors. Pierce knew IGE needed legitimacy."

19   Vanessa Hua, "Engineer Is Programmed for Success," *Los Angeles Times*, 30 Mar 1998, Page 166.

20   Danny Vincent, "China used prisoners in lucrative internet gaming work," The *Guardian*, 25 May 2011. https://www.theguardian.com/world/2011/may/25/china-prisoners-internet-gaming-scam

21   https://ag.ny.gov/press-release/2021/attorney-general-james-ends-virtual-currency-trading-platform-bitfinexs-illegal

22   Shawn Boburg and Emily Rauhala, "Stephen K. Bannon once guided a global firm that made millions helping gamers cheat," *Washington Post*, August 4, 2017. https://www.washingtonpost.com/investigations/steve-bannon-once-guided-a-global-firm-that-made-millions-helping-gamers-cheat/2017/08/04/ef7ae442-76c8-11e7-803f-a6c989606ac7_story.html

Chapter Twenty-nine

Sarasota – A Republican Sanctum

The MAGA synergy in Sarasota County is not just about building alternative institutions that empower the faithful to live their truth, self-segregated from the mainstream, but also about bringing existing institutions more in line with the convictions and anxieties of the modern right. Welcome to Sarasota County, a cradle – and a proving ground – for the MAGAmerican dream.

– Kara Voght, Washington Post[1]

"An area native was one of four men arrested on federal charges of allegedly being a part of a scheme to bilk funds from proponents of building a wall along the U.S.-Mexico border," reported the *Venice Gondolier*.

At 56 the former Venice resident appeared in federal court in Tampa after being arrested earlier in the day and took part in a virtual hearing based in the Southern District of New York.

To me, who had followed Badolato and his frauds for years, it was big news.

Three years after the turn of the century, 2003, Bannon and Badolato jointly launched second careers in serial stock fraud. All of this was well-known in Sarasota, Florida by Joey Barquin, an investor who had a front-row seat as much of it transpired. Defrauded by Andy Badolato, Joey played along for 25 years, determined to get his investment back. All for nought.

He held a grudge. He held nothing back.

The Barquin Revelations

Joey found me after I wrote my first story about Andy Badolato in September 2016, not long after the *Guardian* broke the story of Bannon's connection to Sarasota – or actually to Casey Key Island just west of Venice and Nokomis, Florida. My own turf. Of course I'd paid attention. It was like déjà vu all over again – like when I'd first heard the name Huffman Aviation at Venice Airport in the news. That had also taken place on my turf.

The *Guardian* reported: "Donald Trump's campaign chief has moved his voter registration to the home of one his website's writers, after the *Guardian* disclosed that he was previously registered at an empty house in Florida where he did not live."[2]

Finally, I thought, something local to investigate. Before that, if you check my website, you'll see that, ever since Trump "descended into the Abyss," I'd been focused backward on such things as my 2000 investigation of voting systems and on Donald Trump himself.[3] This new twist on Trump's campaign promised to bring Sarasota, "the meanest city in America," back into the limelight.[4]

I interviewed Joey several times to try to learn what he'd witnessed over the years, first as a tagalong pal of Jonathan Curshen in the late '90s. He'd been introduced to Bad0lato a few years later when the two fraudsters began working together.

What gave Joey the status as an investor was a sad tale of abuse he'd suffered in the early '50s at the hands of nuns at a Catholic orphanage in Vermont. His birth parents' family had dropped him there when he was three, and he was abused there until his adoption at age five by the Barquins, a good family with a heritage from Spain.

He was operating a dive shop in Venice, Florida – called Dolphin Encounters – in 1991 when he married Pamela Lesemann, a professional therapist. Pam helped him find the source of his marital problems, which then led him to sue the orphanage and the unknown nuns for sexual, physical and emotional abuse. He and Pam divorced in 1997. Once Joey collected the money from his settlement, he had no need to work, but he felt a need to put the money to good use. How he got sucked into Curshen's orbit he never explained.

Joey may have first contacted me in 2008, after Curshen was arrested in Florida. The first time Curshen's name appeared at my website was just after his office in Costa Rica was raided in connection with Industrial Biotechnology Corp. (IBC), which I'd inaccurately connected to Stuart Burchill.[5]

My bad. Joey may have contacted me at that time to correct my assumption – to tell me IBC had nothing to do with Wally Hilliard's former treasurer. However, at that time my one focus was directed only on Donna Blue – Cocaine Two.

Due to my diagnosis, as mentioned previously, of ADD (without the hyperactivity component) and Adderall, prescribed to counteract my attention deficit component, I was focused on only one task at a time. In a way, that's a good thing.

463

In the case of Curshen and Badolato, though, it kept me from zeroing in on Badolato until years later, after Steve Bannon "moved into" Andy's beach house on Casey Key.

Roots of Industrial Biotechnology

Michael Pollick of the *Sarasota Herald Tribune* had interviewed Andy Badolato in June 2007. Badolato told him he had filed a lawsuit against Yung Huoy Mark Truei from Taiwan, who had been CEO of Industrial Biotechnology Corp., with which Badolato was affiliated, but who had been fired.

Badolato had smiled broadly and convinced the reporter he was only a "budding capitalist" who'd been "taken for a ride" by Truei, who had damaged IBC, but the company had moved on and still expected great things to happen. We were, however, unable to find any lawsuit in Sarasota County under the name mentioned in Pollick's article.[6] Nevertheless, we did find a few press releases from the time Truei was in charge, dating back to May 2006.

"IBC is honored to include Dr. Kung-Ta Lee as a member of IBC's highly qualified and respected team of Scientific Advisors," said Mark Truei, Vice President of Production and Manufacturing for IBC. Mark continued, "Dr. Lee possesses the knowledge and experience necessary to execute the optimization, scale-up and commercialization of the numerous compounds in IBC's pipeline scheduled for roll-out."[7]

We were impressed. Science, experience, commercialization. Who wouldn't perk up to those words and ask where to sign up to buy shares?

A plethora of press releases were being pumped out around that time by PR firm Biospace, listing names of persons to contact about the products offered by various subsidiaries of UTEK Corporation.[8]

One of the first press releases listed the name David L. West as the contact person.[9] So we began there.

David West had formed IBC as a public corporation in the state of Washington on August 2, 2005. At that time John R. Doran, [J. Ronald Doran] was chairman of the board of IBC, claiming to have acquired its technology from Oxford University for UTEK in Tampa. J. Ronald "Ron" Doran, Sr. was born in New Jersey in 1937.

According to his 2021 obituary in the Asbury Park, *New Jersey Press* on October 24, 2021, Ron was "an advertising sales pro in New York City. In 1993, he founded JRD Associates where he worked until retirement."[10] Doran was a merchant banker who also claimed to have "overseen development, financing, and strategic relationships for various healthcare and technology companies including Uniphyd Corporation, Milcom, and Terranex."[11]

Intriguingly, he had attended St. Thomas of Villanova University, the same university in Miami, Florida where Andy Badolato got his degree. The two would later be associated together in White Knights and Vultures, LLC beginning in 2011.

On August 6, 2005, IBC owned ten million preferred shares of stock issued in its name, as well as 100% of the issued and outstanding shares of common stock of Advanced Bioscience, Inc. (ABI), its wholly owned subsidiary. UTEK acquired ABI one day earlier and changed its management at that time from the Oxford University chemists who'd developed the technologies to Doran and David L. West, at 2033 Main Street, Suite 400 in Sarasota (where Andy had recently moved).

Badolato first became involved with "green energy fuels" through David Lloyd West, a CPA with an MBA in finance, who procured a shell corporation used by Clifford Mark Gross, Ph.D. at the University of South Florida.

Gross, a New Yorker, had spent a year or more in England at Oxford University, where he devised a mechanism to transfer technology, financed with government grants, from university researchers to businesses willing to use the technology in the manufacture of actual products. Gross acquired the patents through his corporation, UTEK. West then acquired a public shell, changed its name and started a business to sell off. West was previously involved with International Diversified Industries, Inc. (IDII), which, in 2004 changed its name to E-4 Music Network, Inc., with a second change in July 2006 to Uniphyd Corp. – a Medicare Advantage plan traded on pink sheets.[12]

LYING AS SERIOUS BUSINESS

This may have been Andy Badolato's first introduction to reverse mergers using shell corporations. But they've been around a few years.

It was then that the business of lying seriously began:

"Aggressive investors and traders will want to watch Uniphyd Corporation (Pink Sheets:UPHD) this morning! Yesterday after the markets closed, the company issued a press release announcing it has reached a definitive agreement for the introduction of its first Medicare managed care plan in Florida!"[13]

Surprise! Just another pump and dump scheme.

Legal documents were drafted by attorney Michael G. Brown, the brother-in-law of Jonathan Curshen. Previous corporate filings were handled by a paralegal named Michael W. Hawkins, who for a time used an address in Melbourne, Florida in the historic Melbourne Hotel. It was Hawkins who had set up the first corporation on which Badolato was first involved with Steve Bannon in 2003 – Donna Messenger Corp.

Chris Anderson discovered the connection in his story for the *Sarasota Herald Tribune* on April 24, 2018.[14]

Hawkins also filed documents on behalf of Sargon-Uniphyd LLC in 2004, and for Galen Uniphyd Health Plan Corporation for Robert L. Trinka. Although the filing stated Galen Uniphyd was being filed in Florida, other provisions of the articles of incorporation stated it was consistent with the laws of the state of Washington, by The Otto Law Group, LLC, of Seattle. David M. Otto was an associate of Badolato's mentor, Gerald C. Parker.

David Otto and a different attorney in his office would later be sued by the SEC in Seattle on behalf of innocent shareholders of MitoPharm Corporation.[15]

The SEC's complaint excoriated the lawyers, the client, their PR firm and anyone else in sight. MitoPharm, as David Baines of the *Vancouver Sun* explained in 2009, "traded on the Pink Sheets, rose to $2.30, then plunged to a nickel."[16]

It was a Pump and Dump extravaganza.

The SEC alleged Otto had directed "an aggressive public relations campaign premised on the misleading promotion of a product that did not exist."[17] It was promoted as an anti-aging cream supposedly invented by its CEO, Pak Peter Cheung of Vancouver – whose name was very similar to Dr. Peter Pak-Hang Cheung, a chemistry professor in Hong Kong.[18]

While Otto advised MitoPharm's CEO how to rip off members of the public who bought shares, he busily figuratively raped his own client all the while through a complicated financing scheme where portions of the promissory note were partially transferred to nominee entities he controlled.

In a different SEC filing we are told: "Under the services of Banyan Capital Partners and Sargon Capital, Inc., Mr. Hawkins assisted SinoFresh HealthCare, Inc., in securing funding through its 'C' and 'D' rounds of private funding and provided administrative oversight during a reverse merger into a publicly held company in October 2003."[19]

In yet another corporate filing, Hawkins claimed to have been "Human Resource Manager for Boeing Corporation, under the Delta IV Rocket Program."[20]

Hawkins was the Manager in 2004 for Sargon Holding Group LLC, as well as with Sargon Holdings II, LLC, founded in 2003 as DM-Sargon LLC, using Andy Badolato's previous address of 7820 S. Holiday Drive, Suite 320 in Sarasota. The DM in the name was short for "Donna Messenger," a client who was a cosmetologist.

Andy Badolato was assisted in his corporate endeavors by business associates that date back to 1996, the year he met Gerald C. Parker. Formerly from Orlando, Parker had successfully created a credit reporting firm and sold it to Equifax in 1988 – just after the housing market crash. Soon after that, the money he'd made was all gone.

Foreclosures hounded him out of Orlando. First they came for his red Mercedes, then his home. By 1998 Gerald Parker was looking for a safe harbor.

There's a proviso used to warn investors who buy securities called "safe harbor."

"When used in this filing, the words 'believe,' 'anticipate,' 'endeavor,' 'estimate,' 'expect,' objective,' 'projection,' 'forecast,' 'goal' and similar expressions are intended to identify forward-looking statements."

In other words, let investors beware of optimistic predictions about anything they buy. The proviso is supposed to protect the seller of the securities, but it won't work if they actually lie.

FINDING SAFETY HARBOR

When he relocated to Safety Harbor, Florida, Parker had just sold his interest in Smart Choice Automotive Group – a chain of used car companies. With Finova as his primary lender, he could sell used cars with financing in place to people with rotten credit.

That, among other things – like financing CIA-owned airplanes that had a habit of being stolen – explains why Finova didn't survive long after that.[21]

Safety Harbor sounded like an ideal destination. As its name implies, the town is the most sheltered area on Old Tampa Bay. In 1995 Parker incorporated in Delaware a new vehicle for what was seen as his future trading empire – Investment Management of America. Andy Badolato helped him get it authorized for business in Florida.

New participants were continually moving in and out. Situated halfway between Tampa and Clearwater, Parker attracted quite a few ne'er-do-wells, including Larry G. Rightmyer, added as secretary for Investment Management in its April 2000 report shown at "Sunbiz." He and

Andy shared the same office address that year on recorded documents – 7820 S. Holiday Drive in Sarasota, just north of Osprey.

Rightmyer's parents lived in Sarasota, and he'd finished college and law school in Florida in 1965. By 1973 he was a partner in the politically connected firm of Republican lawyers – Goldner, Marger, Davis & Rightmyer.

A SMATTERING OF REPUBLICAN POLITICIANS

The senior partner, Herman W. Goldner, mayor of St. Petersburg, had actually founded the Republican Party in Pinellas County in 1947 and helped get his first law partner, William C. Cramer, elected as a Republican to the Florida state house in 1950 – at a time when all other elected officials in Florida were Democrats. Cramer was the first Florida Republican elected to the U.S. Congress in 1954.

He lost in 1970 to Democrat Lawton Chiles for the U.S. Senate, even though President Nixon came to Florida to campaign for him. Cramer then opened a lobbying law firm in Washington, D.C., serving as general counsel to the Republican National Committee. It was still two years before the Watergate break-in.

Could that be when Republicans first discovered how to funnel drug money into political campaigns?

Anastasio Somoza became a client of the Goldner, Marger firm even before Nixon resigned the Presidency. Cramer got assistance for Somoza's LaNica Airline from federal aviation regulators. Herman Goldner's eldest son, Brian, was a 1965 graduate of the Air Force Academy, a former pilot in Vietnam, and soon developed a business relationship with Somoza – both in fishing and in boat building.

You may recall hearing the name Marger in an earlier chapter about Mitchell WerBell's trial. Edwin Marger, the lawyer in that case was a cousin of Bruce Marger, who lived in St. Petersburg.

Rightmyer must have had lots of tales to share with Badolato, assuming they had time to "chew the fat" at the office they shared. Such as the time he served as Percy Foreman's local counsel, representing what the papers called the "Steinhatchee 7" bust.

Seven fishermen from Pass-a-Grille Beach, arrested in March 1973 after a barge carrying nine tons of Jamaican marijuana ran aground. It was not Percy's best work, obviously, judging from the fact that six of the seven got 20 years in prison. Hanging Judge Middlebrooks earned his name that day.

468

Percy accepted none of the blame of course. The reporter quoted him barking at the oldest defendant, "'Shut up,' he hissed at Capo one morning before the jury appeared. 'I swear to God you've got the brain of a chicken.' Later outside the courtroom, Foreman, a jovial man with a quick wit, admitted he had made the statement. 'My only hope is that I haven't offended any of the poultry interests.'"[22]

Rightmyer – before he became an alcoholic lawyer, sued for malpractice and convicted of perjury – had a few drug stories he could have regaled the young Andy with, while they both officed at 7820 S. Holiday Drive in Sarasota. Rightmyer had been the attorney involved in "the largest single seizure of marijuana in Florida's history."[23]

NIXON'S WAR ON DRUGS

Rightmyer also drew up corporate papers for two men from Argentina and Peru for a company called O and M Realty. The idea was to acquire land in the Florida panhandle near the Georgia state line to lease to an American couple, Raymond Hawkins and his wife, who claimed to be using the land to raise appaloosa horses.

Unbeknownst to the Feds at this crucial time, Florida had been so concerned about the upswing in drug smuggling, a statewide grand jury had been formed to hear drug cases. Rightmyer's clients were caught up in this web. The timing was critical because Nixon's war on drugs had just begun – emasculating whatever powers the state once had in such matters.

Rightmyer lost his job, while his firm brought in outside counsel to fight having to transfer his file to the IRS. The Federal judge rubber-stamped that action, and there was no looking back to state control of drug crimes.

Rightmyer's client Hawkins and his wife were arrested for storing 25 tons of weed on their farms, along with Raymond Grady Stansel, Jr., a Tarpon Springs fisherman, who imported 20 tons of weed at Port St. Joe. Though he denied knowing Stansel, Rightmyer's firm's business card was found on the smuggler during an arrest search, and, what's more, Hawkins' phone number at a third farm in Georgia was also in Stansel's wallet.

A statewide Florida grand jury indicted the Stansel crew one year after the bust, the same month, coincidentally, that the indictment of Kenny Burnstine, was unsealed by a Federal grand jury. Just two different competing gangs, of which there are thousands in Florida.

Was something sinister going on to create all that demand in Florida, just as President Nixon announced his War on Drugs?

The "horse farm," actually owned by the South American clients of Rightmyer, was said to have been the ultimate destination for Stansel's busted cargo of Colombian cannabis. It clearly wasn't the first load, simply judging from the fact the Hawkins couple went down for possession of dope from previous deliveries.

Stansel put up a bond of half a million in cash and was scheduled for a hearing in the summer of 1974.

Rightmyer didn't know it then – he may have felt it somewhere in his gut – that his best days were already behind him. He resigned, leaving files behind that proved his complicity. That was the beginning of his decline, bottoming out in 1993 with his disbarment.

Stansel, for his part, claimed to be merely a fisherman, but passports in his possession showed he had been to 12 countries – including Jamaica, Colombia, Japan, Hong Kong, Panama, and the Cayman Islands – within a 30-day window.

Although he took the Fifth 25 times during the 12-hour interview, he did tell police "of more than $850,000 funneled through three of his accounts by Central and South American businesses he said he represents but gets no salary from. He said none of the money is his but is used to purchase and renovate boats to begin a fishing fleet for the companies ...."[24]

"Stansel said he is agent for three companies that list Nicaraguan leader Gen. Anastasio Somoza Jr. as a partner. Each company channels money internally on a regular basis, and most purchases are made in cash with no checks available to trace the cash flow, he said.... All the companies are linked to Blue Chip Fisheries, Inc. in Tarpon Springs," a Florida corporation set up in April 1972.[25]

When the date he was supposed to appear in court came, Stansel didn't show up. Rumor was he'd drowned in Honduras. That excuse persisted until a May 2015 obituary for a gator-swamp tour guide, Dennis Lee Lafferty, disclosed Lafferty was in fact Stansel, who'd faked his death and lived another 40 years in Queensland, Australia.

Just another unheralded American Drug Lord.

NEW MILLENNIUM MEDIA

Badolato's trail shows up among a series of lowlifes from the first corporations he got involved with once he met Gerry Parker. In addition to Rightmyer's influence for a time, he was introduced to an ex-cop who called himself John "JT" Thatch, though his real name was John David Thatch.

Thatch was ejected from the Tampa police department for use of excessive force while arresting an alleged cocaine dealer in 1986. That led him into owning an "adult" bookstore (Pussycat Books) in Largo, where a police raid in 1990 brought him new unwelcome headlines.

By the end of the decade, he had set up shop with Gerald Parker in Safety Harbor, where together with Andy Badolato they created New Millennium Media, Inc. – a Florida company originally chartered in Colorado. It was somehow connected to another grifter named David Otto of the state of Washington – a source for shells – many of which were the mummified remains of Vancouver penny stocks.

Gerald Parker was chairman, Badolato vice chairman, and Thatch filled all the other offices of New Millenium. Its business was to provide outdoor and indoor advertising including "light emitting diode" signage to businesses, according to their filing documents.

We get the sense Parker was running a training school for new venture capitalists, with the older man teaching newbies the practical side of acquiring shells, doing reverse mergers and the like. Some of the businesses they built during that time were legitimate ones with a real but low-cost product, such as the blinking signs on wheels in this case. Another example was turning a small restaurant into a chain, as in Crabby Bill's seafood a few years later.

In time, however, it became easier to just form businesses which had no product at all, only an excuse to claim that one existed. That change occurred around 2003, the year Badolato first worked with Steve Bannon and the same time he changed his address to 2033 Main Street, Suite 400, in Sarasota.

INFINIUM PHANTOMS

Much of what Joey had to say involved people who shared the 2033 Main address with Andy Badolato. People involved in Infinium Labs on the third floor of what was known then as the Infinium Building moved in and out like so many phantoms. They even changed the name of their company to Phantom Entertainment, which seemed appropriate. Like Brent Kovar of Skyway, they claimed to be electronic geniuses, but in the business of gaming – building a mystical little white box, in this case, supposedly superior to Nintendo or X-Box. When I started researching these guys seriously, spooky shivers ran down my spine. "Who are these guys?" I found myself asking.

Timothy Munro Roberts was one of the phantom stars, who were said to be creating the Phantom gaming console, raising millions for a product that never quite went into production.

He later controlled a company called Savvis, that became Savtira. Bankruptcy resulted in 2012 after raising money while promising "astronomical, risk-free returns."[26]

But it took the Feds five years to indict him. Another two years lapsed before he ended up in a cell – the kind with bars for windows – not a phone.

* * *

Many of Badolato's former associates are currently incarcerated, at least one of them for threatening his life. As they headed for the joint, they left strewn behind them the wreckage of plundered public companies.

Joey once told me, "Somehow I happened to be in the office with Badolato on the day two FBI agents out of FBI Tampa came in. Younger agents. They sat him down and informed Badolato that it was basically a coin flip between him and Jonathan Curshen to see which of them would be spending the next 20 years in prison."

"They decided Curshen was the bigger fish to take down. He had extensive international ties. So, the agents flipped Andy Badolato. He started wearing a wire."

Barquin was referring to a conversation that took place years ago, a time before Jonathan Curshen's 2008 arrest.

"Badolato is a close friend and associate of Steve Bannon's," Joey told me. "He's worked for and with Bannon. But Badolato is really a professional con man.

"What I knew about Badolato – well before the feds busted him – was that for years he'd been secretly recording all his phone calls with Bannon. He has the goods on Bannon. It was his insurance policy. He thought it made him bulletproof," Joey said.

Badolato had surreptitiously taped phone conversations with the President's chief advisor. Anytime but now, and anywhere but here, that would be a big story.

Joey continued. "And he was right. Because he'd already been secretly busted by the FBI, and then cut a deal. So, they already knew about the recordings."

"Also," Joey leaned toward me, whispering, "he's a known sexual predator who preys on underage girls. This is not acceptable."

There was strong evidence indicating Joey was telling me the truth. Sarasota police reports detailed his often-abusive behavior with women. He'd been accused of rape on several occasions. But nothing ever stuck.

"When the Trump family heard that Badolato had secretly been tap-ing Bannon," Joey continued, with some satisfaction, "Bannon's days were numbered, and they soon got rid of him." He was fired on August 18, 2017.

"EL PADRONE"

Financial fraud and drug trafficking have long and storied histories in Sarasota. When Steve Bannon and Andy Badolato's crew of alt-right grifters started racking up big financial fraud scores in the early 2000's, they were simply following a well-rehearsed pattern.

When Donald Trump unexpectedly won in 2016, Joey told me, he'd been shocked, quickly deciding he had a civic duty to warn the FBI and other law enforcement agencies about Steve Bannon's lowlife Sarasota as-sociate Badolato. Plus, it was fun.

Joey told them Badolato represented a real security risk to the incom-ing Administration. But it took a while before the fireworks exploded.

The Bannon-Badolato bust was a stark reminder of how much you can get away with – and for how long – when you're a well-connected white guy engaging in organized white-collar crime.

During Watergate, the villains looked like ordinary businessmen. That standard appears to no longer apply. "Bannon looks like a guy selling ex-otic reptiles on the Venice Beach boardwalk," said *Late Night* host Seth Myers. "Or like a guy who lists his home address as the swim-up bar at the Mirage." He reminds me of the kind of guy featured on "Airplane Repo." Bannon and Badolato both look like guys who have just lost their ride.

Andy Badolato had been industrious in the early days. Having just learned about a successful market test conducted by Largo-based Eck-erd drug in 2002, he discovered the product was being made in his own hometown. Charles Fust, the patent owner, called it SinoFresh, a "mouth-wash for the sinuses."

Its factory was housed a few hundred yards from the train depot where the Ringling circus had arrived in Venice every winter, only a short drive from Andy's office at the time. He approached Fust "at the ideal time," the inventor would later tell a reporter, when Fust was seeking ideas for a na-tional branding campaign. His hope was to raise funds to hire a big name like Rush Limbaugh to advertise for him. [27]

That gives you an idea of their politics, maybe what attracted them to each other.

Fust revealed that Badolato brought Steve Bannon on board, along with David Otto of Seattle – whose job it was to take SinoFresh public.

He did so by doing a reverse merger with a Florida corporation called E-Book Networks, Inc., one of thirteen shells created after e-Miracle Network.com of Miami filed for bankruptcy.

That may have been Badolato's first contact with Bannon – an introduction from mutual associate David Otto. It didn't take long for Steve's influence to rub off on Andy. Together they also attracted a host of others like themselves with Steve Bannon as "El Padrone." From that point on the pack became industrious about serial stock fraud.

One of their operations was International Business Ventures Group (IBVG), incorporated in 2001 by Michael Brown, Jonathan Curshen's brother-in-law, who was a lawyer in Sarasota. The business address was the same address initially used for Bannon's Victory Film Project, LLC, set up in Florida on December 30, 2010.

A year later Bannon changed the address to 8383 Wilshire Blvd, Suite 1000 in Beverly Hills CA 90211 – where his company, Bannon Strategic Advisors, was registered. According to the *Daily Beast* in 2017, payments to Bannon from the wealthy and extremely secretive Mercer family, who also financed Breitbart News and Cambridge Analytica, were funneled to that same address.[28]

Mike Muzio of Tampa didn't limit himself to trading with these pals. He also hooked up with a trio calling themselves Homepals Investment Club in North Miami Beach.

Muzio bought the shell company after Michael Brown had set it up for Curshen, using the same address Badolato operated out of in Sarasota. By then Curshen was in jail and had no need of it anymore. Muzio began trading IBVG's worthless stock with Homepals, which was itself nothing but a ponzi scheme. The *New Times* of Broward-Palm Beach said it best in a 2010 headline, "*A Poor Man's Bernie Madoff Screws Haitian-Americans.*"[29]

It wasn't pretty.

Muzio, who served six years of his 163-month federal prison sentence for that crime, had previously been a musician who "owned" Blue Moon Group, a subsidiary of GenesisIntermedia, the company Adnan Khashoggi and Ramy El-Batrawi used in their own scams.

Though Blue Moon had no obvious revenue, it nonetheless issued a press release announcing it had purchased, for three-quarters of a million dollars, a white grand piano Elvis Presley had owned. He spent a total of $1.3 million at the auction, including, among other things, the "Memphis Music" label owned by Robert A. Johnson – the same guy, incidentally, who more recently has been marketing the rock version of "Make America Great Again" on You Tube. These guys all seem to support the same candidate.

Politically speaking, Steve Bannon rose to power first as Breitbart News chairman, becoming Donald Trump's chief strategist after Paul Manafort experienced a spot of bother because of his relationship with Russian oligarch Oleg Deripaska, from whom he's received more than $18 million for unspecified services.

Less well known is the fact that Bannon spent much of the past two decades using complex financial mechanisms – the kind ordinarily employed by only the largest financial services firms – to help him as an investor in penny-stocks.

An experienced Goldman Sachs investment banker in Beverly Hills for several years after completing his master's degree, Bannon also became something of an expert in media packaging – old movies and TV shows produced by various studios that could be resold to cable TV and other re-run networks. Bannon himself made a personal small fortune off *Seinfeld*.

What he's never seemed to brag about is that he also spent several years as CEO of a strange corporation called Biosphere 2, which *Wired* magazine discovered in 2016: "Twenty-five years ago, a New Agey-experiment called Biosphere 2 set out to recreate life on another planet with eight people locked in a giant glass habitat. But it ended bitterly with allegations of financial fraud, scientific goof-ups, and a power struggle outside the dome."[30]

Wired even linked its article to a clip of Steve Bannon on You Tube talking about the science of global climate change. Bannon looked almost halfway presentable at the time. That was long before one of his ex-wives got hooked on meth.

By 1995 Biosphere's owner, Ed P. Bass, Texas oil heir, sold the project to Columbia University of New York, which continued to manage it through Bannon's brother, Christopher, and a corporation he operated through at least 2005.[31]

By then Bannon's focus had shifted. Thereafter, he steered clear of anything that looked even remotely liberal.

Politico reported, "In the years before Bannon emerged as a populist critic of financial wizardry run amok, most of his companies failed to take off, and were often in the throes of legal troubles."[32]

The Bannon group's penny-stock companies were instantly recognizable. Though Lilliputian in size, they employed complex corporate maneuvers favored by the financial masters of the universe, including transnational acquisitions, reverse mergers, and asset purchase agreements – as if they were real companies, which they were not.

"THE THROES OF LEGAL TROUBLES"

Then there's Andrew M. Badolato, whose relationship with former presidential adviser Steve Bannon goes back decades. By a tender age, Andy had already founded and helmed numerous public companies, which all floundered, like unwanted babies exposed on a cliff in Sparta.

Henry Ford brought technology to bear on the problem of mass-producing cars. Badolato performed a similar feat. He brought modern management concepts to bear on a problem in serial financial fraud, of people feeling that paydays took too long, and were too far apart.

Andy's answer was speed. He had companies circling overhead, ready to land whenever a previous flight crashed and burned, which they always did.

Badolato's "The Renewable Corporation" was a Washington company with a Utah transfer agent. With Badolato presiding at all times, The Renewable Corp had formerly been known as Industrial Biotechnology Corporation. Industrial Biotechnology Corporation, which Jonathan Curshen had been flogging when he was arrested in New York in 2008.

Other pump-and-dump schemes the network was involved with are presented to show how industrious Andy Badolato et al were about serial stock fraud. There were too many for us to name here.

After bad publicity and his embarrassing penchant for running public companies into the ground scuppered his dreams of a role in the Trump Administration, Andy Badolato was crushed. Any title at all would have been acceptable. There were plenty of things he was good at. "Procurement Officer in charge of walking around money" would have been ideal.

But what's important about Andy Badolato is: He's no ordinary grifter. Many of his biggest scams have had quasi-official sanction. One example: He partnered with Lockheed and Raytheon – companies Adnan Khashoggi started brokering deals for as early as 1964 – and helmed a company which got a $200 million loan from Florida Governor Jeb Bush's business initiative, "Enterprise Florida." Alas, "Enterprise Florida," and Florida taxpayers, both took a bath on that loan.

But by far Badolato's most fascinating quality was that he was coated with Teflon. Shielded from indictment, even in cases in which ordinary mortals did serious time.

Andy faced failure like a trouper. It was almost as if he expected it. He never batted an eye. Eventually, however, his behavior began reflecting poorly on Steve Bannon, who was much more of a public figure, and already looking more than usually disheveled.

There were obvious clues pointing to transnational organized crime, which no one in Republican circles in Sarasota wanted to face.

"Where We Go One, We Go All"

Steve Bannon and Andy Badolato's alt-right Sarasota criminal network, which successfully stole hundreds of millions of dollars, was held together by allegiance to Trump, and some of this hot money, presumably, wormed its way into Trump's presidential campaign coffers. Sarasota wasn't where the stupid started. But it was where it was funded, at least in part.

Cambridge Analytica (CA) was a U.S. subsidiary of SCL Elections, a British corporation whose shareholders "have social and business links to the heart of the Conservative Party, royalty and the British military," according to David Brown of *The Times*.[33]

We think of them as pretty classy folks. Maybe they were too classy to stay linked with Trump for very long.

Cambridge Analytica was, however, linked to Facebook in a data-mining scandal shortly before the 2018 mid-terms, which provided the opportunity to sever the parent from the subsidiary that got Trump elected. Both corporations quickly filed bankruptcy once the scandal became public.

Cambridge had been "bankrolled by Robert Mercer, a wealthy Republican donor who invested at least $15 million, offered tools that it claimed could identify the personalities of American voters and influence their behavior," according to the *New York Times*.[34]

The Trump campaign relied on those tools in creating Trump's political brand and identifying his base. Although he already seemed to fit the demographic model voters wanted, Trump's strategists, like Bannon, were able to tweak the model by using the profile to write Trump's speeches for his endless rallies.

The brand cared not whether the voters' allegiance was to the U.S. Constitution or the White Nationalist Manifesto.

Winning was all that mattered. It still is.

They may have thought it would be easy to control and manipulate this voter bloc later, but we've all begun to suspect that's by no means true. The tail has taken control of the dog, and it can't be swayed by truth or facts.

Endnotes

1   Kara Vogt, "The MAGAmerican dream lives in Sarasota," *Washington Post*, Sept. 30, 2023. https://www.washingtonpost.com/style/power/interactive/2023/sarasota-maga-dream/

2   Jon Swaine, "Steve Bannon moves Florida voter registration to home of Breitbart writer," *The Guardian*, 26 August 2016. https://www.theguardian.com/us-news/2016/aug/26/steve-bannon-florida-voter-registration-home-breitbart-writer

3   https://www.madcowprod.com/previousstories/

4   https://www.madcowprod.com/2012/04/02/sarasota-florida-meanest-city-america/

5   https://www.madcowprod.com/5126-2/

6   Michael Pollick, "Business in Sarasota says it was taken in by a promised breakthrough," *Sarasota Herald Tribune*, June 8, 2007. https://www.heraldtribune.com/story/news/2007/06/08/business-in-sarasota-says-it-was-taken-in-by-a-promised-breakthrough/28552622007/

7   Press Release, "Industrial Biotechnology Corporation Appoints National Taiwan University Professor, Dr. Kung-Ta Lee, To Scientific Advisory Board," Biospace, May 25, 2006. https://www.biospace.com/article/releases/industrial-biotechnology-corporation-appoints-b-national-taiwan-university-b-professor-b-dr-kung-ta-lee-b-to-scientific-advisory-board-/

8   https://www.biospace.com/employer/512186/industrial-biotechnology-corporation/

9   https://www.biospace.com/article/releases/industrial-biotechnology-corporation-adds-biological-manufacturing-and-production-expertise-/

10   https://www.findagrave.com/memorial/234444607/j.-ronald-doran

11   Disclosure Statement for The Renewable Corporation, July 7, 2010. http://www.otcmarkets.com/financialReportViewer?symbol=RNWB&id=33861

12   "Uniphyd Reaches Definitive Agreement For Medicare Managed Care Plan In Florida," Biospace, October 19, 2005. https://www.biospace.com/article/releases/-b-uniphyd-b-reaches-definitive-agreement-for-medicare-managed-care-plan-in-florida/

13   Wall Street News Alert--Breaking Market News! April 28, 2004, Part 2, April 28, 2004. https://www.globenewswire.com/en/news-release/2004/04/28/309650/1538/en/Wall-Street-News-Alert-Breaking-Market-News-April-28-2004-Part-2.html

14   Chris Anderson, "Steve Bannon, Andrew Badolato, Casey Key and a questionable association," *Sarasota Herald-Tribune*, August 20, 2020. https://www.heraldtribune.com/story/news/local/2020/08/20/steve-bannon-andrew-badolato-and-sarasota-connection/5616202002/

15   Otto would get his comeuppance of a sort in 2011 when allowed by the SEC to enter into a consent decree. https://www.sec.gov/litigation/litreleases/lr-21945

16   David Baines, *Vancouver Sun*, 15 Jul 2009, Page 23.

17   Securities and Exchange Commission v. David M. Otto, Todd Van Siclen, MitoPharm Corporation, Pak Peter Cheung, Wall Street PR, Inc., Charles Bingham, Case No. CV-09-0960 RAJ (WD Wa. filed July 13, 2009). https://www.sec.gov/litigation/litreleases/lr-21126

18   Complaint filed at https://www.sec.gov/files/litigation/complaints/2009/comp21126.pdf Form SB/2A (amendment 4), Alternative Construction Company, Inc.,

19   Form SB/2A (amendment 4), Alternative Construction Company, Inc., March 2006. https://www.sec.gov/Archives/edgar/data/1337566/000114420406013064/0001144204-06-013064.txt.

20   Ibid.

21   Finova had previously been known as Greyhound Leasing. https://www.sec.gov/Archives/edgar/data/883701/000089843001500244/d10k405a.htm

22   Eleanor Randolph, "Steinhatchee 7: Little slips greased the way to cells," *Tampa Bay Times*, St. Petersburg, Florida, 14 Oct 1973, Page 42, Philip Morgan, "Order halts records turnover in IRS probe of Hawkins,"

23, *Tampa Tribune*, 04 Sep 1974, Page 26.

24   Allen Cowan, "Reduction in bond argued," *Tampa Bay Times*, St. Petersburg, Florida, June 09, 1974.

25   Ibid.

26   "Tim Roberts faces fraud charges over failed Tampa startup," *St. Louis Post-Dispatch*, Sep

11, 2015.

27   Alex Leary and Adam C. Smith, "Bannon's Florida footprint full of mystery," *Miami Herald*, 13 Mar 2017, Pages A1-2.

28   Lachlan Markay, "Complaint: Bannon, Mercer Dodged California Taxes," *Daily Beast*, May 05, 2017. https://www.thedailybeast.com/complaint-bannon-mercer-dodged-california-taxes

29   Gus Garcia-Roberts, "A Poor Man's Bernie Madoff Screws Haitian-Americans," *Broward-Palm Beach New Times*, April 15, 2010.https://www.miaminewtimes.com/news/a-poor-mans-bernie-madoff-screws-haitian-americans-6366640

30   Eric Miller, "Trump's Chief Strategist Steve Bannon Ran a Massive Climate Experiment," *Wired*, Dec 7, 2016. hmate-experiment/

31   David Safier, "Chris Bannon: 'We Are Coming For You!'" *Tucson Weekly*, Tue, Nov 14, 2017. https://www.tucsonweekly.com/TheRange/archives/2017/11/14/chris-bannon-we-are-coming-for-you

32   Ben Schreckinger, "Steve Bannon's adventures in penny stocks," Politico, 11/29/2016. https://www.politico.com/story/2016/11/stephen-bannon-stock-market-trump-231915

33   David Brown, "SCL Group's founders were connected to royalty, the rich and powerful," *The Times*, March 21 2018. https://www.thetimes.com/uk/article/scl-group-s-founders-were-connected-to-royalty-the-rich-and-powerful-3pxhfvhlh

34   Nicholas Confessore, "Cambridge Analytica and Facebook: The Scandal and the Fallout So Far," *New York Times*, April 4, 2018. https://www.nytimes.com/2018/04/04/us/politics/cambridge-analytica-scandal-fallout.html

Chapter Thirty

Bust of The MSC Gayane

You're a lost sailor
You've been too long at sea
Now the shorelines beckon
Yeah, there's a price for being free
– "Lost Sailor/Saint of Circumstance" Grateful Dead

It was the second biggest drug bust in American history.

On the evening of June 16, 2019, as skies grew cloudy over Delaware Bay, a giant container ship lumbered towards the Port of Philadelphia.

Longer than three football fields laid end to end, the Mediterranean Shipping Company's MSC *Gayane* (2nd largest in the world) is one of the world's newest classes of ships, the ULCVs – Ultra-Large Container Vessels.

But before arriving at the Port, the ship was intercepted by boats carrying armed agents from a multi-agency task force, who climbed rope ladders and then swarmed aboard the giant ship. Before they were done, they'd seized almost 20 tons of cocaine.

According to the *Philadelphia Inquirer*, "They (the agents) were there, they said, to check to see if locks on the steel containers that hold millions of dollars' worth of goods were intact. "The seals on some boxes didn't look right," stated someone with direct knowledge of the matter."

It was a fig leaf attempting to hide their secret knowledge. But it didn't work. In a matter of months, the top two leaders of a Mafia clan in Kotor, Montenegro would be dead.

The dead men were assassinated in front of their families in a restaurant in Athens, suspected of having "snitched out" the massive cocaine move underway on the container ship, because it belonged to the other Mafia clan in Kotor, with whom they are in the middle of a long and very bloody civil war, with murders and assassinations taking place across Europe from Berlin to Vienna to Valencia, Spain.

It wouldn't seem like the tiny town of Kotor, population 30,000 in the middle of tourist season, would need, or be large enough, to support two feuding Mafia clans.

"ALL QUIET ON THE PHILLY FRONT"

In Europe, the war rages on. But in Philadelphia, where the 20 tons came to rest, things are remarkably quiet. The U.S. Attorney's investigation has produced just one arrest of any consequence, and that came at the time of the seizure, when they busted the ship's Second Mate, Ivan Durasevic.

Ivan Durasevich hardly looks the part of a drug kingpin. He doesn't look really menacing. But he had to suffice. Because, other than a trainee, and the ship's fourth electrician, who both recently pled guilty, he's all U.S. Attorney William M. McSwain had left to show for his year-long investigation.

Moving seven shipping containers bursting with coke across three continents is clearly a bigger logistics task than anything anyone in Second Mate Durasevic's pay grade is ever asked to do.

That fact alone should raise skepticism of the U.S. investigation. However, the government's case also suffers from a number of omissions, falsehoods, and deliberate lies, as well as the inordinate level of secrecy which permeates the case.

Ivan Duresevic, 29, and Fonofaavae Tiasaga, 28, almost immediately confessed to helping load the cocaine onboard. Their names were both visible in the Federal criminal complaint. Until, suddenly, they weren't.

Durasevic, the first crewman to "roll" on his fellows and plead guilty, was suddenly "disappeared" from the government's own Public Access to Court Electronic Records site, called PACER.[1]

A Federal Court Clerk later told me that – in an unprecedented move – the entire case had been sealed retroactively. But copies of the Complaint were visible in local TV news coverage in the days after the seizure. I got my copy from Philadelphia's NBC-10 assignment editor John Taylor, whose station had aired screen grabs from the indictment, which was eventually published on the internet.

The identity of people charged with felony crimes is public record in American courts. But all court documents in the case were sealed, including the names of the defendants. The criminal charges were being treated as a matter of grave national security.

Three days after the massive cocaine bust aboard the container ship, someone leaked the names of three sailors from Kotor, Montenegro, being charged: Aleksandar Kavaja (25), Boško Marković (37), and Nenad Ilić (39). Their names were published by the *Philadelphia Inquirer*.[2]

It also didn't help that the former U.S. Attorney wrote a letter dated June 9, 2021, to former President Trump, asking for his support in a possible run for governor of Pennsylvania, which Trump made public.[3]

The Philly paper then reported, McSwain, "now appears perplexed and speechless as the ex-president uses him as a cudgel to bash Barr and the Justice Department for not fighting to overturn a free and fair election."[4]

Serb Newspapers Cover What U.S. Papers Won't

One crucial piece of evidence did come to light after Aleksander Kavaja, 27, became the third person to plead guilty in the case. His plea shed light on the case, thanks to Serbian-language newspapers, which follow the case the way the *New York Post* would cover a World Series between the Mets and the Yankees.

That's because at least half of the crewmen on the ship, including the captain, are from Kotor, Montenegro, in the former Yugoslavia of Slobodan Milosevic.

The same Kotor, Montenegro, that hosts two feuding Mafia clans? The very same… And U.S. Attorney William M. McSwain never breathed a word of it. Nor will he.

The leader of "Group America," Mileta Miljanic, was the first from Montenegro to enter the big-time narcotics business with the Colombian cartels.

Serb news tends to lean towards the tabloid end of the spectrum. "SHOCK DISCOVERY! A Montenegrin Sailor Who Was Arrested During the Largest Cocaine Seizure in History is a Relative of a Man Who Tried to KILL TITO 3 Times!"[5]

The guilty crewman, Alexandar Kavaja, belonged to a Mafia clan in Kotor, Montenegro, which for decades had been led by a close relative with a famous history as an anti-communist.

Nikola Kavaja spent several decades allegedly working as an assassin for the CIA, during which he made no fewer than four assassination attempts on the life of Yugoslav communist strongman Marshal Tito. But even though he was useful to the CIA, his primary loyalty was to Group America, a Serbian terrorist group formed by Yugoslav ex-pats, which also has been linked to the U.S. Central Intelligence Agency.

"I believe the CIA stands behind them. That is why we gave them the name Group America," one official told OCCRP. [6]

Back in 2003 prosecutors indicted Miljanić on charges of conspiring to distribute narcotics, but the case remains sealed, meaning that we have no idea what they relate to.

GROUP AMERICA

Transnational organized crime is everywhere. But there's a taboo against acknowledging it. Group America represents the seamless integration of transnational organized crime. Here it is in a nutshell:

A Serb underboss (Radonjić) in an Irish-American gang headed by Jimmy Coonan called the "Westies," which dominated New York's old Hell's Kitchen in the late 1980's, becomes the gang's head after Coonan goes to prison. Then the Westies get close to the Italian-American Mafia family the Gambinos, led by John Gotti. When Gotti faces racketeering charges in 1986, the Serb Radonjić fixes the jury. Can't get much more transnational than that.

GUILTY SAILOR FROM FAMOUS CRIME FAMILY

According to Serbian newspaper *Express*, sailor Aleksander Kavaja is a close relative – and maybe even the grandson – of a famous Serbian mobster named Nikola Kavaja, founder of a criminal Serbian brotherhood.

The family surname, Kavaja, is famous in Montenegro and across the former Yugoslavia. Nikola Kavaja, deceased since 2008, was famous in Yugoslavia, where he was known as "Enemy of the State Number One" for attempting to assassinate Marshal Josip Broz Tito on four separate occasions.

Kavaja was described by journalists as an assassin who worked for the CIA, as well as the godfather of a famous Serbian Don in New York named Boško Radonjić. He was also close with Majko Miljanić and Zoran Jakšić, the leaders of a drug network known as "Group America."[7]

While Nikola Kavaja may not have had a parking pass on his windshield for CIA headquarters in Langley, Virginia, he didn't need one. His fame preceded him wherever he went.

A 1997 document released by the CIA after a FOIA request included "excerpts from extensive source reporting over the years." [8]

Kavaja was described as "an opportunist, a bully, and an untrustworthy type of person primarily interested in himself." [9] Whether those qualities were viewed by the CIA as good or bad remained unclear when the assassin, Nikola Kavaja, sat down in 2006 for an interview with the venerable Paris Review, known back in the day as a cover for CIA assets. [10]

Here's how it began:

> **Interviewer:** You were a World War II prisoner, a Communist soldier, a CIA hit man, a hijacker, and now you're a fugitive on the run. Where to begin?
>
> **Nikola Kavaja:** Write down my name. N-i-k-o-l-a. K-a-v-a-j-a. You can call me Nik. Do you want some schnapps?

Who is Nikola Kavaja?

It was a salubrious opening. Over a period of three days, and, what the writer said were "quite a few shots of Schnapps," Nikola Kavaja described his career to author Christopher Stewart, in a profile titled "Assassin," broadcast on National Public Radio in 2006.[11]

Stewart said he had been writing a book on Serbian warlord Arkan when he met Kavaja, a 73-year-old fugitive from the U.S. government, then living in Belgrade in what had once been Yugoslavia.[12]

Remember the war in the Balkans while Bill Clinton was President? It had been like visiting some earlier more primitive time where "warlords" like Arkan committed acts of genocide against their neighbors for ostensibly religious reasons that had been stifled by autocratic Marshal Tito for generations.

The hatred between Muslims and Catholics still seethed unabated below the surface when Kavaja left home to join a Serb emigre terrorist group. He initially got in trouble by bombing Yugoslavia's embassies and consulates abroad – a series of six bombs in in the US and Canada – for this group.

"The six bombs lit our hearts on fire," chanted the group's members during Tito's visit to the US in 1971, when Richard Nixon was President. "The last time the assassination of Tito by Kavaja was attempted in Maryland, when Tito came at the invitation of Richard Nixon. Kavaja was disguised in the uniform of the state guards. He climbed a tree with a sniper. He waited all day and night," but Tito had left two days earlier, Kavaja later said."[13]

Kavaja either joined or helped to found the Serbian liberation movement – "Otadžbina" or SOPO – in America, which on January 29, 1967, set off bombs in Yugoslav embassies in Washington and Ontario and consulates in New York, Chicago, San Francisco and Toronto.[14]

"I don't know how many people were killed. But after that, Tito put pressure on the State Department to find us," Kavaja told his interviewer in 2006, saying he was arrested in New York in 1978 along with more than a hundred others from SOPO.

A court in Chicago found them guilty and then all were released on bond pending appeal except Stojiljko Kajević, a Serbian Orthodox priest the others called Pop, who had no money for his bond.[15]

Kavaja, who clearly did not understand the American system of justice, swore he would not leave Pop behind.

He stood ready to hijack the plane, as they had planned. He'd promised "to land in Chicago, pick up Pop and then fly to Belgrade and crash him into the building of the Central Committee of the Union of Communists (the CC building)."[16]

Kavaja returned home to Paterson, New Jersey, where he sometimes worked as a painter in construction. He devised a plan to free his friend Pop. He'd shared his dream with Pop numerous times and had never been told to put it behind him. He thought the priest would be happy and hail him as a hero.

He'd strapped the homemade bombs to his legs and boarded the flight to Chicago, then overtook the pilots just before landing. He let all 288 passengers leave, keeping three crew members. A lawyer was allowed aboard, who told the FBI and police circling the plane Kavaja only wanted one thing, his friend and priest called Pop. It took awhile for them to locate him in prison. When the call came, Kavaja put the handset to his ear. "Brother Nikola," Pop said, "I will not go with you." Kavaja all but breaks down. In the end, he was flown to Ireland, promised by the lawyer they could not extradite him.

Kavaja realized once they landed, he'd been played. Ireland sent him back to the US, where he was sentenced to 40 years for his crimes – terrorism, carrying explosives, hijacking a plane and trying to kill Tito. He was in prison from 1979 to 1997, paroled after 18 years on condition he remain in America.

Kavaja told the interviewer he'd immediately left the US without a word to anyone – traveling to Mexico, Brazil and South Africa, then to Athens. From there he went to Serbia on a JAT Airlines plane to Belgrade dressed as a flight attendant.

After 9/11 he tried to think of how he could make Al Qaeda pay him royalties for coming up with the scheme. After all, he'd been "the first idiot to try hijacking a plane and flying it into a building."[17]

Nikola Kavaja's less-headline-worthy accomplishments included being known as the godfather of Boško Radonjić, a famous don of the New York Serbian underground.

He was a close friend and mentor to Mile Majko Miljanić, the Drug Kingpin of an up-and-coming narco-trafficking clan in Montenegro called "Group America."[18]

That's what first brought me up short. "Group America?"

"Another Way of Saying CIA"

In international diplomatic and law enforcement circles, newspapers in Europe and South America have reported, there is considerable opinion that "Group America" was just another way of saying "CIA."

I learned that the Organized Crime and Corruption Reporting Project – the network of investigative journalists that exposed money laundering and the trillions parked illegally offshore in the Panama Papers – had done a whole series of reports on Group America, which it called "A U.S.-Serbian Drug Gang with Friends in the Shadows."[19]

But thankfully, there are still contributions to be made, especially since the OCCRP stories add the disclaimer "It's unlikely that Group America had anything to do with the [MSC] Gayane – it's not their style."[20]

Because of my investigations into drug trafficking through Florida while researching "Gangster Planet," I have some insight into who some of Group America's friends in the shadows might be. One man in particular has a half-billion-dollar investment right next door to Kotor, has experience with drug trafficking, and influence with the Serbia Mafia. No one has yet mentioned Oleg Deripaska in connection with Group America, and the omission speaks volumes.

Back to the Future

The story began simply enough. By the time authorities finished searching the MSC Gayane three days after it was interdicted, it had been scoured with fiber optic scopes, x-ray scanning trucks, and drug sniffing dogs. They'd carted off nearly 20 tons of cocaine.

Friday was to be the Big Reveal. But the news conference announcing the massive drug bust vibed hinky from the start. Representatives from a half dozen local state and federal law enforcement agencies had been posed in a wedge-like formation standing in front of a wall made up of bricks of bubble-wrapped cocaine piled artfully behind them.

They were taking a bow. Displaying the goods. It's called "drug porn."[21] They probably learned it from the Mexicans, who have more drugs to display at news conferences than we do.

They took turns at the podium. But, oddly, the authorities didn't have much to say. They wouldn't tell how they found the coke, or if the big bust had been the result of a tip.

The ship had been pulled in for a secondary inspection Sunday night. It was routine. Things evolved from there. The *Philadelphia Inquirer* was the first to notice.

"Officials demurred from saying what had led them to the MSC GUY-ANE, the international cargo freighter on which they made their record-breaking discovery."[22]

Reporter Jeremy Roebuck from the *Inquirer* was clearly annoyed. "They cited routine port inspections, and made vague references to intelligence partners," he wrote. "Authorities also remained circumspect about the role of the six members of ship's crew they've placed under arrest."[23]

Three days later, when the U.S. Attorney announced two seamen from the ship had confessed, and pled guilty, the confessions and guilty pleas were immediately sealed.

"MASSIVE AND STUNNING"

The massive and stunning drug seizure is one of the largest in our nation's history," said U.S. Attorney William W. McSwain. Casey Durst, director of U.S. Customs at the Baltimore Port (CBP), said, "The seizure of a record amount of cocaine sent messages to all seafarers and others that serious consequences awaited them if they tried to smuggle narcotics through the United States."[24]

US Attorney William M. McSwain said mega-dittos to that.

Durst helpfully added, "Laid end-to-end, the packaged bricks of cocaine would cover a distance of about two-and-a-half miles."[25]

"This investigation is ongoing," said U.S. Attorney William W. McSwain. "The situation is very fluid."

Was that why the case was totally sealed?

What I had a hard time visualizing wasn't a yellow brick road two-and-a-half miles long. It was what a government law enforcement official looks like when he's "demurring."

"What we do investigatively is part of our tradecraft, so I can't go into that," explained Marlon Miller, special agent in charge of Homeland Securities Investigations.[26]

U.S. Attorney William M. McSwain's strategy appears to have resulted in a deliberate cover-up of officially sanctioned drug trafficking, larger than any seen in the U.S. since the days of Oliver North and Iran Contra. One goal was to put the case on the back burner until after the election.

No MORE MISUNDERESTIMATION

U.S. Attorney McSwain, a staunch Trump supporter and law & order Republican, used the news conference to get a few things off his chest. Speaking directly to whoever had been responsible for the 20 tons of cocaine, he taunted them for their loss.

"You thought you could breeze into our port and then leave with enough cocaine to destroy millions of lives without getting caught," McSwain sneered. "You thought you were clever. You were wrong."[27]

"You underestimated our city, you underestimated our law enforcement capabilities, and our commitment to decimating the illegal and immoral drug trade."[27]

It was mis-underestimation all around.

McSwain was steaming the next day as well. Stung by the apparent lack of enthusiasm shown by the general public for the massive coke bust, he took to Twitter.

"This is a massive, stunning amount of cocaine," U.S. Attorney William M. McSwain enthused. "One of the largest drug seizures in United States history. This volume of cocaine could kill millions – MILLIONS – of people."

Well, yeah, some skeptic tweeted back, if you do it all at once.

QUESTIONS WERE RAISED

I began to keep track of "anomalies" in the case. They weren't difficult to find.

Ivan Durasevic's Facebook profile, for example, said he's from Kotor. His role was discovered after authorities found traces of cocaine on his hands. He admitted to investigators that he'd been recruited by the ship's "chief officer," though the name of the ship's captain was not disclosed.

Both he and the Samoan crewmen who immediately pled guilty with him told authorities the scheme was led by Darko Roganovich, the ship's captain.

Yet authorities released Roganović almost immediately after the seizure, and he hopped a plane back to Montenegro. One newspaper there reported: "The captain of the ship 'MSC Gajan' [sic] on which more than 16 tons of cocaine was found in Philadelphia, Darko Roganović, is not suspected of smuggling and is returning home, his lawyer Aleksandar Đurišić told 'Dan'.[28]

That's a pretty big anomaly right there.

Nor has there been any mention by the U.S. Attorney, in either court filings or press briefings, of any connection between the massive seizure and any of the other MSC container ships which have been caught recently committing indiscretions.

When the container ship MSC Gayane was busted in Philadelphia, it marked the fourth time an MSC Mediterranean Shipping Company vessel has been involved in a major drug bust … just since the beginning of the year.

Another MSC cargo vessel, the MSC Desiree, "was caught while calling at Philadelphia," carrying a stash of cocaine worth $38 million.

That's two … just at the Port of Philadelphia.

Almost 1.5 tons of cocaine was found on another MSC container ship, the MSC Carlotta, at the port of Newark. Months later, the MSC Carlotta was caught again … this time in Callao, Peru, carrying 2.2 tons of cocaine.

"It Was A Container Ship Crime Wave"

Was a single drug trafficking organization responsible for the recent drug moves on MSC container ships? Was the question even being asked?

Mediterranean Shipping Company is a private company, owned by a private party, who lives in Naples, Italy. His name is Gianluigi Aponte, and, according to the Journal of Commerce, "Mediterranean Shipping is private company with "no annual reports, no filing, or worries about off-hand remarks moving the stock and bringing in government lawyers."[29]

Aponte was also said to be "one of the most secretive tycoons in the world with the company's income a closely guarded secret from the time he acquired his first vessel, Patricia, in 1970 to the present day." The secret was revealed, however, when a leak occurred, showing Aponte to have a net worth of around $9 billion.[30]

Aponte was also at the heart of an influence scandal in France which embroiled French President Emmanuel Macron's chief of staff, who was accused of influence-peddling in cases involving the Mediterranean Shipping Company.[31]

Alexis Kohler was indicted in September 2021 for breaking conflict of interest rules on contracts awarded to MSC, and Bloomberg News conducted an investigation to discover how cocaine traffickers infiltrated the Italian-Swiss shipping company owned by Alexis Kohler's cousins.

In the summer of 2019 Claudio Bozzo, Chief Operating Officer of MSC was ordered by the ship's owner to travel from Geneva to Washington DC, to meet with US Customs and Border Protection, which had seized not only 20 tons of cocaine, but the ship that carried it.

Bozzo could have been Bozo the clown, for all the Customs men cared. His comments tried to show MSC as a major victim, but U.S. Customs didn't buy it.

A VOX Albanian editorial reported: "For the American authorities, the ignorance of the company 'didn't drink water.'"[32]

We think they got the idiom a little mixed up. The story revealed authorities had not been surprised by the drug shipment at the time. Instead, they'd been expecting it.

> "Bloomberg Businessweek investigation found that years before the Gayane inspection, law enforcement authorities in several countries were monitoring MSC ships and crews. US authorities had not only followed the Gayane long before it entered US waters, but they had also boarded and searched several other MSC ships as part of a wider investigation into an international cocaine-trafficking ring that had infiltrated the company of maritime transport. "Through data gathered during these inspections, as well as information gathered in Eastern Europe, they identified a powerful Balkan cartel as the source of these massive shipments."[33]

They said the cartel had been infiltrating the ships' crews for a decade or more to help the cartel build an empire. MSC was its favorite shipping line, leading authorities to ask: "Why have criminal organizations apparently been able to control key operations aboard some of the company's ships for so long?"[34]

It certainly never helped that MSC's freight business does not publish financial statements. It's a family business. Much like the Trump business in America, only different.

According to "court documents" reviewed by the *Vox* article, it was mid-April 2019 when Kavaja was having lunch at a coffee bar, a few days before he was to board the *Gayane* at Antwerp. He's approached by a man he doesn't know, but who knows Kavaja.

The stranger says, "We know who you are, we know who your family is," the man told him, according to US court documents. The man was holding what prosecutors called a "narco" cell phone. "You have a choice," the man told Kavaja. "You can pick up the phone and agree to follow orders, or you can leave now without it," but you will be risking your own safety and your family's. If you accept, we'll pay you $50,000" – nearly a year's salary.[35]

Kavaja picked up the phone. The prosecutors said it may not have been a good choice, but it was a choice he made.

DUBIOUS AND DUBIOUSER

Now we come to the most dubious allegation in the government indictment. How a go-fast boat was supposed to pull alongside a mas-

490

sive cargo ship in open seas – and in the dark, yet! – is a mystery to anyone who's ever been to sea.

"Ivan Durasevic admitted his role to authorities in bringing cocaine onto the vessel after being offered $50,000 by the chief officer. Others assisted in loading the cocaine into containers. The whole process took approximately 30 to 40 minutes," stated the criminal complaint, continuing with the following:

> According to Durasevic, upon leaving Peru he got a call from the chief officer to come down to the deck, where he saw nets on the port side stern by the ship's crane. Durasevic and four others, some wearing ski masks, pushed the nets, containing blue or black bags with handles, into two of the holds.
>
> Durasevic used the ship's crane to load cocaine in bags onto the ship from a flotilla of go-fast speedboats. after the MSC Guyane left the port of Barranquilla, Peru.[36]

The Samoan crewman, Tiasaga said six boats approached the MSC Gayane during the night. Durasevic operated the crane, swinging bag after bag of cocaine onboard.

The two men's stories seem to match. So, too, does the one told by the third crewman to plead guilty, Vladimir Penda, according to a statement released by the U.S. Attorney's office, alleging:

> On multiple occasions during the MSC Gayane's voyage at sea, crew members, including Penda, helped load bulk cocaine onto the vessel from speedboats that approached under cover of darkness, traveling at high speeds.
>
> Crew members used the Gayane's crane to hoist cargo nets full of cocaine onto the vessel and then stashed the drugs in various shipping containers," said the plea filing by Penda, who was part of the team bringing the drugs aboard.
>
> Under cover of darkness, Penda helped load bulk cocaine onto the vessel from speedboats that approached at high speeds. Crew members hoisted the cocaine from cargo nets filled with cocaine onto the deck of the ship, and then stashed the drug in various containers.[37]

Also matching the others was the story told by Aleksander Kavaja:

> Using the ship's crane, they pulled duffel bags filled with wrapped cocaine off the smaller boats and onto the Gayane's deck before splitting the individual bricks among seven cargo containers car-

rying wine, vegetable extract, Chilean dried nuts, scrap metal, and other legitimate goods bound for Europe, Africa, and Asia.[38]

To recap: According to the criminal complaint, the *Gayane's* crew brought the drugs aboard during rendezvous with small fast boats at sea, then concealed the narcotics in containers.

Neither Aleksander Kavaja nor the court documents shed any light on who was ultimately behind the shipment.

And while Aleksander Kavaja faced a maximum sentence of lifetime imprisonment, with a mandatory minimum of 10 years, his plea agreement included no requirement that he cooperate with the ongoing probe.

That's way beyond strange.

The China Syndrome Option

We also considered the possibility of the China connection, which at the time was the option I would have put my money on. The ships MSC *Gayane*, MSC *Carlotta*, and MSC *Desiree* had previously been bought by SinOceanic Shipping – whose initials "SOS" give off quite a pessimistic vibe.

SOS was a wholly owned subsidiary of the Chinese conglomerate called the HNA group, which transferred two of the ships to Blue Star Shipping and JP Morgan a year before the drug seizure as collateral for a loan. Remember how we talked in previous chapters about Adnan Khashoggi "borrowing" stock of various corporations so he could use them for "pump-and-dump" maneuvers?

This is similar to that same legal fiction.

Providing crew and management services to all three ships still fell under the purview of SinOceanic, whose parent company – HNA Group – desperately needed money, as it teetered on the edge of bankruptcy.

While ship ownership ricocheted back and forth between Bermuda, Norway, Switzerland, and God knows where else ... if we dig deep enough, all indications point to the Chinese as having culpability for the ships busted for transporting cocaine.

My money, if I had any, would be on the Chinese. At the time, it appeared Steve Bannon felt the same.

Steve Bannon was cruising off the coast of Connecticut on a $28 million-dollar mega-yacht belonging to a shady business partner, when it was boarded by federal agents who arrested him for looting the Build the Wall Foundation.

The *New York Times* identified the yacht's owner as "Chinese billionaire Guo Wengui." That – the "Chinese billionaire" appellation – is just the first big problem with the story.

They were taking Steve Bannon downtown… to the Federal Courthouse in Manhattan. There, the circumstances of his arrest lit him up like one of the Federal agents had pyrotechnic experience.

Call the yacht Bannon was lounging aboard Exhibit A.

It belongs to a man the *New York Times* identified as "Chinese billionaire Guo Wengui."

Which is actually the first big problem with the story. Tagging Guo Wengui as a "Chinese billionaire" is like calling famous bank robber John Dillinger a specialist in "unauthorized withdrawals."

It may be true, as far as it goes. But it's not an accurate description. So if there is one place where the *New York Times* regularly is guilty of "fake news," this is it. From Mexico's Carlos Slim to Russia's Oleg Deripaska and Dmitry Rybolovlev, gangsters-turned-oligarchs are invariably referred to by the Times as billionaires, or business tycoons, or (my favorite) "billionaire philanthropists."

The *Times* has a hard time calling something what it really is. For example, evidence exists indicating the company that made Guo a billionaire may have been – or may be still – involved in global drug trafficking.

The circumstances of Steve Bannon's arrest offer a clue about RussiaGate. Example: Bannon is a professed anti-globalist. It's his schtick. Yet he was taken into custody on the yacht of a Chinese billionaire who is one of globalization's biggest winners. "Guo Wengui, also known under the Cantonese name Ho Wan Kwok, Miles Guo, and Miles Kwok, is an exiled Chinese billionaire businessman who became a political activist and controls Beijing Zenith Holdings, and other assets. At the peak of his career, he was the 73rd richest person in China," we learn from Wikipedia.

Miles Guo once walked away with a big fat juicy piece of what until recently was one of the world's fastest-growing corporations: China's HNA Group.

A few weeks before Bannon was busted, the two men made an audacious pitch for a Chinese government-in-exile on his podcast over the July Fourth weekend. In a livestream, with Bannon alongside him and the Statue of Liberty in the background, Guo said "From today the Chinese Communist Party (CCP) will no longer be the lawful government of China!"

493

Bannon in the Docks

And, by the by, Steve Bannon never had to stand trial. He made sure to wave his "get out of jail free" card in front of prosecutors and judges.

We can be grateful for one thing, however. Bannon never convinced his benefactor, Donald J. Trump, to pardon himself.

Thanks to Trump's arrogance, he's defending himself in four courts of a total of 91 felony indictments. But that's not to say Bannon got off scotfree. Bannon was convicted on two counts of contempt for ignoring subpoenas and sentenced to four months in jail. The federal sentence is on appeal. But on May 28, 2024 we're hoping to see him in court on his New York case on which his partners in crime, Andy Badolato and have already been serving their time.[39]

Stay tuned.

Endnotes

1   https://www.madcowprod.com/wp-content/uploads/2019/06/drug-shipment-charges.pdf

2   by Jeremy Roebuck, "4 more crew members arrested in record-breaking 16-ton, $1B cocaine bust at Philly port," *Philadelphia Inquirer*, Jun. 19, 2019. https://www.inquirer.com/news/philly-cocaine-drug-bust-gayane-port-arrests-investigation-20190619.html

3   https://cdn.donaldjtrump.com/djtweb/general/Letter_to_President_Trump.pdf

4   Chris Brennan, "Trump is putting Bill McSwain in the hot seat with his election lies. And he just turned up the heat," *Philadelphia Inquirer*, Updated Jul. 12, 2021. https://www.inquirer.com/politics/clout/donald-trump-bill-mcswain-cpac-20210712.html

5   https://volimpodgoricu.me/novosti/sok-otkrice-crnogorski-mornar-koji-je-uhapsen-tokom-najvece-zaplijene-kokaina-u-istoriji-rodjak-covjeka-koji-je-3-puta-pokusao-da-ubije-tita [ENGLISH TRANSLATION: https://volimpodgoricu-me.translate.goog/novosti/sok-otkrice-crnogor-ski-mornar-koji-je-uhapsen-tokom-najvece-zaplijene-kokaina-u-istoriji-rodjak-covjeka-koji-je-3puta-pokusao-da-ubije-tita?_x_tr_sl=auto&_x_tr_tl=en&_x_tr_hl=en&_x_tr_pto=wapp

6   "Who is Mileta Miljanić? The Serbian-American Drug Lord and Leader of 'Group America,'" OCCRP, 15 March 2021. https://www.occrp.org/en/group-america/who-is-mileta-miljanic-the-serbian-american-drug-lord-and-leader-of-group-America

7   A video can be viewed on YouTube: https://www.youtube.com/watch?v=P6Ae8zYw-6zc&t=3704s

8   https://www.archives.gov/files/research/jfk/releases/104-10326-10022.pdf

9   Ibid.

10   https://www.salon.com/2012/05/27/exclusive_the_paris_review_the_cold_war_and_the_cia/

11   Christopher Stewart's interview of Serbian assassin Nikola Kavaja, "Profile of a Serbian Assassin," NPR, July 22, 2006. https://www.npr.org/2006/07/22/5575308/profile-of-a-serbian-assassin

12   *Hunting the Tiger* was published by Thomas Dunne Books; First Edition (January 8, 2008).

13   Citing a 2006 interview with the *Paris Review*, two years prior to Kavaja's death. Cited reference quoted from *Paris Review*: https://volimpodgoricu-me.translate.goog/novosti/ sok-otkrice-crnogorski-mornar-koji-je-uhapsen-tokom-najvece-zaplijene-kokaina-u-istoriji-rodjak-covjeka-koji-je-3-puta-pokusao-da-ubije-tita?_x_tr_sl=auto&_x_tr_tl=en&_x_tr_hl=en&_x_tr_pto=wapp

An obituary appeared in the *New York Times*: Bruce Weber, "Nikola Kavaja, Anti-Tito Hijacker of Jet, Dies at 75," *New York Times*, Nov. 12, 2008. https://www.nytimes.com/2008/11/12/ world/europe/12kavaja.html.

14   Nina Bunjevac, author of the graphic novel and *New York Times* best seller *Fatherland*, wrote about these days in her book, reviewed by Dragana Obradovic "I Only Belong to One Tribe. The Displaced Children of Yugoslavia" *Balkanist Magazine*, May 14, 2015. by https://balkanist.net/profile-nina-bunjevac-author-of-fatherland/

15   Jack Lesar, UPI interview of Stojilko Kajevic, "Violence ruled his life," UPI, Nov. 5, 1981. https://www.upi.com/Archives/1981/11/05/Stojilko-Kajevic-violence-ruled-his-life/7821373784400/

16   https://volimpodgoricu-me.translate.goog/novosti/sok-otkrice-crnogorski-mornar-koji-je-uhapsen-tokom-najvece-zaplijene-kokaina-u-istoriji-rodjak-covjeka-koji-je-3-puta-pokusao-da-ubije-tita?_x_tr_sl=auto&_x_tr_tl=en&_x_tr_hl=en&_x_tr_pto=wapp

17   Note from editor: Daniel Hopsicker put quotes around this phrase, citing "another source" which the editors have not been able to trace. We suspect Daniel thought the quote should exist and was too good not to use. See https://www.madcowprod.com/2020/09/22/cia-law-order-u-s-attorney-20-tons-cocaine/

18   https://www.occrp.org/en/group-america/

19   https://www.occrp.org/en/group-america/#interactive

20   https://www.occrp.org/en/group-america/the-hardest-working-drug-gang-youve-never-heard-of

21   https://abcnews-wsdynamic.aws.seabcnews.go.com/ABC_Univision/News/analy-

sis-drug-porn-exciting-anymore/story?id=18015892

22   Jeremy Roebuck, "17.5 tons of cocaine: Search yields more as feds probe ship they busted at Port of Philadelphia," *Philadelphia Inquirer*, Published Jun. 21, 2019. https://www.inquirer.com/news/philly-port-cocaine-seized-arrests-gayane-largest-drug-busts-mediterannean-shipping-co-20190621.html

23   Ibid.

24   "U.S. Customs and Border Protection Seizes MSC Gayane following Record Cocaine Seizure," 07/08/2019. https://www.cbp.gov/newsroom/local-media-release/us-customs-and-border-protection-seizes-msc-gayane-following-record

25   "Philadelphia cocaine haul is largest in U.S. history: 35K pounds and $1.1B," Associated Press, June 21, 2019. https://www.usatoday.com/story/news/2019/06/21/philadelphia-drug-bust-largest-cocaine-haul-u-s-history/1526399001/

26   Jeremy Roebuck, "17.5 tons of cocaine: Search yields more as feds probe ship they busted at Port of Philadelphia," *Philadelphia Inquirer*, Published Jun. 21, 2019. https://www.inquirer.com/news/philly-port-cocaine-seized-arrests-gayane-largest-drug-busts-mediterannean-shipping-co-20190621.html

27   "Philadelphia cocaine haul is largest in U.S. history: 35K pounds and $1.1B," Associated Press, June 21, 2019.

28   Mirjana Dragaš, "Roganović is not suspected of smuggling 16 tons of cocaine in Philadelphia," Antenna M, 15.07.2019. https://www-antenam-net.translate.goog/drustvo/126603-roganovica-ne-sumnjice-za-sverc-16-tona-kokaina-u-filadelfiji?_x_tr_sl=auto&_x_tr_tl=en&_x_tr_hl=en&_x_tr_pto=wapp

29   Bruce Barnard, "Diego Aponte succeeds father as head of MSC," *Journal of Commerce*, Oct 2, 2014.

30   "Leak reveals Aponte is one of world's richest men," *Container News*, October 13, 2023. https://container-news.com/leak-reveals-aponte-is-one-of-worlds-richest-men/

31   "President Macron's Chief of Staff Indicted Over MSC Links," Reuters, October 3, 2022. https://gcaptain.com/brief-president-macrons-chief-of-staff-indicted-over-msc-links/

32   Redasksia, "INVESTIGATION: Emanuel Macron's boss's ties to cocaine trafficking," Kosova & Bota VOX, 2023-04-03. https://www.voxnews.al/english/kosovabota/investigimi-fijet-e-she- fitte-emanuel-macron-me-trafikun-e-kokaines-i36391

33   Ibid.

34   Ibid.

35   Ibid.

36   hcharges.pdf

37   "MSC Gayane Crew Member Sentenced to 5+ Years for Conspiracy to Smuggle $1 Billion Worth of Cocaine into the United States," Tuesday, April 13, 2021. https://www.justice.gov/usao-edpa/pr/msc-gayane-crew-member-sentenced-5-years-conspiracy-smuggle-1-billion-worth-cocaine

38   "Two MSC Gayane Crew Members Sentenced for Conspiracy to Smuggle $1 Billion Worth of Cocaine into the United States," Monday, August 2, 2021. https://www.justice.gov/usao-edpa/pr/two-msc-gayane-crew-members-sentenced-conspiracy-smuggle-1-billion-worth-cocaine-united

39   Michael R. Sisak, "Steve Bannon's trial in 'We Build the Wall' scheme set for May 2024," Associated Press, May 25, 2023. https://apnews.com/article/steve-bannon-border-wall-trump-trial-eebaec6c851ad88029fd8e4bd48cc77b

Index

Addendum

About The Authors

Scandal in contemporary U.S. life is an institutionalized sociological phenomenon. It is not due primarily to psychopathological variables, but it is due to the institutionalization of elite wrongdoing which has occurred since 1963. Many of the scandals that have occurred in the U.S. since 1963 are fundamentally interrelated: that is, the same people and institutions have been involved.
　　　　　　　　　　　　—Prof. David Simon, *Elite Deviance* (6th edition)

By Linda Minor

Gangster Planet* is Daniel Hopsicker's third and final book. It was researched and written for his website between 2006 up until his death on August 22, 2023, and it covers more years of work than his first two books combined.

Needless to say, it took a great deal of thought and work to organize all the threads that went into it. Although the book was, unfortunately, delayed numerous times, the publication of Daniel's magnum opus completes his mission in life.

Daniel was born on July 16, 1951, at Grant Hospital in Chicago, Illinois, to Harold J. "Harry" and Rita Jean Garry Hopsicker, who had married eleven months earlier. A year later a sister, Carol, was born, followed in 1959 by the youngest, David Hopsicker.

Harry had joined the U.S. Navy on his 18th birthday and returned from World War II after an eventful year. His rating changed several times between the dates of May 5, 1945, and his discharge at San Diego the following year. He rose from Hospital Apprentice, 2nd Class to 1st Class while berthed on the USS *Haven*, a hospital ship which sailed for Pearl Harbor, Hawaii, on July 6, 1945.

From there, the ship departed for Japan, assigned to pick up Allied troops, who had been prisoners of war held by the Japanese, in Okinawa. From there the *Haven* advanced to Nagasaki, Japan, by September 11, taking on new patients suffering from the effects of the atomic blast. Once these troops were added to the hospital ship's patient list, the Haven began its return voyage to San Francisco, stopping at Guam, Saipan, and Pearl Harbor, on its way to San Francisco on January 31, 1946 .

Harry Hopsicker by then was looking forward to his 19th birthday. During the months at sea, he added Pharmacy Mate 3rd class to his rating.

Along with a teen-age Harold Hopsicker, the USS *Haven* also carried, on that same voyage that left San Francisco, radiological equipment and scientific researchers to participate in "atomic tests" in the Pacific as part of Operation Crossroads. The tests were part of a high-level plan being set up by the future head of the Atomic Energy Commission, Lewis Strauss, and Secretary of the Navy James Forrestal, according to a declassified memo in which Strauss wrote:

> If such a test is not made, there will be loose talk to the effect that the fleet is obsolete in the face of this new weapon and this will militate against appropriations to preserve a postwar Navy of the size now planned.

In other words, Harry was being used as a pawn of elite world leaders even at his young age and patriotic stance. Even without a college education, Harry qualified for a good job with Victor Chemical Works at its headquarters plant in Chicago Heights, once he returned to Chicago. It would be the only job he had until his retirement in 1980. Initially, the only chemical the plant produced was monocalcium phosphate, one form of baking powder, but the company also had other agricultural uses as well.

Harry Hopsicker's only background in chemistry was what he'd been taught while he was in the Navy, but he did qualify to be Victor's personnel director and hiring manager. He was also used to resolve disputes in the event of a threatened strike.

Harold and Rita had undoubtedly become familiar with southwest Florida as a result of his inspection of a Tarpon Springs, Florida, plant, which had been built by Victor as early as 1947 "to burn phosphate ore and turn it into elemental phosphorus for use in foods, fertilizers and ammunition," according to a story by Diane Steinle, published in the Tampa Bay Times in 2014, who added that the "furnace produced toxic smoke and radioactive slag. The plant, purchased by Stauffer Chemical in 1960, shut down in 1981."

Harry, as a member of Victor Chemical's inspection committee, had made trips to inspect plants during the '50s. Photos of the committee appeared in newspapers in cities with phosphate plants during the years before Victor merged into Stauffer Chemicals. Harry's last ten years with the company—after it became Stauffer—could not have been pleasant, though Daniel had no idea what his father may have been dealing with.

Here's an example that would have caused Harry Hopsicker some stress: The Agency for Toxic Substances and Disease Registry (ATSDR) called the Tarpon Springs site "a public health hazard due to harmful levels of air pollutants, primarily sulfur dioxide and particulate matter, released from the Stauffer plant while it was in operation."

DANIEL'S HERITAGE

Whether or not Daniel Hopsicker had any inkling of the problems within the company where his father spent thirty years, we don't know. He was aware, as he indicated in one letter back home while he was a student at UCLA that he had noticed remarks they had made about money being tight.

Dan always felt closer to his mom than to his dad, repeating what he'd been told by his aunts that he had the same temperament. As the youngest of four girls and one boy, Rita, as Danny was told by his aunts, "was always a little flighty," especially while she was pregnant with him. Although online Ancestry.com military records don't seem to support it, Daniel had been told his dad was away in Korea during that pregnancy, which, in his mind at least, partially explained symptoms that stemmed from his 1987 diagnosis of ADD.

Rita and her siblings, 100% Irish, were, actually reared by their mother and stepfather, John Slepicka – from a family mix of Austrian, German, Polish and Czech ancestry. Rita's Irish birth dad died in 1932 at the young age of 36, leaving Rita fatherless when she was three. Her mom, Myrtle Garry, married Slepicka in 1938, and he was the only father Rita remembered. He was a Swift Meatpacking Co. employee and supported all five children to adulthood, dying in 1966 after all were married.

Two years later, Danny's family left their comfortable Chicago Heights home, where he'd played basketball, baseball and football at Marian Catholic high school. Harry was transferred to Concord, California eight years after his long-time employer, Victor Chemical Works, merged into Stauffer Chemical Co. of San Francisco.

The move placed Dan in public school at Ygnacio Valley High, the most profound change of his life up to that point. California represented freedom to him, as he landed near the hub of the counterculture movement in the late 1960s.

"Haight-Ashbury was the most notable San Francisco neighborhood that drew in almost 100,000 youths during the summer of 1967, who soon became the heart and soul of the counterculture movement. This summer of youth migration became known as the Summer of Love, which marked the prominence of a movement that would impact decades to come," Wikipedia tells us.

After two years in Concord, Harry told his son he'd been transferred again, and the family would be moving to the East Coast. Dan wouldn't accept it. "I came up with this plan," he told his coauthor. "San Francisco and Berkeley were the center of the peace movement, so I decided I'd lobby to go to UCLA. It didn't have all the hippie connotations that UC Berkeley did."

Then he cajoled, begged, and promised that he would be an ideal son. He'd do anything if his parents would just let him stay in California. His mother saved every letter he wrote home during that time. One was postmarked Jan. 24, 1972, with the only return address: "Heir Apparent."

He argued his case:

> Dear Folks,
>
> Just a quick note to let you know what's happening. Not too much. The weather today [remember it's January, and he's writing to people in Connecticut] is beautiful. I'm sitting out on the grass in front of the Theater Arts building basking in the 65-degree sunshine and hoping it will stay like this for awhile.
>
> I happened to think of something last night which I thought I'd pass along to you. I figured it out, and you are paying not one cent more for the move [to an apartment from a frat house], you are also not paying it one second <u>sooner</u>! So where's the gripe?— except that my residency at any one place is somewhat more than unstable. Well, I've got to go to class. Will give you a fuller review of things later in the week.
> Love, Dan"

When he'd started UCLA in the fall of 1970, his parents had him safely ensconced at the Zeta Beta Tau Fraternity house across the street from the campus. But during his second year he moved unannounced with his then-best friend Rick to a house "in the hills" a mile and a half north of campus. A letter he wrote home tried to put what he'd done in a positive light:

> And now here's the financial news. Hopsicker, Very Limited, a subsidiary of the parent company Hopsicker Enterprises, Inc., is presently at 50, with a forecast of slow dissipation for the next two weeks until a consolidation takes place with a food concern known as The Great American Food & Beverage Co. Hopsicker, Sr. preferred stock, on the other hand, has shown definite upswing due to the liquidation and transfer of 125 shares from Hopsicker, Limited to the parent company.

Inside the envelope was a carbon copy of his list of classes, which included History of Art, an English class on Shakespeare, another called Special Studies English, Introduction to Theater, and a Workshop in Theater. He had already developed an interest, it seems, in becoming a playwright.

He got his degree in English Lit, participating in the Creative Writing program. He'd loved books and reading all his life, but he was also introduced to music by his friend Tommy Kane in Chicago Heights. Not classical music, of course. It was the '60s and '70s when rock and roll became every Baby Boomer's passion.

He would visit the family from that point in Westport, Connecticut, until his father retired ten years later. After that, he would visit them at their retirement community in Venice, Florida, where Rita's three older sisters, each living with her respective spouse, had small retirement homes.

COAUTHOR, LINDA MINOR

I first met Daniel online through Kris Millegan, around 1996. The Internet was then newish. At my job as an Assistant County Attorney in Houston, Harris County, Texas, I had just received my first ever computer, loaded with Windows 95. A few months later, a county official I represented, taught me how to use the Internet, probably calling it the Worldwide Web.

One of the first people I discovered after buying my own PC shortly afterwards was Kris Millegan, who had set up a couple of "list-servs": Conspiracy Theory Research List (CTRL) and CIA-Drugs List. Suddenly, my life began to take on two separate personas – (1) family life, which was real enough; and (2) "research reality" – my ability to discover how the world really operates.

This new faceless phenomenon had brought together many diverse individuals, all looking for answers to myriad questions we wondered about – contradictions between what we saw with our own eyes and what we were being told.

The first member I met in person was Catherine Austin Fitts, who was then crisscrossing the country in an effort, she said, to stay alive. She had been impressed by my ability to do research online and asked me to help her figure out who had destroyed an investment business she had created. I was happy to do so, even though much of what she told me I did not understand.

Over a period of years beginning in 2000, Catherine would stop off at our small home to stay and visit, sometimes for up to a week at a time.

Even though her priorities were not the same as mine, I felt we had the same goal – "seeing the world whole," as she phrased it.

I interpreted that to mean she wanted to integrate the reality we found in our research into our personal lives. The last time I saw her was just before the election in 2016. She was coming through my town, and we met at Starbucks. When she left after an hour of talking, I was crying. She told me reluctantly that she would be voting for Donald Trump, but the explanation she gave me for doing so has since been forgotten. That was the last time we spoke, other than a possible email or two she forwarded to me. Today she has a podcast that informs listeners about "financial transaction freedom and the building of wealth." The goal we did not share was her desire to be rich.

It was through Catherine, however, that I met Lois Battuello, whom Catherine called "the Goddess of Research." Lois wrote an anonymous column posted at Newsmakingnews.com and helped other members of Kris' CIA-Drugs list with research projects. She did research with Sander Hicks for a time, Craig Unger, and even the notorious Gerald Posner.

Michael Ruppert, a former Los Angeles Police Department detective, was also a member of CIA-Drugs. He attended a town hall meeting in South Central Los Angeles and confronted CIA Director John Deutsche about the CIA's involvement with selling drugs in that community.

Kris Millegan hosted "CIA-Drugs Symposium" in Eugene, Oregon on Saturday, June 10, 2000, to allow the various email acquaintances to finally put a face to the folks they'd been in contact with for the previous three years.

I did not attend. Daniel did, along with an assortment of other members of the internet-based email group called CIA-Drugs.

Daniel was introduced for the symposium with these words:

> Daniel Hopsicker has spent a career in business television, producing "Inside Wall Street" and "The Emerging Growth Stock Report," among others. He was the executive producer of a business news magazine airing on NBC internationally when he went to Bill Clinton's Arkansas to film a story for a new series pilot and discovered that "things ain't always been jes' right down here," in the words of a famous Mississippi lawman.
>
> The initial result was a two-hour TV special, "The Secret Heartbeat of America," which he was told "would not air while Clinton was President."
>
> ("They" were right: it airs next winter, after Clinton leaves office.)
> He has just completed the first full-length look at the career of

CIA agent/drug smuggler Adler Berriman Seal called "Barry and 'the boys,'" as well as a TV documentary detailing some of his findings called "In Search of the AMERICAN Drug Lords."

The shocking true story of American 'super-spy' Barry Seal – the inspiration for the 1966 hit "Secret Agent Man," written by his long-time friend Johnny Rivers – is the story of what happens when guys we pay to protect us – CIA guys– go into business with guys we're paying them to protect us against: "Made" guys. Mobsters ... Organized Crime."

As the years went by, Daniel, Kris and I remained friends. I first met Kris in person in Toronto in 2011 where he was doing a conference with Judyth Vary Baker. Judyth and I were good friends for several years until I attended a conference to which she had invited Roger Stone to be a presenter, possibly in 2015. That was the end of my relationship with Judyth, who did not understand what a pimp and fraud Stone has always been.

In 2018 Daniel sent me a chapter of a proposed book to be titled "Krysha," which I read. He knew then that RussiaGate was not a hoax. Parts of that chapter ended up in *Gangster Planet*. Daniel was a true genius, whose instincts were phenomenally accurate.

As he studied Wallace Hilliard, he was sure Wally fit the mold for CIA tells. He was right about that. Only problem was, most intelligence groups fit the same mold. Daniel had been told by Lois Battuello that Khalid bin Mahfouz was the man Europeans suspected of being the financier for Bin Laden. These unnamed Europeans had been after him since BCCI's collapse in 1991, and they had set up the European Union Agency for Criminal Justice Cooperation (Eurojust for short) in March 2002 to co-ordinate investigations into global terrorism.

She said – whether true or not – that George W. Bush, after being given Daniel Hopsicker's book, *Welcome To TerrorLand*, had changed his previous position and allowed the FBI and DEA to work with Eurojust.

A man named Stephan, she said – knowing Stephan had sued Daniel, forcing him to remove his name from the Mad Cow website – was a pilot for Mahfouz in Ireland in 2009. The implication was that Stephan was working uncover for either the FBI or DEA or possibly even Eurojust. She also implied that Wally Hilliard helped Eurojust take out the Uzbek heroin network used to finance bin Laden. Good for him.

In so doing, though, he operated his own drug network, which we revealed in the book. Lois did state that Wally served warrants on behalf of

Interpol in 2009. She said in her email that she was mailing the evidence. Daniel never received it. It was not among his personal effects.

Maybe Lois and Daniel have met up in the Afterlife and are having a good laugh about it all.

Those of us left here on *Gangster Planet* are looking for a reason to laugh. So far, we haven't found one.